L E A D E R S H I P

Resources

A GUIDE TO TRAINING AND DEVELOPMENT TOOLS

7th Edition

LEADERSHIP
Resources

A GUIDE TO TRAINING AND DEVELOPMENT TOOLS

Edited by

Mary K. Schwartz

Kristin M. Axtman

Frank H. Freeman

Center for Creative Leadership
Greensboro, North Carolina

The Center for Creative Leadership is an international, nonprofit educational institution founded in 1970 to advance the understanding, practice, and development of leadership for the benefit of society worldwide. As a part of this mission, it publishes books and reports that aim to contribute to a general process of inquiry and understanding in which ideas related to leadership are raised, exchanged, and evaluated. The ideas presented in its publications are those of the author or authors.

The Center thanks you for supporting its work through the purchase of this volume. If you have comments, suggestions, or questions about any Center publication, please contact John R. Alexander, President, at the address given below.

Center for Creative Leadership
One Leadership Place
Post Office Box 26300
Greensboro, North Carolina 27438-6300

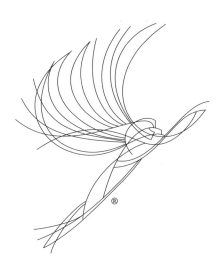

CCL No. 340

ISSN No. 1062-1474
ISBN No. 1-882197-42-9

ABOUT THE EDITORS

Mary K. Schwartz is a librarian at the Center for Creative Leadership. She provides general library services to CCL staff and has worked on four editions of the *Leadership Education Source Book*. Schwartz holds an M.L.S. in library and information science from the University of North Carolina at Greensboro.

Kristin M. Axtman is a program coordinator at the Center for Creative Leadership, where she works with The Women's Leadership Program and client-specific leadership programs. Her own experience with student programs includes coauthoring a national high school leadership curriculum and managing a Colorado College community service program. In addition, Axtman has worked with local, regional, and national nonprofit leadership programs. She is completing her M.A. in organizational design and effectiveness at the Fielding Institute.

Frank H. Freeman directs the library at the Center for Creative Leadership. He develops and oversees information technologies that connect staff and CCL program participants to a wide array of information sources and services on management development and related areas. Freeman has coedited seven editions of the *Leadership Education Source Book*. He received his M.L.S. in library and information science from the University of Maryland.

ACKNOWLEDGMENTS

The production of this book requires a team effort to gather, review, edit, check facts, check again, and assure the readability of an enormous amount of information. Many thanks to:

Shelley Jarrad for combing hundreds of reading lists, writing bibliography annotations, calling vendors, and organizing mountains of information into coherent files.

Sherri Ruffle for helping with the survey of source book users, borrowing hundreds of books and articles through interlibrary loan, writing bibliography annotations, and keeping us supplied with chocolate chip cookies.

Jonathon Bradsher for helping with the survey of source book users and for identifying and contacting many new organizations.

Dena Harris for writing bibliography annotations and for verifying and editing information about organizations and Internet resources.

Carol Keck for sharing multitudinous publisher, instrument, exercise, and video catalogs and for obtaining books as well as identifying and obtaining films.

Peggy Cartner for suggesting new places to search and conducting searches for obscure facts when all other sources had been exhausted.

Kelly Lombardino for planning the strategy around the book's concept, audience, production, and availability.

Lynne Dardanell and **Chris Wilson** for conceiving and designing a classy and appealing cover.

Marcia Horowitz and **Martin Wilcox** for planning the strategy around the book's concept, audience, criteria for selection, and production.

Karen Hardie for thorough copyediting with an eagle eye for details and consistency.

Joanne Ferguson for doing the page layout and proofreading, and for creating an attractive and easy-to-read book.

Jessica Crawford and **Tom Kealey** for helping with bibliographic annotations.

Contributors to the *Leadership Education Source Book* for recommending their favorite classroom-tested resources.

And a most heartfelt thanks to:

Kinsey Gimbel for writing hundreds of new bibliography annotations, gathering and editing information in several other sections, and contributing creative ideas. Without her keen mind, natural talent for writing, and dedication to work above and beyond her many other duties in the Center for Creative Leadership library, this book would not be possible.

CONTENTS

INTRODUCTION

Leadership Resources: A Guide to Training and Development Tools is for people who are responsible for or interested in leadership development, including HRD professionals, corporate trainers and consultants, educators, student activity directors, and organizers of youth and community leadership programs.

It continues the resource descriptions of reading materials, instruments, exercises, videos, Internet resources, organizations, and conferences in six previous editions of the *Leadership Education Source Book.* First published in 1986, the source book has been a forum for providing comprehensive and current information on leadership resources and for sharing examples of leadership courses and programs. As the field of leadership education grows, so do the number and quality of resources that support it. Beginning with this edition, *Leadership Resources* becomes a separate book. (For more information about *Leadership Education: A Source Book of Courses and Programs,* see the Order Form at the back of this book.)

Sources of Information

The resources described in this book were suggested by contributors to the *Leadership Education Source Book* and the Center for Creative Leadership staff, and were also selected through a thorough search of library sources. These include:

- Databases such as Psychlit®, ABI/Inform®, Books In Print, ERIC, and PAIS International.
- Standard reference materials.
- Catalogs from book publishers, film distributors, and vendors of instruments and exercises.
- Tables of contents of more than 100 journals and newsletters and numerous reviews.
- Listserv discussion groups and Internet websites.

The editors examined hundreds of articles, books, instruments, exercises, and Internet resources. From the enormous amount of material found, we selected about sixty percent for inclusion in this book. As such, these resources provide a relevant core, not an exhaustive list, of materials available.

Criteria for Selection

Annotations of each resource are descriptive rather than evaluative. However, an element of evaluation may be assumed as each item must meet certain criteria to be included in the book. Some criteria apply more to some sections than others. To be selected, items must:

- Be explicitly related to leadership theory or practice or be implicitly related to leadership learning.
- Have a sound conceptual base and accurately reflect the concept that it claims to teach.
- Be clearly and interestingly presented.
- Conform to one of the book's subject headings.
- Include appropriate support materials for facilitators.
- Be easily available.

New Materials

Materials that appeared in previous editions but are still referenced and widely used remain in this edition. However, about one-third of the book is new. Dated items have been removed and replaced with more current information. The *New* tag above a title identifies an item that is new to this edition.

Changes in This Edition

When planning each edition, we survey readers to learn what changes could improve the book's usefulness. Based on readers' recommendations, there is no longer a directory of Resource Persons. This section too often duplicated information found in *Leadership Education: A Source Book of Courses and Programs* as well as in such books as the *ASTD Buyer's Guide and Consultant Directory.* Added to the book is an annotated list of core journals and newsletters. We also included more material on hot topics such as multicultural diversity, service learning, coaching, 360-degree feedback, spirit, and learning.

The editors invite your suggestions for improving the next edition. We are especially interested in short film clips that illustrate a leadership lesson. Please send recommendations for format changes or favorite resources to:

Mary Schwartz, Editor/Librarian
Center for Creative Leadership
One Leadership Place
Post Office Box 26300
Greensboro, NC 27438-6300
Phone: (336) 286-4086
Fax: (336) 286-4087
E-mail: schwartzm@leaders.ccl.org

BIBLIOGRAPHY

The annotations in this section describe textbooks, research reports, conference proceedings, essays, program models, debates of existing theory or introduction of new theory, training materials, fiction, biographies, and self-development tools. The annotations are organized by subject headings, then by the first author's last name using American Psychological Association-style citations.

The materials on diversity and leadership research have expanded since the last edition and have been reclassified.

Diversity materials are organized as:
• General
• Multicultural and Global
• Gender
• Ethnic

The materials on leadership research are organized as:
• General (overviews of the field of leadership research).
• Theories and Models – Traits and Behaviors (discussions of the Great Man theory, traits, competence, or intelligence.
• Theories and Models – Situational and Positional (discussions of situational or contingency theories, differences between leaders and managers, substitutes for leadership, or the emergence of leadership).
• Theories and Models – Relational (discussions of the leader-member exchange, path-goal theory, transformational leadership, charisma, influence, power, the dark side of leadership, and other relationship theories).
• Development of Leadership (research items about development processes, selection, succession, derailment, diversity, and assessment).
• Trends and New Frameworks (research items about global and intercultural leadership, call to leadership, spirit, or strategic leadership).

See the Contents below for an outline of subject headings or use the Index for a more detailed guide to subjects and authors.

CONTENTS

GENERAL LEADERSHIP

New

Alvesson, M. (1996). **Leadership studies: From procedure and abstraction to reflexivity and situation.** *Leadership Quarterly, 7*(4), 455-485.

Conventional approaches to leadership research have used positivistic methods, often quantitative and hypothesis-based, that emphasize objectivity and procedure. Alvesson believes that these methods are so removed from everyday life that they are of little use, and criticizes mainstream research and its search for "objective reality." He advocates using a reflexive, situational approach that recognizes the biases of the researcher and opens up new ways of understanding. This style, according to the article, is more appropriate for studying something as subjective as leadership.

New

Association of Leadership Educators. (1997). *Leaders in leadership education: Proceedings of the annual conference.* Columbus, OH: Author. Available from ALE, c/o Larry Wilson, University of Illinois, 2320 West Peterson Avenue, Suite 200, Chicago, IL 60659. Phone: (773) 761-5099. Fax: (773) 761-6955. E-mail: wilson@idea.ag.uiuc.edu

This book contains the proceedings from the Association of Leadership Educators (ALE) 1997 annual conference. The 25 speeches and workshop descriptions include "Developing Leadership with Multi-National Audiences," "Growing Our Own Future Leaders: A Case Study in Texas Leadership Training," "Mastering Leadership from a Distance: A Revolutionary Doctoral Program from the University of Phoenix," "Community Team Leadership: A Systems Approach to Sustainable Community Development," and "Leadership Attaining Strategies: A Dramatistic Taxonomy." The articles contain, variously, appendices, inventories, and bibliographical references. There is also a section summarizing the conference roundtable discussions.

Astin, A. W. (1993). *What matters in college? Four critical years revisited.* San Francisco: Jossey-Bass.

Written for faculty and student-affairs professionals, this book presents a study of the impact of college on students. In 1985, data were collected from 300 four-year institutions and their 27,000 incoming freshmen. Four years later, 4,000 of those students responded to a survey to determine their changed cognitive abilities, self-concepts, and behaviors. Leadership opportunities and growth in leadership skills were among the college-environment and student-involvement measures on the survey. Includes bibliographical references and index.

Barnard, C. (1968). *The functions of an executive: Thirtieth anniversary edition.* Boston: Harvard University Press.

This is a path-breaking book on the analysis of business organizations and the functions of the executives in them. Barnard presents his theory of cooperative behavior in the formal and informal organization. He takes that which has been developed at the level of theory and abstraction and puts it in the perspective of the practicing executive.

Bass, B. M. (1990). *Bass and Stogdill's handbook of leadership: Theory, research, and managerial applications* (3rd ed.). New York: Free Press.

Intended for students of leadership, this edition of the handbook covers a broad range of leadership definitions, concepts, and theories. Shifts in the content and method of leadership studies resulted in new chapters on executive studies, leader-follower relations, and women in leadership. Also featured are chapters on personal traits, charisma, intellect, and political tactics. Seventy-five hundred references include some unpublished reports that offer fresh ideas. Includes bibliographical references, a glossary of terms, and author and subject indexes.

Bennis, W. (1993). *An invented life: Reflections on leadership and change.* New York: Addison-Wesley.

In his autobiographical first chapter, Bennis reflects on leadership lessons learned from his older brothers, his World War II post as a 19-year-old infantry commander, and shoe polish. Personal stories in each chapter illustrate how to invent a rewarding career and a fulfilling life by learning to lead. Old and new essays on ethics, change, group behavior, and democracy provide a historical perspective on the character of leadership. New essays provide a vision of future challenges. In his foreword, Tom Peters calls Bennis the "guru of modern management." Includes bibliographical references and index.

New

Bennis, W. (1997). *Managing people is like herding cats.* Provo, UT: Executive Excellence Publishing.

Bennis says that cats, like people, "won't allow themselves to be herded. They may, however, be coaxed, cajoled, persuaded, adored, and gently led." Bennis applies these principles in the three sections of this book, which address the leadership crisis, what makes a leader, and leading change. The book's chapters originally appeared as articles in *Executive Excellence*, and include such titles as "Leadership Pornography and Optional Ethics," "Four Competencies of Great Leaders," "Ten

Traits of Dynamic Leaders," "Dealing with the Way Things Are," and "Winning and Losing." Includes index.

Bennis, W. G. (1994). *On becoming a leader* (2nd ed.). Reading, MA: Addison-Wesley.

From the author of *Why Leaders Can't Lead*, this report examines the dynamics and difficulties in becoming a leader. Bennis presents the idea that every person has the capacity for leadership. Discussions with leaders in politics, business, and the arts include such topics as knowing oneself, knowing the world, moving through chaos, and creating change. Includes a bibliography and index.

Bolman, L. G., & Deal, T. E. (1991). **Leadership and management effectiveness: A multi-frame multi-sector analysis.** *Human Resource Management, 30*(4), 509-534.

Four perspectives of organizational leadership are defined as structural, human resource, political, and symbolic frames. A qualitative study, using narrative reports written by managers about critical incidents, analyzes their use of the four frames. A quantitative study, using the instrument *Leadership Orientations*, measures managers' use of the four frames. Gender differences in frame orientation and effectiveness are also reported.

Boone, L. E., & Bowen, D. D. (1987). *The great writings in management and organizational behavior* (2nd ed.). New York: Random House.

An anthology of seminal essays written by individuals whose works have become the cornerstones for contemporary management and organizational theory. From pioneers Weber, Fayol, and Follet, to second-generation contributors Mayo, Barnard, and Maslow, the text is chronological and gives the reader a historical point of reference. Part three, "The Paradigm Creators," includes McGregor's "The Human Side of Enterprise," "One More Time: How Do You Motivate Employees" by Herzberg, and Likert's "An Integrating Principle and an Overview." The final section, "Major Current Contributions," includes essays by McClelland, Vroom, and Schein. Includes indexes.

Burns, J. M. (1978). *Leadership.* New York: Harper & Row.

The "dynamic reciprocity" theme is presented in a highly readable volume of leadership analysis. History, biographies, and a sociopsychological approach combine to provide a highly innovative study of the elements of leadership. Teaching and learning leadership are discussed in narrative format. This book could well be used as a follow-up text to the study of leadership theory. Includes bibliographical references and index.

Clark, K. E., & Clark, M. B. (Eds.). (1990). *Measures of leadership.* West Orange, NJ: Leadership Library of America.

This is an introduction to a wide variety of measures of leadership, with detailed information on their characteristics and their validity. The book includes 29 research reports from well-known contributors to the study of leadership; they describe leaders' abilities, personalities, and behaviors. Included are an introduction that summarizes and interprets the findings and a report of the proceedings of the conference on which the book is based. Includes bibliographical references and index.

Clark, K. E., & Clark, M. B. (1996). *Choosing to lead* (2nd ed.). Greensboro, NC: Center for Creative Leadership.

Those who aspire to lead must be aware of the responsibilities involved and must make a conscious decision to commit. The Clarks call this "choosing to lead." The key is to identify and develop leaders who will choose to be dedicated. The authors review 15 years of theory and research to support this premise. They analyze existing leadership programs and discuss the role of experience and cultural differences in leadership development. Includes bibliographical references and index.

Clark, K. E., Clark, M. B., & Campbell, D. P. (Eds.). (1992). *Impact of leadership.* Greensboro, NC: Center for Creative Leadership.

The impact of leadership was the subject of a 1991 conference sponsored by the Center for Creative Leadership. The 42 research papers in this book represent the range of discussion at that conference from the outcomes of good leadership to the ways of producing those effects. Other leadership impact issues include power, influence, authority, perceptions, stereotypes, customs, and expectations. Includes bibliographical references and index.

Cleveland, H. (1985). *The knowledge executive: Leadership in an information society.* New York: Dutton.

This book builds on the premise that more than half of all work now done in the United States is information work, and discusses the differences between information and other kinds of resources. Cleveland says that "tomorrow's leaders will be those with a taste for paradox, a talent for organizational ambiguity, and the capacity to hold new and dissimilar ideas comfortably in the managerial mind." Includes bibliographical references and index.

Conger, J. A. (1990). **The dark side of leadership.** *Organizational Dynamics, 19*(2), 44-55.

The same behaviors that distinguish leaders from managers can create negative outcomes. Conger examines three

skill areas that can contribute to negative outcomes:
1) strategic vision can fail when the vision reflects
personal rather than organizational needs, markets are
unrealistically assessed, or resources are miscalculated;
2) communication skills are misused when a leader is
manipulative, takes undue credit, or fails to recognize
others; 3) poor general management skills include
creating rivalries, creating dependency, absence from
operations, and autocratic leadership.

New
Crosby, P. B. (1996). *The absolutes of leadership.* San
Diego, CA: Pfeiffer.

Crosby shares the leadership insights he gained through
his experience in the military, as an executive, and as a
consultant of quality management. He believes that what
a leader is matters more than what a leader does. He
defines leadership as "deliberately causing people-driven
actions in a planned fashion for the purpose of accom-
plishing the leader's agenda." Citing historical and current
events, newsmakers, work scenarios, and cartoons,
Crosby illustrates how to know a leader when you see
one. This book is part of the Warren Bennis Executive
Briefing Series.

New
Culp, K., & Cox, K. J. (1997). **Leadership styles for the
new millennium: Creating new paradigms.** *Journal of
Leadership Studies 4*(1), 3-17.

This literature review provides an overview of both the
study of leadership and of the development of leadership
practices throughout history. The authors profile the
different ways scholars have defined leadership, explain
different theories of how leadership is developed, and
present a table of the evolution of leadership, from
Genghis Khan to Ronald Reagan. Also included is a table
showing the effects of time and environment on leadership styles. Seven leadership paradigms are then presented as alternative styles of leadership that may arise in
the next century: administrative, catalytic, collegial,
humanitarian/activist, innovative, religious, and visionary.
Includes references.

Cummings, L. L., & Staw, B. M. (Eds.). (1990). *Leadership, participation, and group behavior.* Greenwich, CT:
JAI Press.

This is a collection of articles on social behavior. One
reviews a decade of leadership literature. Another
discusses routinization of charisma with examples from
two charismatic leaders. Two address participation in
decision making and worker participation in management.
Yet another reports that researchers have used committee
meetings as tools for analysis; the authors suggest that the

committee meeting in itself is a topic worthy of study.
The final article examines basic concepts, assumptions,
and models of group effectiveness. The authors outline
current concepts of group technology, cohesiveness, and
norms and then offer new alternatives. Includes bibliographical references and index.

DeVries, D. L. (1993). *Executive selection: A look at what
we know and what we need to know.* Greensboro, NC:
Center for Creative Leadership.

In 1992, the Center for Creative Leadership brought
together researchers, human resource executives, executive recruiters, and practicing executives to discuss the
key issues around executive selection. This conference
report examines the realities of organizational performance that have led to the growing interest in this area.
Nine observations are explored in depth, relevant literature is surveyed, and recommendations are offered for
how executive selection can be improved. There are also
appendices that contain conference information, a
glossary, and key questions concerning the observations
and an extensive bibliography.

New
Drucker, P. F., Dyson, E., Handy, C., Saffo, P., & Senge,
P. M. (1997). **Looking ahead: Implications of the present.**
Harvard Business Review, 75(5), 18-32.

To commemorate the 75th anniversary of *Harvard
Business Review*, five noted business writers—Peter
Drucker, Esther Dyson, Charles Handy, Paul Saffo, and
Peter Senge—were asked to describe the problems and
challenges they see for executives in the next century.
Drucker discusses the demographic changes taking place
that will result in the "collective suicide" of the world's
developed nations and a rapid rise in the power of current
Third World countries. Dyson says that the Internet has
narrowed the boundaries of what can be held private and
shrunk the distance between a company and its employees
and customers. She says companies must learn to accept
and use the "involuntary feedback" the Internet allows.
Handy describes a model for a "citizen contract," in
which corporations are not considered the property of
stockholders but communities of common purpose. Saffo
addresses the need for new technology that not does not
simply produce more information, but helps us make
sense of it. Finally, Senge discusses the need to abandon
hierarchical leadership and develop a community of
leaders through research, capacity building, and practice.

Du Brin, A. J. (1995). *Leadership: Research, findings,
practice, and skills.* Boston: Houghton Mifflin.

This textbook is intended for use in undergraduate and
graduate leadership courses in business management or

public administration. It reviews basic leadership theories, emphasizes skill development, and suggests effective leadership practices. Each chapter includes self-assessments, case studies, skill-development exercises, and questions to initiate discussions.

New
Farson, R. E. (1996). *Management of the absurd: Paradoxes in leadership.* New York: Simon & Schuster.

Farson draws on his experience as a psychologist, naval officer, and CEO to examine the dilemmas faced every day by managers and leaders. Farson's long-time collaboration with famed psychologist, Carl Rogers, taught him that life is difficult, that human relations are complex, and that for every action there is an opposite reaction. He expects readers to be disturbed by the paradoxes here, but hopes that disagreement will lead to thought and discussion. The paradoxes include: effective managers are not in control; people we think need changing are pretty good the way they are; we learn not from our failures but from our successes; and individuals are very fragile.

New
Fitton, R. A. (Ed.). (1997). *Leadership: Quotations from the world's greatest motivators.* Boulder, CO: Westview Press.

Fitton has compiled memorable words spoken by leaders and about leadership. Statesmen, military leaders, executives, philosophers, and poets from ancient history through the present day are represented. For example, Napoleon Bonaparte said, "A leader is a dealer in hope." Quotations are arranged by subject and indexed by author for easy access. Subjects include: adversity, boldness, character, duty, humor, mistakes, physical presence, truth, and victory. This book is a handy reference for writers, researchers, speakers, or leaders who practice reflection.

New
Fulmer, R. M. (1997). **The evolving paradigm of leadership development.** *Organizational Dynamics, 25*(4), 59-72.

Fulmer states that leadership programs are moving away from "management training" on a university campus to customized "executive education" offered at schools, training centers, and at corporate facilities. He sees seven trends that will drive the future of leadership programs. Participants will grow from passive listeners to active learners. Development will evolve from one-time events to an ongoing process. The purpose of leadership development will change from knowledge to action. Study of cases and best practices will switch focus from past performance to the future. Those who plan, design, deliver, and select development programs will move from specialists in their field into partnerships that pool their

expertise. Trainers will concentrate on substance more than style. Finally, leadership development will move from "ivory tower to factory floor."

Gardner, J. W. (1990). *On leadership.* New York: Free Press.

John Gardner has put together his series of leadership papers with some additional material to produce a book that explores the multifaceted nature of leadership. The strength of the book is his ability to explicate this complexity while keeping the reader's attention with enlightening anecdotes and a studied optimism. Commenting on leadership development, Gardner states, "Fortunately, the development of leaders is possible on a scale far beyond anything we have ever attempted. . . . The reservoir of unused human talent and energy is vast, and learning to tap that reservoir more effectively is one of the exciting tasks ahead for mankind." Includes bibliographical references.

Glazer, J. W. (1995). **The call for leadership.** *Journal of Leadership Studies, 2*(4), 111-121.

Leadership educators commonly engage in dialogue and research. Glazer states that it's time to take the next step—action. The need for leadership is critical in today's society, and leadership educators and students are well positioned to create positive changes. Some ways to take action are: improve institutions of higher learning, identify community problems and suggest solutions, replace existing mental models of society's expectations with innovative models, and raise the moral consciousness of ourselves and others.

Hesselbein, F., Goldsmith, M., & Beckhard, R. (Eds.). (1996). *The leader of the future: New visions, strategies, and practices for the next era.* San Francisco: Jossey-Bass.

This is a collection of original essays written by the most recognized names in the field of leadership. Future visions of our schools, our jobs, and our society are described in works by: Peter Senge, "Leading Learning Organizations: The Bold, the Powerful, and the Invisible"; Stephen Covey, "Three Roles for the Leader in the New Paradigm"; James Kouzes and Barry Posner, "Seven Lessons for Leading the Voyage to the Future"; David Noer, "A Recipe for Glue"; and many others. The Drucker Foundation supported the creation of this book, which leads off with a foreword by Peter Drucker. Includes an index.

Hitt, W. D. (Ed.). (1992). *Thoughts on leadership: A treasury of quotations.* Columbus, OH: Battelle Press.

This anthology of quotations supports the theory that leaders are fully functioning persons. In a generic leadership model, 25 competencies are presented in five leadership dimensions: reasoning, coping, knowing, believing, and being. Ideas regarding creative thinking, excellence, integrity, knowing the organization, visioning, team building, valuing, responsibility, and courage are capsulized in the words of original authors. Quotations are indexed by author and by subject. Includes bibliographical references.

New
Hodgetts, R. M. (1996). **A conversation with Warren Bennis on leadership in the midst of downsizing.** *Organizational Dynamics, 25*(1), 72-78.

In this interview, presented in question-and-answer format, Hodgetts asks Bennis about downsizing, value-based leadership, and the timelessness of good leadership. Bennis believes the three biggest challenges facing organizations today are globalization, technology, and employee empowerment, but that downsizing is not the answer. He describes the negative effect downsizing has had on the workplace, and reiterates the need, stronger today than ever, for leaders to create an environment of trust and offer their followers a sense of meaning and vision.

Hodgkinson, C. (1983). *The philosophy of leadership.* New York: St. Martin's.

This work is a companion to Hodgkinson's *Towards a Philosophy of Administration* (1978). He argues that leadership is essentially a philosophical activity that must deal with values because they "impinge upon every phase of the administrative process." The relationship of administration and leadership is one of identity. Includes bibliography and index.

Hogan, R., Curphy, G., & Hogan, J. (1994). **What we know about leadership: Effectiveness and personality.** *American Psychologist, 49*(6), 493-504.

After reviewing current literature and contemporary definitions of leadership, the authors offer their own definition. "Leadership involves persuading other people to set aside for a period of time their individual concerns and to pursue a common goal that is important for the responsibilities and welfare of a group." An overview of the literature describing personality/leadership theories, what leaders do, teamwork, if leadership really matters, and how leaders are chosen helps lay people put the mosaic of leadership into context. A review of personality/leadership theories, forecasting, failure, and teamwork completes the picture.

Howell, J. P., Bowen, D. E., Dorfman, P. W., Kerr, S., & Podsakoff, P. M. (1990). **Substitutes for leadership: Effective alternatives to ineffective leadership.** *Organizational Dynamics, 19*(1), 21-38.

When a leadership problem occurs, is the source of the problem the leader or the situation? When a leader's traits and behavior don't fit a situation, the leader can be replaced, he or she can change the behaviors, or the situation can be changed. The authors suggest the alternatives of leadership substitutes. Group decision making and goal setting, peer review, consistent feedback, rewards, and intrinsic satisfaction motivate subordinates to self-manage effectively.

Hunt, J. G., & Larson, L. L. (Eds.). (1974). *Contingency approaches to leadership.* Carbondale, IL: Southern Illinois University Press.

In this second leadership symposium volume, 16 outstanding scholars in the field of administrative sciences review and discuss recent contingency approaches to leadership. It is extensively illustrated with tables, graphs, and sample scale items. Includes a bibliography.

Hunt, J. G., & Larson, L. L. (Eds.). (1979). *Crosscurrents in leadership.* Carbondale, IL: Southern Illinois University Press.

This book, the fifth volume in the Leadership Symposia Series originating in 1971, examines the variety of leadership approaches that are characteristic of the field today. This series covers the content of biennial symposia held at Southern Illinois University. The symposia were established to provide in-depth consideration of current and future leadership directions and to provide an interdisciplinary perspective for the scholarly study of leadership. Includes a bibliography and index.

Hunt, J. G., Sekaran, U., & Schriesheim, C. A. (Eds.). (1982). *Leadership: Beyond establishment views.* Carbondale, IL: Southern Illinois University Press.

This book is the sixth volume of the Leadership Symposia Series originating in 1971 and covering the content of biennial symposia held at Southern Illinois University. This volume joins the earlier ones in charting the state of the field. Includes bibliography and index.

New
Insch, G. S., Moore, J. E., & Murphy, L. D. (1997). **Content analysis in leadership research: Examples, procedures, and suggestions for future use.** *Leadership Quarterly, 8*(1), 1-25.

Content analysis, a method for analyzing contextual material, is not often used by organizational researchers.

This article gives a brief background to the method and summarizes leadership studies that have used it. The authors believe that the main strength of content analysis is its ability to combine quantitative and qualitative techniques. An 11-step process for using content analysis is also provided, which includes: identifying texts, generating a coding system, assessing reliability, and assessing construct validity.

Kellerman, B. (Ed.). (1984). *Leadership: Multidisciplinary perspectives.* Englewood Cliffs, NJ: Prentice Hall.

This book represents cooperative work in leadership studies. It provides a comprehensive range of perspectives on the interactions between those labeled leaders and those labeled followers. It serves as both an introduction to the subject and as a forum for related ideas that may be expected to stimulate more advanced discussion and study. The volume consists of a series of original essays by scholars from different disciplines, each considering leadership issues. Includes bibliographical references and index.

Kerr, S. (1977). **Substitutes for leadership: Some implications for organizational design.** *Organization and Administrative Sciences, 8*(1), 135-146.

Kerr utilizes a sociological perspective to establish the wide variety of characteristics (individual, task, and organizational) influencing leadership strategies.

Kets de Vries, M. F. R. (1993). *Leaders, fools, and impostors: Essays on the psychology of leadership.* San Francisco: Jossey-Bass.

From a psychoanalytic viewpoint, Kets de Vries offers a collection of essays on the leader-follower relationship. Beginning in childhood, we all seek leaders in life. When called upon to lead, we often fall into traps. Examples of successful and failed leaders in history, literature, the arts, and business help to define several leader types. Mirroring, narcissism, disengagement, and emotional illiteracy are among the leadership pitfalls to avoid. Includes bibliographical references and index.

Kouzes, J. M., & Posner, B. Z. (1995). *The leadership challenge: How to keep getting extraordinary things done in organizations* (2nd ed.). San Francisco: Jossey-Bass.

In this revision of the popular 1987 work, Kouzes and Posner continue to explore the practices and commitments of exemplary leaders. Chapters include: "Confronting the Status Quo," "Learning from Mistakes and Successes," "Inspiring a Shared Vision," "Sharing Power and Information," and "Building a Commitment to Action." The work is research-based, with data originating from the authors' collaborative leadership project begun in 1983

and resulting in the instrument, *The Leadership Practices Inventory.* Includes bibliographical references and index.

Krantz, J. (1990). **Lessons from the field: An essay on the crisis of leadership in contemporary organizations.** *Journal of Applied Behavioral Science, 26*(1), 49-64.

Krantz notes a shift from centralized leadership to a broader focus on the context of leadership. His article explores common themes in leadership and discusses three books in depth. Using systems thinking and psychodynamic theory, Krantz explains the effects of our change to a postindustrial society; the emergence of global competition; and a continuously changing, unstable environment. Effective leadership involves setting direction, providing vision, facilitating intergroup relations, and distributing authority to all levels of an organization.

Krantz, J., & Gilmore, T. N. (1990). **The splitting of leadership and management as a social defense.** *Human Relations, 43*(2), 183-204.

Organizations respond with social defenses to the challenges of a new society: mergers, acquisitions, cutbacks, downsizing, technology, global competition, increased complexity, and continuous change. One method of social defense is managerialism, or implementing the magic of technique as a tool for organization. Another defense is heroism, or assigning heroic qualities to one leader. Effective leadership combines creative, visionary, and mission-setting style with management skills.

New
Krause, D. G. (1995). *The art of war for executives.* New York: Perigree.

Twenty-five hundred years ago, a Chinese warlord collected the teachings of a military strategist named Sun Tzu. In this book, Krause applies a modern translation of those teachings to the business world, explaining that "today's battlefields are not physical places . . . today's battles occur within the minds of those who comprise the constituents of an organization." Sun Tzu's writings address subjects including planning, gathering intelligence, and maneuvering, and are based on his ten basic principles: learn to fight, show the way, do it right, know the facts, expect the worst, seize the day, burn the bridges, do it better, pull together, and keep them guessing.

Locke, E. A., Kirkpatrick, S., Wheeler, J. K., Schneider, J., Niles, K., Goldstein, H., Welsh, K., & Chah, D. (1991). *The essence of leadership: The four keys to leading successfully.* New York: Lexington Books.

Dealing with essentials rather than minute details, the authors present their leadership model. Drawn from a 1989 graduate seminar on leadership, the work begins by redefining leadership versus management, and transformational versus transactional leadership. The resulting model demonstrates how four key areas (motives and traits; knowledge, skills, and ability; vision; and implementation of vision) play key roles in effective leadership. Includes bibliographical references and index.

Lord, R. G., & Hall, R. J. (1992). **Contemporary views of leadership and individual differences.** *Leadership Quarterly: Special Issue: Individual Differences and Leadership: III, 3*(2), 137-157.

Previous articles on individual differences in leadership studies are summarized. Four themes emerge: creative problem solving, experience as a predictor, intelligence and leader effectiveness, and the social nature of leadership. Each of these themes holds implications for selection, training, and development of leaders. The authors conclude that mistakes have been made in previous work on leadership by the oversimplification of complex issues.

New
Maxwell, J. C. (1995). *Developing the leaders around you.* Nashville, TN: Thomas Nelson Publishers.

Maxwell states the "truly successful leaders who are in the top 1% . . . know that acquiring and keeping good people is a leader's most important task." He argues that the key to great leadership is developing the good people around you into leaders who will contribute to your vision. The material in this book is taken from his sermons and lectures at the Skyline Wesleyan Church in San Diego and INJOY, a leadership development institute. The chapters include: "The Leader's Toughest Challenge: Creating a Climate for Potential Leaders," "The Leader's Primary Responsibililty: Identifying Potential Leaders," and "The Leader's Greatest Joy: Coaching a Dream Team of Leaders."

McFarland, L. J., Senn, L. E., & Childress, J. R. (1993). *21st century leadership: Dialogues with 100 top leaders.* New York: Leadership Press.

In personal interviews, 100 CEOs, university presidents, authors, and journalists share their wisdom and their vision of the future of leadership. Warren Bennis, Distinguished Professor of Business Administration, USC, and John Sculley, Chairman and CEO of Apple Computer, Inc., share their insights in the book's foreword. The authors contribute this book as a gift to business schools, colleges, universities, community groups, libraries, and other educational institutions. Includes index.

McGregor, D. (1966). *Leadership and motivation: Essays.* Cambridge, MA: MIT.

This collection of essays by McGregor was edited and compiled by Warren Bennis, Edgar Schein, and Caroline McGregor. It covers the various periods in his career: Industrial Relations days at MIT, Antioch College presidency days, and then his return as Sloan Professor to MIT's Sloan School of Management. The essays reflect McGregor's ability to change an entire concept of organizational man and to replace it with a theory that stressed individual potential, emphasized personal growth, and elevated the employee's role in industrial society. Includes a bibliography.

New
Micklethwait, J., & Wooldridge, A. (1996). *The witch doctors: Making sense of the management gurus.* New York: Times Books.

Economist editor, Micklethwait, and writer, Wooldridge, contend that much management theory is driven by fear and greed. The motivational speakers, heavily hyped consultants, and business school professors who promote trite theories obscured in jargon are witch doctors. The authors examine recent management ideas of witch doctors and other theorists by asking three questions: Is it intelligible? Does it add more than common sense? Is it relevant? The result is an analysis of management fads and genuine management initiatives. Includes bibliographical references and index.

Mintzberg, H. (1975). **The manager's job: Folklore and fact.** *Harvard Business Review, 53*(4), 49-61.

The author examines common misconceptions, myths, and rumors that dominate average managers' concepts of their jobs. He bases his article on many recent studies and tries to define a set of usable and well-defined components for managers. The author feels managers play a complex, intertwined combination of interpersonal, informational, and decisional roles. He hopes to enable managers to better understand their jobs.

Morgan, G. (1988). *Riding the waves of change: Developing managerial competencies for a turbulent world.* San Francisco: Jossey-Bass.

Gareth Morgan argues that it is not enough to look at what organizations and managers are doing well; rather, it is critical to see how managerial skills can enhance one's ability to anticipate change. The competent manager needs to have one foot in tomorrow's business. He defines the ways managers can look for what is changing in new technologies, market conditions, management trends, and employees' values and expectations. Morgan sets out a program for cultivating a "proactive mindset" to managing. Includes bibliography and index.

New

Nahavandi, A. (1997). ***The art and science of leadership.*** Upper Saddle River, NJ: Prentice Hall.

This textbook presents a broad review of leadership not limited to business organizations. The author's basic assumption is that leadership can be learned, focusing this book on practical application. He looks at various definitions of leadership and effectiveness, the wave of organizational change in recent years, individual attributes, the link between power and leadership, contingency theories, and leadership training and development. Each chapter contains tables and models, discussion questions, and exercises. Includes bibliographical references and index.

National Forum Staff. (1991). **Leadership for a new millennium.** *National Forum, 71*(1), 2-32.

Articles in this special issue focus on contemporary issues in leadership: "Leadership for an Uncertain Century" by S. W. Morse; "Leadership for America's Third Century" by J. A. Joseph; "Leadership for a Shrinking Planet" by B. Kellerman; "Leadership: The Public and the Expert" by D. Yankelovich; "Learning Some Basic Truisms About Leadership" by W. Bennis; "A Single Voice: The Writer as Leader" by N. Cousins; "A New Look at Leadership Styles" by C. Desjardins and C. O. Brown; "Teaching and Assessing Leadership Styles" by R. Heifetz; "Future Leaders in Higher Education" by M. W. Tack. See the separate entry for "Leadership Education: A New Threshold" by R. L. Morrill and J. A. Roush.

New

Perreault, G. (1996). **Metaphors for leadership: Military battle and friendship.** *Journal of Leadership Studies, 3*(1), 49-63.

Perreault uses two metaphors to describe leader-follower dyads—military battle and friendship. Military battles evoke images of competition and blind obedience. In contrast, friendships evoke images of inspiration and interdependence. Perreault cites leadership literature that supports these metaphors and compares the leader-follower relationships, use of language, and bases of power. Includes bibliographical references.

Reckmeyer, W. (Ed.). (1995). ***Leadership readings.*** Stanford, CA: American Leadership Forum.

This volume includes the essays and writings of some of the world's foremost thinkers on leadership. Authors include Stephen Covey, *The Seven Habits of Highly Effective People* (1989); John Gardner, *On Leadership* (1990); Robert Greenleaf, *The Servant as Leader* (1990);

Barbara Kellerman, *Leadership for a Shrinking Planet* (1991); Deborah Tannen, *You Just Don't Understand* (1990); Peter Vaill, *Managing as a Performing Art* (1989); and Margaret Wheatley, *Leadership and the New Science* (1992). The collection also includes Martin Luther King's "I Have a Dream" speech (1963) and his "Letter from a Birmingham Jail" (1963).

Rosenbach, W. E., & Taylor, R. L. (Eds.). (1993). ***Contemporary issues in leadership*** (3rd ed.). Boulder, CO: Westview.

The purpose of this book is to describe the phenomenon of leadership and to identify what it is that makes a person an effective leader. Articles cover an interdisciplinary overview of the key issues in leadership at different organizational levels from a variety of perspectives. Includes bibliographical references.

Rustow, D. A. (1970). ***Philosophers and kings: Studies in leadership.*** New York: George Braziller.

Through essays on James, Mill, and Newton, as well as essays on more explicitly political leaders, this collection seeks to explore the phenomenon of leadership. The approaches vary from historical analyses of leaders and their times, to psychological analyses of leaders and their followers, to theoretical analyses of leadership demands inherent in certain political movements. There are also essays dealing with conceptual approaches to leadership.

Safire, W., & Safire, L. (Eds.). (1990). ***Leadership.*** New York: Simon & Schuster.

This is a collection of leadership quotations from ancient Greek and Chinese philosophers, former and current politicians, executives, and sports heroes. The editors suggest searching for the verb or action in each bit of wit and wisdom. Quotations are arranged by leadership traits such as excellence, intelligence, loyalty, and strength. Names of leaders quoted are indexed.

New

Shepard, I. S., Farmer, R. F., & Counts, G. E. (1997). **Leadership definitions and theorists: Do practitioners and professors agree?** *Journal of Leadership Studies, 4*(1), 26-45.

Countless definitions of leadership exist. The authors of this study identified 11 definitions, developed by Fielder, Zaleznik, Rost, Sergiovanni, Bennis, Burns, Nicoll, Hersey and Blanchard, Covey, and Bates, and then asked professors and practitioners of leadership programs whether or not they agreed with the definitions. Five tables present the results, but ultimately the authors concluded that no one definition has widespread support. The authors argue that developing an accepted definition of leadership within a school or organization is essential, or serious conflicts can emerge over hiring, policy development, and policy implementation. Includes references.

New
Shriberg, A., Lloyd, C., Shriberg, D. L., & Williamson, M. L. (1997). *Practicing leadership: Principles and applications.* New York: Wiley.

This textbook uses the metaphor of a journey to move students through the evolution of leadership theory. The technique of parable is woven throughout the text to illustrate the journey and leadership development of fictional college students. Each chapter employs a variety of teaching tools: book summaries, questions to spark discussion, cases, exercises, and biographical sketches of people who exemplify one leadership style. The subjects of globalism and diversity are integrated throughout the book to affirm their importance throughout all theories, attributes, and applications. Some chapters are: "Pre-Industrial Paradigms of Leadership," "The Disciplinary Roots of Leadership," "Modern Leadership Theories," and "The Hero's Journey: A New Leadership Model." Includes bibliographical references and index.

New
Sleeth, R. G., & Johnston, W. R. (1996). **The effective leader as a link between tasks and people.** *SAM Advanced Management Journal, 61*(2), 16-21.

Sleeth and Johnston have blended six different theories on leadership into their own Leadership Link Model (LLM). They argue that "people are the focus for skills and motivations, and tasks require tools and structure of activities." The job of a leader is to bridge the gap between people and tasks, and link the psychological and physical elements of work together. When managers practice effective "gap-filling," they allow both themselves and their employees to develop new skills and talents, according to the authors.

Sooklal, L. (1991). **The leader as a broker of dreams.** *Human Relations, 44*(8), 833-856.

Vision, or a leader's dream, develops in three stages. It begins as a personal vision, poorly articulated and tenuously connected to reality. It grows into a leader's dream, generating excitement and becoming more rational. Then it emanates excitement to the organization and society. A support system, inside and outside the organization, helps to produce, script, and implement the dream into a corporate entity.

Tannenbaum, R., & Schmidt, W. H. (1973). **How to choose a leadership pattern.** *Harvard Business Review, 51*(3), 162-175, 178-180.

This is a *Harvard Business Review* classic, reprinted from 15 years earlier. For this reprint the authors have added a commentary examining the nature of leadership from the perspective of the 1970s. They capture the main ideas involved in the question of how a manager should lead the organization.

Taylor, R. L., & Rosenbach, W. E. (1989). *Leadership: Challenges for today's managers.* New York: Nichols Publishing.

Composed of 22 articles written by nationally recognized authorities on management, this book is aimed at practicing managers "who are doing leadership or aspire to be leaders." John Gardner, Robert Kaplan, Peter Drucker, Bernard Bass, and others write about leadership. The purpose of the book is to stimulate thought and to help provide a framework for understanding the multifaceted nature of executive leadership.

Terry, R. W. (1993). *Authentic leadership: Courage in action.* San Francisco: Jossey-Bass.

Dichotomies of international peace and war are mirrored in our communities, schools, businesses, and families. Unprecedented crises are met by challenges and reforms. Within this framework of dichotomies, Terry uses diverse leadership theories to build a perspective of leading as a subset of action joined with authenticity. This principle incorporates courage, vision, ethics, and spirituality. Includes bibliographical references and index.

Timpe, A. D. (1987). *Leadership: Volume 3 in Facts on File's series: The art and science of business management.* New York: Facts on File.

This compendium provides access to a broad range of practical information, theory, and research associated with leadership ability and how to develop it. The variety of insights, experience, and concepts presented offer many useful approaches for human resource planning. The sources represented in this volume cover a wide range of professional publications, including a number not readily available to most executives. And, for those wanting a more expanded discussion on a particular component, the bibliography is a valuable resource. This book is organized into six sections, including: leadership—the effective traits; perceptions of power and authority; and leadership styles. Includes bibliography and index.

New
Tulgan, B. (1995). ***Managing Generation X: How to bring out the best in young talent.*** Santa Monica, CA: Merritt Publishing.

A Generation X'er himself, Tulgan interviewed over 100 up-and-coming workers born between 1963 and 1981 to find out if the "slacker" stereotypes are true, and to determine how mangers can best handle this new population of workers. Quotes from his subjects on issues such as technology, corporate culture, career security, and their best and worst managers fill the book. Tulgan shares a list of recommendations for managers who supervise X'ers. Includes index.

New
Ulmer, W. F. (1997). ***Inside view: A leader's observations on leadership.*** Greensboro, NC: Center for Creative Leadership.

Ulmer, a retired U.S. Army three-star general and former president of the Center for Creative Leadership, shares his insight on the subject of leadership. This book is a compilation of *Inside View* columns that Ulmer wrote for CCL's quarterly newsletter *Issues & Observations* and an adapted essay written for the Kellogg Leadership Studies Project. Ulmer addresses the difficulty of defining leadership, the differences between military officers and civilian leaders, current selection and promotion systems, assessment, change, and his passion—learning. Includes bibliographical references.

Vaill, P. B. (1989). ***Managing as a performing art: New ideas for a world of chaotic change.*** San Francisco: Jossey-Bass.

This publication is intended for practicing managers who want a fresh look at organizations and how to manage them. The book's two concurrent themes are introduced in the title. First "performing art" is Vaill's metaphor representing "dynamism, fluidity, extraordinary complexity and fundamental personalness of all organizational action." The second concept of "chaotic change" describes "a system of problems or instabilities," which Vaill sees in today's corporate environment. These two themes are brought together in a series of chapters meant to challenge and stimulate the reader to new levels of management innovation and effectiveness. Includes bibliography and index.

New
Wells, S. (1997). ***From sage to artisan: The nine roles of the value-driven leader.*** Palo Alto, CA: Davies-Black.

"Leadership opportunities are inevitably embedded in the context of management issues." Wells argues that no distinction should exist between managers and leaders,

and describes nine roles in which the leadership process intersects with the focused responsibilities of a manager—Sage, Visionary, Magician, Globalist, Mentor, Ally, Sovereign, Guide, and Artisan. Both a self-scoring role assessment and a free mail-in assessment are included with the book. The chapter on each role includes tables of ways to identify a person's role, tips for learning the skills of a specific role, and warning signs to indicate if you have gone overboard in a role. Includes bibliographical references and index.

New
White, R. P. (1997). **Seekers and scalers: The future leaders.** *Training & Development, 51*(1), 20-24.

White dismisses the idea that leadership can be learned by following a set of simple steps, arguing instead that leadership and innovation come from "difficult learning," or searching for knowledge without having a specific goal or "right answer" in mind. White says that children are the best role models for leaders because they are not afraid of difficult learning. He also offers a whimsical scale for assessing leadership and learning potential, with couch potatoes on the bottom, passengers in the middle, and explorers on top.

Wren, J. T. (Ed.). (1995). ***The leader's companion: Insights on leadership through the ages.*** New York: Free Press.

This is a collection of the principal works on leadership, which are assigned readings in the Foundations course at the Jepson School of Leadership Studies at the University of Richmond. Included are excerpts from the classic writings of James MacGregor Burns, Robert Greenleaf, Bernard Bass, Plato, Ann Morrison, Geerte Hofstede, John Gardner, Warren Bennis, and many others. Wren's selection and organization of these readings supports his premise that leadership is central to the human condition, that leadership is timeless and current—not a fad, and that leadership should be understood and practiced by all—not by a privileged few. Includes bibliographical references and index.

New
Zand, D. E. (1997). ***The leadership triad: Knowledge, trust, and power.*** New York: Oxford University Press.

Triadic leadership combines the forces of knowledge, trust, and power in equal measure. When properly exercised, triadic leadership is: having access to knowledge and putting it into action, giving loyalty and asking for commitment, understanding when to use power and when to give it away. Cases and charts throughout the book illustrate a variety of situations in which leaders may integrate the triad. Includes index.

RESEARCH

GENERAL

Dansereau, F., Yammarino, F. J., & Markham, S. E. (1995). **Leadership: The multiple-level approaches.** *Leadership Quarterly (Special Issue: Leadership: The Multiple-level Approaches [Part I]), 6*(2), 97-109.

This article introduces a series on classic and contemporary leadership theory in two special issues of *Leadership Quarterly (LQ)*. Part I, in *LQ 6*(2), includes essays on: the Ohio State approach, contingency, participative decision making, charismatic leadership, transformational leadership, and leader-member exchange. Part II, in *LQ 6*(3), contains essays on: information processing, substitutes for leadership, romance of leadership, self-leadership, multiple-linkage model, multilevel theory, and individualized leadership. The introduction compares the major theories to find various methods of analysis and various assumptions about leadership characteristics, situations, and relationships with followers.

New
Greenwood, R. G. (1996). **Leadership theory: A historical look at its evolution.** *Journal of Leadership Studies, 3*(1), 3-16.

This is a reprint of an article that appeared in the initial issue of *The Journal of Leadership Studies* (1993). Greenwood examines the historical evolution of leadership theories, searching for and not finding a unified definition of leadership. He cites the *Oxford English Dictionary* (1993), which traces the word "leader" to the 14th century and the word "leadership" to the 19th century. He discusses Frederick Taylor's *Shop Management* (1911), Henri Fayol's *Bulletin de la Société de l'industrie minérale* (1916), Mary Follet's *Creative Experience* (1924), Chester Barnard's *Functions of the Executive* (1938), and more current theorists. This journal issue is dedicated to the memory of Ronald G. Greenwood.

Hunt, J. G. (1991). *Leadership: A new synthesis.* Newbury Park, CA: Sage.

Hunt suggests a new synthesis, an expanded framework for scholarly study of leadership-knowledge content and orientation. His multiple-level leadership model includes studies from high levels of management down through organizations and across time. Hunt investigates varying concepts of leadership as reality and as perception, assumptions, definitions, purposes, and measurements. Includes bibliographical references and indexes.

Hunt, J. G., Baliga, B. R., Dachler, H. P., & Schriesheim, C. A. (1988). *Emerging leadership vistas.* Lexington, MA: Lexington Books.

This review of leadership research covers the various, and sometimes controversial, perspectives of researchers across the subject. The research examined here attempts to find answers to "What is meant by leadership?" Beginning in Part 1, the first four chapters examine the concept of charismatic leadership. The focus is on how this form of leadership shapes individual motivation and behavior. In Part 2, three chapters measure the activities of leadership within the organization. Examples are shown of how leadership runs deep within the functioning of the organization. Part 3 reviews the theories of leadership research. The concluding chapters look at some overlooked research plus new, emerging findings.

Jago, A. G. (1982). **Leadership: Perspectives in theory and research.** *Management Science, 28*(3), 315-336.

The author reviews prominent trends in leadership research and constructs a typology based on the themes in the research. He makes the point that existing research has covered only a part of the wide domain of leadership phenomena.

New
Kellogg Leadership Studies Project (1996, 1997). *KLSP working papers.* College Park, MD: KLSP. To order, contact the James MacGregor Burns Academy of Leadership, University of Maryland, College Park, MD 20742-7715. Phone: (301) 405-7920. Fax: (301) 405-6402. E-mail: kellogg@umdd.umd.edu.

The Kellogg Leadership Studies Project (KLSP) is an attempt to enrich the theory and practice of leadership through a four-year project funded by the W. K. Kellogg Foundation. Fifty leadership practitioners and scholars participate in focus groups to find intellectual breakthroughs and rid leadership studies of any existing superficial, "quick fix" elements. Working papers are available from the focus groups on leadership and followership, ethics and leadership, and transformational leadership. The citizen leadership group is preparing case studies of ten U.S. cities and regions that support collaborative citizen leadership. Another group is studying the purpose and recommended practices of leadership in the 21st century. The papers include bibliographical references.

New

Kenney, R. A., Schwartz-Kenney, B. M., & Blascovich, J. (1996). **Implicit leadership theories: Defining leaders described as worthy of influence.** *Personality and Social Psychology Bulletin, 22*(11), 1128-1143.

The authors report on three studies of followers' expectations for leaders worthy of influence (LWI). In the first two, participants were asked to rank order the influence-rendering traits and behaviors of appointed leaders (study 1) and elected leaders (study 2). Both study groups were asked to judge all of the traits and behaviors to determine if they are most often exhibited by appointed leaders, elected leaders, or equally by both kinds of leaders. The authors were surprised to find a wide difference between followers' influence expectations of appointed and elected leaders. The third study tested participants' cognition of LWI prototypes. Results indicated that follower expectations are based on memory, context, and labels assigned by others. The authors call for additional research to be done on followers' perceptions and expectations of leaders who are worthy of influence. Includes bibliographical references.

King, A. S. (1990). **Evolution of leadership theory.** *Vikalpa, 15*(2), 43-54.

King offers a model of evolutionary stages of leadership theory. Nine eras reflect specific themes, beginning with the early *Great Man* and *Trait* periods that make up the Personality Era. Leadership theory progresses through eras called Influence, Behavior Situation, Contingency, Transactional, Anti-leadership, Culture, and Transformational. King prescribes a future Integrative Era which adopts the most relevant concepts from the past to develop leaders who are visionary; take risks; exemplify the values, goals, and culture of their organizations; think strategically; energize people into action; and develop followers into leaders.

Klenke, K. (1993-1994). **Meta-analytic studies of leadership: Added insights or paradoxes?** *Current Psychology, 12*(4), 326-343.

A literature search yielded 14 meta-analytic studies in three areas of leadership: theories, small groups, and gender differences. Klenke points out that various research techniques, criteria, coding, and moderators cause inconsistent results, suggesting that meta-analysis be conducted on the large body of research of leadership practices and behaviors to establish a sound methodology.

Knoop, R. (1994). **A model of universal leadership based on psychological type.** *Journal of Social Behavior and Personality, 9*(1), 43-62.

The Jungian theory of personality types and universal theories of two-dimensional leadership style are merged to form a new model. Knoop illustrates the expectations for thinking-, feeling-, sensing-, and intuitive-type leaders in task-oriented or people-oriented situations.

New

Northouse, P. G. (1997). *Leadership: Theory and practice.* Thousand Oaks, CA: Sage.

This textbook is intended for students in graduate and advanced undergraduate leadership courses in business, communication, political science, and health services. It is divided into sections that describe leadership theories and their relative merits. Each section provides case studies, a bibliography, an instrument, and suggestions for applying each theory to practice. Sections and their accompanying instruments are: the trait approach with the *Leadership Trait Questionnaire (LTQ)*; the style approach with the *Style Questionnaire*; the situational approach with *Situational Leadership: A Brief Questionnaire*; contingency theory with the *Least Preferred Co-worker (LPC) Measure*; path-goal theory with the *Path-Goal Leadership Questionnaire*; leader-member exchange theory with the *LMX 7 Questionnaire*; transformational leadership with the *Multifactor Leadership Questionnaire Form 6S*; team leadership theory with the *Team Effectiveness Questionnaire*; the psychodynamic approach with the *Psychodynamic Styles Checklist*; and women and leadership with the *Attitudes Toward Women as Managers (ATWAM) Scale*. Includes bibliographical references and indexes.

Pfeiffer, J. W. (Ed.). (1991). *Theories and models in applied behavioral science.* San Diego, CA: Pfeiffer.

This four-volume reference tool is available in hardbound or loose-leaf format. Theories and models used in applied behavioral science, social science, human resource development, industrial/organizational psychology, training, and consulting are organized by their application to individuals, groups, leadership, or organizations. The third volume focuses on leadership issues, including conflict resolution, gender-related politics, organizational power, situational leadership, total quality management, goal analysis, coaching, and influence. Reproducible visual aids are included throughout. Includes bibliographical references and index.

Podsakoff, P. M., MacKenzie, S. B., Ahearne, M., & Bommer, W. H. (1995). **Searching for a needle in a haystack: Trying to identify the illusive moderators of leadership behaviors.** *Yearly Review of Management: A Special Issue of the Journal of Management, 21*(3), 423-470.

The authors review 25 years of leadership theory, specifically path-goal and substitutes-for-leadership theories. They identify many moderators of leadership behavior including subordinate characteristics, supervisor traits, tasks, role perceptions, and organizational characteristics. They also analyze research methods, the percentage of moderators actually identified, and the nature of the moderating effects. Little support to validate a large amount of the research was found.

New
Rejai, M., & Phillips, K. (1997). *Leaders and leadership: An appraisal of research and theory.* Westport, CT: Praeger.

This book briefly reviews leadership theories over time, including those that identify leadership skills, types of leaders, and functions of leadership. The authors recommend areas for future leadership research: gender issues, minority and Third World leadership, crisis leadership, and the tenure of leaders. Includes bibliographical references and index.

New
Sivasubramaniam, N., Kroeck, K. G., & Lowe, K. B. (1997). **In the eye of the beholder: A new approach to studying folk theories of leadership.** *Journal of Leadership Studies, 4*(2), 27-41.

This case study uncovers the folk theory of leadership, which is the popular press or general public's view of leadership constructed from personal experience. Participants at a university leadership training program answered a questionnaire before the program to survey their beliefs about leadership. In this three-part survey, attendees were asked to identify words and phrases relating to leadership, to rate those words, and to provide personal information. The findings suggest that individuals have different construct systems for receiving and categorizing leadership information. Common folk-theory constructs are: task master, insightful expert, value-centered individual, and visionary.

Yammarino, F. J., & Bass, B. M. (1991). **Person and situation views of leadership: A multiple levels of analysis approach.** *Leadership Quarterly, 2*(2), 121-139.

Yammarino and Bass present a multiple-levels-of-analysis approach to integrate the vast literature on leadership. Theories and models are categorized broadly as person, situation, or person-situation. Charts illustrate how theories affect the views of individuals, views between individuals, and views between or within groups or collectives. Implications for research and practice are discussed.

Yukl, G. (1989). **Managerial leadership: A review of theory and research.** *Journal of Management, 15*(2), 251-289.

This article is a review and evaluation of leadership theories and research findings. Major topics and controversies are: leadership versus management, leader traits and skills, leader behavior and activities, leader power and influence, situational determinants of leader behavior, situational-moderator variables, transformational leadership, importance of leadership for organizational effectiveness, and leadership as an attributional process. A notable emerging concept is leadership as a shared process.

THEORIES AND MODELS – TRAITS AND BEHAVIORS

Ashour, A. S., & Johns, G. (1983). **Leader influence through operant principles: A theoretical and methodological framework.** *Human Relations, 36*(7), 603-626.

Literature on learning and leadership is reviewed. This article discusses a leader's influence on subordinate motivation and behavior acquisition. Operant theory is used to explain leader influence. Suggestions for research in leader reinforcement are discussed.

New
Chemers, M. M. (1997). *An integrative theory of leadership.* Mahwah, NJ: Lawrence Erlbaum Associates.

In this book, Chemers attempts to review the literature on leadership and integrate and reconcile the existing theories and the empirical findings. He addresses transactional and exchange theories, the contingency model, and transformational leadership, and includes chapters on the influence of culture on leadership processes and women in leadership. Includes bibliographical references and indexes.

New
Neck, C. P., & Milliman, J. F. (1994). **Thought self-leadership: Finding spiritual fulfillment in organizational life.** *Journal of Managerial Psychology, 9*(6), 9-16.

Although spirituality is rarely discussed in business, the authors says that "work is intended to be one of the most profound ways of experiencing the divine presence in the world." This article defines what spirituality means in a corporate context and how it positively affects job performance. The authors then describe the thought self-leadership theory, which proposes that workers can lead themselves by using specific cognitive strategies, including mental imagery and directed thought patterns. A strategy that uses this theory to enhance spirituality on the job is also offered. Includes bibliographical references.

Offermann, L. R., Kennedy, J. K., Jr., & Wirtz, P. W. (1994). **Implicit leadership theories: Content, structure, and generalizability.** *Leadership Quarterly, 5*(1) 43-58.

Implicit leadership theory is a term used to describe the perception shared by the general public regarding attributes of typical leaders. The authors examine the perceptions of male and female subjects when considering the leadership characteristics of leaders, effective leaders, and supervisors. They identified eight significant factors: sensitivity, dedication, tyranny, charisma, attractiveness, masculinity, intelligence, and strength. Gender perceptions were not significantly different.

Smoll, F. L., & Smith, R. E. (1989). **Leadership behaviors in sport: A theoretical model and research paradigm.** *Journal of Applied Social Psychology, 19*(18), 1522-1551.

The athletic environment is a natural setting for observational research because many psychological processes are involved. Learning, perception, attention, motivation, emotion, developmental processes, memory, problem solving, and social interaction can all be studied. A *Coaching Behavior Assessment System* has been designed for research between youth coaches and players. A model is offered to measure and define relationships between what coaches actually do, how these behaviors are perceived and recalled by players, and children's attitudinal responses to the total situation.

RESEARCH THEORIES AND MODELS – SITUATIONAL AND POSITIONAL

Blank, W., Weitzel, J. R., & Green, S. G. (1990). **A test of the situational leadership theory.** *Personnel Psychology, 43*(3), 579-597.

The authors challenge the validity of Hersey and Blanchard's situational leadership theory (SLT). At two universities, hall directors' leadership task behaviors and relationship behaviors are measured. Subordinate resident advisors' psychological maturity and job maturity are measured. When results are charted to determine leader effectiveness, SLT is not supported. Authors suggest future research and theory development.

Chemers, M. M., & Ayman, R. (Eds.). (1993). *Leadership theory and research: Perspectives and directions.* San Diego, CA: Academic Press.

This volume is a tribute to Fred Fiedler, in honor of his 40 years of research in the field of leadership. His contingency theory, regarding the interaction of leader qualities with situation, revolutionized the study of leadership. His associates pay tribute to Fiedler's emphasis on the future and his groundbreaking theories and models of integrated training, leader behavior, and leader intelligence. In this vein, contributors present their visions for future leadership research. Includes bibliographical references and index.

New
Fernandez, C. F., & Vecchio, R. P. (1997). **Situational leadership theory revisited: A test of an across-jobs perspective.** *Leadership Quarterly, 8*(1), 67-84.

Hersey and Blanchard's Situational Leadership Theory is based on the idea that leaders should use different levels of task and relationship behavior for different followers, depending on the followers' readiness/maturity levels. Though popular, the theory is backed by little empirical evidence. This study criticizes the readiness/maturity factor for being imprecise, and asks whether job level could be used as a measure instead when testing the validity of the theory within a university. The authors found that "supervisor monitoring and considerateness may be differentially related to outcome variables as a function of job level."

Fiedler, F. (1967). *A theory of leadership effectiveness.* New York: McGraw-Hill.

This book presents a theory of leadership effectiveness that takes account of the leader's personality as well as the situational factors in the leadership situation. This theory attempts to specify, in more precise terms, the conditions under which one leadership style or another will be more conducive to group effectiveness. The book summarizes the results of a 15-year program of research on leadership and a theory of leadership effectiveness, and integrates the findings. Includes bibliographical references and index.

Fiedler, F. E. (1971). **Validation and extension of the contingency model of leadership effectiveness: A review of empirical findings.** *Psychological Bulletin, 76*(2), 128-148.

This paper reviews studies that tested and extended the contingency model of leadership effectiveness. The model predicted a curvilinear relationship such that leaders with low least preferred co-worker (LPC) scores ("task-oriented") would perform more effectively in very favorable and unfavorable situations, while high LPC leaders ("relationship-oriented") would perform more effectively in situations intermediate in favorableness.

Fiedler, F. E. (1995). **Reflections by an accidental theorist.** *Leadership Quarterly, 6*(4), 453-461.

When asked to write an article on theory building, Fiedler decided not to do a philosophical essay or a meta-theory. Instead, he chose to share his personal experience with three theories in a 45-year career. His dissertation research, *The Critical Element in the Therapeutic Relationship* (1950), measures a therapist's expertise to determine the successful outcome of treatment. The *Contingency Model* (1964, 1967) measures the task- or relationship-motivation style of leadership most desired in different situations. The Cognitive Resource Theory (1986, 1987) identifies conditions that are conducive to leadership. Fiedler explains the messy process of wading through data, reformulating hypotheses, and bearing criticism. He concludes that theory building is a creative process and, therefore, a lengthy, painstaking, and sometimes painful experience that eventually makes a valuable contribution.

Graeff, C. L. (1983). **The situational leadership theory: A critical view.** *Academy of Management Review, 8*(2), 285-291.

Theoretical issues undermining the robustness of the situational leadership theory and the utility of its prescriptive model are discussed. More specifically, conceptual ambiguity associated with the mechanics of applying the concept of job-relevant maturity and other problems with the normative model are seen as seriously limiting its pragmatic utility. In addition, problems with the *Leader Effectiveness and Adaptability (LEAD)* instrument are identified and discussed.

Hersey, P., & Blanchard, K. (1996). **Revisiting the life-cycle theory of leadership development.** *Training & Development, 50*(1), 42-47.

A condensed version of a 1969 article introducing situational leadership theory is presented. At the same time, this article brings readers up-to-date with Hersey and Blanchard's recent commentary on the progress of leadership theorizing in the past 25 years.

Jackson, C. N. (1993). **On linking leadership theories.** *Journal of Management Education, 17*(1), 67-78.

Different styles of leadership require different amounts of structure initiated by a leader or substitutes for leadership. Autocratic and consultative styles require high leader initiation for inexperienced followers with low growth needs. Participative and delegative styles require less

leader initiation and more worker initiation. Jackson contends that a leader must identify how much structure is needed in order to encourage job satisfaction and growth among subordinates, and initiate only that much and no more.

Kerr, S., & Jermier, J. M. (1978). **Substitutes for leadership: Their meaning and measurement.** *Organizational Behavior and Human Performance, 22*(3), 375-403.

Current leadership theories and models are reviewed. This article stresses that some leadership styles can be effective, regardless of the situation. A number of substitutes for leadership can be found to give guidance and promote good feelings within an organization.

Norris, W. R., & Vecchio, R. P. (1992). **Situational leadership theory: A replication.** *Group & Organization Management, 17*(3), 331-342.

Recent research studies on Hersey and Blanchard's situational leadership theory have attempted to measure optimal supervision and follower maturity. Norris and Vecchio studied 91 nurses and their supervisors in a three-way interaction involving structuring, consideration, and maturity. Followers with low maturity required high task-supervision and low relationship-supervision. Followers with high maturity required low task- and low relationship-supervision.

Podsakoff, P. M., MacKenzie, S. B., & Fetter, R. (1993). **Substitutes for leadership and the management of professionals.** *Leadership Quarterly, 4*(1), 1-44.

Kerr and Jermier's substitutes-for-leadership model (1978; see above) is discussed and modified. Leader behaviors, leadership substitutes, and criterion variables were tested in professional and nonprofessional groups. Variance in employee attitudes, role perception, and employee performance indicates that the theoretical basis for a leadership-substitutes model needs additional refinement.

Smith, P. B., & Peterson, M. F. (1988). *Leadership, organizations, and culture: An event management model.* Newbury Park, CA: Sage.

The authors have designed their own research model to show that being able to read the culture of an organization is central in all types of leadership functions. With the expansion of multinational corporations, this ability has become increasingly crucial to corporate survival. Chapters 1 through 4 focus on a historical analysis of leadership research, beginning with studies in the 1940s, up to contemporary research. Chapters 5 through 7 present the authors' research model. Chapters 8 through 10 develop this model further by discussing its three-tiered perspective. The final chapter contrasts the authors' model with five other models analyzed in the book. Includes bibliographical references and index.

New
Widgery, R. N., & Tubbs, S. L. (1997). **Leadership and attitude change theory.** *Journal of Leadership Studies, 4*(2), 3-17.

This article explains the dynamics behind attitude change theory and its relevance to the persuasive practice of leadership in the workplace. Changing attitudes can help a manager communicate more effectively by increasing awareness of employees' perspectives. To explain attitude change theory, the author uses Heider's Balance Theory, which utilizes triangles to illustrate the algebraic product of task, supervisor, and employee. If the product is positive, the employee's attitude is balanced. If the product is negative, the employee's attitude is unbalanced. Guidelines are given for leaders who have to delegate unattractive tasks.

THEORIES AND MODELS – RELATIONAL

Aktouf, O. (1992). **Management and theories of organizations in the 1990s: Toward a critical radical humanism.** *Academy of Management Review, 17*(3), 407-431.

Theories developed over the past 20 years contribute to Aktouf's conclusion that a radical-humanistic position is the basis of successful management. This person-centered theory relies on developing an employee's desire to belong and encouraging the use of his or her intelligence. He recommends a neo-Marxist humanist ideology to foster creativity and productivity through the willing participation of all parties in a common endeavor.

Alvesson, M. (1992). **Leadership as social integrative action: A study of a computer consultancy company.** *Organization Studies, 13*(2), 185-209.

A case study of 35 managers and employees of a Swedish computer-consultancy company supports the concept of leadership as social integrative action. Corporate culture, values, norms, and symbolic guidelines reflect and are reflected by the company's leadership. Alvesson states this constitutes a professional-service "adhocracy," which ties employees closely to the company, influences projects through informal discussions, anchors values and principles, and strengthens the sense of community.

Bass, B. M. (1995). **Theory of transformational leadership redux.** *Leadership Quarterly, 6*(4), 463-478.

Bass recounts the birth and growth of transformational leadership theory beginning with his graduate-student

days cleaning the cages of laboratory rats. Ideas about behavior inspired many research projects that provided data for the theory presented in *Leadership and Performance Beyond Expectations* (1985). Bass credits early researchers and world-class leaders with creating the framework for his research. He regrets that much of the new leadership research is based on criticism of old theories rather than the creation of new theories.

New
Bass, B. M. (1998). *Transformational leadership: Industrial, military, and educational impact.* Mahwah, NJ: Lawrence Erlbaum.

Bass synthesizes research on transformational leadership to help the U.S. Army Research Institute develop a relevant military theory of leadership. He includes the findings from business, education, government, and health care organizations to create an overview of transformational leadership that inspires subordinate commitment, involvement, loyalty, and performance. Issues of importance to military leadership are: stress among followers; the contingencies of emergency, conflict, and crisis; organizational culture; gender differences; policy implications; predicting and developing leadership; and substitutes for leadership. Includes bibliographical references, author index, and subject index.

New
Blake, R. B., & McCanse, A. A. (1991). *Leadership dilemmas: Grid solutions.* Houston: Gulf.

This book updates the Grid tool introduced in Blake and Mouton's *The Managerial Grid* (Gulf, 1964). Using the terms *leadership* and *management* interchangeably, the Grid is a framework for plotting an individual's approaches to performing tasks and relating with other people. The five styles on the original grid are: impoverished management (low task, low relationship); country club management (low task, high relationship); authority compliance (high task, low relationship); middle of the road (mid-task, mid-relationship); and team management (high task, high relationship). Added to the grid in this edition are: paternalistic management (reward and punishment) and opportunistic management (what's in it for me?).

Conger, J., & Kanungo, R. (1994). **Charismatic leadership in organizations: Perceived behavioral attributes and their measurement.** *Journal of Organizational Behavior, 15*(5), 439-452.

This article reports on the development of a questionnaire intended to measure the perceived behavioral dimensions of the Conger and Kanungo charismatic leadership model (1987, 1988). Data were collected from 488 managers belonging to four organizations located in the U.S. and Canada. Analysis of the results and implications for future research and practice are discussed.

Dansereau, F. (1995). **A dyadic approach to leadership: Creating and nurturing this approach under fire.** *Leadership Quarterly, 6*(4), 479-490.

As a graduate student in the 1960s, Dansereau questioned why some individuals formed leadership relationships with some followers and not with others. The immense popularity of Martin Luther King, Jr., John F. Kennedy, and Robert Kennedy and their tragic assassinations put Dansereau's question into a personal context. Dansereau developed a theory to explain such differences in response, called *leadership dyads.* Following criticism and new development, Dansereau's most recent conclusion is that leaders who support their followers' self-worth have loyal followers while those who lead with impersonal attachment spawn anger and hatred.

Drath, W. H., & Palus, C. J. (1994). *Making common sense: Leadership as meaning-making in a community of practice.* Greensboro, NC: Center for Creative Leadership.

A common way of viewing leadership has been to see it as a process of social influence. In this report, the authors offer a new perspective—seeing it as a process in which people engaged in a common activity create shared knowledge and ways of knowing. Taking this perspective makes it possible to gain a new understanding of such concepts as influence, individual action, motivation, and the relationship between authority and leadership. The implications of this shift for the practice of leadership and leadership development are discussed. Includes bibliographical references.

Graen, G. B., & Uhl-Bien, M. (1995). **Relationship-based approach to leadership: Development of leader-member exchange (LMX) theory of leadership over 25 years: Applying a multi-level multi-domain perspective.** *Leadership Quarterly, 6*(2), 219-247.

LMX theory dictates that leaders exist only in relation to their followers. Without that relationship, leadership doesn't exist. The LMX theory has evolved from a vertical leader-follower dyad to an analysis of relationships in groups and networks. The authors discuss the development of this theory as a comprehensive approach to leadership study. They examine issues of measurement and dimension, and compare LMX, transformational, and transactional leadership theories.

Hollander, E. P. (1992). **Leadership, followership, self, and others.** *Leadership Quarterly: Special Issue: Individual Differences and Leadership: II, 3*(1), 43-54.

Rather than focus solely on leaders' attributes and effect on others, this paper focuses on followers' perceptions and expectations. Hollander refers to prior research and models to illustrate interpersonal relationships, mutual identification, bases of power, giving and taking credit for good and bad leadership behavior, and charisma. A perceptual/attributional perspective credits or blames the leader for group outcomes.

House, R. J., & Mitchell, T. R. (1974). **Path-goal theory of leadership.** *Journal of Contemporary Business, 3*(4), 81-94.

This article states that an integrated body of conjecture by students of leadership, referred to as the *path-goal theory of leadership*, is emerging. It attempts to describe the theoretical framework for understanding the effect of leadership behavior on subordinate satisfaction and motivation.

Hunt, J. G., Boal, K. B., & Sorenson, R. L. (1990). **Top management leadership: Inside the black box.** *Leadership Quarterly, 1*(1), 41-65.

Leadership models often use an input/throughput/output conceptualization, with the throughput demonstrated as a black box. This model looks inside the black box to determine matches between leader and subordinate prototypes. The authors recommend further research to support this model.

New
Jackson, S. E., & Ruderman, M. N. (Eds.). (1995). *Diversity in work teams: Research paradigms for a changing workplace.* Washington, DC: American Psychological Association.

The editors see a need for understanding diversity in work teams, based on two significant changes in the American workforce at the end of the 20th century. First, the face of the workforce is changing. Women and people of color represent a source of growth. At the same time, corporate globalization brings together colleagues from various cultures. The second change is a structural reorganization from hierarchical to flatter, more flexible organizations that rely on teamwork. In response to these changes, social scientists are seeking and substantiating new theories that integrate organizational demography, social identity, psychological distance, intergroup competition, and negotiation. The term *diversity* is used broadly to include demographic differences (gender, ethnicity, age), psychological differences (knowledge, values), and organizational differences (tenure, level). J. E. McGrath, J. L. Berdahl, and H. Arrow present a map of this concept and describe four theoretical approaches for understanding work team diversity. G. B. Northcraft, J. T. Polzer, M. A. Neale, and R. M. Kramer examine the interpersonal dynamics of multidisciplinary teams through social identity theory and the principles of negotiation. A. S. Tsui, K. R. Xin, and T. D. Egan study age, tenure, educational, and social differences between employees and their supervisors. D. J. Armstrong and P. Cole use social distance theory to analyze the difficulties that arise from geographically dispersed work teams. Includes bibliographical references and index.

Jung, D. I., Bass, B. M., & Sosik, J. J. (1995). **Bridging leadership and culture: A theoretical consideration of transformational leadership and collectivistic cultures.** *Journal of Leadership Studies, 2*(4), 3-18.

This paper reviews the four I's of transformational leadership: idealized influence (charisma), inspirational motivation, intellectual stimulation, and individualized consideration. These characteristics are considered in the context of collectivism, as in the cultures of Japan, China, or Israel, as opposed to the individualism predominant in American culture. Because collectivistic cultures have higher levels of group orientation and commitment to collective accomplishment, there appears to be a conceptual bridge between these cultures and transformational leadership. The authors present a theoretical intersection where the two concepts meet and recommend this as an area for future research.

New
Lipman-Blumen, J. (1996). *The connective edge: Leading in an interdependent world.* San Francisco: Jossey-Bass.

Today's leaders face two opposing forces, interdependence and diversity, that are making old forms of leadership obsolete. Lipman-Blumen proposes a new model of *connective leadership*, based on the idea that since physical and political boundaries no longer restrict us, connections between people are tightening. She identifies three types of connective leadership—direct, relational, and instrumental—and then applies her model to research on managers and executives, and to women in leadership positions. Includes bibliographical references and indexes.

Loye, D. (1977). *The leadership passion.* San Francisco: Jossey-Bass.

This book surveys 180 years of thought and research bearing on the relationships between ideology in the individual, social leadership, and management styles. Variables receiving major attention include liberalism-conservatism, risk taking, alienation, anomie, extremism, activism, Machiavellianism, locus of control, as well as

leader-follower, parent-child, and age-generational relationships. Findings support new models of ideological functioning. Includes bibliographical references and index.

New
Podsakoff, P. M., MacKenzie, S. B., & Bommer, W. H. (1996). **Transformational leader behaviors and substitutes for leadership as determinants of employee satisfaction, commitment, trust, and organizational citizenship behaviors.** *Journal of Management, 22*(2), 259-298.

In this study, data were collected on over 1,500 employees from different industries and job levels to determine whether a connection exists between two theories of leadership—the transformational leader theory and the "substitutes for leadership" theory. Extensive statistical analysis resulted in the authors' finding little support for the substitutes theory, but they advocate more research. Tables and graphic representations of the findings accompany the article.

Podsakoff, P. M., MacKenzie, S. B., Moorman, R. H., & Fetter, R. (1990). **Transformational leader behaviors and their effects on followers' trust in leader, satisfaction, and organizational citizenship behaviors.** *Leadership Quarterly, 1*(2), 107-142.

Over 900 petrochemical employees answered questionnaires about their superiors' six transformational leadership behaviors and one transactional leadership behavior. Superiors answered questionnaires about their employees' citizenship behaviors. Scales measured the direct and indirect effects of transformational behaviors on organizational citizenship. Results indicated that employee citizenship is mediated by followers' trust in their leader.

New
Schnake, M., Dumler, M. P., & Cochran, D. S. (1993). **The relationship between "traditional" leadership, "super" leadership, and organizational citizenship behavior.** *Group & Organization Management, 18*(3), 352-365.

This article describes the five behaviors of organizational citizenship behavior (OCB). They are: 1) altruism—an employee helping another employee voluntarily, 2) conscientiousness—doing more than is necessary, 3) sportsmanship—refraining from complaining or causing annoyances, 4) courtesy—keeping others informed, and 5) civic virtue—keeping oneself informed and participating responsibly in decisions and meetings. The authors report on a study of these five behaviors measured against traditional leadership and super leadership in one organization. Contrary to their expectations, the traditional leadership characteristics of initiating structure and consideration had higher correlation to OCB than did the super leadership characteristics of self-goal-setting, self-observation, and self-expectation.

Shamir, B., House, R. J., & Arthur, M. B. (1993). **The motivational effects of charismatic leadership: A self-concept based theory.** *Organization Science, 4*(4), 577-594.

The authors present a new theory of charismatic leadership based on the motivation of self-interest. A model depicts the organizational conditions and follower attributes that frame leader behaviors, effects on followers' self-concepts, effects on followers, and motivational mechanisms.

Sims, H. P., Jr., & Lorenzi, P. (1992). *The new leadership paradigm: Social learning and cognition in organizations.* Newbury Park, CA: Sage.

Using social learning and cognition (SLC), Sims and Lorenzi offer a new framework for dealing with the accelerated change in relationships between managers and employees. Admitting that there are no quick fixes, the authors offer SLC as a viable method to collect, organize, and present management concepts that are theoretically sound and eminently practical, because they come from both the academic and business communities. Includes bibliographical references and index.

Wofford, J. C., & Goodwin, V. L. (1994). **A cognitive interpretation of transactional and transformational leadership theories.** *Leadership Quarterly, 5*(2), 161-186.

A model is proposed to provide a framework for managers to determine the appropriate situations for implementing transformational or transactional leadership styles. Understanding follower expectations and needs for a vision, goals, intellectual stimulation, self-consideration, and rewards helps a leader to respond appropriately. Implications for further research are discussed.

Yammarino, F. J. (1995). **Dyadic leadership.** *Journal of Leadership Studies, 2*(4), 50-74.

Analysis of leadership literature examines the patterns of leader-follower agreement in three broad categories. Transformational, charismatic, and visionary theories are grouped as inspirational leadership. Transactional, exchange, contingent reward-and-punishment theories are grouped as instrumental leadership. Emergent, elected, and nonappointed theories are grouped as informal leadership. Yammarino proposes a multiple-level conceptualization of these three categories and dyads at various levels to integrate a framework for theories and models of dyadic leadership.

Yammarino, F. J., & Dubinsky, A. J. (1994). **Transformational leadership theory: Using levels of analysis to determine boundary conditions.** *Personnel Psychology, 47*(4), 787-811.

Sales personnel and their managers participated in a study to determine four dimensions of transformational leadership: charisma, inspiration, intellectual stimulation, and individualized consideration. Thirty-three managers and 105 salespeople responded to the *Multifactor Leadership Questionnaire* (Bass, 1990), reporting the perceived behaviors in superior/subordinate relationships. A within-and-between analysis led to the conclusion that transformational leadership theory holds more strongly at the individual level than at dyad, group, or cross levels.

DEVELOPMENT OF LEADERSHIP

New

Allred, B. B., Snow, C. C., & Miles, R. E. (1996). **Characteristics of managerial careers in the 21st century.** *The Academy of Management Executive, 10*(4), 17-27.

The authors conducted an analysis of organizational trends, a survey of managers in order to predict what managerial careers will be like in the next century. They begin by tracing the development of managerial positions within the hierarchical organizations that developed after World War II to the present-day model of managing in network organizations. They then predict that the dominant organizational model will soon shift to a cellular structure, in which "people will be responsible for managing themselves while collaborating with others." These predictions are based on three basic ideas of organizational studies: 1) organizational structure dictates core managerial competencies, 2) different organizational structures require a different mix of managerial competencies, and 3) organizational structure dictates how careers are managed. Includes bibliographical references.

Bryson, J., & Kelley, G. (1978). **A political perspective on leadership emergence, stability, and change in organizational networks.** *Academy of Management Review, 3*(4), 713-723.

A political approach to leadership in organizational networks is presented. From a review primarily of the political-science and public-administration literature, a theoretical perspective is developed suggesting individual, procedural, structural, and environmental variables affecting leadership emergence, stability, and change. A list of hypotheses describes much of the political dynamics of organizational leadership.

New
Csoka, L. S. (1997). ***Bridging the leadership gap.*** New York: Conference Board.

This is a Conference Board report on a study of 400 *Fortune* 1,000 companies and their leadership practices. Significant findings are: 1) only 8% rated their company's leadership capacity as excellent, 2) there is little emphasis on leadership development for frontline managers, 3) content and delivery of leadership training is outdated, and 4) team performance is the most frequently used measure of performance. The companies with the most favorable leadership ratings placed more emphasis on leadership at all levels and less on only senior managers.

New
Fitzgerald, C., & Kirby, L. K. (Eds.). (1997). ***Developing leaders: Research and applications in psychological type and leadership development: Integrating reality and vision, mind and heart.*** Palo Alto, CA: Davies-Black.

This edited book begins with an overview of the Myers-Briggs Type Indicator® (MBTI) for those not familiar with it. Mary McCaulley of the Center for Psychological Type explains the link between personality types and leadership development. John Fleenor and Ellen Van Velsor report on the Center for Creative Leadership's research of the MBTI's use with group performance and 360-degree feedback. Paul Roush reports on the U.S. Naval Academy's research using MBTI data to effect behavior changes. Fitzgerald and Kirby describe the methods for applying MBTI dynamics to leadership development. Other researchers and practitioners write about the application of the MBTI in simulations, feedback instruments, organizational change, and strategic planning. Includes bibliographical references and indexes.

New
Fleenor, J. W., McCauley, C. D., & Brutus, S. (1996). **Self-other rating agreement and leader effectiveness.** *Leadership Quarterly*, *7*(4), 487-506.

Multi-perspective rating instruments, which solicit information on an individual's performance from various sources, offer researchers the opportunity to compare the differences between self-ratings and the ratings of others. Past work created four categories for the levels of self-other agreement: over-estimators (who rated themselves higher than others rated them), under-estimators (who rated themselves lower than others rated them), in-agreement/good raters, and in-agreement/bad raters. In this study, the authors asked whether adding more categories allowed for a more detailed analysis of self/other ratings. They found that adding the two further distinctions of over-estimators/good and under-estimators/poor helped compare agreement groups more effectively.

New
Guastello, S. J. (1995). **Facilitative style, individual innovation, and emergent leadership in problem solving groups.** *Journal of Creative Behavior*, *29*(4), 225-239.

After reviewing recent literature, the authors determined that little research had been done on the leadership of creative groups. In this article they review what theories do exist on leading creative teams, and then describe their study, in which a group of university security officers were observed playing the Island Commission game, an exercise in teamwork. The research asked whether facilitative leadership style and individual creative contribution were related to emergent leadership in a leaderless situation. Analysis of the guards' interaction and their responses afterwards show that both factors were positively related to perceptions of leadership.

Kaplan, R. E., Drath, W. H., & Kofodimos, J. R. (1991). ***Beyond ambition: How driven managers can lead better and live better.*** San Francisco: Jossey-Bass.

The authors' research with senior executives reveals that leadership development is based more on personal growth than on behavioral change. Executives were analyzed by themselves, co-workers, current families, and original families to determine inner character. The authors explain the challenge of gaining self-awareness and how expansive character and elevated position can create executive-performance problems. Through stories of real people and three case studies, they describe how a process of character shift can result in more effective leadership and greater personal happiness. Includes bibliographical references and index.

Neider, L. L., & Schriesheim, C. A. (1988). **Making leadership effective: A three stage model.** *Journal of Management Development*, *7*(5), 10-20.

Building on existing leadership research, the authors introduce a three-phase diagnostic model of leadership effectiveness. The model is intended as a pragmatic and useful tool designed for practicing managers to assess and increase their effectiveness as leaders. Expectancy, path-goal theory, and transactional perspectives are used to illustrate the model.

New
Proehl, R. A., & Taylor, K. (1997). **Leadership, cognitive complexity, and gender.** *Leadership Journal: Women in Leadership—Sharing the Vision*, *1*(2), 39-48.

The authors combine two theories of adult development to create their own model of good leadership using gender as one factor. The first theory is introduced in R. Kegan (1982), *The Evolving Self: Problem and Process in Human Development,* Cambridge: Harvard University

Press. The second theory comes from J. Rosener (November/December 1990), "Ways Women Lead," *Harvard Business Review,* 119-125. In this theoretical work, Kegan's thoughts on complexity of mind are blended with more recent work on women's capacity for a relational-based approach to knowing. The authors ultimately believe that cognitive complexity, not gender, is the basis for good leadership. Includes bibliographical references.

New
Rohs, F. R., & Langone, C. A. (1997). **Increased accuracy in measuring leadership impacts.** *Journal of Leadership Studies, 4*(1), 150-158.

While instructional programs in leadership development are becoming more and more common, little research exists on how to measure the impact of these programs. This study surveyed Georgia community leaders before and after they completed a 12-week leadership development program to determine the best way to measure the impact of the experience. The results showed that a then/ posttest method was more effective than a traditional pretest/posttest model, because it accounted for the response shift that occurred as the subjects' understanding of leadership changed. Includes bibliographical references and tables of the results.

Ruderman, M. N., & Ohlott, P. J. (1990). *Traps and pitfalls in the judgment of executive potential.* Greensboro, NC: Center for Creative Leadership.

Ruderman and Ohlott report on the process of identifying high-potential employees. Organizations can profit from early identification by offering these employees enhanced developmental opportunities. Supervisors' personal values or employees' personal traits are among common biases that lead to misidentification. Suggested are objective criteria for identification, such as job-behavior categories, internal talent scouts, multiple data, and appropriate framing of screening questions. Includes a bibliography.

New
Walter, G. M. (1997). *Corporate practices in management development.* New York: Conference Board.

This is a Conference Board report of a survey and interviews conducted to determine the training and development practices in large organizations. Findings indicate that the future of management development will: link development efforts to organizational strategy, focus heavily on experience-based development, involve university-and-business partnerships, provide high-potential managers with risks as well as challenges,

institutionalize systems of management development, and invest in pre- and post-training efforts.

New
Wheelan, S. A., & Johnston, F. (1996). **The role of informal member leaders in a system containing formal leaders.** *Small Group Research*, 27(1), 33-55.

In this exploratory field study, researchers observed attendees at a group relations conference to examine the emergence of informal leaders in a temporary group that already has formal leaders. The Group Development Observation System was used to analyze the verbal interaction patterns of subjects. Earlier research found that informal leaders typically behaved as extensions of formal leaders, but Wheelan and Johnston found that when member leaders emerged they often acted in opposition to formal leaders.

TRENDS AND NEW FRAMEWORKS

New
Chen, C. C., & Van Velsor, E. (1996). **New directions for research and practice in diversity leadership.** *Leadership Quarterly: Special Issue: Leadership and Diversity (Part II), 7*(2), 285-302.

In this conclusion to the two-part special issue on Leadership and Diversity, Chen and Van Velsor examine the intersection between the two. First, they identify four areas for further study: the impact of social-group identities on organizations, the unconscious sociopsychological processes, the political aspects of leadership, and follower perspectives. Then they offer four leadership frameworks that can be further developed to address diversity: attribution theories of leadership and followership, theories of leadership prototypes, the leader-member exchange model, and the behavioral complexity model. Finally, practical implications are addressed, including how to understand the unique strengths and needs of diverse leaders and how to develop global leaders.

Gerstner, C. R., & Day, D. V. (1994). **Cross-cultural comparison of leadership prototypes.** *Leadership Quarterly*, 5(2), 121-134.

Graduate students from France, Germany, Honduras, India, Taiwan, China, Japan, and the U.S. participated in a sample survey to determine business leadership prototypes in their countries. The subjects rated 59 leader attributes including decisiveness, goal-orientation, education, and trust. Results indicate significant differences in leadership prototypes among cultures. No single attribute appeared in the top five lists of all countries. Determination rated high among the responses of Western students, and intelligence rated high among the responses of Eastern students.

New

Hausken, K., & Plumper, T. (1996). **Hegemonic decline and international leadership.** *Politics & Society, 24*(3), 273-295.

In the past few decades the world has changed faster than the theory on international political economy. Increased globalization, the decline of the U.S. as a coercive power, and the rise of the European Community and Japan have made past assumptions about hegemonic stability outdated. This article offers a new theory to explain how nations determine the appropriate means for producing international public goods in today's world order. Four possibilities emerge in this model: hegemonic leadership (which is becoming less common), voluntary joint leadership, coercive leadership, or a situation in which the public goods are not produced.

New

Lake, D. A. (1993). **Leadership, hegemony, and the international economy: Naked emperor or tattered monarch with potential?** *International Studies Quarterly, 37*(4), 459-489.

The theory of hegemonic stability has brought the link between international political structures and the international political economy to the attention of scholars, but has been widely criticized. Lake says that this theory is actually made up of two distinct theories: leadership theory, which focuses on public goods and international stability, and hegemony theory, which examines the policy preferences of states within an economic system. While attempting to build and expand on this now out-of-favor theory, Lake also calls for more empirical research to test hegemonic stability and its components.

New

Leavy, B. (1996). **On studying leadership in the strategy field.** *Leadership Quarterly, 7*(4), 435-454.

Is a strategy a plan or a past pattern of action? Leavy argues that it is both, a mixture of intended and emergent processes, in which leadership is constantly changing with time and context. This article offers a three-part conceptual framework for viewing strategic leadership: the situational leadership challenge; the leader's personal ability and convictions; and the symbolism, image, and credibility inherent in the leader's role. These three factors determine an individual's leadership capacity, which will decide a group's performance and strategic impact over time. Political and business leaders, from Margaret Thatcher to Anita Roddick, founder of The Body Shop, are used to illustrate the framework.

New

Luke, J. S. (1998). *Catalytic leadership: Strategies for an interconnected world.* San Francisco: Jossey-Bass.

In today's complex world, an effective public leader is not a hierarchical authority figure, but an individual who can bring together "diverse individuals from multiple agencies to address interconnected public problems and work together towards solutions." Luke develops a framework for this new style of leadership, dividing his book into three sections—challenges facing leaders, the catalytic tasks of public leaders, and foundational skills for public leaders. An appendix offers advice on establishing criteria based on desired outcomes, which Luke says reduces political bargaining and improves group decision making. Includes bibliographical references and index.

New

Reed, T. K. (1997). **Leadership to match a new era: Democratizing society through emancipatory learning.** *Journal of Leadership Studies, 4*(1), 58-77.

Changes in American society are transforming the qualities that make an effective leader. In this article Reed first describes seven of these changes, including the rise of the information age, an increased awareness of diversity, growing ecological concerns, and changing demographics. She then outlines a transformational-learning model of leadership, in which leaders create "learning collaboratories" with their followers where team members learn about themselves. An appendix lists the four stages of transformational learning: 1) beliefs are unveiled and come into conflict with others' beliefs, 2) discomfort arises from this conflict, 3) old ways of thinking are released and new insights are developed, and 4) the learners accept themselves and their new insights. Includes bibliographical references and four graphic figures that illustrate this learning process.

Wheatley, M. J. (1992). *Leadership and the new science: Learning about organization from an orderly universe.* San Francisco: Berrett-Koehler.

How does "new science"—revolutionary discoveries in quantum physics, chaos theory, and molecular biology—affect the fundamental issues of organizing work, people, and life? Wheatley suggests we tear down 17th-century Newtonian thinking about our universe and adopt new perspectives from our natural world. A new perspective can help to find order in a chaotic world; differentiate order from control; create more participative, open, and adaptive organizations; and reconcile individual autonomy and organizational control. Includes bibliographical references and index.

GLOBAL AND SOCIAL ISSUES

New

Aburdene, P., & Naisbitt, J. (1992). *Megatrends for women.* New York: Villard.

Aburdene and Naisbitt focus their predictions for the future on the increasing power that women exercise in politics, sports, business, religion, health care, and social activism. There will not be a reversal from patriarchy to matriarchy and an oppression of men. Rather, there will be a partnership—a sharing of power and expression of full potential. A lengthy chapter describes women in the workplace of the future, their opportunities, leadership style, and ability to balance work and family. Leadership traits that will thrust women ahead are: strategic risk-taking, consensus building, creativity, flexibility, facilitation, and welcoming change. Includes bibliographical references and index.

Albaum, G., Murphy, B. D., & Strandskov, J. (1990). **A note on cross-cultural perceptions of influence of leadership groups.** *Journal of Managerial Issues, 2*(3), 337-344.

University students from the U.S., Denmark, and New Zealand were surveyed about the level of influence among nine different leadership groups. U.S. students perceived feminists as actually having the greatest influence and as being the preferred group to have influence. Students from New Zealand perceived the military as having the greatest influence and feminists as their preferred group. Danish students perceived religion as the group with actual influence and also their preferred group.

New

Ali, A. J. (1996). **Organizational development in the Arab world.** *Journal of Management Development, 15*(5), 4-21.

Ali is guest editor of this special issue on management development in the Middle East. His article analyzes the various Islamic schools of thought on such OD applications as: change, self-development, training, and conflict. Other articles in this special issue are: A. Reichel, "Management Development in Israel: Current and Future Challenges"; H. S. Atiyyah, "Expatriate Acculturation in Arab Gulf Countries"; D. M. Hunt and M. I. At-Twaijri, "Values and the Saudi Manager: An Empirical Investigation"; and A. Al-Meer, "A Comparison of the Need Importance Structure Between Saudis and Westerners: An Exploratory Study."

New

Barnett, J. H., Weathersby, R., & Aram, J. (1995). **Shedding cowboy ways for global thinking.** *Business Forum, 20*(1&2), 9-13.

"Cowboy ways" is a term used to reflect the nationalistic mind-set of many American executives. Executives' attitudes of individualism, simplicity, and superiority may be circumventing their efforts to globalize American businesses. To break cultural barriers, the authors recommend a new mind-set: Change from an individual to a systemic viewpoint. Move from simplistic, short-term goals to more complex, multidimensional strategies. Learn to understand and appreciate cultural values outside one's national boundaries.

Baumol, W. J., Blackman, S. A. B., & Wolff, E. N. (1989). *Productivity and American leadership: The long view.* Cambridge, MA: MIT.

Is the United States really the leaderless, lackluster, unproductive society it has often been made out to be? The authors take a second look at the numbers and courageously proclaim American productivity is alive and well. When taking a long view of things—ignoring short-term blips of greater concern to politicians and macro-economists—the United States compares favorably to other industrialized nations. The authors explore the impacts of international convergence, our change to an information society, education, and natural resources on productivity. New "yardsticks" are offered for measuring future economic growth and productivity. Includes bibliographical references and index.

Bennis, W. (1991). **Managing the dream: Leadership in the 21st century.** *Antioch Review, 49*(1), 22-28.

Transnational challenges, the opening of the European Common Market, the power of the yen, and constant change mark our entry into the 21st century. Leaders must embrace their ambiguous, yet turbulent environments to define new dreams or visions that will guide the way. Bennis outlines five basic parts to managing the dream: communicating, recruiting, rewarding, retraining, and reorganizing. He offers examples of leaders who have used metaphors, global alliances, and other tactics to manage their dreams.

New

Bennis, W., Parikh, J., & Lessem, R. (1996). ***Beyond leadership: Balancing economics, ethics and ecology*** (Rev. ed.). Cambridge, MA: Blackwell Business.

Written for practitioners and students of leadership, this revised edition focuses on a global approach to management, with a concern for a balance of ethical, economic, and ecological managerial skills. The American, Asian, and Afro-European roots of the authors are reflected in a marriage of Eastern and Western philosophies in this book. The authors present an ethical paradigm with four elements: personal development, group synergy, organizational learning, and sustainable development. The philosophy behind the paradigm is that organizations are living systems where every individual depends on the whole and the whole depends on every individual. Includes index.

New

Brake, T. (1997). ***The global leader: Critical factors for creating the world class organization.*** Chicago: Irwin.

To understand global leadership, one must consider environment, key competencies, and organizational support. Global environment is composed of those who buy (the ten largest emerging markets are China, Indonesia, India, South Korea, Turkey, South Africa, Poland, Argentina, Brazil, and Mexico) and the companies with goods and services to market. Key competencies—business acumen, relationship management, and personal effectiveness—form the model Global Leadership Triad. Organizational support builds onto the triad adding strategy, architecture, culture, education, and performance systems. Brake reports on his interviews with leading global companies such as Avon, Colgate-Palmolive, and NYNEX. Includes bibliographical references and index.

Bryson, J. M., & Crosby, B. C. (1992). ***Leadership for the common good: Tackling public problems in a shared-power world.*** San Francisco: Jossey-Bass.

Massive and complex public problems, such as homelessness, urban crime, AIDS, drug abuse, domestic violence, and global warming, are the shared responsibility of many organizations that must pool power and resources to get things done. Government, nonprofit organizations, and business leaders, joining together in a public leadership network, could identify the problems, explore solutions, facilitate policy change, and mobilize collective action. Examples of civic reform in Minneapolis-St. Paul and the dispute over federal abortion laws illustrate shared power, which creates policy change. Includes bibliographical references and index.

Burns, J. M. (1972). ***Uncommon sense.*** New York: Harper & Row.

Burns's treatise asserts that the domestic- and foreign-policy troubles he identifies as confronting the U.S. are rooted in the habits of those who preserve outmoded myths and shibboleths that blind citizens and presidents alike to the necessity for creative governmental change. The central argument of the book concerns means and ends; it is an examination of the capacity of the nation to define its fundamental values and to transform them into guides to action.

Childs, J. B. (1989). ***Leadership, conflict, and cooperation in Afro-American social thought.*** Philadelphia: Temple University Press.

Writing from the view of an anthropologist, not a political scientist or historian, Childs compares two philosophies toward human equality. The vanguard perspective claims access to special knowledge, believes that energy flows from a dominant center in every society, believes that the sleeping masses can be exploited, and strives to lift people out of their dormant stage into awareness of their own strength. Mutuality seeks to expand the recognition and interaction of a multitude of groups without boundaries or perceptions of superiority among groups. Case studies contrast the philosophical working styles of Booker T. Washington and W. E. B. DuBois, and George W. Ellis and Arturo (Arthur) Schomburg. Includes bibliography and index.

Cleveland, H. (1993). ***Birth of a new world: An open moment for international leadership.*** San Francisco: Jossey-Bass.

As a political scientist and public executive, Cleveland has formed an extensive alliance with leaders of international peacekeeping organizations. From 1986 to 1989, this alliance, informally called The Group and formally titled the International Governance Project, met to discuss the requirements for international cooperation through the prisms of scientific discovery, technological innovation, and the rapid delivery of information. In this book, Cleveland reports on The Group's conclusions for shared responsibility, lessons learned from history, the success of democracy, the necessity of private enterprise, and the roles of the United States and the United Nations. Includes bibliographical references and index.

Dechant, K., & Altman, B. (1994). **Environmental leadership: From compliance to competitive advantage.** *Academy of Management Executive, 8*(3), 7-27.

In the 1970s environmental efforts were driven by government regulations and a desire to avoid penalties. Since then, major corporations such as Johnson &

Johnson, The Body Shop, and Procter & Gamble have found that linking business strategy to "green" objectives is good for the bottom line. This article shares the experiences of these and other companies in planning, problem solving, product development, legal and financial liabilities, and total quality programs.

New
Dell, T. (1996). *The corporate environmental leader: Five steps to a new ethic.* Menlo Park, CA: Crisp.

Written by the president of an environmental research firm, this book describes five steps that corporate leaders can take to make their business environmentally friendly: ground yourself in nature's principles, respect the tide of history, expand the vision, emulate the principles, and neutralize negatives with positives. Chapters include an extensive environmental timeline, checklists of the positive steps both companies and individuals can take and their results, and an appendix that gives environmental case studies of 30 major corporations, including Coca-Cola, Procter & Gamble, and Wal-Mart. Includes bibliographical references.

Etzioni, A. (1993). *The spirit of community: Rights, responsibilities, and the Communitarian agenda.* New York: Crown.

A Communitarian movement, founded by Etzioni (a former White House Fellow), proposes that Americans strive to balance the rights of individuals with social responsibilities. The author presents a case for a new moral order without government oppression, law and order without a police state, and free speech without hate and hostility. In a Communitarian society, the institutions of families, schools, and neighborhoods are strengthened, while special-interest groups and politics are checked. Includes bibliographical references and index.

New
Etzioni, A. (1996). *The new golden rule: Community and morality in a democratic society.* New York: BasicBooks.

What makes a good society? According to Etzioni, founder of the Communitarian Network, it requires a balance between individual rights and social responsibilities. Contrary to Western beliefs, freedom and morality do not have to conflict, but can reinforce each other. In this "positive doctrine" of communitarianism, Etzioni addresses the two founding principles of a good society—social order and autonomy—how they interact, and how they have emerged in Western society. The concept of society is examined from both a historical and sociological perspective, and each chapter includes "implications for practice and policy." Includes bibliographical references and index.

New
Freire, P. (1993). *Pedagogy of the oppressed* (Rev. ed.). New York: Continuum.

Educator Paulo Freire was exiled from Brazil in 1964 for his radical ideas on teaching illiterate adults to learn and to speak out on social issues. This book, originally written in 1973, explains his theory and method for enabling oppressed citizens of the Third World to assume political power and improve conditions in their homelands. The first stage develops a consciousness of oppression and a commitment to change. The second stage encourages organization of nonviolent action, dialogue, and reflection to confront an oppressive culture. Includes bibliographical references.

Gardner, J. W. (1964). *Self-renewal.* New York: Harper & Row.

The author brings together the topics of moral decay and renewal and the individual's capacity for lifelong learning. Gardner feels that unless we attend to the requirements of renewal, aging institutions and organizations will eventually bring our civilization to ruin. This is a call to foster versatile, innovative, and self-renewing men and women who share a vision of something worth saving. Includes bibliographical references in notes.

Gardner, J. W. (1965). **The antileadership vaccine.** *Carnegie Corporation of New York, Annual Report.*

There are many leaders in our society. The author discusses what he calls an "antileadership vaccine," meaning that a larger number of young people are being steered away from leadership roles. The process begins in society itself. Individuals do not envision themselves as individuals but rather as anonymous members in a mass of people. Stereotypes of leaders enhance the unattractiveness of leadership positions. The necessity of leaders in our society is discussed.

Gardner, J. W. (1978). *Morale.* New York: Norton.

Hope, but not blind optimism, is applauded by the founder of Common Cause and former secretary of Health, Education, and Welfare in an essay on the attitudes and values in contemporary society. Gardner offers encouraging thoughts on renewing a belief in ourselves. Includes index.

Gemmill, G., & Oakley, J. (1992). **Leadership: An alienating social myth?** *Human Relations, 45*(2), 113-129.

Are leaders really necessary? Or has society locked itself into the idea that leaders are necessary in order to repress uncomfortable and often painful needs and emotions that emerge when people work together? Gemmill and Oakley contend that our concept of leadership has become a psychic prison, which has induced massive learned helplessness and feelings of alienation. They detail the mythologizing of leadership and suggest possibilities for restructuring to promote creativity and self-actualization.

Golding, W. (1962). *The lord of the flies.* New York: Putnam.

This is a parable about the breakdown of civilized restraints under extreme circumstance. A nuclear war forces the evacuation of children from Britain. One airplane filled with prep-school boys is wrecked on an uninhabited island. All adults on board are killed; only the boys remain alive. What ensues is the boys' attempt to create a society according to their sense of order based on a combination of their education and character.

New
Grobler, P. A. (1996). **In search of excellence: Leadership challenges facing companies in the new South Africa.** *SAM Advanced Management Journal, 61*(2), 22-34.

Major political transitions in South Africa have also thrown the country's business community into turmoil. In the past, many South African corporations were "overmanaged and underled . . . floating in an ocean of authoritarianism and bureaucratic hierarchies." Grobler maintains that South Africa's greatest weakness is its lack of human capital, and emphasizes the importance of developing more leaders with new leadership styles. He advocates a form of transformational leadership, in which leaders challenge their subordinates to learn new skills. A number of visual aids and graphs are used to illustrate the concepts.

Heifetz, R. (1994). *Leadership without easy answers.* Cambridge, MA: Belknap Press.

As the Director of the Leadership Education Project at the Kennedy School of Government, Harvard University, Heifetz reflects on teaching leadership. His experience includes teaching undergraduate, for-credit, noncredit, master's level, mid-career, executive, and military leadership courses. From this varied background, Heifetz draws conclusions about the role of leadership in a complex society. It has become common to blame leaders for the ills of society and to expect leaders to solve our problems. Heifetz suggests that it's time to redefine citizenship and let everyone, those with and without authority, take leadership roles to strengthen our democratic society. Includes bibliographical references and index.

Hofstede, G. (1980). **Motivation, leadership, and organizations: Do American theories apply abroad?** *Organizational Dynamics, 9*(1), 42-63.

It is important to remember that management theories developed and studied in one country may be of little use in other countries, due to differences in culture. National culture has been divided into four dimensions: power distance, uncertainty avoidance, individualism-collectivism, and masculinity-femininity. Differences in employee motivation, attitudes, management styles, and organizational structures between countries can be traced to differences in mental programming. Includes bibliography and index.

Hofstede, G. H. (1980). *Culture's consequences: International differences in work-related values.* Beverly Hills, CA: Sage.

This book explores the differences in thinking and behavior in 40 countries. Surveys of 116,000 employees of multinational companies and studies of children's literature in each society identify four dimensions of personal values and collective cultures. Power distance is defined as dominance and the distance between worker and boss. Uncertainty avoidance deals with rule orientation, anxiety, security, and dependence. Individualism is the relationship between individual and society or between personal time and work commitment. Masculinity addresses the duality of the sexes, assertiveness versus nurturing qualities, and their value in a society. There are implications for policy-making and research, but this is also a valuable tool for those studying global business concerns.

Howe, W. (1995). **Leadership and spun leadership in the O. J. Simpson case: Towards an ecology for leadership studies.** *Journal of Leadership Studies, 2*(1), 13-35.

Spun leadership is that which evolves from an individual or local situation into a societal issue. A prime example is the "case of the century" that captured the attention of millions of American citizens. Conversations about the control of courtroom proceedings could be overheard almost everywhere. The behavior of the trial's key players, from attorneys to witnesses and family members, has been judged as credible, charismatic, or unethical. Issues raised in this trial rippled into larger issues of race relations, police competence, and media ethics.

New
Ikenberry, G. J. (1996). **The future of international leadership.** *Political Science Quarterly, 111*(3), 385-402.

This article addresses the concerns of political scientists who see the end of U.S. leadership and world dominance. Ikenberry argues that the concept of world leadership has changed in the past 50 years. There is no longer a need for ideological heroism, military dominance, or economic control. Rather, world leadership now requires an ability to foster communication and commonality of social purpose among nations. It is evident in several forms. Structural leadership directs the distribution of capital, natural resources, and military might. Institutional leadership refers to relations among nations, trade agreements, and peace treaties. Situational leadership happens when a head of state uses personal power or charisma to transform the capacity of his or her nation. Ikenberry concludes that American structures and relationships are strong enough to maintain a position of world leadership.

New
Jaeger, A. M., & Kanungo, R. N. (Eds.). (1990). ***Management in developing countries.*** New York: Routledge.

This book provides a comparative analysis of the management techniques that work in Western cultures and those in developing countries. Major obstacles to organizational management in Third World countries are: 1) deficiency of financial and human resources, 2) turbulence of the political and legal environment, and 3) differences in cultural values. Situations in China, India, and East Africa are specifically addressed. Contributing authors suggest that Western managers offer training and education, foster stable organizational climates, form links with technologically advanced partners, and develop indigenous managers. Includes bibliographical references.

Kingston, R. J. (Ed.). (1993, Summer). *Kettering Review*.

The *Kettering Review* is published quarterly by the Kettering Foundation, an organization that supports individuals and groups who are actively trying to solve the problems of communities, government, and education. This issue is dedicated to the issues of leadership, followership, and power. Classic essays from *The Hero in History* by Sidney Hook (1943), *The Human Condition* by Hannah Arendt (1958), and *The Knowledge Executive* by Harlan Cleveland (1985) are reprinted. Original essays address the delicate balance between public leadership and a shared public power.

Kotter, J. P. (1995). ***The new rules: How to succeed in today's post-corporate world.*** New York: Free Press.

A tracking study of 115 MBAs from the Harvard Class of 1974 reveals changes in the path to a successful career. Over 20 years, the study participants responded to annual questionnaires indicating their personal and professional choices, actions, successes, and failures. Kotter's assessment of the data indicates that career paths have changed drastically in 20 years. The globalization of markets and competition has caused a huge shift in economic forces,

the structure and function of organizations, and wage levels. The path to a successful career has shifted away from big business toward entrepreneurship. Currently, the requirements for success are speed and flexibility, exceedingly high standards, a strong competitive nature, and lifelong learning. Includes bibliographical references and index.

New
Lappe, F. M., & Du Bois, P. M. (1994). ***The quickening of America: Rebuilding our nation, remaking our lives.*** San Francisco: Jossey-Bass.

The authors are a husband-and-wife team who direct the Center for Democracy. Through the Center's seminars, Lappe and Du Bois have compiled a report of the key insights of successful Americans regarding the state of our democracy. They claim that we are in a period of quickening, a phase of active growth and development. This workbook helps readers learn ten arts of democracy: active listening, creative conflict, mediation, negotiation, political imagination, public dialogue, public judgment, celebration and appreciation, evaluation and reflection, and mentoring. There are activities that allow readers to explore and practice the ten arts. Includes bibliographical references and index.

New
Leicester, G. (1996). **From dominance to leadership: America's place in the world.** *Political Quarterly, 67*(1), 36-45.

Leicester offers a British point of view on Henry Kissinger's remarks at the 1995 conference of the Royal Institute of International Affairs. Kissinger discussed a power shift following the Cold War that changed Britain's role from power to influence and America's role from dominance to leadership. Leicester argues that leadership is a more challenging role than dominance and he doubts that America can achieve it. He comments on ally relations that are approaching instability and new, softer forms of power: economic weight, trading relations, diplomacy, culture networks, and ideology.

New
Lessem, R., & Neubauer, F. (1994). ***European management systems: Towards unity out of cultural diversity.*** London: McGraw-Hill.

Four of the seven leading industrial nations of the world are in Western Europe: Germany, France, Italy, and the U.K. But leading management theory and practice come from the other three: U.S., Canada, and Japan. Lessem and Neubauer suggest that the advances in political and economic unification in Western Europe will enable the synergy of once-diverse management systems. Four philosophies are evident in the European businessphere. According to Lessem and Neubauer, the British pragmatic, action-oriented, experiential philosophy is most closely aligned with American business practices. The German holistic, idealistic, reflective philosophy is closer to Japanese management theory. The French are rational and the Italians are humanistic. The authors compare these four cultural philosophies to Carl Jung's four psychological types and suggest a model in which each culture contributes its strength. Includes bibliographical references and index.

Lobel, S. (1990). **Global leadership competencies: Managing to a different drumbeat.** *Human Resource Management, 29*(1), 39-47.

Expatriate managers have a 70% failure rate in developing countries due to an inability of the manager or spouse to adjust to a new culture. Lobel identifies managerial competencies for global leadership and analyzes how these competencies can be taught. Competencies include technical skill, verbal and nonverbal communication, behavioral flexibility, cultural empathy, low ethnocentrism, and a curious nature. Lobel suggests that a manager can be taught to step out of his or her comfort zone and adapt to a new reality.

New
Lodge, G. C. (1995). *Managing globalization in the age of interdependence.* San Diego, CA: Pffeifer.

Lodge defines globalization as "the process forced by global flows of people, information, trade, and capital." In this book, he attempts to "view globalization holistically," with chapters addressing the historical and cultural elements as well as business aspects of the new global paradigm. Each chapter uses visual aids, including graphs, charts, pictures, pulled quotes, statistics, and cartoons to illustrate concepts. Includes bibliographical references and index. This book is part of the Warren Bennis Executive Briefing Series.

Maynard, H. B., Jr., & Mehrtens, S. E. (1993). *The fourth wave: Business in the 21st century.* San Francisco: Berrett-Koehler.

Applying Toffler's concept of historical waves of change (*The Third Wave*, 1984), this book envisions a future where the health and well-being of the earth and its inhabitants are secure. This vision is framed by the world of business, because its magnitude of power is enormous and the need for a shift in attitudes is critical. Maynard and Mehrtens hope this vision will spark dialogue and serve as a road map toward a fourth wave, an integration of all dimensions of life and a responsibility for the whole. Includes bibliographical references and index.

Mead, R. (1994). *International management: Cross cultural dimensions.* Cambridge, MA: Blackwell.

This textbook was written for MBA students or others wanting to learn interpersonal skills for managing across national borders. Chapters address analysis of cultural differences, structures for decision making, patronage relationships, cross-cultural communication, motivation, dispute and negotiation, expatriate staff assignments, and planning change. Each chapter contains a discussion of theory and exercises to practice new learnings. Includes bibliographical references and index.

Mills, C. W. (1956). *The power elite.* New York: Oxford University.

The power elite, those men and women whose positions enable them to transcend the ordinary environments of ordinary people, are in positions to make decisions having major consequences. This book studies the hierarchies of state, corporation, and army that constitute the means of power. It offers a sociological key to understanding the role of higher circles in America.

Moore, P. (1994). **Voices on change: Hard choices for the environmental movement.** *Leadership Quarterly: Special Issue: Leadership for Environmental and Social Change, 5*(3/4), 247-252.

One of the founders of the Greenpeace movement describes the differences between confrontation and acceptance at the policy-making table. For over 20 years, Moore has moved between the role of alarmist to that of collaborator between governments, corporations, public institutions, and environmentalists. His efforts at sustained development and collaboration are viewed as treasonous by some ecoextremists who favor anti-development and zero-tolerance attitudes.

New
Naisbitt, J. (1996). *Megatrends Asia: Eight Asian megatrends that are reshaping our world.* New York: Simon & Schuster.

Futurist John Naisbitt predicts a shift of power from the Western world to the Pacific Rim. The World Bank declares that the emergence of Asian business is an economic miracle. Naisbitt agrees that there's a miracle occurring in the East, but believes it's more than economic growth—it's a miracle of human spirit. He predicts an Asian renaissance during which Asia will dominate the world economically, politically, and culturally. Very briefly, Naisbitt discusses the new breed of leaders emerging in Asia. Includes bibliographical references and index.

Naisbitt, J., & Aburdene, P. (1990). ***Megatrends 2000: Ten new directions for the 1990s.*** New York: William Morrow.

Megatrends are large social, economic, political, and technological changes that influence society for a decade or beyond. Naisbitt and Aburdene refer to the year 2000 as the arrival of the future and a deadline for solving our current problems of hunger, disease, drugs, and pollution. They identify ten megatrends of the 1990s to use as a frame of reference for measuring new information and for making business choices. Among the trends are global economy, women in leadership, and the triumph of the individual. Includes bibliographical references and index.

Nanus, B. (1989). ***The leader's edge: The seven keys to leadership in a turbulent world.*** Chicago: Contemporary Books.

By the coauthor of *Leaders: The Strategies for Taking Charge*, this book was written as a progress report on the effects of change on the leadership function in the U.S. Nanus's research with 200 leaders in politics, business, education, media, religion, and environmental protection, combined with readings on U.S. leadership, provides an analysis of where we are, where we should be headed, and how to get there. Seven megaskills are identified to provide a clear sense of direction, restore a sense of purpose, catalyze people to act enthusiastically, and align their energies toward a common goal. Includes index.

Norris, M. (1992). **Warren Bennis on rebuilding leadership.** *Planning Review, 20*(5), 13-15.

In a keynote address to the Planning Forum's International Conference, Bennis outlined the changing role of leaders in a rapidly changing world. Technology, globalization, and demographic diversity are the forces to which organizations must respond in the 1990s. Bureaucratic organizations cannot survive these tumultuous changes. Organizations must flatten and they must empower leaders at all levels. Leadership in the 1990s requires a strong sense of purpose, conceptual skills, technical competence, people skills, judgment, taste, and character.

Plato. *Republic.*

The ancient Greek philosopher, Plato, wrote his most enduring work, *Republic,* around the year 387 B.C. The story is of a fictional character called Socrates, as was Plato's teacher and mentor, in a fictional republic named Athens. Socrates shares his philosophy on the nature of justice and his vision of an ideal society. In the story, Socrates argues with the citizens of Athens on the question of restructuring society to allow each man the opportunity to achieve his highest potential.

Portugal, E., & Yukl, G. (1994). **Voices on change: Perspectives on environmental leadership.** *Leadership Quarterly: Special Issue: Leadership for Environmental and Social Change, 5*(3/4), 271-276.

Growing environmental concerns affect organizational policies, programs, and budgets. How do individual and organizational leaders influence a broad assortment of stakeholders to consider the complex issues of environmental responsibility? The authors address this concern with a two-dimensional framework for environmental leadership process. This transformational style of leadership involves visioning, consensus-building, sense-making, and symbolic action.

Pucik, V., Tichy, N. M., & Barnett, C. K. (Eds.). (1992). ***Globalizing management: Creating and leading the competitive organization.*** New York: Wiley.

Doing business across national boundaries creates the need for new organizational structures and processes. Members of INSEAD/European Institute of Business Administration and a team of multinational human resource management scholars and researchers have been studying this phenomenon for over ten years. At annual symposia, they share ideas for researching global-management needs and teaching new management styles. In this book, the authors summarize the trends they have witnessed. Some keys for successful global management are: early cross-cultural experience through assignments in other countries, global networking, cross-cultural team building and problem solving, and the ability to continuously transform. Includes bibliographical references and index.

New

Reichel, A. (1996). **Management development in Israel: Current and future challenges.** *Journal of Management Development, 15*(5), 22-36.

Reichel reports on a study of 217 top-level Israeli executives. His research examines executive training and development needs relative to Israel's size and location. These executives are also affected by Israeli-Arab relations, military activity, immigration, technology, and tourism. Reichel concludes that Israeli executives need training programs that focus on service, entrepreneurial skills, research and development, and a combination of nationalism and multiculturalism.

Rogers, J. L. (1988). **New paradigm leadership: Integrating the female ethos.** *Initiatives, 51*(4), 1-8.

Rogers suggests that a major shift is occurring in Western culture. The patriarchal world with its emphasis on male-oriented values of rationality, competition, and independence is shifting toward a new paradigm. The values of the female ethos—mutuality, cooperation, and affiliation—are becoming recognized as a transformational and empowering leadership style. This article examines the values of the female ethos, their connection with the shift in Western culture, and their influence on the practice of leadership.

Shareef, R. (1991). **Ecovision: A leadership theory for innovative organizations.** *Organizational Dynamics, 20*(1), 50-62.

Ecovision is a leadership theory merging corporate and environmental goals. Ecovision invests in R&D and is moral, creative, and intuitive. It borrows from social psychology and ecology. It encourages innovation and flexibility. Examples of ecovision leaders are Ted Turner of CNN, Al Neuharth of *USA Today*, and Vincent Lane of the Chicago Housing Authority.

Shrivastava, P. (1994). **Ecocentric leadership in the 21st century.** *Leadership Quarterly: Special Issue: Leadership for Environmental and Social Change, 5*(3/4), 223-226.

The world is facing ecological crises at a rapidly increasing rate. The depletion of the ozone layer, species extinction, air pollution, acid rain, and toxic waste threaten the world's resources for future generations. Economic development, public policy, and individual behavior are all responsible for the problem and the solution. As the engineers of economic development, the corporate sector holds the largest share of responsibility and the greatest promise for resolution. The author warns corporate leaders to not tack ecological concerns onto their decisions as afterthoughts. He encourages decision-makers to promote sustainable economic development and the quality of life for all the world's inhabitants at the center of corporate planning.

New
Slowinski, G., Chatterji, D., Tshudy, J. A., & Fridley, D. L. (1997). **Are you a leader in environmental R&D?** *Research-Technology Management, 40*(3), 47-54.

Industrial R&D leaders can be pivotal in determining their organizations' environmental awareness and policies. This article offers a self-assessment questionnaire for R&D directors to use to evaluate the environmental policies of their organizations. R&D factors measured include environmental policies, strategic planning, the organizational approach, environmental training, and management processes. This questionnaire was previously given to 30 major companies and the authors list the five that scored highest, including Dow Chemical and Clorox, and identify management characteristics that these companies share.

Swierczek, F. W. (1991). **Leadership and culture: Comparing Asian managers.** *Leadership and Organization Development Journal, 12*(7), 3-10.

In Western culture, leadership theory is of an individualistic nature. In Asian culture, the unit of society is the family or one's extended relationships. Swierczek compares leadership in 11 Eastern cultures to U.S. culture. Areas of comparison are: power distance, individualism, and Confucian dynamism (which consists of persistence, status of relationships, thrift, and a sense of shame). He concludes that leadership should adapt to the culture in which the leader operates.

Toffler, A. (1991). *Powershift: Knowledge, wealth and violence at the edge of the 21st century.* New York: Bantam.

The third in Toffler's trilogy, including *Future Shock* (1970) and *The Third Wave* (1984), *Powershift* presents a new theory of social power and shifts in economy, business, politics, education, religion, the media, and global affairs. Toffler argues that power was once obtained through wealth or violence. But the future of power belongs to knowledge and the systems that create, enhance, and exchange knowledge. Tempered with an emphasis on relationships, ethics, and appreciation of the individual, Toffler's vision encourages the use, not abuse, of knowledge as power. Includes bibliographical references and index.

Torbert, W. R. (1991). *The power of balance: Transforming self, society, and scientific inquiry.* Newbury Park, CA: Sage.

Torbert offers a new theory of power, a new practice of management, and a new approach to conducting social science. Autobiographical cases illustrate stages of moral development and organizational reform. In the foreword, D. A. Schon states that this is "a document of shocking grandiosity," yet "Torbert's theory is notable because of the depth and breadth of its aspirations." Includes bibliographical references and index.

Urquhart, B., & Childers, E. (1990). *A world in need of leadership: Tomorrow's United Nations.* Uppsala, Sweden: Dag Hammarskjold Foundation.

The unique leadership demands of the United Nations are studied in this presentation of papers. U.N. leadership responsibilities include peacemaking, safeguarding the environment, management of world economy, and coordination of member states that have political differences. The authors study historical and current U.N. organizational structure and leadership-selection processes. They report that new leadership demands have evolved, and offer recommendations for organizational restructuring and a new leadership-selection process.

New
Van Belle, D. A. (1996). **Leadership and collective action: The case of revolution.** *International Studies Quarterly, 40*(1), 107-132.

In a collective action, such as a revolution, there are the activists who pay a high price, the free riders who reap benefits without paying the price, and the leaders who do both—pay the price and receive the benefits. Van Belle explains that individuals enter collective action with the intent of assuming leadership and reaping the greatest rewards. He presents formulas and models that illustrate the rational choice, success threshold, and relative deprivation in a revolutionary situation. Strategies employed by the revolutionary leader include altering the value of the status quo and creating safety buffers. Van Belle hopes that this examination of leadership in the context of revolution will aid the understanding of leadership in all collective action. Includes bibliographical references.

Weisbord, M. R. (1992). *Discovering common ground: How future search conferences bring people together to achieve breakthrough innovation, empowerment, shared vision, and collaborative action.* San Francisco: Berrett-Koehler.

Based on his chapter "Inventing the Future" in *Productive Workplaces* (Jossey-Bass, 1987), Weisbord shares his visionary concept of future-search conferences, a shift from expert problem solving to shared responsibility for our world's problems. Business, government, education, and all sectors of society meet for three-day conferences to discover common ground, imagine ideal futures, expand horizons, and build democratic social values. He describes successful conferences, potential pitfalls, and planning advice for practitioners. Includes bibliographical references and index.

Westley, F. (1991). **Bob Geldof and Live Aid: The affective side of global social innovation.** *Human Relations, 44*(10), 1011-1036.

In 1984-1985, Irish singer/songwriter Bob Geldof organized the largest charity event in history with a benefit recording and Live Aid, a two-continent, 17-hour global rock telethon. His efforts raised 75 million pounds for famine relief in Ethiopia. Geldof's visionary leadership resulted from his personal background, moral disposition, sense of timing, and ability to motivate others into action. Geldof's unique ability to integrate visual imagery of famine with popular music created a global philanthropic passion.

HISTORY AND BIOGRAPHY

New
Ashby, R., & Ohrn, D. D. G. (Eds.). (1995). *Herstory: Women who changed the world.* New York: Viking.

Herstory details the historical and social significance of over 100 women and gives overviews of the times in which they lived. It contains diverse women from all areas of the world with political, religious, social, and artistic influence. Some of the more well-known women are: Sappho, Sojourner Truth, Susan B. Anthony, Eleanor Roosevelt, and Bessie Smith. Some less recognizable women are: The Trung Sisters, who led a Vietnamese uprising against the Chinese in A.D. 39; Sister Juana Ines de la Cruz of Mexico, who entered a convent in order to continue her broad education and defend the right of women to pursue a scholarly life; and Mairead Corrigan and Betty Williams, who won the 1976 Nobel Peace Prize for their efforts to stop the violence in Northern Ireland. The book includes a selected bibliography and suggested further reading, as well as geographical, alphabetical, and occupational indexes.

New
Barber, J. D. (1992). *The presidential character: Predicting performance in the White House* (4th ed.). Englewood Cliffs, NJ: Prentice Hall.

Barber draws on political psychology and history to explain how citizens can determine a potential president's character, worldview, and leadership style. Key factors include the candidate's personality, centers of power and national climate at time of election, and the candidate's affinity for action and enjoyment of the presidency. The media, although exercising much influence, provides less actual information. Barber analyzes the character of presidents from William Howard Taft to George Bush. Includes bibliographical references in notes and an index.

Boyes, R. (1994). *The naked president: A political life of Lech Walesa.* London: Secker and Warburg.

Boyes chronicles the political rise and fall of a revolutionary-turned-president. Walesa's charismatic, street-style leadership qualities met the needs of the

Polish working class in 1990. But when his Solidarity Party couldn't influence parliament sufficiently to serve effectively, he lost popularity and his bid for reelection. Includes bibliographical references and index.

Burns, J. M. (1956). *Roosevelt: The lion and the fox.* San Diego, CA: Harcourt-Brace Jovanovich.

This is a highly readable, two-volume biography (the second volume is *Roosevelt: Soldier of Freedom*). Burns describes the 32nd president as a man of "no fixed convictions about methods and policies" whose chief tenet was "improvise."

Caro, R. (1975). *The power broker: Robert Moses and the fall of New York.* New York: Random House.

This book reveals the singular public service, achievements, foresight, and egotism of Robert Moses and attacks the type of urban planning that Moses personified. The author contends his planning was dehumanizing, insensitive toward the poor and minority groups, and more concerned with parks and parkways than people, which has paved the way for much of today's urban ills. Includes bibliography and index.

Caro, R. A. (1984). *The years of Lyndon Johnson: The path to power.* New York: Random House.

This is the first of a three-volume biography of the 36th president of the United States. It begins with Johnson's boyhood and concludes with his defeat in his first race for the Senate in 1941. "The more one thus follows his life, the more apparent it becomes that alongside the thread of achievement running through it runs another thread, as dark as the other is bright, and as fraught with consequences for history." Includes bibliographical references and index.

Carpenter, D. A. (1991). **Simon de Montfort: The first leader of a political movement in English history.** *History*, 76(246), 3-23.

In the 13th century, de Montfort was the first political opponent of the king of England to seize power and to govern England in his own name. Carpenter examines the personal characteristics that caused this unprecedented rise to power. De Montfort is described by chroniclers as a military expert, consistent in the face of danger, a glamorous personality, influential, religious, tenacious, principled, and confident.

New
Chandler, J. B. (1996). **An interview: John W. Gardner, leader of leaders.** *Journal of Leadership Studies*, 3(1), 17-24.

This is a brief but revealing interview with John Gardner, former Secretary of Health, Education, and Welfare during the Lyndon Johnson administration; founder of Common Cause; Centennial Professor in Public Services at the Graduate School of Business at Stanford University; and author of *Self-Renewal* (1964) and *On Leadership* (1990). Gardner shares his insights on leadership development across the lifespan, continued vitality, and personal growth among senior citizens. He promotes optimism, learning through change and challenge, and collaborative governance to enrich communities. Chandler finds that Gardner, in his nineties, represents the lifelong leader about whom he writes.

Clemens, J. K., & Mayer, D. F. (1987). *The classic touch: Lessons in leadership from Homer to Hemingway.* Homewood, IL: Dow Jones-Irwin.

This book taps the collective wisdom found in the classic works of Western philosophy, history, biography, and drama and applies it to the problems of modern managers and leaders. It addresses such issues as how to build a team and keep it together, how to manage an acquisition once it's in place, how to eliminate daily distractions, and how to better trust your intuition. Includes bibliography and index.

New
Davis, M. A., Jr. (1997). **Matilda of Tuscany and Daimbert of Pisa: Women's leadership in medieval Italy, 1054-1092.** *Leadership Journal: Women in Leadership— Sharing the Vision*, 1(2), 31-38.

In this brief look at the political life of Maltilda, Marchioness of Tuscany (1054-1116), the author makes two main points about leadership in the Middle Ages: women were key players in the political events of the time and the "great person" theory of history has been overused in medieval studies. By describing the complex alliance that Matilda formed with Tuscan nobility, the papacy, and Daimbert, the archbishop of Pisa, Davis illustrates both Matilda's political power and the complex interplay of people and circumstances that determined the course of history. Includes bibliographical references.

De Gaulle, C. (1975). *The edge of the sword* (2nd ed.). Westport, CT: Greenwood Press.

This book is essentially a selection of essays in which De Gaulle presents his personal philosophy of the meaning of leadership, World War II, and France's role in the war's history. These elements are woven together by discussions of character, prestige, military doctrine, the conduct of war, and politics and the soldier. The historical insights De Gaulle offers here carry greater meaning for his having lived through so many of the important events he discusses.

DeMause, L. (1984). **The making of a fearful leader: "Where's the rest of me?"** *Journal of Psychohistory, 12*(1), 5-21.

This article is from *Reagan's America* by Lloyd DeMause. It deals with Ronald Reagan's personal anxieties and how those anxieties affected his politics. This chapter evaluates Reagan's phobias and explains why he developed them. The author states the reason for Reagan's success in 1980 was not so much his abilities but his promises that psychologically dealt with the same inner turmoils that Americans were experiencing during that time.

New
Enkelis, L., Olsen, K., & Lewenstein, M. (1995). *On our own terms: Portraits of women business leaders.* San Francisco: Berrett-Koehler.

The authors highlight the careers and personal development of 14 women, including: Ruth Owades, president of Calyx & Corolla, a florist catalog company; Wilma Mankiller, principal chief of the Cherokee Nation; Elaine Chao, president and CEO of United Way of America; Marjorie Silver, president of Pinsly Railroad Company; and Carol Bartz, president, CEO, and chairman of the board of Autodesk, Inc., a computer software company. In their own words, each woman documents her climb to a position of power, sharing her experience to serve as a model and source of advice. The authors fill in appropriate details, such as company history and revenues. Photographs help complete the portrait of each woman at work and home.

Erikson, E. H. (1970). *Gandhi's truth: On the origins of militant nonviolence.* New York: Norton.

Erikson reveals that what has always been thought of as a relatively minor episode in Gandhi's life—the Abmedabad Mill strike of 1918 and Gandhi's first fast—was, in fact, an event of crucial importance in his rise as a natural leader and as the originator of militant nonviolence. Bibliographical references included in notes.

Freeman, D. S. (1942). *Lee's lieutenants.* New York: Scribner.

This is a three-volume study of the Confederate commanders who served with and under General Robert E. Lee in the Civil War. "The necessary qualities of high military command manifestly are military imagination,

initiative, resourcefulness, boldness coupled with a grasp of practicality, ability to elicit the best of men, and the more personal qualities of character, endurance, courage and nervous control." Includes bibliography and index.

Gaventa, J. (1980). *Power and powerlessness: Quiescence and rebellion in an Appalachian valley.* Champaign, IL: University of Illinois.

The author presents systematic research on the history of coal and people in the Appalachian valley, and raises the question of why the local people haven't put up greater and more frequent resistance to King Coal. The documentation includes the periods of powerful rank-and-file resistance that swept through the valley. Includes bibliographical references and index.

Gilbert, B. (1983). *Westering man: The life of Joseph Walker.* New York: Atheneum.

This book presents a history of the frontier and pioneer life of Joseph Reddeford Walker (1798-1876). Walker was characterized as exceptional for his physical prowess, intellect, and talents, and because of a consistent pattern of decent, principled behavior, which men of great strength and self-confidence can sustain—an example of what a frontier hero could and should be. Includes bibliography and index.

Greenstein, F. I. (1982). *The hidden-hand presidency: Eisenhower as leader.* New York: BasicBooks.

This is an analysis of Eisenhower's policies and strategies. Greenstein establishes that the president practiced "public vagueness" and "private precision." Eisenhower purposely projected the image of being a politically benign, folksy leader who reigned but did not rule, so as to publicly accent the head-of-state role of the president, thus garnering public support. Greenstein draws together the lessons that contemporary and future presidents can learn from Eisenhower's style. Includes bibliographical references and index.

Greenstein, F. I. (1991). **The president who led by seeming not to: A centennial view of Dwight Eisenhower.** *Antioch Review, 49*(1), 39-44.

In polls following his presidency, experts ranked Eisenhower 29th in terms of greatness. In the 1980s another poll ranked Eisenhower in the top ten. Newly acquired documents reveal that Eisenhower intentionally played up his role as head of state, while downplaying his role as political leader. He greeted the public and press with great warmth, muddled speech, scrambled syntax, and sparse substance. Yet his official papers indicate that he was shrewd, well informed, analytical, and on top of the issues. His hidden-hand style of leadership was employed to keep his strategies private and to avoid blame for unpopular decisions.

Greenstein, F. I. (1994). **The two leadership styles of William Jefferson Clinton.** *Political Psychology, 15*(2), 351-361.

President Clinton exhibits two distinct styles—one is a passion to make numerous sweeping policy changes without attention to detail and the other is salesmanship to gain support for a pet project with infinite attention to detail. Greenstein analyzes the factors contributing to these alternate styles: the policy issues during Clinton's term, his political drive, fluency, charm, energy, intelligence, lack of discipline, and his capacity to learn from his mistakes.

Gyatso, T. (Dalai Lama XIV). (1990). *Freedom in exile: The autobiography of the Dalai Lama.* New York: HarperCollins.

In 1940 a six-year-old child was proclaimed the 14th Dalai Lama of Tibet. He served as a spiritual and political leader until an army of the People's Republic of China forced his exile in 1959. He has continued to lead the 100,000 refugees who followed him to India as the Tibetan Government in Exile. His Five-Point Peace Plan in 1987, proposing the restoration of Tibet and the protection of its citizens' fundamental human rights, earned him the Nobel Peace Prize in 1989.

Halberstam, D. (1983). *The best and the brightest.* New York: Penguin.

This is a study of the people who filled cabinet and other high government positions in the administration of John F. Kennedy. It questions why so many of their decisions and policies were later proved to be wrong.

Heifetz, R. A. (1994). **Some strategic implications of William Clinton's strengths and weaknesses.** *Political Psychology, 15*(4),763-768.

Heifetz comments about William Clinton's presidential style. He states that Clinton's ebullience and dynamism reflect a belief in an enormous personal power to solve complex problems and heal others' personal pain. Clinton's desire to be up close and personal with the public, his verbal and organizational skills, and his persistence are considered both strengths and weaknesses. Heifetz notes that President Clinton's style during his first nine months in office closely parallels his style during his first term as governor of Arkansas, which was consumed with setbacks but served as a valuable learning experience.

Iacocca, L., & Novak, W. (1984). *Iacocca: An autobiography.* New York: Bantam Books.

This book provides an autobiographical account of Lee Iacocca's life in leadership, from his 32 years with Ford Motor Company to his taking over the helm of Chrysler. It is filled with personal reflections on his experiences and views of corporate and national leadership. Includes index.

Isaacson, W. (1992). *Kissinger: A biography.* New York: Simon & Schuster.

Henry Kissinger has as many critics as admirers. This biography attempts to remain unbiased in the account of the teenage refugee who fled Nazi Germany and became Richard Nixon's secretary of state. He is an undisputed political genius and statesman, but his role in the public spotlight made him a celebrity with enormous power in domestic and foreign affairs. Extensively researched, this book describes Kissinger's influence on the Vietnam War; on peace summits in Moscow, Beijing, and the Mideast; and on Watergate. Includes bibliographical references and index.

James, D. C. (1982). **Command crisis: MacArthur and the Korean War.** *Harmon Memorial Lectures in Military History, 24,* 1-16.

The controversy surrounding the dismissal of MacArthur by Truman is explored.

Kearns, D. (1976). *Lyndon Johnson and the American dream.* New York: New American Library.

Kearns has taken her observations and what LBJ told her during their years together as part of the White House Fellows Program and distilled them into an anecdotal-analytical picture of his personality and his accumulation of power. The author discusses how this power was put to use in light of the nature of political power in general and the changing character of U.S. government since the 1930s. Includes bibliographical references and index.

Keegan, J. (1987). *The mask of command.* New York: Viking.

Historian Keegan recognizes "the leader of men in warfare can show himself to his followers only through a mask, but a mask made in such form as will mark him to men of his time and place as the leader they want and need." It is the intent of the author to penetrate behind the mask. The following are discussed: "Alexander the Great and Heroic Leadership"; "Wellington: The Anti-hero"; "Grant and Unheroic Leadership"; and "False Heroic: Hitler as Supreme Commander." He concludes with a provocative "Post-heroic: Command in the Nuclear World." Includes bibliography and index.

King, M. L., Jr. (1964). *Why we can't wait.* New York: Harper & Row.

An inside account of the nonviolent movement for Civil Rights, which achieved its greatest victory to date with the demonstration in Birmingham in the summer of 1963. Rejecting both planned gradualism and unplanned spontaneity, King here reveals himself as a master strategist in conducting Civil Rights demonstrations.

Lansing, A. (1976). *Endurance.* New York: Avon.

This is an account of Sir Ernest Shackleton's Imperial Trans-Antarctic Expedition of 1915. "For scientific leadership give me Scott; for swift and efficient travel, Amundsen; but when you are in a hopeless situation, when there seems no way out, get down on your knees and pray for Shackleton."

LeVeness, F. P., & Sweeney, J. P. (Eds.). (1987). *Women leaders in contemporary U.S. politics.* Boulder, CO: Lynne Rienner.

Based on personal interviews, this book is a collection of biographical sketches of nine women who have achieved success in politics. It focuses on their career paths, their unique areas of involvement, and their positions on women's issues. Shared character traits are identified as supportive families, strong values, religious upbringing, and educational achievements. Among the women studied are Shirley Chisolm, Dianne Feinstein, Geraldine Ferraro, and Sandra Day O'Connor. Includes bibliographical references and index.

Little, M., & Haley, A. (1965). *The autobiography of Malcolm X.* New York: Grove Press.

Malcolm X describes the brutalities suffered by his family and himself, but also comments on his own degeneracy and his two conversions.

Luecke, R. A. (1994). *Scuttle your ships before advancing: And other lessons from history on leadership and change for today's managers.* New York: Oxford University Press.

Luecke differentiates between the hard sciences, which accumulate knowledge from each generation, and the moral sciences, which need to be continually relearned. The moral sciences—leadership, diplomacy, and negotiation—occur in difficult and ambiguous situations. Luecke's historical references to leaders in such situations provide lessons for today's leadership studies. Included are Hernán Cortés, Aztec emperor; Louis XI, king of France; Martin Luther, religious reformer; Hadrian,

Roman emperor; Thomas Hutchinson, British loyalist; and Lyndon Johnson, U.S. president. Includes bibliographical references and index.

Manchester, W. (1978). *American Caesar: Douglas MacArthur, 1880-1964.* Boston: Little, Brown.

General of the Army, Douglas MacArthur "was a great thundering paradox of a man, noble and ignoble, inspiring and outrageous, arrogant and shy, the best of men and the worst of men, the most protean, most ridiculous, and most sublime." Includes bibliographical references and index.

Manchester, W. (1983). *The last lion: Winston Spencer Churchill.* Boston: Little, Brown.

Working with diaries, memoranda, government documents, the private correspondence of Churchill and others, and interviews with Churchill's surviving colleagues and members of his family, the author provides a narrative recreating the past and private life of Churchill. This is the first of a two-volume biography. Includes bibliography and index.

New

Mankiller, W., & Wallis, M. (1993). *Mankiller: A chief and her people.* New York: St. Martin's Press.

Wilma Mankiller tells the story of the Cherokee people and of her emergence as their first female chief. Like her ancestors before her, Mankiller was forced to leave her family home in Oklahoma during a government relocation program. And, like her ancestors, she returned to her ancestral home. Her journey in the years between reflects the history of her people—facing prejudice and fighting for their heritage. During the Native American occupation of Alcatraz from 1969 to 1971, Mankiller experienced a political awakening and began her work in the revitalization of tribal communities. She later raised funds for Native American causes, formed government relations, met her mentor Ross Swimmer, and rose through the leadership ranks of the Cherokee Nation. In 1985, Mankiller became chief of the Cherokees upon Swimmer's resignation and was subsequently reelected to serve two more terms. Her leadership resulted in the legal and moral recognition of Native American nations and their self-governance.

McFeely, W. S. (1981). *Grant: A biography.* New York: Norton.

This biography of Ulysses S. Grant, Union Army Commander and 18th president of the United States, tells "a story of the quest of an ordinary American man in the mid-nineteenth century to make his mark. Grant failed as a peacetime army officer, a farmer, a minor businessman, a store clerk—and still he wanted to be taken into account." Includes bibliography and index.

Meier, A. (1965). **On the role of Martin Luther King.** *New Politics, 4*, 52-59.

Martin Luther King, Jr.'s combination of militancy and conservatism led to his great success. King better than anyone else could articulate the desires of blacks both to the blacks and to white America. This, along with his ability to hold the center position between conservative and radical groups, made King an effective leader.

Morgenthau, H. J., & Hein, D. (1983). *Essays on Lincoln's faith and politics: Volume 4.* Lanham, MD: University Press of America.

Morgenthau approached Lincoln's view of ethics and religion from the vantage point of the political scientist and historian. Hein has approached the study of Lincoln's faith as a theologian and religious historian. Lincoln's religious and political ethics represented the core values in the American political tradition.

Nair, K. (1994). *A higher standard of leadership: Lessons from the life of Gandhi.* San Francisco: Berrett-Koehler.

Although he never held public office, Gandhi had enormous influence on his country. His religious principles drove him to seek equality for the millions of "untouchables" at the bottom of India's caste system. Nair believes that Gandhi's heroism, which stemmed not from violence but from bravery and moral purpose, provides a fine example for young people. Gandhi's higher standard of leadership was based on fundamental values and commitment to his fellow citizens. Includes bibliographical references and index.

Oates, S. B. (1983). *Let the trumpet sound: The life of Martin Luther King, Jr.* New York: New American Library.

This is a magnificent recreation of a life—of a boy dominated by the minister father who "ruled his home like a fierce Old Testament patriarch"; of a young scholar passionately caught up in the teachings of Thoreau and Gandhi; of a man driven by his vision of racial equality. Stephen Oates portrays the forces that shaped "a very human man"—parental, cultural, spiritual, and intellectual—into the right person for a crucial moment in American history. Includes bibliographical references and index.

Phillips, D. T. (1992). *Lincoln on leadership: Executive strategies for tough times.* New York: Warner Books.

Taking a historical perspective in search for tomorrow's leadership solutions, Phillips explores the qualities that

made Abraham Lincoln one of America's most revered leaders. Lincoln's talent with people, his character, management style, and communicative abilities are analyzed to identify keys that will serve today's leaders. Phillips explains why we should seize the initiative and never relinquish it, wage only one war at a time, encourage risk-taking while providing job security, make requests or suggestions instead of issuing orders, and, once in a while, let things slip. Includes bibliographical references and index.

New
Phillips, D. T. (1997). *The founding fathers on leadership: Classic teamwork in changing times.* New York: Warner.

Phillips combines history lessons with examples of team leadership in this book on America's founding fathers. Samuel Adams is described as a rabble-rouser whose passionate indignation painted a vision for America's independence. George Washington inspired followers when he read the Declaration of Independence to the soldiers of the Continental Army. Benjamin Franklin built strong alliances to shore up the new country's weaknesses and lift morale. These leaders and dozens more provide leadership lessons for present-day executives and teams. Includes a bibliography and an index.

New
Powell, C. (1995). *My American journey.* New York: Ballantine.

Colin Powell is one of this country's premier military leaders. In this book he tells the story of his life, from his childhood in Harlem to his marriage, to his experiences in Vietnam, Panama, and Desert Storm. Includes index and photographs.

Prewitt, K., & Stone, A. (1973). *The ruling elites: Elite theory, power, and American democracy.* New York: Harper & Row.

The authors present a brief examination of elite theory through both a philosophical and historical summary of the elitist position. Includes a bibliography.

Renshon, S. A. (Ed.). (1995). *The Clinton presidency: Campaigning, governing, and the psychology of leadership.* Boulder, CO: Westview Press.

During the 1992 presidential campaign, American voters appeared to be more interested in the candidates' personalities than their platforms. In this book, Renshon and other political-science scholars analyze the distinct personalities and perceived leadership styles of George Bush, Bill Clinton, and Ross Perot. Discussion progresses through the post-election/pre-inauguration time period and Clinton's first year in the White House, to assess the relationship between campaign psychology and in-office performance. Includes bibliographical references and index.

Roberts, W. (1985). *Leadership secrets of Attila the Hun.* New York: Warner Books.

The history books describe Attila the Hun as a 5th-century tyrant who ruled a band of rapists and murderers as they plundered their way across the Roman Empire. Roberts suggests that we view Attila as an entrepreneur who forged a cohesive team from an uncivilized horde of barbarians. Roberts explains why he considers Attila to have been a successful negotiator, field marshal, and visionary leader.

New
Salinger, P. (1997). *John F. Kennedy, Commander in Chief: A profile in leadership.* New York: Penguin Studio.

Salinger, former press secretary to President Kennedy, shares his account of Kennedy's military leadership. In this book, he tells how it felt to be an insider at the behind-the-scenes decision making during the Bay of Pigs, the building of the Berlin Wall, the beginnings of U.S. involvement in Vietnam, the space race, and the Cuban missile crisis. Salinger tells his stories through fond memories, excerpts from speeches, and many photographs. Includes index.

Schlesinger, A. M., Jr. (1985). *Robert Kennedy and his times* (2nd ed.). New York: Ballantine.

Historian Schlesinger writes as an admirer and friend of Robert Kennedy in this massive biography. Granted free access to the Kennedy family papers and other documents, he combines a thorough review of Kennedy's public career with a more intimate record of his private life. Includes bibliographical references and index.

Schwartz, B. (1983). **George Washington and the Whig conception of heroic leadership.** *American Sociological Review, 48*(1), 18-33.

The author discusses the transformation of George Washington from a military hero to a moral symbol and how he demonstrated the Whig conception of heroic leadership. Leadership is discussed in the Republican tradition.

Scott, R. F. (1923). *Scott's last expedition: Captain Scott's own story.* Philadelphia: Transatlantic.

This work contains the personal journals of Captain Robert Falcon Scott on his 1910 to 1912 expedition to the South Pole. "Had we lived, I should have had a tale to tell of the hardihood, endurance, and courage of my compan-

ions which would have stirred the heart of every Englishman." Includes charts and illustrations.

Silk, L., & Silk, M. (1981). *The American establishment.* New York: Avon.

The establishment as the third important force in American society—following democracy and capitalism—is the subject of this study of the U.S. power structure. What the establishment is, how it operates, and the powerful role it plays in U.S. history today are examined in minihistories of what the authors believe to be the nation's most influential organizations. Includes bibliographical references and indexes.

Simonton, D. K. (1994). *Greatness: Who makes history and why.* New York: Guilford Press.

This book is grounded in the psychology of history. The author considers psychological factors such as birth order, personality, madness, and genius to identify characteristics of those who influence society. Artists, authors, composers, politicians, scientists, inventors, military heroes, movie stars, and criminals serve as examples to support his theories. Includes bibliographical references and indexes.

New
Skowronek, S. (1997). *The politics presidents make: Leadership from John Adams to Bill Clinton* (New ed.). Cambridge, MA: Belknap Press.

Originally published in 1993, this new edition has an updated preface and afterword with insights on President Bill Clinton's leadership. The book examines recurring leadership patterns in presidential history and links modern presidents to their predecessors by similarity of political style or situation. In particular, presidents are considered as agents of change. Three types of presidential change agents are discussed in detail. *Reconstruction* represents an opposition to the previous administration and the most promising of all situations for the exercise of political leadership. Thomas Jefferson, Abraham Lincoln, and Franklin Roosevelt fall into this category. *Articulation* represents a stable situation in which a president has the opportunity to be innovative. James Monroe, Theodore Roosevelt, and Lyndon Johnson are examples in this category. *Disjunction*-type presidents assume power in impossible situations. Their affiliation with failed commitments can lead only to lost credibility. John Quincy Adams, Herbert Hoover, and Jimmy Carter are described as disjunction-type presidents. Includes bibliographical references in notes and an index.

Terrill, R. (1980). ***Mao: A biography.*** New York: Harper & Row.

Terrill's biography of the late Chinese leader is imbued with his familiarity with and respect for Chinese culture. He shows how Mao identified his own suppression as a boy under an unrelenting, dictatorial father with the suppression of the peasants and consequently forged strength and lessons useful in his complex future. Includes bibliographical references and index.

Thompson, K. W. (Ed.). (1983). ***Ten presidents and the press.*** Lanham, MD: University Press of America.

This volume brings together the work of leading presidential interpreters and scholars who met for extended discussions at the Miller Center. It contains presentations and discussions on ten presidents and their relations with the press: Woodrow Wilson, Franklin Roosevelt, Harry Truman, Dwight Eisenhower, John Kennedy, Lyndon Johnson, Richard Nixon, Gerald Ford, Jimmy Carter, and Ronald Reagan. Includes a bibliography.

Verma, M. M. (1990). ***Gandhi's technique of mass mobilization.*** New Delhi, India: R. K. Gupta.

Gandhi led 400 million people from tyranny and poverty toward self-respect, self-reliance, and socioeconomic justice. He had deep insight into mass psyche and its collective strength. To fight a despotic government, he transformed his people's passive acceptance into organized, nonviolent withdrawal of cooperation and support. His integrated technique incorporated religious, intellectual, moral, social, political, economic, and psychological approaches.

New
Washington, J. M. (1986). ***I have a dream: Writings and speeches that changed the world.*** San Francisco: HarperCollins.

This is a collection of Martin Luther King, Jr.'s most famous speeches and critiques. It includes: *I Have a Dream, Letter from a Birmingham Jail, The Drum Major Instinct,* and *Pilgrimage to Nonviolence.* Washington provides a chronology of King's life and has arranged the speeches in sequence with an introduction on the time period and significance.

Wecter, D. (1972). ***The hero in America: A chronicle of hero-worship.*** New York: Charles Scribner's Sons.

With this 1941 book, Dixon Wecter was the first historian to undertake the task of examining the impact of the

known political, military, and celebrated leaders/heroes of American history. He asks the question, "How do Americans choose their heroes?" Throughout its 18 chapters, Wecter examines the public personalities who have come to represent the symbols of government, our national ideals, and what is best about being American. This is a classic presentation of our past leaders. Detailed profiles cover the pilgrim founders to the architect of the New Deal. Includes bibliography and index.

Williams, T. H. (1969). ***Huey Long.*** New York: Knopf.

This is the biography of a Louisiana governor and U.S. Senator and a study of Southern and national politics. Williams maintains that Long in the beginning reached for power in order to do good and that "finally the means and the end became so entwined in his mind that he could not distinguish between them, could not tell whether he wanted power as a method or for its own sake." It is based on nearly 300 interviews, manuscripts, documents, newspapers, periodicals, and secondary sources. Includes bibliographical references.

Wills, G. (1994). ***Certain trumpets: The call of leaders.*** New York: Simon & Schuster.

Wills, the Pulitzer Prize-winning author of *Lincoln at Gettysburg: The Words That Remade America* (Touchstone Books, 1992), reexamines the nature of the leader-follower partnership in this book. He claims that leadership is the reciprocal engagement of two wills, "one leading (often in disguised ways), the other following (often while resisting)." Through biographical sketches of 16 leaders and 16 antileaders, Wills paints a portrait of leadership through history and across the range of human experience. Representing politics is a discussion of Franklin D. Roosevelt as an elected leader and Adlai Stevenson as an antitype. Other portraits include: religious leader, King David and antitype, Solomon; military leader, Napoleon and antitype, George McClellan; business leader, Ross Perot and antitype, Roger Smith; artistic leader, Martha Graham and antitype, Madonna. Includes bibliographical references and index.

Wofford, H. (1980). ***Of Kennedys and Kings: Making sense of the sixties.*** New York: Farrar, Straus and Giroux.

Wofford combines memoirs and narrative in this book, mingling others' opinions with his own to give balanced assessments of people and events. Wofford is positive about the accomplishments of the decade and remains committed to public service and responsible political action. Includes index.

DIVERSITY

GENERAL

New
Abramms, B., & Simons, G. F. (Eds.) (1996). *Cultural diversity sourcebook.* Amherst, MA: HRD Press.

Barbara Ehrenreich, Robert Fulghum, bell hooks, Maya Angelou, George Bush, and Elie Wiesel are among the contributors to this anthology of writings, speeches, poems, magazine articles, and short stories addressing diversity. Abramms and Simons take the unusual step of structuring their book around the issue of class, although some chapters also address race, gender, diversity under fire, applications, spirit, alternative models and visions, and affirmative action.

New
Andrews, E., Riley, F., & Yarborough, D. (1997). **The diversity council.** *Diversity Factor, 5*(4), 21-26.

This article describes how diversity councils provide structured, consistent leadership to change the culture in three companies. At GE, diversity activities have graduated from awareness issues to competencies in team building and communication among people of other races or genders, with different physical abilities, or with a different sexual orientation. GTE is striving to remove barriers through recruitment and hiring practices, development and mentoring, training, and flexibility in work-and-family issues. Top-level executives serve on the diversity councils at both companies. A virtual diversity team leads the effort at Silicon Graphics. All employees with a passion for and commitment to diversity contribute to the initiatives, which include training programs, lunchtime seminars, and shared celebrations sponsored by affinity groups.

New
Blank, R., & Slipp, S. (1994). *Voices of diversity: Real people talk about problems and solutions in a workplace where everyone is not alike.* New York: AMACOM.

Blank and Slipp wrote this book in response to "the urgent managerial appeal: 'What should I know about the experience of the diverse groups?' and 'What should I do about it?'" After a brief introduction to group identity and dynamics, the book profiles different "diverse voices," including African Americans, Asian Americans, Latinos, recent immigrants, women, workers with disabilities, and white men. Each group's description includes statistical information, examples of "scenes from the workplace," and quotes from members of that group. A final section offers suggestions of how managers can best handle

conflicts with diverse employees, and "guidelines for better relationships" for workers in both the minority and dominant groups. Includes index and suggested readings.

Carnevale, A. P., & Stone, S. C. (1995). *The American mosaic: An in-depth report on the future of diversity at work.* New York: McGraw-Hill.

Research sponsored by the U.S. Department of Labor, the American Society for Training and Development, and the Joyce Foundation is reported in this volume of data and description. The authors analyze the cultural implications, wage issues, and demographic trends for racial and ethnic groups, men and women workers, disabled persons, gay and lesbian workers, and older workers. Historical references, the current debate over affirmative action, and projections for the future are presented. Includes bibliographical references and index.

New
Cox, T., Jr. (1993). *Cultural diversity in organizations: Theory, research, and practice.* San Francisco: Berrett-Koehler.

Cox defines cultural diversity as the "representation, in one social system, of people with distinctly different group affiliations of cultural significance." He argues that managers who maximize the advantages of diversity will profit from innovation and improved communication. A model for planning organizational change contains five parts: 1) leadership must commit to change and map a strategy for communication; 2) there should be assessment of organizational culture, experiences, and attitudes; 3) educational programs should increase awareness and build communication skills; 4) human resource departments should recruit, develop, compensate, and promote without bias; and 5) accountability and evaluation of the change efforts should be ongoing. Concepts covered in this book include: group identities, prejudice, stereotyping, ethnocentrism, organizational culture, acculturation, and informal integration. These concepts are summarized in proposition statements that may be used by teachers and trainers to frame class discussions or exam questions. Includes bibliographical references and index.

New
Cox, T., Jr., & Beale, R. L. (1997). *Developing competency to manage diversity: Readings, cases and activities.* San Francisco: Berrett-Koehler.

Cultural Diversity in Organizations: Theory, Research and Practice was published in 1993, and Cox calls this book the "action" sequel to his original "theory book." He and Beale provide managers with the tools they needs to successfully manage a diverse workforce, including 31 activities, 23 readings, and six case studies. The tools are divided into three categories—those that will provide a foundation for competency in diversity, tools that develop individual competency, and tools that develop organizational competency. Includes bibliographical references and index.

New

DiTomaso, N., & Hooijberg, R. (1996). **Diversity and the demands of leadership.** *Leadership Quarterly: Special Issue: Leadership and Diversity (Part II)*, 7(2), 163-187.

In the past, diversity literature and leadership literature have been connected only minimally, and studies of diversity have considered leaders "the targets of influence rather than the agents of change." This introduction to Part II of the special Leadership and Diversity issue argues that diversity and leadership must be connected on multiple levels and in multiple dimensions. The authors begin making these connections by dividing the existing diversity literature into four parts: interpersonal and intergroup interaction, the impact of organizational transformation on diversity, social-science studies of inequality, and the morality and ethics of diversity and multiculturalism.

New

Dobbs, M. F. (1996). **Managing diversity: Lessons from the private sector.** *Public Personnel Management*, 25(3), 351-367.

Dobbs describes successful diversity programs at three major companies, including the Xerox Corporation, and identifies the qualities that make them successful. These include having top management commitment, employee support, a variety of interventions, and a supportive corporate culture. These programs are then compared with the city of San Diego's diversity program. Dobbs describes a new framework, modeled on corporate diversity programs, that public agencies can use. Advice on integrating diversity into organizational practice, dealing directly with resistance, and using evaluations is included.

Ferdman, B. M. (Ed.). (1994). *A resource guide for teaching and research on diversity.* St. Louis, MO: American Assembly of Collegiate Schools of Business.

This guide is designed for faculty and program directors who plan and teach courses on diversity. Educators and researchers share perspectives on the definition of diversity, course content and philosophy, pedagogical approaches, and management theory. Syllabi of 27 courses focus on diversity in undergraduate, master's level, and doctoral programs. Eight more syllabi illustrate

how diversity can be integrated into other courses. Reading lists and two additional bibliographies suggest books, articles, and films to supplement coursework. A list of 193 teachers, researchers, and consultants working on diversity includes name, address, phone number, area of expertise, current projects, and publications for each. Includes bibliographical references and index.

Gardenswartz, L., & Rowe, A. (1993). *Managing diversity: A complete desk reference and planning guide.* San Diego, CA: Pfeiffer.

By the turn of the century, 70% of new entrants to the workforce will be women and minorities. Diverse cultures within organizations will require that leaders learn to: communicate cross-culturally, conduct diversity audits, build teams, plan meetings, and create corporate cultures that embrace diversity. Worksheets and activities support the text for implementation of techniques suggested throughout the book. Includes bibliographical references and index.

New

Gentile, M.C. (1994). *Differences that work: Organizational excellence through diversity.* Boston: Harvard Business School Press.

Gentile has brought together 16 articles on diversity from the *Harvard Business Review.* Together they present the idea that new growth, learning, and innovation can come from taking another perspective on the differences among people in the workforce. The book begins with a historical look at discrimination and the demographics of those who work. It then focuses on the issues of harassment and the limitations in job advancement faced by minorities. Other topics discussed are AIDS, aging, and family life and their relationship to the workplace. Gentile stresses that differences among people can enhance success because they channel new learning both in individuals and in organizations. Includes bibliographical references and index.

New

Hooijberg, R., & DiTomaso, N. (1996). **Leadership in and of demographically diverse organizations.** *Leadership Quarterly: Special Issue: Leadership and Diversity (Part I)*, 7(1), 1-19.

This article introduces a special issue on leadership and demographically diverse organizations. The authors review current knowledge of male/female, white/non-white, and U.S./non-U.S. differences and their relevance to leadership. They propose six areas for further research: 1) use a leader-member exchange model to examine racially mixed dyads; 2) explore various ethnocentric views; 3) learn the effect that a leader from one demographic group has on all members of a team; 4) study the impact of integrated leadership at the top of an organization; 5) explore the characteristics of masculine, feminine, and androgynous behaviors and the indication of leadership emergence; and 6) study influence tactics.

New
Kossek, E. E., & Lobel, S. A. (Eds.). (1996). *Managing diversity: Human resource strategies for transforming the workplace.* Cambridge, MA: Blackwell Business.

Scholars in human resource management contribute essays on the subject of diversity at work. They acknowledge the complexities of designing HR practices for nonhomogeneous groups, which include persons of different genders, ethnicity, functions, nationality, language, ability, religion, lifestyle, or tenure. Increased diversity in the workforce combined with the turbulence caused by downsizing and rapidly changing technology together increase the importance of developmental relationships and activities. The authors recommend strategies for recruiting and selection, mentoring, and training. Includes bibliographical references and index.

Morrison, A. M., & Crabtree, K. M. (1992). *Developing diversity in organizations: A digest of selected literature.* Greensboro, NC: Center for Creative Leadership.

Descriptions and analyses of 85 articles are organized according to the five-step action process introduced in Morrison's *The New Leaders* (1992). The five steps are: discover diversity problems, strengthen top management commitment, choose solutions that fit a balanced strategy, demand results and revisit goals, and use building blocks to maintain momentum. There are several case studies and articles about "best companies." Includes bibliographical references and index.

Morrison, A. M., Ruderman, M. N., & Hughes-James, M. (1993). *Making diversity happen: Controversies and solutions.* Greensboro, NC: Center for Creative Leadership.

This is a report from the 1992 CCL conference, "Leadership Diversity: Beyond Awareness Into Action." The conference format included concurrent sessions, a scenario-based panel discussion, interactive theater, and small-group discussions. Four major themes emerged and provided the basis for this report: 1) What does diversity mean to organizations? 2) How can organizational commitment to diversity be developed? 3) How should a diversity initiative proceed? 4) What are some important diversity practices? Includes bibliographical references.

New
Rusaw, A. C. (1996). **All God's children: Leading diversity in churches as organizations.** *Leadership Quarterly: Special Issue: Leadership and Diversity (Part II), 7*(2), 229-241.

How do pastors, as leaders without formal authority, inspire their congregations to support diversity and integration? Rusaw conducted a case-study analysis of pastors at three urban churches to discover how they created follower commitment to desegregation. Four leadership strategies pastors use in response to diversity issues are identified: raising awareness and support for subgroups within the organization, modulating change in small-group settings, giving voice to different stories, and mediating transcendent vision and experiences.

New
Scandura, T. A., & Lankau, M. J. (1996). **Developing diverse leaders: A leader-member exchange approach.** *Leadership Quarterly: Special Issue: Leadership and Diversity (Part II), 7*(2), 243-263.

The leader-member exchange theory, a much-studied approach to leadership, focuses on the working relationship between leaders and followers. However, LMX literature has not addressed the role that diversity due to race or gender may play in these relationships. This article attempts to integrate the existing LMX and diversity literature to show how diversity affects the stages of the leader-follower relationship, including the role-taking, role-making, and role-routinization stages. The authors believe that understanding how differences affect the success of leader-member relationships will greatly enhance the promise of the LMX model.

New
Thackray, C., & McCall, M. (1997). **Women evolving as leaders.** *Journal of Leadership Studies, 4*(2), 18-26.

Thackray and McCall researched leadership from women's perspective to see if women were evolving through time as leaders. They studied ten women—five from the pre-Civil War era and five from the 20th century. Women in the first group included Frances Wright, the first woman to deliver a publicly recorded speech, and Elizabeth Stanton, the first woman to publicly call for the elective franchise. They were found to be more action-oriented and to use greater emotion than 20th-century women. Women leaders of the 20th century included Barbara Jordan, the first black woman to serve on the Texas State Senate, and Geraldine Ferraro, the first female vice-presidential nominee. The findings suggested that women as leaders were evolving through time, although there were not significant differences among the women studied.

New

Thomas, D. A., & Ely, R. J. (1996). **Making differences matter: A new paradigm for managing diversity.** *Harvard Business Review, 74*(5), 79-90.

In the past, companies have viewed diversity two ways, through either the discrimination-and-fairness paradigm or the access-and-legitimacy paradigm. In these two frameworks, say Thomas and Ely, people often feel exploited, and while the staff get diversified, the work does not. They advocate a third paradigm, in which diversity is connected to work perspectives, so that "we are all on the same team, *with* our differences—not *despite* them." After researching organizations across the country, the authors have defined the preconditions and actions necessary for companies to transform their vision of a diversified workplace.

MULTICULTURAL AND GLOBAL

New

Adler, N. J. (1997). *International dimensions of organizational behavior* (3rd ed.). Cincinnati, OH: South-Western College Publishing.

This textbook is based on the premise that "global complexity is neither unpredictable nor random. Variations across cultures and their impacts on organizations follow systematic, predictable patterns." A learning module is included in each chapter. Some examples of chapters are: "Creating Cultural Synergy"; "Multicultural Teams"; and "Global Leadership, Motivation, and Decision Making." Each includes charts, exercises, questions for reflection, cases, and bibliographical references. Adler describes three videos that she produced to supplement lessons in the study of work beyond national boundaries. The most relevant to leadership is the two-part series that follows the development of a multinational team on a project in Africa. *It's a Jungle Out There* and *The Survival Guide* document the team's experience and analyze their problems with cross-cultural communication and decision making. Includes index.

Adler, N. J., & Izraeli, D. N. (1994). *Competitive frontiers: Women managers in a global economy.* Cambridge, MA: Blackwell.

Although women represent over 50% of the world population, in no country do women represent even close to half of the corporate managers. This book presents a cross-national comparison of the cultural, social, legal, economic, and political history of domestic business and management hiring practices. Professors, researchers, and human resources practitioners contribute essays on women in management roles in 21 countries including

Japan, China, Germany, Great Britain, Israel, South Africa, Canada, and the U.S. Includes bibliographical references and index.

Ayman, R., Kreicker, N. A., & Masztal, J. J. (1994). **Defining global leadership in business environments.** *Consulting Psychology Journal, 46*(1), 64-77.

The authors distinguish between international and global leadership. The differences stem not from the activities but from the cross-cultural interaction of a firm's leaders. Internationalism is defined as an exchange across nations. Globalism is defined as a sense of unity across multiple borders. The authors present two training models for teaching global leadership.

New

Dorfman, P. W., Howell, J. P., Hibino, S., Lee, J. K., Tate, U., & Bautista, A. (1997). **Leadership in Western and Asian countries: Commonalities and differences in effective leadership processes across cultures.** *Leadership Quarterly: Special Issue: International and Cross-Cultural Leadership Research (Part I), 8*(3), 233-274.

Can the effectiveness of specific leadership behaviors be generalized across cultures? This study surveyed over 1,500 managers and professionals in five countries—Japan, South Korea, Taiwan, Mexico, and the United States—to determine the effectiveness of six leadership behaviors: directive leadership, leader-contingent rewards, leader-contingent punishment, supportive leadership, participative leadership, and charismatic leadership. Visual models of the results and theoretical descriptions of leadership in each country are given. Overall, the study found that three behaviors (supportive, contingent reward, and charismatic) were culturally universal, while the effectiveness of the other behaviors was culturally specific. Includes bibliographical references.

New

Earley, P. C., & Erez, M. (Eds.). (1997). *New perspectives on international industrial/organizational psychology.* San Francisco: The New Lexington Press.

Do national differences in people's values and beliefs affect their work behavior? This compendium addresses that question by examining recent developments in cross-cultural industrial/organizational psychology around the themes of theory, motivation and values across cultures, working across cultural borders, and power relationships. The chapters, often written by colleagues from different cultures working together, address specific issues that include: organizational justice, decision making, cross-cultural leadership, communication difficulties, and individual-union-organization relationships. Includes bibliographical references and index.

Elashmawi, F., & Harris, P. R. (1993). *Multicultural management: New skills for global success.* Houston: Gulf.

As part of a series on managing cultural differences, this book serves as an orientation to American, Japanese, and Arab business cultures. Space and time, introductions, telephone calls, presentations, training, and group composition are perceived differently in each culture. Appropriate communication is illustrated by situations in a domestic work environment compared to situations in an integrated marketplace. Quizzes throughout each chapter test the reader's understanding of strategies and skills. Includes bibliographical references and index.

New
Harris, P. R., & Moran, R. T. (1996). *Managing cultural differences* (4th ed.). Houston: Gulf.

As part of a series on managing cultural differences, this book serves as a resource for both practitioners and students on how to develop cross-cultural expertise in a global market. Unit I focuses on the worldwide influences impacting leaders and management efforts. Topics include the globalization of economies, challenges in global communications, and creating synergistic relationships amid cultural differences. Unit II focuses on how leaders can understand, analyze, cope with, and become more sensitive to cultural differences while improving interactions in a global market. Unit III offers cultural specifics for doing business in North America, Latin America, Asia, Europe, the Middle East, and Africa. Backgrounds, customs, negotiating strategies, and business courtesies for each region are provided. The authors stress that cultural differences can and should be seen as a resource, not an impediment. An accompanying *Instructor's Guide* for both professors and human resource development professionals is available. Includes index.

New
Hunt, J. G., & Peterson, M. F. (1997). **Overview: International and cross-cultural leadership research.** *Leadership Quarterly: Special Issue: International and Cross-Cultural Leadership Research (Part I), 8*(3), 201-202.

This introduction to the first part of a special issue on international leadership poses the questions the authors hope the issue can answer. Does "leadership" have meaning outside the English language? How can leadership theories with an American bias apply to other countries? Is international leadership an oxymoron? Hunt and Peterson also provide a brief overview of the articles that follow, which address how to adapt American leadership measures to other countries, the problems of a culturally diverse workforce, influence, and motivation.

New
Lewis, R. D. (1996). *When cultures collide: Managing successfully across cultures.* London: Nicholas Brealey.

Lewis addresses both the theoretical and practical aspects of cultural diversity. The first section of his book examines how people are culturally conditioned at an early age and the interrelatedness between language and thought, and later chapters address specific cultural differences and how to handle them. Lewis divides the world's cultures into three rough categories: linear-actives (including Germans and Swiss), multi-actives (including Italians and Latin Americans), and reactives (including Chinese and Finns). A final section offers specific cultural information on more than 20 countries, including Spain, Russia, Italy, Sweden, China, and France. Includes index.

New
Moya Ah Chong, L., & Thomas, D. C. (1997). **Leadership perceptions in cross-cultural context: Pakeha and Pacific Islanders in New Zealand.** *Leadership Quarterly: Special Issue: International and Cross-Cultural Leadership Research (Part I), 8*(3), 275-293.

In New Zealand, citizens of European heritage, mainly descendants of British immigrants, are called Pakeha. This study surveyed Pakeha and Pacific Islander supervisors and employees of major public organizations to determine whether the two ethnic groups view leadership differently. The results support the researchers' hypotheses: leader and follower ethnicity interact to affect follower satisfaction, and leadership prototypes held by members of the two groups seem to have culturally based differences. Includes bibliographical references.

New
Odenwald, S. B. (1996). *GlobalSolutions for teams: Moving from collision to collaboration.* Chicago: Irwin.

Multinational corporations have become a mainstay of today's global economy, and this book is a reference for such corporations and their leaders, offering resources and advice. Chapters address issues such as multinational corporate culture, competencies for global teams, and transformation; and a practical model for global teams is presented. Case studies from companies including Ford, Apple, National Semiconductor, and Motorola follow each chapter. A reference list of assessments, books, videos, and games on international business is included, along with an index and references.

New

Peterson, M. F., & Hunt, J. G. (1997). **International perspectives on international leadership.** *Leadership Quarterly: Special Issue: International and Cross-Cultural Leadership Research (Part I), 8*(3), 203-231.

Peterson and Hunt begin by saying that they hope to offer a context for the work in this special issue on international leadership. They then address four basic questions: Is leadership a global idea? Why study leadership internationally? Why study leadership "scientifically"? Does leadership have a technological/modern U.S. bias? After discussing the existing theories around these themes, the article offers a brief history of the study of leadership from the 19th century through the current status of the discipline, specifically focusing on international studies and international management. Includes bibliographical references.

Punnett, B. J. (1991). **Language, cultural values and preferred leadership style: A comparison of Anglophones and Francophones in Ottawa.** *Canadian Journal of Behavioral Science, 23*(2), 241-244.

In a multicultural country, such as Canada, there are several similarities and differences between those who speak different languages. A study of 319 Anglophone and 126 Francophone middle managers used the *Value Survey Module* and the *Ohio Leadership Behavior Description Questionnaire*. Results suggest that organizational influence has a greater impact on cultural values than does language difference.

New

Rao, A., Hashimoto, K., & Rao, A. (1997). **Universal and culturally specific aspects of managerial influence: A study of Japanese managers.** *Leadership Quarterly: Special Issue: International and Cross-Cultural Leadership Research (Part I), 8*(3), 295-312.

Noting that most measures of managerial influence have been developed in the U.S., the authors developed their own instrument to survey managers in a large Japanese corporation. Their research found that Japanese managers use some culturally specific influence tactics, including sanctions, appeals to higher authority, and socializing, that are not found in American measures. The implications of these findings are also discussed, including the possibility that Japanese managers may have difficulty influencing subordinates from other cultures. Includes bibliographical references.

New

Rhinesmith, S. H. (1993). *A manager's guide to globalization: Six keys to success in a changing world.* Alexandria, VA: American Society for Training and Development.

Rhinesmith believes that any person or organization hoping to compete on the global field must be able to manage the following six areas: 1) the competitive process, 2) complexity, 3) organizational adaptability, 4) multicultural teams, 5) uncertainty, and 6) personal and organizational learning. Each competency has its own action mind-set, personal characteristic, and key practices and tasks (all of which are summarized in an index). A final chapter discusses how to integrate these skills into a cohesive leadership style. Includes bibliographical references and index.

Ritvo, R. A., Litwin, A. H., & Butler, L. (Eds.). (1995). *Managing in the age of change: Essential skills to manage today's diverse workforce.* New York: Irwin.

This book addresses the issues of organizational change and multicultural diversity. Educators, CEOs, policymakers, and researchers share their insights on growth, downsizing, conflict management, and the demographics of the new American workforce. Bob Lee, then president of the Center for Creative Leadership, explains how to accept resistance and turn it into energy. Other chapters include "Sensitizing Managers to Asian-American Diversity Issues," "Hispanics in the Workplace," "The Clonal Effect in Organizations," and "Cross-Cultural Mentoring." Includes index.

New

Sai, Y. (1995). *The eight core values of the Japanese businessman: Toward an understanding of Japanese management.* New York: International Business Press.

Based on a literature review and interviews, Sai's book attempts to explain the complicated values of Japanese businesspeople. The eight core values that are most commonly shared by Japanese in the business world are: group orientation, diligence, aesthetics and perfectionism, curiosity and emphasis on innovation, respect for form, a mind for competition and emphasis on innovation, the importance of silence, and perceptions of time. Each broad value is discussed in more specific terms and illustrated with examples. Includes bibliographical references and index.

New

Seelye, H. N., & Seelye-James, A. (1995). *Culture clash: Managing in a multicultural world.* Chicago: NTC Business Books.

Multicultural business situations are becoming more common, but they can still be difficult to negotiate. This book offers concrete advice to executives and managers who are dealing with other cultures. Each chapter includes case studies, maps, and "toolboxes" containing activities that can help smooth intercultural business dealings. Chapters address issues such as language barriers, developing rapport, protocol, communication styles, and negotiation. Includes bibliographical references and index.

Simons, G. F., Vasquez, C., & Harris, P. R. (1993). *Transcultural leadership: Empowering the diverse workforce.* Houston: Gulf.

"In the new global and domestic workplace we are all immigrants, experiencing culture shock on a daily basis." Ethnic and gender diversity is a growing phenomenon that affects everyday activities, such as conversations, meetings, decision making, training, and resolving disputes. The authors promote a positive attitude toward dealing with diversity through listening to verbal and nonverbal messages, encouraging feedback, relieving stress and prejudice, and managing by values. Achieving acculturation can stimulate high performance and enhanced quality of life at work. Includes bibliographical references and index.

New
Valikangas, L., & Okumura, A. (1997). **Why do people follow leaders? A study of a U.S. and a Japanese change program.** *Leadership Quarterly: Special Issue: International and Cross-Cultural Leadership Research (Part I),* 8(3), 313-337.

What motivates people to follow a leader? The authors argue that this answer differs across cultures. This article examines major change initiatives in two companies, GE in the U.S. and Japanese pharmaceutical manufacturer Eisai, and determines that the two CEOs used very different methods to motivate their employees. The American leader emphasized the consequences of the changes for employees and appealed to the shared values of all employees, and the Japanese leader focused on developing a corporate identity that would inspire followers to change in order to remain a part of their social group. Appendices describe the two companies, their histories, and their change plans in detail. Includes bibliographical references.

New
Wilson, M. S., Hoppe, M. H., & Sayles, L. R. (1996). *Managing across cultures: A learning framework.* Greensboro, NC: Center for Creative Leadership.

The multicultural team of authors combine their education, research, and experience to design a framework for U.S. managers who are confronted with cross-cultural business interactions. The framework is composed of seven dimensions that describe workplace dilemmas experienced in every culture: identity, goals, authority, ambiguity, knowledge acquisition, time, and outlook on life. Each chapter discusses one dilemma in the form of a continuum with two opposing choices. First, the authors provide a description of values for each pole. Then, examples from the workplace reveal how those values affect specific situations. Finally, the authors present four steps to apply the framework and improve cross-cultural understanding: observe your own and others' behavior, construct a provisional hypothesis or stereotype for behaviors in other cultures, constantly revise your hypothesis based on your experiences, and challenge yourself to grow. Includes bibliographical references.

New
Yoshimura, N., & Anderson, P. (1997). *Inside the Kaisha: Demystifying Japanese business behavior.* Boston: Harvard Business School Press.

A Japanese middle manager and an American professor collaborate in this effort to describe the internal workings of large Japanese companies (*kaishas*). Based on interviews with Japanese salarymen, the book challenges the idea that Japanese business practices are based on traditional cultural values. Rather, Yoshimura and Anderson argue that Japanese businesses have developed "organizational mechanisms" that dictate behavior. They use these mechanisms to explain six apparent contradictions that exist in Japanese companies; for example, harmony is emphasized, yet workers are fiercely competitive. Includes bibliographical references and index.

GENDER

New
Adler, N. J. (1996). **Global women political leaders: An invisible history, an increasingly important future.** *Leadership Quarterly: Special Issue: Leadership and Diversity (Part I),* 7(1), 133-161.

Adler draws a historic pattern of women's global leadership with a list of 25 women who have led modern governments. She compares their paths to power, high visibility, and inconsistent support to find similarities across time and cultures. When compared to the experiences of men in global leadership positions, a pattern emerges. Among the women on her list are: Indira Gandhi, former Prime Minister of India; Golda Meir, former Prime Minister of Israel; Aung San Suu Kyi, Opposition Leader in Burma; Margaret Thatcher, former Prime Minister of Great Britain; and Isabel Perón, former President of Argentina.

Albrecht, L., & Brewer, R. M. (Eds.). (1990). ***Bridges of power: Women's multicultural alliances.*** Philadelphia: New Society Publishers.

Growing out of a conference held in 1988 by the National Women's Studies Association, this book reflects the many perspectives of the diverse conference participants on ways to enhance women's power and leadership through alliances and coalitions. Representative chapter titles include "American Indian Women: Diverse Leadership for Social Change," "African-American Women Leaders and the Politics of Alliance Work," "Conflict and Cooperation Among Women in the Welfare Rights Movement," and "Feminist Alliances: A View from Peru."

Astin, H. S., & Leland, C. (1991). ***Women of influence, women of vision: A cross-generational study of leaders and social change.*** San Francisco: Jossey-Bass.

Astin and Leland profile 77 women in education who provided leadership in the modern women's movement of the 1960s through the 1980s. This book documents key experiences, formative influences, role models, perspectives, and accomplishments of the women who initiated and sustained a major social movement. The intent of this book is to provide a conceptual model for future studies of leadership and social change. Practical strategies are offered for emerging leaders to overcome discouragement, avoid burnout, and find time for personal lives. Includes bibliographical references and index.

Barrentine, P. (Ed.). (1993). ***When the canary stops singing: Women's perspectives on transforming business.*** San Francisco: Berrett-Koehler.

Early in the century, miners would send a canary below ground to test the environment. When the canary stopped singing, the miners knew the air was toxic. Barrentine suggests that, as the canaries were to the miners, women are harbingers of needed transformation in today's business environment. Fifteen women entrepreneurs, executives, and consultants contribute essays about the need for more humane and nurturing workplaces. They recommend a harmony between men and women to achieve a full and productive work environment that benefits everyone. Includes bibliographical references and index.

New
Berdahl, J. L. (1996). **Gender and leadership in work groups: Six alternative models.** *Leadership Quarterly: Special Issue: Leadership and Diversity (Part I), 7*(1), 21-40.

Berdahl compares six models to determine the emergence of task-oriented (masculine) or social (feminine) leadership. The first model, No Sex Differences, assumes that personal differences in abilities or behavior have no

connection to one's gender. The second model, Stereotypical Sex Differences, asserts that social differences have biological origins. The third model, Gender Schema, claims that gender role identity is a psychological choice. The fourth model, Status Roles, relates to expected competence or dominance in group interaction. The fifth model, Social Roles, emphasizes the social expectations of men and women. Finally, the Multicultural Model suggests that cultural and experiential differences, more than sex differences, account for individual task-oriented or social-leadership behaviors. Berdahl recommends that gender/leadership researchers study groups over time and use a variety of models.

Bilimoria, D., & Piderit, S. K. (1994). **Board committee membership: Effects of sex-based bias.** *Academy of Management Journal, 37*(6), 1453-1477.

Member characteristics of Fortune 300 board committees were considered for gender, experience, occupation, tenure, and business affiliation to find evidence of sex discrimination. Results indicated that the low numbers of women on corporate boards, in general, and on influential committees, specifically, are related to lack of board experience. This lack of experience is related to the difficulty women have in breaking into the circle of power that provides board experience.

New
Catalyst. (1996). ***Women in corporate leadership: Progress and prospects.*** New York: Author.

In 1995, Catalyst surveyed 461 female executives about their career paths and strategies. They found that successful women's career paths were spread across industries and functions. Their critical career strategies were: 1) exceed performance expectations, 2) develop a style with which male managers are comfortable, 3) seek difficult assignments, and 4) have an influential mentor. In related research, Catalyst surveyed 325 CEOs of Fortune 1000 companies on the subject of female executives. The CEOs cited lack of experience as the primary reason why so few women achieve top-level positions. They considered appropriate efforts to support female leadership development: 1) giving women high visibility assignments, 2) ensuring that diverse candidates are considered in succession plans, and 3) mentoring programs.

Denmark, F. L. (1993). **Women, leadership, and empowerment.** *Psychology of Women Quarterly, 17*(3), 343-356.

This literature review first summarizes the changing definition of leadership and its early focus on men. Recent studies discuss how and why women have been slow to enter the executive arena, and the assigned characteristics of feminine and masculine styles. Denmark's research, in progress at the time of this article, views leadership from a feminist perspective and calls for women in positions of leadership to empower other women to break the glass ceiling.

Eagly, A. H., & Johnson, B. T. (1990). **Gender and leadership style: A meta-analysis.** *Psychological Bulletin, 108*(2), 233-256.

Research comparing the leadership styles of women and men is reviewed. Almost 400 organizational studies, laboratory experiments, and assessment studies provide evidence of a presence and absence of differences between the sexes. Comparisons are measured between interpersonal versus task styles and between democratic versus autocratic styles. This quantitative review has established a complex set of findings and the authors recommend further scrutiny.

Eagly, A. H., & Karau, S. J. (1991). **Gender and the emergence of leaders: A meta-analysis.** *Journal of Personality and Social Psychology, 60*(5), 685-710.

Reviews of 75 research findings on the emergence of male and female leaders in leaderless groups are analyzed. Characteristics analyzed are date of research publication, author gender, age of subjects studied, group size, gender typing of task, social complexity of task, and amount of interaction. The results indicate that males focus on instrumental behaviors and females focus on expressive behaviors. Thus, the tendency is for men to lead and for women to serve as social facilitators.

Eagly, A. H., Karau, S. J., & Makhijani, M. G. (1995). **Gender and the effectiveness of leaders: A meta-analysis.** *Psychological Bulletin, 117*(1), 125-145.

The authors aggregated the results of 76 laboratory and organizational studies on gender and leader effectiveness. Although some differences in behavior were reported, no difference was found in the general tendency of men and women leaders. Conditions that favored one gender over another were the type of organization, the level of leadership, and the prejudicial attitudes about specific leadership roles. Leaders received higher ratings in roles that were congruent with masculine/feminine expectations. Male leaders were rated higher in task-related roles, while women received higher ratings in relationship roles.

Eagly, A. H., Makhijani, M. G., & Klonsky, B. G. (1992). **Gender and the evaluation of leaders: A meta-analysis.** *Psychological Bulletin, 111*(1), 3-22.

This review of research examines whether women are evaluated less favorably than their male counterparts in leadership roles. Leadership characteristics are held constant, using only gender as a variable. Outcomes

indicate a small tendency to devaluate female leaders overall. But in situations of autocratic or nonparticipatory leadership style, women are devalued significantly more than their male counterparts.

Fagenson, E. A. (1993). ***Women in management: Trends, issues, and challenges in managerial diversity.*** Newbury Park, CA: Sage.

Fagenson traces women managers' experiences using an interdisciplinary analysis. The book begins with an examination of historical and global perspectives. The issues of ethnicity, health, and family responsibilities are addressed. It concludes with a look at future trends in job discrimination and the restructuring of organizations from a feminist perspective. Includes bibliographical references and index.

New

Fitzgerald, L. (1997). **Women in leadership: A student's perspective.** *Leadership Journal: Women in Leadership—Sharing the Vision, 1*(2), 137-141.

Written by a senior majoring in Leadership Studies at the University of Richmond, this article describes the author's experiences as a woman in leadership positions, including president of the student government. She also lists three traits that she has observed in women leaders—the Wonder Woman mind-set, the relationship-oriented nature of women's leadership, and the fact that women expect emotional satisfaction from their leadership positions. Fitzgerald believes that, taken to extremes, these can be counterproductive, and she offers suggestions on how women can best manage these traits.

Gibson, C. B. (1995). **An investigation of gender differences in leadership across four countries.** *Journal of International Business Studies, 26*(2), 255-279.

Over 200 male and female managers in Norway, Sweden, Australia, and the U.S. were surveyed about leadership styles and behaviors to determine gender and cultural differences. In all four countries, results showed that males placed the strongest emphasis on goal-setting behavior and females emphasized interpersonal-facilitation behavior. One significant difference in style preference emerged from the Australian subjects who preferred a directive style of leadership, whereas all others preferred a nondirective style. The authors suggest that their findings serve as a base for further research on global and gender differences.

Glaser, C., & Smalley, B. S. (1995). *Swim with the dolphins: How women can succeed in corporate America on their own terms.* New York: Warner Books.

Being female is an advantage in today's workplace. The desired behaviors for today's managers are: empowering, nurturing, and consensus building—behaviors that come naturally to many women. This book presents a balanced management style, the style of a dolphin manager—decisive, flexible, confident, and caring. Today's manager won't get far behaving as a shark—commanding and controlling—or as a guppy—powerless and ineffective. Thirteen dolphin-women who swam to positions of power share their stories. Not only women can be dolphins, though. The authors include tips for men who are seeking a balanced management style. Includes bibliographical references and index.

Guy, M. E. (1993). **Three steps forward, two steps backward: The status of women's integration into public management.** *Public Administration Review, 53*(4), 285-292.

Guy outlines the pattern of women's integration into public management and contrasts it to women's integration into society at large. High or low opportunity, power, and numerical representation combine to produce self-perpetuating cycles. Career development, workplace policies, personal background, family obligations, and mentoring are factors that explain women's periodic surges forward and periodic lack of progress in public management and management in general.

Haslett, B. J., Geis, F. L., & Carter, M. R. (1992). *The organizational woman: Power and paradox.* Norwood, NJ: Ablex.

Opportunities are increasing for women to enter managerial positions, but their advancement and their salaries are not keeping pace with the potential. Factors that affect the success and status of women within organizations are analyzed. Readers are encouraged to identify barriers and practice power-building behaviors and communication skills. Case studies illustrate the issues and the suggested methods for resolution of problems and professional growth. Includes bibliographical references and indexes.

Helgesen, S. (1990). *The female advantage: Women's ways of leadership.* New York: Doubleday.

This book is not about what women can learn from business but what business can learn from women. Contemporary organizations are eliminating pyramids and trimming bureaucratic structures at the same time that women are increasingly pressed into the workforce for economic reasons. Women constitute 45% of the total workforce. Eighty percent of female college graduates work. One-third of all new businesses are started by women. Helgesen reports on her diary studies of female executives in four organizations: Girl Scouts of U.S.A., Western Industrial Contractors, Ford Motor Company, and Brunson Communications. Includes bibliographical references.

Jacobs, R. L., & McClelland, D. C. (1994). **Moving up the corporate ladder: A longitudinal study of the leadership motive pattern and managerial success in women and men.** *Consulting Psychology Journal, 46*(1), 32-41.

A 12-year study followed the careers of 211 men and 180 women in a large utility company. Subjects took the *Thematic Apperception Test* (Murray, 1943), participated in behavioral simulations, and were interviewed. They were reevaluated every two years. A Leadership Motive Pattern (LMP) placed the subjects into achievement, affiliation, power, and activity-inhibition categories. Subjects with higher LMP scores—images of resourceful power as opposed to relative or helpless power—achieved higher management positions.

Kanter, R. M. (1993). *Men and women of the corporation* (2nd ed.). New York: BasicBooks.

Kanter introduces readers to the male executives and female aspirants in the Industrial Supply Corporation (pseudonym for a never-revealed company). Structural and cultural factors in the company, especially the distribution of power, have enormous influence on the men's and women's careers and self-images. This updated edition considers the paradigm shift that has changed the world of business in the 15 years since original publication. A new preface, afterword, and chapter describe new roles for women, expanded opportunities, and new workplace issues for men and women in the 1990s. Two appendices report on Kanter's field study and observations of women's leadership in organizations. Includes bibliographical references and index.

New
Karnes, F. A., & Bean, S. M. (1993). *Girls and young women: Leading the way: 20 true stories about leadership.* Minneapolis, MN: Free Spirit.

This is a book for and about very young leaders. Stories about girls who assumed leadership roles in their schools and communities are meant to inspire other young girls. Five-year-old Isis Johnson organized a food drive for the poor and hungry people of New Orleans. Fourth-grader Jennifer Kyer implemented a recycling program at her school. Fifth-graders Lee Palmer and Janine Givens gained equal access to library materials previously unavailable to elementary school students. A leadership bibliography suggests more books for young leaders.

New

Klenke, K. (1996). *Women and leadership: A contextual perspective.* New York: Springer.

In Chapter 1, Klenke uses a metaphor of lenses or prisms for the interactions of leadership, gender, context, and culture. In Chapter 2, she suggests that leadership in history has been shaped by contexts such as religion or politics. Portraits of women such as Joan of Arc, Mary Baker Eddy, Elizabeth I, Harriet Tubman, and Alice Paul reinforce Klenke's belief in contexts as shaping. Chapter 3 is a discussion of several leadership theories such as the trait approach, followed by applications using Margaret Thatcher, Debbie Fields, and Candy Lightner as examples. In Chapter 4 the difference and need for balance between management and leadership is discussed. Janet Reno is Klenke's example of a woman manager, and Mary Kay Ash is her example of a woman leader. Portrayals and coverage of women leaders in the media are analyzed in Chapter 5. In Chapter 6 gender differences in leadership are debunked, as are barriers to women's development. Chapter 7 examines the visible and not-so-visible barriers to women's leadership. In Chapter 8, Klenke examines women leaders in the contexts of sports, religion, and politics. Cross-cultural differences in worldwide context are examined in Chapter 9. European leaders include: Mary Robinson of Ireland; Tansu Ciller of Turkey; Aung San Suu Kyi, Burmese dissident; Eva Perón of Argentina; and Isabel Perón, also of Argentina. The final chapter is on leadership education and new programs. Includes bibliographical references and index.

New

Klenke, K. (1997). **Women in the leadership and information labyrinth: Looking for the thread of Ariadne.** *Leadership Journal: Women in Leadership—Sharing the Vision, 1*(2), 57-70.

Klenke uses the metaphor of the labyrinth to describe how women, although they may have gained entry into the worlds of leadership and information technology (IT), will not rise to the top without a societal change. Leadership and IT may not seem related, but Klenke argues that they are both complex fields with strong gender-based hierarchies that exclude women. She proposes an alternate model, illustrated here, in which gender, leadership, and IT interact and, at the same time, offer guidance to women working in these traditionally male-dominated arenas. Includes bibliographical references.

Komives, S. R. (1991). **Gender differences in the relationship of hall directors' transformational and transactional leadership and achieving styles.** *Journal of College Student Development, 32*(2), 155-165.

A seven-campus study of hall directors (supervisors) and resident assistants (subordinates) revealed significant gender differences in self-perceptions of leadership and achieving styles. Seventy-four hall directors and 602 resident assistants responded to parallel 70-item questionnaires. Transformational traits measured were charisma, individual consideration, intellectual stimulation, and inspiration. Transactional traits measured were contingent rewards and management by exception.

New

Lauterbach, K. E., & Weiner, B. J. (1996). **Dynamics of upward influence: How male and female managers get their way.** *Leadership Quarterly: Special Issue: Leadership and Diversity (Part I), 7*(1), 87-108.

Do male and female managers use different strategies to influence their superiors? Based on Nancy Chodorow's theory of gender formation, Lauterbach and Weiner hypothesized that female managers' influence processes would be characterized by interdependence and social connection, while men's processes would be based on independence and autonomy. Their study, consisting of interviews and surveys of male and female managers in a Fortune 100 company, supported this hypothesis. Women were more likely than men to act out of organizational interest, not self-interest; to involve others in planning; and to consider others' viewpoints and feelings.

Leavitt, J. A. (1985). *American women managers and administrators: A selective biographical dictionary of twentieth-century leaders in business, education and government.* Westport, CT: Greenwood Press.

While many women are still striving to reach top-management ranks and equal pay, this collection of biographical sketches informs the reader of 226 women who have achieved positions of leadership. Family, education, and career information is provided, highlighting honors and "firsts." Bibliographical references about and by the subjects follow each entry. This book is intended to create visibility for these role models as an inspiration for some and an indication of their authority for all. Includes bibliography and index.

Melcher, D., Eichstedt, J. L., Eriksen, S., & Clawson, D. (1992). **Women's participation in local union leadership: The Massachusetts experience.** *Industrial & Labor Relations Review, 45*(2), 267-280.

A 1989 survey of union leaders indicates that women hold leadership roles proportionate to the female percentage of union membership. But they are overrepresented in marginal roles, such as secretaries, and underrepresented in influential roles, such as presidents. Women chair many committees but rarely serve in the positions of visibility and influence that lead to high-level office or national recognition. Minority women have less representation than white women. Both male and female union leaders agree that increasing women's leadership roles is desirable.

Moen, J. K. (1995). **Women in leadership: The Norwegian example.** *Journal of Leadership Studies, 2*(3), 3-19.

Norwegian women hold a large number of political leadership positions including prime minister, cabinet members, and 40% of the parliament. Moen conducted interviews with 15 of these women to gain insight into social and political conditions, leadership styles, and the difficulties they face. Cultural and geographic factors unique to Norway that contribute to a national sense of equality are identified. Pertinent to women everywhere, Moen finds the recurring themes of leadership based on strong interpersonal relationships, team-building skills, and advocacy for human rights.

Morrison, A. M. (1992). *The new leaders: Guidelines on leadership diversity in America.* San Francisco: Jossey-Bass.

How can companies adopt diversity as a powerful competitive strategy? Morrison, lead author of *Breaking the Glass Ceiling* (Addison-Wesley, 1992), shares her findings after probing 16 private and public organizations to identify practices that obstruct or encourage the advancement of white women and people of color into executive ranks. By adopting a leadership-diversity strategy, procedures, and actions, companies can reach broader markets, improve employee satisfaction, and increase productivity. Keys to making diversity work are rotational assignments, mentoring programs, and internal networks that develop careers of high-potential managers. Morrison also offers specific guidance via a five-step diversity plan to help companies assess diversity needs, design programs, and measure results. Includes bibliographical references and index.

Morrison, A. M., Schreiber, C. T., & Price, K. F. (1995). *A glass ceiling survey: Benchmarking barriers and practices.* Greensboro, NC: Center for Creative Leadership.

This report presents the results of a survey conducted by the Human Resource Planning Society and the Center for Creative Leadership involving more than 300 human resource managers. They were asked: 1) What barriers exist today that prevent women and people of color from reaching senior management? 2) What key practices does your organization use to overcome these barriers? Results include the most prevalent, critical, and effective practices. Includes bibliographical references.

Morrison, A. M., White, R. P., Van Velsor, E., & the Center for Creative Leadership. (1992). *Breaking the glass ceiling: Can women reach the top of America's largest corporations?* (Updated ed.). New York: Addison-Wesley.

Since 1987, when the first edition of this book was published, the term *glass ceiling* has become a symbol of inequality for women, and recently for people of color. In this updated edition, much of the original text is kept intact. New research, based on interviews with 100 executives, provides a look at progress over five years and implications for further strides. A new chapter describes techniques organizations are using to remove barriers that prevent women and other nontraditional managers from advancing. Includes bibliographical references and index.

New
Nichols, N. A. (Ed.). (1994). *Reach for the top: Women and the changing facts of work life.* Boston: Harvard Business School Press.

This book is a collection and examination of *Harvard Business Review*'s most controversial articles on women in the workplace. The 12 articles present analyses of women's issues, including job opportunities and limitations, balancing work and motherhood, sexual harassment, and the undermining of women's managerial skills. Nichols states that there are no swift solutions to solve these problems but rather a variety of alternatives: fighting discrimination, becoming an entrepreneur, or turning a deaf ear. She encourages women to "reach for the top" to fulfill themselves, contribute to the well-being of their families and their employers, and to reap financial rewards that have previously eluded women. The book closes with three stories of women who each made a difference in a male-dominated workplace by reaching for the top. They are: Rosemarie B. Greco, president, CEO, and director of CoreStates First Pennsylvania Bank; Kye Anderson, president, CEO, and chairman of Medical Graphics Corporation; and Lore Harp, the CEO of Vector Graphic Design Inc. Includes bibliographical references and index.

Noe, R. A. (1988). **Women and mentoring: A review and research agenda.** *Academy of Management Review, 13*(1), 65-78.

Mentors provide sponsorship, exposure, counseling, and role clarity. They help protégés develop career plans and increase the probability of success. Women have difficulty establishing mentor relationships due to late entry into the workforce, frequent career interruptions, and the small number of female mentors available in executive positions. Noe suggests future research topics: cross-gender mentors, formal mentoring relationships assigned by organizations, access to information networks, tokenism, powerbases, and the sexual perceptions of cross-gender mentoring.

New
Oberst, G. F., & Wanke, J. (1997). **Women are citizen leaders: The citizen leadership training program.** *A Leadership Journal: Women in Leadership—Sharing the Vision, 1*(2), 81-89.

In 1993 Florida's Gulf Coast Community College founded the Citizen Leadership Institute, designed to build community by developing and strengthening the leadership skills of community members. This article discusses how the Institute's programs have been specifi-cally adapted to address leadership skills and roles for women. The authors describe the gender-specific needs of women and how programs are modified around them, offer examples of historic female community leaders including Rosa Parks, and describe women who have gone through CLI's programs and the community work they do. Includes bibliographical references.

Offermann, L. R., & Beil, C. (1992). **Achievement styles of women leaders and their peers: Toward an understand-ing of women and leadership.** *Psychology of Women Quarterly, 16*(1), 37-56.

Women's achievement style and leadership outcomes were examined in two studies. In the first study, female college leaders were compared to male college leaders. In the second study, female college leaders were compared to a control sample of undergraduate men and women. The *Power Apprehension Scale, Texas Social Behavior Inventory,* and *Achieving Styles Inventory* were completed by all participants. Some findings were: female leaders scored high in achievement orientations and lower than male counterparts in power or competitive orientations.

New
Parker, P. S., & ogilvie, d. t. (1996). **Gender, culture, and leadership: Toward a culturally distinct model of African-American women executives' leadership strategies.** *Leadership Quarterly: Special Issue: Leadership and Diversity (Part II), 7*(2), 189-214.

According to the authors, current literature describes two distinct models of leadership—the Anglo-American male hierarchical model and the "distinctly female" model. But neither applies to African-American women executives (AAWEs), who face the interactive effects of sexism and racism. The authors propose a third model of leadership that takes into account the unique social location of

AAWEs within the dominant culture. In this model, simultaneous race and gender oppression force AAWEs to create their own leadership strategies, which include risk taking, campaigning, networking/mentoring, and maintaining a sense of biculturalism.

Richter, L. K. (1990). **Exploring theories of female leadership in South and Southeast Asia.** *Pacific Affairs, 63*(4), 524-540.

This paper explores the historical, contextual, and environmental parameters of leadership among highly placed, elected and appointed female Asian officials. Key variables include ideology of patriarchy, social class, and martyrdom. Richter posits that Asian women rise to power through family connections rather than through Western-style influences, such as education, public policy, and public support.

Rizzo, A., & Mendez, C. (1990). *The integration of women in the workplace: A guide for human resources and management development specialists.* New York: Quorum.

Do gender-based differences exist in the workplace? Rizzo and Mendez examine how stereotypes have historically caused the underutilization and devaluation of women in the workplace. Case studies present a new perspective of women emerging as a rapidly growing segment of the professional and managerial population. This practical handbook offers strategies for human resource and management-development specialists to find, hire, and keep talented women. Workshops, tools, and strategies outline a model for organizational integra-tion. Includes bibliographical references.

Rosener, J. (1990). **Ways women lead.** *Harvard Business Review, 68*(6), 119-125.

Rosener conducted a survey of International Women's Forum members and organizational male counterparts. Respondents were asked questions about their leadership styles, their organizations, work-family issues, and personal characteristics. Survey results indicated that women in leadership positions earn the same amount of money as male counterparts. Women tend to use a transformational leadership style and men tend to use a transactional style. Women tend to use personal power based on charisma, work record, and contacts. Men tend to use structural power based on organizational position, title, and the ability to reward and punish.

New
Ruderman, M. N., Ohlott, P. J., & Kram, K. E. (1996). *Managerial promotion: The dynamics for men and women.* Greensboro, NC: Center for Creative Leadership.

The authors interviewed men and women who had been promoted within a Fortune 500 company in order to analyze the gender differences in promotion dynamics. Reasons for promotion, such as a record of success and good interpersonal skills, are identified, and ways the promotion process can undermine women's advancement are discussed. The authors also outline strategies companies can use to make more balanced promotion decisions. Includes references and an appendix of interview questions.

Singer, M. (1990). **Cognitive correlates of adolescents' aspirations to leadership: A developmental study.** *Journal of Adolescence*, *13*(2), 143-155.

This study of 52 14-year-old and 78 17-year-old high school students measures age and gender differences in leadership aspirations. The subjects completed a questionnaire measuring overall leadership aspirations, 13 valence-instrumentality expectancies for 13 leadership outcomes, self-efficacy perceptions, and attributions of effective leadership. The results indicated significant gender differences in valence scores and significant age differences in self-efficacy and attribution measures.

New
Slack, J. D., Myers, N., Nelson, L., & Sirk, K. (1996). **Women, research, and mentorship in public administration.** *Public Administration Review*, *56*(5), 453-458.

This study examined the rate at which women's research was published in *Public Administration Review*, and found that female researchers publish at lower rates than men and tend to enter into fewer joint research ventures than men do. One reason offered for this is that few women have mentors in the field because men occupy most of the senior positions in public administration and tend to offer their advice and support to other men. The study did show that the number of women publishing in the field seems to be increasing in the 1990s.

Smith, P. L., & Smits, S. J. (1994). **The feminization of leadership.** *Training & Development*, *48*(2), 43-46.

To test assumptions of gender differences in work experience and leadership style, the authors conducted a survey of male and female business owners. All businesses were traditionally male-dominated—construction, manufacturing, and wholesale distribution. Same- and opposite-sex groupings of owners and employees were compared in the areas of owners' characteristics, personnel practices, and employee attitudes. They found that

male and female owners shared personal characteristics such as age, education, and experience. Both genders instituted similar personnel practices, but those practices were better understood by the employees of female owners. Female owners hired more female employees and had happier employees in general.

Touchton, J. G., Shavlik, D., & Davis, L. (1993). *Women in presidencies: A descriptive study of women college and university presidents.* Washington, DC: American Council on Education.

In 1985, the ACE Commission on Women in Higher Education launched a study of women CEOs in higher education. The results of 230 responses profile the personal and professional development of these successful women. Data were collected on: 1) identification for presidential roles; 2) education and professional experience; 3) demographic information such as ethnicity, marriage, and children; 4) perceptions on women's and minority issues; 5) institutional data; and 6) advice for women seeking presidential roles. One significant result of this study was the 1990 Women Presidents' Summit. The other was this report, which serves as baseline data for future studies of women in presidencies. Includes a bibliography.

Troemel-Ploetz, S. (1994). **"Let me put it this way, John": Conversational strategies of women in leadership positions.** *Journal of Pragmatics, 22*(2), 199-209.

The author takes a linguistic approach to women's leadership. A review of literature reveals that women address others by name, give positive mirroring, save face (their own and others'), and show respect. How do women exercise authority, give directives, or criticize when necessary? Troemel-Ploetz cites conversational examples to answer these questions. She concludes that women are perceived as egalitarian and humane in leadership conversations.

Van Nostrand, C. H. (1993). *Gender-responsible leadership: Detecting bias, implementing interventions.* Newbury Park, CA: Sage.

In spite of recent efforts to eradicate sexism in the workplace, other biases against women, both subtle and not so subtle, still persist. Using examples from personal experience, dialogues with and observations of other professionals, as well as more formal research methods, Van Nostrand endeavors to make readers more aware of these biases and then offers specific intervention techniques that can be used to help eliminate them. Includes bibliographical references and index.

White, B., Cox, C., & Cooper, C. (1992). *Women's career development: A study of high flyers.* Cambridge, MA: Blackwell.

An in-depth study of 48 women executives and entrepreneurs in journalism, banking, law, accounting, manufacturing, and marketing provides insight into women's career development. Data on childhood, education, personality, motivation, work history, family history, and power are measured against a career development model to determine career success. Career success is defined as "both being able to live out the subjective and personal values one really believes in and to make a contribution to the world of work." Includes bibliographical references and index.

Whitt, E. J. (1994). **"I can be anything!": Student leadership in three women's colleges.** *Journal of College Student Development, 35*(3), 198-207.

Interviews of 200 students were conducted at Wellesley College, Randolph-Macon Woman's College, and Westhampton College. Students were asked: How do women lead? Describe leadership experiences. How do learning environments affect leadership experiences? Answers to the questions reveal women's aspirations, available opportunities to learn and practice leadership, their role models, and the different opportunities in women's versus coeducational institutions.

ETHNIC

New

Bonilla-Santiago, G. (1992). *Breaking ground and barriers: Hispanic women developing effective leadership.* San Diego, CA: Marin Publications.

This book reports on the Hispanic Women Leaders' Project, a collection of oral histories from 99 Hispanic women who have made significant contributions despite the challenges they faced in a racist and sexist society. Their stories reveal common attitudes toward family values, education, challenges, aspirations, authority, and leadership style. Seventeen stories are shared in detail. Among them are: Miriam Colon, Artistic Director and Founder of the Puerto Rican Traveling Theater in New York; Polly Baca, former Colorado State Senator; Patricia Diaz-Dennis, former Federal Communications Commissioner; Esther Novak, Director of Urban Affairs at AT&T; Lena Guerrero, former Texas Commissioner of Railroads and Transportation and legislator in the Texas State House of Representatives; Nelly Galan, Manager of WNJU TV in New York; and Iliana Ros-Lehtinen, U.S. Congresswoman.

New

Caudron, S., & Hayes, C. (1997). **Are diversity programs benefiting African Americans?** *Black Enterprise, 27*(7), 121-132.

The authors state that corporate efforts to decrease prejudice and increase sensitivity have become diluted and ineffective. Early diversity programs addressed racism, sexism, and homophobia. Current diversity programs have grown to include religious intolerance, agism, education, and even family birth order. The authors agree that sensitivity to all groups is important, but that catch-all diversity programs are not meeting the needs of African Americans. They also agree that training alone is not the solution—corporate culture must change. Examples of corporations with successful diversity programs are: SC Johnson Wax; TIAA-CREF; Texas Instruments, Inc.; and Ameritech Corp.

Chatterjee, P. (1993). **The observer as an instrument in qualitative community studies.** *Journal of Sociology and Social Welfare, 20*(4), 29-50.

Chatterjee reports on studies of black leadership in Cleveland, Ohio, from 1967 to 1971 and 1989 to 1991. As an Asian Indian, Chatterjee claims to have a unique perspective as a man of color studying men of a different color. He interviewed and observed subjects who were organizational and elected leaders to identify their constituencies and the issues that led to mobilization of leadership behavior. He asked questions about identity, integration, confrontations, political power, and goals. One conclusion from this study is that in qualitative research, the researchers themselves become important instruments.

Donelan, R. W. (1993). **African and African-American voices on educational leadership: Counter cultural images and narratives.** *International Journal of Educational Reform, 2*(4), 418-424.

To understand African and African-American leadership, one must understand the traditional African concept of leader as both servant and shepherd of the people, and the value of community over individual. Donelan submits excerpts from a century of African and African-American philosophy to illustrate a sense of leadership. He encourages minority participation in education, both in teaching and in content design for historical identity.

New

Gaines, K. K. (1996). *Uplifting the face: Black leadership, politics, and culture in the twentieth century.* Chapel Hill, NC: University of North Carolina Press.

The author describes American society in the late 20th century as subtly racist. Post-civil rights neoliberal goals have fallen short of a color-blind society with equal

justice and equal opportunities. This book explains how
that happened through a historical perspective of what it
means to be black or white in America. Discourses on
racist and anti-racist theories are compared. The ideology
of racial uplift is discussed in terms of the black middle
class who align with conservative mores and of the blacks
trapped in poverty who embrace optimistic liberal ideals.
Writings of black social scientists throughout the century
document the struggles and the leadership that made
progress toward civil rights and racial uplift. Includes
bibliographical references and index.

New
Hackel, S. W. (1997). **The staff of leadership: Indian
authority in the missions of Alta California.** *William and
Mary Quarterly*, 3rd Series, *54*(2), 347-376.

Hackel examines a period in the history of California. To
protect the Spanish interest in the new world, 18th-
century Spanish authorities established Franciscan
missions from San Diego to San Francisco. Native
Americans who converted were given homes and work
inside the missions. Within their ranks, leaders emerged
to run the communities of 500 to 1,000 residents. Scholars
have long argued whether the missions and their Indian
leaders were protective or committing cultural genocide.
Hackel's essay doesn't moralize. Instead, it describes the
selection of Indian leaders and their responsibilities as
well as the Spanish influence of leadership style and its
adaptation to native culture. He identifies patterns of
leadership that eventually led to a successful rebellion
against the Franciscans.

New
Harvey, S. (1996). **Two models to sovereignty: A comparative history of the Mashantucket Pequot Tribal
Nation and the Navajo Nation.** *American Indian Culture
and Research Journal*, *20*(1), 147-194.

Harvey presents two sides to the issue of gaming as a
means to economic independence and self-sufficiency for
Indian nations. About one-third of the 500 tribes in the
U.S. currently offer some form of gaming—casinos or
bingo parlors—as a form of economic enterprise, resulting in several billion dollars of profit. The small Pequot
tribe of Connecticut owns the largest casino in the
Western hemisphere and uses its profits to rebuild the
tribe. The larger Navajo tribe of New Mexico resists the
lure of gaming money, preferring to build the tribe
through traditional means—at home and school. Harvey
examines each tribe's style of leadership, culture, and
pursuit of sovereignty. Includes bibliographical references
in notes.

Hill-Davidson, L. (1987). **Black women's leadership:
Challenges and strategies.** *Signs: Journal of Women in
Culture and Society*, *12*(2), 381-385.

Reflections on the Black Women's Leadership Symposium, held at the University of North Carolina at Chapel
Hill in the spring of 1986, are documented. Divergent
views of feminism, sexism, racism, class, and relationships among groups in the U.S. and the Third World
created a climate of energy and creative thinking. Research questions surfaced at the symposium to launch the
systematic exploration of oppression, expanded consciousness, and the eradication of systems of domination.

New
James, J. (1997). *Transcending the talented tenth: Black
leaders and American intellectuals.* New York: Routledge.

The ongoing presumption in American politics, according
to the author, is that "there are leaders, and then there are
black leaders." This book examines how historically
"leadership has been articulated in and for black communities" and how those communities approach leadership
today. First, James shows how women and radicals have
been erased from the history of black leadership. Then she
addresses contemporary crises, including racial violence,
intellectual elitism in the black community, and the
intertwined oppressors of race, class, and gender. Extensively researched, the book includes quotes and poems
from W. E. B. Du Bois, James Baldwin, and Audre Lorde.
Includes bibliographical references and index.

Jules, F. (1988). **Native Indian leadership.** *Canadian
Journal of Native Education*, *15*(3), 3-23.

Jules examines the relevant features of leadership in
Native Indian context. A review of the literature and
interviews with three Indian leaders reveal dissatisfaction
with the quality of education for Indian children. Jules
applies a model of Native Indian leadership to educational
administration. Native Indian groups have linguistic and
geographic differences but common values and spiritual
identity. Knowledge of Indian culture, group decision
making, respect for elders, wisdom, integrity, and
humility are essential for educational leadership in a
Native Indian context.

Lusane, C. (1994). *African Americans at the crossroads:
The restructuring of Black leadership and the 1992
elections.* Boston, MA: South End.

Lusane frames the concept of black leadership within the
political, social, and economic context of American
society from 1965 through 1992. The growth of conservative intolerance, end of the Cold War, escalating national
debt, health care crisis, and increase in crime have all
affected the black community. A variety of leadership

responses have emerged ranging from grassroots activism to presidential campaigning. Lusane describes former Los Angeles gang members who have stepped into leadership positions in an effort to negotiate peace treaties between warring gangs. In addition to these and other grassroots leadership efforts, he discusses the Congressional Black Caucus, Nation of Islam Minister Louis Farrakhan, Supreme Court Justice Henry Thomas, and the Reverend Jesse Jackson. He closes his book with a call to the black community to exhibit and demand leadership actions. Includes bibliographical references and index.

New

Martinez-Cosio, M. (1996). **Leadership in communities of color: Elements and sensitivities of a universal model.** *Journal of Leadership Studies*, *3*(1), 65-77.

This article considers the definition of leadership presented in Rost's *Leadership for the Twenty-first Century* (Praeger, 1993) and applies that definition to communities of color. Rost says that leadership is "an influence relationship among leaders and followers who intend real changes that reflect their mutual purposes." Martinez-Cosio believes that this definition provides a framework for people of various ethnic and cultural backgrounds to participate fully in the dominant society while maintaining their cultural differences. She describes many examples of Hispanic leaders whose work supports this definition. Includes bibliographical references.

Miller, D. I. (1978). **Native American women: Leadership images.** *Integrated Education*, *6*(1), 37-39.

Miller contrasts the role of female leaders played out in Native American culture with that found in the majority culture. She notes that although there are wide differences in Native American societies, certain central value themes typify most Native American people, including cooperation, cohesiveness, concern for others, and "scorn toward egotistical or self-seeking behavior on the part of one as against the group." The difficulties of modern Native American women, who must straddle two cultures and who also have to deal with the distorted images that whites have of Native Americans, are addressed.

New

Millner, S. Y. (1996). **Recasting civil rights leadership: Gloria Richardson and the Cambridge Movement.** *Journal of Black Studies*, *26*(6), 668-687.

This article documents the emergence and leadership style of Gloria Richardson, who was one of only a few women to transform the Civil Rights movement. Richardson was a middle-aged mother and member of an elite African-American family when she responded to recruiters from the Student Nonviolent Coordinating Committee. Within

a year, Richardson was co-chair of the Cambridge branch and a nationally recognized spokesperson. Much of the media attention she received focused on her class status and her gender, discounting her message in sexist, racist, and paternalistic tones. In this article, Millner sifts through the language to identify the leadership characteristics that enabled Richardson to assume power easily, take risks readily, and have enough impact to move the Civil Rights movement north of the Mason-Dixon line. Includes bibliographical references.

Morrison, M. K. C. (1987). ***Black political mobilization, leadership power and mass behavior.*** Albany: State University of New York.

The term *black political mobilization* describes the political victories of black Americans in the South. The author returned to Mississippi to examine the many advances in black electoral involvement in the years after the passage of the Voting Rights Act of 1965. The book focuses on three rural Mississippi towns. The towns are agriculture-based and poor, with populations around 2,000 and significant African-American voting majorities. Influenced by the Civil Rights era of the 1960s, they have elected black mayors since the early 1970s. An excellent example of minority electoral politics, this region has become a rich environment for a new class of black leaders. Includes bibliography and index.

Nance, E. E. (1989). **The Black community and the leadership dilemma.** *Community Education Journal*, *16*(4), 10-11.

In the 1960s and 1970s, black leadership was focused on civil rights. As a result, the gap between black and white income levels narrowed, education levels increased, and blacks succeeded in elective politics. In the late 1980s these trends reversed. Nance recommends a strategy shift toward internal reconstruction of the black community. Empowering many leaders would unite the complex structure and create a large vision for urban design. Three hundred or more persons together would select key issues, develop goals, and implement physical and social strategic plans.

New

Preparing future leaders today. (1997). *Black Enterprise*, *27*(7), 92-108.

Twelve deans from historically black colleges and universities (HBCUs) convened at a business education roundtable to discuss the challenges and opportunities available for African-American business students. The deans challenged faculty to develop case studies based on African-American leaders. They identified a need to educate corporate America about the strengths of HBCUs, which include: mentoring graduates, small-business support for student businesses, campus leadership opportunities, and international internships. HBCUs encourage students to consider both corporate and entrepreneurial career paths.

Santellanes, D. (1989). **Leadership in the Hispanic community: The importance of context.** *Community Education Journal, 16*(4), 12-13.

Community educators succeed in direct relation to their training. This article suggests a new training design for Hispanic-community educators, one that is sensitive to social, economic, and cultural factors. Conceptual skills would familiarize educators with Hispanic values, cultural mores, and the extended-family support system. Technical skills would include unobtrusive needs assessments. Human skills would stress the importance of verbal communication, particularly listening.

New
Smith, E. (1997). **Leader or manager: The minority department chair of the majority department.** *Journal of Leadership Studies, 3*(1), 79-94.

This article asks whether minorities can lead or manage, or do both, as department chairs of colleges and universities. Smith suggests that chairpersons are managers who make a department function, and they are also leaders who establish a vision for their departments. Actions to increase the inclusiveness of minorities are: allowing a three-month training period before one assumes the chair position and training for gender equity and diversity.

New
Xin, K. R. (1997). **Asian American managers: An impression gap?** *Journal of Applied Behavioral Science, 33*(3), 335-355.

Why are there so few Asian Americans in leadership positions? Xin hypothesizes that this is partly due to differences in Asian Americans' impression management style, or the way they present themselves to their superiors. She surveyed a group of Asian-American managers and their supervisors, and a group of European-American managers and their supervisors, and found that both the managers and supervisors viewed the impression management behavior of Asian Americans and European Americans differently—with Asian Americans losing out in the process. The article also includes background on the theory of impression management and how Asian cultural roots may affect this.

New
Xin, K. R., & Tsui, A. S. (1996). **Different strokes for different folks? Influence tactics by Asian-American and Caucasian-American managers.** *Leadership Quarterly: Special Issue: Leadership and Diversity (Part I), 7*(1), 109-132.

This article reports on a survey of 141 Caucasian-American and 196 Asian-American managers who live and work in Southern California, their superiors, and their direct reports. All participants were asked about the managers' behaviors when exerting influence. The study finds almost no cultural differences between the two groups of managers, although the authors suggest that may be because they live and work in the same culture. Both groups used different tactics when influencing upward (with their superiors) and downward (with their direct reports). Also in both groups, raters' perceptions differed from managers' perceptions in terms of rationality, ingratiation, and upward appeal. The authors suggest that diversity issues may be more relevant to position than to ethnicity.

ORGANIZATIONS

Alexander, J., Fennell, M., & Halpern, M. (1993). **Leadership instability in hospitals: The influence of Board–CEO relations and organizational growth and decline.** *Administrative Science Quarterly, 38*(1), 74-99.

There has been a great deal of interest in recent years on the issue of managerial succession because of its potential effect on organizational strategy, performance, and change. This study tested whether frequent succession in the top management position of an organization was associated with the political structure defining the relationship between the Board and the CEO. Results of the study concluded that high CEO turnover was related

in a greater degree to the relationship with the Board than with organizational growth or decline.

New
Ashkenas, R., Ulrich, D., Jick, T., & Kerr, S. (1995). *The boundaryless organization: Breaking the chains of organizational structure.* San Francisco: Jossey-Bass.

This book is written by the team that designed and executed GE's successful change process called Work-Out. Here, they don't describe the GE program, but they do present the model that resulted from their experience. The model contains four boundaries that constrain traditional organizations: vertical (hierarchy), horizontal (barriers between internal work functions), external (barriers between the organization and external groups), and global differences. There are methods to measure an organization's degree of involvement and practical steps to break old patterns.

Bass, B. M., & Avolio, B. J. (Eds.). (1994). *Improving organizational effectiveness through transformational leadership.* Thousand Oaks, CA: Sage.

In 1985, Bernard Bass presented a theory of transformational leadership that employed four behaviors: idealized influence, inspirational motivation, intellectual stimulation, and individualized consideration. In this book, ten years later, leadership theorists discuss the application of the transformational theory in real organizations. They address the issues of delegation, culture, teams, decision making, quality, and human resources practices. Includes bibliographical references and index.

New
Belbin, M. (1996). *The coming shape of organization.* London: Butterworth-Heinemann.

Belbin shares his observations on the demise of organizational design. Based on his experience with personnel selection and team building, he predicts a trend toward teamwork as the predominant organizational structure of the future. In such a structure, leadership is shared. Belbin offers a new organizational model, the progression helix, a continuous upward process with varied entry points. Participants represent strategic team members, professionals on cross-functional teams, and operational team members. The participants move forward and upward according to their contributions to their teams. In the appendices are exercises to support teamwork and a handout on team roles. Includes bibliographical references and index.

New
Bolman, L. G., & Deal, T. E. (1997). *Reframing organizations: Artistry, choice, and leadership* (2nd ed.). San Francisco: Jossey-Bass.

The authors of *Modern Approaches to Understanding and Managing Organizations* (1984) have written again about enriched managerial thinking. From a large and complex body of leadership theory, they present a simple four-frame model for understanding organizations. The structural frame is a factory with a task-oriented structure, rules, and goals. The human resource frame is a family in which relationships are most important. The political frame is a jungle where power and conflict reign supreme. The symbolic frame is a temple filled with culture, rituals, heroes, and inspiration. Learning to look through multiple lenses, or reframing, allows managers to broaden their

repertoire. New to the second edition are: discussions of organizational structure in response to technology and the global economy; a new chapter on the relationship among ethics, soul, and spirit in organizations; and a new case that explores the reframing process in action. Includes bibliographical references and index.

New
Bowles, M. (1997). **The myth of management: Direction and failure in contemporary organizations.** *Human Relations, 50*(7), 779-803.

According to the author, "the Myth of Management refers to those core beliefs, values and meanings which underpin the exercise of the contemporary management of organizations" and "amounts to a religious fundamentalism [that] has largely monopolized the goals of (late) twentieth century societies." This myth specifically emphasizes: a belief in internal and external competition; the primacy of growth over community, individuals, ecology; and the pursuit of "functional rationality." Bowles believes that the myth is "a means of symbolizing the dilemmas which we face in the modern age," and that it shows how people have tried to find meaning in the business world at the expense of both individuals and society.

New
Brion, J. M. (1996). *Leadership of organizations: The executive's complete handbook.* Greenwich, CT: JAI Press.

This three-volume set may be used by practitioners or students who want to learn about leadership, executive ability, and organizational behavior. Volume 1 contains information on the social aspects: the human factor, learning, behavior, values, motivation, appraisal, and management by objectives. Volume 2 covers technical issues: power, communication, participation, decision making, planning, structure, and the human resources department. Volume 3 is about integrating the first two: change, leadership roles and responsibilities, leadership training and development, managing conflict, justice, and problem solving. All subjects are treated with overviews of major theories as well as practical suggestions for implementation. Charts and models throughout support the text. Appendices include summaries and questions to clarify the lessons in each volume. An extensive bibliography, a name index, and a subject index are in Volume 3.

Carlopio, J. R. (1994). **Holism: A philosophy of organizational leadership for the future.** *Leadership Quarterly: Special Issue: Leadership for Environmental and Social Change, 5*(3/4), 297-307.

As organizations struggle to adapt to an increasingly chaotic, globally interdependent society, traditional leadership philosophies are being rewritten. Carlopio suggests that the time is right for a holistic approach to leadership. This approach gives equal credence to whole organizations and the individuals within. Like the yin and the yang, holistic leadership depends on the balance of two seemingly diverse yet actually connected forces: making a profit and serving the community, leaders who are really supporters, and employees who are empowered decision-makers. The Body Shop is described as an example of a holistic organization.

Connor, P. E., & Lake, L. K. (1988). *Managing organizational change.* New York: Praeger.

The authors have written this book to help readers understand change management. Throughout its ten chapters, the results of extensive research are presented. The book describes how organizational change, though destabilizing and somewhat scary, can be managed with positive outcome. The first chapters discuss how the need for change is usually recognized by foresight of events or by reaction to surprises. Later chapters illustrate how to proceed with organizational change and how to navigate change effectively. The final chapters discuss the ethical issues involved in organizational change. A selected bibliography and list of tables, figures, and questionnaires, plus an index to the text, are included.

Czarniawska-Joerges, B., & Wolff, R. (1991). **Leaders, managers, entrepreneurs on and off the organizational stage.** *Organization Studies: Special Issue: Interpreting Organizational Leadership, 12*(4), 529-546.

Using a theater metaphor, the authors explore three roles within organizations: managers, leaders, and entrepreneurs. Changes in the debate about organizational theory and in organizational practice put different roles in focus at different times. The authors illustrate the contexts in which a given role acquires dominance. "Leadership is seen as symbolic performance, expressing the hope of control over destiny, management as the activity of introducing order by coordinating flows of things and people toward collective action, and entrepreneurship as the making of entire new worlds."

Darling, J. R. (1992). **Total quality management: The key role of leadership strategies.** *Leadership and Organization Development Journal, 13*(4), 3-7.

This article presents a model of keys to organizational quality that includes two components, care of customers and constant innovation, built on a foundation of committed people. Four strategies are used by leaders to achieve this model. Gaining attention through a shared vision creates a quality focus. Communicating the meaning behind the vision helps unite the team in identification and solution of problems. Positioning for trust implies

integrity, accountability, persistence, and reliability. Confidence through respect, for self and for others, seeks and develops talent to its fullest potential.

Egan, G. (1993). *Adding value: A systematic guide to business-driven management and leadership.* San Francisco: Jossey-Bass.

In an era of abounding management advice, why is mismanagement so often responsible for the failure of businesses and the tremendous waste of resources by government agencies? Egan asserts that the fault lies not with individual managers but with the entire system of management. Managers are not the culprits. They are the victims of selection-and-development processes. Egan offers three models for managers to capitalize on the best ideas within their own organizations. Model A reflects leadership and organizational processes. Model B provides a framework for managing change. Model C suggests methods for dealing with the shadow side of the organization, the messiness of business, organizational politics, culture, and employee idiosyncracies. Includes bibliographical references and index.

Eggleston, K. K., & Bhagat, R. S. (1993). **Organizational contexts and contingent leadership roles: A theoretical exploration.** *Human Relations, 46*(10), 1177-1192.

The authors present a model of symbolic and substantive leadership roles in the context of organizational stages. During the convergent state, the symbolic leader dominates through efforts to build legitimacy. During a transition state, symbolic and substantive leaders hold equal power. During a period of reorientation, the substantive leader dominates as major shifts occur in strategy, processes, and technology. Because business success or failure depends on the outcome of reorientation, the implications of this study are important to businesses in transition who need to plan a reorientation.

Feyerherm, A. E. (1994). **Leadership in collaboration: A longitudinal study of two interorganizational rule-making groups.** *Leadership Quarterly: Special Issue: Leadership for Environmental and Social Change, 5*(3/4), 253-270.

This article reports on year-long case studies of two environmental agencies as they developed new rules for the control of air pollution. South Coast Air Quality Management District established a market-based incentive program to control California smog. The Environmental Protection Agency sought a regulation to control volatile organic compounds in paint, lacquer, and varnish. Interviews and observation of meetings with multiple stakeholders provided context to view the leadership behaviors that influenced collaboration. Three behaviors emerged as most influential: surfacing the underlying assumptions of group members, creating new ideas, and initiating collective action.

Gibbons, P. T. (1992). **Impacts of organizational evolution on leadership roles and behaviors.** *Human Relations, 45*(1), 1-18.

Are firms the masters of their own destinies by strategic choice or does environment determine leadership decision making and behavior? Gibbons offers a contingency theory that incorporates environmental and task-design forms of leadership. He suggests the underlying managerial approach should move from a control to an involvement paradigm.

Graham, J. W., & Havlick, W. C. (1994). *Mission statements: A guide to the corporate and nonprofit sectors.* New York: Garland.

Mission statements from 622 organizations include a very brief description of each business and its primary purpose, goals, and long-range objectives. This book was compiled for use by business leaders and students who are writing mission statements or researching organizational culture. Includes bibliographical references, company name index, location index, and industry index.

New
Greenberg, J. (1996). *Managing behavior in organizations: Science in service to practice.* Upper Saddle River, NJ: Prentice Hall.

This is a textbook for undergraduate, MBA, and executive students of organizational behavior. Greenberg reviews organizational-behavior theories and their relevance to actual organizational practices. The 12 chapters cover: historical background, psychology and social perception, motivation, job satisfaction, organizational culture, communication and influence, group dynamics, leadership, decision making, organizational structure, change, and today's challenges. Each contains explanations of major theories and their application, an example of best practice in a major company, a brief self-assessment, a group exercise, and a case study. Personal name, company name, and subject indexes are included.

New
Guns, B. (1996). *The faster learning organization: Gain and sustain the competitive edge.* San Diego, CA: Pfeiffer.

Guns has developed a model for a faster learning organization (FLO), specifically one that learns more quickly than its competitors. He describes how an organization can become a FLO by simultaneously implementing three strategies: "surge learning" around a few key points, cultivating human resources, and transforming the

organizational environment into one that challenges and supports faster learning. Examples from Xerox, Toyota, and NASA, as well as charts, pictures, and cartoons, illustrate the concepts. This book is part of the Warren Bennis Executive Briefing Series.

New
Handy, C. (1995). *Gods of management: The changing work of organizations.* New York: Oxford University Press.

This is an updated version of Handy's 1978 classic management book of the same name. The author describes four organizational cultures as represented by four gods from Greek mythology. An organization led by Zeus has a club culture, one that is defined by functions or products. An organization led by Apollo has a culture of rules and order. Athena is task oriented and manages through the continuous and successful solution of problems. Dionysus rules the existential organization where cooperation and consensus prevail. Handy suggests that managers understand the four cultures for two reasons. First, to be most effective they should work in organizations that match their personal preferences. Second, the work of management requires a full battery of styles to apply in different situations. Includes bibliographical references and index.

Herriot, P., & Pemberton, C. (1995). *New deals: The revolution in managerial careers.* New York: Wiley.

In middle-class Europe and America, one's career is the foundation of one's identity, lifestyle, and status. Organizational changes over the past 15 years have drastically altered the security and confidence of middle-class careers. Two British career researchers wrote this book to explain the revolution taking place among professionals, their managers, and organizations. Long-term relational contracts that implied trust and commitment over the long term no longer exist. The authors explain how we arrived where we are and how to cope with the new rules for both organizations and individuals. For each stage, they offer a case study to show how theory is translated into practice. Includes bibliographical references and index.

Hersey, P., Blanchard, K. H., & Johnson, D. E. (1996). *Management of organizational behavior: Utilizing human resources* (7th ed.). Upper Saddle River, NJ: Prentice Hall.

Almost 30 years ago, this book was introduced to help managers, parents, teachers, human resource professionals, and students to understand behavioral science. Each chapter has been revised for this new edition and there is increased focus on the issues of quality and the international dimension of management. Chapters discuss theories in management, motivation, group dynamics, and leadership with heavy emphasis on situational leadership.

Blanchard's concept of the one-minute manager is recapped. Charts throughout each chapter compare different theories as well as simplify and summarize the lessons. Includes bibliographical references and index.

New
Hesselbein, F., Goldsmith, M., & Beckhard, R. (Eds.). (1997). *The organization of the future.* San Francisco: Jossey-Bass.

Thirty-eight leadership and organization scholars and practitioners share their thoughts on the future of American business organizations. Chapters include: "How Generational Shifts Will Transform Organizational Life" by Jay Conger; "Will the Organization of the Future Make the Mistakes of the Past?" by Jeffrey Pfeffer; "The Circular Organization" by Frances Hesselbein; "The Mondragon Model: A New Pathway for the Twenty-first Century" by Joel Barker; "Restoring People to the Heart of the Organization of the Future" by Rosabeth Moss Kanter; "Competitiveness and Civic Character" by Philip Kotler; "Creating Sustainable Learning Communities for the Twenty-first Century" by Stephanie Pace Marshall; "Self-Esteem in the Information Age" by Nathaniel Branden; "Leading Across Cultures: Five Vital Capabilities" by John Alexander and Meena Wilson; and "The Next Challenge" by Chris Argyris. Includes index.

New
Hirschhorn, L. (1997). *Reworking authority: Leading and following in the post-modern organization.* Cambridge, MA: MIT Press.

Hirschhorn uses the term "post-industrial" to signify an era of technological and economic change and the term "post-modern" to signify recent changes in organizational climates and work relationships. Individuals are relying more on personal authority than hierarchical authority. The benefit is that individuals bring more ideas, feelings, and values to their jobs. The problem is that individuals lack respect for those in positional power. Hirschhorn recommends building a culture of openness to encourage risk-taking, forgive failures, stimulate creativity, and establish a sense of community. Includes bibliographical references and index.

Hofstede, G. (1994). *Uncommon sense about organizations: Cases, studies and observations.* Thousand Oaks, CA: Sage.

Reprints of 17 articles are presented to share obvious and not-so-obvious insights into the behavior of people who work within large organizations. Three themes evolve: 1) the impact of jobs on people, 2) power and control in organizations, and 3) training. Because these articles were originally published for teaching purposes, there is a list

of questions following each chapter, intended to initiate discussion. Includes bibliographical references and index.

Howard, A., & Associates. (1994). *Diagnosis for organizational change: Methods and models.* New York: Guilford Press.

Thirteen behavioral scientists contribute essays on the complex process of organizational change. Ann Howard introduces a framework to analyze jobs and determine training needs. Warner Burke outlines the pros and cons of some prominent diagnostic models for organizational development. Edward Lawler shares his research on reward systems and business strategy. Together, they explain how organizational change leads to a high-involvement workplace where motivated individuals and small groups contribute to the success of the organization as a whole. Includes bibliographical references and index.

Kanter, R. M., Stein, B. A., & Jick, T. D. (1992). *The challenge of organizational change: How companies experience it and leaders guide it.* New York: Free Press.

The "big three" model of organizational change connects the internal and external forces that set change into motion (environment, life cycle, and political dimensions) with new forms of identity and new management roles. Growth, downsizing, technological advancements, and competition create dramatic changes. Changes at IBM, GM, GE, Motorola, Sears, BancOne, Apple, and other world-class organizations are analyzed to illustrate motion, form, and role. Includes bibliographical references and index.

Kets de Vries, M. F. R. (1995). *Life and death in the executive fast lane: Essays on irrational organizations and their leaders.* San Francisco: Jossey-Bass.

Organizational leaders have two roles to fill—the charismatic role that envisions, empowers, and energizes and the instrumental role that structures the organization and rewards followers. Each leader brings with him his past, his inner needs, conflicts, and dreams. Kets de Vries explains how leaders influence corporate culture with their distinctive personal styles. CEO succession, downsizing, mergers, international assignments, gender issues, family businesses, and bad bosses all add to the complexity of leadership style and its effect on corporate culture. Includes bibliographical references and index.

Lantis, M. (1987). **Two important roles in organizations and communities.** *Human Organization, 46*(3), 189-199.

The author discusses the anthropologist's role in providing research in the area of the relation between leader and follower. The author argues that the literature has come primarily from social psychology, applied psychology, and political science. She feels the anthropologist can make an important contribution in this area and that the time has come for anthropologists "to delve further into this subject." She identifies the usefulness of this research as it relates to contemporary organizations and community programs.

New
Lawler, E. E. (1996). *From the ground up: Six principles for building the new logic corporation.* San Francisco: Jossey-Bass.

Lawler uses examples from major companies, including Procter & Gamble, United Airlines, and IBM, to illustrate his belief that organizations should be based on six principles: 1) organization is the ultimate competitive advantage, 2) involvement is the most effective source of control, 3) all employees must add significant value, 4) lateral processes are the key to organizational effectiveness, 5) organizations should be designed around products and customers, and 6) effective leadership is the key to organizational effectiveness. Chapters address the issues of teams, rewards, communication and measurement, and human resources. Includes bibliographical references and index.

Lawler, E. E., III. (1994). *Motivation in work organizations.* (Classic ed.). San Francisco: Jossey-Bass.

This classic work from 1973 has been re-released with a new introduction. Lawler's original research explains why motivation is based on people's needs. Extrinsic rewards such as pay and intrinsic rewards such as a sense of achievement continue to motivate employees. Lawler's theories on personal drive, job design, and job performance have stood the test of time and have served as a base for job motivation research in the past 20 years. Includes a bibliography.

New
Maghroori, R., & Rolland, E. (1997). **Strategic leadership: The art of balancing organizational mission with policy, procedures, and external environment.** *Journal of Leadership Studies*, 4(2), 62-81.

This article examines strategic leadership and the assessment of the right leadership style for an organization's condition. Strategic leadership is defined as the art of creating a balance between external environment, corporate mission, and the corresponding system of implementation. External effectiveness occurs when an organization's mission is congruent with its external environment. Internal effectiveness suffers when policies and procedures are not aligned with the mission. Four leadership strategies for internal effectiveness are: status quo, total quality management, reengineering, and

mission institutionalization. Four strategies for external effectiveness are: long-term survival, mission maintenance, mission realignment, and mission creation.

New
McDaniel, R. R. (1997). **Strategic leadership: A view from quantum and chaos theories.** *Health Care Management Review*, 22(1), 21-37.

Most organizations, including HMOs, are based on Newtonian principles of an orderly and predictable world governed by concrete and discernible natural laws. But recent quantum and chaos theories from the sciences can be used to describe another model of leadership and management in the health care field. These new theories explain that the world is inherently unpredictable and is incredibly sensitive to the smallest change in initial conditions. Based on these theories, McDaniel argues that rather than trying to plan and control their organizations, health care leaders should facilitate the inevitable change. Ways McDaniel suggests to do this include: complicating an organization, rather than simplifying it; developing a collective organizational mind; and allowing for self-organization.

New
Melum, M. M., & Collett, C. (1995). *Breakthrough leadership: Achieving organizational alignment through hoshin planning.* Chicago: American Hospital Publishing.

Hoshin planning, derived from the Japanese term *hoshin kanri*, is a sort of management compass that points everyone in an organization toward a common destination. The authors claim that hoshin planning can help executives achieve business breakthroughs and long-term success. Although the proposed audience is top executives, this book is a thorough guide to understanding and implementing the concept of hoshin planning and could be used by educators as well. Case studies, figures, and tables help to illustrate concepts and to provide clear definitions and comparisons with other management strategies.

New
Morgan, G. (1997). *Images of organization* (2nd ed.). Thousand Oaks, CA: Sage.

Morgan visualizes organizations as metaphors, and uses these characterizations to understand organizations' structures, how they identify problems, and how they implement solutions. Metaphors are used to describe organizations as machines, organisms, cultures, political systems, instruments of domination, and psychic prisons. The second edition includes an expanded section on the implications for practice and how readers can use "metaphor to negotiate the demands of a paradoxical world." Includes bibliographical references and index.

Nadler, D. A., Shaw, R. B., Walton, A. E., & Associates. (1995). *Discontinuous change: Leading organizational transformation.* San Francisco: Jossey-Bass.

Over a ten-year period, the authors have noted increased efforts at organizational change and shifts in the type of change desired. They share their experiences and observations for the benefit of executives who are responsible for large-scale changes, consultants who work with these executives, and students of change theory and practice. This book provides a framework for recognizing the need for change before a crisis erupts, the types of change and action strategies to deal with them, and the methods to build the leadership capability for a change-capable organization. Includes bibliographical references and index.

Natemeyer, W. E. (1978). *Classics of organizational behavior.* Oak Park, IL: Moore.

As stated in the title, this volume is a classic. From Maslow on motivation to Hersey and Blanchard on the life-cycle theory, this book is a foundational presentation of organizational behavior. The 32 individual essays and articles are some of those we see over and over again. It is nice to have them all in one volume. Includes bibliographical references.

Oakley, E., & Krug, D. (1993). *Enlightened leadership: Getting to the heart of change.* New York: Simon & Schuster.

Poor quality, decreased productivity, and low profits signify a need for organizational change. Rather than provide a cookie-cutter solution, the authors recommend that you trust the real experts of your organization—its employees. Poor quality, productivity, and profits are not the problems to be addressed. They are merely the symptoms. The real problems come from the human issues of mind-set and performance. The authors present a framework for generating a continuous-improvement mind-set adaptable to any organization's unique circumstances. Includes bibliographical references and index.

Ott, J. S. (1989). *The organizational culture perspective.* Chicago: Dorsey Press.

This is a careful examination of the procedural difficulties and concerns in defining an organizational culture. Ott pinpoints where the organizational culture viewpoint fits into organization theory, and why it differs from the other aspects of human organization. He also provides a description of the uses, procedures, concepts, language, and theories of organizational culture. A historical analysis on the growth of organizational culture perspective is combined with viewpoints drawn from cultural anthropology, sociology, and ethno-archeology. In

addition to an extensive bibliography, charts, tables, and a subject index are included with the text.

New
Pauchant, T. C., & Associates. (1995). *In search of meaning: Managing for the health of our organizations, our communities, and the natural world.* San Francisco: Jossey-Bass.

The volume and variety of changes facing organizations today cause changes in the way managers and employees make sense of their organizations. The essays in this book suggest a new way of understanding organizations and a new way of making sense called *organizational existentialism.* This concept is described in the essays: "Existential Addiction: A Model for Treating Type-A Behavior and Workaholism" by P. E. Bracke and J. F. T. Bugental; "Organizations as Existential Creations: Restoring Personal Meaning While Staying Competitive" by N. Aubert; "Acknowledging the Dark Side of Organizational Life" by H. Schwartz; "The Four Questions of Life: Their Effect on Human Motivation and Organizational Behavior" by F. I. Herzberg; and others. Includes bibliographical references, name index, and subject index.

Peters, T. J. (1992). *Liberation management: Necessary disorganization for the nanosecond nineties.* New York: Knopf.

Is the business organization as we know it on the decline? According to Peters the answer is a resounding "yes." Citing a 1991 headline—"IBM to Start Announcing Its Fall Line"—Peters sees a shift to fashion orientation for business marked by need for greater flexibility than ever before. Successful organizations will have to reevaluate their organizational structures, learn to hustle, make better use of information technology, and thrive in an atmosphere of seeming disorganization. Utilizing small, task-oriented groups, companies must develop strategies that enhance speed and responsiveness, thus improving competitiveness. Includes bibliographical references and index.

New
Phillips, R. L., & Hunt, J. G. (Eds.). (1992). *Strategic leadership: A multiorganizational-level perspective.* Westport, CT: Quorum Books.

This book is based on the proceedings of a 1991 conference sponsored by the U.S. Army Institute for the Behavioral and Social Sciences and the U.S. Army War College. Military and civilian leadership experts gathered to explore the complexities of top-level leadership in stratified systems. Several essays address the issue of environment and its impact on different levels of organizational strategy. Others address organizational structure and restructuring, particularly downsizing. Also discussed are stakeholder management, critical tasks and competencies of top-level leaders, selection, and development. Most essays discuss leadership in a military context but insist that the issues are relevant to top-level leaders in all organizations. Includes bibliographical references and index.

New

Rago, W. V. (1996). **Struggles in transformation: A study in TQM, leadership, and organizational culture in a government agency.** *Public Administration Review, 56*(3), 227-234.

Written by the director of quality services for the Texas Department of Mental Health and Mental Rehabilitation, this article describes the process the department went through when it implemented a TQM model. The author found that the key to a successful organizational transformation was for senior managers to both personally transform the way they work and to create goals and a vision for the organization that are communicated to the employees. To help readers see the role of their individual change in the larger context, several charts are included that parallel the leadership activity, organizational barriers, and personal struggles that accompany organizational transformation.

New

Ritti, R. R. (1998). *The ropes to skip and the ropes to know: Studies in organizational behavior* (5th ed.). New York: Wiley.

This book is useful to organizational newcomers. Its 55 allegorical stories and cautionary tales demonstrate in a narrative fashion the "real" things that happen to managers and employees in organizations. Ritti offers insights about the unwritten protocols that exist in all organizations. These protocols about how people behave are never found in staff procedures manuals or company histories. Ritti sees survival and success in any organization as being dependent upon the ability of a person to read the invisible definitions to which the organization subscribes. Includes bibliographical references.

Schein, E. H. (1992). *Organizational culture and leadership* (2nd ed.). San Francisco: Jossey-Bass.

This updated version deletes some original chapters, expands others, and includes new materials on the culture concept. There is increased emphasis on the leadership-culture relationship. New chapters explore subgroup culture, the role of the founder, and the impact of information technology. Schein discusses organizations in midlife and turnaround periods of changing culture. This volume is intended to be a supplement to, not a replace-

ment of, the original. Includes bibliographical references and index.

New

Schein, E. H. (1996). **Three cultures of management: The key to organizational learning.** *Sloan Management Review, 38*(1), 9-20.

While many people have talked about the importance of organizational culture, Schein argues that every organization contains three distinct cultures—the community of executives, of engineers, and of day-to-day operators. Schein believes that most organizations cannot effectively learn and move forward because these cultures work against, not with, each other. This article describes each culture and its assumptions, and the implications of these differences. Schein also briefly outlines a plan for creating dialogue and cooperation across an organization's cultures. Includes bibliographical references.

Senge, P. M. (1990). *The fifth discipline: The art and practice of the learning organization.* New York: Currency/Doubleday.

Successful organizations tap people's commitment and capacity to learn at all levels. Senge teaches the theory and techniques of team learning. A team using interactive dialogue can achieve greater results than any one individual effort. At the same time, each individual on the team learns and grows beyond his or her ability to do so alone. Senge also teaches the theory and technique of systems thinking, and the ability to see a vision and to implement the forces necessary to get there. A learning organization fosters reciprocal commitment between individual and organization. Includes bibliographical references and index.

Senge, P. M., Roberts, C., Ross, R. B., Smith, B. J., & Kleiner, A. (1993). *The fifth discipline fieldbook: Strategies and tools for building a learning organization.* New York: Currency/Doubleday.

Senge, Director of the Center for Organizational Learning at the MIT Sloan Business School of Management, first introduced his theory of learning organizations in *The Fifth Discipline* (1990). Based on that theory, Senge, his coauthors, and 67 contributors have organized a collection of tools, methods, stories, ideas, exercises, and resources into a fieldbook for businesses, schools, community agencies, or any organizations wishing to overcome their learning disabilities. This fieldbook is intended to be written in during meetings, conflicts, or whenever ideas occur. Cross-references, margin icons, and an index help the reader easily access topics of current interest.

Srivastva, S., Cooperrider, D. L., & Associates. (1990). ***Appreciative management and leadership: The power of positive thought and action in organizations.*** San Francisco: Jossey-Bass.

This book is the result of a 1988 symposium of organizational-behavior scholars and doctoral students at Case Western Reserve University. Fourteen essays explore new perspectives on the appreciation of diversity, creativity, cooperation, and values within individuals and organizations. The authors suggest that appreciative management will create shared responsibility, opportunity for growth, and a new sense of purpose to meet the challenges of our changing society. Includes bibliographical references and index.

New
Stacey, R. D. (1996). ***Complexity and creativity in organizations.*** San Francisco: Berrett-Koehler.

Complexity, a field of study that has developed from the chaos theory, describes systems that "operate in an intermediate phase between stability and instability." Stacey believes that this also describes human organizations, and he has developed a new complex model of organizational behavior, which he compares to the traditional model. His book describes the science of complexity in depth, shows how complexity can be "mapped onto" organizations, and discusses the implications that the complexity theory may have for organizations. Examples from the European Technology Transfer Committee and companies including British chemical company Enigma, illustrate the complex ideas. Includes references, index, and a glossary of terms.

Tompkins, J. (1995). ***The genesis enterprise: Creating peak-to-peak performance.*** New York: McGraw-Hill.

Tompkins declares that peak performance alone cannot guarantee success. The process of continuously beginning anew and climbing to new peaks is the route to success that he calls *Genesis Leadership*. To lead a Genesis organization, Tompkins recommends shifting from management to leadership by shaping organizational culture and understanding the tenets of motivation. He also suggests shifting from individual responsibilities and recognition to teamwork and shifting from customer/supplier relationships to true partnerships. Includes index.

Trice, H. M., & Beyer, J. M. (1991). **Cultural leadership in organizations.** *Organization Science, 2*(2), 149-169.

Leadership affects organizational culture by innovating or by maintaining the status quo. The authors discuss a typology that distinguishes the different kinds of leadership by the consequences produced. Nine elements of cultural leadership, derived from concepts of charisma,

are linked to innovation or maintenance consequences. Changing organizational needs determine the varying needs for specific types of leaders.

Vicere, A. A. (1992). **The strategic leadership imperative for executive development.** *Human Resource Planning, 15*(1), 15-31.

The strategic leadership model indicates an organizational time/life cycle from emergence, growth, and maturity to decline and decay. Organizations move through stages of innovation and creativity, organizing structure, opportunity and growth, control, and adaptation to survive competition. Some organizations reach a crisis stage of reaction that usually leads to bureaucracy. The model depicts the challenges of dealing with the aftermath of an organization's growth and success.

Vroom, V. H. (1995). ***Work and motivation.*** San Francisco: Jossey-Bass.

This updated version of Vroom's 1964 *Work and Motivation* is part of the Jossey-Bass management series of classic works. The original work was an attempt to develop a theoretical structure for research in industrial and organizational psychology. Twenty-eight pages of preface and introduction explain the author's new perspectives on the subjects of job performance, work satisfaction, and occupational choice. If he were to rewrite his expectancy theory 30 years after the original, Vroom states that his own life experiences, changes in scientific reporting, and new research discoveries would alter the model. This book remains a classic for the student of organizational psychology. Includes bibliographical references and index.

Waldman, D. A. (1993). **A theoretical consideration of leadership and total quality management.** *Leadership Quarterly, 4*(3), 65-79.

This article focuses on the mutual influence of leadership and organizational culture on TQM policies and practices. Waldman applies situational and transformational leadership theories to the TQM practices of teamwork and continuous improvement. Learning and information-sharing cultures contribute to the TQM practice of cooperative problem solving. Waldman presents a model that illustrates the TQM outcomes resulting from transformational leadership and a learning culture.

New
Weick, K. E. (1995). ***Sensemaking in organizations.*** Thousand Oaks, CA: Sage.

Weick describes sensemaking as "a developing set of ideas with explanatory possibilities," rather than a body of established knowledge, to understand the complexities and ambiguities of life. Weick draws heavily on the research of organizational theorists to introduce the concept of sensemaking in organizations. Analysis of scholarly discussion reveals the concept's seven distinguishing characteristics. Sensemaking is: 1) grounded in identity construction, 2) retrospective, 3) enactive of sensible environments, 4) social, 5) ongoing, 6) focused on and extracted by cues, and 7) driven by plausibility rather than accuracy. Understanding the framework of sensemaking can enable leaders to deal with complexity, ambiguity, surprise, discrepancy, emergency, or excess information. Includes bibliographical references, author index, and subject index.

Weisbord, M. R. (1987). *Productive workplaces: Organizing and managing for dignity, meaning and community.* San Francisco: Jossey-Bass.

In this excellent work the author offers fresh thinking and new approaches to making businesses and organizations more effective, satisfying, and rewarding environments for employees. Weisbord revisits the histories and theories of organizational development, and gives new interpretations. In later chapters he examines the application of these theories through case-study profiles. Finally he presents new applied theories, thoroughly documenting their operation. His intention is to move beyond the intellectual developments of current organizational theory toward developing new humanistic solutions to real organizational problems. Includes bibliography and index.

New
Wheatley, M. J., & Kellner-Rogers, M. (1996). *A simpler way.* San Francisco: Berrett-Koehler.

The authors, who research nature and human nature and their influence on organizational development, share their unique philosophy about life-giving organizational forms. "There is a simpler way to organize human endeavor. It requires a new way of being in the world. . . Being in the world with play and creativity. . . Being willing to learn and to be surprised." They believe that leadership evolves from how people agree to be together and behavior is rooted in these agreements. Photographs and poetry supplement the message in this optimistic book. Includes bibliographical references and index.

New
Yukl, G. A. (1998). *Leadership in organizations* (4th ed.). Upper Saddle River, NJ: Prentice Hall.

The focus of this textbook is managerial leadership of formal organizations. A balanced presentation of application and theory helps leaders deal with their immediate challenges and understand the concepts behind the methods. This new edition emphasizes leadership effectiveness and highlights guidelines for improving effectiveness throughout. There are new and expanded chapters on team leadership, change, strategic leadership, followership, distributed leadership, influence process, and developing leadership. Thirty-three cases of actual and modified business situations support the lessons. Includes extensive bibliographical references and author and subject indexes.

TEAMS AND GROUPS

Beck, J. D., & Yeager, N. M. (1994). *The leader's window: Mastering the four styles of leadership to build high-performing teams.* New York: Wiley.

A new leadership theory is based on Hersey and Blanchard's Situational Leadership Theory. Leadership "L4" is represented in a model with four windows. Each window represents levels of giving direction and giving support. The authors discuss why each level is appropriate in a specific situation. To illustrate effective and ineffective leadership at various levels of direction and support, the authors reference leadership literature and use colorful examples from popular television programs. This book is intended for executives to use for self-development.

New
Bennis, W., & Biederman, P. W. (1997). *Organizing genius: The secrets of creative collaboration.* Reading, MA: Addison-Wesley.

Successful groups aren't just trying to fix a problem, they're trying to "put a dent in the universe." Bennis, an expert in leadership issues, collaborates with writer Biederman to explain why certain teams are able to produce greatness, and why "none of us is as smart as all of us." After describing seven "Great Groups," from the Manhattan Project to the 1992 Clinton campaign, the book offers "take-home lessons" on the characteristics of a successful team. These include that Great Groups think they are on a mission from God; they see themselves as winning underdogs; and they are optimistic, not realistic. Includes bibliographical references and index.

Cannella, A. A., Jr., & Rowe, W. G. (1995). **Leader capabilities, success, and competitive context: A study of professional baseball teams.** *Leadership Quarterly, 6*(1), 69-88.

To study leadership succession in a situational context, the authors studied baseball field managers. Characteristics of this group are: high visibility during the decision-making process, their function as targets for criticism, high compensation, competitive intensity, and the perceived value of their experience. All major league teams from 1951 to 1980 were analyzed for performance, manager ability, rivalry, reorganization, and player turnover. The implications for business are discussed.

Carew, D. K., Parisi-Carew, E., & Blanchard, K. H. (1986). **Group development and situational leadership: A model for managing groups.** *Training & Development Journal, 40*(6), 46-50.

This article reviews the concepts of situational leadership and group development and functioning and combines them into a single leadership model, with the premise that there is no one best leadership style for all situations.

New
Carley, M. S. (1996). **Teambuilding: Lessons from the theatre.** *Training & Development, 50*(8), 41-43.

The author, a trainer and veteran stage director, describes how a great theatrical production is a model of teamwork, using his experience directing the show *Noises Off* as an example. The article includes a list of the qualities that both a successful team and stage production need, including a clear focus on task, mutual trust, well-defined roles, flexible leadership, innovation and improvisation, and closure.

New
Daniels, D. (1996). **Leadership lessons from championship basketball.** *Journal for Quality and Participation, 19*(3), 36-48.

Daniels calls basketball "a metaphor for today's marketplace and society. It is characterized by constant movement . . . and winning demands teamwork." He parallels the positions on a basketball team and the roles in organizations: the human resources group is like a point guard, production is like a power forward, and senior management is comparable to a center. The importance of transition and how companies can create transition and proactive behavior in their workers is also discussed. Examples from recent Chicago Bulls teams and compa-

nies including FedEx and Motorola illustrate Daniels' ideas.

New
Donnellon, A. (1996). *Team talk: The power of language in team dynamics.* Boston: Harvard Business School Press.

Donnellon calls this a "sociolinguistic look at teams," because she analyzes not just the actions of teams but their conversation, stories, and jargon, and uses this information to differentiate between real teams and teams in name only. Teams from four Fortune 200 companies are analyzed in depth, and they form the basis for chapters on hierarchy, leadership, and personal commitment. Donnellon also offers "Advice to Teams" and "Advice to Managers," and a "team talk audit" is included so readers can analyze their own teams' conversation and exchanges. Includes index and appendices that describe Donnellon's research methods.

New
Fisher, B., & Thomas, B. (1996). *Real dream teams: Seven practices used by world class leaders to achieve extraordinary results.* Delray Beach, FL: St. Lucie Press.

To discover how real "dream teams" are created, Fisher and Thomas identified 12 "world-class team leaders": coaches Lou Holtz, John Wooden, Jody Conradt; business leaders Don Tyson and Donald Petersen; author Norman Vincent Peale; scientist Gertrude Elion; university dean Sybil Mobley; Major General Patrick Henry Brady; mountain climber Lou Whittaker; musician Carl Schiebler; and pilot Steve Trent. Based on interviews with these leaders, the authors define seven practices essential to effective teams: 1) commitment to a clear mission; 2) mutual support, respect, and encouragement; 3) clearly defined and accepted roles; 4) win-win cooperation; 5) individual competency; 6) empowering communication; and 7) a winning attitude. Each practice is illustrated by quotes from the leaders, graphs, and figures. Includes references.

New
Francis, D., & Young, D. (1992). *Improving work groups: A practical manual for team building* (Rev. ed.). San Diego, CA: Pfeiffer.

The authors suggest that a team-management approach is powerful and flexible as they guide readers through practical team-building steps. The first step is taking the *Team Review Survey* to identify strengths and weaknesses. Then the team is ready to work on: effective team leadership, commitment, positive climate, effective meetings, role clarity, personal development, creativity, and interteam relationships. There are 25 structured activities for developing group and member skills.

Glacel, B. P., & Robert, E. A., Jr. (1994). *Light bulbs for leaders: A guide book for leaders and teams.* Burke, VA: VIMA International.

The first section of this book describes the fictional FULCRUM Corporation, which is in a state of decline. Its fictional senior managers learn to motivate their workforce, change the organizational culture, and lead through collaboration rather than control. The lessons they learn are summarized at the end of each chapter. The second part of the book explains 12 behaviors for learning creative new ways to lead. The authors have taught business, political science, and leadership, and currently coach teams at the Department of Defense, NASA, and major corporations.

Hackman, J. R. (Ed.). (1990). *Groups that work (and those that don't): Creating conditions for effective teamwork.* San Francisco: Jossey-Bass.

Developed as a result of a group study on group performance, this book offers insights for those who design, lead, serve in, or research groups. Twenty-seven task-performing teams were evaluated for effectiveness, using as measures: quality of product or service, ability to regroup after task completion, and the growth of individual members as a result of their participation. Groups studied were top management, task forces, professional support groups, performing groups, human-service teams, and production teams.

New
Hallam, G. L. (1996). *The adventures of Team Fantastic: A practical guide for team leaders and members.* Greensboro, NC: Center for Creative Leadership.

At CCL, Hallam has researched and trained hundreds of teams and has coauthored instruments for developing teams and team leaders. In this book, he introduces Team Fantastic, a virtual team that travels through time and space. Each adventure presents a new challenge and suggested actions for team success. When Team Fantastic lands on the moon, they manage their time carefully to finish assignments before running out of oxygen. In New York City, empowered team members operate equipment and direct traffic to repair a water main before rush hour. They practice feedback skills before their opening performance of a Shakespearean play. This fantastic team travels through 15 more scenarios to demonstrate commitment, organizational support, conflict management, and innovation.

Hare, A. P. (1976). *Handbook of small group research.* New York: Free Press.

This book contains 15 chapters, as well as appendices, indexes, and a 323-page bibliography on small-group research studies. The chapters fall into three basic categories: group process, structure-interaction variables, and performance characteristics. This is primarily a reference resource that summarizes the major trends and findings on small groups from 1898 through 1974. It is suitable for the serious reader interested in small-group dynamics and leadership.

New
Hare, A. P., Blumberg, H. H., Davies, M. F., & Kent, M. V. (1994). *Small group research: A handbook.* Norwood, NJ: Ablex.

This handbook supplements, not replaces, the 1976 *Handbook of Small Group Research.* Together they report what is known on this subject from the beginning of small-group research until 1988. Of particular interest are the sections on influence, leadership, group decision making, and conflict. Includes extensive bibliographical references, name index, and subject index.

Harrington-Mackin, D. (1994). *The team-building tool kit: Tips, tactics, and rules for effective workplace teams.* New York: AMACOM.

This resource is intended for start-up and existing teams that are developing their own set of rules. Chapters include starting up, meetings, team behavior, how to handle team members' fear and control, decision making, problem solving, evaluation, performance rewards, and training. Real team scenarios emphasize each rule in each chapter. Questions most frequently asked by teams in progress are listed at the end of each chapter to reinforce the text. Includes bibliographical references and index.

Hirschhorn, L. (1991). *Managing the new team environment: Skills, tools, and methods.* Reading, MA: Addison-Wesley.

This book was written as a text for an IBM training video. Based on case studies, it teaches managers the process of building a team and authorizing team members to act. Managers' daily behaviors create the balance between authority and empowerment, discipline and freedom, intimacy and distance. If managers are willing to take on "learner roles," they can create effective triangles between themselves, individual team members, and the team as a whole.

Johnson, D. W., & Johnson, F. P. (1991). *Joining together: Group theory and group skills* (4th ed.). Englewood Cliffs, NJ: Prentice Hall.

Each chapter defines a group-related concept with discussion of theory and research findings. Chapters include group dynamics, experiential learning, controversy and creativity, conflicts of interest, leading learning and discussion groups, leading growth and counseling groups, team development, and the psychological benefits of group membership. Coordinator instructions are detailed for over 100 exercises teaching effective group behaviors. Includes bibliographical references, a glossary of terms, and index.

Kolb, J. A. (1992). **Leadership of creative teams.** *Journal of Creative Behavior, 26*(1), 1-9.

Forty teams from manufacturing, aerospace, and health services organizations provided data on the correlation between leader behavior and team performance. Results suggest that an important function of a team leader is public relations. The leader provides boundary management to obtain organizational support and resources, allowing team members the freedom to concentrate on their creative efforts.

New
Kostner, J. (1994). *Virtual leadership: Secrets from the Round Table for the multi-site manager.* New York: Warner Books.

In this unique business novel, King Arthur offers a modern-day businessman advice on how to effectively lead geographically dispersed teams. The author uses Merlin, Excalibur, Lancelot, and the Round Table as metaphors for how modern-day leaders can bridge both physical and interpersonal distances and become more effective "virtual leaders."

Laiken, M. E. (1994). **The myth of the self-managing team.** *Organization Development Journal, 12*(2), 29-34.

Laiken reports on two studies of team management in large organizations. In the first, three scenarios were observed. Traditional, highly directive team leaders had dependent and angry team members. Team leaders who assumed no management role had chaotic and dysfunctional team members. Facilitative team leaders who adapted their behavior to the teams' stage of development had high-performing and satisfied team members. In the second study, team leaders received training to anticipate role changes and all teams reported satisfaction. Laiken concludes that conflict resolution is the toughest challenge facing team management and that a trained, facilitative leader is a necessary element for team success.

New
Manion, J., Lorimer, W. L., & Leander, W. J. (1996). *Team-based health care organizations: Blueprint for success.* Gaithersburg, MD: Aspen.

This book for health care administrators promotes a transformation of the health care system through the use of teams and shared leadership. The authors build a strong

case for the cost benefits, work performance, individual commitment, and job satisfaction that exist in team-based organizations. Chapters explain the planning process, stages for implementing teams, perils and pitfalls, leading change, and lessons from teamwork in the corporate sector. Teamwork among health care providers raises special issues. Cross-functional teams of specialists have different levels of skill and responsibility yet must coordinate among themselves and with other cross-functional teams to provide continuity of care for patients. Tips, techniques, and case studies illustrate how it can be done. Includes bibliographical references and index.

New
Mankin, D., Cohen, S. G., & Bikson, T. K. (1996). *Teams and technology: Fulfilling the promise of the new organization.* Boston: Harvard Business School Press.

This book introduces a framework called mutual design and implementation (MDI). MDI links teams and the information systems they need to enhance knowledge and improve performance. This framework makes it possible to pool knowledge quickly around complex issues. MDI's basic principles are: using conflict creatively, flexible planning that allows for serendipity, inviting cross-functional and multi-level involvement, and creating learning systems. The authors fit the framework to five kinds of teams: work teams, project teams, parallel teams, management teams, and ad hoc networks. In each case, the team composition, leadership, external connections, information resources, and suggested training programs are described. Includes bibliographical references and index.

New
Mulvey, P. W., Veiga, J. F., & Elsass, P. M. (1996). **When teammates raise a white flag.** *Academy of Management Executive, 10*(1), 40-49.

Although the strength of teamwork is the diversity of perspectives that team members bring, too often members censor their opinions and simply go along with the group. As a result, teamwork can result in a flawed decision-making process, in which not all team members are heard. This article lists six reasons "why team members give up," including pressure from others to conform to the team's decision and lacking confidence in one's ability to contribute. The authors then suggest ways that team leaders can prevent this before, during, and after a meeting, including such recommendations as setting a tone for the meeting and encouraging self-feedback. Includes bibliographical references in endnotes.

Nirenberg, J. (1993). *The living organization: Transforming teams into workplace communities.* San Diego, CA: Pfeiffer.

Nirenberg's blueprint for reform aligns organizational change to those changes now transforming our society making workplaces more personally satisfying. To succeed, reforms must not be considered benevolent acts implemented only when convenient. Reforms must be substantiated by top management, board approval, legislation, and employee acceptance. Every member of an organization needs to share the pain and the gain as performance rises and falls in the marketplace. Includes bibliographical references and index.

Nurick, A. J. (1993). **Facilitating effective work teams.** *SAM Advanced Management Journal, 58*(1), 22-27.

Effective project teams are characterized by task factors, such as timely performance, staying within budget, and achievement of quality, and by relationship factors, such as conflict resolution, trust, and communication. Group dynamics that can derail a team are: different points of view, role conflict, implicit power struggles, and groupthink. A strategy for development of effective teams is selecting team members with good interpersonal skills and offering additional communication-skills training.

New
Odenwald, S. (1996). **Global work teams.** *Training & Development, 50*(2), 54-57.

Leading global teams requires a unique combination of skills. In this article, team leaders from international companies list the competencies they believe are necessary, including physical stamina; a sense of humor; excellent interpersonal skills; a tolerance for ambiguity; and loyalty to family, country, and organization. The author uses examples from Egypt and China to further describe the challenges of global teams, and discusses the role of HR in forming and maintaining these teams.

Ray, D., & Bronstein, H. (1995). *Teaming up: Making the transition to a self-directed, team-based organization.* New York: McGraw-Hill.

On their own time, most people manage homes, families, and community service. At work, they would manage their own time, productivity, and service if allowed. Ray has learned this firsthand as he assisted hundreds of organizations' transitions from traditional management to team-based organizations. Bronstein conducted interviews with many of the managers and employees who completed the transition. Their experiences serve to teach organizations how to prepare, design, and implement empowerment through self-directed teams. Includes bibliographical references and index.

Reddy, W. B., & Jamison, K. (1988). *Team building: Blueprints for productivity and satisfaction.* Alexandria, VA: NTL Institute for Applied Behavioral Science.

In this comprehensive work, 19 chapters address a wide range of team-building issues. Written for the team builder and the manager, the material covered represents what has been currently written on the subject. The book has five sections: Part 1 provides the basic elements of team building; Part 2 explores a broader view of the theories of team building; Part 3 shows various applications for building teams; Part 4 illustrates how team building is a manageable activity; and Part 5 looks at the social issues involved in building teams. The final chapter has biographical summaries of the 23 contributors to this text. Includes a bibliography.

Rossy, G. L., & Archibald, R. D. (1992). **Building commitment in project teams.** *Project Management Journal, 23*(2), 5-14.

Project managers depend on schedules, contractors, suppliers, and various functional contributors to achieve their project objectives. Getting commitment and then getting all parties to fulfill their commitments is a unique challenge. Using a balance of supporting and innovating skills, a project manager can develop commitment in an environment with many conflicting demands. Examples of these skills are: leading by example, encouraging continuous feedback, supporting current plans while striving for improvement, and maintaining a balance among priorities.

New
Shields, D. L. L., Gardner, D. E., Bredemeier, B. J. L., & Bostro, A. (1997). **The relationship between leadership behaviors and group cohesion in team sports.** *Journal of Psychology, 131*(2), 196-210.

This article reports on an analysis of leadership behavior and group cohesion in two natural groups—baseball teams and softball teams. The authors intend to prove that leadership in natural groups is different and less well researched than leadership in military and therapeutic groups. More than 300 athletes completed the *Multidimensional Model of Leadership* (Chelladurai & Carron, 1978), the perceived and preferred versions of the *Leadership Scale for Sports* (Chelladurai & Saleh, 1980), and the *Group Environment Questionnaire* (Carron, Widmeyer, & Brawley, 1985). Twenty-three coaches completed the self-perceived version of the *Leadership Scale for Sports.* The authors conclude that team cohesion occurs when athletes and coaches agree on what is actually happening in instruction—democratic or autocratic behavior, social support, and positive feedback—

not when they agree on what should be occurring. Includes bibliographical references.

Tjosvold, D., & Tjosvold, M. M. (1993). *The emerging leader: Ways to a stronger team.* New York: Lexington.

This book is written for those who want to lead their task forces, departments, and organizations through times of change. These individuals practice a learning style of leadership in which they are willing to begin with their own personal changes, confront their blind spots, and build on their strengths. They challenge others to do the same and create environments in which people support each others' efforts to be effective. Where this learning style of leadership exists, successful teamwork results. Includes bibliographical references and index.

Torres, C. (1994). *The Tao of teams: A guide to team success.* San Diego, CA: Pfeiffer.

The *Tao Te Ching*, an ancient Chinese philosophy, inspired this collection of poetic images. Applied to teamwork, this philosophy teaches self-knowledge and respect for others. Aligning with forces of the universe, the negative yin and the positive yang, allows teams to accept change as a natural event. Eighty-one passages reinforce lessons on trust, flexibility, diversity, intuition, power, and conflict resolution. Includes bibliographical references.

Torres, C., & Spiegel, J. (1991). *Self-directed work teams: A primer.* San Diego, CA: Pfeiffer.

A brief overview of changes needed to implement self-directed teams explains a new leadership need. Team members are empowered to contribute to product and service improvements, experience greater job satisfaction, and feel like partners in their organization. Includes bibliographical references.

Weiss, J. C. (1988). **The D-R model of coleadership of groups.** *Small Group Behavior, 19*(1), 117-125.

This article is concerned with the coleadership of citizen groups, groups for teaching and training, and work groups in general. The author has developed a model of co-leadership referred to as the "D-R" model, which focuses on five overlapping processes: develop/relationship; discuss/roles; divide/responsibility; defer/respect; and debrief/review. The model is intended to be used as a practical guide and is designed to improve group relationships.

Wellins, R. S., Byham, W. C., & Wilson, J. M. (1991). *Empowered teams: Creating self-directed work groups that improve quality, productivity, and participation.* San Francisco: Jossey-Bass.

Self-directed work teams—groups empowered to manage themselves and their work on a day-to-day basis—are different from other groups in that they are formal, permanent organizational structures. Self-directed teams work best because they are closest to the work and know best how to improve job performance. Team atmosphere enhances the feeling of "owning" jobs and making a meaningful contribution to the organization, and team empowerment offers possibilities not available to individual employees. Drawing on a national survey, research, literature review, and experience, the authors provide information on the mechanics of getting started. Includes bibliographical references and index.

New
Wheelan, S. A., & Kaeser, R. M. (1997). **The influence of task type and designated leaders on developmental patterns in groups.** *Small Group Research, 28*(1), 94-121.

This field study explored the development patterns of groups that did not have formal leaders and were performing different tasks. Small groups of attendees of a group relations conference were observed and their verbal interactions were examined using the Group Development Observation System. Statistical analysis, presented here in tables, showed that in this setting group duration, rather than group task type or the presence or absence of designated leaders, accounted for differences in groups.

New
Wilson, G. L. (1996). *Groups in context: Leadership and participation in small groups* (4th ed.). New York: McGraw-Hill.

This book aims to help readers become productive members of groups and enjoy their interactions with other group members. It is written as a textbook—each chapter states its objectives at the beginning; discusses theory, research, and practice throughout; and summarizes ideas at the end. There are exercises, journal-writing assignments, and models. New topics in the 4th edition include: ethics and responsibility in group communication, advantages and disadvantages of group work, critical thinking and quality of information, and gender and cultural differences in language. Includes a glossary, bibliographies, indexes, and a quick-reference guide to troubleshooting solutions for typical group problems.

New
Wilson, J. M., George, J., Wellins, R. S., & Byham, W. C. (1994). *Leadership trapeze: Strategies for leadership in team-based organizations.* San Francisco: Jossey-Bass.

The authors, who all work for the human resources trainer Development Dimensions International, acknowledge that leading teams can be as scary as flying on a trapeze. Part One of this book describes how the roles of leaders are changing as more companies shift to a team system, and includes case studies and flow charts to illustrate the new model. Part Two is prescriptive, detailing a course of action, complete with discussion plans and self-checks, for managers in team situations and for organizations hoping to support their team leaders.

Zenger, J. H., Musselwhite, E., Hurson, K., & Perrin, C. (1994). *Leading teams: Mastering the new role.* Homewood, IL: Business One Irwin.

Easily readable and bottom-line practical, this book is written for managers who want to utilize or strengthen teams at work. It opens with the argument that teams work better, faster, cheaper than traditional employer/employee relationships. It follows with an outline of a team's life cycle—its phases of forming, storming, norming, and performing. Finally, excerpts from interviews with managers who survived team building at work discuss issues of building trust and dealing the loss of positional power.

SETTINGS OF LEADERSHIP

COMMUNITY, VOLUNTEER, AND NONPROFIT

New
Bargen, D. (1996). **Community visioning and leadership.** *Journal of Leadership Studies, 3*(3), 135-162.

The most important factor in building and strengthening healthy communities is *community visioning,* a process of effectively stating what the collection of individuals and organizations really wants to be. This paper identifies the process of building healthy, strong communities. The process is developed with the premise that communities are unique, and that applying the visioning process presents profound challenges.

Boyte, H. C. (1989). *Commonwealth: A return to citizen politics.* New York: Free Press.

American democracy is intended to be a government of the people, by the people, and for the people. The United States was built on a commonwealth of active citizenry. But the problems faced by the founders were different from the enormous societal problems faced today. A restored interest in citizen involvement is at work to protect the environment, offer help to troubled people, build homes, improve education, and promote public safety. Boyte reports on the efforts of some grassroots organizations that have successfully effected change through active citizenship. Includes bibliography and index.

New
Brown, M. J. (1996). **What can community organizers teach us?** *Journal for Quality and Participation, 19*(5), 78-84.

Recently, how to empower workers has become a popular topic for books and seminars, but Brown argues that community organizations have been empowering their volunteers for years. He encourages business leaders to learn how volunteer coordinators recruit community members, spur them to take on leadership responsibility, and maintain relationships with these newly empowered volunteers. The article provides suggestions for how to apply these tactics to the business world, such as conducting one-on-one interviews with workers and appealing to their self-interest to inspire action.

Center for Leadership Excellence of the Catholic Health Association. (1994). *Transformational leadership for the healing ministry: Competencies for the future: A report on the findings.* St. Louis, MO: Author.

The Catholic Health Association used focus groups, sampling, interviews, and data analysis to determine the key situations facing leaders today and the competencies needed to provide the best health care possible within the identified situations. Among the 15 situations facing leaders are: change, diversity, values, and fiscal responsibility. Among the competencies are: spirituality, respect for others, moral wisdom, organizational awareness, and interpersonal understanding. A Model of Outstanding Leadership integrates the competencies and service to the community.

Chrislip, D. D., & Larson, C. E. (1994). *Collaborative leadership: How citizens and civic leaders can make a difference.* San Francisco: Jossey-Bass.

Three challenges facing communities are: complex societal issues such as poverty and crime, frustrated citizens, and bureaucratic gridlock. Chrislip and Larson share case studies to demonstrate how five communities faced these challenges with collaborative leadership and achieved successful results. Baltimore organized BUILD (Baltimoreans United in Leadership Development) to deal with its overwhelming poverty, illiteracy, school dropout, teen pregnancy, unemployment, and housing problems. Its mission is to prepare young people to be responsible, contributing citizens. Phoenix, Newark, Denver, and Roanoke also addressed and overcame their communities' problems through collaboration. Includes bibliographical references and index.

Clary, E. G., Snyder, M., & Ridge, R. (1992). **Volunteers' motivations: A functional strategy for the recruitment, placement, and retention of volunteers.** *Nonprofit Management & Leadership, 2*(4), 333-350.

Understanding the personal motivations of volunteers is examined from a psychological framework. Six motivational functions are identified: social, value, career, understanding, protective, and esteem. A volunteer-function inventory may be used to identify and measure the motivations of volunteers and is recommended to administrators for use in planning recruitment, placement, and retention strategies.

Cohen, M. B. (1994). **Who wants to chair the meeting? Group development and leadership patterns in a community action group of homeless people.** *Social Work with Groups, 17*(1/2), 71-87.

Cohen reports on a community-action group sponsored by a food, clothing, and shelter agency for the homeless in a New England city. Staffed by four employees, social-work students, and volunteers, this agency empowered its clients to provide feedback for the agency. An open-ended, task-centered group was initially chaired by agency staff members. Over the course of 18 months, eight individuals emerged as group leaders to plan a fund-raising event, establish guidelines for acceptable behavior, write a newsletter, and organize recreational activities. Leadership changed hands over issues of group dynamics and due to the unpredictable nature of the group members.

Cusack, S. A. (1994). **Developing leadership in the third age: An ethnographic study of leadership in a seniors' center.** *Journal of Applied Gerontology, 13*(2), 127-142.

Following retirement, one moves into the third age of life, which is often a time of personal growth and service to the community. Using observation, interviews, and focus groups, Cusack examines the potential for developing leadership ability among retirees for the benefit of community seniors' centers. She was surprised to learn some of the assumptions that her subjects had about the concepts of leadership and influence. She concluded that the unique culture of a senior center and the needs and skills of its members affect the potential for leadership development among retirees.

New
Dart, R., Bradshaw, P., Murray, V., & Wolpin, J. (1996). **Boards of directors in nonprofit organizations: Do they follow a life-cycle model?** *Nonprofit Management & Leadership, 6*(4), 367-379.

Several theoretical models exist that apply a life cycle to nonprofit boards. This study used survey data from 1,200 Canadian nonprofits to empirically test these models. Results showed that some of the broader life-cycle hypotheses did apply to most boards—boards tended to grow in size and use more structure and formal procedures as they aged. However, the authors found that their research did not support more specific hypotheses about board behavior, and they caution against applying these models without considering more variables than just board age.

New
De Pree, M. (1997). *Leading without power: Finding hope in serving community.* San Francisco: Jossey-Bass.

De Pree says that for-profit companies could learn from America's nonprofit community, because volunteers "allow no room in their work for the deceptive simplicity of the single bottom line." Instead nonprofits are places where people "realize their potential and do so continually." This collection of essays offers leaders inspiration and advice on how to transform their organizations into "movements" that attract people not with money, but with the promise of meaningful work and a fulfilled life. DePree's topics include potential, service, vision, and moral purpose.

New
Eadie, D. C. (1997). *Changing by design: A practical approach to leading innovation in nonprofit organizations.* San Francisco: Jossey-Bass.

Written for the leaders of nonprofits, this book offers a model for designing and implementing change initiatives. The author focuses on three key areas: coordinated leadership on the part of the chief executive and the board, creative innovation in establishing what needs to be changed and how, and effective implementation of new ideas and programs. Real-life case studies are used to illustrate concepts, and chapters address issues including building boards, nurturing creativity, and strategic management.

New
Eisenhower Leadership Group. (1996). ***Democracy at risk: How schools can lead.*** College Park, MD: Author. To get a copy of this report, contact the James MacGregor Burns Academy of Leadership, University of Maryland, 1107 Taliaferro Hall, College Park, MD 20742. Phone: (301) 405-0390.

Scholars from the University of Maryland, Harvard University, and Washington State University collaborated on this report that describes how to help students become citizen leaders. Based on an assessment of the 38 college and university projects funded by the federal Department of Education Dwight D. Eisenhower Development Program, the scholars conclude that leadership learning can light the fire of democracy in the next generation of students and reverse the trend toward apathy.

New
Ellis, S. J. (1996). ***From the top down: The executive role in volunteer program success*** (Rev. ed.). Philadelphia: Energize.

This book addresses leadership issues for organizations that depend on volunteers to deliver service. This revised edition designates different types of volunteers: student interns, stipended workers, corporate volunteers, technical assistance volunteers, groups, those who give a few hours of support, court-refereed community service workers, residents of community homes, those with vested interest in a program, national service workers, unemployed or disabled volunteers, and virtual volunteers. Ellis makes recommendations about how to handle legal issues, determine the dollar value of volunteer work, and foster volunteer/staff relationships. One appendix outlines the major functions of volunteer administration. Another appendix lists resources including support organizations and a bibliography. Includes index.

Ellis, S. J., & Noyes, K. H. (1990). ***By the people: A history of Americans as volunteers*** (Rev. ed.). San Francisco: Jossey-Bass.

Three centuries of volunteer action in America are recorded in this history. Mass movements for abolition, women's suffrage, and Civil Rights have pioneered social change. Self-help groups like the Grange, the PTA, and the Red Cross have shaped us as a people. Recent developments, such as care for AIDS patients and the presidential "thousand points of light" community service initiative, are analyzed. The authors explore prospects for

the future of volunteerism. Includes bibliographical references and index.

New
Firstenberg, P. B. (1996). ***The 21st century nonprofit: Remaking the organization in the post-government era.*** New York: Foundation Center.

Firstenberg, a long-time nonprofit executive and board member, applies his years of experience to developing a plan for managing tax-exempt organizations. He addresses the importance of accountability and describes a way that nonprofits can prove their productivity to the public. Other chapters address how to expand an organization's revenue base and managing human resources in nonprofits. Three leaders of nonprofits are also profiled—McGeorge Bundy, former president of the Ford Foundation; former Princeton president William Bowen; and Joan Ganz Cooney, a founder of *Sesame Street*. Includes index.

New
Gabelnick, F. (1997). **Educating a committed citizenry.** *Change, 29*(1), 30-35.

According to Gabelnick, the responsibility for developing committed leaders of the 21st century belongs in higher education. Curricula must include courses on multiculturalism and social responsibility. Campuses must encourage dialogue on the tough subjects of injustice and societal change. Campus programs must integrate service and learning. Gabelnick cites examples of socially responsible courses and programs. Some involve students in local politics and environmental campaigns. Others address gender issues, racism, and poverty. Organizations that support educational-community leadership initiatives include the Washington Center, The Greenleaf Center, the Kellogg Foundation, the Ford Foundation, and Campus Compact.

New
Green, J. C., & Griesinger, D. W. (1996). **Board performance and organizational effectiveness in nonprofit social services organizations.** *Nonprofit Management & Leadership, 6*(4), 381-402.

The authors surveyed the leaders and board members of 16 nonprofits serving developmentally disabled adults to determine whether board performance was related to organizational effectiveness. Itemizing board activities and using accreditation surveys to determine effectiveness, the study found a significant relationship between the two factors. Board activities most strongly correlated with effectiveness included policy formation, financial planning and control, program monitoring, resource development, and dispute resolution.

New

Henton, D., Melville, J., & Walsh, K. (1997). ***Grassroots leaders for a new economy: How civic entrepreneurs are building prosperous communities.*** San Francisco: Jossey-Bass.

Joint Venture: Silicon Valley was a collaborative regional alliance, formed in 1992, that united business, government, education, and community leaders for the purpose of strengthening the economy and improving the area's quality of life. Three Joint Venture advisors wrote this book to describe their efforts and other examples of civic entrepreneurship around the country. They explain how any community can implement a program like theirs, outlining the steps of initiation, incubation, implementation, and improvement. Includes bibliographical references and index.

Herman, R. D. (Ed.). (1994). ***The Jossey-Bass handbook of nonprofit leadership and management.*** San Francisco: Jossey-Bass.

Nonprofit scholars and executives write about the unique management skills necessary in nonprofit organizations. Their intent is to provide a comprehensive and in-depth picture of this sector. They discuss the nature of philanthropy, political influence, legal issues, lobbying, program development, fund-raising and financial management, recruiting and retaining volunteers, staff and board relationships, and the future of nonprofits. Includes bibliographical references.

New

Herman, R. D., Renz, D. O., & Heimovics, R. D. (1997). **Board practices and board effectiveness in local nonprofit organizations.** *Nonprofit Management & Leadership, 7*(4), 373-385.

How do nonprofits judge the effectiveness of their boards? This study of 64 Kansas City agencies examined the relationship between the extent to which boards used prescribed board practices and stakeholder judgments of their effectiveness. The prescribed practices, drawn from the growing literature on boards, include having a board manual, holding an annual board retreat, and using a board self-evaluation. The study found that the methods used to evaluate boards vary so widely that making any generalizations is dangerous, but the authors believe that using prescribed board practices may increase overall effectiveness.

New

Houle, C. O. (1997). ***Governing boards: Their nature and nurture.*** San Francisco: Jossey-Bass.

A project of the National Center for Nonprofit Boards, this book is a basic manual for board members and

nonprofit leaders. Chapters address issues including how to think about a board, its structure, its human potential, its operations, and the external relationships of a board. Also included are a list of books for further reading, an 1890 article offering fund-raising advice that still applies today, and a rating scale for boards. Includes bibliography and index.

Ilsley, P. J. (1990). ***Enhancing the volunteer experience: New insights on strengthening volunteer participation, learning, and commitment.*** San Francisco: Jossey-Bass.

Ilsley's four-year study of volunteers in organizations such as hospitals, political groups, and museums provides insight into the volunteer perspective. The primary motivation for volunteering is not altruism, but the opportunity to learn. Giving volunteers a voice in recruitment, placement, and training leads to high morale and better performance. Ilsley offers strategies for balancing organizational, staff, and volunteer needs to avoid conflicts and burnout. Includes bibliographical references and index.

New

Jack, E. T. (1996). **Philosophical foundation of citizen leadership.** *Journal of Leadership Studies, 3*(4), 54-60.

Jack claims that in the last 25 years, Americans have distanced themselves from their neighbors by being less involved in civic associations and religious communities. He believes that it is this distancing that causes the social problems of divorce, alcoholism, poverty, and crime. Jack recommends that citizens join forces to solve local problems and cites several historical and current examples of successful citizen action. Public benefits of such citizen leadership are: strangers meeting on public ground, mutual responsibility for our world, the fear of strangers faced and dealt with, and conflict resolution.

Jones, B. D., & Bachelor, L. W. (1993). ***The sustaining hand: Community leadership and corporate power*** (2nd ed.). Lawrence, KS: University Press of Kansas.

The authors revised their 1986 edition of this book to reinforce the premise that politicians and business executives in any community have fundamentally different agendas yet are interdependent. An additional case study, the Chrysler Jefferson project, chronicles Detroit's effort to revitalize the industry that supports the city. Includes bibliographical references and index.

Kaagan, S., Stovall, B., Hesterman, O., & Catala, Y. (1995). **Bonding two cultures, university and community, through leadership development.** *Journal of Leadership Studies, 2*(3), 75-90.

CLIMB (Community Leadership Initiative—Michigan's Best) partners Michigan State University Extension and community leaders throughout the state of Michigan. The authors credit the success of this joint program on a shared vision, self-reflection in the academic community, and the wealth of resources in the academic community for conducting research and designing innovative new courses and programs.

Kahn, S. (1991). *Organizing: A guide for grassroots leaders* (Rev. ed.). Silver Spring, MD: NASW Press.

As a songwriter and folksinger, Si Kahn focuses on struggle and social change in America. This written guide teaches how to unite people to effect change and existing power structures. Social workers set the example, serving as agents of change and preserving the worth, dignity, and uniqueness of each individual. Kahn calls for grassroots organizations to address the issues of homelessness, violence, drug abuse, poverty, and health care. Includes bibliographical references and index.

Kettering Foundation. (1992). *Community politics.* Dayton, OH: Author.

This is a working paper from the Kettering Foundation's projects, including the National Issues Forum, the Negotiated Investment Strategy, and studies of American politics. Described are some "dangers of politics as usual and the benefits of moving citizens into constructive choicework."

New
Kroll, K., & Vandenberg, L. (1996). **Community centered organizational leadership: Challenges for practice.** *Journal of Leadership Studies*, *3*(4), 117-128.

This articles describes the shared leadership style of a service organization called Food for the Hungry/Kenya. This nongovernmental organization helps the rural and urban poor citizens of Kenya in emergency situations and through self-development programs. What makes this organization "leaderful," or a practitioner of shared leadership, is the sense of personal calling that each member feels, their commitment to the organization's purpose, and their desire to be servant leaders. Each works to build community with each other and the people they serve. A strong Christian philosophy runs throughout the program.

New
Lakey, B., Lakey, G., Napier, R., and Robinson, J. (1995). *Grassroots and nonprofit leadership: A guide for organizations in changing times.* Philadelphia: New Society Publishers.

The authors believe that social change is like a river, at various times running fast, slow, dangerous, and calm. They use this metaphor to structure their book, which addresses the organizational issues nonprofits face.

Chapter topics include starting a social movement (gathering the rafting party), handling growth (finding a big enough raft), developing a board (coordinating paddling), and avoiding burnout (pacing yourself for the journey). Includes index.

New
Leitch, D. (1997). **Society in motion: Russia's emerging voluntary sector.** *Nonprofit Management & Leadership*, *7*(4), 421-433.

A former consultant and trainer for independent social organizations in central Russia, Leitch describes voluntary agencies in the city of Voronezh within a historical context. Although the Soviet government discouraged independent associations, many community leaders gained experience during the 1960s and 1970s in neighborhood organizations and underground "informals." With the coming of *glasnost* in the late 1980s, these grassroots leaders began openly addressing the dire social needs in Russia. A large number of voluntary groups in Voronezh are self-organizing, which Leitch attributes to the community leadership that developed in the pre-Gorbachev period, despite heavy state oppression.

New
Lewis, P. V. (1996). *Transformational leadership: A new model for total church involvement.* Nashville, TN: Broadman & Holman.

Lewis addresses the need for change in the leadership of today's churches. He outlines leadership traits and styles to help pastors identify their current practices and learn new ones. Transformational leadership style is most closely aligned with Christian leadership. It builds on the strength of others, raises awareness about issues of consequence, and enables people to transcend their own self-interest. Lewis cites examples of transformational leadership from business, sports, music, and scripture. At the end of each chapter are questions to encourage discussion and reflection.

Littrell, D. W., Karns, L., & Wilson, V. R. (Eds.). (1992). *Developing community leadership: The EXCEL approach.* Missouri Rural Innovation Institute, 529 Clark Hall, University of Missouri, Columbia, MO 65211. Phone: (314) 882-5859.

The W. K. Kellogg Foundation and University Extension funded EXCEL, a leadership program in 60 communities throughout Missouri. Citizen groups volunteered more than 100 hours in a one-year program to study local cultural, economic, political, and social forces and to study strategies for community development. In this notebook, the Missouri Rural Innovation Institute shares its process for organizing this successful community leadership-development program. Chapters include: concept, budget planning, program content, recruiting, publicity, and evaluation. Includes bibliographical references.

New
Marano, R. (1997). ***Young volunteers: Providing service and making an impact on communities.*** *NASSP Bulletin, 81*(591), 45-48.

Marano describes the Prudential Spirit of Community Awards, created in partnership with the National Association of Secondary School Principals in 1995. The awards recognize young heroes who initiate outstanding volunteer projects. So far, 10,000 young people have been honored. Every U.S. school may name one honoree per every 1,000 students. From that pool, each state selects two winners who each receive $1,000, a silver medal, and an expense-paid trip to the national awards in Washington, DC. Five national winners each receive $5,000 and a gold medal. One 1997 winner is Brian Harris of Cypress, California, who paired 20,000 global pen pals to promote interracial understanding. Another is Kristin Deaton of Putnam City, Oklahoma, who founded a softball league for children with special needs. More than fame or prizes, the awards serve to focus on the contributions of young people and to encourage all citizens to get involved in their communities.

New
Mason, D. E. (1996). ***Leading and managing the expressive dimension: Harnessing the hidden power source of the nonprofit sector.*** San Francisco: Jossey-Bass.

Mason states that voluntary, nonprofit organizations are "instruments for people who want something done and arenas for people who seek expressive involvement." This expression may take the form of fostering innovation, the pleasure of performing, socializing, or alignment with an ideology. Among the competencies for developing an organization's expressive dimension are: forming and articulating a vision, building trust, communicating, innovating, understanding political activity, persuading, recruiting, fund-raising, emphasizing ethics, inspiring, exploiting opportunities, and maximizing cohesion. This book is written for leaders, volunteer coordinators, board members, researchers, educators, and consultants in the independent sector. Includes bibliographical references, name index, and subject index.

New
Matusak, L. R. (1997). ***Finding your voice: Learning to lead—Anywhere you want to make a difference.*** San Francisco: Jossey-Bass.

This book is written for people who do not hold positions of power but who do choose to lead. Matusak states that

every day we all have opportunities to be creative, act with purpose, and encourage others to work together toward positive change. Through her work at the Kellogg Foundation, Matusak has identified hundreds of people who make a difference in their communities without getting their names in the headlines. In this book, she shares many of their stories. A resource section recommends leadership development programs, books, and films for people who want to find their voices and begin leading. Includes index.

Miller, L. C. (1991). ***Citizen-directed futures assessments.*** Department of Rural Sociology, University of Wisconsin–Extension, 1450 Linden Drive, Madison, WI 53706. Phone: (608) 262-3913.

Using future-needs assessment techniques developed for the space industry, Miller suggests that citizen groups can envision the future of their communities. She offers exercises to develop image thinking for those accustomed to linear thinking. Outlines are provided for analysis of needs, participant workshops, and action-planning. "Almost any change can be accomplished in the long-term if sufficient will and energy are mobilized."

Nygren, D. J., Ukeritis, M. D., McClelland, D. C., & Others. (1993, May-June). **Religious-leadership competencies.** *Review for Religious*, pp. 390-417.

The authors used competency-assessment methods to determine the competencies critical to outstanding performance in religious leadership positions. In a study of Roman Catholic congregational leaders, they identified threshold competencies—those necessary for anyone aspiring to meet at least typical standards for congregational leadership—and excellence competencies. Outstanding leaders are characterized by being more concerned than typical leaders with exerting power and influence to attain congregational goals, and are less concerned with supervising and counseling individual members of the congregation.

O'Brien, D. J., & Hassinger, E. W. (1992). **Community attachment among leaders in five rural communities.** *Rural Sociology, 57*(4), 521-534.

Leaders in rural communities must feel strong personal attachments to invest the effort necessary to mobilize community members toward social change. They also need to form networks outside the community to draw resources and assistance for local programs. A study of leaders in five rural communities measures the sociodemographic and social-network characteristics of rural leaders.

New

Perlmutter, F. D. (1995). **Nonprofit social services in Moscow: Leadership and administrative issues.** *Nonprofit Management & Leadership*, *6*(1), 39-54.

Based on interviews collected in Moscow during 1992, this article surveys the state of the nonprofit sector in Russia after the fall of the Soviet Union, specifically leadership and governance in the country's newly emerging social service organizations. Perlmutter found that many nonprofits were led by charismatic figures, and that essentially no organizations had professionally trained leaders or boards. She encourages Western organizations to help train Russian nonprofit leaders, and also surveys state laws governing nonprofits and the various resources available.

Pollio, D. E. (1994). **Wintering at the Earle: Group structures in the street community.** *Social Work with Groups, 17*(1/2), 47-70.

This case study presents a group of Richmond, Virginia, homeless people to provide an insider's view of life on the streets. The author met 11 men and women living in the deserted Earle Hotel through his work at a drop-in center. He documents the group dynamics, sense of belonging, and leadership that evolved in this group over a two-year period. Pollio discusses the implications of this insider's view for the provision of psychological services to homeless populations.

New

Pynes, J. E. (1997). *Human resources management for public and nonprofit organizations.* San Francisco: Jossey-Bass.

Written by a professor of public administration, this is the first book to address integrating human resources management and strategic mission in the context of public and nonprofit agencies. In addition to discussing recruitment, performance evaluation, and compensation, the author addresses issues unique to nonprofits, such as managing volunteers. Figures and exhibits provided include wage schedules, sample interview questions, National Labor Relations Board Standards, and a grid for matching present and potential board members.

New

Reed, T. K. (1996). **A new understanding of "followers" as leaders: Emerging theory of civic leadership.** *Journal of Leadership Studies, 3*(1), 95-104.

Reed presents the new theory of civic leadership and how it has transformed the shape of leadership and democratized society. During the last three decades social movements have fostered civic learning among followers of grassroots leaders. This learning has equipped followers

to take a critical look at the world around them and to take action against injustice. In this article, civic leaders are defined as are the differences between civic participation and civic leadership. One impact of civic leadership is that leaders are no longer universally trusted simply by virtue of position. Reed challenges leadership study programs to learn more about this emerging leadership role and the new theory of societal leadership.

Selsky, J. W., & Smith, A. E. (1994). **Community entrepreneurship: A framework for social change leadership.** *Leadership Quarterly: Special Issue: Leadership for Environmental and Social Change, 5*(3/4), 277-296.

Community entrepreneurship occurs when a community-based leader organizes a group that influences social change. These situations are characterized by turbulent social environments, temporary and fluid alliances, and fast-paced events. Three qualities coexist in community entrepreneurs: the ability to envision and articulate a multiframe perspective, an entrepreneurial spirit, and a reflective and learning nature. Two case studies are documented in this research report, both concerned with community development in Philadelphia's nonprofit sector in the 1980s.

New

Thompson, A. M. (1995). **The sexual division of leadership in volunteer emergency medical service squads.** *Nonprofit Management & Leadership, 6*(1), 55-66.

According to the author, "although women constitute a relatively greater proportion of the nonprofit and voluntary work force . . . women continue to be underrepresented among leadership ranks." This study statistically analyzed survey data from New York EMS teams to determine whether these teams, which elect their leaders, showed a sexual division of leadership. Results show that while there was no aggregate sex bias, women were mainly elected staff or administrative leaders, while most of the head line officers were men.

New

Tropman, J. E. (1997). *Successful community leadership.* Washington, DC: NASW Press.

Social services and community organizations are rapidly and profoundly changing. Tropman uses practical how-to advice to explain how to take leadership in community groups, how to conduct effective community group meetings, and the rewards of community leadership. Chapters are divided to quickly find information about group leadership, community group membership, the community facilitator, decision management, discussions, evaluations, and other subjects. A section is also devoted to using the library and the Internet to search for information about the community and leadership issues. The appendices show a sample agenda, sample options memo, and sample minutes from a meeting. Includes bibliographical references and index.

New
Tschirhart, M. (1996). *Artful leadership: Managing stakeholder problems in nonprofit arts organizations.* Bloomington: Indiana University Press.

This book explains how and why leaders of nonprofit arts organizations choose their strategies for dealing with stakeholders. Predictors and themes in problem management are analyzed, and insight is given into why specific problems arise, why certain strategies are chosen, and how effective those strategies are. Although targeted primarily toward students and scholars, this book may also be used by the practitioners in nonprofit organizations. There are chapters on managing relationships with stakeholders, predicting responses to problems with stakeholders, finding patterns in the management of problems, and exploring challenges associated with stakeholder groups. Appendices explain study methodology and tables used throughout the book. Includes bibliographical references and index.

Van Orman, J. R. (1989). **Leadership and grassroots development: Reflections of an IAF representative.** *Grassroots Development, 13*(2), 3-7.

As a project manager for the Inter-American Foundation, Van Orman summarizes the qualities necessary to lead grassroots programs in impoverished communities. One must understand that the root of a program is hope, that a mechanism for coping with reality is sometimes mistaken for passivity, and that leaders must bridge two cultures. When naturally charismatic leaders emerge, IAF offers leadership training, program support, and funding.

Weems, L. H., Jr. (1993). *Church leadership: Vision, team culture, and integrity.* Nashville, TN: Abingdon Press.

Pastors are leaders, and their leadership takes on greater significance in difficult times. If the task of leadership is change, what are the stages of the journey for the leader to become change master? Weems suggests the first stage is creating a vision that embodies people's hopes and desires, where imagination and courage are essential. Next, change masters must have the power to advance their vision by involving and influencing a team culture where people will devote their considerable time and energy to make the vision a reality. Finally, change masters must maintain the momentum and keep faith and hope alive during the inevitable frustrations inherent in execution. Weems asserts the best way for institutions to endure and prosper is to encourage leaders who will build

on the past by envisioning an even better future. Includes bibliographical references.

Wells, R. (1991). **Leadership and community: Partners for empowerment.** *Campus Activities Programming, 24*(5), 33-38.

Society endures a paradox—our need for individuality and our need for community. Leaders face the challenge of bringing together socially interdependent people who share certain practices and are nurtured by community. Wells offers ten principles for building communities: inclusion, caring, respecting differences, safety, common purpose, commitment, self-examination, decision making by consensus, decentralization of authority, and celebration.

New
Wood, M. M. (Ed.). (1996). *Nonprofit boards and leadership: Cases on governance, change, and board-staff dynamics.* San Francisco: Jossey-Bass.

This book is made up of 13 teaching cases based on real-life leadership issues faced by nonprofit organizations. Each case includes exhibits, an annotated bibliography, and discussion questions, and requires the reader to make a decision based on the information provided. Organizations described in the cases include a United Way allocations committee, a nonprofit hospital, a museum, a university, a women's shelter, and AIDS Project Los Angeles. Includes index.

Zander, A. (1990). *Effective social action by community groups.* San Francisco: Jossey-Bass.

Self-starting groups working toward social reform are unique and have not been widely researched. Zander examines their nature, motivation, objectives, and methods for achieving goals and facing resistance. Eleven methods are discussed, ranging from permissive to coercive. This book is intended for citizen groups wishing to increase their power and influence and for researchers of groups in general. Includes bibliographical references and index.

CORPORATE

New
Bahrami, H., & Evans, S. (1997). **Human resource leadership in knowledge-based entities: Shaping the context of work.** *Human Resource Management, 36*(1), 23-28.

A growing number of companies today are knowledge-based entities, organizations characterized by intensity, novelty, and collaborative teamwork. What role can HR play in these organizations? This article argues that HR should take an active leadership role based on a new model for HR teams. The model identifies four roles HR needs to play in these knowledge-based entities: 1) the "orgitecht" who leads organizational design, 2) the vendor who handles HR transactions, 3) the hub who acts as an information base, and 4) the glue who handles communications and executive development.

Bateman, T. S., Sakano, T., & Fujita, M. (1992). **Roger, me, and my attitude: Film propaganda and cynicism toward corporate leadership.** *Journal of Applied Psychology, 77*(5), 768-771.

Two studies were conducted on viewers of *Roger & Me,* a 1989 feature film about Roger Smith, CEO of General Motors, and the layoffs of 30,000 auto workers. In Durham, North Carolina, 106 movie patrons were asked to complete questionnaires prior to viewing the movie. Following the film, 162 were asked to complete the same questionnaire. In Japan, 542 university students were divided into four groups to complete the same questionnaire, some pre-viewing, some post-viewing, and some never viewing the film. In both studies, results indicated that the film created an attitude change of increased cynicism toward General Motors specifically and U.S. business in general.

New
Bennis, W., & Townsend, R. (1995). *Reinventing leadership: Strategies to empower the organization.* New York: William Morrow.

This book is for companies seeking new leadership styles to suit their new downsized status. It probes the old command-and-control style of leadership that no longer works and suggests ways to create guiding visions and to empower employees. Bennis and Townsend present their ideas in dialogue form and offer dialogue starters at the end of each section to stimulate new ideas. There are role-playing dialogues, partner analyses, debate questions, what-if discussions, management evaluations, and group dialogues. At the end of the book, a 21-day planner helps readers transfer new learnings into practical application.

Bridges, W. (1994). **The end of the job.** *Fortune, 130*(6), 62-74.

It is argued that jobs discourage accountability because they reward people, not for getting the necessary work done but for "doing their jobs." Now the world of work is changing. The conditions that created jobs 200 years ago—mass production and large organizations—are disappearing. Organizations, like individuals, will have trouble shifting their expectations and habits to fit the new post-job world. At a future-oriented organization like

Intel, you can see the future role of the worker. A person is hired and assigned to a project, it changes over time, then the person is assigned to another (well before the first is finished), and then to another. This requires working under several team leaders, keeping different schedules, being in various places, and performing a number of different tasks. Hierarchy implodes and individuals "report to each other."

Bruce, J. S. (1992). *The creative opportunists: Conversations with CEOs of small businesses.* Greensboro, NC: Center for Creative Leadership.

As a follow-up to his study of CEOs of large corporations, Bruce reports on his study of CEOs of small businesses. He states that there are some fundamental challenges faced by all CEOs, regardless of the size of their organizations. In comparison, he found that CEOs of small businesses have four distinct attributes: they are creative, their creativity exceeds their resources, they are willing to take risks, and they are able to seize opportunities quickly.

New
Collins, J. C., & Porras, J. I. (1994). *Built to last: Successful habits of visionary companies.* New York: HarperBusiness.

Collins and Porras researched 18 companies they define as visionary, including 3M, American Express, Nordstrom, and Walt Disney, and identified the factors that made them successful. These include establishing a company's core values and sticking to them, setting "Big Hairy Audacious Goals," and being willing to both experiment and fail. Very reader friendly, the book includes interviews with the CEOs of visionary companies, charts, graphs, an index, and Frequently Asked Questions.

Drucker, P. F. (1969). *The effective executive.* New York: Harper & Row.

Drucker presents findings of a systematic study on what effective executives do that the rest do not do, and what they do not do that the rest tend to do. Findings show that effectiveness can be learned and, more importantly, that it must be learned. This book presents, in simple form, the elements of this practice.

Drucker, P. F. (1982). *The changing world of the executive.* New York: Times Books.

This book provides insights into, and an understanding of, the world of the executive. It also provides a useful "executive agenda" to stimulate both thought and action. The book should be read with this overriding question in mind: "How can I, and we in my organization, use this idea or these insights to perform more effectively—to do a better job, and above all, to welcome and accommodate the new and the different?"

Dunphy, D., & Stace, D. (1993). **The strategic management of corporate change.** *Human Relations, 46*(8), 905-920.

Thirteen Australian service companies participated in a research study of organizational change. Banking, insurance, aviation, and telecommunications companies responded to the Dunphy/Stance change matrix, which is described in this article. The matrix considers which style of leadership (coercive, directive, consultative, or collaborative) achieved the desired change results (fine tuning, incremental adjustment, modular transformation, or corporate transformation). Four summary case studies illustrate the effectiveness of each leadership style during the course of organizational change.

New
Dutton, G. (1996). **Future shock: Who will run the company?** *Management Review, 85*(8), 19-23.

Many companies have no formal succession plan, and if top-management members leave suddenly, the organization can be thrown into turmoil. Dutton recognizes that succession plans can cause problems within the organization if they become political, but she emphasizes their necessity. Four types of succession plans are described— simple replacement of the CEO, full replacement of top management, creating an internal talent pool, and creating an extended talent pool both inside and outside the organization. The succession plans of companies including Wal-Mart, Coca-Cola, Goodyear, and Texas Instruments are described.

New
Ettorre, B. (1996). **Changing the rules of the board game.** *Management Review, 85*(4), 13-17.

Corporate governance, according to the author, has long consisted of "rubber-stamp boards, overpaid directors, and interlocking directorships." This article outlines some of the recent reforms that companies have instituted to make their boards more accountable and more effective. Type of compensation, board diversity, self-evaluation, the mission and values of a board, and board size are all addressed. Examples of board reforms from companies such as American Express, General Electric, and Kimberly-Clark are included.

New
Farkas, C. M., & De Backer, P. (1996). *Maximum leadership: The world's leading CEOs share their five strategies for success.* New York: Henry Holt.

After interviewing more than 160 CEOs of multinational corporations, Farkas and De Backer identified the five approaches to leadership used most by executives: strategic, human assets, expertise, box, and change agent. The strengths and weaknesses of each approach are addressed, and examples of leaders, from companies including Gillette and ITT, who succeeded and failed with each strategy are given. Includes index.

Farquhar, K. W. (1995). **Leadership transitions: Current issues, future directions.** *Human Resource Management: Special Issue on Leadership Transitions, 34*(1), 3-10.

As guest editor of this special issue, Farquhar provides an overview of the current trends in leadership research, the impact on the inner organization, implications for career development, and strategic perspectives. Each article in this issue includes a case study.

Farquhar, K. W. (1995). **Not just understudies: The dynamics of short-term leadership.** *Human Resource Management: Special Issue on Leadership Transitions, 34*(1), 51-70.

Interim and acting CEOs—are they junior leaders? Do they aspire to reach the top without much chance of actually getting there? Or is temporary leadership a strategic window to practice skills in crisis management, support of organizational goals, and paving the way for new leadership? Farquhar defines the three styles of interim leadership and their potential for success. A case study of interim leadership in an educational setting illustrates Farquhar's model of the dynamics of short-term leadership.

New
Floyd, S. W., & Wooldridge, B. (1996). *The strategic middle manager: How to create and sustain competitive advantage.* San Francisco: Jossey-Bass.

Traditional definitions of middle managers focus on their operating responsibilities and management duties, but Floyd and Wooldridge argue that in today's business world middle managers must take on more strategic leadership roles. They recount the history of middle management from World War II on, describe the possibilities for leadership that exist in mid-level positions today, and then offer hands-on advice on applying the book's ideas. Specific chapters address issues faced by those in middle management, how top managers can better work with middle managers, and how those aspiring to middle-management positions can use leadership skills. Includes two self-assessment tests and an index.

Fuller, T. (1995). **Does business need leaders?** *Business Horizons, 38*(4), 1-9.

Fuller reports that the fascination with leadership is strictly an American phenomenon, not shared by European or Japanese management. He also reports that charismatic leadership gets the most attention in the press, but may be less deserving of publicity than other styles of leadership. He questions cultural differences and need for leadership, infatuation with the glamour of leadership, and ambiguous definitions of leadership.

Ghoshal, S., & Bartlett, C. A. (1995). **Changing the role of top management: Beyond structure to processes.** *Harvard Business Review, 73*(1), 86-96.

The hierarchical management structure that built large corporations in the 1970s no longer works in the competitive business environments of the 1980s. This article discusses 20 U.S., European, and Japanese companies that changed their vertical structures and reaped rewards. Three processes highlight their success stories: an entrepreneurial process, a competence-building process, and a renewal process.

Goss, T., Pascale, R., & Athos, A. (1993). **The reinvention roller coaster: Risking the present for a powerful future.** *Harvard Business Review, 71*(6), 97-108.

Reinvention is defined as "not changing what is, but creating what isn't." In the age of downsizing, turnarounds, and reengineering, the authors claim that reinvention is the difference between short- and long-term success. To succeed in the long run, a CEO must communicate a strategic vision for change beyond lowering costs and improving productivity. A company must alter its basic premise. The reinvention stories of British Airways, Haagen-Dazs, Ford, Honda, and Nordstrom illustrate the concept.

New
Grove, A. S. (1996). *Only the paranoid survive: How to exploit the crisis points that challenge every company and career.* New York: Doubleday.

Grove, a manager at Intel, shares his experiences with what he calls "strategic inflection points," which are ". . . the times in the life of a business when its fundamentals are about to change." Although these changes are often brought on by technological changes, they are not restricted to technological industries; they can affect any business. Grove tries to teach leaders and others to cope with such change by ". . . shaping an energetic and

efficient team that is capable of responding to the unanticipated as well as to any ordinary event."

Harris, P. R. (1994). *High performance leadership: HRD strategies for the new work culture* (Rev. ed.). Amherst, MA: HRD Press.

Each chapter of this book introduces a learning module for changing behavior, a summary of behavioral-science theory, exercises for teaching and practicing new behavior, and instrumentation for data gathering and personal development. Some of the behaviors discussed are improving communication skills, enhancing team relations, and leading change. Appendices include a directory of HR organizations and publications. Also includes a bibliography and index.

Hill, L. A. (1993). *Becoming a manager: Mastery of a new identity.* Cambridge, MA: Harvard Business School Press.

A study of 19 newly appointed front-line managers follows the expectations, frustrations, and attitude changes they experience in their first year on the job. Based on extensive observation; interviews with managers, subordinates, and superiors; then considerable follow-up, Hill reports her findings using the actual words and feelings of her subjects. One major change in new managers is role growth from task control to personal-relationship influence. Includes bibliographical references and index.

New
Hodgetts, R. M. (1996). **A conversation with Steve Kerr.** *Organizational Dynamics, 24*(4), 68-79.

In a question-and-answer format, Kerr, the director of GE's leadership education center, discusses his book *The Boundaryless Organization* and his work with GE and Jack Welch. He talks about the challenges he faced implementing changes at GE and cites a number of trends in today's economy. Kerr advocates a business world that is less hierarchical and less focused on vertical promotions, and is more oriented toward a global economy.

Hollenbeck, G. P. (1994). *CEO selection: A street-smart review.* Greensboro, NC: Center for Creative Leadership.

Although selecting a CEO may be the single most important event an organization must face, there is little practical literature available on the subject. In this report, the author, a management psychologist specializing in executive development and succession planning and former human resources executive, reviews several practically oriented books and articles on CEO selection. The reviews are critical and evaluative and reflect the author's own views, tempered by his experience. Includes bibliographical references and index.

New
Isachsen, O. (1996). ***Joining the entrepreneurial elite: Four styles to business success.*** Palo Alto, CA: Davis-Black.

Isachsen identifies four styles of entrepreneurs, two who do the work of managers and two who are leaders. The *administrator* and *tactician* are responsible, persistent, and know how to best deliver goods and services. The *strategist* and *idealist* are spiritual, maintain their sense of purpose, build trust, and enable their employees to deliver superior performance. There is a brief self-scored test for the reader to determine his or her dominant entrepreneurial style. To support his framework, Isachsen tells the stories of entrepreneurs who became successful. Some of them are: administrator Bob Lowe, CEO of Lowe Enterprises, a real-estate firm; tactician Beverly Trupp, CEO of Color Design Art, Inc., one of the largest interior decorating firms in the U.S.; strategist Delores Kesler, Chair of Accustaff temporary employment agency; and idealist Barbara Edwards, CEO of the public relations firm California Host. Includes index.

New
James, G. (1996). ***Business wisdom of the electronic elite: 34 winning management strategies from CEOs at Microsoft, COMPAQ, Sun, Hewlett-Packard and other top companies.*** New York: Times Business.

From industry-wide research and personal interviews with leaders of successful high-tech companies, James describes what the *electronic elite* have to teach other business leaders. He reveals their management strategies that unleash creativity, increase responsiveness, respect individuals, and build communities. The new corporate culture practiced by the electronic elite can be adopted by traditional organizations if leaders and employees shift into six new mind-sets: 1) business is an ecosystem, not a battlefield; 2) the corporation is a community, not a machine; 3) management is service, not control; 4) employees are peers, not children; 5) motivate with vision, not fear; and 6) change is growth, not pain. Throughout the book are quotations—tidbits of wisdom from the electronic elite, exercises, and self-assessments to test the reader's alignment with the new culture. Includes bibliography and index. Appendices summarize key learnings.

Joiner, C. W. (1987). ***Leadership for change.*** Cambridge, MA: Ballinger.

Drawing on his own experiences with the auto industry and as head of Mead Imaging, Joiner presents a thoughtful amalgam of theory and experience, logic and practice. It is designed to provide a framework for planning and leading individuals through the step-by-step process that builds a competitive organization. Some of the key ingredients for successful change include: building a top-management team, selecting a strategic issue, identifying one key change, and establishing strong personnel support systems.

New
Kanter, R. M. (1989). ***When giants learn to dance.*** New York: Simon & Schuster.

The weakening of corporate hierarchies opens opportunities for new leaders who are disciplined, pragmatic, collaborative, and who can get the job done. At the same time, resources such as time and money become more precious and increased competition appears locally and globally. All of these conditions remind Kanter of the Olympic Games. In her sports/business metaphor, Kanter claims that large corporations must get lean and agile, form alliances, and learn creative maneuvering. In other words, to survive in a rapidly changing business environment, giants must learn to dance. To compete successfully, corporations must foster new streams for innovative ideas and must be person-centered and creation-oriented. Kanter cites examples of giants, such as Eastman Kodak, B. F. Goodrich, and Bank of America, who have learned to dance. Includes bibliography and index.

New
Kanter, R. M. (1997). ***Rosabeth Moss Kanter on the frontiers of management.*** Boston: Harvard Business School Publishing.

Kanter, former editor of the *Harvard Business Review*, presents her classic essays as a refresher course for managers who are scrutinizing their organizational structures and aspiring to innovative futures. The essays cover a variety of topics: strategy, innovation, global trends, strategic alliances, and community responsibility. But there is a unifying theme: "the importance of providing the tools and conditions that liberate people to use their brainpower to make a difference in a world of constant change and challenge." In Chapter 5, Kanter describes six certainties for CEOs to achieve success in an uncertain world: keep learning, focus on processes—not products, maintain standards of excellence, understand the politics of business, develop interdependent and intercompany relationships, and be prepared for rising levels of discomfort. Chapter 19 describes the 1991 *World Leadership Survey* distributed through business journals in 25 countries. Responses came from 11,678 managers, representing all 25 countries. Includes index.

New

Klagge, J. (1996). **The leadership role of today's middle manager.** *Journal of Leadership Studies, 3*(3), 11-19.

In preparation for identifying the tasks of the middle manager in today's organizational environment, the author examines some of the costs associated with the loss of middle managers. He concludes with an exploration of their varied roles, including integrating organizational unity, facilitating human diversity, and implementing support systems for recognizing best practices.

Koestenbaum, P. (1991). *Leadership: The inner side of greatness.* San Francisco: Jossey-Bass.

Based on dialogues with managers and CEOs over ten years, Koestenbaum recommends a philosophical application to leadership. His leadership diamond model frames personal and organizational situations into four elements of greatness: vision, reality, ethics, and courage. Nine keys to business wisdom are offered with practical steps to develop a leadership mind, helpful tips, and affirmations. Includes bibliographical references and index.

Kotter, J. P. (1982). *The general managers.* New York: Free Press.

This book seeks to report and discuss the implications of a study of a group of executives in generalist or general-management jobs. Conducted between 1976 and 1981, this investigation employed multiple methods to look in depth at 15 general managers from nine different corporations spread out across the U.S. Includes bibliography and index.

Kotter, J. P. (1988). *The leadership factor.* New York: Free Press.

In a very precise and direct manner the components that allow effective leadership to occur are presented. This book covers such factors as: why effective leadership is increasingly important today, and, within today's corporate world, what does effective leadership really mean to business outcomes, profits, and products? Companies that have shown superior leadership are presented to illustrate the elements present in real situations that promote the growth of effective leadership. The appendix offers an *Executive Resources Questionnaire* helpful to those who may be curious to know where their business falls in the effective leadership spectrum. Includes bibliography and index.

Kotter, J. P. (1990). *A force for change: How leadership differs from management.* New York: Free Press.

Kotter reports on a two-phase research program to determine the differences between leadership and man-

agement. First, 200 senior executives from 12 successful organizations were interviewed and surveyed regarding executive history and behavior. Then, 12 cases of "highly effective leadership in business" were identified and studied. Kotter indicates that early experiences form intelligence, drive, mental health, and integrity—factors that separate leaders from managers. Vision, alignment, and motivation are defined. Examples illustrate what these factors look like in practice and how they are created. Includes bibliographical references and index.

McCauley, C. D., Eastman, L. J., & Ohlott, P. J. (1995). **Linking management selection and development through stretch assignments.** *Human Resource Management: Special Issue on Leadership Transitions, 34*(1), 93-115.

Matching the right person to the right job depends on a candidate's competencies and on his or her ability to stretch to meet the job requirements. The authors discuss the organizational benefits of developing employees through stretch assignments. A factor analysis of the *Developmental Challenge Profile®* resulted in a framework with 15 developmental components that include: unfamiliar responsibilities, handling external pressure, managing diversity, influencing without authority, and dealing with a difficult boss.

New

Miles, R. H. (1997). *Leading corporate transformation: A blueprint for business renewal.* San Francisco: Jossey-Bass.

According to Miles, the corporate transformation process can be broken down into four steps: generating energy for transformation, developing a vision of the future, aligning the organization and culture, and orchestrating the transformation. The author also divides corporate transformations into four categories—repositioning, revitalizing, merging businesses and cultures, and managing leadership succession—which he illustrates with case studies of organizations including National Semiconductor and the PGA Tour. Includes bibliographical references and index.

New

Miller, W. H. (1996). **Leadership at a crossroads.** *Industry Week, 245*(15), 42-57.

As the 21st century approaches, five major forces are changing the traditional role of an industry leader—employee empowerment, corporate restructuring, the information explosion, globalization, and the rapid pace of change. This article analyzes these forces and describes the new skills leaders will have to learn, including relational skills to help persuade employees to buy into corporate goals, and how to be a follower and work in a team. A box within the article contains a brief interview with Colin Powell on leadership.

Odiorne, G. S. (1987). *The human side of management: Management by integration and self-control.* Lexington, MA: Lexington Books.

In light of the transition in our economy from industrial-goods producing to information producing, managers increasingly find themselves concerned with the motivation of a workforce that is well educated and highly talented. These "knowledge workers" require ongoing intrinsic incentives to commit to the organization's mission. The author aims to show managers how they can act as the integrators of their staffs. Throughout the book's 14 chapters, each component of managing, from hiring, training, development, appraisal, and mentoring to firing can be approached to cultivate the talents and strengths of one's staff, while achieving the mission and goals of the larger organization. Includes bibliography and index.

Ouchi, W. (1981). *Theory Z.* Reading, MA: Addison-Wesley.

Ouchi shows how American corporations can meet the Japanese challenge with a highly effective management style that promises to transform business in the 1980s. Theory Z management takes the best of Japanese business techniques and adapts them to the unique corporate environment of the United States. The book goes behind the scenes at several U.S. corporations making the Theory Z change and shows step-by-step how the transition works. Corporate philosophies are examined.

Peters, T. J. (1987). *Thriving on chaos: Handbook for a management revolution.* New York: Knopf.

Tom Peters, well-known lecturer and coauthor of *In Search of Excellence* (1982), stirs the waters of the status quo by calling for revolution in American management. According to Peters, his book "challenges everything we thought we knew about managing, and often challenges over a hundred years of American tradition." Peters recognizes "chaos" as an inherent element in any competitive situation. Chaos must be addressed and dealt with proactively if American business and industry want to remain key players in the global marketplace. Peters prescribes what changes are necessary for positive results. Includes bibliography and index.

Peters, T. J., & Waterman, R. H., Jr. (1982). *In search of excellence: Lessons from America's best-run companies.* New York: Harper & Row.

Tom Peters is a frequent speaker at business conferences and seminars telling American management how to lead

effectively. Peters and Waterman studied 43 successful American companies and found eight basic principles shared by all of them. *The Wall Street Journal* called it "Exuberant and absorbing—one of those rare books on management that is both consistently thought provoking and fun to read." Includes bibliographical references and index.

Pfeffer, J. (1994). *Competitive advantage through people: Unleashing the power of the workforce.* Boston: Harvard Business School Press.

Traditional determinants of an organization's competitive advantage are: 1) difficulty for new businesses to enter, 2) competitors and substitutes for your product or service, and 3) bargaining power of buyers and suppliers. Pfeffer points out that the five top-performing firms in the past 20 years broke the old rules. While facing tough entry, enormous competition, and buyer/supplier advantages, these five firms grew by 15,000% and more. How? Rather than depending solely on technology or strategic positioning, these companies concentrated on managing their workforces. Pfeffer illustrates the strategic advantages of training permanent employees and utilizing contingency employees. Includes bibliographical references and index.

Reimann, B. C. (1992). **The 1992 strategic management conference: The new agenda for corporate leadership.** *Planning Review, 20*(4), 38-46.

America's leading strategic thinkers met in May 1992 to inspire and teach managers how to meet corporate challenges in our changing world. Henry Kissinger warned of a lack of stability in "the new world order." Robert Long, of Kodak, taught that a decision-maker must be a sower of seeds, leader of learning, purveyor of philosophies, and a doer of deals. James Houghton of Corning, Inc., endorsed the success of empowerment. Warren Bennis identified technology, globalization, and diversity as tomorrow's greatest corporate challenges. Other themes included moving from hard techniques to soft intangibles and from total quality to process redesign.

Scully, J. A., Sims, H. P., Jr., Olian, J. D., Schnell, E. R., & Smith, K. A. (1994). **Tough times make tough bosses: A meso-analysis of CEO leader behavior.** *Leadership Quarterly, 5*(1), 59-83.

Mid-level managers at 56 technology firms were asked to rate their CEOs' leadership behaviors. When compared to each firm's financial data, the study showed that CEOs respond to the bottom line with specific leadership styles. In firms with low performance, CEOs acted as tough bosses utilizing instruction-, command-, and reprimand-type behaviors. In firms with high performance, CEOs practiced encouraging, motivating, and inspiring behaviors.

New
Sessa, V. I., & Campbell, R. J. (1997). *Selection at the top: An annotated bibliography.* Greensboro, NC: Center for Creative Leadership.

In this era of rapidly changing organizational environments, the task of executive selection is critical. Compiled by researchers at the Center for Creative Leadership, these summaries direct the reader to over 100 books and articles on such issues as how to do selection, how to avoid costly mistakes, and how to predict executive success. Includes bibliographical references and index.

Sherman, S. (1994). **Leaders learn to heed the voice within.** *Fortune, 130*(4), 92-100.

In today's fast-moving, ever-changing business atmosphere, leaders need to experience and practice a surprising skill: reflection. Business schools from Harvard to USC are including work exercises in reflection as required courses, and corporations such as AT&T, PepsiCo, and Aetna are integrating various forms of introspection training into management development programs. Corporations need people to act independently, be accountable, and take responsibility for managing their piece of the business. With this in mind, Sherman charts the goals of introspection, which include objectivity, self-confidence, tolerance, action, creativity, and intuition.

New
Sifonis, J. G., & Goldberg, B. (1996). *Corporation on a tightrope: Balancing leadership, governance, and technology in an age of complexity.* New York: Oxford University Press.

Sifonis and Goldberg identify three major forces that affect corporations—governance, technology, and leadership—and describe how businesses must confront these factors aggressively and concurrently. Chapters address how governing boards can help and hurt a company, how CEOs must lead technological changes, and how to build multilevel leadership. Examples from companies including Motorola, General Electric, and Federal Express illustrate the concepts. Contains an index and bibliography.

New
Smilor, R. W., & Sexton, D. L. (Eds.). (1996). *Leadership and entrepreneurship: Personal and organizational development in entrepreneurial ventures.* Westport, CT: Quorum Books.

This collection of writings examines the entrepreneurial leader from the personal, organizational, and multidimen-

sional perspectives. Chapters include "Leadership Skills of Entrepreneurs," "Leading the Virtual Corporation," and "Making the Entrepreneurial Team Work." Includes index.

Snyder, N. H., Dowd, J. J., Jr., & Houghton, D. M. (1994). *Vision, values, and courage: Leadership for quality management.* New York: Free Press.

This book attempts to simplify the concept of total quality management. The authors claim that customer-driven quality has been the key to success for the smaller companies who forced General Motors, IBM, and Sears from their pedestals. But they also claim that it's quality leadership, not quality management, that will be the key to future successes. The leadership practices of Walt Disney, Michael Eisner, Ray Kroc, and Sam Walton demonstrate how to grow a business that delights its customers, embraces change, empowers employees, and prospers over the long term. Includes bibliographical references and index.

Spechler, J. W. (1993). *Managing quality in America's most admired companies.* San Francisco: Berrett-Koehler.

Since 1987 the National Institute of Standards and Technology, an agency of the Department of Commerce, has presented the Malcolm Baldrige Award for excellence in quality management and achievement. Up to two awards each year are given in three categories: manufacturing companies, service companies, and small business. This book, which describes the requirements, evaluation process, and criteria for selection, may be used as preparation for application, a basis for local awards, self-assessment, goal setting, or training. Success stories of previous winners reveal quality at work. Includes bibliographical references.

New
Steers, R. M., Porter, L. W., & Bigley, G. A. (1996). *Motivation and leadership at work* (6th ed.). New York: McGraw-Hill.

Previous editions of this graduate-level textbook were titled *Motivation and Work Behavior.* The new title and contents reflect an increased interest in the relationship between leadership and organizational behavior (OB), particularly leadership and motivation. The text focuses on a blend of theoretical frameworks, major research, real-world applications, and selections authored by leading OB scholars. They explain the nature of work, goal-directed work attitudes and performance, the fairness of reward systems, social interaction, personal identity, and the development of employees as learners. Includes bibliographical references and indexes.

Tichy, N. (1986). ***Transformational leader.*** New York: Wiley.

The authors describe transformational leaders as actors in a three-act play. In Act I, they recognize the need for organizational change. In Act II, they create a new vision. The play ends as change is institutionalized and the vision becomes a reality. Examples of real-life leaders illustrate transformational leadership at work. Includes bibliography and index.

Tichy, N. (1993). **Revolutionize your company.** *Fortune, 128*(15), 114-118.

Excerpted from Tichy's book, *Control Your Destiny or Someone Else Will*, this article describes the process of revolutionizing using Jack Welch's approach at reinventing GE as a case study. "A Handbook for Revolutionaries" begins with the examination of the corporation as it is. The agents of revolution must ask themselves: 1) What is the hand you have been dealt? 2) What are the company's core problems? 3) Where are the transformational leaders you will need for your team? The handbook is divided into three sections: awakening, envisioning, and re-architecting.

New
Tichy, N. (1996). ***Simultaneous transformation and CEO succession: Key to global competitiveness.*** *Organizational Dynamics, 25*(1), 45-59.

A change in leadership and organizational transformation are two of the biggest challenges a company can face, especially when they occur at the same time. This article illustrates this with the story of Ameritech, a company that both named a new CEO and completely reorganized its internal structure between 1991 and 1995. As Tichy relates the process Ameritech went through, he also describes old and new frameworks for CEO succession and the "three-act drama" of organizational change—awakening, envisioning, and re-architecting.

New
Tichy, N. M., & Cohen, E. (1997). ***The leadership engine: How winning companies build leaders at every level.*** New York: HarperBusiness.

Tichy uses examples from companies including GE and Ameritech to illustrate how good leaders develop more leaders within their organization, creating an ever-turning "leadership engine." He identifies four areas in which good leaders help others develop: generating positive energy, making tough decisions, developing good business ideas, and instilling values that will help support those ideas. A "Handbook for Leaders Developing Leaders" also offers over 100 pages of hands-on development activities leaders can use in their organizations. Includes bibliographical references and index.

New
Ulrich, D. (1997). ***Human resource champions: The next agenda for adding value and delivering results.*** Boston: Harvard Business School Press.

This book doesn't address the tasks of human resources professionals. Rather, it studies the challenges they face and the results they must deliver. One important challenge is the development of intellectual capital. Businesses must become learning organizations that can respond quickly to rapidly changing environments. To achieve this, HR professionals act as change agents. Another challenge is balancing the tension between serving as a strategic management partner and as an employee champion. To achieve this, HR professionals must facilitate communication, build trust, and offer development opportunities. Includes bibliographical references and index.

New
Verespej, M. A. (1996). **Lead, don't manage.** *Industry Week, 245*(5), 55-60.

Peter Neff, CEO of chemical manufacturer Rhone-Poulenc, Inc., is profiled. In the last five years Neff has streamlined the company, eliminated top-down management practices, and placed more authority and responsibility on the employees who work directly with customers. This article explains how Neff did this, specifically describing the reorganization of Rhone-Poulenc's customer service department, a resource center set up to offer employees training and skills assessment, and the company's policies for rewarding innovation.

New
White, M. C., Smith, M., & Barnett, T. (1997). **CEO succession: Overcoming forces of inertia.** *Human Relations, 50*(7), 805-828.

An earlier study by Smith and White (1987) of executive succession from 1957 to 1981 found that the career specializations of new CEOs tended to be the same as their predecessor's, and were typically in line with the company's past strategies. The current study analyzed the succession of 138 CEOs of *Business Week 1000* companies between 1981 and 1990. The authors found that these CEOs were more likely to have different career specializations than their predecessors, and past corporate strategy had less influence on their selection. The authors believe that as technology and globalization forced industries to change quickly in the 1980s, many companies used the entrance of a new CEO to facilitate organizational adaptation.

New
White, R. P., Hodgson, P., & Crainer, S. (1996). ***The future of leadership: Riding the corporate rapids into the 21st century.*** London: Pitman.

The authors assert that the days of corporate certainty, when leaders understood their roles and direction was predictable, are gone. Leadership in the 1990s and beyond is more about responding to change and learning to balance. They suggest five key skills necessary for leaders of the future: 1) learning the difficult lessons means seeking change and taking risks; 2) maximum energy helps when trial-and-error approaches drain physical and emotional energy; 3) simplicity is essential to deliver important messages in times of chaos and complexity; 4) multiple focus allows leaders to balance multiple objectives that are often in opposition; and 5) trusting one's inner sense (a combination of experience, timing, instinct, and flexibility) enables leaders to respond quickly and with confidence. Includes bibliographical references.

Wiersema, M. F. (1992). **Strategic consequences of executive succession within diversified firms.** *Journal of Management Studies, 29*(1), 73-94.

This study focuses on executive succession across a sample of Fortune 1000 firms. The findings confirm that recruiting top management from outside the organization is likely to result in significantly changed corporate strategy. Promoting from within is likely to result in maintaining the status quo.

Yeung, A. K., & Ready, D. A. (1995). **Developing leadership capabilities of global corporations: A comparative study in eight nations.** *Human Resource Management, 34*(4), 529-547.

More than 1,200 managers from large corporations around the world responded to a survey about leadership competence. There was general agreement in the areas of facilitating strategic change, articulating a vision, and empowering others. In other areas, cultural influences affected perceptions of leadership competence. French, Italian, and Australian managers rated a leader's ability to be a catalyst of cultural change as most important. German and Korean managers emphasized integrity and trust. Japanese managers stressed empowerment, British managers stressed quality, and American managers stressed action to get results.

Zaleznik, A. (1989). ***The managerial mystique.*** New York: Harper & Row.

Zaleznik asserts that business has developed a managerial mystique that emphasizes order, efficiency, and predictability, and has given rise to the importance of form,

rather than the substance of business. He admonishes today's business schools and MBA programs, asserting they are preparing their students to fit a mold and they are not preparing them for leadership roles. He explains why this is so and illustrates how business needs leaders who are visionary and willing to challenge the status quo. Includes bibliographical references.

Zaleznik, A. (1992). **Managers and leaders: Are they different?** *Harvard Business Review, 70*(2), 126-135.

While performing very different roles, managers and leaders are vital to the success of business. They must be cultivated and trained to achieve success. Managers defuse conflict and ensure day-to-day business gets done. Their goals arise from necessity rather than desires. Leaders define goals from personal attitudes, inspire creativity, and seek new opportunities for organizations. A solid organizational framework must be in place to realize the potential of our most gifted leaders. This article originally appeared in the May-June 1977 issue of *Harvard Business Review, 55*(3), 67-78.

EDUCATIONAL

Appleton, J. R. (1991, Fall). **The context.** *New Directions for Student Services, 55*, 5-15.

Political behavior within colleges and universities, specifically student affairs, is the result of a complex set of constituencies and organizational patterns. Teaching and learning, research, scholarly activity, and community service are more difficult to define than manufacturing a product. Goals are determined by conflicting interests of students, faculty, parents, alumni, community, donors, and government agencies. This paper describes six kinds of power, various members' expectations, and the importance of a leader's vision in creating congruence among the many groups.

Apps, J. W. (1994). ***Leadership for the emerging age: Transforming practice in adult and continuing education.*** San Francisco: Jossey-Bass.

Apps claims that our society is entering an emerging age of confusion, frustration, and lightning-fast change. The old leadership rules don't work and the new ones haven't been written yet. Adult- and continuing-education organizations must understand traditional leadership and, at the same time, practice and teach a new approach. Apps recommends that educators and leadership students develop their own personal philosophies to discover the deepest dimensions of who they are and then rely on their self-knowledge during times of chaotic change. This personal approach to leadership development is an ongoing learning process that encourages reframing problems and exploring new assumptions. Includes bibliographical references and index.

New
Ashbaugh, C. R., & Kasten, K. L. (1995). *Educational leadership: Case studies for reflective practice* (2nd ed.). White Plains, NY: Longman.

This book presents 62 case studies based on educational leaders who have experienced value conflicts and controversies due to differences in beliefs and attitudes. The cases are written for graduate students who are planning administrative careers in levels from kindergarten through high school. The authors give procedures for analyzing and reflecting on situations dealing with culture, program design, resources, and politics. The importance of values in decision making is stressed, along with the idea that educational administration can be never be value-free. Includes bibliographical references and index.

New
Bennett, C. K. (1996). **Schools, technology, and educational leadership: A framework for change.** *NASSP Bulletin, 80*(577), 57-65.

In an increasingly technological era, U.S. public schools have done little to integrate computers into students' learning. In this article Bennett places the responsibility for doing so on principals, suggesting a framework that educational leaders can use to implement a technological learning program. Five categories of actions principals must complete, including defining a mission, are listed, as well as 13 specific questions that principals should ask themselves when managing a technology program, such as "Do teachers and students have adequate access to hardware and software?"

New
Bensimon, E. M., & Neumann, A. (1993). *Redesigning collegiate leadership: Teams and teamwork in higher education.* Baltimore: Johns Hopkins University Press.

Bensimon and Neumann report on their study of team-oriented leadership at 15 U.S. colleges, universities, and community colleges. At each school, they interviewed the president and his or her top leadership team of administrators, academic deans, student affairs directors, and development officers. The results of 70 interviews reveal the nature of "presidential team" organization, working relationships, diversity, and conflict. The advantages of team leadership are: accessing diverse thinking styles to solve problems, understanding cognitive complexities, providing peer support, and increasing accountability. The disadvantages of team leadership are: becoming isolated from the rest of the institution, falling into groupthink,

sacrificing minority opinions to group consensus, and consuming large blocks of time. The authors offer suggestions for team self-study. Includes bibliographical references and index.

Birnbaum, R. (1988). *How colleges work: The cybernetics of academic organization and leadership.* San Francisco: Jossey-Bass.

The author's purpose is to provide new thoughts about university and college leadership. In an effort to shed light on the primary dimensions of every university and college, Birnbaum has studied four models: bureaucratic, political, organized anarchy, and collegial. He describes why systems of organization that consider all four aspects are necessary in higher education. In an effort to synthesize these four dimensions, Birnbaum has integrated the best parts of each model into a new model of organization. He illustrates how this model can help academic leaders understand the nature of colleges as organizations, which in turn will enhance their leadership abilities. Includes bibliography and index.

Birnbaum, R. (1992). *How academic leadership works: Understanding success and failure in the college presidency.* San Francisco: Jossey-Bass.

Findings are reported on the Institutional Leadership Project, a five-year longitudinal study of formal leaders in 32 colleges and universities. Three-day interviews with presidents, senior administrative officers, committee chairs, trustees, and faculty leaders were conducted, then repeated two years later. Perceptions on morale, financial status, governance, quality, and general change were identified as improved, remaining the same, or worsened. Includes bibliographical references and index.

New
Bogue, E. G. (1994). *Leadership by design: Strengthening integrity in higher education.* San Francisco: Jossey-Bass.

Bogue's belief is ". . . that the principal challenge to leadership effectiveness in colleges and universities is more than a challenge of intellect—to acquire and use good ideas. It is a challenge of character—to learn and apply constructive ideals." An aspect of his thesis is that leaders are designers. Each chapter of the book centers on a design ideal: honor, dignity, curiosity, candor, compassion, courage, excellence, and service. Bogue also believes that effective leadership is a "conceptual, moral, and performing art form—one in which ideas and ideals are tested, integrated, and utilized in the act, the performance." His audience is academic administrators, mentors for collegiate leaders, those selecting collegiate leaders, and leaders in corporate and civic sectors. Includes bibliography and index.

New
Bolman, L. G., & Deal, T. E. (1994). ***Becoming a teacher leader: From isolation to collaboration.*** Thousand Oaks, CA: Corwin Press.

Bolman and Deal, authors of *Reframing Organizations: Artistry, Choice and Leadership* (1991), expand their theory of reframing into the field of education. They believe that new and veteran teachers can become more successful when they divide their classroom perspectives into four frames: structural, human resource, political, and symbolic. Using several frames helps a teacher view a situation from different angles and find new ways to deal with issues of power or relationships. For example, teachers can use the human resource frame to bond with troublesome students or balance work and family responsibilities. They can use the political frame to view conflict as a source of energy and renewal rather than a source of stress. Includes bibliographical references.

New
Boyd, B. (1996). **The Principal as Teacher: A model for instructional leadership.** *NASSP Bulletin, 80*(580), 65-73.

This article proposes a model of the Principal as Teacher, in which a principal teaches one class during the school year, which the author believes can greatly enhance his or her instructional leadership. The three dimensions of leadership this model can address—the physical-sensory, the symbolic, and attitudes and assumptions—are given, and the author includes a list of practical requirements needed for this model to work, including a firm commitment of the principal's time and a strong support staff.

New
Brubaker, D. L., & Coble, L. D. (1997). ***Staying on track: An educational leader's guide to preventing derailment and ensuring personal and organizational success.*** Thousand Oaks, CA: Corwin Press.

This guide is an assessment tool for educational leaders who want to avoid derailment and, at the same time, develop in their career. Brubaker and Coble discuss real issues that face leaders in education, which potentially could result in a response that leads them to derailment. The authors present cases built around themes of avoiding or dealing with derailment, which can be thought through individually or discussed in a group. Lessons learned through this guide enable leaders to get on the right track, as well as help their staff and colleagues stay on track. Includes bibliographical references and indexes.

Campbell, D. W., & Greene, D. (1994). **Defining the leadership role of school boards in the 21st century.** *Phi Delta Kappan, 75*(5), 391-395.

The National School Boards Association formed a task force with the California School Boards Association to develop a definition of the governance responsibilities of school boards. The task force determined that content function should be: vision and climate for excellence, superintendent appointment and evaluation, budget adoption and fiscal accountability, curriculum development and program accountability, governance and policy, and collective bargaining. Tenets of effective boardsmanship are: understanding, teamwork, support, respect, trust, communication, professionalism, and fairness.

New
Carter, G. R., & Cunningham, W. G. (1997). ***The American school superintendent: Leading in an age of pressure.*** San Francisco: Jossey-Bass.

The authors, one of whom is a former Superintendent of the Year, talked to over 40 superintendents of school districts around the nation in preparation for writing this in-depth look at the challenges faced by the leaders of American schools. Sections of the book address current dilemmas for superintendents, responses and remedies, and new directions and responsibilities in the schools. In addition to describing the current situation of school superintendents, the book also tries to "chart the way for pioneers, champions, and catalytic agents to create the future of American education." Includes bibliographical references and index.

Chaffee, E. E., & Tierney, W. C. (1988). ***Collegiate culture and leadership strategies.*** New York: Macmillan.

This text is based primarily upon interviews conducted with over 400 academic administrators from a cross section of schools—small rural colleges to major research universities. Seven case studies are presented to provide researchers and administrators with documented information about the complex dynamics of culture and leadership. The authors consider three key issues: 1) how culture is important in shaping the organizational life of colleges and universities, 2) how academic leaders match decision-making strategies to their organizational cultures, and 3) how executives can develop strategies to address issues in their organizations. Includes bibliography and index. Four appendices provide documents, surveys, interviews, and tables.

New

Clark, D. C., & Clark, S. N. (1997). **Addressing dilemmas inherent in educational leadership preparation programs through collaborative restructuring.** *Peabody Journal of Education, 72*(2), 21-41.

Major research universities face a dilemma: Are they preparing students to be leaders or researchers? This article tells how one school shifted its focus to a more practical, hands-on leadership approach, by describing the restructuring process that occurred in the University of Arizona's Educational Administration Program. Intending to offer a model to other schools facing program restructuring, the authors relate the history of the program, the task force created to change the program, the actions of the task force, and the resulting curriculum. Includes bibliographical references.

Clement, L. M., & Rickert, S. T. (1992). *Effective leadership in student services.* San Francisco: Jossey-Bass.

Clement and Rickert reveal attributes necessary for successful leadership in student services. Based on a study of more than 200 presidents, deans, and directors of student programs, personal qualities such as integrity, commitment, and tenacity are examined. Practical strategies are offered for forging meaningful relationships and dealing with confidentiality and favoritism, budgets, and even campus crises such as protests or the death of a student. Includes bibliographical references and index.

Cohen, M. D., & March, J. G. (1986). *Leadership and ambiguity: The American college president* (2nd ed.). Boston: Harvard Business School Press.

This book examines some general ideas about leadership and ambiguity in the context of the American college president. The second edition adds short commentaries plus brief empirical addenda to the chapters on presidential activities and careers—also an essay on administrative leadership. Includes bibliography and index.

New

Cunningham, W. G., & Gresso, D. W. (1993). *Cultural leadership: The culture of excellence in education.* Needham Heights, MA: Allyn and Bacon.

Cunningham and Gresso provide an overview of school reform through success stories from several school districts. Instead of providing a formula for success, they support the idea that every community is unique and needs to formulate its own success story. The school culture, not the structure, must change to bring reform. There are examples of successful school reform through such program themes as Quality, Information and Improvement; School-University Partnerships; and Visioning in Schools. In Norfolk, Virginia, public schools were successful using visioning techniques to change the way administrators, teachers, and students viewed each other. At the same time, they were able to raise test scores and attendance levels. Includes bibliographical references and indexes.

New

Deal, T. E., & Peterson, K. D. (1994). *The leadership paradox: Balancing logic and artistry in schools.* San Francisco: Jossey-Bass.

Deal and Peterson bemoan the changing roles of school principals. In years past, a principal was a community figure of moral authority who exerted positive influence on young minds. In recent years, principals have become disciplinarians who run schools like assembly lines. The leadership paradox in this book refers to a principal's need to rely on both knowledge and wisdom—knowing about and knowing how—to run schools and impact young minds at the same time. They compare management and leadership issues, as well as technical and spiritual methods, that a principal may employ to balance dual roles. Includes bibliographical references and index.

New

Dunlap, D. M., & Schmuck, P. A. (Eds.). (1995). *Women leading in education.* Albany: State University of New York Press.

Essays in this book urge women to take leadership positions in the field of education where women dominate the workforce. Personal narratives of women who have risen to leadership roles tell of their journeys of struggle and success. Other essays describe successful mentoring programs, the glass ceiling, gender consciousness, advocacy organizations, accounts of women of color in educational leadership, and feminist leadership theories. A ten-year study of 142 female administrative aspirants reports that 58% of the women achieved their career goals. Dunlap proposes a new agenda for a new century. She suggests that educational leadership practice, policy, and research focus on: gender and leadership, schools as organizations, social congruence, support, and action. Includes bibliographical references and index.

Fisher, J., & Koch, J. V. (1996). *Presidential leadership: Making a difference.* Phoenix: Oryx Press.

The authors recommend a transformational style of leadership in institutions of higher learning. They explain how a charismatic president with a powerful vision can transform a university. They also discuss total quality management in the context of higher education, race and gender issues, fund-raising, presidential searches, and salary negotiation. Includes bibliographical references and index.

Fisher, J. L., & Tack, M. W. (Eds.). (1988). *Leaders on leadership: The college presidency.* San Francisco: Jossey-Bass.

Asked to speak from their own unique perspective, 18 college presidents have consented to write about the characteristics that promote effective, successful leadership. From institutions such as Notre Dame University, Johns Hopkins University, Boston University, and the University of California, each leader writes from a personal perspective about the energy, commitment, vision, courage, and personal style demanded of their position. Compiled to function as a sourcebook providing valuable insights about the highest ranks of leadership in educational administration, this text offers a view of the problems and issues from leaders' desktops. Includes bibliographies and index.

Gezi, K. (1990). **The role of leadership in inner-city schools.** *Educational Research Quarterly*, *12*(4), 4-11.

This paper reviews research on effective schools and examines the role of leadership in inner-city schools. Gezi concludes that effective principals have positive attitudes toward compensatory education and students, understand cultural pluralism, and are committed to the goal of helping each student succeed. Inner-city principals, teachers, administrators, parents, and communities should work together as a team to set goals and develop strategies for achieving goals.

New
Glasman, N. S., & Glasman, L. D. (1997). **Connecting the preparation of school leaders to the practice of school leadership.** *Peabody Journal of Education*, *72*(2), 3-20.

The authors believe that the behaviors that characterize school leadership should be the focus of training programs for educational leaders, and in this article they provide a theoretical background for their argument. First they offer common definitions of leadership and the behaviors associated with those definitions, and then they describe the content and history of educational leadership training programs. One element—problem solving—is identified as a link between preparation and practice, and a problem-solving module worksheet is included as an appendix. Includes bibliographical references.

Green, M. F. (Ed.). (1988). *Leaders for a new era: Strategies for higher education.* New York: American Council on Education/Macmillan Publishing.

Leadership is contextual. A leader is a product of his era, culture, and organizational setting. College and university administrators, faculty leaders, and department chairs face unique leadership challenges due to diminished resources and conflicting constituencies. The context of academic leadership is examined and potential leaders are recommended. New models are offered for the selection and training of leaders who will lead in different capacities, with different backgrounds, different styles, and different skills. Includes bibliographies.

Green, M. F., & McDade, S. A. (1991). *Investing in higher education: A handbook of leadership development.* Washington, DC: American Council on Education.

Directed to governing boards, chief executive officers, senior administrators, faculty, and others who make decisions about duties, performance, and professional lives of faculty and staff, this book serves as a guide to developing individuals who can lead institutions of higher education in their quest for excellence. It focuses on a very practical question: How can colleges and universities develop leadership capacity and effectiveness to the fullest extent possible? With chapters organized by specific positions (academic deans, department chairs, faculty, etc.), it is well suited for selective reading. Includes bibliographical references and index.

New
Guarasci, R., Cornwell, G. H., & Associates. (1997). *Democratic education in an age of difference: Redefining citizenship in higher education.* San Francisco: Jossey-Bass.

Over the past 20 years the growing social diversity at American colleges and universities has created a firestorm of debates over multiculturalism and free speech. This book examines the ideas of identity and difference, and also offers an in-depth look at programs around the country that are attempting to help undergraduates develop "democratic sensibility, citizenship skills, and multicultural fluency." These programs include learning communities, public-service learning, and residential communities. Includes bibliographical references and index.

New
Gullatt, D. E. (1997). **Teachers taking the lead.** *Schools in the Middle*, *6*(5), 12-14.

Gullatt states that teachers play key leadership roles when developing programs, climate, and curriculum that help students learn to their maximum capability. Predictors of teacher leadership are: a broad range of skills, interests, and experiences; involvement in curriculum teaching and development; administrative and organizational experience; knowledge of community concerns; risk-taking temperament; and interpersonal skills. Gullatt suggests methods for developing leadership skills in middle school teachers. Includes bibliographical references.

Hahn, R. (1995). **Getting serious about presidential leadership: Our collective responsibility.** *Change, 27*(5), 12-19.

Hahn reports that there is a demand for educational leaders with strong skills in public relations, administration, fund-raising and fiscal management, scholarship, vision, and sensitivity to students. Do such leaders exist? Hahn says they do not. He claims that the success of educational leaders depends on the support they receive from boards, faculty, executive officers, students, alumni, staff, and the community. To identify educational leaders who can win that support, look for the following qualities: understanding, values, calm behavior in the face of crisis, courage, and fairness.

Hall, D. T. (1995). **Unplanned executive transitions and the dance of the subidentities.** *Human Resource Management: Special Issue on Leadership Transitions, 34*(1), 71-92.

Hall shares his personal experience with leadership transitions in an academic setting. As a management professor, Hall had many years of experience studying and teaching about succession planning and executive development. When he was appointed Acting Dean of the School of Management at Boston University, he had the opportunity to practice what he had taught.

Hamel, A. (1992). **A portrait of youthful leadership.** *Journal of Applied Behavioral Science, 28*(2), 224-237.

Author Hamel spent three months investigating the leadership philosophy and practices of a young elementary school principal. Through observation, interviews with the principal's colleagues, and talks with students, Hamel found him to be both an instigator of change and a force for stability. Leadership was based on collaborative relationships that empowered others.

Hart, A. W. (1991). **Leader succession and socialization: A synthesis.** *Review of Educational Research, 61*(4), 451-474.

Based on an estimated 7% to 10% annual principal turnover, leadership succession is an important factor in the social dynamics of schools. "Succession is a disruptive event that changes the lines of communication, realigns relationships of power, affects decision making, and generally disturbs the equilibrium of normal activities." Studying succession and its interaction with formal and informal social mechanisms offers a new perspective.

New
Heslep, R. D. (1997). **The practical value of philosophical thought for the ethical dimension.** *Educational Administration Quarterly, 33*(1), 67-85.

Heslep suggests that educational leaders who take a philosophical approach to solving ethical problems will achieve practical wisdom. He claims that the first tendency is to rely on tradition, standards, research, and personal experience. But principals and superintendents who also employ inquisitive, reflective, and critical techniques add a philosophical dimension to their problem-solving and decision-making tasks. The use of these techniques can help educational leaders turn their institutions into moral agencies that support knowledge, interaction, freedom, and purpose.

New
Hodgkinson, C. (1991). *Educational leadership: The moral art.* Albany: State University of New York Press.

Hodgkinson claims that ". . . values constitute the essential problem of leadership and that the educational institution is special because it both forms and is formed by values." The special problem for educational leadership is a lack of goal specificity, or divergent interests at two levels—the personal level where the teaching-learning process occurs and the organizational level that determines collective purpose and achievement. The solution for educational leadership lies in the theory and practice of values, which Hodgkinson calls the moral art. In the final chapter, "Prescriptions and Practicalities," Hodgkinson suggests that educational leaders observe leaders in other fields to understand personal values and those in other contexts. Includes bibliographical references and index.

Jacobson, S. L., & Conway, J. A. (Eds.). (1990). *Educational leadership in an age of reform.* New York: Longman.

This collection of articles addresses the changing role of educational leaders. Three recent waves of educational reform are: reordering priorities, restructuring the teaching profession, and rethinking administrator preparation. Four undercurrents of reform are: empowerment, restructuring school governance, politics, and emerging technologies. These themes are analyzed and integrated to present an agenda for research and educational-leadership development. Includes bibliographical references.

Kirby, P. C., Paradise, L. V., & King, M. I. (1992). **Extraordinary leaders in education: Understanding transformational leadership.** *Journal of Educational Research, 85*(5), 303-311.

Two investigations relate leader characteristics and behaviors with extraordinary performance. Quantitative results were obtained, using Bass's *Multifactor Leadership Questionnaire*, from a study of 103 educators who associated leader effectiveness with charisma and intellectual stimulation. Qualitative results were obtained from analysis of narratives describing educational leaders perceived to be extraordinary. The qualitative results emphasized professional-development opportunities for followers and suggested that leader behaviors, rather than personality, inspire followers to higher levels of performance.

Krug, S. E. (1993). **Leadership craft and the crafting of school leaders.** *Phi Delta Kappan, 75*(3), 240-244.

Essential functions of a school principal are: defining a mission, managing curriculum and instruction, supervising teaching, monitoring student progress, and promoting an effective instructional climate. Rather than a skill-building, mastery-learning approach, Krug suggests a cognitive apprenticeship for school principals. Participants complete a self-assessment, are observed by analysts, receive feedback, and frame their knowledge of skills into contexts of practice.

Lewis, P. H. (1994, Fall). **Implementing the culture of leadership.** *New Directions for Higher Education, 87,* 93-99.

To ensure success, a campus leadership program needs the involvement of its chief executive officer. Lewis cites examples from Boston College, Western Kentucky University, the University of North Carolina at Chapel Hill, and Kennesaw State College.

New
Lucas, A. F. (1994). *Strengthening departmental leadership: A team-building guide for chairs in colleges and universities.* San Francisco: Jossey-Bass.

Lucas offers advice for those who move from subject-specific faculty positions into roles as department chairs with leadership responsibilities. She outlines nine key responsibilities: creating a shared vision, motivating faculty to enhance productivity, motivating faculty to teach effectively, handling faculty evaluation and feedback, motivating faculty to increase scholarship, motivating faculty to increase service, building a creative climate for communication, managing conflict, and developing chair survival skills. She suggests a method to rate individuals, then use the feedback to build skills. A Leadership

Matrix graphs an individual's skill development against each skill's importance to the department. Using the matrix allows an individual to see strengths and weaknesses and to plan opportunities for leadership development. Includes bibliographical references and index.

McCauley, C. D. (1990). *Effective school principals: Competencies for meeting the demands of educational reform.* Greensboro, NC: Center for Creative Leadership.

Within the next ten years, half of all current principals will retire. The next generation of school principals faces new challenges to meet educational reform. Research on school-based management, teacher empowerment, parental choice, and school/business partnerships was evaluated along with research on corporate management to determine competencies needed by effective school principals. This report serves as a guide for selecting and developing principals who can set direction, motivate, build teams, create networks, and handle pressure. Includes a bibliography.

Murphy, J. (1992). *The landscape of leadership preparation: Reframing the education of school administrators.* Newbury Park, CA: Corwin Press.

Addressing the question of how best to prepare tomorrow's school leaders, Murphy reviews the strengths and weaknesses of current programs to form a vision about the future of school-leadership preparation. He suggests that our infatuation with specialization may prove counterproductive, and that we should opt instead for an interrelatedness of curriculum leading to administrators who are competent scholars, teachers, counselors, researchers, field workers, and professional leaders. Includes bibliographical references and index.

New
Murphy, J. A., & Pimentel, S. (1996). **Grading principals: Administrator evaluations come of age.** *Phi Delta Kappan, 78*(1), 74-84.

This article examines a results-based, profit-sharing evaluation program used in the Charlotte-Mecklenburg Schools (CMS), North Carolina. It is similar to evaluation programs found in the corporate world. CMS moved from evaluations based on a principal's compliance, to a checklist of rules, to a system that focuses on a principal's effectiveness. The system is based on performance incentives—bonuses for staff who have made improvements or have met set goals. Examples of questions from evaluation surveys given to teachers, staff, parents, and students are provided. Addie Moore and Fred Slade, two CMS principals, share their personal accounts of the new evaluation system's effect on their work.

Myers, M. R., Slavin, M. J., & Southern, W. T. (1990). **Leadership and attitudes: Emergence and maintenance of leadership among gifted students in group problem solving.** *Roeper Review, 12*(4), 256-261.

Tenth- and eleventh-grade student groups were assigned to identify a problem, to seek resolution, and to develop a multimedia statement. Internal and external assessments determined quality of leadership in relation to group project success. Students perceived fluent and verbally aggressive leaders as effective with no correlation to project success. Staff perceived participative leaders, who used restatement and focus to lead the group, as the most effective leaders with the most successful projects. Passive leaders, who organized to meet deadlines with no focus on quality, were judged least effective.

New
Nemerowicz, G., & Rosi, E. (1997). *Education for leadership and social responsibility.* Washington, DC: Falmer Press.

The authors present a new leadership paradigm that they call inclusive leadership. It's based on their experimental Women's Leadership Institute at Wells College. The institute grew from a traditional program serving only the school's undergraduate students to a larger nontraditional program serving community and business leaders, alumnae, teenagers, and young children. The authors' research is based on interviews with children and with artists and a content analysis of *Fortune* magazine. From their experience and research emerged a framework for teaching leadership at all levels, beginning with very young children and continuing through all arenas of one's life. This inclusive leadership is a process in which all citizens have a right and a responsibility to participate. Includes bibliographical references and index.

New
Parkay, F. W., & Hall, G. E. (1992). *Becoming a principal: The challenges of beginning leadership.* Needham Heights, MA: Allyn and Bacon.

This book presents the findings of the Beginning Principals Study (BPS) through case studies on 12 first-year principals. The purpose of the BPS is to show the development of a principal's professional identity. It also describes his or her expectations, fears, and common problems. Directed to graduate students, the discussion questions and activities at the end of each chapter examine the basics of a successful foundation: visibility, communication, and an effective administrative team. The authors offer advice for new principals on decision making, relationships with staff, and empowerment. Veteran principals share their reflections. The experiences of principals in Canada, the United Kingdom, and

Australia are compared to those in the U.S. Includes bibliographical references and index.

New
Parry, A. E., and Horton, M. J. (1997). **Board leadership when there is no leader.** *Journal of Leadership Studies, 4*(2), 55-61.

This case study is a model for universities that are facing the crisis of operating without a president and with only a board of directors. Friends University, a small private university in Kansas, shares its story of finding a replacement for a resigned president and dealing with the challenge of balancing the budget and reducing the deficit at the same time. The college approached the situation by learning how the outside world perceived the school and accepting the results of this critical research. Then, the board worked together to find a qualified president while successfully reducing the school's deficit.

Perlman, B., Gueths, J., & Weber, D. A. (1988). *The academic intrapreneur: Strategy, innovation, and management in higher education.* New York: Praeger.

As defined in this book, intrapreneurship is entrepreneurship turned inward; it is the new venture within an organization. The authors have investigated how it works in the academic community. They begin with an overview of the concept of intrapreneurship and its process, then go on to describe the intrapreneurial world. Later chapters examine a model of intrapreneurship and delve further into the meaning and use of intrapreneurship to the growth of organizations. The book concludes with a look at the future possibilities for intrapreneurship. Includes bibliography and index.

New
Phay, R. E. (1997). **Learning to be effective CEOs: The Principals Executive Program.** *NASSP Bulletin, 81*(585), 51-57.

This article describes the Principals Executive Program (PEP), a state-mandated professional development program for North Carolina principals modeled on Harvard's leadership training program for business executives. Founded in 1984, PEP is considered highly successful by principals, legislators, and consultants, and nearly half of the state's principals have completed it. The history, content, and future of PEP are discussed here.

Plough, T. R. (1995). **Fostering leadership development and professionalism for university department heads.** *Journal of Leadership Studies, 2*(1), 142-148.

Two hundred department heads have participated in the Academic Leadership Workshop Series at the Rochester Institute of Technology. The annual series consists of eight seminars for academic and administrative leaders. Evaluation interviews are conducted before, during, and after the series to determine the effectiveness of the program and the changes leaders perceived in their understanding and practice of leadership skills. Over eight years, the evaluation shows increased morale, networking inside and between departments, and increased appreciation for leadership competence at all levels, from administration to support staff.

Reissman, R. (1995). **In search of ordinary heroes.** *Educational Leadership*, *52*(8), 28-31.

A group of children from an inner-city, multiethnic middle school set out to identify ordinary heroes. After reading *The Diary of Anne Frank*, the students defined heroes in a variety of ways: someone who helps a stranger, a person who bounces back after a tragedy, or someone who helps another person even when it puts the helper at risk. This article is authored by the children's teacher who discusses the development of the Ordinary Hero Hall of Fame.

Reitzug, U. C. (1994). **A case study of empowering principal behavior.** *American Educational Research Journal, 31*(2), 283-307.

An elementary school principal named as "best principal" by colleagues in his school district was selected for this study. Observations, interviews, and feedback from teachers were compiled over a three-month period. The types of empowering behavior exhibited by the principal were chronicled as: creating a supportive environment, honoring teachers' opinions, providing opportunities for staff development, and acquiring resources.

New
Restine, N. (1997). **Learning and developing in the context(s) of leadership preparation.** *Peabody Journal of Education*, *72*(2), 117-130.

This article explores four aspects of learning and development in leadership preparation: preparing leaders for schools; learning, development, and forms of knowledge; the logic of activity and experience; and mentoring, partnerships, and networking. The authors say that educational leaders need to be less concerned with theoretical purity and focus more on the direct benefits that leadership development has for students. Includes bibliographical references.

Roach, K. D. (1991). **University department chairs' use of compliance-gaining strategies.** *Communication Quarterly, 39*(1), 75-90.

This reports on 130 university faculty members who responded to a questionnaire about compliance-gaining

techniques used by department chairs. The techniques, categorized as expectancies, relationships, or values, were ranked for effectiveness, faculty job satisfaction, and chair performance evaluation.

New
Sergiovanni, T. J. (1992). ***Moral leadership: Getting to the heart of school improvement.*** San Francisco: Jossey-Bass.

Sergiovanni introduces the idea of building school leadership on the basis of moral authority. This book for school administrators and principals examines a traditional view of leadership called direct leadership and its failure to improve schools. Sergiovanni suggests using substitutes for direct leadership such as creating a sense of community and promoting professionalism as a virtue. He believes that leaders should be servants and ministers to those whom they lead. Leadership needs to be based on shared values—in the sense of a community rather than an organization. Community leadership builds motivation through emotions, values, and connections with other people. Includes bibliographical references and index.

New
Sergiovanni, T. J. (1994). ***Building community in schools.*** San Francisco: Jossey-Bass.

Sergiovanni focuses on the theory of community in schools as an alternative to a traditional, formal organizational structure. Community is a sense of connection and commitment. It binds teachers and students together with shared values and ideals. Educators interested in community are introduced to ideas for building relationships, transforming discipline policies, and encouraging citizenship. Key elements for a curriculum that supports community are: setting educational priorities, the social significance of students' learnings, and school climate. Principals and teachers who are struggling to build community share their ideas and stories. Includes bibliographical references and index.

Shoenberg, R. E. (1993, September 1). **Developing informed, effective campus leaders.** *Chronicle of Higher Education*, p. A68.

With more and more stakeholders participating in the campus leadership process, Shoenberg suggests that "all members of the campus then, not just those with formal authority, need the skills and information necessary to exercise supportive leadership." He describes a project he directed whereby 11 colleges and universities experimented with an array of leadership development opportunities for administrators, faculty, staff, and students.

New

Short, P. M. (1997). **Reflection in administrator preparation.** *Peabody Journal of Education*, 72(2), 86-99.

This article identifies reflection as a tool that school administrators can use to improve their leadership skills. After reviewing the literature and research on reflection, Short describes techniques that can promote it, including group reflection, reflective journals, educational platforms, case stories, and reflective shadowing and interviewing. Includes bibliographical references.

New

Short, P. M., & Greer, J. T. (1997). *Leadership in empowered schools: Themes from innovative efforts.* Upper Saddle River, NJ: Merrill.

This is a report of two studies that examined leadership and empowerment in 26 newly restructured schools. The chapters describe the dimensions of leadership identified in the research and the specific behaviors of teachers and principals who exhibited or failed to exhibit each leadership dimension. Examples of these dimensions are: leading change, focusing on structure, building trust, stimulating risk, empowering teachers and students, and evaluating empowered leadership. Following most of the case studies are discussion questions for students of educational leadership. The authors recommend two assessment instruments for practitioners who want to identify their school's leadership strengths and weaknesses. Includes index.

New

Smith, S. C., & Piele, P. K. (Eds.). (1997). *School leadership: Handbook for excellence* (3rd ed.). Eugene, OR: ERIC Clearinghouse on Educational Management.

The essays in this book suggest how a leader, especially a principal, can inspire all members of a school community to work toward the goal of excellence in education. It approaches leadership from four perspectives: the person, the values, the structure, and the skills. Chapters include: "Portrait of a Leader"; "Leadership Styles and Strategies"; "Ethical Leadership"; "Cultural Leadership"; "School-based Management"; and "Building Coalitions." The authors synthesize theoretical literature on school leadership and interviews with practitioners to recommend action and continuous learning. Includes bibliographical references.

New

Teitel, L. (1997). **Understanding and harnessing the power of the cohort model in preparing educational leaders.** *Peabody Journal of Education*, 72(2), 66-85.

In 1995 the University of Massachusetts at Boston began using the cohort model, in which students are admitted in groups and work together toward their degrees, in all of their educational leadership programs. This article describes the change, using quotes from students and faculty, to illustrate the benefits and drawbacks of the cohort model. The author identifies five issues this model raises, including increased connections among students and unbalanced power relationships with faculty members, and offers recommendations on how schools and students can deal with them. Includes bibliographical references.

Thurston, P., Clift, R., & Schacht, M. (1993). **Preparing leaders for change-oriented schools.** *Phi Delta Kappan*, 75(3), 259-265.

Four researchers from the National Center for School Leadership at the University of Illinois, Urbana-Champaign, conducted simultaneous case studies in distributed leadership at four schools. They found four attributes that characterize school leaders as agents of change: being child-centered, collaboration with multiple constituencies, ability to process a wide variety of information, and effective communication skills. To meet the demand for educational reform, the authors suggest that school principals practice this distributed style of leadership.

Wingspread Group on Higher Education. (1993). *An American imperative: Higher expectations for higher education: An open letter to those concerned about the future.* Racine, WI: Johnson Foundation.

This is a report of a Wingspread working group that examined the question, "What does society need from higher education?" The group was chaired by William Brock, former congressman, senator, Secretary of Labor, and head of the Workforce 2000 study. The group identified three fundamental issues for colleges and universities that wish to graduate students who are able to assume leadership roles: 1) take values seriously, 2) put student learning first, and 3) create a nation of learners. The report itself and 32 essays contributed from corporate, nonprofit, and educational CEOs support the Wingspread recommendations. Includes bibliographical references.

New

Zellner, L. J. (1997). **Leadership laboratories: Professional development and national teaching standards.** *NASSP Bulletin*, 81(585), 45-50.

The responsibilities of principals have increased over the past 30 years, so that today's principals need training and education to most effectively lead their schools. This article describes the School Leadership Initiative (SLI) started by the Texas Education Collaborative, an infrastructure of social networks offering professional development opportunities to educators. SLI developed a list of primary goals for principals, given here, based on the idea that the duty of principals is to develop leadership among their students and teachers. The establishment of "leadership laboratories," in which principals came together to work on these goals, is also described.

New
Zlotkowski, E. (1996). **Linking service-learning and the academy: A new voice at the table?** *Change, 28*(1), 20-27.

The interest in service learning on college campuses has grown in recent years, but this kind of experience has not yet been effectively linked to traditional academic learning. Do service-learning proponents, asks the author, "represent a movement of socially and morally concerned activists operating from an academic base or a movement of socially, morally, and pedagogically concerned academicians?" He believes there is a place on campus for both civic/moral concepts and the academic, but says that service-learning enthusiasts have not successfully presented their case to academia. Leaders in this area must now establish pedagogical rationales for service learning in specific disciplines and integrate the movement into all areas of higher education.

MILITARY

Atwater, L. E., & Yammarino, F. J. (1992). **Does self-other agreement on leadership perceptions moderate the validity of leadership and performance predictions?** *Personnel Psychology, 45*(1), 141-164.

A study of 91 U.S. Naval Academy students and 158 naval officers investigated self- and other ratings to predict leadership and measure leader behavior. Those with inflated self-ratings and low other ratings were found to possess a lower measurement of leadership behavior. Those with self- and other ratings in agreement were found to possess a higher measure of leader behavior.

New
Baldwin, J. N. (1996). **The promotion record of the United States Army: Glass ceilings in the officer corps.** *Public Administration Review, 56*(2), 199-206.

Baldwin studied the promotion records of over 123,000 Army officers between 1980 and 1993 and compared the promotion rates of female and minority officers with those of male and white officers. He found that "those promoted and considered for promotion in the Army are disproportionately men and Caucasian." Relative to the Army's "Uniform Guidelines on Employee Selection Procedures," the promotion rates are respectable, but

when compared to other public agencies the Army's record is not good. Baldwin attributes the inequality in promotion not only to gender and race issues, but to the interactions of "socioeconomic, educational, cultural, and institutional factors."

New
Barber, H. F. (1992). **Developing strategic leadership: The U.S. Army War College experience.** *Journal of Management Development, 11*(6), 4-12.

The senior institution in the Army educational system, the U.S. Army War College is the culmination of formal military education for most officers. This article describes the College and its students, and details the shift that took place in the late 1980s and early 1990s from teaching about leadership in a general sense to teaching mainly strategic leadership. Barber first describes the process of implementing this shift, including a conference held in 1991 to design the new program. He then explains how learning about strategic leadership is especially beneficial for the high-ranking military leaders who typically attend the College.

Cohen, W. A. (1990). *The art of the leader.* Englewood Cliffs, NJ: Prentice Hall.

Cohen states that leaders are not born; leadership is learned. Leaders always have sponsors to support their rise to the top. In turn, leaders always become sponsors, enabling others to rise to the top. His nine techniques propose to enable readers to become leaders who are satisfactorily compensated, who reach their full potential, and who enjoy their work. Military examples demonstrate how to take charge of any situation, how to win loyalty and respect, and how to develop self-confidence. Cohen teaches seven steps to achieve "charisma." Includes bibliographical references.

Jaques, E., & Clement, S. D. (1991). *Executive leadership: A practical guide to managing complexity.* Arlington, VA: Cason Hall.

This book defines what leadership is, who can be a leader, and how managerial leadership affects the success or failure of an organization. Jaques and Clement examine the internal, personal world of human intent and the external world of human interaction in the workplace. They offer five components of capability to evaluate effective and accountable leaders. Examples are drawn from the U.S. Army leadership training and doctrine. Includes bibliographical references and index.

New

Keithly, D. M. (1996). **Leadership in doctrine.** *Journal of Leadership Studies, 3*(4), 129-138.

Keithly, an associate professor at the National Defense University, explains the U.S. Navy's military doctrine for learning and practicing leadership. During times of peace, Naval commanders have little opportunity to practice the skills necessary for combat leadership. They rely on a leadership doctrine, a set of standards written by senior officers. Recognizing that leadership is complex, the standards are not commandments. They are a touchstone from which an officer may use personal judgment, take initiative, and develop a personal style. The doctrine recognizes that leadership hinges on personalities and situations.

New

Mazur, A., & Mueller, U. (1996). **Channel modeling: From West Point cadet to general.** *Public Administration Review, 56*(2), 191-198.

The U.S. Army and Air Force are considered meritocracies, where advancement depends solely on competency. But do other factors also determine who will assume leadership roles in the military? This study examined the careers of the West Point class of 1950 to determine whether "visibility factors," including appearance and sociability, helped predict which cadets would become leaders. The authors found that personal factors, including whether the man "looks like a leader," whether he came from a family that was "a model of American tradition," and whether he was an athlete, particularly a football player, ultimately differentiated the men who became generals from lower-ranking officers.

McGuire, P. (1983). **Desegregation of the armed forces: Black leadership, protest and World War II.** *Journal of Negro History, 68*(2), 147-158.

The Selective Service and Training Act of 1940 enabled blacks to enlist in the armed forces. But they were met with discrimination at many levels: draft rejection, segregated units, segregated training and facilities, lesser assignments. At the urging of Mary McLeod, director of the Division of Negro Affairs, Mrs. Roosevelt persuaded the President to appoint black advisors to the Selective Service and War Department. These advisors labored throughout World War II on behalf of desegregated units, black officer selection and training, acceptance of black blood donations to the Red Cross, and the assignment of black pilots on combat missions.

New

McNally, J. A., Gerras, S. J., & Bullis, R. C. (1996). **Teaching leadership at the U. S. Military Academy at West Point.** *Journal of Applied Behavioral Science, 32*(2), 175-188.

The authors, professors in the Department of Behavioral Sciences and Leadership at West Point, describe their method for teaching their cadets leadership. They teach the Intellectual Procedure, in which cadets identify what is happening, account for what is happening, and formulate leader action. The course also includes a theoretical section that addresses individuals, groups, leadership, and organizational systems. In addition, the article describes the West Point grading and course-evaluation procedure, and the seven-week workshop on teaching military leadership that new faculty must attend. The authors have used the Intellectual Procedure when training police departments around the country and believe that it applies in both civilian and military settings.

Newman, A. S. (1981). *Follow me: The human element in leadership.* Novato, CA: Presidio Press.

This is a collection of columns written for *ARMY* magazine by retired U.S. Army Major General Aubrey S. "Red" Newman. The recollections and anecdotes explain Newman's theory of motivating people through command presence, command techniques, and command in battle. The colorful stories in this book serve to illustrate how commanders can be effective in directing their followers and at the same time encourage independent thought and action. *Follow Me II: More on the Human Element in Leadership* (Presidio Press, 1992) offers 51 more columns of wit and wisdom.

Oliver, D., Jr. (1992). *Lead On! A practical approach to leadership.* Novato, CA: Presidio Press.

Drawing on years of experience in America's nuclear-powered submarine fleet, Rear Admiral Dave Oliver's leadership successes have far-reaching implications for civilian management. His stories and examples of leadership at work in military situations show how leadership makes individual efforts better and melds individuals into superior teams. The final chapter encapsulates the book with a checklist for leadership effectiveness. Includes bibliographical references.

Pagonis, W. G., & Cruikshank, J. L. (1992). *Moving mountains: Lessons in leadership and logistics from the Gulf War.* Boston: Harvard Business School Press.

Pagonis recounts his logistical operation that moved unprecedented numbers of people, vehicles, fuel, ammunition, food, shelters, medical supplies, and mail during the Gulf War. Citing Alexander the Great as his inspiration, Pagonis describes the leadership lessons found in logistical operations. He credits his success on building blocks—leadership support from many directions: 1) the civilian leadership of President Bush and Secretary of Defense Cheney; 2) military leadership of Generals Schwartzkopf, Powell, Yeosock, Luce, and Franks; 3) corporate leadership of the 12,000 Americans working in Saudi Arabia; 4) global leadership of the host country; and 5) the hands-on leadership among his troops. Includes bibliographical references and index.

Popper, M., Landau, O., & Gluskinos, U. M. (1992). **The Israeli Defense Forces: An example of transformational leadership.** *Leadership and Organization Development Journal, 13*(1), 3-8.

Regular motivation is behavior resulting from perceived rewards, whereas normative commitment is behavior resulting from values and personal meaning. The Israeli Defense Forces use leadership training at all levels to build strong normative commitment. Officers learn to meet their followers' basic human needs of personal meaning and identity. The results indicate that followers are more willing to commit personal sacrifices and achieve exceptional goals.

Puddington, A. (1991). **Black leaders vs. Desert Storm.** *Commentary, 91*(5), 28-34.

While blacks make up 13% of the general population in the U.S., they constituted 20% of the armed services in Desert Storm. Black Congressional leaders voiced opposition to the war based on disproportionate risk, while black soldiers reported feelings of respect and equality. Puddington relates the statements of Congressional leaders, Reverend Jesse Jackson, and General Colin Powell about the high number of blacks in our volunteer military forces.

New
Rejai, M., & Phillips, K. (1996). *World military leaders: A collective and comparative analysis.* Westport, CT: Greenwood.

This analysis covers 45 military leaders from 13 countries. Rejai and Phillips look at sociodemographic, psychological, and situational variables that accounted for the development of each military leader, using a quantitative and qualitative approach. Some of the variables analyzed are: urban or rural birthplace; number of siblings and age rank among them; ethnicity; religious affiliation; education level; father's primary occupation; membership in legal or revolutionary organizations; arrest, imprisonment, or exile; and foreign travel. The authors also look at six psychological or motivational dynamics that propel men toward military careers: nationalism; conservative

(or ultra-) nationalism; relative deprivation; love deprivation; marginality; and vanity, egotism, and narcissism. Includes bibliographical references and index.

Stevens, G., & Gardner, S. (1987). **But can she command a ship? Acceptance of women by peers at the Coast Guard Academy.** *Sex Roles, 16*(3&4), 181-188.

In the Coast Guard, team effort is required to perform necessary tasks: navigating through rough seas, rescuing sailors in peril, apprehending smugglers, and protecting the shores of the U.S. Early studies of Coast Guard males indicated nonacceptance of women leaders in these situations. A more recent study indicated that attitudes are changing. Using two instruments, *Attitudes Toward Women Scale* at a private college and *Attitudes Toward Women in the Military Scale* at the Coast Guard Academy, 222 students indicated that Coast Guard males have increased positive attitudes toward women as leaders.

New
Sullivan, G. R., & Harper, M. V. (1996). *Hope is not a method: What business leaders can learn from America's Army.* New York: Times Books.

The authors are former U.S. Army senior officers and are currently affiliated with Boston University's CEO Leadership Forum. They played key roles in reinventing Army leadership from the command-and-control style that served the military so well during World War II and then corporate America during the 1950s and 1960s. They lay out five challenges that needed to be addressed: 1) the competitive environment changed rapidly, 2) emerging technology posed new opportunities and problems, 3) teamwork and technical skills needed to be upgraded, 4) stakeholders demanded new and unexpected tasks, and 5) financial pressure forced massive cost cutting and downsizing. Sullivan and Harper believe these challenges can be met by "creating the future" through strategic leadership. They share their guidelines for leading change, emphasizing values, building teams, being flexible, and developing leaders. Appendices chart the changes in Army personnel and budgets since 1989. Includes bibliographical references and index.

New
Taylor, R. L., & Rosenbach, W. E. (Eds.). (1996). *Military leadership: In pursuit of excellence* (3rd ed.). Boulder, CO: Westview Press.

Contributing authors from within and outside the military compare the special nature of military leadership with the universal concept of leadership in general. In his foreword, Walter Ulmer states that "warfare and the institutions dedicated to preparation for war have given us the richest lode to mine in our quest for understanding . . .

routinely exposing the bedrock of character that underlies leader behavior." Essays stress the importance of followership, credibility, and personal values in concert with organizational values. New to this edition are portraits of military heroes of the past and leadership lessons learned from current events. New images of leadership have emerged from downsized corporate America, the end of the Cold War, technological innovations, and women in the military. Lee Smith describes how the "new" U.S. Army is adapting. Includes bibliographical references.

Van Fleet, D. D., & Yukl, G. A. (1986). *Military leadership: An organizational behavior perspective.* Greenwich, CT: JAI Press.

Concepts and research from organizational behavior are employed in an effort to further our understanding of military leadership. In addition, a more complex framework for the study of leadership is presented and its utility is illustrated through actual experiences of research based on military samples—from general to specific. Includes bibliographical references and index.

Yammarino, F. J., Spangler, W. D., & Bass, B. M. (1993). **Transformational leadership and performance: A longitudinal investigation.** *Leadership Quarterly, 4*(1), 81-102.

This is a report on the longitudinal research of 186 Naval Academy midshipmen who were later assigned to the warfare fleet. School records and superior/subordinate feedback were compiled over a 14-year period to study the relationship between previous performance and subsequent leadership. The authors found that the academic achievement, conduct, and military competence of midshipmen were predictive of transformational-leadership style in naval officers.

POLITICAL

New
Abbott, P. (1996). *Strong presidents: A theory of leadership.* Knoxville: University of Tennessee Press.

Abbott presents a theory of an imaginary belated president, one who emulates the behavior of a successful predecessor yet strives to surpass him. A belated president understands that the legendary achievements of his predecessors and poetic distance elevates the memory of heroic presidents of the past. Each president struggles, in his own time, with the dichotomies of strength and weakness, benevolence and self-interest, power and restriction, approval and criticism. Abbott describes the strengths and weaknesses of history's most memorable

presidents, whom he calls poet presidents: George Washington, Abraham Lincoln, Franklin Roosevelt, Andrew Jackson, Theodore Roosevelt, and John Kennedy. He also describes the lessons to be learned from the failures of Woodrow Wilson, Herbert Hoover, and Richard Nixon; as well as the irony of Thomas Jefferson, who embodied extreme strength and weakness. Includes bibliographical references and index.

Alinsky, S. (1972). *Rules for radicals.* New York: Random House.

Alinsky draws on his extensive experience as an organizer of community groups to define areas of emphasis for potential activists and sets forth a method he believes is most successful in effecting social reform. Alinsky weights arguments on means and ends, examines the use of words in influencing people, and describes tactics he found viable and that can be employed to change society. Includes bibliographical references.

New
Appleby, R. S. (Ed.). (1997). *Spokesmen for the despised: Fundamentalist leaders of the Middle East.* Chicago: University of Chicago Press.

In his introduction, Appleby defines fundamentalism as "the blending of traditional religion and its politicized, ideological defense." This book's contributors examine its occurrence in the Middle East by profiling eight fundamentalist leaders. In chapters based largely on interviews with the leaders or their followers, the authors attempt to "test the theoretical constructs 'fundamentalism' and 'charismatic authority' against the theory-confounding particulars of human life." Leaders profiled include the Ayatollah Khomeini; the founder of Hamas, Shaykh Ahmad Yain; and Sayyid Muhammad Husayn Fadlallah, a leader of the Shi'ite group Hizbullah. Includes bibliographical references and index.

Barber, J. D., & Kellerman, B. (Eds.). (1986). *Women leaders in American politics.* Englewood Cliffs, NJ: Prentice Hall.

This book illustrates the roots and contemporary emergence of women from outsiders to insiders in the political system. Examples of women who led themselves and others to influence and achievement are cited through key passages of their own writings and essays of political context. Abigail Adams, Harriet Beecher Stowe, Margaret Chase Smith, Eleanor Roosevelt, Sandra Day O'Connor, and Elizabeth Dole are among the women featured. Includes a bibliography.

Beyle, T. L. (Ed.). (1992). *Governors and hard times.* Washington, DC: CQ Press.

Leading political science scholars write about the 1989 and 1990 gubernatorial elections. Ten of the 21 new governors elected during that period are profiled. Each faced issues of a falling economy, unpopular tax and program decisions, legislative power struggles, or scandal. When studying how inexperienced governors face the demands of their office, some common themes emerge: state government is rapidly changing, public opinion often distracts governors from important issues, the governor's personality affects the ability to lead, and changes at the federal level cause greater changes at the state level. Includes bibliographical references and index.

Burns, J. M. (1977). **Wellsprings of political leadership.** *American Political Science Review, 71*(1), 266-275.

This paper, presented as the Presidential Address at the American Political Science Association meeting held in Chicago in September 1975, is an exploration of sources of leadership that lie in areas that are to some degree outside the traditional boundaries of political science. It is excerpted and summarized from a larger work in progress.

Burns, J. M. (1980, July/August). **Political leadership in America.** *Center Magazine*, 10-18.

Burns is interested in the relationship between values reduced to purpose, on the one hand, and intended social change, on the other. Leadership can be crucial in bringing about intended social change. He explores political leadership and political conflict by interviewing a number of professors of political science and sociology, directors of institutions, and other prominent leaders.

New
Burns, J. M. (1990). *Cobblestone leadership: Majority rule, minority power.* Norman: University of Oklahoma Press.

Burns presents an agenda for reforming American politics and government. In this lecture from the Julian J. Rothbaum distinguished lecture series, Burns calls for grassroots activism, which he calls "cobblestone leadership." In addition, there is urgent need for a reexamination of the Constitution, a strengthening of the Democrat and Republican parties, reduction in campaign spending, congressional term limits, and an end to corruption in politics. Includes index.

Campbell, C. (1986). *Managing the presidency: Carter, Reagan, and the search for executive harmony.* Pittsburgh, PA: University of Pittsburgh Press.

Campbell argues that too many studies of U.S. chief executives have focused on personalities and styles without adequately taking into account the president's relationship to his advisors and the machinery of the office. Campbell describes the institutional development of the presidency in recent years with particular emphasis on the Carter and Reagan administrations. Campbell draws on interviews with nearly 200 officials, including senior members of the White House staff. Includes bibliographical references and index.

New
Campbell, C., & Rockman, B. A. (Eds.). (1996). *The Clinton presidency: First appraisals.* Chatham, NJ: Chatham House.

Contributing authors share their assessments of President William Clinton's first presidential campaign and first term in office. Barbara Sinclair describes Clinton's relationship with Congress. David O'Brien writes of Clinton's effect on the judicial arm of government. Joel Aberbach analyzes the executive branch through selection of political appointees and the use of permanent officials. Other essays describe Clinton's ability to mobilize support, his domestic and foreign policy, his lack of influence on mid-term elections, and the state of executive leadership in the U.S. Includes bibliographical references in chapter notes and an index.

Cantor, D. W., Bernay, T., & Stoess, J. (1992). *Women in power: The secrets of leadership.* Boston: Houghton Mifflin.

To research the phenomenon of women politicians, the authors interviewed 25 female, high-level, elected officials. They found evidence that empowerment messages, confidence building, and relationships between mothers and daughters are relevant to a woman's success. With a foreword by Dianne Feinstein, an afterword by Geraldine Ferraro, and interviews with Ann Richards and Pat Schroeder, this book presents the most powerful women in today's political arena as they share their secrets for success. Includes bibliographical references and index.

New
DeGregorio, C. A. (1997). *Networks of champions: Leadership, access, and advocacy in the U.S. House of Representatives.* Ann Arbor: University of Michigan Press.

The author states that lawmaking is a team effort among legislators, their staffs of experts, and the lobbyists who seek to influence them. In the U.S. House of Representatives, where each team member has personal interests to protect, the teams must work together against incredible odds. While researching this book, the author discovered that congressional leadership emerges from obscure positions. Those who possess substantive knowledge and informal influence, but do not hold positions of power, practice an "earned style of leadership." These are the leaders who can "turn warring factions into winning coalitions" and who "champion policy in the face of adversity." Legislators seek alliances with, and lobbyists are quick to ferret out, these leaders. To illustrate congressional team leadership in context, DeGregorio cites several recent policy issues including: welfare reform, international trade policy, farm credit, nuclear test ban, and the anti-drug bill. Includes bibliographical references and indexes.

New
Deluga, R. J. (1997). **Relationship among American presidential charismatic leadership, narcissism, and rated performance.** *Leadership Quarterly, 8*(1), 49-65.

This study uses historical data to rate the narcissism and charisma of U.S. presidents from Washington to Reagan. Deluga hypothesized that narcissism would be positively related to charismatic leadership and rated performance, and the research supports this. However, the study warns that this shows only a correlational, not a causal, relationship between narcissism and performance, and that narcissistic charismatic leadership can have negative consequences.

New
Denton, R. E., Jr., & Holloway, R. L. (1996). *The Clinton presidency: Images, issues, and communication strategies.* Westport, CT: Praeger.

Contributing authors analyze William Clinton's skills as a "rhetorical president." Beginning with the 1993 inaugural address, they examine town hall meetings, political advertising, unsuccessful health care reform, and a roller coaster relationship with the media throughout his first term in office. Craig Allen Smith's essay suggests that Clinton's middle-class appeal is based on his message that we can make tomorrow better than today and we all have a responsibility to make it happen. The Republican cry for family values is described as using a passive noun. In contrast, Clinton used active verbs when demanding a government that values families and promotes family leave, health care, and job training. The book also includes content analysis of political cartoons, an essay on the communication style of Hillary Rodham Clinton, and a critique of the Clinton administration e-mail system. Includes bibliographical references and index.

New
Duerst-Lahti, G., & Kelly, R. M. (Eds.). (1995). *Gender power, leadership, and governance.* Ann Arbor: University of Michigan Press.

This book merges theory with empirical research and incorporates feminism into political ideology. The primary concept is gender power—"the power that results from our gendered (e)valuation of things and behaviors, our ways of being, behaving, and structuring social relations." Contributing authors link power and traditional leadership to masculinity and link sex-role identity to decision-making style. There is an analysis of the 1992 elections and a popular media slogan, "the Year of the Woman." Authors examine the number of times during this "year" that women were represented as leaders in articles of the *New York Times* and *The Washington Post.* The editors conclude that acceptance of gender power would contribute to the understanding of public governance and leadership. Includes bibliographical references.

Eldersveld, S. J., Stromberg, L., & Derksen, W. (1995). *Local elites in Western democracies: A comparative analysis of urban political leaders in the U.S., Sweden, and the Netherlands.* San Francisco: Westview Press.

The authors tested the premise that in a healthy society, political elites form strong relationships with community groups to help them understand the communities' problems and values and to respond with the appropriate actions. Intermediate-sized cities—population 29,000 to 163,000—were selected for comparison: 20 in the U.S., 15 in Sweden, and 20 in the Netherlands. Interviews were conducted with the top public administrators in each city to determine their evaluation of and effectiveness in dealing with their city's problems. Cultural diversity, the power of local leaders in business and other institutions, and the variations between the cities themselves complicated efforts at generalization. The research did identify some uniformity in the areas of perceived problems and priorities. Includes bibliographical references and index.

New
Ellis, S., Nadler, A., & Rabin, A. (1996). **Political leaders in the SYMLOG space: Perceptions of right and left wing leaders by right and left wing constituencies.** *Leadership Quarterly, 7*(4), 507-526.

This study used the *Systematic Multiple Level Observation of Groups* (SYMLOG®) measure to determine how different constituent groups felt about the friendliness, task-orientation, and dominance of right- and left-wing Israeli politicians. Right-wing voters rated right-wing leaders higher on friendliness and task-orientation, while left-wing voters rated left-wing leaders higher on those traits. Each group of constituents saw leaders affiliated with their political party as closer to their image of the ideal leader than leaders from the opposing party.

Europe's diminished leaders. (1995, January 21). *Economist, 334,* 51-56.

The primary reason why Europe's leaders seem diminished is that no one can find answers to the difficult problems facing the European Union, most notably the war in Bosnia, political upheaval in Northern Africa, and the political and military debacle in Russia. Democracies expect their leaders to make hard choices and to explain them to the electors. There seems to be very little of these activities among the leaders of France, Germany, and Italy. The political problems of each country, along with those of Russia, Croatia, and Poland, are discussed.

Folkertsma, M. J., Jr. (1988). *Ideology and leadership.* Englewood Cliffs, NJ: Prentice Hall.

From four modern political ideologies, American Liberalism, Marxism, Fascism, and Islamic Fundamentalism, the author has selected seven political leaders who exemplify and embody the essence of these ideologies. The leaders surveyed are James Madison, Franklin D. Roosevelt, Martin Luther King, Jr., Joseph Stalin, Mao Zedong, Adolf Hitler, and Ruhollah Khomeini. It is the author's goal to "explain what these leaders believe, how they acted upon their beliefs, what difference it made to their country and where relevant, to the world about them." Includes bibliographies and index.

New
Geer, J. G. (1996). *From tea leaves to opinion polls: A theory of democratic leadership.* New York: Columbia University Press.

Geer examines the relationship between politicians and public opinion, arguing that "polls have altered in systematic and important ways the behavior of elected politicians." Although the book includes many examples from American presidential politics, this is mainly a theoretical examination of how public opinion has affected democracy and political leadership. Figures and probability tables help illustrate philosophical concepts, including public mandate and independence. Includes bibliographical references and index.

Genovese, M. A. (Ed.). (1993). *Women as national leaders.* Newbury Park: Sage.

Historically, most political leaders have been men. Since World War II, a few women have emerged as heads of national government and have given researchers an opportunity to study gender and political leadership. Contributing authors focus on seven women leaders: Golda Meir, Indira Gandhi, Margaret Thatcher, Isabel

Perón, Corazon Aquino, Benazir Bhutto, and Violeta Chamorro. Each case of a woman's rise to power traces her encounters with obstacles and the skills acquired to circumvent them. Includes bibliographical references and index.

New
Gertzog, I. N. (1995). *Congressional women: Their recruitment, integration, and behavior* (2nd ed.). Westport, CT: Praeger.

In Gertzog's first edition of this book, published in 1984, he examined the women who served in Congress from 1916 to the late 1970s. He updated his study with new interviews after the 1992 "Year of the Woman" elections, and in great detail describes the background and experiences that successive generations of Congresswomen have brought to their offices. There are direct quotes from past and present Congresswomen and charts showing the most common characteristics of Congresswomen and the issues they have faced. Includes bibliographical references and index.

Greenstein, F. I. (Ed.). (1988). *Leadership in the modern presidency.* Cambridge, MA: Harvard University Press.

The author acknowledges two premises that underlie the leadership of the nine presidents who held office from 1933 to 1988. First, presidents influence public policy, and, second, the impact of their presidency is a function of their personal leadership qualities. In Chapters 1 through 9, scholars on each of the presidents from Franklin D. Roosevelt through Ronald Reagan provide insight into the nature of each president's leadership qualities and discuss the impact these qualities have had on policy-making decisions. Greenstein concludes with his own analysis and observations on modern presidential leadership. Includes bibliographical references and index.

Haas, E. F. (1988). *Political leadership in a Southern city: New Orleans in the progressive era, 1896-1902.* Ruston, LA: McGinty.

Although urban political machines rarely characterize the South, rapid population growth and ethnic diversity based on an influx of immigrants and blacks drove turn-of-the-century New Orleans to preserve white supremacy and Democratic party control. The author sheds light on the ensuing power struggle and how Regular Democrats organized working-class whites and immigrants into tight-knit wards and precincts to dominate the more reform-minded business and professional Citizens' Leaguers until the advent of Huey Long in 1928. Includes bibliography and index.

Hastedt, G. P., & Eksterowicz, A. J. (1993). **Presidential leadership in the post Cold War era.** *Presidential Studies Quarterly, 23*(3), 445-458.

World War II and the Cold War and their subsequent threat to national security created a need for supreme executive authority in foreign affairs. In *Presidential Government* (1973), Burns defined this need as the "Presidential Government Model of Leadership." After the Cold War, political scientists are considering the possibilities of other models. The "Executive/Party Model of Leadership" emphasizes a Jeffersonian style of teamwork, majority rule, and party responsibility. The "Executive/Congressional Model of Leadership" emphasizes a Madisonian style of checks and balances, protection of minority rights, and limited government.

New

Havel, V. (1991). *Open letters: Selected writings 1965-1990.* New York: Knopf.

In editing this series of writings, Paul Wilson hopes to ". . . present the reader with Havel the man, not just Havel the dissident thinker." The book includes many of Havel's lesser known pieces such as a 1969 letter to Alexander Dubcek one year after the Soviet invasion of Czechoslovakia. It also includes Havel's most influential works such as the 1978 essay "The Power of the Powerless," which inspired the working class to support the Solidarity movement, and his 1990 New Year's Address, his first speech as the new president of Czechoslovakia. Includes index.

Hunt, R. G., & Meindl, J. R. (1991). **Chinese political economic reforms and the problem of legitimizing leader roles.** *Leadership Quarterly, 2*(3), 189-204.

Caught in the crosscurrent of decentralizing economic power and deconcentrating political power, Chinese enterprise is experiencing significant changes in leadership. Efforts are underway to reduce the Communist Party's role in administrative affairs and to institute a system of managerial responsibility. Surveys of 94 Chinese and 154 American junior managers identify attitudes toward work values, indicating variance in several areas.

Juckes, T. J. (1995). *Opposition in South Africa: The leadership of Z. K. Matthews, Nelson Mandela, and Stephen Biko.* Westport, CT: Praeger.

This book presents a sociopsychological retrospective of 20th-century political activities in South Africa. Three key individuals led an apartheid-opposition movement that restructured a society and earned one of them a Nobel Peace Prize. Zachariah Matthews led the intellectual movement that stressed liberation through education.

Nelson Mandela, who was imprisoned for his leadership of the militant movement, became a symbol of black hope and strength. Stephen Biko's dedication to integrated education spawned the Black Consciousness movement. A chronology of events runs from the 1652 settlement of Dutch colonists to Nelson Mandela's 1990 release from prison, 1993 Nobel Peace Prize, and 1994 election as president of South Africa. Includes bibliographical references and index.

Kellerman, B. (Ed.). (1986). *Political leadership.* Pittsburgh, PA: University of Pittsburgh Press.

This is a sourcebook for the study of political leadership. All of the essays address some aspect of leadership, even though some of the authors are philosophers, psychologists, sociologists, political scientists, historians, mythologists, literary figures, activists, and public officials. The collection is particularly rich in political psychology—work that explicitly connects political life to the psychology of individuals and groups. Includes bibliographies.

Kellerman, B. (1991). **The president abroad: Leadership at the international level.** *Leadership Quarterly, 2*(1), 1-7.

Major foreign-policy initiatives of presidents Kennedy, Johnson, Nixon, Carter, and Reagan are discussed. Kellerman reports that three out of five presidents successfully achieved their foreign-policy goals, resulting in their recognition as world leaders. The four tasks that facilitated success are identified as: formulating goals clearly and consistently; employing power, authority, and influence energetically and effectively; motivating domestic and foreign constituencies to follow their lead; and overseeing implementation.

McCann, S. J. (1992). **Alternative formulas to predict the greatness of U.S. presidents: Personological, situational, and zeitgeist factors.** *Journal of Personality and Social Psychology, 62*(3), 469-479.

What defines a president as a great leader? Simonton (1988; see below) devised a five-variable formula incorporating years in office, war years, scandal, assassination, and war hero to create a predictor of presidential greatness. Personological variables were added: IQ, drive, wit, tidiness, height, and attractiveness. Three zeitgeist variables weighted each president's tenure in office. Situational variables weighted events during administrations. The above criteria were used to rank data on 29 presidents from Washington to Lyndon Johnson.

McFarland, A. S. (1969). *Power and leadership in pluralist systems.* Stanford, CA: Stanford University Press.

This book creatively synthesizes all relevant works on the nature of power in pluralist systems including such diverse works as Dahl's *Who Governs?* (1961), K. Mannheim's *Ideology and Utopia* (1936), and Easton's *The Political System* (1953). It is an analysis of the differing approaches to problem solving in the political arena. Includes bibliography.

New
McGovern, S. J. (1997). **Mayoral leadership and economic development policy: The case of Ed Rendell's Philadelphia.** *Policy and Politics, 25*(2), 153-172.

McGovern describes the popularity and success of Philadelphia mayor Ed Rendell as a leadership phenomenon. Rendell was responsible for leading his city out of a fiscal crisis and pursuing economic growth, gaining an exceptional 80% approval rating among constituents. He has consulted with mayors throughout the country to share his leadership expertise. His methods include: collaboration with the city council and state legislature, personal involvement in large and small community affairs, bringing an influx of state aid and HUD money, and eliminating budget deficits without raising taxes. Rendell's leadership style served his city well in times of crisis. McGovern examines Rendell's ability to lead the city in *normal* times. Includes bibliographical references.

New
Michaels, J. E. (1997). *The president's call: Executive leadership from FDR to George Bush.* Pittsburgh, PA: University of Pittsburgh Press.

Arguing that presidents are "judged by the company they keep," Michaels examines presidential leadership in the context of Senate-confirmed presidential appointees (PASs). She surveyed and interviewed current and former PASs, mainly from the Bush administration, and uses the responses to analyze the leadership both of presidents and PASs within their departments. Chapters describe the people who become PASs, the nomination and confirmation process, interbureaucratic relations, and how presidents use political appointments. Advice is also offered to future PASs. Includes bibliographical references and index.

Morris, T. D. (1984). **Taking charge in Washington.** *Harvard Business Review, 62*(4), 24-40.

The author discusses the leadership of McNamara, Staats, and Califano while they were in federal-government leadership positions. The experiences of these individuals show that to be an effective federal manager one must: bring "zest" for new career experiences, be able to make contributions quickly because of the limited appointment, be an effective communicator, have strategies for attaining goals, and develop long-range objectives.

Neustadt, R. E. (1990). *Presidential power and the modern presidents: The politics of leadership from Roosevelt to Reagan* (Rev. ed.). New York: Free Press.

The president is vested with the powers of our country's highest office. How does he make those powers work for him? Neustadt defines power in politics: what it is, how to get it, how to keep it, how to lose it. This revised edition reexamines Franklin Roosevelt, Truman, and Eisenhower and then examines Kennedy, Johnson, Nixon, Ford, Carter, and Reagan. It is intended as a learning device for corporation presidents, union leaders, clergy, and students of government and politics. Includes bibliographical references and index.

Neustadt, R. E., & May, E. R. (1986). *Thinking in time: The uses of history for decision-makers.* New York: Free Press.

This is a book about time and high-level political actions, but it is not a book on time management. The authors' focus is time past, and they offer stories and suggest tools with the hope that they can illustrate "how to use experience, whether remote or recent, in the process of deciding what to do today about the prospect for tomorrow." Includes bibliography and index.

Olshfski, D. (1990). **Politics and leadership: Political executives at work.** *Public Productivity & Management Review, 13*(3), 225-243.

This is not about the bureaucratic politics of getting control of power, policy, or resources. Nor is it about the politics of getting elected to public office. This analysis examines appointed executives and their own perceptions of their work inside partisan environments. They define politics as an understanding of one's environment and knowing how to operate in it. Politics is also advancing a particular issue or the gaining of support for a particular person or program.

New
Peters, R. M., Jr. (Ed.). (1994). *The speaker: Leadership in the U.S. House of Representatives.* Washington, DC: Congressional Quarterly.

In the foreword, former speaker Tom Foley describes changes in the U.S. House of Representatives over the past 30 years. Primarily, there has been a movement away from a monopoly of power in the hands of senior members to a distribution of power to all members. Ironically, as power was redistributed in the House, the role of the speaker grew more influential. This book provides a history and insightful analysis of this role. Topics include: selecting a speaker, the speaker as party leader, the speaker's relationship with the minority party, and the speaker's influence on the national budget and foreign policy. Former speakers Carl Albert, Thomas P. "Tip" O'Neill, Jr., and Jim Wright share their insights and advice to those who follow in their footsteps. Includes bibliographical references and index.

Rejai, M., & Phillips, K. (1988). **Loyalists and revolutionaries: Political elites in comparative perspective.** *International Political Science Review, 9*, 107-118.

Based on the examination of 50 well-known revolutionary and loyalist leaders, Rejai and Phillips reveal the results of their comparative analysis of these two political elite populations. Their study examines the historical, situational, social, and psychological condition of these leaders. Questions raised include: Do the two groups differ in social-background attributes, political patterns, situational encounters, and psychological dynamics? The study identified cluster traits that applied to both populations. However, at a second level of analysis, traits and characteristics emerged that significantly separated the groups. A list of loyalists and revolutionary leaders is included.

New
Rockman, B. A. (1997). **The limits of executive power.** *The World & I, 12*(1), 22-31.

Rockman claims that the American president appears to be more powerful than he really is. In public, he is surrounded by media and Secret Service personnel. Streets are blockaded to let his motorcade pass. When he approaches a podium to speak, a band plays "Hail to the Chief." These symbols create an illusion of power for a president who is head of state but limited by constitutional checks and balances. Rockman compares the real power of modern American presidents to past presidents and to heads of state in other countries. In other countries, heads of state do not have the same constraints imposed by the American Congress and Supreme Court.

New
Rose, G. L. (1997). *The American presidency under siege.* Albany: State University of New York Press.

Rose observes that, in the past 25 years, presidential elections have become a routine exercise in politics more than "a coming to power of a new national leader." He contends that presidential candidates no longer touch the hearts and souls of American citizens, not because of voter apathy, but because of a post-Watergate phenomenon—a decline in presidential power. Rose sees the American presidency as under siege by special interest groups, the media, an oversized federal bureaucracy, and a reactionary Congress. He documents this hostile environment, describes the contributions of America's best presidents, and proposes the restoration of creative

presidential leadership. An appendix suggests debate issues for students of political science. Includes bibliographical references and index.

New
Scharfstein, B. (1995). *Amoral politics: The persistent truth of Machiavellism.* Albany: State University of New York Press.

The author uses the term *Machiavellism* to represent a "disregard of moral scruples in politics, that is, the political use . . . of every kind of deception and force." A comparison of political practice in Ancient China and India, Renaissance Italy, tribal cultures, and the 20th century indicates that Machiavellism is fundamental to societies and a human condition as common as love and hate. Scharfstein questions citizen acceptance of amoral politicians and some scholars' reluctance to include Machiavellism in studies of politics and ethics. He struggles with the question, "Does the prevalence of Machiavellism rule out the likelihood of a better political future?" but determines that it is impossible to answer. Includes bibliographical references and index.

New
Scher, R. K. (1997). *Politics in the new South: Republicanism, race and leadership in the twentieth century.* Armonk, NY: M.E. Sharpe.

While Scher disputes the existence of a "New South," in this book he describes three political changes that have shaped the South this century: the rise of the Republican party (and consequently two-party politics), the entry of blacks into mainstream politics, and the changing nature of gubernatorial leadership. In the section on Southern governors, Scher offers both a historical background of the office and a theoretical model for Southern gubernatorial leadership. Charts, tables, and figures are included in this extensively researched book. Includes bibliographical references and index.

Sheehy, G. (1988). *Character: America's search for leadership.* New York: William Morrow.

Well known for her previous works, *Passages* (1976) and *Pathfinders* (1982), Gail Sheehy profiles the top political figures of our recent past and on the current scene. In an effort to reveal the elements of leadership and character that propel one to the top, Sheehy has chosen such men as Jesse Jackson, Bob Dole, Gary Hart, Mike Dukakis, and George Bush. Each individual's profile is presented in a clear, if not always flattering, light. As the author puts it, "Readers should feel the same cold slap of insight, awakening them from conventional thinking, that I feel each time I study the character of a leader as it has developed."

Sheffer, G. (Ed.). (1993). *Innovative leaders in international politics.* Albany: State University of New York Press.

Sheffer notes that political leaders often respond to social problems with piecemeal solutions and marginal changes. In this book, guest authors discuss eight political leaders who responded to the needs of their societies with broad, sweeping innovative changes. Each author addresses the importance of personality, intuition, intellect, and the relationship between domestic policy and international acceptance. The leaders discussed are: French Prime Minister, Charles De Gaulle; Israeli Prime Minister, Moshe Sharett; German Chancellor, Konrad Adenauer; King Juan Carlos of Spain; Indian moralist, Mohandas Gandhi; Soviet President Mikhail Gorbachev; and Egyptian President, Anwar Sadat. Includes bibliographical references and index.

Shogan, R. (1991). *The riddle of power: Presidential leadership from Truman to Bush.* New York: Dutton.

For the past 50 years, the president of the United States has been both the most powerful man in the world and a figure of doubtful authority in the U.S., struggling with broken promises, failed policies, and political deadlock. Shogan examines the ideology, values, and character of nine postwar presidents and the events that marked their terms. Written from the perspective of a Washington political journalist, this book explores "how the individual shapes the presidency and how the presidency provides the ultimate revelation of the man." Includes bibliographical references and index.

Simonton, D. K. (1987). *Why presidents succeed: A political psychology of leadership.* New Haven, CT: Yale University Press.

This book examines the four standards of presidential success: success in presidential elections, popularity in the polls, performance in the White House, and presidential greatness. As a political psychologist, the author looks at the presidency and the appearance of personal qualities that may contribute to effective leadership. Such factors as attitudes, intelligence, childhood experiences, age, environment, motivation, and cognitive style are measured in winning an election, acting as commander-in-chief, and carrying out legislative programs. The author's use of empirical methods to analyze the relationships of traits to effective leadership lend credibility to his conclusions. Includes bibliography and index.

Simonton, D. K. (1988). **Presidential style: Personality, biography, and performance.** *Journal of Personality and Social Psychology, 55*(6), 928-936.

The author used biographical information on 39 U.S. presidents as a basis for assessments of presidential style by seven raters. Five basic style dimensions were delineated: interpersonal, charismatic, deliberative, creative, and neurotic. These styles were shown to be related both to objective and subjective indicators of presidential performance.

New

Sinclair, B. (1995). *Legislators, leaders, and lawmaking: The U.S. House of Representatives in the postreform era.* Baltimore: Johns Hopkins University Press.

Sinclair discusses the changing role of congressional leadership following reforms of the past 25 years. In the 1970s, both parties lost identity and power, leaving congressional candidates to win elections and develop leadership on their own rather than depending on party loyalty. In the 1980s, House majority-party leadership developed its own cohesion and regained lost power. When the 1994 elections put Republicans in the majority seat for the first time in 40 years, political scholars predicted a show of strong leadership. Sinclair analyzes the "anomaly of strong congressional party leadership in an era of relatively weak parties." She describes House leadership functions and their considerable influence on the legislative process. Analysis of leadership function and influence are reported in tables throughout the text. Includes bibliographical references and index.

Smith, C. A., & Smith, K. B. (1994). *The White House speaks: Presidential leadership as persuasion.* Westport, CT: Praeger.

Persuasive speech is central to the position of president. Speech is used to unify varied interests, legitimize the president's power, resolve conflicts, and implement policies. To illustrate the persuasive power of presidential speechmaking, the authors discuss Gerald Ford's pardon of Richard Nixon, Ronald Reagan's debate over the Panama Canal treaties, Jimmy Carter's energy program, and William Clinton's 1992 campaign. Includes bibliographical references and index.

Thompson, K. W. (Ed.). (1985). *Essays on leadership: Comparative insights.* Lanham, MD: University Press of America.

Six studies of important world leaders, including Winston Churchill, Dwight Eisenhower, and Adlai Stevenson, are presented. Their direction has had a lasting effect, especially on leadership in the Cold War. Each essay looks at the background, philosophy, and charisma of these very different leaders from across the world. The purpose is to draw out principles of leadership by focusing on the political practices of these statesmen. A thoughtful reflection and a review of the historical facts dominate these essays. Includes a bibliography.

Tucker, R. C. (1995). *Politics as leadership* (Rev. ed.). Columbia: University of Missouri Press.

The original edition (1981) was based on a series of lectures on leadership ethics. The lectures are reprinted in this revised edition with additional commentary on key events of the past 15 years in which political leadership caused sweeping reform. Tucker cites Mikhail Gorbachev and Nelson Mandela as recent political leaders who effected positive change and Rwandan President Habyariamana as a political leader responsible for the genocidal slaughter of one million of his compatriots. Includes bibliographical references and index.

Walsh, D. F., Best, P. J., & Rai, K. B. (1995). *Governing through turbulence: Leadership and change in the late twentieth century.* Westport, CT: Praeger.

In the past three decades, major political and economic changes have compounded the difficult task of leading a national government. In this book, the authors present case studies of seven world leaders who have governed in times of turbulence. Three were leaders of communist states undergoing transitions: Lech Walesa, president of Poland; Mikhail Gorbachev, president of the Soviet Union; and Boris Yeltsin, president of the Russian Republic. Two were leaders of Third World countries: Deng Xiaoping, de facto leader of the Communist Party of China; and Rajiv Gandhi, prime minister of India. Two were leaders of advanced industrial nations: Margaret Thatcher, prime minister of the United Kingdom; and Helmut Kohl, chancellor of Germany. Includes bibliographical references and index.

Willner, A. R. (1984). *The spellbinders: Charismatic political leadership—A theory.* New Haven, CT: Yale University Press.

The author has attempted to unravel and explain the spells exerted by political leaders who have succeeded in inspiring, swaying, or seducing multitudes and holding their minds and emotions in control. This work was originally begun in 1964 as a comparative study of the leadership strategies of Sukarno, Nasser, and Nkrumah. Weber's concept of political charisma is used as the general theme relating these three leaders. Includes bibliographical references and index.

New
Woodward, B. (1991). *The commanders.* New York: Simon & Schuster.

Woodward chronicles in great detail U.S. military decision making from the election of George Bush as president in 1988 until 1991, when the Persian Gulf War began. The relationships between leaders including Bush, Dick Cheney, Colin Powell, and James Baker are de-scribed, and their decisions in military actions including the invasion of Panama are explained. Based mainly on interviews with people involved in these decisions, Woodward says that "this book falls somewhere between newspaper journalism and history." Includes index and photographs.

New
Young, O. R. (1991). **Political leadership and regime formation: On the development of institutions in international society.** *International Organization, 45*(3), 281-308.

Establishing agreements between international regimes requires extensive negotiation. Young defines leadership within the context of institutional bargaining and argues that it is a necessary element in successsful negotiation. He identifies three types of leadership—structural, entrepreneurial, and intellectual—and clarifies the role individuals play in international affairs. Concepts are illustrated with political examples, including Woodrow Wilson's 1918 attempt to form the League of Nations and modern-day international cooperation in the Arctic.

Zoll, D. (1989, Summer). **On political leadership.** *Modern Age, 32*, 215-223.

Zoll contends that the most able, intellectual, and politically talented individuals do not run for the office of president of the United States. Do we, as a society, prefer mediocrity? Or does the role require cleverness over intellect? Zoll suggests that society demands puritanical presidential candidates with no eccentricities. These demands eliminate many intellectuals and innovators who, by their nature, are nonconformists.

PUBLIC SERVICE AND GOVERNMENT

Behn, R. D. (1991). *Leadership counts: Lessons for public managers from the Massachusetts welfare training and employment program.* Cambridge, MA: Harvard University Press.

The author describes the first five years of a Massachusetts program, ET CHOICES, which in 1988 was able to successfully achieve its goal to educate, train, and place into jobs 50,000 welfare recipients. Not a historical chronicle of the program, the book instead attempts to extract from the program lessons about public management. Behn's analysis spans the spectrum of managerial tasks—from the responsibility to create and communicate a public mission to the more mundane problem of motivating individuals to accomplish specific tasks. Includes bibliographical references and index.

New

Beyle, T. L. (1995). **Enhancing executive leadership in the states.** *State and Local Government Review, 27*(1), 18-35.

Beyle explains three decades of reform in state governments that has led to increased gubernatorial authority— greater power to make appointments in executive positions, veto legislation, and write state budgets. Two polls, one of constituents and one of political scientists and journalists, report on the job performance of 50 governors serving in the summer of 1994. When the numbers were correlated, six governors received exceptionally high ratings and five received very low ratings. Beyle analyzes the factors that determine good job performance at this level: the institutional powers of governorship in a given state; a governor's personal power; and how a governor works with administrators, the state legislature, and the media. Includes bibliographical references.

New

Card, M. A. (1997). **Toward a middle-range theory of individual-level strategic leadership transitions.** *Leadership Quarterly, 8*(1), 27-48.

Case studies of three state-level agency directors, including the directors of Ohio's Departments of Health and Employment Services, are used to examine the importance of the initial actions of a new official. Card identifies three stages in the leadership transition process: the crisis of appointment as a new leader tries to secure his or her position, the crisis of leadership as the leader tries to establish influence and authority with subordinates, and the crisis of autonomy and control as the new leader arrives on the job. This article attempts to offer potential agency leaders a guide for easing these difficult organizational transitions.

New

Carver, J. (1997). *Boards that make a difference: A new design for leadership in nonprofit and public organizations* (2nd ed.). San Francisco: Jossey-Bass.

Carver presents his policy governance model and explains how nonprofit and public agency leaders can implement it in their organizations. Carver defines four categories of policies that boards should focus on: 1) ends to be achieved, 2) means to those ends, 3) the board-staff relationship, and 4) the process of governance itself. The second edition includes updated policy samples and a chapter on the process of policy development. Includes bibliographical references and index.

New

Clingermayer, J. C., & Feiock, R. C. (1997). **Leadership turnover, transaction costs, and external city service delivery.** *Public Administration Review, 57*(3), 231-239.

A major concern for any city government is delivering municipal services in the most efficient and cost-effective manner, and many cities use external service delivery methods. This study examined whether turnover in city leadership affected these delivery choices. Statistical analysis of national data on cities showed that mayoral turnover discouraged out-sourcing of social services, which the authors speculate required hands-on management because they were politically sensitive. However, turnover of city leadership encouraged out-sourcing of less politically sensitive services, including support staff, regulatory functions, and public works programs.

Denhardt, R. B., & Stewart, W. H. (1992). *Executive leadership in the public service.* Tuscaloosa: University of Alabama Press.

This collection of essays commissioned in memory of University of Alabama professor Coleman B. Ransone, Jr., explores the important link between executive and administrative levels in the public sector. Striking a reasonable balance between leadership in the abstract and specific power centers, the essays address such topics as political professionalism, presidential and gubernatorial persuasiveness, developmental perspectives on public leadership, and finding new professionalism in city management. Includes bibliographical references and index.

Doig, J. W. (1987). *Leadership and innovation: A biographical perspective on entrepreneurs in government.* Baltimore: Johns Hopkins University Press.

This book is about men and women who have held top positions in public organizations. From these positions, each individual made a mark on the world, an innovative change; they each had an influence on what their office did. In brief, they fashioned formal authority into effective influence. Using a biographical approach, the authors have selected a number of extraordinary government leaders. Profiles include: "David Lilienthal and the Tennessee Valley Authority," "Admiral Hyman Rickover: Technological Entrepreneurship in the U.S. Navy," and "The Politics of Art: Nancy Hawks and the National Endowment for the Arts." Includes bibliographical references and index.

Fairholm, G. W. (1991). *Values leadership: Toward a new philosophy of leadership.* New York: Praeger.

How can government attain excellence while confronted with such problems as multiple goals, complex organizational structure, and enormous physical and scheduling coordination? In government, group dynamics involves citizen-consumers, executives, administrators, legislators, employees, and the media. This book proposes a new values-driven, change-oriented, and developmental leadership for government. Chapter 2 reviews current and past leadership theories and their applications in public bureaucracies. Includes bibliographical references and index.

Garner, L. H., Jr. (1989). *Leadership in human services: How to articulate and implement a vision to achieve results.* San Francisco: Jossey-Bass.

This book addresses the unique demands imposed on leaders working in the field of human services. Drawing on case studies and based on the principles of "result-oriented management," the author outlines how human-services practitioners must learn to articulate a vision and then translate their vision into specific objectives. Includes bibliography and index.

New
Goodsell, C. T., & Murray, N. (Eds.). (1995). *Public administration illuminated and inspired by the arts.* Westport, CT: Praeger.

Fifty years ago, a commentary in the journal *Public Administration Review* suggested that novels provide a useful medium for deeper understanding of public administration. This book takes that idea further by recommending novels, short stories, poetry, classical literature, films, and paintings to enhance leadership lessons in public administration. These works of art reflect the complexities of human nature and provide opportunities to learn about unfamiliar cultures. The editors call these connections "bridges." Some chapters are: "Leadership Lessons from Shakespeare" by C. R. Gira, "How Imagination Transforms Leaders" by S. R. Kuder, "Art and Transformation in *Murder in the Cathedral*" by M. R. Carey, "Poetry and Leadership" by D. H. Nelson, and "Lessons in Leadership from *Lonesome Dove*" by P. R. Russell and D. B. Tinsley. An index guides readers to subjects, authors, artists, and works of art. Includes bibliographical references and index.

Grover, H. L. (1994). **Transition leadership and legacies.** *Public Manager, 23*(2), 9-12.

Current national and international pressures make it imperative that the American government undergo a significant strategic transformation from bureaucracy to responsive organization. This strategic challenge of transformation must be addressed by a new generation of federal executives. Strategies for executive-development providers are discussed.

Heimovics, R. D., Herman, R. D., & Jurkiewicz, C. L. (1993). **Executive leadership and resource dependence in nonprofit organizations: A frame analysis.** *Public Administration Review, 53*(5), 419-427.

Political and funding challenges in nonprofit organizations create complex and volatile administrative responsibilities. Responsibility for obtaining needed resources is often beyond the scope of the board and falls to the chief executive, giving the executive a position of centrality. Research using a multiple-frame orientation, including structural, human resource, political, and symbolic frames, coded data from 52 executives in successful and unsuccessful events. Results indicated that executives who effectively use a political frame have greater success in mobilizing constituencies, forming coalitions, creating obligations, negotiating, and bargaining.

Johnson, A. L., & Luthans, F. (1990). **The relationship between leadership and management: An empirical assessment.** *Journal of Managerial Issues, 2*(1), 13-25.

In two studies, 166 managers and 522 subordinates in finance, manufacturing, retail, service, and the public sector responded to a leadership-behavior scale and a standardized questionnaire on outcome variables. Results indicated that additional information about managerial activities increased the relevance of outcome variables such as performance, satisfaction, and commitment.

New
Koehler, J. W., & Pankowski, J. M. (1997). *Transformational leadership in government.* Delray Beach, FL: St. Lucie Press.

This book is a response to public cynicism of government bureaucracies that consume tax dollars, stifle innovation, and deliver far fewer outcomes than citizens demand. The authors draw parallels between government agencies and corporations and their leadership. Corporations have been moving toward smaller, more responsive, and efficient organizational structures with empowered employees. The authors suggest that government agencies implement such transformational style leadership to improve their own organizations. This book outlines the principles, skills, and behaviors of transformational leadership. It suggests steps for creating a vision, empowering employees, and inspiring change. Includes bibliography and index.

Lowry, P. E. (1995). **The assessment center process: Assessing leadership in the public sector.** *Public Personnel Management, 24*(4), 443-450.

Organizations using assessment centers to determine the best candidates for hiring and promotion have been stymied by the complexity of leadership definitions. Lowry suggests using a task assessment rather than a dimension assessment. When based on an individual's job analysis, assessment can be more easily measured and feedback can be more easily interpreted.

Lynch, R. (1993). *Lead! How public and nonprofit managers can bring out the best in themselves and their organizations.* San Francisco: Jossey-Bass.

Managers are often so overwhelmed by everyday tasks that they forget the more fundamental task of leadership. Lynch describes how the leadership role transcends managerial tasks and explains how public and nonprofit leaders can enhance their organizations through bringing out the best in themselves, their organizations, and their people. Case studies are used to illustrate how managers can optimize their personal influence, establish a sense of collective purpose, design jobs that reward employees for meaningful tasks, create a more streamlined organizational structure, foster and sustain meaningful values, keep employees hopeful in hard times, and create a positive organizational climate. Includes bibliographical references and index.

New
Menzel, D. C. (Ed.). (1996). *The American county: Frontiers of knowledge.* Tuscaloosa: University of Alabama Press.

Most studies of leadership in public administration avoid discussion of county governments. This level of public administration is responsible for unglamorous services such as corrections, welfare, indigent health care, road maintenance, vital statistics, property taxes, and garbage collection. The essays in this book address a transformation of county governments in recent decades. They acknowledge that counties have rapidly growing populations to serve, are moving away from old-style political machines to new-style management structures, and are initiating coordinated services across intergovernmental boundaries. Challenges that face the elected and appointed officials who want to modernize county governments are: partisanship, fragmented authority, and the relationship between county commissioners and county managers. Includes bibliographical references and index.

New
Menzel, D. C. (1997). **Teaching ethics and values in public administration: Are we making a difference?** *Public Administration Review, 57*(3), 224-230.

Beginning in the 1970s, many schools offering master's degrees in public affairs/administration began requiring students to take ethics courses. This study surveyed the graduates of four such schools to determine whether they faced ethical dilemmas on the job, and whether their ethics education helped them resolve these dilemmas. The

author concluded that although students at three of the schools reported that their classes had helped them resolve ethical problems, overall these classes are not doing enough to address the real-life issues that public administration leaders face.

Morgan, D. R., & Watson, S. S. (1992). **Policy leadership in council-manager cities: Comparing mayor and manager.** *Public Administration Review, 52*(5), 438-446.

A 1987 International City Management survey analyzed the leadership roles and relationships of mayors and managers in more than 1,500 council-manager cities. Power was measured by responsibilities such as: appointing department heads, veto rights, preparing budgets, preparing agendas, and conferring with community leaders. Also considered were roles such as: ceremonial representative, media representative, negotiator, and policy director. It was determined that most mayor-manager relationships worked closely as a team, with mayors dominating in larger cities and managers dominating in smaller cities.

Nutt, P. C., & Backoff, R. W. (1993). **Transforming public organizations with strategic management and strategic leadership.** *Journal of Management, 19*(2), 299-347.

Public-sector organizations are under pressure to initiate changes in their missions and practices. At the same time, their agencies are often politically protected or riddled with inertia. Nutt and Backoff outline strategic management and leadership approaches in actual cases of transformation in a public library, a state bureau of worker's compensation, and other public-sector organizations.

New
Rough, J. (1996). **The wisdom council and responsible leadership.** *Journal for Quality and Participation, 19*(7), 74-79.

According to the author, "government employees are managed by the hardest and most autocratic boss you could imagine"—the public. He suggests that one way government employees can address the public's harmful style of leadership is by forming *Wisdom Councils*—small, randomly selected groups of workers who meet for a short time, dialog, and develop *Statements of Unanimity* for the organization. Examples of Wisdom Councils from a high school, manufacturing plant, and a public works department are used to illustrate how developing an organizational consensus helps workers communicate more effectively with the public.

Schneider, M., Teske, P., & Mintrom, M. (1995). ***Public entrepreneurs: Agents for change in American government.*** Princeton, NJ: Princeton University Press.

Public entrepreneurs are political leaders who spearhead sweeping movements, introduce new policies, and create dynamic change. Entrepreneurs see unfilled needs and create new ways to meet those needs. Entrepreneurs seize opportunities even when the outcome is uncertain. And entrepreneurs assemble teams that have the talents and resources necessary to create a desired change. Includes bibliographical references and index.

Selznick, P. (1983). ***Leadership in administration: A sociological interpretation.*** Berkeley: University of California Press.

This book has become a classic in the art of executive leadership. Selznick's reminder that the true exercise of leadership transcends a concern with mere efficiency is even more appropriate in today's era of quasi-scientific thought about organizations.

Sherwood, F. P. (1992). **Institutionalizing executive development and attendant problems.** *Public Productivity & Management Review, 15*(4), 449-461.

Because of high costs and the limited audience they serve, executive-development programs are highly vulnerable. Comparing state leadership programs in Virginia, Texas, and North Carolina, Sherwood suggests that gubernatorial support makes the difference between success and failure. Getting top-level executives as participants and a leader with expertise in public-sector management create an aura of success. Universities are important resources for collaboration.

Sigelman, L., Sigelman, C. K., & Walkosz, B. J. (1992). **The public and the paradox of leadership: An experimental analysis.** *American Journal of Political Science, 36*(2), 366-385.

Over the years, polls have questioned the public about their preference for leaders who serve as delegates or leaders who serve as trustees. Time, issues, trust, and acceptance of long-standing policies affected responses. A new study asks, "When an elected official's independent judgment conflicts with the desires of his or her constituents, how do people think the official should and will respond?" The study reveals the unavoidable paradox of leaders who are, in reality, followers of their constituents.

New
Smith, G. E., & Huntsman, C. A. (1997). **Reframing the metaphor of the citizen-government relationship: A value-centered perspective.** *Public Administration Review, 57*(4), 309-318.

Past theories of the relationship between citizens and government have included the citizen-as-customer and citizen-as-owner models. Both of these have been criticized—the customer model limits citizens to the role of passive consumers, and government is too large for most individuals to relate to it as owners. The authors propose a value-centered model, which emphasizes the worth of government to its citizens and the investments citizens make. A study of the city government of a Northeast city illustrates how public administrators and leaders can reframe their view of government services and think in terms of their value, not their cost.

Svara, J. H., & Associates. (1994). ***Facilitative leadership in local government: Lessons from successful mayors and chairpersons.*** San Francisco: Jossey-Bass.

In a city run by a council-manager style of government, a mayor has little official power. The same is true for the chairperson of a county commission. Svara shares actual cases where chief elected officials exhibited leadership skills to become more than figureheads in: Decatur, Georgia; Greensboro, North Carolina; Montgomery County, Ohio; Roanoke, Virginia; College Station, Texas; and San Diego, California. Svara's Facilitative Model ranks a mayor's or chairperson's perception as a ceremonial figure, spokesperson, educator, goal setter, and team builder. Includes bibliographical references and index.

New
Terry, L. D. (1995). ***Leadership of public bureaucracies: The administrator as conservator.*** Thousand Oaks, CA: Sage.

Bureaucratic leadership is defined as "institutional leadership in the administration of public bureaucracies within the executive branch of all levels of government." The American public has lost faith in many of these bureaucracies, giving way to discussions about reorganization and privatization. In this book, Terry affirms the legitimacy of bureaucratic leadership by drawing on research from law, management, and sociology. He believes that, when guided by constitutional principles, public administrators can earn public trust and maintain governmental stability. A model of administrative conservatorship defines how bureaucrats can conserve institutional mission, integrity, stakeholder support, and authority. Some of the agencies discussed are: FAA, FBI, Federal Reserve Bank, IRS, NASA, and HUD. This book is part of the "Advances in Public Administration Series," which encourages critical rethinking of public administration. Includes bibliographical references and index.

New
Terry, L. D. (1997). **Public administration and the theater metaphor: The public administrator as villain, hero, and innocent victim.** *Public Administration Review, 57*(1), 53-61.

The theater metaphor has always been a powerful tool in American political discourse. This article describes how Ronald Reagan used the metaphor during the 1980s to portray public administrators as evil villains. The supporters of the administrative state fought back by casting civil servants in the roles of hero and innocent victim, but the author believes that all of these characterizations are dangerous. He says that they limit the abilities of public administrators because "the villain is incapable of positive action, the hero lacks an understanding of limitations to power, and the victim is ignorant of responsibility."

Thomas, J. C. (1995). *Public participation in public decision: New skills and strategies for public managers.* San Francisco: Jossey-Bass.

Since the 1960s, American citizens have become increasingly involved in managing public organizations, and Thomas states that this trend is growing. He wrote this book primarily for public managers seeking guidelines for grassroots collaboration and also for citizen leaders who want to learn about policy-making. He reviews the history of the public-participation movement, theories of public management, and mechanisms for gaining public acceptance. An *Effective Decision Model* suggests criteria for collaboration. Case studies in each chapter enhance the lessons on how to and how not to collaborate. Includes bibliographical references and index.

Van Wart, M. (1993). **Providing a base for executive development at the state level.** *Public Personnel Management, 22*(2), 269-282.

Four levels of training and development—employee, supervisory, management, and executive—have different needs, commitment issues, design concerns, and evaluation problems. Management development programs must be sophisticated, integrating theory and practical examples. Executive development programs are often expensive and handicapped by time pressures. Both levels of programming need to focus on interpersonal and conceptual skills. Existing state programs for managers and executives are briefly described with emphasis on their relationship to the overall human-resource-development system.

Whitaker, G. P., & Jenne, K. (1995). **Improving city managers' leadership.** *State and Local Government Review, 27*(1), 84-94.

In 28,000 American municipalities, the city manager is the top administrator. This article reviews the power of authority typically held by city managers, challenges to their roles as leaders, and the results of sharing authority. The authors suggest that city managers who practice facilitative leadership are most effective. The key elements of facilitative leadership are: promoting staff development, cooperating with elected officials, championing change, committing to community awareness and responsiveness, and facilitating the flow of information.

Young, D. R., Hollister, R. M., Hodgkinson, V. A., & Associates. (1993). *Governing, leading, and managing nonprofit organizations: New insights from research and practice.* San Francisco: Jossey-Bass.

The 1991 Spring Research Forum, cosponsored by Independent Sector, the United Way Strategic Institute, and the Mandel Center for Nonprofit Organizations, examined current research on management and leadership in nonprofit organizations. Board structure and functions, missions, board/staff relations, volunteerism, resource development, public policy, and managing change were the major topics of discussion. The authors of this book are the scholars, educators, and practitioners who shared their research at the forum. Includes bibliographical references and index.

LEADERSHIP PROCESSES AND SKILLS

GENERAL

Agor, W. H. (Ed.). (1989). *Intuition in organizations: Leading and managing productively.* Newbury Park, CA: Sage.

Intuition is not magical or paranormal. It is a brain skill integrating physical, emotional, mental, and spiritual functions. Executives use intuition to create visions, make decisions, predict trends, and solve problems. The *Agor Intuitive Management Survey* evaluates individual intuition level. Charts compare national norms by management level, sex, ethnic group, and occupation. There are case studies, practical guidelines for developing intuitive skills, and an agenda for future research. Includes bibliographical references and index.

Atwater, L. E. (1988). **The relative importance of situational and individual variables in predicting leader behavior: The surprising impact of subordinate trust.** *Group & Organization Studies, 13*(3), 290-310.

Drawing on earlier studies, Atwater's research assesses "the relative influence of personality traits of leaders, job characteristics, expectations of supervisors and subordinates, and trust and loyalty upward upon leader behavior." Examining 98 triads, comprised of a first-line supervisor, the supervisor's immediate supervisor, and one or two subordinates, the research revealed that subordinates' levels of trust and loyalty toward leaders were predictive of supportive leader behavior and that personality traits were predictive of demanding leader behavior. The importance and positive results of developing an atmosphere of trust and loyalty are examined.

Autry, J. A. (1991). *Love and profit: The art of caring leadership.* New York: William Morrow.

A workplace is a neighborhood with interpersonal relationships and the full range of human emotions. A manager who creates a caring environment has employees who grow personally, contribute creatively, and share in the psychic and financial rewards of a job well done. Autry's 28 years of management experience and his poems emphasize success through love and caring. "The more people you take with you, the faster you'll get there and the longer you'll stay."

Autry, J. A. (1994). *Life and work: A manager's search for meaning.* New York: William Morrow.

Autry states that for many years as a manager, he struggled to keep his life and work properly separated.

The realization that a better solution was integration of life and work, of family and employees, led to *Love and Profit: The Art of Caring Leadership* (1991). In this new book, he shares essays, poems, and letters of advice to his children, who are at various stages in their careers. Includes index.

Avolio, B. J., Waldman, D. A., & Yammarino, F. J. (1991). **Leading in the 1990s: The four I's of transformational leadership.** *Journal of European Industrial Training, 15*(4), 9-16.

Transformational leaders promote change to stay competitive. They influence their followers by practicing the four I's: *Individualized consideration* is listening, nurturing, and mentoring followers. *Intellectual stimulation* is using reason to solve problems and valuing followers' creative contributions. *Inspirational motivation* is generating enthusiasm, setting an example as a hard worker, and remaining optimistic through times of crisis. *Idealized influence* is building confidence and trust, achieving desired results, and serving as a behavioral role model.

Bellingham, R., & Cohen, B. (1989). *Leadership: Myths and realities.* Amherst, MA: Human Resource Development Press.

Bellingham and Cohen explore ten myths of old-style leadership and organizational effectiveness. They then offer ten corresponding realities of new-style leadership for comparison. Trends indicate that managers are progressing from doing more to doing better. New leadership skills include thinking creatively, initiating strategic change, and doing the right things right. "Individuals with new ideas and access to information will be the resources of prominence." Includes bibliographical references and index.

Bennis, W. G. (1989). *Why leaders can't lead: The unconscious conspiracy continues.* San Francisco: Jossey-Bass.

"What prevents leaders from taking charge and making changes?" Bennis writes here about the dark side of leadership, especially the problems a leader encounters in attempting to take charge of an organization. He believes we are presently lacking any true leaders. By the author's definition true leaders embody six important virtues: integrity, dedication, magnanimity, humility, openness, and creativity. Includes index.

Benton, P. (1990). ***Riding the whirlwind: Benton on managing turbulence.*** Cambridge, MA: Basil Blackwood.

Benton contrasts today's turbulent environment with historical periods of struggle and change. He examines the leadership skills that brought us from feudalism to the Renaissance to the industrial revolution and those that will take us to the next frontier. Leadership through turbulence requires a calm intellect and a dedication to humane values. Those who can understand new conditions will be the innovators of new approaches and will emerge as the successful leaders of the future. Includes bibliographical references and index.

Bigelow, J. (1992). **Developing managerial wisdom.** *Journal of Management Inquiry, 1*(2), 143-153.

Wisdom is an elusive concept, difficult to define and often not addressed in management development programs. As a management educator, Bigelow strives to incorporate issues regarding wisdom into his courses. In this article, he examines historical attitudes through quotations from high achievers and classic literature. He examines personal growth from naiveté to wisdom and offers a model of wisdom development.

Boyatzis, R. E. (1982). ***The competent manager: A model for effective performance.*** New York: Wiley.

The purpose of this study was to determine which characteristics of managers are related to effective performance in various management jobs in a variety of organizations. An additional purpose was to investigate how managerial competencies affect each other and relate to other aspects of management jobs. Includes bibliographical references and index.

New
Cabana, S., & Parry, C. (1996). **Leadership for turbulent times.** *Journal for Quality and Participation, 19*(2), 76-79.

Leadership and authority are two different things, and in times of change it is essential to maintain your authority while taking leadership actions. This article explains the differences between the two and describes the pitfalls of leading change: how exercising leadership can put your authority at risk, and how more traditional leaders may disagree with your actions. Tips for evaluating whether you have the authority to lead change and how to spot others who see the need for change are also given.

Campbell, D. (1993). **Good leaders are credible leaders.** *Research Technology Management, 36*(5), 29-31.

Credibility is defined as being believable and worthy of trust and is considered the most significant determination of good leadership. A study of 55 R&D managers, using self- and other *Campbell Leadership Index* assessments, indicates that R&D managers are more credible than average managers. But in some cases a considerable gap exists between self- and other ratings. Adjectives describing credible managers are: *considerate, cooperative, optimistic, resilient,* and *well-adjusted.* Adjectives describing those with low credibility are: *cynical, depressed, moody, sarcastic,* and *self-centered.*

Chary, S. N. (1990). **New concepts in leadership effectiveness.** *Leadership and Organization Development Journal, 11*(2), i-iii.

Chary recommends a new model of the effective leader. Important characteristics are commitment to the task at hand and clarity of goals. A leader's style depends on subordinates' commitment and perception of goals, and on the organizational and social environments. A leader's style changes with new tasks, different subordinates, different environments, and changes in commitment.

Clemens, D. S. (1992). ***Leadership literacy: The solution to our present crisis.*** Englewood, CO: Leadership America.

Clemens explores the importance and benefits of a leadership-literate society and identifies particular leadership traits by examining the characteristics of Susan B. Anthony, Harry S. Truman, John F. Kennedy, Lee Iacocca, and Martin Luther King, Jr. He points out that all were goal oriented, looked to themselves to make things happen, believed in the need to break from the status quo, and believed an integral part of human nature is an inherent desire for self-improvement. Includes an index.

New
Davis, B. L., Hellervik, L. W., Skube, C. J., Gebelein, S. H., & Sheard, J. L. (1996). ***Successful manager's handbook: Development suggestions for today's managers*** (1996 ed.). Minneapolis: Personnel Decisions International.

This book contains suggestions for developing competencies in nine areas: administrative skills, communication, interpersonal skills, leadership, motivation, organizational knowledge, organizational strategy, self-management, and thinking skills. The leadership competencies include: providing direction, influence, fostering teamwork, coaching, and championing change. The book is organized around PDI's Wheel of Managerial Success so that it may be used alone or in conjunction with their *Profilor®* 360-degree instrument. Each of the nine sections offers tips for good practice, actions to take in current positions or stretch assignments, recommended readings, and suggested seminars. A section on international resources describes one U.S. seminar with a global focus and 35 management seminars in Canada, Europe, Australia, and Mexico.

Ekvall, G. (1991). **Change-centered leaders: Empirical evidence of a third dimension of leadership.** *Leadership and Organization Development Journal: Special Issue: Leadership and Personal Creativity, 12*(6), 18-23.

This report of a study among 130 Swedish white-collar employees analyzes several dimensions of followers' attitudes toward leadership, including security, satisfaction, and commitment. Three styles of leadership are identified: employee-centered, change-centered, and structure-centered. Each style results in varying attitudes among employees; thus, different styles are needed in different situations.

Evans, P. (1992). **Developing leaders and managing development.** *European Management Journal, 10*(1), 1-9.

Evans divides leaders into two groups: experts who lead by technical authority, and generalists who lead by management skills. Cross-functional mobility, or transferring technical experts into management positions, creates layered career development. By learning to delegate technical functions, a leader can be free to build the business, tackle the competition, and improve organizational performance. Evans determined that successful leaders use their first 100 days to actively listen to subordinates, build relationships, develop goals, and test alternative plans.

Fairholm, G. W. (1994). *Leadership and the culture of trust.* Westport, CT: Praeger.

Fairholm describes leadership as "a process of building a trust environment within which the leader and follower feel free to participate toward accomplishment of mutually valued goals using agreed-upon processes." This book teaches how to build organizations in which work is done collectively and all parties contribute to an ever-changing culture that responds to organizational needs. Chapters include: "Defining Culture," "The Process of Developing Trust," "Shared Governance," and "Integrating Quality." Includes bibliographical references and index.

New
Flin, R. (1996). *Sitting in the hot seat: Leaders and teams for critical incident management.* New York: Wiley.

This book is for and about leaders in life-threatening crisis situations. There are three scenarios: 1) leaders have prior warning as in the cases of riots or storms; 2) they are on-site when the crisis occurs as in ship and plane accidents or industrial disasters; or 3) leaders are called to the scene as in the cases of fires, hostage situations, or explosions. In all cases, Flin claims that leadership training is as important as the planning of mobilization procedures. Military models of command-and-control are

most often used, but Flin recommends that crisis leaders understand and employ other styles such as consultative, coaching, situational, and team leadership. Flin describes some leadership training techniques in the military, aeronautical, fire, police, offshore oil, and nuclear power industries. Includes bibliographical references and index.

New
Fuller, T. (1995). **Does business need leaders?** *Business Horizons, 38*(4), 1-4.

The author addresses the hottest commodity in business today—leadership. Consultants teach it, business periodicals celebrate it, and companies seek it. But the question that is seldom addressed is, "What is the actual value of leadership?" or, stated more clearly, "Is leadership more important or necessary than competent management?" Fuller discusses this question in a guest editorial.

Gabarro, J. J. (1987). *The dynamics of taking charge.* Boston: Harvard Business School Press.

For the new manager, the elements involved in managing an organization, office, department, or special project are explored here. The author has distilled the factors that he suggests make a difference to the new manager in any job situation. The stages of taking charge are also pointed out. The final chapter addresses the pitfalls and stumbling blocks that may occur in the process of taking charge and highlights ways to enhance the process. Appendices offer research studies and information on research methodology and design. Includes bibliography and index.

Good guru guide: Take me to your leader. (1993, December 25; 1994, January 7). *Economist, 329,* 21-26.

The Economist humorously states that the guru profession has become overcrowded. To separate the seers from the charlatans, the writers provide a guide of today's most popular gurus and rate them on the following qualities: influence, originality, intellectual coherence, and the devotion of followers. On the list are Tom Peters, Peter Drucker, Rush Limbaugh, and assorted business notables, scientists, economists, philosophers, and academicians.

Gray, J. W., & Pfeiffer, A. L. (1987). *Skills for leaders.* Reston, VA: National Association of Secondary School Principals.

This book is designed for secondary-school student leaders as a manual for enlarging on and developing leadership potential and skills. This straightforward guide is composed of the following chapters: "The Challenge of Leadership," "Understanding Communication," "Understanding Followers," "Understanding Yourself as a Leader," and "Communication Skills for Leaders." This book could have broad application for educators, management trainers, and human resources personnel who seek a concise and easy-to-follow introduction to leadership programming. Includes a bibliography.

Hackman, M. Z., Furniss, A. H., Hills, M. J., & Paterson, T. J. (1992). **Perceptions of gender-role characteristics and transformational and transactional leadership behaviours.** *Perceptual and Motor Skills, 75*(1), 311-319.

Using the leadership model of Bass (1985) and the gender model of Bem (1974), this study compares perceived gender-role characteristics with two leadership styles. A questionnaire was answered by 71 men and 82 women students enrolled in an undergraduate management course. Results indicate that transformational leadership requires a balance of masculine traits such as task awareness and feminine traits such as interpersonal awareness.

Hitt, W. D. (1993). *The model leader: A fully functioning person.* Columbus, OH: Battelle Press.

The idea that a theory is only valuable when it can be put into practice is once again evident in Hitt's latest work. He defines "the model leader" (first and foremost a fully functioning person) in terms of 25 competencies, each brought to life through quotations from leading thinkers on leadership and through anecdotes. After defining the "model leader," he presents a Leadership Agenda to help readers develop a personal action plan to improve their own leadership competency. Includes bibliographical references and index.

New
Hooijberg, R. (1996). **A multidirectional approach toward leadership: An extension of the concept of behavioral complexity.** *Human Relations, 49*(7), 917-946.

This is a report of a study done on 534 middle managers in a large manufacturing firm and in the public utility industry. Peers, subordinates, and superiors responded to a questionnaire about each manager's behavior repertoire and leadership effectiveness. The behavior repertoire includes four functions: people leadership, adaptive leadership, stability leadership, and task leadership. Data imply that effective leaders need to have a broad repertoire of leadership functions and the ability to vary their behavior depending on their various interactions.

Javidan, M., & Dastmalchian, A. (1993). **Assessing senior executives: The impact of context on their roles.** *Journal of Applied Behavioral Science, 29*(3), 328-342.

The authors cite previous executive leadership research that used context-free methodologies. In this study, 1,687 mid- to senior-level managers in three Canadian organizations were examined through a multiple-contingency approach. Participants were asked to rate their superiors'

competence in five roles: mobilizer, ambassador, driver, auditor, and servant. Results indicated that senior managers were perceived to be more competent in the five roles than mid-level managers. Results also indicated no difference between perceptions of senior managers in public versus private organizations.

Kets de Vries, M. F. R. (1989). **Leaders who self-destruct: The causes and cures.** *Organizational Dynamics, 17*(4), 5-17.

The author identifies three psychological forces (transference, fear of success, and isolation from reality) that may occur when an individual assumes a position of leadership. Aggressive behavior, paranoid reaction, depression, and substance abuse are among the stress reactions discussed. To prevent the occurrence of harmful reactions, the author suggests that executives learn to identify potential signs of trouble and that board members take an active role in noting warning signs. He also recommends that executives have access to training programs that provide nonthreatening environments for individuals to discuss their working experiences.

Kets de Vries, M. F. R. (1989). *Prisoners of leadership.* New York: Wiley.

Kets de Vries explores the inner world of the leader, probing into the psychoanalytical side of leadership behavior. Using a "psycho-biographical" approach and drawing on case illustrations and studies of leaders in action, his book examines leadership success and failure at the psychic level. "I want the reader to understand that the leader's task is paradoxical: at one level the leader appeals to the rational capacities of the followers, while at another his or her message is aimed directly at their unconscious." Includes bibliography and index.

Kim, W. C., & Mauborgne, R. A. (1992). **Parables of leadership.** *Harvard Business Review, 70*(4), 123-128.

The Asian technique of using parables to teach the essential wisdom of life is employed here to teach the essential qualities of leadership. Five one-page parables tell of characters who learn to listen beyond spoken words to the hearts of others, to remain humble, to commit to a purpose, to see truth from different viewpoints, and to trust in the strength of a team.

Kouzes, J. M., & Posner, B. Z. (1993). *Credibility: How leaders gain and lose it, why people demand it.* San Francisco: Jossey-Bass.

Based on surveys of more than 15,000 people, 400 case studies, and 40 in-depth interviews, this book explains why leader credibility is the cornerstone of corporate performance and global competitiveness. Built on the relationship between leader and constituents, credibility results from honesty, boldness of vision, courage of conviction, understanding, respect, and energetic involvement. Six disciplines help a leader achieve credibility: self-discovery, appreciating others' differences, shared values, competence, purpose, and hope. Includes bibliographical references and indexes.

Leslie, J. B., & Van Velsor, E. (1996). *A look at derailment today: North America and Europe.* Greensboro, NC: Center for Creative Leadership.

The Center for Creative Leadership has been studying executive derailment for 12 years, first among U.S. executives and most recently among executives from the European Union. This book compares the factors that contribute to derailment and success over time and across cultures. Four enduring themes have emerged as predictors of derailment: 1) problems with interpersonal relationships, 2) failure to meet business objectives, 3) failure to build and lead teams, and 4) inability to change during times of transition. Includes bibliographical references.

McCall, M. W., Jr., & Lombardo, M. M. (1983, February). **What makes a top executive?** *Psychology Today*, 26-31.

This article looks at reasons why executives derailed: inability to adapt to a new boss, overdependence on a mentor, inability to think strategically, and failure to staff effectively. The authors further compare the behavioral differences between the arrivers (people who make it to the top) and the derailers.

Mintzberg, H. (1973). *The nature of managerial work.* New York: Harper & Row.

Mintzberg has sought to identify the whole range of relationships that constitute the manager's world in the contemporary organization, and as a result his conclusions have great worth in a world dependent on leadership skills. An identification of the behavioral skills combined with an overview of how managers manage is presented. Characteristics of managerial work, work roles, variation in work, science and the manager's job, and the future of managerial work are topics covered. Includes a bibliography.

Mitrani, A., Dalziel, M., & Fitt, D. (1992). *Competency based human resource management: Value-driven strategies for recruitment, development and reward.* London: Kogan Page.

Competencies are the motives, attitudes, knowledge, and behavior found in superior performers. In the workplace, management competencies lead to continuous improvement and organizational success. In this book, leading

European HRD specialists define the competencies of budding managers for the purpose of identification and management development. This book received the 1993 European Management Book of the Year award. Includes bibliographical references and index.

Mumford, M. D., Gessner, T. L., Connelly, M. S., O'Connor, J. A., & Clifton, T. C. (1993). **Leadership and destructive acts: Individual and situational influences.** *Leadership Quarterly, 4*(2), 115-147.

A leader's personality, values, and beliefs affect decision making, organizational goal setting, and long-term performance. Situational forces may exert a strong influence on destructive acts, but an individual chooses whether to act destructively. A study reveals characteristics that contribute to destructive behavior: low self-esteem, negative belief in humanity, lack of empathy, narcissism, self-aggrandizement, fear, dominant power motives, and social alienation.

Nanus, B. (1986). **Leadership: Doing the right thing.** *Bureaucrat, 15*(3), 9-12.

This article explores the differences between leadership and management. Findings from interviews with 90 well-known leaders from business and the public sector led to the formulation of four major skills shared by effective leaders: a results orientation, articulating and communicating meaning, earning trust by taking stands and sticking to them, and knowing one's own strengths and weaknesses.

Nanus, B. (1992, September/October). **Visionary leadership: How to re-vision the future.** *Futurist, 26,* 20-25.

Leaders must be committed to their vision, but they must be equally committed to meeting change. Nanus offers suggestions that help leaders devise and revise visions. He recommends that leaders: 1) recruit a vision task force, 2) be realistic, 3) reduce the possibility of unpleasant surprises, 4) be on the lookout for organizational inertia, 5) concentrate on things other than the bottom line, 6) be flexible and patient in implementing the vision; and 7) never become complacent.

New
Posner, B., & Kouzes J. (1996). **Ten lessons for leaders and leadership developers.** *Journal of Leadership Studies, 3*(3), 3-10.

The authors of *The Leadership Challenge* and *Credibility* discuss ten lessons in leadership for individuals and organizations. Based on a personal-best leadership study, the conclusions of the lessons reveal not only that leadership is an observable, learnable set of practices, but also that the belief that leadership can't be learned is a far more powerful deterrent to development than is the nature of the leadership process itself.

New
Prestwood, D., & Schumann, P. (1997, January/February). **Seven new principles of leadership.** *Futurist, 31,* 68.

Leadership is no longer a position, it is a state of mind. We must all develop our leadership capability to its fullest in order for our organizations and institutions to be transformed. Developing leadership in ourselves and other individuals requires an understanding of seven basic principles, which are listed and discussed in this short article.

Quigley, J. V. (1993). *Vision: How leaders develop it, share it, and sustain it.* New York: McGraw-Hill.

The subject of corporate vision is a hot topic for the 1990s, but many corporations still lack a vision that has broad-based commitment. Quigley outlines a plan for the formation of a new corporate vision, widespread communication techniques, stewardship, renewal, and sustaining strategy. He addresses the basic human need for meaning and fulfillment in the workplace. Solutions called *Rx for Leaders* throughout each chapter offer quick tips for easy reference. Examples of successful visions at work highlight the lessons. Includes an index.

New
Richardson, J. (1997). **Strategic leadership: From fragmented thinking to interdisciplinary perspectives.** *Leadership Journal: Women in Leadership—Sharing the Vision, 1*(2), 91-100.

According to Richardson, a community activist and professor of environmental studies, leaders today have "developed fragmented perspectives" and lack a "comprehensive understanding" of the problems they face. She uses examples from her experience in the environmental movement, including the debate over the management of Lake Champlain, to illustrate how destructive a fragmented approach can be. This article encourages leaders to use a holistic, strategic approach to solving problems and offers ten suggestions on how to do this, including know thyself, share knowledge with others, and know the local culture. Includes bibliographical references.

New
Robbins, S. P., & Hunsaker, P. L. (1996). *Training in interpersonal skills: TIPS for managing people at work* (2nd ed.). Upper Saddle River, NJ: Prentice Hall.

This textbook supports the notion that skills training supersedes theoretical understanding. The TIPS learning model contains ten actions: assess basic skill level, review key concepts, test knowledge, identify behaviors to learn,

observe behaviors, practice behaviors, assess deficiencies, test understanding, do experiential learning exercises, and develop an action plan. These actions are applied to leadership skills in the chapters: "Self-awareness," "Providing Feedback," "Empowering," "Coaching," and "Building Teams."

Rodrigues, C. A. (1993). **Developing three-dimensional leaders.** *Journal of Management Development, 11*(3), 4-11.

Rodrigues proposes that three basic leadership styles are required for the varying situations encountered by leaders on a daily basis. The *innovator* is dominated by a need for achievement, exhibits entrepreneurial behaviors, is a nonconformist, and performs well in a start-up or crisis situation. The *implementor* is assertive, confident, a systematic and methodical planner, and brings necessary structure for growth and renewal. The *pacifier* maintains the status quo and offers support and development to staff. Rodrigues shares a questionnaire for measuring leadership abilities in each of these three styles.

New
Rosen, R. H., & Brown, P. B. (1996). *Leading people: Transforming business from the inside out.* New York: Viking.

The authors contend that leading is hard work made possible by adopting eight principles: vision, trust, participation, learning, diversity, creativity, integrity, and community. In-depth interviews with 36 leaders and reviews of their organizations' documents, awards, speeches, and videos paint profiles of each leader's unique strengths. James DePreist, conductor and music director of the Oregon Symphony Orchestra, serves as an example of a visionary leader. Douglas G. Myers, executive director of the San Diego Zoo, provides a lesson in trust. The story of Alan Mulally, senior vice president of Boeing's Airplane Development division, illustrates the value of participation and teamwork. The work of Shirley DeLibero, executive director of the New Jersey Transit Corporation, provides a lesson in building community. The remaining leaders each have a leadership lesson to teach based on one of the eight principles. Includes index.

New
Rothwell, W. J. (1994). *Effective succession planning: Ensuring leadership continuity and building talent from within.* New York: AMACOM.

For any organization to survive, it must have competent and continuous leadership. In this book, Rothwell presents a seven-step plan for ensuring systematic succession: 1) make the case for change, 2) get started, 3) refine the program, 4) appraise the short-term needs,

5) project long-term needs, 6) build from inside, and 7) build from outside. A case study from a major insurance company, recommended book and software lists, and over 60 worksheets, graphs, and forms are included to make this book a practical guide for companies planning to create their own leadership-succession program. An index is also included.

New

Sapienza, A. M. (1995). *Managing scientists: Leadership strategies in research and development.* New York: Wiley-Liss.

This book is for managers who administer R&D organizations and direct the work of creative scientists. Their leadership challenges are unique—the cognitive work of scientists is unpredictable, and scientists are often trained to be solo contributors. Sapienza discusses methods for improving human interaction and, thus, inspiration and collaboration among these knowledge workers. There are techniques for communicating, understanding organizational culture, designing systems to foster innovation, and managing change. Exercises help the reader identify personal leadership styles as well as strengths and weaknesses. Includes bibliographical references and index.

Sayles, L. R. (1989). *Leadership: Managing in real organizations.* New York: McGraw-Hill.

Although many aspiring managers and business school graduates develop an understanding of the goals of management and their outcomes within the dynamics of an organization, the *how* of pursuing goals and outcomes is often the stumbling block for managers. The author provides a detailed examination of managing in the real world. He points out the intricate navigational skills required in managing within assigned areas of responsibility, as well as the negotiating skills needed for working with other divisions of an organization, which may indirectly contribute to one's success or failure. Includes bibliographical references and index.

Sayles, L. R. (1993). *The working leader: The triumph of high performance over conventional management principles.* New York: Free Press.

Astute working leaders do not presume systems are designed efficiently, nor do they see "customer consciousness" or "quality consciousness" as compartmentalized activities. Through case studies, Sayles shows that leaders who concentrate on work-flow relationships between jobs, functions, and departments can increase the sense of responsibility and motivation among subordinates. This effective management of work systems leads to high performance in quality, efficiency, and service. Includes bibliographical references and index.

Sayles, L. R. (1995). *Leadership for turbulent times.* Greensboro, NC: Center for Creative Leadership.

This report is an outcome of a 1994 Center for Creative Leadership conference, "New Demands for Leadership: Responding to Turbulence." The behavioral-science researchers, leadership trainers, corporate executives, and consultants who attended the conference identified new leadership skills and perspectives for a radically changing business environment. Eight themes emerged: teamwork, removing boundaries, the employer-employee relationship, values, technology, strategic planning, learning, and culture. From these themes, Sayles draws implications for research and training agendas. Includes bibliographical references.

New

Sayles, L. R. (1996). *High performance leadership: Creating value in a world of change.* Portland, OR: Productivity Press.

This pocket-sized book imparts leadership advice in a one-hour read. It is an updated and synthesized version of Sayles's book *The Working Leader* (McGraw-Hill, 1993). The reader is reminded of commonsense "old style" leadership skills and introduced to new competencies for changing work environments. Includes brief bibliographical notes.

Stumpf, S. A., & Mullen, T. P. (1991). **Strategic leadership: Concepts, skills, style and process.** *Journal of Management Development, 10*(1), 42-53.

Based on teaching experience, research, observation, and discussions with thousands of managers, the authors have identified four elements of strategic leadership. The first element includes the concepts of mission, vision, and strategy. The second element includes skills and competencies, knowing the market, and overcoming threats. Personal style and the process of strategic leadership make up the final element. In a metaphor, each element represents a leg supporting the table that holds a business plan. With any leg missing, the table is not supported.

New

Wall, B., Solum, R. S., & Sobol, M. R. (1992). *The visionary leader: From mission statement to a thriving organization, here's your blueprint for building an inspired, cohesive customer-oriented team.* Rocklin, CA: Prima Publishing.

An organization's vision, clearly defined in a mission statement, has increased importance in the chaos of organizational flattening and downsizing. The authors first examine the economic and sociological changes that are currently affecting American business. Then they offer practical advice for designing and communicating a vision that defines shared purpose, shared values, and guidelines for action. Each chapter includes a leadership action plan to guide readers along each step. Once an organization's vision is in place, leaders must promote continuous cultural improvement that includes: measuring how well the organization works with the vision, management-team action planning that solves problems in cultural issues, and task-force problem solving that helps build participation. Includes an index.

Whetten, D. A., & Cameron, K. S. (1984). *Developing management skills.* Glenview, IL: Scott, Foresman.

This textbook was written for management courses that combine conceptual learning with practical, interpersonal experience. Chapters focus on nine critical management skills, including developing self-awareness, gaining power and influence, and managing conflict. Each chapter includes a pre-assessment (test or role play), conceptual text material explaining behavioral guidelines, case studies, exercises, and assignments. Includes bibliographies and index.

Wofford, J. C. (1994). **Getting inside the leader's head: A cognitive processes approach to leadership.** *SAM Advanced Management Journal, 59*(3), 4-9.

Cognitive processes are important functions for managers, especially in performance appraisal, reward, discipline, communication, interpersonal conflict, and training. This case study follows a newly appointed manager of a spinning mill in India. His negotiations and policy development with union leaders are used to follow the cognitive processes of management.

Zaccaro, S. J., Gilbert, J. A., Thor, K. K., & Mumford, M. D. (1991). **Leadership and social intelligence: Linking social perspectives and behavioral flexibility to leader effectiveness.** *Leadership Quarterly: Special Issue: Individual Differences and Leadership: I, 2*(4), 317-342.

Successful leaders have two characteristics of social intelligence: social perceptiveness and behavioral flexibility. This paper proposes that those who are considered successful leaders: 1) have increased knowledge structures regarding people and situations, 2) better understand and respond to the critical social elements of organizational problems, and 3) grasp more quickly the implications of social affordances inside and outside the organizational environment.

Zimmerman, J. H. (1993). **The demand of the future: "The complete executive."** *Human Resource Management, 32*(2&3), 385-397.

To deal with rapid technological change and increased information availability, executives of the future must

combine leadership and management competencies. This complete executive will provide an organizational road map and motivate employees to maximize their contributions at every level of the organization. Zimmerman recommends setting aside time for reflection to gain understanding of oneself and others.

CHARISMA

New
Aberbach, D. (1996). *Charisma in politics, religion and the media: Private trauma, public ideals.* Washington Square: New York University Press.

This book describes the public images, often created by the media, of famous people who have or had charismatic appeal. The author draws surprising parallels in the lives of individuals who have nothing in common except their charismatic personalities. Among the people studied are: Adolph Hitler; Marilyn Monroe; Charlie Chaplin; John Lennon; Indian religious leader, Krishnamurti; German philosopher and author, Martin Buber; and Hebrew poet, Chaim Nachman Bialik. Includes a bibliography, name index, and subject index.

Barnes, D. F. (1978). **Charisma and religious leadership: An historical analysis.** *Journal for the Scientific Study of Religion, 17*, 1-18.

A theory of charismatic leadership is proposed that explores conditions under which it emerges. Leaders arise in periods of social change when new religious beliefs may be formalized. Biographies of 15 charismatic leaders are included in this article.

Bass, B. M. (1985). *Leadership and performance beyond expectations.* New York: Free Press.

Bass discusses the role of the transformational or charismatic leader—who these leaders are, how they get results, and why their leadership often exceeds all expectable limits. He attempts to close the gap between the work of social and organizational psychologists, whose focus has been on small groups and institutional settings, and that of political scientists and psychohistorians, who have done most of the important studies of world-class leaders. Includes bibliography and index.

Bass, B. M., Waldman, D. A., Avolio, B. J., & Bebb, M. (1987). **Transformational leadership and the falling dominoes effect.** *Group & Organization Studies, 12*(1), 73-87.

This investigation examined the practice of transformational leadership (TL) at two levels of management in a New Zealand government agency. TL was defined as the extent to which a manager is seen as charismatic, as treating each subordinate as an individual, and as intellectually stimulating. Implications were drawn concerning the importance of developing TL abilities at upper levels of management to enhance the likelihood of such leadership at lower levels.

New
Behling, O., & McFillen, J. M. (1996). **A synchretical model of charismatic/transformational leadership.** *Group & Organization Management, 21*(2), 163-191.

This article offers a synchretical model, a model that reconciles differences among existing models, of charismatic/transformational leadership. Six attributes of leader behavior are generally agreed upon: displaying empathy, dramatizing mission, projecting self-assurance, enhancing image, assuring followers of competency, and providing opportunities to experience success. When these leader attributes are combined with three key followers' beliefs —inspiration, awe, and empowerment—a charismatic/transformational relationship emerges. The authors describe the development, validity, and reliability of paper-and-pencil instruments they designed to empirically test the model. In the appendices are the *Follower Belief Questionnaire–Form II* and *Attributes of Leader Behavior Questionnaire–Form II.* Includes bibliographical references.

Bryman, A. (1992). *Charisma and leadership in organizations.* Newbury Park, CA: Sage.

Bryman reviews charisma theory and research from Weber to the "New Leadership" perspective. Physical characteristics, the exchange between leader and follower, vision, and routinization are illustrated by examples. Bryman cautions against embracing the New Leadership approach and suggests areas for future research. Includes bibliographical references and index.

Conger, J. A., & Kanungo, R. N. (1987). **Toward a behavioral theory of charismatic leadership in organizational settings.** *Academy of Management Review, 12*(4), 637-647.

The authors identify a lack of serious research in the area of charismatic leadership. They feel that a systematic conceptual framework is required. Drawing from political science, sociology, social psychology, and research in the field of organizational leadership, the authors developed a model "linking organizational contexts to charismatic leadership." As in any form of leadership, charismatic leadership is considered an observable behavioral process. The model is constructed on the belief that charisma is an attribution made by followers who observe the role of leader within the context of the organization. Thirteen research hypotheses are presented for future study.

Conger, J. A., & Kanungo, R. N. (1992). **Perceived behavioural attributes of charismatic leadership.** *Canadian Journal of Behavioural Science, 24*(1), 86-102.

A study of eight behaviors attributed to charismatic leadership in organizational settings supports a model proposed in 1987 (see above). Behaviors include: reforming, sensing needs, advocating visions, inspiring, taking risks, demonstrating initiative. Over 100 mid-level supervisors completed a survey of 41 questions on a six-point scale. Results indicate that charismatic leadership can be studied as a dimension of leadership and also demonstrate the validity of the behavioral model, providing both predictive convergent and discriminant validity tests of the construct.

Conger, J. A., Kanungo, R. N., & Associates. (1988). *Charismatic leadership: The elusive factor in organizational effectiveness.* San Francisco: Jossey-Bass.

This work is a gathering of thoughts and research by experts from various fields: organizational development, management, psychology, and sociology. The rationale: to provide a broad analysis of the concept of charismatic leadership. The contributors attempt to bring clarity to the problems and differences in understanding the meaning of charismatic leadership. What is it? How does it develop? How might it be cultivated? The authors argue that charismatic leadership can be trained. They offer training approaches and provide a questionnaire that can be used to identify individuals, in any setting, with the potential for charismatic leadership. Includes bibliographies and index.

Den Hartog, D. N., Koopman, P. L., & Van Muijen, J. J. (1995). **Charismatic leadership: A state of the art.** *Journal of Leadership Studies, 2*(4), 35-49.

The authors examine controversial arguments of charisma by asking: Does charisma exist only in the eye of the beholder? Can charisma be learned or measured? Is charisma a phenomenon of exceptional persons or is there such a thing as everyday charisma? Is charisma always beneficial or is there a dark side? They conclude that there are significant differences in the perception of charisma and that additional research is needed in the area of rhetoric and situational analysis.

New
Downton, J. V., Jr. (1973). *Rebel leadership: Commitment and charisma in the revolutionary process.* New York: Free Press.

Downton explains leadership in social systems in this early work about followers searching for identity through transactional relations with charismatic leaders. Rebel leaders who influence mass movements gain authority from the commitment and trust of their followers. Downton compares his theory with Weber's theory of charismatic heroes, which is described in Gerth and Mills, *From Max Weber: Essays in Sociology* (Oxford, 1946). Includes a bibliography.

Fagen, R. R. (1965). **Charismatic authority and the leadership of Fidel Castro.** *Western Political Quarterly*, *18*(2), 275-284.

Fagen notes that the appellation of *charismatic* has been applied quite freely to various leaders with a variety of meanings. His purpose in this article is to take a first step toward rational explication of the concept of charisma and to show, using Fidel Castro as an example, how the concept might be used in empirical inquiry.

New
Gabriel, Y. (1997). **Meeting God: When organizational members come face to face with the supreme leader.** *Human Relations*, *50*(4), 315-342.

This article focuses on the religious or literary theme of meeting God and relates that theme to the experience of an organizational member who meets the organization's top leader. From a psychoanalytic view, Gabriel describes the primal fantasies that organizational members project onto their leaders. He finds four core fantasies: 1) the leader cares for his or her followers, 2) the leader is accessible, 3) the leader is omnipotent and omniscient, and 4) the leader has a legitimate claim to lead others. Includes bibliographical references.

Hogan, R., Raskin, R., & Fazzini, D. (1990). **How charisma cloaks incompetence.** *Personnel Journal*, *69*(5), 73-76.

Employees promoted into management positions or applicants who interview well share common personality traits. Intelligence, confidence, charm, energy, and assertiveness are apparent. The authors describe three types of ineffective managers with personality traits that are not so easily apparent. The *betrayer* uses negative information against associates. The *high likability floater* has no agenda and accomplishes little. The *narcissist* is motivated by a need for recognition, not achievement.

Hopfl, H. (1992). **The making of the corporate acolyte: Some thoughts on charismatic leadership and the reality of organizational commitment.** *Journal of Management Studies, 29*(1), 23-33.

Corporate acolytes are middle managers who are expected to serve and reinforce their corporate culture. Charismatic leaders ask for total commitment from these acolytes. In reality, middle managers shift between identification with and rejection of their organizations and conflicting life worlds.

House, R. J., & Howell, J. M. (1992). **Personality and charismatic leadership.** *Leadership Quarterly: Special Issue: Individual Differences and Leadership: III, 3*(2), 81-108.

Personalized charisma is self-aggrandized, non-egalitarian, and exploitive. Socialized charisma is collectively oriented, egalitarian, and non-exploitive. Machiavellian, narcissistic, and authoritarian personalities seek power for personal motives at the expense of others. Self-confident, nurturing, sensitive, and considerate personalities can transform followers' needs and aspirations from self to the greater good of the whole.

House, R. J., Spangler, W. D., & Woycke, J. (1991). **Personality and charisma in the U.S. presidency: A psychological theory of leader effectiveness.** *Administrative Science Quarterly, 36*(3), 364-396.

A study of 39 U.S. presidents tests a general model of leader effectiveness by measuring personality characteristics, charisma, crises, age, and need for power. Results indicate that personality and charisma do affect leader effectiveness. The authors discuss the organizational implications of their findings.

Howell, J. M., & Avolio, B. J. (1992). **The ethics of charismatic leadership: Submission or liberation?** *Academy of Management Executive*, *6*(2), 43-54.

Why are some charismatic leaders beneficial to their followers while others are destructive? Charismatic leaders powerfully communicate their vision, inspire extraordinary performance, build trust, and promote creativity. Yet ethical standards vary. In-depth interviews were conducted with 25 leaders regarding values, ethics, attitudes toward followers, use of power, communication, and consideration.

Johnson, D. P. (1979). **Dilemmas of charismatic leadership: The case of the People's Temple.** *Sociological Analysis, 40*, 315-323.

A proposed model of charismatic leadership is used to interpret the power of Jim Jones's People's Temple, which ended in a mass suicide in Jonestown, Guyana. Charismatic leaders are continually seeking ways in which to reinforce their power.

New
Kirkpatrick, S. A., & Locke, E. A. (1996). **Direct and indirect effects of three core charismatic leadership components on performance and attitudes.** *Journal of Applied Psychology, 81*(1), 36-51.

This article reports on a laboratory simulation designed to determine if charismatic leadership positively affects follower outcomes. The authors studied seven theories of transformational and charismatic leadership to identify three core competencies: vision, vision implementation through task cues, and communication style. Two actors portrayed leaders—one as a charismatic leader and one without vision, task cues, or charismatic communication style. University students participated as followers of both leaders. The most significant finding is a leader's vision strongly affects a follower's intellectual stimulation, inspiration, congruence with a leader's values, trust in a leader, and perception of a leader as charismatic. Includes bibliographical references.

Lindholm, C. L. (1990). *Charisma.* Cambridge, MA: Basil Blackwell.

Adolph Hitler, Charles Manson, and Jim Jones. These three were able to transform the lives of their followers and to change the course of history. What power was present in all three that allowed them to lead others past the fundamental laws of self-preservation? Lindholm uses the theories of Hume, Mill, Weber, Durkheim, and Freud to explore the depths of the human agency and social change. He argues that there is a deep human desire to escape from the limits of self and that charismatic leaders provide the avenue required. The question becomes how to harness the positive, productive potential of this power to effect constructive change. Includes bibliographical references and index.

Newman, R. G. (1983). **Thoughts on superstars of charisma: Pipers in our midst.** *American Journal of Orthopsychiatry, 53*(2), 201-208.

This article discusses the effects of charisma in the use and misuse of power, using R. Browning's (1895) version of *The Pied Piper*. The interdependent relationship between a leader and his or her followers is explored, and the psychological implications of these forces for society and its institutions are addressed.

O'Connor, H., Mumford, M. D., Clifton, T. C., Gessner, T. L., & Connelly, M. S. (1995). **Charismatic leaders and destructiveness: An histriometric study.** *Leadership Quarterly, 6*(4), 529-555.

A discussion of personalized versus socialized charisma and a sampling of real-world leaders identifies traits of destructive charismatic behavior: high need for power,

object beliefs, negative life themes, outcome uncertainty, narcissism, and fear. Speeches of 82 national leaders were analyzed and compared to the subjects' psychological profiles of behavior and harm or influence on society. Examples of socialized leaders are: Andrew Carnegie, Sir Winston Churchill, Martin Luther King, Jr., and Joseph Pulitzer. Examples of personalized or destructive leaders are: Idi Amin, Jim Bakker, Fidel Castro, John DeLorean, Adolph Hitler, and Jimmy Hoffa.

Pauchant, T. C. (1991). **Transferential leadership: Towards a more complex understanding of charisma in organizations.** *Organization Studies: Special Issue: Interpreting Organizational Leadership, 12*(4), 507-527.

The author introduces a concept for researching the subjective and affective relationship established in the leader-follower dyad. A model of self-psychology, incorporating self-deflating, self-inflating, and positive self-regard structures, indicates leader-follower transference with successful or problematic outcomes. The author suggests future research to establish a methodology and a framework for understanding charismatic leadership.

New
Pillai, R. (1996). **Crisis and the emergence of charismatic leadership in groups: An experimental investigation.** *Journal of Applied Social Psychology, 26*(6), 543-562.

Pillai claims that many theories of charismatic leadership focus too heavily on the personal attributes of the charismatic leader and not enough on the situation that fosters the leader's emergence. He believes that crisis situations are important to the emergence of charismatic leadership. This article reports on a laboratory study of 96 undergraduate university students. Sixteen groups of six members each participated in a simulated crisis situation to provide data on leader emergence and follower reactions. Pillai concluded that a crisis highlights the inferential and attributional process among followers. Includes bibliographical references.

Puffer, S. M. (1990). **Attributions of charismatic leadership: The impact of decision style, outcome, and observer characteristics.** *Leadership Quarterly, 1*(3), 177-192.

One hundred three observers participated in a case study of one manager's decision style and the outcome of his decision. Observers rated the manager's expertise, risk-taking, and charisma against the final outcome. Puffer concluded that intuitive decision style and successful outcome have great impact on observers' attribution of charismatic leadership.

Richardson, R. J., & Thayer, S. K. (1993). *The charisma factor: How to develop your natural leadership ability.* Englewood Cliffs, NJ: Prentice Hall.

This blueprint outlines the steps to take for developing a charismatic aura. Skills that can be learned are: communicating with the whole body, inspiring emotions, and creating a link with others. Speeches, stories, and experiences of charismatic leaders throughout history are used to illustrate each step. The authors insist that goal setting, corporate support, and ethics are prerequisites to influencing others.

New
Sankowsky, D. (1995). **The charismatic leader as narcissist: Understanding the abuse of power.** *Organizational Dynamics*, 23(4), 57-71.

Research on leadership today often focuses on the empowerment of followers, but here Sankowsky describes how leaders can misuse their power. This article concentrates on one form of power, symbolic status, in which leaders act as parent figures and guide the belief systems of their followers. Sankowsky defines symbolic status, explains how leaders use it to manipulate their followers, and describes typical follower response to these charismatic leaders. Examples of such leaders, from Steve Jobs at Apple to Michael Eisner at Disney, are used to illustrate the concepts. Includes bibliographical references.

New
Sellers, P. (1996). **What exactly is charisma?** *Fortune*, 133(1), 68-75.

This article attempts to answer the question: Why is charisma so important, and what can someone do to have more of it? The answer to the second half is—probably not much, you either have it or you don't, but defining what it is and measuring its importance is relatively easy. This *Fortune* article provides examples from NetScape, Sears, and the NBA.

Shamir, B. (1991). **The charismatic relationship: Alternative explanations and predictions.** *Leadership Quarterly*, 2(2), 81-104.

Various theories explain the effects of charismatic leaders on their followers. Psychoanalytic theories assume that early family experiences cause adults to manifest early parental relationships later in adult relationships. Sociological-symbolic theories are based on values, the need for order and meaning, and one's connection to society. Attribution-based theories posit that a leader's behavior has a profound effect on followers. Self-concept theories propose transformational processes to increase the intrinsic value of effort, empowerment, goal accomplishment, and commitment.

Tommerup, P. (1990). **Stories about an inspiring leader: "Rapture" and the symbolics of employee fulfillment.** *American Behavioral Scientist*, 33(3), 374-385.

The staff at a university conference and catering department is identified as having an exceptionally high degree of job satisfaction, labeled as "rapture." Staff members experience a sense of order, appreciation for their individual and collective efforts, and effective leadership. The head of this department is perceived by his employees as a leader with a deep sense of values, a catalyst for inspiration and ideas, and a source of energy. Employees enjoy telling stories of their leader's actions, which are "behavioral recipes" for success.

Weed, F. J. (1993). **The MADD queen: Charisma and the founder of Mothers Against Drunk Driving.** *Leadership Quarterly,* 4(3/4), 329-346.

Candy Lightner, the charismatic founder of MADD, is featured in this examination of the pros and cons of charismatic leadership. Lightner's personal tragedy fueled the growth of an active and well-funded national organization. Lightner became a symbol of bereavement turned into moral mission. The same traits that helped her inspire others to build a large, complex organization are the traits that interfered with the routine management of that organization and caused Lightner's loss of influence and leadership position.

COMMUNICATION, FEEDBACK, AND NEGOTIATION

Armstrong, D. M. (1992). *Managing by storying around.* New York: Doubleday.

At Armstrong International, Inc., management by storytelling had been used with success for five years. Armstrong shares his philosophy for this simple, fun, and memorable way to pass along corporate traditions, train new employees, recognize special efforts, recruit, and sell. He shares many of his favorite stories, including the morals of each story, to prove that there are valuable lessons to be learned from this method of management.

Barge, J. K. (1989). **Leadership as a medium: A leaderless group discussion model.** *Communication Quarterly*, 37(4), 237-247.

A study of 190 undergraduate students analyzed the relationship between leader behavior and group productivity and compared that to group leadership behavior and group productivity. Rated on task orientation, dynamism, goal formulation, direction, and other leader behaviors, the study found that no individual leader behavior significantly influenced productivity at a greater level than the behavior of groups without leaders.

Caroselli, M. (1990). *The language of leadership.* Amherst, MA: Human Resource Development Press.

Fortune 500 executives claim the most important skill for leadership success is the ability to communicate well. Caroselli analyzes the language of ten leaders, including Lee Iacocca, Mario Cuomo, Peter Drucker, and Tom Peters. Exercises and checklists at the end of each chapter serve as reference and review. Diagrams illustrate leadership concepts. Caroselli asserts that communication skills can be acquired through practice.

Conger, J. A. (1991). **Inspiring others: The language of leadership.** *Academy of Management Executive, 5*(1), 31-45.

There's a critical link between a leader's vision and his or her ability to powerfully communicate its essence. To motivate and inspire, a leader must be a rhetorician. Conger recommends that executives learn basic rhetorical skills. Framing is the process of defining the purpose of an organization in a meaningful way. Rhetorical crafting is the skill of using symbolic language to give power to a message. Using stories, metaphors, and rhythm generates excitement.

Couto, R. A. (1993). **Narrative, free space, and political leadership in social movements.** *Journal of Politics, 55*(1), 57-79.

Interviews were conducted with 50 Civil Rights leaders to determine the power of narratives in political communication. It was determined that stories of evil oppression circulating through a community can fuel social movement. Stories of wisdom and virtue lend credibility to leaders of social movements.

Crawford, C. B. (1994). **Theory and implications regarding the utilization of strategic humor by leaders.** *Journal of Leadership Studies, 1*(4), 53-68.

Of all the communication tools that leaders use, humor is one of the most promising and one of the least understood. Humor can be used to contrast two incongruent ideas or to release tension. It can increase the popularity or influence of a speaker. It links people together in a positive environment and communicates organizational culture. On the darker side, humor may be employed to suggest superiority or to disparage others. Crawford's research examines the purpose and appropriateness of humor in the context of leadership.

Cunningham, I. (1992). **The impact of leaders: Who they are and what they do.** *Leadership and Organization Development Journal, 13*(2), 7-10.

Language pattern analysis is explored to determine its role in increasing leader effectiveness in organizations. Patterns can be seen as verbalizations (doing) emanating from deeper underlying patterns (being). In addition to being centered and focused, leaders must be grounded physically, spiritually, and professionally to achieve peak performance. Through exploration and challenge, the microlevel activity of language pattern analysis can help leaders increase their positive impact on organizations.

Dinkmeyer, D., & Eckstein, D. (1993). *Leadership by encouragement.* Dubuque, IA: Kendall/Hunt.

An encouraging leader listens, focuses on strengths, utilizes humor, and is communicative and honest. An encouraging organization builds trust, communicates a shared vision, empowers associates, and practices equality. This hands-on guide outlines the skills to master and presents exercises to facilitate mastery for the encouraging leader.

Fairhurst, G. T. (1993). **The leader-member exchange patterns of women leaders in industry: A discourse analysis.** *Communication Monographs, 60*(4), 321-351.

Through taped conversations between six female leaders and their male and female employees, certain patterns of discourse emerged. High-level leader-member exchanges were marked by patterns of values-convergence, problem solving, humor, support, and coaching. Low-level exchanges included face-threatening acts, competitive conflict, and power games. Gender issues appeared more often in cases where age, education, and technical experience were also factors. Includes bibliographical references and index.

New
Fairhurst, G. T., & Sarr, R. A. (1996). *The art of framing: Managing the language of leadership.* San Francisco: Jossey-Bass.

Framing is about the leadership opportunities that exist in the many conversations of everyday work situations. Leaders use communication tools such as metaphors, jargon, contrast, spin, and stories to clarify and influence. Selecting the proper tool for each situation is called framing. To determine the extent that framing is used and that opportunities for framing are lost, the authors conducted communication research. In a successful company, 200 work-related conversations lasting 30 minutes each were taped and analyzed. They concluded that leadership situations are often spontaneous and cannot be scripted in advance, but leaders can learn to send thoughtful messages by framing.

New
Felton, K. S. (1995). ***Warriors' words: A consideration of language and leadership.*** Westport, CT: Praeger.

Felton examines the public discourse of history's great communicators to examine their rhetoric, impact on listeners, and influence on society. Featured are Gandhi's "doctrine of the sword," Clarence Darrow's defense summation in a murder trial, Winston Churchill's speeches to Parliament, Franklin D. Roosevelt's fireside chats, Martin Luther King, Jr.'s Nobel Prize acceptance speech, and others. Felton also acknowledges the negative impact of persuasive speech from demagogues such as Adolf Hitler and Joseph McCarthy. Includes bibliographical references and index.

Fisher, R., & Ury, W. (1991). ***Getting to yes: Negotiating agreement without giving in*** (2nd ed.). Boston: Houghton Mifflin.

This book is about the method of principled negotiation. It describes the problems that arise in using standard strategies of positional bargaining and explains the four principles of this method of negotiation: 1) separate people from the problem; 2) focus on interests, not positions; 3) invent options for mutual gain; and 4) insist on using objective criteria. The second edition remains unchanged except for minor updates and a new section with questions frequently asked of the authors and their answers.

New
Hackman, M. Z., & Johnson, C. E. (1996). ***Leadership: A communication perspective*** (2nd ed.). Prospect Heights, IL: Waveland.

This textbook assumes that "leadership is best understood as a product of symbolic communication." Leaders use symbols, both in words and actions, to create visions, build trust, and influence others. The first section of the book introduces the fundamentals of leadership and its link to communication. The second section discusses leadership in different contexts: teams, organizations, politics, diversity, creativity, and ethics. Chapters contain theoretical background, cases, and exercises to illustrate the practical application of each lesson. Contains bibliographical references and index.

Harvey, J. B. (1988). ***The Abilene paradox and other meditations on management.*** Lexington, MA: Lexington Books.

Here, through a series of essays, Harvey contemplates the organizational behaviors in business life that unintention-

ally set up obstacles to success, growth, and innovation. The title essay, "The Abilene Paradox," illustrates how people in organizations take part in projects or assignments in which there is unspoken agreement that an idea won't work, and yet they proceed to pour valuable time, effort, and money into it. Harvey's parables about human behavior in organizations are insightful and engaging. Includes a bibliography.

Hazucha, J. F., Hezlett, S. A., & Schneider, R. J. (1993). **The impact of 360-degree feedback on management skills development.** *Human Resource Management, 32*(2&3), 325-351.

To determine the impact of 360-degree feedback, 48 managers were retested two years following feedback. Results indicated an increase in management skills, greater self-other agreement, and organizational advancement. Other findings indicate that younger managers demonstrated more changed skills and that review, coaching, and ongoing training are necessary to prevent feedback from being a one-time event.

New
Hinck, E. A. (1993). ***Enacting the presidency: Political argument, presidential debates, and presidential character.*** Westport, CT: Praeger.

Hinck sees presidential debates not as a discussion of position or policy but as forums for creating an image of leadership. The debate forum is not suited to analytic, detailed presentation of platform. It is suited to observe a candidate defend a broad platform while under the attack of his opponent. Studying the alignment between how a candidate argues and the content of his argument reveals much about that candidate's character. Aristotle's theories of politics and rhetoric serve as a basis for Hinck's review of nine 20th-century presidential debates and the character of the candidates in each. Includes bibliographical references and index.

New
Kaye, B., & Jacobson, B. (1996). **Reframing mentoring.** *Training & Development, 50*(8), 44-47.

The authors challenge the traditional view of mentoring as a one-on-one process, developing instead a model in which groups of employees are taught by "learning leaders." Advice on how to be an effective learning leader is offered, including how to determine an employee's learning needs, how to lead group discussions, and how to give learning assignments.

New

Kritek, P. B. (1994). *Negotiating at an uneven table: A practical approach to working with difference and diversity.* San Francisco: Jossey-Bass.

Kritek, a nurse and professor of nursing, examines the process of resolving conflict in which unacknowledged inequality influences the situation and its outcome. She compares traditional approaches to an uneven table with more constructive approaches and offers ten "ways of being" that can positively affect inequality and diversity. These include: be a truth teller, honor your integrity, find a place for compassion, draw a line in the sand without cruelty, know what you do and do not know, and know when and how to leave the table. Exercises and personal stories from Kritek's nursing experience accompany each chapter. Includes bibliographical references and index.

New

Kunich, J. C., & Lester, R. I. (1996). **Leadership and the art of feedback: Feeding the hands that back us.** *Journal of Leadership Studies, 3*(4), 3-22.

This article focuses on leaders and their ability to provide and receive feedback, especially in a supervisor/subordinate relationship. Feedback from a supervisor to an employee helps to inform and motivate the employee. The word feedback can be used as an acronym that defines leadership: Frequent, Early, Evidence-based, Dialogue-oriented, Beneficial, Accurate, Clear, and Kind. For example, frequent means that an employee is not just receiving a yearly report card but, instead, is receiving feedback as needed. Discussion questions are provided.

Likert, R., & Likert, J. G. (1976). *New ways of managing conflict.* New York: McGraw-Hill.

The authors have written a highly detailed text on the methodology, principles, and step-by-step procedures for managing social conflict within organizations, referred to as "System 4." The basic strategy to the Likert method is to change the "win-lose" approach to a "win-win" philosophy. The text provides administrators in business, government, education, and community groups a clearly detailed presentation on how to reduce internal and external conflict. This book has special relevance for social-science educators and students. Includes bibliography and index.

Linver, S. (1994). *The leader's edge: How to use communication to grow your business and yourself.* New York: Simon & Schuster.

This book is intended for organizational leaders who need to effectively address large groups, who wish to express thoughts and feelings openly, who believe they can reach out and connect with others. Linver identifies several

links between leaders and effective communicators. Both have vision and passion. Both bridge the gap between self and audience/followers. Both are keenly aware that behavior speaks as clearly as verbal communication. Linver's work as a speech consultant to Coca Cola and Arthur Andersen provides the anecdotes throughout the book.

New

Lumsden, G., & Lumsden, D. (1997). *Communicating in groups and teams: Sharing leadership* (2nd ed.). Belmont, CA: Wadsworth.

This is a textbook for courses in communication and teamwork with a focus on shared leadership. It is written for the student, moving from personal experience to theories to practical applications. Most of the book suggests that all team members assume leadership responsibility, but one chapter focuses on the special skills needed by a designated leader. This new edition provides information on computer-assisted techniques—electronic meetings, also called GDSS or group decision support systems—that foster interaction and eliminate domination by any one member. Chapters include excerpts from articles, cases, assessments, learning activities, cartoons, models, writing exercises, and reflections. Appendices provide suggestions for doing team projects, planning meetings, and making presentations. Includes a glossary, bibliographical references, name index, and subject index.

Morton, T. M. (1990). **Leadership.** *Business Horizons, 33*(6), 3-7.

In a leadership course at the University of Louisville, students improve communication skills by using practical techniques. Creating one-page memos forces students to write clearly and concisely. Oral presentations are videotaped and followed by feedback. Listening exercises and questioning guest speakers sharpen skills. Students make genograms, which are psychological family trees of patterns and problems handed down from one generation to another. Morton encourages students to know themselves, their values, their visions, and their potential contributions to society.

Pearce, T. (1995). *Leading out loud: The authentic speaker, the credible leader.* San Francisco: Jossey-Bass.

The nature of leadership communication has moved away from pre-television delivery of information to a more personal style—an authentic, heartfelt call for commitment. Pearce teaches the reader to articulate basic values and to understand the basics of speechwriting and presentation. He shares his personal experiences as a former

IBM executive and a current corporate communication coach. Includes bibliographical references and index.

Tannen, D. (1994). *Talking from 9 to 5: How women's and men's conversational styles affect who gets heard, who gets credit, and what gets done at work.* New York: William Morrow.

This is the third book in Tannen's implicational hierarchy on communication (*That's Not What I Meant!: How Conversational Style Makes or Breaks Your Relations with Others* [1986] and *You Just Don't Understand: Women and Men in Conversation* [1991]). For this book, Tannen collected transcripts of business conversations, both one-on-one and in groups, to research how conversational style at work determines credibility. Discussion of conversational style remains focused on personal influences such as gender differences, geographic region, ethnicity, class, and age. Includes bibliographical references and index.

Theus, K. T. (1995). **Communication in a power vacuum: Sense-making and enactment during crisis-induced departures.** *Human Resource Management: Special Issue on Leadership Transitions, 34*(1), 27-49.

The case of American University President Richard Berendzen's 1990 resignation following his arrest for making obscene telephone calls is presented. That kind of sudden departure can have numerous disruptive influences on an organization, such as emotional instability, damaged reputation, and a power vacuum. Theus compares Berendzen's case to similar situations at Kodak and American Express to frame a model for leading effectively during times of transition.

Van Velsor, E., Taylor, S., & Leslie, J. B. (1993). **An examination of the relationships among self-perception accuracy, self-awareness, gender, and leader effectiveness.** *Human Resource Management, 32*(2&3), 249-263.

A study of 648 randomly selected managers, 168 senior executives, and 79 hospital administrators provided data on self- and subordinate-rating discrepancies compared to performance. Self-awareness was negatively related to self/other rating discrepancy. Those who underrated their own leadership abilities received high subordinate ratings in self-awareness and effectiveness. Overraters received low ratings from their subordinates. Gender analysis revealed few differences between men's and women's ratings.

Wallace, M. D., Suedfeld, P., & Thachuk, K. (1993). **Political rhetoric of leaders under stress in the Gulf Crisis.** *Journal of Conflict Resolution, 37*(1), 94-107.

The Gulf Crisis and War serves as a social-science laboratory for the study of crisis behavior. A study of leaders' utterances before, during, and after the crisis and war analyzes integrated complexity of communication and its association with behavior. The study concludes that environmental stress, risk, or crisis result in lower-complexity information processing and communication. Leaders in successful situations tend to process information and communicate with increased complexity.

Walton, R. E. (1987). *Managing conflict: Interpersonal dialogue and third-party roles* (2nd ed.). Reading, MA: Addison-Wesley.

Conflict resolution is an important skill necessary at all levels of management. The author has developed an outline for diagnosing continuing conflicts, and offers several options for resolving them. Methods and concepts are presented here that can be applied to various types of conflict, including both interpersonal and inter-system. Topics span fundamental steps of managing conflict, skills for facilitating open dialogue, and third-party advantages of consultants. Examples of conflict resolution are provided through three case studies and through a presentation of an international workshop on the dialogue of conflict over border disputes. Includes bibliographies.

Wills, G. (1992). *Lincoln at Gettysburg: The words that remade America.* New York: Touchstone.

The Civil War battle at Gettysburg, Pennsylvania, was a military disaster for both the North and South. Each side lost several thousand soldiers and suffered severe psychological defeat. Bodies were hastily buried in shallow, unsuitable graves. In time, proper arrangements were made for reburial in a new national cemetery. The dedication ceremony became a symbol of healing the pain of a war-torn country. President Abraham Lincoln's three-minute speech on that occasion convinced his listeners that America was founded on the principle that all men are created equal. His brief words had the power to bring the nation together. In this Pulitzer Prize-winning book, Wills examines Lincoln's personal history and the speech itself to understand the power of communication. Includes bibliographical references and index.

New
Witherspoon, P. D. (1997). *Communicating leadership: An organizational perspective.* Needham Heights, MA: Allyn & Bacon.

This is a textbook for students of organizational leadership and speech communication. It covers the topics of organizational theory; leadership trait, behavior, situational, and humanistic theories; communication style and technology; change; and diversity. Witherspoon believes that leadership is a set of behaviors displayed in a proactive process and is also a communication process. This communication process allows a leader to develop shared meanings, to search for and use information effectively, and to create and communicate visions. Following each chapter is a summary, discussion questions, and a case study problem. Includes bibliographical references and index.

New

Yammarino, F. J., & Atwater, L. E. (1997). **Do managers see themselves as others see them? Implications of self-other rating agreement for human resources management.** *Organizational Dynamics*, *25*(4), 35-44.

The authors estimate that 10 to 15% of today's organizations use multi-rater feedback instruments for performance evaluations or to plan their managers' developmental learning. In this article, Yammarino and Atwater discuss the rationale for gathering 360-degree feedback from a manager, peers, subordinates, and superiors. The important data are found in the agreement between the self-rating and the feedback from others. A manager who overestimates his or her abilities has a high need for development. This person is a candidate for derailment. One who gets negative feedback from self and others may be a poor performer who has a high need for development. A manager who underestimates his or her talents may need to set higher aspiration levels and has only a moderate development need. The manager who gets favorable feedback and has a positive self-image is a high performer with the lowest need for development.

CREATIVITY, INNOVATION, AND CHANGE

Beatty, C. A., & Lee, G. L. (1992). **Leadership among middle managers: An exploration in the context of technological change.** *Human Relations*, *45*(9), 957-989.

Based on studies of three companies implementing CAD-CAM, computer-aided design and manufacturing systems, a model is offered for leadership during technical change. Linking market pressure to types of strategy for change provides a picture of the social dynamics of technological change. Exercising leadership skills of pathfinding, people problem-solving, and technical problem-solving is effective in overcoming barriers to change.

New

Beckhard, R., & Pritchard, W. (1992). *Changing the essence: The art of creating and leading fundamental change in organizations.* San Francisco: Jossey-Bass.

This book is directed toward organizational leaders who feel a need for redirection. Reasons for seeking redirection may include a change in identity or changed relationships with key stockholders. Beckhard believes there are four aspects to vision-driven change: 1) creating and setting the vision, 2) communicating the vision, 3) building commitment to the vision, and 4) organizing people and what they do so that they are aligned with the vision. Ways to implement a new vision include charting responsibility and developing a commitment plan. Includes bibliographical references and index.

New

Blank, W. (1995). *The nine natural laws of leadership.* New York: AMACOM.

By applying quantum mechanics to the business world, Blank has developed a new paradigm that he calls *quantum leadership*, based on the premise that "at the deepest levels, reality is a field, an interaction that cannot be understood in terms of separate parts." Central to this paradigm are the "nine natural laws of leadership," which include: a leader has willing followers, leaders use influence beyond formal authority, and leadership involves risk and uncertainty. Based on these laws, Blank offers over 150 "Action Ideas," practical suggestions on how to use quantum leadership in everyday situations. Includes bibliographical references and index.

New

Bryner, A., & Markova, D. (1996). *An unused intelligence: Physical thinking for 21st century leadership.* Berkeley, CA: Conari Press.

Physical thinking integrates mind and body to create a natural source of vitality. It allows one to deliver and receive messages through verbal communication and body language. The authors explain how to understand physical thinking in learning organizations, job stress, trust, respect of other people's limits, vision, and collaborative leadership. Physical practice exercises with instructions and photographs accompany each chapter. There is a useful chart that helps readers relate theory to practice. Includes bibliographical references, an index, and an appendix explaining the five disciplines of a learning organization.

New
De Ciantis, C. (1996). **What does drawing my hand have to do with leadership? A look at the process of leaders becoming artists.** *Journal of Aesthetic Education: Special Issue: The Aesthetic Face of Leadership, 30*(4), 87-97.

Teaching leaders the process of making art enlarges their perceptual universe and enhances their competency to thrive in a chaotic world. De Ciantis describes how art and leadership are linked in the touchstone exercise, part of the LeaderLab® program at the Center for Creative Leadership. Participants use found materials to create three-dimensional artworks to represent their most deeply-rooted sense of purpose. They keep their artwork in a place where, in the chaos of their daily lives, they can see it and be reminded of what is most important. De Ciantis also describes the methods for teaching art-making in the Center's Leading Creatively program. Includes bibliographical references.

De Pree, M. (1989). *Leadership is an art.* New York: Doubleday.

In the artistic industry of furniture design and manufacturing, Max De Pree leads his company, Herman Miller, to success through several measures. Practicing the art of leadership, De Pree supports the ideas of all employees, from designers to workers on the line. As a result, Herman Miller has won awards for innovative designs including the Eames chair, which is in the permanent collections of New York's Museum of Modern Art and the Louvre. Herman Miller is consistently chosen as one of the best companies to work for in America, cited for its Scanlon Plan, which rewards employees for their suggestions to improve productivity, quality, and customer service. It ranks among the top ten companies in return to investors and investment in R&D.

De Pree, M. (1992). *Leadership jazz.* New York: Currency/ Doubleday.

In a surprising look at the tough challenges facing today's leaders, De Pree identifies two difficult concepts successful leaders must perfect: voice, the ability to express one's beliefs; and touch, the ability to demonstrate competence and resolve. These concepts, mastered in jazz, have never before been acknowledged in business. De Pree urges leaders to find their own voices and reconsider every assumption they hold on leadership. He compares leadership to an inspired jazz performance, dependent on environment, fellow players and their need for individual expression as it benefits the group, and the absolute dependence on the leader for guidance.

Ellis, R. J. (1983, March). **Organizational leadership in turbulent times.** *Management Review, 72,* 59-61.

In turbulent times a manager must be able to stimulate problem-solving activities to generate as many innovative ideas as possible. Three aspects present in an organization may help stimulate new ideas: "free atmosphere," a "supportive environment," and a "loose structure." Ideas must not only be stimulated but also supported through the use of reinforcement or disapproval and the manipulation of the organization and information flow.

Feldhusen, J., & Pleiss, M. (1994). **Leadership: A synthesis of social skills, creativity, and histrionic ability?** *Roeper Review, 16*(4), 293-294.

In this short article based on the authors' study, 54 students from four distinct regional areas were rated by their teachers on the basis of leadership behavior, creative ability, and dramatic skill. Significant correlation was found between leadership and dramatic skills and between creativity and dramatic skills. Surprisingly, there was no correlation between leadership and creativity.

Fernald, L. W., Jr. (1988). **The underlying relationship between creativity, innovation and entrepreneurship.** *Journal of Creative Behavior, 22*(3), 196-202.

The author identifies the creative, innovative, and entrepreneurial characteristics found in common in the lives of seven individuals who exemplify these important attributes. Individuals identified are: Stanford Ovhinsky, Steven Wozniak, Wally Amos, Helen Smith, Jerome Lemelson, Bob Gundlach, and Wilson Greatbatch.

New
Galpin, T. J. (1996). *The human side of change: A practical guide to organizational redesign.* San Francisco: Jossey-Bass.

Galpin asserts that organizational change is not new. Organizations have merged, downsized, and restructured with a focus on technical and financial issues. Many of these changes have resulted in lost talent and bad relations. He states that a new kind of change is in order—one that combines the technical with the human side—to create a lasting transformation. This nonacademic, nontheoretical book is written for working leaders who seek a framework and the techniques to achieve such a change. A nine-step change-management process is designed to be achieved in 13 to 20 months. Galpin bases his framework and techniques on his experience as an organizational development consultant who has helped government and commercial organizations plan and achieve positive change. In the appendices, two toolkits help the reader apply the chapter lessons to real-life situations: a strategic toolkit for executives and an implementation toolkit for supervisors and mid-level managers. Includes a glossary, bibliographical references, and index.

Gardner, H., & Laskin, E. (1995). *Leading minds: An anatomy of leadership.* New York: BasicBooks.

Gardner's research of the human brain and his passion for history and current events led to this study of the mind of the leader. He questions which type of leadership has greater influence, the direct leadership of a president or prime minister or the indirect leadership of a creative mind. For example, during World War II, were Franklin Delano Roosevelt's and Winston Churchill's creation of an allied force more influential than Albert Einstein's theory of nuclear reaction? Gardner examines other great minds in politics, religion, anthropology, business, and the military. Includes bibliographical references and index.

New
Heifetz, R. A., & Laurie, D. L. (1997). **The work of leadership.** *Harvard Business Review, 75*(1), 124-134.

Heifetz, Director of Harvard University's Leadership Education Project, and Laurie address leadership in situations of *adaptive change*—how to mobilize people throughout an organization to develop new strategies and learn new ways of operating. They identify "six principles for leading adaptive work: 'getting on the balcony,' identifying the adaptive challenge, regulating distress, maintaining disciplined attentions, giving the work back to people, and protecting voices of leadership from below." Recent changes at KPMG Netherlands illustrate the concepts.

Heil, G., Parker, T., & Tate, R. (1995). *Leadership and the customer revolution: The messy, unpredictable, and inescapably human challenge of making the rhetoric of change a reality.* New York: Van Nostrand Reinhold.

This book presents a challenge to leaders facing rapid-fire organizational and personal change. It suggests that leaders reinvent themselves as revolutionaries, systems architects, customer advocates, and heroes. To meet customer demands for service and quality, the authors recommend actions for building a loyal workforce that delights in delighting customers. Includes bibliographical references and index.

New
Howard, V. A. (1996). **The aesthetic face of leadership.** *Journal of Aesthetic Education: Special Issue: The Aesthetic Face of Leadership, 30*(4), 21-37.

Howard claims that artistry and leadership are complex subjects, about which much has been written but little is agreed. He finds that books written by historians, journalists, and biographers, not by social scientists, reveal the "emotionalized thinking" that link artistry and leadership, the aesthetic face of leadership. This emotionalized thinking is represented by the sensitivity, judgment, persuasiveness, imagination, and timing exemplified in the actions, decisions, rhetoric, and public presence of great leaders. He argues that, while some leadership skills can be taught, leadership itself can only be achieved through painful refinement of one's sensibilities. Includes bibliographical references.

Hoyle, J. R. (1995). *Leadership and futuring: Making visions happen.* Thousand Oaks, CA: Corwin Press.

Hoyle, a professor of organizational theory and future studies at Texas A&M University, wrote this short book on visionary leaders. In it, he describes his six favorites and their common characteristics: concern for others, a clear message, and persistence. He applies future theory to the visioning process to explain how to motivate others to embrace a cause beyond themselves. Hoyle suggests techniques for developing and practicing the skills to shape and share visions. Includes bibliographical references.

Ijiri, Y., & Khun, R. L. (Eds.). (1988). *New directions in creative and innovative management.* Cambridge, MA: Ballinger.

This book asks the questions, "How can we effectively formulate and implement novel ideas into viable products and services?" and "What are the optimal relationships between theory and practice in creative and innovative management?"

New
Katz, R. (Ed.). (1997). *The human side of managing technological innovation: A collection of readings.* New York: Oxford University Press.

The readings presented in this collection focus on "issues critical to the effective management of technical professionals and cross-functional teams through the innovation process." Articles are organized around six themes: the management and motivation of professional performance, managing innovative groups and project teams, the management and leadership of technical professionals, managing professionals within innovative organizations, the management of organizational processes, and managing technological innovation. Includes an index.

New
Katzenbach, J. R., & the RCL Team. (1995). ***Real change leaders: How you can create growth and high performance at your company.*** New York: Random House, Inc.

According to the authors, in between the present and the future is a period of change called the *delta state.* They believe that "real change leaders (RCLs) learn how to survive and win in the delta state." Major change efforts that start at the top of companies often stall midway down, so Katzenbach and his team interviewed 150 mid-level managers they call "down-the-line leaders." These RCLs, from organizations including Compaq, Shell, and the New York City Transit Authority, are able to create change by visualizing what needs to be done and motivating the people around them. The book is aimed at both middle managers who want to develop RCL characteristics and executives who want to recognize the RCLs in their own companies. Includes bibliographical references and index.

Keller, R. T. (1995). **Transformational leaders make a difference.** *Research Technology Management, 38*(3), 41-44.

The transformational leader strives to achieve results by inspiring creative thinking and emphasizing group goals over personal self-interest. A study of 66 industrial R&D project groups found transformational leadership to account for higher quality in research projects. In development projects, however, a more directive style of leadership explained higher quality. Guidelines for effective leadership are suggested.

New
Kotter, J. P. (1996). ***Leading change.*** Boston: Harvard Business School Press.

This book is an extension of Kotter's previous works on change ("Leading Change: Why Transformation Efforts Fail," *Harvard Business Review*, 1995; *A Force for Change: How Leadership Differs from Management,* 1990; *Corporate Culture and Performance,* 1992; *The New Rules: How to Succeed in Today's Post-corporate World,* 1995). The previous works cite empirical evidence and examples of change efforts in real organizations. This book is more personal. It's an analysis formed during Kotter's years as a professor of leadership at Harvard and a scholar of organizational change. He outlines an eight-stage change process. He also forecasts an increasingly important capacity for organizations to continually change and for their leaders to continually learn.

New
Kuczmarski, T. D. (1996). ***Innovation: Leadership strategies for the competitive edge.*** Lincolnwood, IL: NTC Business Books.

Kuczmarski lists four goals for this book: 1) convince CEOs of the power of innovation; 2) increase top management involvement in and commitment to innovation; 3) unleash the power of employees to think creatively and innovate; and 4) provide practical tools, techniques, and guidelines for making innovation work. Each chapter contains figures, self-assessment tests, lists of action steps, and an "innovation checklist." Chapters address kick-starting your organization, the role of shareholders, measuring innovation progress, and developing your personal commitment. Includes an index.

Land, G., & Jarman, B. (1992). ***Breakpoint and beyond: Mastering the future—today.*** New York: HarperBusiness.

All systems in nature, individuals as well as organizations, go through a process of change that can lead to renewal and transformation. Understanding nature's creative process can aid in the understanding and acceptance of change. *Breakpoint* is defined as a break with the past, a push to the edge of an era, and a leap into the unknown. Land and Jarman teach the reader how to recognize personal and organizational breakpoints, to embrace the process of change with creativity, and to build bridges into the future. Includes bibliographical references and index.

Lippitt, G. L. (1987). **Entrepreneurial leadership: A performing art.** *Journal of Creative Behavior, 21*(3), 264-270.

According to the author, entrepreneurial leadership as an art means "orchestrating the totality of the enterprise with energy, self-confidence, persistence and learning capabilities." Lippitt identifies six behavioral characteristics of the entrepreneurial leader: risk taking, divergent thinking, sharp focus, personal responsibility, economic orientation, and learning from experience. Practical guidelines for self-development are provided.

MacKinnon, D. W. (1978). ***In search of human effectiveness.*** Buffalo, NY: Creative Education Foundation.

This publication is based on MacKinnon's research into the nature and nurture of creativity. This collection of papers focuses on the understanding and nurturing of the creative potential in individuals. The major theme of the research and writing is a concern to find ways to help people become as fully functioning as possible. Includes bibliography and index.

McCall, M. W., Jr. (1980). **Conjecturing about creative leaders.** *Journal of Creative Behavior, 14*(4), 225-234, 257.

Creativity is seen as a deviant response by the leader in order to solve some problem. The author sees creative leaders as crafty, contrary, grouchy, dangerous, feisty, inconsistent, evangelistic, prejudiced, and spineless. The creative leader tries to create new ideas and evaluate them.

McCaskey, M. B. (1982). *The executive challenge: Managing change and ambiguity.* Marshfield, MA: Pitman.

This book offers timely suggestions and practical help for managers facing change and ambiguity. Its discussions of mapping, of the stress of ambiguity, of forces that favor or block creativity, of qualities of the creative person—including courage, humility, toleration of disorder, use of intuition, and integration of opposites in the personality—are all valuable to the manager in gaining insight.

New
McLagan, P., & Nel, C. (1996). **A new leadership style for genuine total quality.** *Journal of Quality and Participation, 19*(3), 14-16.

According to the authors, today's "new style of leader-ship" means that everyone in a company, not just upper management, has to practice leadership skills. They list six steps that can help managers who have traditionally been followers develop the new skills: 1) look deep within and transform yourself, 2) create direct relation-ships with employees, 3) help managers and front-line workers change, 4) see the leader as a focused visionary, 5) share information throughout the organization, and 6) support this new definition of leadership.

New
Merritt, S., & DeGraff, J. (1996). **The revisionary vision-ary: Leadership and the aesthetics of adaptability.** *Journal of Aesthetic Education: Special Issue: The Aesthetic Face of Leadership, 30*(4), 69-85.

The authors address the challenge of training leaders to create adaptable, if not predictable, visions in a discon-tinuous, chaotic world where very little is predictable. Merritt, founder of the Polaroid Creativity Lab, shares her insights on developing the aesthetic competencies of her company's leaders. She employs two frameworks: Parson's five stages of aesthetic development in *How We Understand Art* (Cambridge University Press, 1987) and Thompson's *Visionary Leadership Inventory* (Human Factors, 1994). A new model illustrates how leaders can identify where their aesthetic competencies are at a given point and where they can aim to achieve growth from

self-awareness to an awareness of larger, transpersonal forces. Includes bibliographical references.

Mink, O., Rogers, R., & Watkins, K. (1989). **Creative leadership: Discovering paradoxes of innovation and risk.** *Contemporary Educational Psychology, 14*(3), 228-240.

The research reported in this article attempts to explore the paradoxes inherent in the enactment of creative leadership in complex interpersonal situations. The situations in this study were difficult interpersonal interactions faced by public-school superintendents.

New
Moore, R. (1996). **The nightmare science and its daytime uses.** *Journal of Aesthetic Education: Special Issue: The Aesthetic Face of Leadership, 30*(4), 5-20.

Moore explains how, by the early 20th century, the academic discipline of aesthetics achieved a reputation as a "nightmare science," an arcane and impractical version of philosophy. But at the end of the century, scholars perceive aesthetics to make a valuable link between the arts and successful living. The aesthetic principles of analysis, context, perception, and experience have useful application in planning, education, and other practical endeavors.

Morgan, G. (1993). *Imaginization: The art of creative management.* Newbury Park: Sage.

Imaginization is a new way of thinking, organizing, and helping people develop their creative potential. It is a means for finding innovative solutions to difficult problems, and it empowers people to trust themselves in a world of constant change. Morgan demonstrates imaginization in action as an invitation to reimage ourselves and organizational management. Includes bibliographical references and index.

New
National Leadership Institute. (1996). *Proceedings: The 1996 NLI Conference: Leaders and change.* College Park: National Leadership Institute, University of Maryland University College.

Every two years, the National Leadership Institute Conference draws together 200 executives, HRD profes-sionals, OD consultants, and university professors to exchange ideas on the theory and practice of leadership. This book contains the proceedings of the 1996 NLI Conference. Some of the conference speakers were: Peter Vaill, "Leadership Is Not Learned: It Is Learning"; Pamela S. Mayer, "Aesthetic Competencies: The Chang-ing Face of Leadership"; Susan Bethanis, "The Language of Leadership, Linking Metaphors with Organization

Transformation"; Carole Y. Lyles, "Leading in a Postmodern Organization"; and Katherine L. Yocum, "Volunteer Leaders: Frontiers of the Third Age."

O'Toole, J. (1995). *Leading change: Overcoming the ideology of comfort and the tyranny of custom.* San Francisco: Jossey-Bass.

O'Toole uses an artistic metaphor to illustrate how a leader/artist can create order through design, composition, tension, balance, and harmony. James Ensor's painting "Christ's Entry in Brussels in 1889" depicts a community's self-absorption and disrespect for the leader-figure of Christ. After discussion of value-based leadership, O'Toole observes harmony in Georges Seurat's painting "Sunday Afternoon on the Island of La Grande Jatte." Another artistic metaphor describes *Rushmorean* leadership based on the styles of the four U.S. presidents immortalized on Mount Rushmore. O'Toole recommends four candidates who exhibit value-based leadership styles for a Corporate Mount Rushmore. Includes bibliographical references and index.

New
Palus, C. J., & Horth, D. M. (1996). **Leading creatively: The art of making sense.** *Journal of Aesthetic Education: Special Issue: The Aesthetic Face of Leadership, 30*(4), 53-68.

The authors propose that the processes of leadership are fundamentally art-making. They argue that this art-making is an aesthetic competency that enhances other, more rational-analytical competencies so often used to face the complex challenges in organizations. Through collaborative inquiry, or co-inquiry, individuals and communities come together to make meaning around what is real, important, and possible. The authors explain how the Leading Creatively program at the Center for Creative Leadership helps leaders develop these aesthetic competencies: noticing; subtle representation; fluid perspective; right-brain mental processing; personalizing work; skeptical inquiry; shared meaning process; serious play; portraying paradoxes, conflicts, and the unknown; and facility with metaphors. Includes bibliographical references.

Parnes, S. J. (1988). *Visionizing.* East Aurora, NY: D.O.K.

"This book is designed for those interested in encouraging and nurturing creative awareness, attitudes and accomplishments in themselves and others." The book is based on the Osborn-Parnes creative problem-solving process, and can be used as a workbook for individual study or group instruction.

Prince, F. A. (1993). *C and the box: A paradigm parable.* San Diego, CA: Pfeiffer.

This five-minute cartoon-illustrated book is intended to deliver a simple message. *C* goes through life as a conformist until it finds a coil that allows it to spring out of its box and begin a life filled with creativity. The message is to seek a new outlook and new ways to solve problems, overcome conformity and bureaucracy, and discover inner strength and motivation. Also available on video.

New
Quinn, R. E. (1996). *Deep change: Discovering the leader within.* San Francisco: Jossey-Bass.

Quinn describes painful, yet rewarding, experiences of deep personal and organizational change. He argues that every person can be a change agent who demands excellence of self and who improves his or her surrounding systems. Each chapter contains a lesson on how to "walk naked into the land of uncertainty." Some of the leadership lessons are: lifelong learning, finding and maintaining vitality, acting with integrity, and building interdependent relationships. The reflection questions at the end of each chapter are organized into personal and organizational steps to achieve change. Quinn recommends writing responses in a journal to capture key learning moments. Includes brief bibliographical references and index.

New
Ray, M., & Rinzler, A. (Eds.). (1993). *The new paradigm in business: Emerging strategies for leadership and organizational change.* New York: Jeremy P. Tarcher/ Perigee.

Ray and Rinzler argue that the new paradigm developing in business today hinges on "having the freedom to use our highest resources while taking responsibility for ourselves, for others and for the environment in which we live." Their compilation includes chapters by Peter Senge and Warren Bennis, and addresses five themes: the roots of present change, the beginning of new leadership, organizational transformation, social and environmental responsibility, and visions of the future. Businesses operating in this new paradigm, including Ben and Jerry's Homemade Ice Cream, Inc., and the Body Shop, are profiled. Includes bibliographical references.

New
Ready, D. A., Valentino, D. J., & Gouillart, F. J. (1994). *Champions of change: A global report on leading business transformation.* Lexington, MA: International Consortium for Executive Research and Gemini Consulting.

This is a report of the 1994 International Competitive Capabilities Project. More than 1,450 managers and executives from 12 global corporations responded to a survey about organizational effectiveness and leadership competencies. Researchers drew six conclusions: 1) transformation is not a program or a one-time event—it is a regenerative process; 2) sustainable competitive advantage depends on flexibility and on being close to the customer; 3) evidence suggests that we are not prepared for the future; 4) the new leadership challenge is to continually renew organizations; 5) for leaders to develop, they must have opportunity, organizational support, and self-determination; and 6) there is a large gap between the current global mind-set and the one we'll need in the future.

New
Renesch, J. (Ed.). (1994). *Leadership in a new era: Visionary approaches to the biggest crisis of our time.* San Francisco: New Leaders Press.

Twenty-three leadership practitioners and scholars share their expectations for leaders of the near future. The issues new leaders will face are: dealing with challenging times, welcoming change, and seeking responsibility. Essays include: "Cinderella Can Be Tough, John Wayne Can Cry" by Barbara R. Hauser; "Diversity and Leadership Development" by Ann M. Morrison; "An Adventure in Enlightened Leadership" by Ed Oakley; "Leadership Challenges in Technical Organizations" by Peter K. Krembs; "Leading Change: The Leader as the Chief Transformation Officer" by Warren Bennis; "A Sacred Responsibility" by Barbara Shipka; "Servant-Leadership: Toward a New Era of Caring" by Larry C. Spears; "The Innocent Leader: Accepting Paradox" by E. Magaziner; "Leadership: The Values Game" by Carol McCall; "Attributes of Leadership: A Checklist" by Max DePree; and "Winning Trust" by Perry Pascarella.

Russell, P., & Evans, R. (1992). *The creative manager: Finding inner vision and wisdom in uncertain times.* San Francisco: Jossey-Bass.

Change can be an exciting time full of opportunities and a stressful time of uncertainty. To cope with change, we must have an inner sense of stability while keeping a flexible, open mind to see all the possibilities. A creative manager balances stability and flexibility when using the creative process in communications, relationships, team building, empowerment, and dealing with stress. Includes bibliographical references.

New
Schrage, M. (1997, December-January). **The Gary Burton Trio.** *Fast Company, 1*(6), 110-113.

Schrage conducts an interview with Gary Burton, a jazz vibraphonist and educator. They discuss the similarities between jazz combos, known for their creativity and spontaneity, and management teams. Burton compares orchestra conductors to autocratic CEOs. Both jazz combos and management teams need strong leaders to carry the vision and to help musicians and managers learn new riffs or ways of work, discipline, and spontaneity. Burton explains that strong leaders can enable an active flow of creativity as long as the vision of the group is maintained.

Scott, S. G., & Bruce, R. A. (1994). **Determinants of innovative behavior: A path model of individual innovation in the workplace.** *Academy of Management Journal, 37*(3), 580-607.

Engineers, scientists, and technicians in a U.S. industrial corporation's R&D facility participated in interviews and responded to questionnaires about innovation. Questions about problem-solving style, innovative climate, leader-member exchange, and role expectations were asked to determine workplace behavior and support for innovation. A model illustrates the effects that leadership, work group relations, and individual attributes have on individual innovative behavior through climate perceptions.

New
Sheridan, J. H. (1997). **The winds of change.** *Industry Week, 245*(15), 58-65.

Confronting change has become a major challenge for business leaders. This article describes how the CEOs of major companies, including Honeywell, AK Steel Corp., Eastman Chemical, and Chrysler, have dealt with the changes in their markets. John Kotter, a writer on leadership issues, also discusses ways any organization can manage change.

New
Smith, R. A. (1996). **Leadership as aesthetic process.** *Journal of Aesthetic Education: Special Issue: The Aesthetic Face of Leadership, 30*(4), 39-52.

The philosophy of aesthetics considers the nature of art, its interpretation and appreciation, its critical evaluation, and its cultural context. The process of leadership, as defined by Drath and Palus in *Making Common Sense* (Center for Creative Leadership, 1994), considers the efforts of a community of practice to achieve a common understanding. Smith links the two concepts to explain leadership as an aesthetic process. The result is a creative process of continual learning and social responsibility. Includes bibliographical references.

Starratt, R. J. (1993). *The drama of leadership.* Washington, DC: Falmer Press.

As a teacher of aspiring leaders, Starratt regularly addresses the cynicism associated with current business and political leadership. His research on the historical crises of the last century and social organizational theories has led to a fresh perspective on leadership. Rather than write about leaders themselves, he writes here about leadership in the context of social institutions and social movements. Using a theater metaphor, Starratt's leaders are players in comedies and tragedies, struggling over human values. Leaders serve as directors, coaches, stage managers, script writers, and critics. They require more than technical competence as they continually explore new practices. Includes bibliographical references and index.

New

Taormina, T. (1996). *Virtual leadership and the ISO9000 imperative.* Upper Saddle River, NJ: Prentice Hall.

ISO9000 is a quality-management system that was developed in the 1970s in cooperation with the European Community. It transcends language and cultural barriers and establishes a global accreditation system for companies doing international business that is now used in over 80 countries. Taormina explains the fundamentals of ISO9000, details what it means for companies, and describes the leadership necessary to move American companies to this global mind-set. Along with reader-friendly graphs and boxes, this book offers companies a practical strategic implementation plan, sample quality manuals, an internal auditor training course, and an audit checklist. Includes bibliographical references and index.

New

Turner, J. R., Grude, K. V., & Thurloway, L. (Eds.). (1996). *The project manager as change agent: Leadership, influence and negotiation.* New York: McGraw-Hill.

This textbook helps project managers learn to lead in three directions: downward—leading a team to complete a project on time and within budget; outward—influencing and winning support from peers; and upward—serving as project ambassador to win support from those in power. To do this, project managers must understand the nature of change and the culture of projects. Chapters focus on organizational change, teams and team roles, internal marketing, and ethics. Case studies throughout illustrate project managers as change agents. There are tools for diagnosing change and determining the health of a project. Includes bibliographical references and indexes.

New

Von Oech, R. (1986). *A kick in the seat of the pants: Using your explorer, artist, judge, and warrior to be more creative.* New York: Harper & Row.

Von Oech believes that to develop our creative process we must adopt four roles: explorer, artist, judge, and warrior. The explorer searches for new information, and the artist turns resources into new ideas. A judge evaluates the merits of a new idea, and the warrior carries the new ideas into action. When these roles are combined, they form a creative team in the theater of your mind. Von Oech describes how one can expand into unfamiliar roles and be flexible in switching roles through exercises and anecdotes. Includes bibliography and index.

New

Walberg, H. J., & Others. (1996). **Childhood traits and experiences of eminent women.** *Creativity Research Journal, 9*(1), 97-102.

This is a summary of research that examined the early traits, conditions, and experiences of 256 eminent women who influenced their times and achieved importance in their fields. Included are: skater Sonja Henie, blind and deaf educator Helen Keller, painter Grandma Moses, businesswoman Helena Rubinstein, and political leader Eleanor Roosevelt. Historians and practitioners rated each woman on childhood factors such as: alert to novelty, hardworking, persevering, and well traveled. The most common factors were identified as: intelligence, perseverance, and stimulating social environments. The women were found to have been encouraged and stimulated by parents, teachers, and other adults, while living in environments that were receptive to different ideas.

DECISION MAKING AND PROBLEM SOLVING

Axelrod, R. (1984). *The evolution of cooperation.* New York: BasicBooks.

The author conducted a Computer Prisoner's Dilemma Tournament with 14 entries from game theorists in economics, psychology, sociology, political science, and math. The winner was *Tit for Tat*, the simplest entry, which is a strategy of starting with cooperation, and thereafter doing whatever the other player did in the previous move. He conducted a second tournament with 60 entries from around the world. *Tit for Tat* won again. From this experience, Axelrod developed a theory of cooperation. Includes bibliography and index.

New

Black, J. S., & Gregersen, H. B. (1997). **Participative decision-making: An integration of multiple dimensions.** *Human Relations, 50*(7), 859-878.

Participative decision making (PDM) has several components, including the degree of employee involvement and the decision-making process itself. The decision process has five stages: identifying the problem, generating alternative solutions, selecting a solution, planning to implement the solution, and evaluating the implementation. This study of employees at a manufacturing company examined the differential impact of these two aspects of PDM. The authors found that employees with above-average involvement in the decision-making process reported higher levels of satisfaction and performance. Moreover, the more stages of the decision making employees were involved in, the higher their levels of satisfaction.

Calvert, G. (1993). *Highwire management: Risk-taking tactics for leaders, innovators, and trailblazers.* San Francisco: Jossey-Bass.

Risk management has taken on new meaning as organizations face productivity challenges with reduced resources, shorter cycles, and increased workloads. Calvert shares his views on risk taking as a management strategy to help others learn how to welcome risk as a positive force. Three self-assessments, *Risk Attitudes Inventory*, *Risk-taking Control Scale*, and *Risk Success Quiz* provide a foundation for knowing one's strengths and weaknesses. Managers from a variety of industries share their risk-taking experiences, successful tactics, skills and attitudes, and ways to avoid emotional stress and unnecessary costs. Includes bibliographical references and index.

Champion, J. M., & James, J. H. (1989). *Critical incidents in management: Decision and policy issues* (6th ed.). Homewood, IL: Richard C. Irwin.

Designed as an instructional and educational tool for "students in all stages of professional development," this book has application for educators involved in traditional classroom courses as well as management-training and executive-leadership personnel. The book is composed of 50 incidents that illustrate the variety of issues facing today's management. The situations take place in various settings including business, government, health care, and education. The first 40 incidents include: description of the incident, critiques written by academicians, observations made by the authors of the book, discussion items, and suggested readings. The last ten incidents are without critiques. Includes bibliographies.

New

Hale, G. A. (1996). *The leader's edge: Mastering the five skills of breakthrough thinking.* New York: Irwin.

Hale recommends five critical-thinking skills for leaders: 1) situation review, 2) cause analysis, 3) decision making, 4) plan analysis, and 5) innovation. In this practical guide, he explains through anecdotes and hypothetical situations how to master the skills well enough to teach them to others. There are also suggestions for using critical-thinking skills to advocate for new ideas and to solve people problems. Includes an index.

Janis, I. L. (1982). *Groupthink: Psychological studies of policy decisions and fiascoes* (2nd ed.). Boston, MA: Houghton Mifflin.

The author examines five events, from World War II to Watergate, that turned into major fiascoes for five American presidents: Franklin Roosevelt's being unprepared for the attack on Pearl Harbor; Harry Truman and the invasion of North Korea; John Kennedy and the Bay of Pigs invasion; Lyndon Johnson's escalation of the Vietnam War; and Richard Nixon's role in the Watergate cover-up. By a close examination of the group process that led to the course of action taken for each of these events, Janis seeks to answer the question: "How could such bright, shrewd leaders and their advisors arrive at such poor decisions?" The author has developed a convincing and controversial set of dynamics to explain group decision-making strategies and how they can fail. Includes bibliography and index.

Janis, I. L. (1989). *Crucial decisions: Leadership in policymaking and crisis management.* New York: Free Press.

This exhaustive presentation of a constraints model of policy processes extends Janis's earlier work. He examines when and why leaders of large organizations make avoidable errors that result in faulty policy decisions. He offers an integrated, general theory of the conditions under which sound procedures would lead to successful outcomes. References to historical policy decisions serve as examples. Includes bibliography and index.

New

Kahai, S. S., Sosik, J. J., & Avolio, B. J. (1997). **Effects of leadership style and problem structure on work group processes and outcomes in an electronic meeting system environment.** *Personnel Psychology, 50*(1), 121-146.

This article reports on a laboratory study of participative versus directive leadership styles and their effects on problem solving through the use of an electronic meeting system (EMS), also called group decision support systems (GDSS). The anonymity of members using this system enhances participative leadership and group potency when solving unstructured or moderately structured problems. Includes bibliographical references. A similar study is reported in Sosik, Avolio, and Kahai (1997), "Effects of leadership style and anonymity on group potency and effectiveness in a group decision support system environment," *Journal of Applied Psychology*, *82*(1), 89-103.

Maier, N. R. (1963). *Problem-solving discussions and conferences: Leadership methods and skills.* New York: McGraw-Hill.

This book deals with research on improving the effectiveness of a leader's performance in group problem solving and decision making; it integrates these studies with earlier research on problem solving and frustration. It looks at the principles of group behavior that are used by leaders, and how they may serve to improve meetings. Includes a bibliography.

March, J. G., & Weissinger-Baylon, R. (Eds.). (1986). *Ambiguity and command: Organizational perspective on military decision making.* Marshfield, MA: Pitman.

This book is about military decision making under conditions of ambiguity, situations where objective, technology, or experience are unclear and where solutions and problems are joined together. The intent is to explore whether theories of decision making under ambiguity, developed through observations of nonmilitary organizations, might contribute to understanding and improving some aspects of command decision making in the Navy. Includes bibliographies and index.

Martin, C. M. (1993). **Feelings, emotional empathy and decision making: Listening to the voices of the heart.** *Journal of Management Development*, *12*(5), 33-45.

Empirical studies and anecdotal experiences reinforce the legitimacy of the affective dimension of managerial decision making. This dimension reflects sensitivity to the feelings and plight of employees, customers, and others affected by decisions. Martin recommends listening to the voices of the heart rather than basing decisions solely on a rationally analytical level of understanding.

McVey, R. S. (1995). **Critical thinking skills for leadership development.** *Journal for Leadership Studies*, *2*(4), 86-97.

McVey reviews theories on thought process and its influence on behavior. He notes that vertical thinking has been a common practice of business managers who solve immediate problems at the expense of long-term planning. He asserts that lateral thinking better serves the business leader who must create a vision, innovate new processes, and plan strategically. He urges teachers across the curriculum, from elementary school to college level, to develop their students' common sense and teach lateral, critical-thinking skills. He recommends the use of case methods, real or hypothetical, as effective teaching tools.

New
Menke, M. M. (1997). **Essentials of R&D strategic excellence.** *Research Technology Management*, *40*(5), 42-47.

This article reports on a benchmarking study of 45 best decision-making practices in 79 leading R&D organizations. Each organization responded to a questionnaire about the decision-making practices in use, number of new products, sales of new products, and return on R&D investment. The study revealed a top-ten list of best practices: 1) understand the drivers of industry change; 2) coordinate long-range business R&D plans; 3) focus on customer needs; 4) agree on clear, measurable project goals; 5) use a formal development process; 6) use cross-functional teams; 7) coordinate development with commercialization; 8) determine, understand, and measure end-customer needs; 9) refine projects with regular customer feedback; and 10) hire the best and maintain expertise. Includes bibliographical references.

Mintzberg, H. (1994). *The rise and fall of strategic planning: Reconceiving roles for planning, plans, planners.* New York: Free Press.

The former president of the Strategic Management Society concludes that the term *strategic planning* is an oxymoron. Planning is an analytical process while strategy is more intuitive. Mintzberg reviews the origins of strategic planning and models that didn't work. He is convinced that planning can harm an organization by destroying commitment and encouraging politics. The alternative is to reconceive the process of creating strategy through informal learning and personal vision. Includes bibliographical references and index.

Mumford, M. D., & Connelly, M. S. (1991). **Leaders as creators: Leader performance and problem solving in ill-defined domains.** *Leadership Quarterly: Special Issue: Individual Differences and Leadership: I*, *2*(4), 289-315.

Problem solving relies on well-organized knowledge structure and the cognitive processes that contribute to effective solutions. Creative problem solving occurs when a problem is poorly defined, when novelty is needed, and when information structures are reorganized. Because leaders face varying and ever-changing problems, problem construction relates to leader performance more than does knowledge structure.

Quinlivan-Hall, D., & Renner, P. (1990). ***In search of solutions: Sixty ways to guide your problem-solving group.*** Vancouver: Training Associates.

Ways to solve problems in meetings without personality clashes, time wasters, and procedural wrangling are offered. The authors outline three stages of the problem-solving process and roles of key players: facilitator, recorder, and participants. Included are 60 facilitation techniques that assist groups to define issues, generate solutions, make decisions, and devise action plans and follow-up strategies. Includes bibliography and index.

Schrage, M. (1990). ***Shared minds: The new technologies of collaboration.*** New York: Random House.

Schrage describes a new technology for two or more minds to collaborate on problem solving or brainstorming. In a computer-augmented meeting, two or more people exchange ideas while a technographer keys the dialogue into a computer, which instantly transmits the dialogue onto an overhead screen. Examples of successful collaborations exhibit the benefits of joint effort. Schrage details the design, environment, and tools for technological collaboration. This technology is often called group decision support system (GDSS).

New
Sosik, J. J., Avolio, B. J., & Kahai, S. S. (1997). **Effects of leadership style and anonymity on group potency and effectiveness in a group decision support system environment.** *Journal of Applied Psychology, 82*(1), 89-103.

This article reports on a laboratory study of transactional versus transformational leadership style and their effects on group decision making when using a group decision support system (GDSS). The GDSS is an interactive network of computers used to generate solutions to unstructured problems. The anonymity of members using this system enhances transformational leadership and group potency. Includes bibliographical references. A similar study is reported in Kahai, Sosik, and Avolio (1997), "Effects of Leadership Style and Problem Structure on Work Group Process and Outcomes in an Electronic Meeting System Environment," *Personnel Psychology, 50*(1), 121-146.

New
Volkema, R. J. (1997). **Managing the problem formulation process: Guidelines for team leaders and facilitators.** *Human Systems Management, 16*(1), 27-34.

Volkema suggests methods for team leaders to manage the problem formulation process and reduce Type III errors (solving the wrong problem). It is important to involve the right people and to not rush the process. Team leaders need to recognize the biases in human judgment that influence the process such as: personal experiences outweigh more valid data, first or most recent data is given undue importance, aversion to taking risks, and selective perception. When sufficient effort is devoted to formulating a problem, the remainder of the decision-making process is improved. Includes bibliographical references.

Vroom, V. H., & Jago, A. G. (1988). ***The new leadership: Managing participation in organizations.*** Englewood Cliffs, NJ: Prentice Hall.

The significance of leaders sharing power with their constituents and staff members, and its impact upon cultivating participation and influence in organizations, is measurable, say the authors. Intended for use by several different audiences, the book presents a model for measuring situational leadership. Chapters 2 through 4 and 8 through 12 are of particular interest to managers. Academic readers will want to look closely at chapters 6 through 12. Leadership trainers will find chapters 6 and 8 through 13 useful. Appendices expand upon the meaning of measurements and definitions. Includes bibliography and index.

Vroom, V. H., & Yetton, P. W. (1975). ***Leadership and decision making.*** Pittsburgh, PA: University of Pittsburgh.

This book is written for scholars, researchers, managers, and administrators who share an interest in leadership, decision making, and organizational behavior. Central to all the research reported in this book is the role of situational differences as determinants of the choice of a decision process. A summary of the major findings and how they relate to other approaches in the study of leadership is provided. Includes a bibliography.

New
Weber, J. (1996). **Influences upon managerial moral decision making: Nature of the harm and magnitude of consequences.** *Human Relations, 49*(1), 1-22.

This article examines possible ethical dilemmas faced by managers and the moral considerations that affect their decision making. A sample of 259 managers enrolled in an MBA program completed the *Moral Judgment Interview* (Colby & Kohlberg, 1987) to determine how they perceived degrees of harm and consequence. Situations involving physical harm received top priority, followed by economic harm and psychological harm. Life-and-death issues were ranked of greatest consequence, followed by injury and job-termination issues. The results of this study have implications for further research and ethical decision-making models. The *Moral Judgment Interview* is in the appendix. Includes bibliographical references.

Westin, A. F., & Aram, J. D. (1988). *Managerial dilemmas: Cases in social, legal and technological change.* Cambridge, MA: Ballinger.

Authors Westin and Aram address the social, legal, and technological changes that confront modern management decision making. They present 12 fact-based case studies that include such contemporary issues as: medical ethics and business decisions; sexual discrimination and the corporate culture; reproductive risk and EEO; employee protest versus employee loyalty; testing employees for substance abuse; due process in a nonunion firm; and big brother in the automated office. The book is intended to expose the reader to a range of questions facing organizations, to assist in developing diagnostic skills, and to present the management-change processes that are now confronting large corporations. Includes bibliographies.

New
Zeckhauser, R. J., Keeney, R. L., & Sebenius, J. K. (Eds.). (1996). *Wise choices: Decisions, games, and negotiations.* Boston: Harvard Business School Press.

Howard Raiffa is a an applied mathematician who pioneered the fields of decision analysis, game theory, and negotiation. This collection of 23 papers is a tribute to his work, and specific papers address issues as diverse as risk and return on stock portfolios, the selective revelation of product information, and a decision analysis of the prenatal detection of Down's Syndrome. The book's central theme is that the consequences of decisions are important and alternatives are often ambiguous, but "wise choices flow from systematic analysis." Includes index.

EMPOWERMENT AND PARTICIPATION

Alster, J., & Gallo, H. (Eds.). (1992). *Leadership and empowerment for total quality.* New York: Conference Board.

This is a special report marking the 75th anniversary of the Conference Board, whose mission is to improve the business-enterprise system and to enhance the contribution of business to society. The following CEOs share their organizations' experiences with total quality management through empowerment: Jon C. Madonna, KPMG Peat Marwick; Paul Allaire, Xerox Corporation; John Johnstone, Olin Corporation; and Ernest Drew, Hoechst Celanese Corporation.

Barker, J. R. (1993). **Tightening the iron cage: Concertive control in self-managing teams.** *Administrative Science Quarterly, 38*(3), 408-437.

With the demise of bureaucratic systems, the locus of control shifts from management to workers. In self-

managed teams, workers negotiate value-based actions to achieve corporate mission and productivity. Barker contends that this type of concertive control is actually tighter than top-down management control.

Belasco, J. A., & Stayer, R. C. (1993). *Flight of the buffalo: Soaring to excellence, learning to let employees lead.* New York: Warner Books.

Belasco, author of the management best-seller, *Teaching the Elephant to Dance* (1990), and Stayer, the Johnsonville Foods CEO featured in Tom Peters's video *The Leadership Alliance* (1988), share their insights on leadership. Having been autocratic leaders in their own organizations, they each felt like a head buffalo followed blindly by a herd of employees. Using the buffalo herd metaphor, they share the learning processes that allowed them to change their own behaviors. Using another metaphor, they explain how they transferred ownership to employees who now resemble flocks of geese flying in V-formation with every goose responsible for its own flight.

Block, P. (1987). *The empowered manager: Positive political skills at work.* San Francisco: Jossey-Bass.

Block writes about politics in the workplace and their effect on middle managers. His suggestions for controlling one's career destiny include: understanding bureaucracy, making contracts with bosses and subordinates, and developing strategies to deal with adversaries. Includes bibliography and index.

Block, P. (1993). *Stewardship: Choosing service over self-interest.* San Francisco: Berrett-Koehler.

Stewardship replaces top-down control with partnership and choice at all levels. Individuals within an organization take responsibility and hold themselves accountable. Block presents models of stewardship for organizations and for individuals. He states that organizations that practice stewardship will succeed by choosing service over self-interest and by integrating the best of the human spirit with the demands of the marketplace. Includes an index.

New
Case, R. H., & Singer, J. (1997). **Re: Project team empowerment aboard the Starship Enterprise.** *Research-Technology Management, 40*(3), 13-15.

Can you imagine Captain Kirk implementing an empowerment program? This memo from the illustrious starship captain describes what happened when the Federation decided that the crew should be "empowered." Case and Singer use this fictional message from a traditional "old school" leader to describe some of the disadvantages of employee empowerment, such as teams falling behind technically and a loss of objectivity.

Chaleff, I. (1995). ***The courageous follower: Standing up to and for our leaders.*** San Francisco: Berrett-Koehler.

Chaleff introduces the psychological dynamics of the leader-follower dyad. In the worst-case scenarios such as Nazi Germany, followers blindly accept a leader's behavior and are afraid to challenge. In the best-case scenarios, followers are proactive, take responsibility, challenge unethical behavior, and champion change. Being a courageous follower means knowing when to separate from a leader whose purpose or behavior no longer warrants support. Includes bibliographical references and index.

New
Cohen, S. G., Chang, L., & Ledford, G. E., Jr. (1997). **A hierarchical construct of self-management leadership and its relationship to quality of work life and perceived work group effectiveness.** *Personnel Psychology, 50*(2), 275-308.

Self-management, as defined by Manz and Sims's *Self-Management Leadership Questionnaire* (1987, *Administrative Science Quarterly, 32*(1), 106-129), is characterized by self-observation, self-goal setting, incentive modification, rehearsal, and self-expectation. The authors used the *SMLQ* to compare self-managed and traditionally managed employees in a large telephone company. They affirmed the validity of the *SMLQ* and found that self-managing work teams were more effective. The study also showed that when leaders of both kinds of work groups exhibit self-managing behaviors, the quality of work life and effectiveness of the group increased.

Deal, T. E., & Jenkins, W. A. (1994). ***Managing the hidden organization: Strategies for empowering your behind-the-scenes employees.*** New York: Warner Books.

Deal and Jenkins use a theater metaphor to illustrate the value of employees who work quietly backstage to support the star employees who are in the limelight. They suggest strategies for casting the best talent and for giving ovations for outstanding performances. As management/leadership educators and consultants, the authors base their empowerment premise on their consulting work with 500 organizations, several in-depth case studies, interviews, and a study of the literature. Includes bibliographical references.

Drath, W. H. (1993). ***Why managers have trouble empowering: A theoretical perspective based on concepts of adult development.*** Greensboro, NC: Center for Creative Leadership.

This report, based on eight years of research with high-level managers, considers the character factors that enable managers to empower subordinates. Drath argues that the authoritative character factors that help managers achieve their positions are the same ones that cause them to have difficulty sharing authority. The lifelong process of creating personal meaning conflicts with the demands of leadership. The solution lies in creating a balance between these two worlds. Drath defines the strengths and weaknesses of managers who have difficulty empowering subordinates and those who have developed into participative managers. Organizational support plays a key role in this development. Includes bibliographical references.

Fox, W. M. (1987). ***Effective group problem solving: How to broaden participation, improve decision making, and increase commitment to action.*** San Francisco: Jossey-Bass.

The author has examined the ways that one can achieve success by using participative problem solving in the work group, committee, or volunteer group. The many achievements of participation-based programs in industry are described, with gentle reminders to others of the difficulties they may encounter if they fail to understand and learn from such model programs. The Improved Nominal Group Technique (INGT) is presented. This process consists of research-based guidelines that minimize or eliminate the many problems found in conventional group procedures. As a follow-up and review, the appendix includes a test of the concepts of the INGT. Includes bibliography and index.

Gastil, J. (1994). **A definition and illustration of democratic leadership.** *Human Relations, 47*(8), 953-975.

Previous definitions of democratic leadership identify three primary functions: 1) distribution of responsibility, 2) empowering the membership, and 3) participatory decision making. Gastil presents a decision-tree model that promotes shared authority and good group relations. This model is intended for groups of all sizes, from small work teams to large societies. To illustrate the model, he describes the Kettering Foundation's National Issues Forum, a case study in democratic leadership.

Gastil, J. (1994). **A meta-analytic review of the productivity and satisfaction of democratic and autocratic leadership.** *Small Group Research, 25*(3), 384-410.

In a review of the literature on democratic and autocratic leadership, Gastil identifies a lack of commonality between the two styles. He reports on a meta-analysis of 39 studies comparing sample size, context, and the measurable effects of democratic and autocratic leadership styles on group productivity and member satisfaction. His conclusions suggest apparent effectiveness of naturally occurring democratic leadership and limitations of externally imposed democratic methods.

Hirschhorn, L. (1990). **Leaders and followers in a postindustrial age: A psychodynamic view.** *Journal of Applied Behavioral Science: Special Issue: Character and Leadership*, 26(4), 529-542.

To develop a collaborative relationship, a leader must show dependence on followers, exposing vulnerability. Likewise, a follower desiring to collaborate may be seen by a leader as threatening, thus exposing vulnerability. Case studies illustrate the psychological awareness and growth experienced by followers and leaders who have learned to depend on one another by accepting their own vulnerabilities.

Hollander, E. P. (1978). *Leadership dynamics: A practical guide to effective relationships.* New York: Free Press.

This book focuses on effectiveness leadership with an emphasis on leader-follower relations. Hollander defines leadership as an influence process with a variety of styles and situations. He introduces a concept of "social exchange," in which each participant gives and receives something from the relationship and rewarding-type behavior is practiced. Includes bibliography and index.

New
Howard, A., & Wellins, R. S. (1994). *High-involvement leadership: Changing roles for changing times.* Pittsburgh, PA: Development Dimensions International; Tenafly, NJ: Leadership Research Institute.

High-involvement leadership occurs when "organizations empower their employees by pushing down decision-making responsibility to those close to internal and external customers." This study examined the response of over 1,300 workers, from senior managers to associates, to high-involvement leadership. It found that although this leadership style had widespread benefits, many barriers to its implementation still exist, and senior managers often view it "through rose-colored glasses." Based on these results, the authors offer their recommendations for implementing high-involvement leadership, including involving high-level managers in organizational transformation, establishing rewards for employees, and identifying individuals' specific development needs.

New
Hurst, V. (1996). **The nomenclature of leadership.** *Journal of Leadership Studies*, 3(1), 123-129.

Hurst believes that to make a change in an organization, institution, or society, there needs to be collaboration instead of leadership. Collaborative relations allow people to have a social mind-set that is concerned with common welfare. According to Hurst, the words leadership and collaboration have different meanings. Leadership describes position and unequal influence. Collaboration promotes mutuality and equality. Hurst feels that leadership will always have a place in society but that it is collaboration that will ultimately make the monumental changes.

Keller, T., & Dansereau, F. (1995). **Leadership and empowerment: A social exchange perspective.** *Human Relations*, 48(2), 127-146.

To determine an employee's feeling of job control and support from above, 92 dyads completed subordinate/superior feedback questionnaires. Results support the hypotheses that receipt of negotiating latitude and support for self-worth positively relate to subordinates' perceptions of control and fairness. In return, subordinates respond with higher performance and fewer dyadic problems. The authors conclude that empowering leadership practices benefit superiors.

Kelley, R. E. (1992). *The power of followership: How to create leaders people want to follow and followers who lead themselves.* New York: Currency/Doubleday.

"Leaders contribute on the average no more than 20% to the success of most organizations." Kelley's assertion begins a new look at the roles of leaders and followers in organizations. Breaking from the conventional definition of followers as sheep, Kelley defines them as people who know what to do without being told. He also asserts ambition is less and less a correlate of success; groups with many leaders can be chaotic, whereas groups with none can be very productive; there are styles of followership, just as there are styles of leadership. Leaders are urged to understand and embrace shared responsibility and reward. Includes bibliographical references and index.

New
Khan, S. (1997). **The key to being a *leader* company.** *Journal for Quality and Participation*, 20(1), 44-50.

To determine the state of employee empowerment in today's business world, the author surveyed managers and quotes many of their answers here. Khan describes whether managers feel empowered or not, what actions they take to empower their employees, and then develops a definition of empowerment and a list of its benefits. The article includes a list of the risks of empowerment, reasons it can fail, steps companies can take to empower employees, and methods for inspiring employee trust in the empowerment process.

Lawler, E. E., III. (1992). *The ultimate advantage.* San Francisco: Jossey-Bass.

High-involvement management practices—those that foster quick adaptation and change and satisfy work relationships—are not just a good idea; they are an economic necessity. Acknowledging that employees give more to their work when they have a say in how the company is run, Lawler outlines programs that go beyond the total-quality-management approach. Providing a competitive advantage is characterized by diversity, entrepreneurial behavior, and respect for the individual. Organizations encourage innovation, increase cost-effectiveness, deliver enhanced quality, customer service, and speed by setting up work teams. Includes bibliographical references and index.

Lee, C. (1991). **Followership: The essence of leadership.** *Training, 28*(1), 27-35.

Traits of effective followership are independent critical thinking and an active versus passive nature. Lee defines five levels of followership as: "sheep" who are dependent and passive, "yes people" who are active but uncritical, "alienated followers" who are critical and independent but don't act, "survivors" who balance in the middle of both traits, and "effective followers" who think for themselves and carry out tasks with enthusiasm. Effective followers behave like good leaders. Effective followership is exemplified at Lincoln Electric.

Manz, C. C. (1986). **Self-leadership: Toward an expanded theory of self-influence processes in organizations.** *Academy of Management Review, 11*(3), 585-600.

Manz offers the premise that the central control mechanisms within organizations are self-control systems. He outlines strategies commonly used by individuals to manage both boring tasks and intrinsically satisfying tasks. Strategies for self-leadership practice are given.

Manz, C. C. (1992). **Self-leading work teams: Moving beyond self-management myths.** *Human Relations, 45*(11), 1119-1140.

In a self-management situation, an employee determines how to complete a task or meet a standard. In a self-influence situation, an employee determines what should be done and why. Self-managed teams share efforts and decision making to benefit the whole. Self-leading teams

involve the workforce in determining the direction of the organization and then carry out that direction.

New
McLagan, P. A., & Nel, C. (1995). *The age of participation: New governance for the workplace and the world.* San Francisco: Berrett-Koehler.

McLagan and Nel call for a fundamental shift toward participative governance in the workplace. Their four major challenges to leaders are: 1) let go of authoritarian perspectives and behaviors, 2) lead the emotional transition, 3) be accountable stewards of high performance and high involvement, and 4) give leadership away to every member of the organization. Self-management, broad business, understanding, knowledge of business finance and economics, critical-thinking skills, integrative communication skills, mutual learning skills, and flexible decision making are needed from everyone in an organization to achieve successful participative governance. A *Governance Assessment* is included to help organizations evaluate their distribution of authoritarian and participative governance. Includes bibliographical references and index.

Mmobuosi, I. B. (1991). **Followership behaviour: A neglected aspect of leadership studies.** *Leadership and Organization Development Journal, 12*(7), 11-16.

Appointments to leadership positions come from above, but confirmation comes from below. What is appropriate leader behavior when subordinates are uncooperative? A research study controlled subordinate noncooperation in three groups. Mmobuosi reports the research findings and conclusion that leader behavior results partially from relationships with subordinates.

New
Plas, J. M. (1996). *Person-centered leadership: An American approach to participatory management.* Thousand Oaks, CA: Sage.

Despite this country's reverence for the individual, American business has traditionally neglected individuals, paying attention to problems, not people. Plas offers a model of person-centered leadership that "does not just focus on workers, it focuses on the *individual* worker." Plas uses companies including Southwest Airlines, Wal-Mart, and FedEx to illustrate her theory, and offers readers a strategy for making their own organizations person-centered. Information boxes and pulled quotes highlight key concepts and each chapter includes a list of references for further reading. Includes bibliographical references and index.

New

Randolph, W. A. (1995). **Navigating the journey to empowerment.** *Organizational Dynamics, 23*(4), 19-32.

Over the past eight years, Randolph has researched the empowerment programs of ten companies (identified by fictitious names) and has developed a plan for empowering employees based on his experience. His plan includes three steps: share information, create autonomy through structure, and let teams become the hierarchy. Randolph explains why each step is important and offers companies specific ways to put them into action, using examples from the companies he studied. Includes bibliographical references.

Reitzug, U. C. (1992). **Self-managed leadership: An alternative school governance structure.** *Urban Review, 24*(2), 133-147.

The problems facing urban schools—drugs, lack of discipline, declining test scores, and dysfunctional families—require that school leadership be assumed by the frontline members of the educational system, the teachers. Traditionally, limitations have been placed on teachers' authority to solve problems and make decisions. Emerging is a structure to empower teachers through participative decision making. Reitzug suggests an alternative structure of self-management which would utilize individual potential, synergize ideas, build commitment, and create teacher leadership.

Ripley, R. E., & Ripley, M. J. (1993). **Empowerment: What to do with troubling employees?** *Journal of Managerial Psychology, 8*(3), 3-9.

Troubling employees are described as immature, demanding, blaming, incompetent, uncooperative, passive-aggressive, or psychologically unhealthy. In other words, they are employees a manager would be afraid to empower. Ripley and Ripley discuss empowering solutions, such as modeling from the top and concentrating on objective, nonthreatening training in the areas of quality and continuous improvement.

Rost, J. C. (1991). *Leadership for the twenty-first century.* New York: Praeger.

A critique of 150 writings on leadership since 1930, this book explores old definitions of leadership and proposes a new one. Fundamental concepts of great-man theories, facilitators, psychological traits, behavior, situation, and excellence are criticized for oversimplifying a complex set of relationships. Rost suggests that a study of followership will help scholars, trainers, and practitioners to better understand leader-follower relationships. Includes bibliographical references and index.

Rost, J., & Smith, A. (1992). **Leadership: A postindustrial approach.** *European Management Journal, 10*(2), 193-201.

The old, industrial-age, authoritative style of leadership has failed. A postindustrial approach is founded upon leaders and followers in agreement on mutual purposes. The authors propose a model of the five Cs of credibility: character, care, courage, composure, and competence.

Sarros, J. C. (1992). **What leaders say they do: An Australian example.** *Leadership and Organization Development Journal, 13*(5), 21-27.

A Management-Leader Profile (MLP) model is used to illustrate the results of 32 top Australian executives interviewed over a nine-month period during 1990. Executives were selected based on their contributions to management and leadership in Australian public- and private-sector organizations. The MLP indicates that leaders and managers fall into one of two zones, the proactive or reactive. Whatever the organization's leadership-management style, leaders should be proactive and empowering rather than reactive and de-energizing.

New

Schuster, F. E., Morden, D. L., Baker, T. E., McKay, I. S., Dunning, K. E., & Hagan, C. M. (1997). **Management practice, organization climate, and performance: An exploratory study.** *Journal of Applied Behavioral Science, 33*(2), 209-226.

This article reports on a five-year experiment in a Canadian dairy-processing and distribution firm. To develop and sustain competitive advantage, the firm recognized the need for employee-centered management. Over five years, the new structure was implemented in seven steps: 1) develop a baseline of employee participation, performance, and satisfaction; 2) initiate improvements in communication, rewards, and shared decision making; 3) change executive evaluation and reward practices to measure and compensate for human development as well as production; 4) remove barriers to participation; 5) involve employees in planning the changes; 6) measure the changes in participation, performance, and satisfaction; and 7) use criteria to reinforce or modify the strategies. The experiment resulted in a significant growth in operating income as well as significant improvements in employee morale and commitment. Includes bibliographical references.

Semler, R. (1993). *Maverick: The success story behind the world's most unusual workplace.* New York: Warner Books.

Semler's Brazilian company, Semco, has been recognized as a humane and productive manufacturer of industrial machinery. Its employees set their own production quotas, work on their own time without pay, redesign products, and formulate marketing plans. Everyone is taught how to read the balance sheets and cash-flow statements. When Semco considers acquiring a new factory, all employees load onto buses for tours of the new site so they can make informed votes on the decision to acquire. Semler sees his leadership role as that of a catalyst who creates an environment in which others make decisions.

New
Sims, H. P., Jr., & Manz, C. C. (1996). ***Company of heroes: Unleashing the power of self-leadership.*** New York: Wiley.

The authors of *SuperLeadership* (Prentice Hall, 1989) revisit their theory of the enabling leader who teaches others to lead themselves. This book compares super-leadership to other frameworks, especially visionary and heroic leadership. It suggests four steps to apply the superleadership theory and create an organization of self-leaders, a company of heroes. The four steps are: 1) leaders must practice self-leadership behavior, 2) encourage followers to practice self-leadership, 3) foster teamwork, and 4) build a company culture of self-leadership. Examples of superleaders are former U.S. President Jimmy Carter, whose hands-on role with Habitat for Humanity encouraged thousands of new volunteers, and Jack Welch, CEO of GE, whose town meeting-style Work Out sessions broke down barriers between workers and management and revitalized flagging productivity. Includes bibliographical references and index.

New
Spreitzer, G. M. (1996). **Empowering middle managers to be transformational leaders.** *The Journal of Applied Behavioral Science*, 32(3), 237-261.

In the early 1990s Ford Motor Company sent 3,000 of its middle managers through a leadership development program called LEAD, which consisted of an intensive one-week session with a follow-up six months later. This study surveyed a sample of the managers to determine how their leadership styles changed in those six months. The authors first identify the five types of changes the managers initiated—management-style change, transactional within-unit change, transactional organization change, transformational work-unit change, and transformational organization change—and then analyze how the managers' personality characteristics determined what sort of changes they instituted. Includes bibliographical references.

New
Townsend, P. L., & Gebhardt, J. E. (1997). ***Five-star leadership: The art and strategy of creating leaders at every level.*** New York: Wiley.

This book assumes that leadership is a behavior, not a position. It revisits old management theories, total quality management, and military leadership to build a case for the distribution of power, leadership, and development throughout an organization. The authors suggest skills to develop in self and others for empowering leaders at every level. Among the appendices are: the description of a new military philosophy called *Total Quality Leadership;* more than a dozen lists of leadership skills, principles, practices, and competencies drawn from the literature; and an article on love and leadership reprinted from the *Marine Corps Gazette* (1982). Includes a bibliography and index.

Vanderslice, V. J. (1988). **Separating leadership from leaders: An assessment of the effect of leader and follower roles in organizations.** *Human Relations*, 41(9), 677-696.

What are the distinctions between leadership and leadership functions? Can these functions be carried out by other members of the organization? What conditions are necessary to make a "leaderless" organization successful? These are some of the questions addressed in Vanderslice's comparison study, which examines Moosewood Industries, a leaderless-structured enterprise, and another company that has a flat structure. The conclusions of the study raise some basic questions for behavioral scientists about the definition of motivation, power, and responsibility.

Vogt, J. F., & Murrell, K. L. (1990). ***Empowerment in organizations: How to spark exceptional performance.*** San Diego, CA: University Associates.

Empowerment liberates, rather than controls, people. Whether self-initiated or initiated by management, empowerment enables employees to control their own commitment and contribution to an organization. This automatically enlarges the power of an organization. Vogt and Murrell offer a framework for understanding empowerment and practical advice necessary to apply it. There are three management-style surveys: organizational culture, subordinates' perceptions, and managers' perceptions. Includes bibliographical references.

New
Wall, S. J., & Wall, S. R. (1995). ***The new strategists: Creating leaders at all levels.*** New York: Free Press.

The Walls introduce a circular model called *Strategy: A Dynamic Learning Process.* In it, deliberate strategies are based on industry analysis, competitive position, and allocation of resources. As these strategies are tested and fit to customer needs, they change and grow. As front-line employees provide customer feedback, the strategies evolve again. The result is a new set of strategies that uncovers previously unanticipated markets and unarticulated customer needs. The authors explain how to capitalize on the wealth of knowledge at all levels of an organization to achieve the highest level of strategic planning. Appendix A has self-assessment questionnaires for frontline strategists, strategy integrators, strategic leaders, and influence tactics. Appendix B offers a detailed outline of the strategic-planning process. Appendix C explains six steps for developing new skills. Examples of strategic planning in major corporations exhibit good practice. Includes bibliographical references and index.

ETHICS, VALUES, SPIRIT, AND SERVANT LEADERSHIP

Aguilar, F. J. (1994). ***Managing corporate ethics: Learning from America's ethical companies how to supercharge business performance.*** New York: Oxford University Press.

The author does not attempt to answer specific ethical questions. Instead, he suggests ways to motivate ethical behavior—not just to avoid scandals and lawsuits. Ethical behavior can build strong relationships and benefit the bottom line. Examples from Johnson and Johnson, General Mills, Hewlett-Packard, and Texas Instruments reveal how successful companies practice business ethics. Includes bibliographical references and index.

Badaracco, J. L., Jr., & Ellsworth, R. R. (1989). ***Leadership and the quest for integrity.*** Boston: Harvard Business School Press.

This book poses the question, "How do managers deal with the messy realities and trade-offs of today's business world?" Intending to challenge traditional beliefs about leadership, the authors conducted lengthy interviews with the CEOs of Citicorp, Du Pont, Johnson & Johnson, Colgate-Palmolive, and other major companies. Their experiences provide insight into how managers can juggle their responsibilities to the organization, their personal beliefs, their behavior, and their vision for the future of the organization. It is the consistency with which they balance their visions, intentions, and actions that equals integrity. This consistency, claim the authors, is the truest path to leadership. Includes bibliography and index.

Bellingham, R., & Cohen, B. (1990). ***Ethical leadership: A competitive edge.*** Amherst, MA: Human Resource Development Press.

Ethical issues facing businesses today are: protecting the environment; health and safety; quality of product or service; and relations with employees, customers, and community. Based on a 1988 international survey of 300 executives, Bellingham and Cohen have devised a range of ethical goals. At the low end is "staying out of trouble." The ideal is "becoming an ethical exemplar." The authors suggest action steps to achieve the highest goals and list exemplars who have found that ethical practices do result in long-term business success. Includes bibliographical references.

Bolman, L. G., & Deal, T. E. (1994). ***Leading with soul: An uncommon journey of spirit.*** San Francisco: Jossey-Bass.

As social scientists, the authors pursued an uncommon journey of their own to link leadership with spirituality—reclaiming the human capacity that gives lives passion and purpose. Using the ancient literary style of conversations between a troubled leader and a wise guide (in this case, a Japanese guide), this book reveals the process of finding, believing, sharing, and leading with soul. Includes bibliographical references.

New

Briskin, A. (1996). ***The stirring of soul in the workplace.*** San Francisco: Jossey-Bass.

Briskin calls his book "a reality check on management and the workplace: where we are, where we have been, and where we may be going." He uses historical background and real-life stories to develop a theory of the role the soul plays in the workplace, and the role it should play. Chapters address issues including the legacy of efficiency, managing emotions, taking up organizational roles, and how to affirm your experience at work. Includes bibliographical references and index.

Ciulla, J. B. (1995). **Leadership ethics: Mapping the territory.** *Business Ethics Quarterly, 5*(1), 5-28.

In this map, Ciulla explains that the territory of ethics lies in the heart of leadership studies and has veins in research. She discusses where the research on this subject has been, where ethics fits into recent definitions of leadership, and where future research could explore a greater understanding of leadership ethics. The question that Ciulla wants researchers to ask is not "What is leadership?" but "What is good leadership?"

Conger, J. A., & Associates. (1994). *Spirit at work: Discovering the spirituality in leadership.* San Francisco: Jossey-Bass.

With the collapse of traditional sources of support and connectedness (family, church, and community), the workplace has become the primary community for many people. Conger claims that the workplace can and should offer a link to spirituality through leadership practices of integrity, prudence, justice, and fortitude. Chapters cover such issues as the differences between spirituality and religion, dealing with paradoxes of private self and public service, and creating spiritual connectedness through storytelling. Includes bibliographical references and index.

Covey, S. R. (1991). *Principle-centered leadership.* New York: Summit Books.

Principles are "natural laws and governing values that are universally valid," such as fairness, equity, justice, integrity, honesty, and trust. Leadership is the ability to apply these principles to problems, resulting in quality, productivity, profitability, and win-win relationships. Covey explains his concepts of alternative life- and organizational-centers, leadership levels, maturity continuum, power process, conditions of empowerment, management paradigms, and learning environments. At the center of his concepts are principles, like a compass guiding the way. Includes an index.

New
Dehler, G. E., & Welsh, M. A. (1996). **Spirituality and organizational transformation: Implications for the new management paradigm.** *Journal of Managerial Psychology,* 9(6), 17-26.

According to the authors, leaders tend to ignore spirituality as they guide their organizations through change. In this article, Dehler and Welsh attempt to integrate work on spirituality and organizational transformation, discussing topics such as the inspirational side of leadership, Csikzentmihalyi's theory of flow, and work-as-play. They then describe the practical effects that spirituality can have on management and offer managers advice on how to lead in a spiritually aware manner. Includes bibliographical references.

New
Dreher, D. (1996). *The Tao of personal leadership.* New York: HarperBusiness.

Dreher observes that leaders in all fields are informed by ancient principles such as those written two thousand years ago in the *Tao Te Ching* by Lao Tzu. The 81 poems in the *Tao* reveal the wisdom of living systems—in nature, in people, and in relationships. This book draws

leadership lessons from the *Tao,* as well as from Buddhism and the martial art of aikido. In part one, "The Yin of Inner Leadership," Dreher concentrates on the personal elements of leadership and self-development. In part two, "The Yang of Leadership in Action," she focuses on the relationships and responsibilities of leadership. Includes bibliographical references and index.

New
Fairholm, G. W. (1997). *Capturing the heart of leadership: Spirituality and community in the new American workplace.* Westport, CT: Praeger.

Fairholm observes that leaders must bring to their tasks "their whole selves, their knowledge of the spiritual dimension of life that, perhaps, more powerfully than any other force, guides daily action." In this book, he takes a creative approach to building a framework for understanding the spiritual nature of leadership and its potential manifestation in the workplace. Some examples are: spirituality helps leaders understand self and others better, spirituality is a holistic approach that considers the needs of employees and the goals of the organization, spiritual leaders help others reach their highest potential, and spiritual leaders live out their deeply held personal values. Includes bibliographical references and index.

Francis, D., & Woodcock, M. (1990). *Unblocking organizational values.* Glenview, IL: Scott, Foresman.

Managers' values shape the destiny of an organization. Whether success is defined as profitability or as contribution to society, values create a strong foundation for setting and achieving goals. Effectiveness, fairness, economy, teamwork, and opportunism are among the 12 basic values examined. A questionnaire is included to analyze and clarify an organization's values. Practical steps at the end of each chapter guide leaders toward setting values into action. Includes bibliographical references and index.

Graham, J. W. (1991). **Servant-leadership in organizations: Inspirational and moral.** *Leadership Quarterly,* 2(2), 105-119.

Graham outlines four variations of charismatic leadership. *Weberian charismatic authority* is based on a perceived divine gift of the leader and socioeconomic distress of the followers. *Personal celebrity charisma* happens when followers with low self-esteem romanticize a dramatic and forceful leader. *Transformational leadership* is a partnership where the goals of the leader, the followers, and the organization are all met. *Servant leadership* adds moral development, a focus on service, and a spiritual insight for the leader and for followers who progress into leadership positions. Case studies illustrate examples of servant leadership.

Greenleaf, R. K. (1977). *Servant leadership: A journey into the nature of legitimate power and greatness.* New York: Paulist Press.

This book is a constructive and critical examination of leadership and the perversions of leadership in major spheres of American life, including the crucial sphere of the responsibility (and irresponsibility) of boards of trustees. It develops the concept of the servant leader and deals with the structure and mode of government that will favor optimal performance of our many institutions as servants of society. It also gives biographical models of two great servant leaders. Includes index.

Hall, B. P., & Thompson, H. (1980). *Leadership through values: A study in personal and organizational development.* New York: Paulist Press.

Hall has conducted 13 years of research on value theory in personal development, religious and educational organizations, and international management situations. His theory of consciousness and value development has been used in urban planning and human resource development, and in establishment of organizational culture. "Competent, caring persons can humanize our institutions and harness our technologies. In cooperation with others who care, they can seek to restore harmony to our natural world, to our inner worlds, and among our human communities." Seven leader-followership styles are described.

Harrison, F. C. (Ed.). (1989). *Spirit of leadership: Inspiring quotations for leaders.* Germantown, TN: Leadership Education and Development.

Poets, presidents, and philosophers are but a few of the many individuals represented in this collection of quotations that address the multifaceted nature of leadership. Includes an index.

Hawley, J. (1993). *Reawakening the spirit in work: The power of dharmic management.* San Francisco: Berrett-Koehler.

Dharma is a Sanskrit word meaning deep, deep integrity, or living by your inner truth. Dharmic management fuses spirit, character, values, and decency within the workplace. This nonreligious book guides the reader toward achieving purpose, peace, health, and happiness in business life and life in general. Includes bibliographical references and index.

Heider, J. (1985). *The Tao of leadership.* Atlanta, GA: Humanics New Age.

Primarily an adaptation of the Chinese classic tome of wisdom, *Tao Te Ching* by Lao Tzu, Heider has found a new application for this work. As a teacher and trainer of group leaders, Heider has taken the principles set down in the *Tao* and applied them to the leadership process. Based upon the same structure as the *Tao*, each page is the author's version of the meaning of Lao Tzu's own words. This text is meant to provide inspiration and a path to the higher intentions of leadership for those who lead, in whatever context, whether family or group, church or school, business or military, political or administrative. Includes a bibliography.

New
Hendricks, G., & Ludeman, K. (1996). *The corporate mystic: A guidebook for visionaries with their feet on the ground.* New York: Bantam.

The authors claim that real mystics are not found in monasteries, but in corporate boardrooms. To reach this conclusion, Hendricks and Ludeman conducted interviews with several hundred executives who do soul-satisfying work, empower others, and build profits for their companies. These corporate mystics can be identified by 12 characteristics: absolute honesty, fairness, self-knowledge, a focus on contribution, nondogmatic spirituality, getting more done by doing less, calling forth the best of themselves and others, openness to change, a special sense of humor, keen distant vision and up-close focus, an unusual self-discipline, and balance. This little book is sprinkled throughout with quotations by and about mystic leadership. The book ends with four ten-minute exercises to enhance integrity, vision, and intuition and seven radical rules for business success.

Hesse, H. (1956). *The journey to the East.* New York: Farrar, Straus & Giroux.

This classic work of fiction was the inspiration for much of Robert Greenleaf's work with servant leadership. The story follows a group of leaders from different cultures and backgrounds, called the League. They embark on a highly successful expedition until their humble servant disappears. Unable to settle on a common path or pursuit, the league breaks up and the leaders go in their own directions.

Hickman, C. R. (1990). *Mind of a manager: Soul of a leader.* New York: Wiley.

Hickman defines leaders as visionary and creative. Managers are analytical, structured, and turn leaders' visions into commercial successes. Organizations rely on leaders and managers working together toward common goals and avoiding natural conflict. He divides organizational success into five factors: competitive advantage, capability, change, style, and results. Balance between leaders and managers in all factors creates harmony. Questionnaires are provided to assess self, teams, organizations, and attitudes. Includes bibliographical references and index.

Hitt, W. D. (1990). *Ethics and leadership: Putting theory into practice.* Columbus, OH: Battelle Press.

Leaders have considerable influence on the ethical conduct of their people when they transform vision into action, empower others, and use their own power to achieve worthwhile ends. This book is intended to help managers understand ethics, make ethical decisions, and promote ethical conduct. Values are described as beliefs that guide behavior toward meeting goals. Examples, practical suggestions, and exercises illustrate traditional American values, organizational and personal values, ethical conflicts, styles, and systems. An organizational code of ethics is proposed. Includes bibliographical references and index.

New
Hitt, W. D. (1996). *A global ethic: The leadership challenge.* Columbus, OH: Battelle Press.

Hitt examines the need for a global set of core values. Leaders are challenged to: 1) find the common ground by being a citizen of the world, 2) strive to become a fully functioning person, 3) live a life of total dedication to the truth, 4) be truly committed to the good life, and 5) enlist others to be citizens of the world. To live the good life, Hitt believes one should live a life of compassion, contribution, integrity, communication, and cooperation. The book has exercises to help one understand why there is a need for a global ethic and how to live the good life in a global community. Includes bibliographical references and index.

Hosmer, L. T. (1994). *Moral leadership in business.* Boston: Irwin.

This is a textbook for students of leadership ethics. The author defines moral problems, reasoning, and principles and applies those concepts to organizational issues and managerial responsibilities. There are numerous case studies and assignments in each chapter. The leveraged buyout of RJR Nabisco, the wreck of the Exxon Valdez, and Ford versus Greenpeace are among the cases used to illustrate ethical problems in business. Includes bibliographical references and index.

Huey, J. (1994). **The new post-heroic leadership.** *Fortune,* *129*(4), 42-50.

Leadership involves getting things started and facilitating change. In the past, most corporations substituted hierarchy for leadership, but as the power of position continues to erode, corporate leaders are going to face two fundamental tasks: first, to develop and articulate exactly what the company is trying to accomplish, and second, to create an environment in which employees can figure out what needs to be done and then do it well. Examples of this post-heroic, or servant leadership are discussed at W.L. Gore, Levi's, and Johnson & Johnson.

New
Kanungo, R. N., & Mendonca, M. (1996). *Ethical dimensions of leadership.* Thousand Oaks, CA: Sage.

The authors believe that the actions of a leader "are effective only to the extent that they are imbued with sound ethical principles." This book provides both a conceptual framework for ethical leadership and strategies for its practical applications. The first sections analyze the different approaches to leadership, the motivations of a leader, the relationship between leaders and followers, and the nature of altruism as a motivational construct and an ethical justification for a leader's actions. Later chapters focus on how leaders can prepare themselves to function ethically, dismissing standard methods of teaching ethics as an intellectual exercise and focusing instead on spirituality and how individuals develop their moral character. Includes references and an index.

Kelly, C. M. (1987). **The interrelationship of ethics and power in today's organizations.** *Organizational Dynamics,* *16*(1), 4-18.

The focus of this article is on Kelly's analysis of the "destructive achiever." The "destructive achiever has the charisma of a leader, but lacks his operational values; this achiever's net effect on the long-term welfare of the organization is negative." The author identifies three types of destructive achievers and discusses their influence and negative impact on an organization. Kelly concludes that leadership must remain vigilant for counterproductive behaviors. Dialogue, values discussion, and active participation within the organization are required.

Kidder, R. M. (1995). *How good people make tough choices.* New York: William Morrow.

At the Institute for Global Ethics, Kidder hears repeated concerns over the breakdown of morality. In executive ethics seminars for corporate, nonprofit, academic, and governmental clients, he asks participants to bring to the table real ethical dilemmas they have encountered. In this book, Kidder shares these dilemmas without revealing identities. Discussion of ethics paradigms and mental tools for solving dilemmas help the reader understand the decision-making process in situations of truth versus loyalty, individual versus community, and justice versus mercy. Includes bibliographical references and index.

Kiechel, W., III. (1992, May 4). **The leader as servant.** *Fortune, 125,* 121-122.

Twenty years after Greenleaf's book, *The Servant as Leader,* Kiechel reexamines and redefines the role of servant leaders in more proactive language. Servant leaders take people and their work seriously, finding initiatives and direction in group goals and a willingness to share in mistakes and pain. Servant leaders maintain and blend their own vision with those of their subordinates. In addition, servant leaders are self-effacing, do not glorify leadership, and do see themselves as stewards, adopting a long-term perspective.

Kouzes, J. M., & Posner, B. Z. (1992). **Ethical leaders: An essay about being in love.** *Journal of Business Ethics, 11*(5), 479-484.

Love constitutes the soul of ethical leadership. Ethical leaders understand the needs and values of their constituents and raise the level of human conduct. The authors claim that love lights a fire to get things done and that it is healing, supportive, and creative. Love is the power behind individual health; why not organizational health?

New
Kuczmarski, S. S., & Kuczmarski, T. D. (1995). *Values-based leadership.* Englewood Cliffs, NJ: Prentice Hall.

The authors write about their concern over the apparent lack of values in corporate America. They believe the foundation lies in a valueless society of disintegrating families and is reflected in the decreasing productivity of American workers. Interviews with employees from banks, law firms, nonprofit organizations, and restaurants uncovered a general feeling of "anomie," a lack of purpose or an apathetic attitude at work. The authors believe that awareness of this problem is the first step to combating it. They suggest ways for corporate leaders to develop value norms in themselves and their companies and to help employees gain meaning and self-satisfaction at work. Building personal relationships, showing passion, allowing conflict without blaming, encouraging personal success, and building teams are some of the ways to cement values and increase productivity. Includes an index.

Lessem, R. (1990). *Developmental management: Principles of holistic business.* Cambridge, MA: Basil Blackwell.

Lessem suggests that a successfully developed business, like a whole person, has a body, mind, heart, and soul. He equates body with primal management, mind with rational management, and soul with inspirational management. In this book, Lessem concentrates on the heart of business, which he calls developmental management. Drawing upon philosophies from Far Eastern, Middle Eastern, African, European, and American cultures, he explains what developmental management is and how to achieve it. Drexion Group's success is cited as an example. Includes bibliographical references and index.

Lombardo, M. M. (1986). *Values in action: The meaning of executive vignettes.* Greensboro, NC: Center for Creative Leadership.

The premise of this paper is that organizational and individual values are cemented not only through grand events but also through small ones. These vignettes or episodes are vividly remembered even decades later. This paper attempts to show that these vignettes collectively have major significance for organizations, and what they signify needs to be managed to enhance individual and organizational effectiveness. Includes a bibliography.

New
Marcic, D. (1997). *Managing with the wisdom of love: Uncovering virtue in people and organizations.* San Francisco: Jossey-Bass.

According to the author, the root cause of problems in American business today is "lack of love," and this book attempts to operationalize spirituality and teach managers to act with virtue. Quotes from the writings of different religions are used throughout the book to show that spirituality can be inclusive of all, and examples from the business world illustrate the concepts. Marcic includes checklists and charts to help readers apply her theories in their own lives and organizations.

New
McCormick, D. W. (1994). **Spirituality and management.** *Journal of Managerial Psychology, 9*(6), 5-8.

For many managers, incorporating spirituality into their work is a challenge but is necessary for their personal well-being. This article offers a working definition of spirituality, and then explores five themes relevant to an individual leader's relationship with the sacred: compassion, right livelihood, selfless service, work as meditation, and problems with pluralism.

McCoy, B. H. (1983). **The parable of the sadhu.** *Harvard Business Review, 61*(5), 103-108.

McCoy shares his experience when faced with a real life-and-death moral dilemma while climbing in the Himalayas. The author and fellow climbers had a narrow window of opportunity to reach a particular summit and fulfill their mission when they discovered an Indian holy man close to death along the path. Each climber offered food, clothing, water, or brief transport toward a place of safety. Yet, none of them forsook their own goals to carry the holy man down the mountain. McCoy examines the choices he and others made that day and the choices he makes today when confronted with moral dilemmas in his business.

Messick, D. M., & Bazerman, M. H. (1996). **Ethical leadership and the psychology of decision making.** *Sloan Management Review, 37*(2), 9-22.

From a psychological perspective, the authors explain weaknesses in the decision-making process. One can make errors in determining risks or use bias in seeking information to support one side of an issue. Unrealistic beliefs about the world, other people, and themselves can trap executives in ethical dilemmas. The authors explain how to recognize and avoid these traps and to make decisions that pass the sunshine test—decisions that stand up in the light of day and under public scrutiny.

Michalos, A. C. (1995). *A pragmatic approach to business ethics.* Thousand Oaks, CA: Sage.

Is the term "business ethics" an oxymoron? Not so, according to Michalos who is coeditor of the *Journal of Business Ethics*. He argues that ethical behavior is good for business and reaps profits. He examines the ethical issues surrounding the promotion of tobacco products and responsible advertising from a pragmatic perspective. Chapters on trust, taxation, NAFTA, public-opinion polling, and militarism have useful references. Includes bibliographical references and index.

Neville, R. C. (1989). **Value, courage, and leadership.** *Review of Metaphysics, 43*(169), 3-26.

In this presidential address to the Metaphysical Society of America, Neville claims that leadership is obligated by social conditions. He discusses personal virtue, courage, and social responsibility as perceived by Plato and several 20th-century philosophers. He confesses that his view of leadership is moral idealism.

Owen, H. (1987). *Spirit: Transformation and development in organizations.* Potomac, MD: Abbott.

This is a book about spirit and how it changes and develops in organizations. Chapters 1 through 6 lay the groundwork for Owen's thesis that spirit plays an important leadership role within an organization. Chapter 7 describes the need for someone to facilitate the process of infusing the organization with spirit. Chapter 8 considers how the concepts of time, reality, and meaning affect business strategy. Chapters 9 and 10 describe the practice of organizational spirit upon concrete findings extracted from case studies on the Internal Revenue Service; the Eastern Virginia Medical Authority; and the Norfolk, Virginia, Water Management Authority.

New
Perreault, G. (1997). **Ethical followers: A link to ethical leadership.** *Journal of Leadership Studies, 4*(1), 78-89.

Perreault considers followers active participants in the leadership process, saying that followers have an ethical responsibility to do two things: "1) follow a leader whose goals and practices are ethical and 2) carry out the goals and practices in an ethical manner." She then lists four components of ethical decision making that followers must posses: the ethical sensitivity to interpret a situation, the ethical reasoning to figure out what one ought to do, the ethical motivation to decide what one intends to do, and the ability to carry out that decision. Famous cases in which followers both did and did not act ethically, including Watergate, the release of the Pentagon Papers, and the Beech-Nut apple juice scandal, are used to illustrate this decision-making process. Ultimately Perreault argues that both leaders and followers must take ethical responsibility for their behavior. Includes references.

New
Petrick, J. A., & Quinn, J. F. (1997). *Management ethics: Integrity at work.* Thousand Oaks, CA: Sage.

The authors combine a conceptual framework of manage-ment ethics with real-life cases to make this book both practical and theoretically sound. First, they identify four processes of management: ethical planning, organizing, leading, and controlling. They then describe seven management clusters: accounting/auditing, finance/investment, marketing/advertising, business management/human rescues, technology/quality operations/organiza-tional behavior, public/nonprofit/health care, and interna-tional/public policy. Twenty-eight mini-cases, from organizations including Sears, United Way, E.F. Hutton, and Dow Corning, are then used to apply the theories and tools to each process in each cluster. The appendices include six tools and assessment instruments. Also includes index and references.

New
Posner, B. Z., & Schmidt, W. H. (1996). **The values of business and federal government executives: More different than alike.** *Public Personnel Management*, 25(3), 277-289.

Posner and Schmidt surveyed over a thousand business executives and managers in government agencies to determine whether the two groups felt differently on issues like the importance of organizational goals, organizational stakeholders, various personal traits, values issues, and trends of the future. The results of statistical analyses of each variable are given. Among their findings, business leaders were more optimistic about the future and more likely to feel clearly that their personal life takes priority over their professional life. Includes bibliographical references.

Renesch, J. (1992). *New traditions in business: Spirit and leadership in the 21st century.* San Francisco: Berrett-Koehler.

Dedicated "to the men and women in the business community who possess a vision for a better world and the courage to evoke a positive change," this is a collection of writings from 15 leading pioneers of new-paradigm thinking. In a move away from traditional "bottom line" thinking, the work fuels the quest for observing spiritual values, building learning organizations, creating empowered workplaces, and unleashing the full potential of personal creativity and productivity. Part I establishes the groundwork for the new business paradigm and the human factor. Part II explores the methodology required to shift to a new business consciousness that is more inclusive, responsible, and caring. Includes bibliographical references and index.

New
Sanders, J. O. (1994). *Spiritual leadership* (2nd ed.). Chicago: Moody Press.

This book, originally published in 1967, is based on a series of lectures that Sanders delivered to the Overseas Missionary Fellowship in Singapore in 1964 and 1966. It has been updated for a new audience with explanations of references that were timely 30 years ago and are now obscure. Women leaders receive new attention. The 22 lectures are on topics such as: a comparison of natural and spiritual leadership, insights on leadership from Paul and Peter (from Biblical scripture), prayer and leadership, the responsibilities of leadership, and the art of delegation. There are study questions to spark group discussion on common life experiences, lecture themes and their

relevant Bible passages, and suggestions for life applications. There are two indexes, one of scripture and one of persons mentioned in the lectures.

New
Shaw, R. B. (1997). *Trust in the balance: Building successful organizations on results, integrity, and concern.* San Francisco: Jossey-Bass.

According to Shaw, trust is an organizational factor that must be integrated into the very structure of organizations. He addresses trust at four different organizational levels: individual credibility, one-to-one collaboration, team performance, and overall organizational vitality. Two assessment surveys—for organization and leadership—are included to help the reader fulfill the author's three key imperatives: achieving results, acting with integrity, and demonstrating concern. Includes bibliographical references and index.

New
Shelton, K. (1997). *Beyond counterfeit leadership: How you can become a more authentic leader.* Provo, UT: Executive Excellence.

Shelton claims that our society is abundant with counterfeit leaders—executives, politicians, and celebrities who have more visibility than credibility. Counterfeit leaders commit more acts of deceit than great accomplishments. He encourages readers to face their own counterfeit qualities—incapacitation, imitation, ignorance, indolence, irresponsibility, and insecurity—and become authentic leaders who get quality results and build strong relationships. A model of Shelton's leadership cycle shows readers how to enter at any stage of counterfeit leadership, understand the causes, find a cure, and achieve authentic leadership. Warren Bennis wrote the foreword to this book.

New
Shipka, B. (1997). *Leadership in a challenging world: A sacred journey.* Boston: Butterworth-Heinemann.

Shipka calls her book "a walking stick to support your walk on the path of your life's work—the work of providing leadership in the business world during times of enormous change and transition." She describes eight powers—aliveness, passion, integrity, authenticity, relatedness, expression, perspective, and reverence—and how business leaders can harness these powers to make their work benefit humanity. Each chapter contains quotations, illustrations, and questions for reflection. Includes bibliographical references and index.

Spears, L. C. (1995). ***Reflections on leadership: How Robert K. Greenleaf's theory of servant-leadership influenced today's top management thinkers.*** New York: Wiley.

This collection of 27 essays on servant leadership begins with two essays written by Robert K. Greenleaf. "Life's Choices and Markers" describes the five significant influences in Greenleaf's life from which he evolved the philosophy of leadership through service. "Reflections from Experience" is published for the first time in this book. Over the past two decades, the philosophy of servant leadership has been applied in business, trustee-ship, community-leadership programs, leadership studies, and personal growth. Paying tribute to Greenleaf, the man, and servant leadership as an emerging leadership paradigm, are authors such as M. Scott Peck; Peter Senge; the Greenleaf Center's director, Larry Spears; and Robert Greenleaf's son, Newcomb Greenleaf. Includes biblio-graphical references and index.

New
Spears, L. C. (Ed.). (1998). ***Insights on leadership: Service, stewardship, spirit, and servant-leadership.*** New York: Wiley.

Robert Greenleaf's theory of servant leadership has influenced many of today's prominent leadership think-ers. This sequel to 1995's *Reflections on Leadership*, also edited by Spears, contains over 30 essays by respected thinkers in the field, including Stephen Covey, Peter Block, Margaret Wheatley, James Autry, and Ken Blanchard. Essays are organized around the themes of service, stewardship, spirit, and servant leadership. Includes index.

Srivastva, S. (Ed.). (1988). ***Executive integrity: The search for high human values in organizational life.*** San Francisco: Jossey-Bass.

Twelve leading scholars in the field of organizational behavior examine the role integrity plays or could play in contemporary organizational thinking and decision making. From Michael Maccoby's inventive "Integrity: A Fictional Dialogue," to the empirically based "Reciprocal Integrity: Creating Conditions that Encourage Personal and Organizational Integrity" by Chris Argyris and Donald Schon, this collection of original essays should appeal to academics, executives, students, and individuals concerned about ethical thinking in the corporate environ-ment. Includes bibliography and index.

Walton, C. C. (1988). ***The moral manager.*** Cambridge, MA: Ballinger.

How does the ethical manager tackle the hard questions that decision-makers must ask? "If knowing what's right

doesn't necessarily mean doing what's right, how is virtue instilled in managerial development?" "How can we keep vital those organizational values that brought success in the first place?" The author brings to this work two original features that make this book useful. An ethics quiz at the start of each chapter encourages readers to challenge their own belief systems while they feel the pressure of ethical dilemmas. In addition, scenarios found throughout the book draw out the often conflicting values managers must weigh in their work. Includes bibliography and index.

LEARNING AND EXPERIENCE

New
Bell, C. R. (1996). ***Managers as mentors: Building partnerships for learning.*** San Francisco: Berrett-Koehler.

Bell describes mentoring as the "power-free facilitation of learning . . . teaching through consultation and affection rather than constriction and assessment." In this book he identifies these keys to being an effective mentor: push employees to take risks, be known as a dramatic listener, be a model of your own values, and celebrate successes. Chapters also address feedback, remote learning, and mentoring around equipment, and a self-check scale is included so readers can evaluate their mentoring abilities. Includes bibliographical references and index.

Bettin, P. J., & Kennedy, J. K. (1990). **Leadership experi-ence and leader performance: Some empirical support at last.** *Leadership Quarterly*, *1*(4), 219-228.

This study proposes a measure of leader experience based on work history and examines its relevance to leader per-formance. Subjects were 84 U.S. Army company com-manders and battalion staff officers. Work history factors include: length of time served, type of positions held, nature of previous duties, and skills acquired. Results suggest that work experience with relevant previous duties is a valid indicator of future leader performance.

New
Bierma, L. L. (1996). **How executive women learn corporate culture.** *Human Resource Development Quar-terly*, *7*(2), 145-164.

Bierma interviewed and observed 11 female executives in Fortune 500 companies to determine how women learn organizational culture. She discovered that culture learning is a process that includes cognitive, experiential, and collaborative tactics. Cognitive learning experiences such as reading, adjunct teaching, and public speaking helped the women to build confidence and strengthen skills. Observation and reflection were useful experiential techniques for learning office politics. Collaborative tactics such as mentorships, peer support, and networking helped the women learn to function in male-dominated cultures and to develop influence.

Ciofalo, A. (1992). *Internships: Perspectives on experiential learning.* Malabar, FL: Krieger.

This collection of articles by faculty and professionals in business and mass communications offers varying philosophies and techniques on internships, and suggests internships work best when the perspectives of professionals and educators converge. Not promising a how-to book, Ciofalo offers a variety of viewpoints and case histories to help establish and set parameters for measurement of internship programs. Includes bibliographical references.

Compoc, K., Lewis, C., Weaver, M., & Stoneback, S. (1992). *Preparing to lead: The college women's guide to internships and other public policy learning opportunities in Washington, DC.* Washington, DC: Public Leadership Education Network.

This guide is part of the mission of the National Education for Women's Leadership, a program designed to identify, educate, and develop the next generation of women public leaders. The purpose of the guide is to help women students take full advantage of the learning opportunities in the nation's capital. A listing of internships and fellowships in the research, advocacy, political, and government arenas is included. Includes index.

New
Daudelin, M. W. (1996). **Learning from experience through reflection.** *Organizational Dynamics, 24*(3), 36-48.

This article discusses the ancient learning process of reflection as a leadership development tool. It suggests that organizations create formal reflection practices for managers to stop amid their usual frantic pace to consider what has been learned from experience and what are new possibilities. Individual reflection may take the form of spontaneous thinking during routine activities, journal writing, or assessment instruments. Helper or peer-group reflection activities include performance appraisals, mentoring, and feedback discussions. Daudelin reports on her research study that introduced reflective activities to managers and the actions they took following reflection. The managers reported that individual and helper reflection activities significantly improved their management actions. Peer group reflection activities did not affect managers' subsequent actions. Includes bibliographical references.

New
de Woot, P. (1996). **The need for a sustainable learning society.** *European Forum for Management Development, 96*(2), 32-35.

In this presentation from a conference on visions for management development, de Woot challenges the idea that education is a strictly intellectual or finite process. He argues that in a changing and increasingly technological world, education is necessary for the purpose of creating citizens, not automatons or academics removed from everyday life. To do this, primary and secondary education must be improved, and the concepts of adult education and learning as a cradle-to-grave process must be enhanced.

Eichinger, R. W., & Lombardo, M. M. (1990). *Twenty-two ways to develop leadership in staff managers.* Greensboro, NC: Center for Creative Leadership.

This report notes the gap in developmental opportunities between staff (human resources, engineering, R&D, PR) and line (sales, manufacturing, operations, management). Employees in line functions have authority to make final decisions and can measure their output by revenue. They are, therefore, exposed to the experiences that develop successful executives. Staff managers can gain developmental experience by taking challenging jobs, such as start-ups, fix-its, or leaps in responsibility. Lessons can be learned from role models, coursework, and hardships that cause self-examination. A variety of experiences leads to success. A study of 250 executives' most significant learning experiences explains why a gap exists between staff and line development. Twenty-two recommendations are made for closing the gap. Includes a bibliography.

Fiedler, F. E. (1992). **Time-based measures of leadership experience and organizational performance: A review of research and a preliminary model.** *Leadership Quarterly: Special Issue: Individual Differences and Leadership: II, 3*(1), 5-23.

Work experience is composed of time in service, time in a leadership position, time in a work unit, diversity of experience, relevant experience, and overlearned behavior. Leadership experience alone does not correlate to performance. Research indicates that intellectual abilities and effort must correlate to experience for high performance, particularly in times of stress or uncertainty.

Fiedler, F. E. (1995). **Cognitive resources and leadership performance.** *Applied Psychology, 44*(1), 5-28.

Selection and promotion are typically based on one's intelligence, experience, and expertise. Fiedler examines the relationship of these three characteristics with leadership performance. He reviews studies of U.S. Army infantry leaders, fire fighters, U.S. Coast Guard personnel, and ROTC cadets to support the Cognitive Resource Theory and its implications for work environment and training.

New
Finzel, H. (1994). *The top ten mistakes leaders make.* Wheaton, IL: Victor Books.

Finzel believes great leaders are not born to lead, but instead they learn from trial and error. This book presents ten actions of leadership that are negative and then turns them around into a positive experience. Each chapter includes case studies, biblical principles, and powerpoints to help explain the main points. The ten negative actions include: a top-down approach, not focusing on the people, lack of affirmation and praise, not making room for creative people, decision making by dictatorship, failing to delegate, lack of effective communication, not recognizing an organization's culture, success without successors, and a failure to focus on the future. Includes bibliographical references.

Howe, W., & Lipscomb, C. (1995). **The leadership student and the leadership teacher: A trans-role/transatlantic dialogue.** *Journal of Leadership Studies, 2*(3), 91-99.

A professor and a recent graduate of the Jepson School of Leadership Studies at the University of Richmond in Virginia discuss the shifting patterns in a teacher-learner dyad and a leader-follower dyad. Lipscomb's acceptance of a teaching position in Hungary following graduation adds a cultural dimension to the dialogue. Howe, the teacher of the new teacher, describes himself as a great-grandparent of leadership education passing on a legacy from one generation to the next.

New
Hughes, R. L., Ginnett, R. C., & Curphy, G. J. (1996). *Leadership: Enhancing the lessons of experience* (2nd ed.). Boston, MA: Irwin/McGraw-Hill.

This textbook is aimed primarily at undergraduates, but is also useful for professional schools or leadership training programs. Based on a simple model demonstrating the relationship among leader, follower, and situation, the authors take an in-depth look at each variable and how it operates within the framework to enhance or impede leadership abilities. In this second edition, chapters have been consolidated and there is new material on women's leadership and globalization. However, the focus of the text remains on the value of experience in leadership development, and the authors again emphasize that leadership is a process, not a position. Personal anecdotes clarify the text by offering unique insights into developmental aspects of leadership. Each section has a list of

key terms, questions for discussion, and suggested material for further reading. Includes bibliographical references and index.

Lindsey, E. H., Homes, V., & McCall, M. W., Jr. (1987). *Key events in executives' lives.* Greensboro, NC: Center for Creative Leadership.

This report is designed for those individuals who are concerned with the development of executive talent. Drawing on information gathered from over 191 successful executives from six major corporations, this book systematically examines the key events and pivotal experiences that have contributed to these individuals' "high potential" designation. Includes bibliographical references.

New
Maccoby, M. (1997). **Making many Penny's: New management challenge.** *Research Technology Management, 40*(1), 56-58.

This article is adapted from Maccoby's keynote address to the 1996 World Future Society's annual meeting. Maccoby discusses the shifting paradigm from a manufacturing society to a service-oriented, information-dominated society. The new logic is the logic of learning, and it changes the way managers do business. Focus moves away from products and toward people. Some of the shifts are: from continuous improvement to continuous learning, from decentralization to interactivity, from managers as analyzers to leaders as synthesizers, from accumulating knowledge to learning to learn. He describes the value of an AT&T service technician named Penny whose stellar customer service brings several million dollars of business to her company. Maccoby recommends that organizations develop many Penny's by shifting to a learning model.

Martin, G. D., & Baker, B. E. (Eds.). (1993). *The national directory of internships* (1994-1995 ed.). Raleigh, NC: National Society for Experiential Education.

Hundreds of opportunities for on-the-job learning experiences are listed. Internships lasting from one month to two years are available in community organizing, industrial relations, international relations, outdoor adventure, conflict resolution, social-science research, and 79 other areas of interest. Each listing includes the sponsoring organization's information, a description of the internship, eligibility requirements, and application information. The listings are indexed by sponsoring organization, geographic location, and area of interest.

McCall, M. W., Jr., Lombardo, M. M., & Morrison, A. M. (1988). *The lessons of experience: How successful executives develop on the job.* Lexington, MA: Lexington Books.

"Where do successful business leaders come from?" "How do they learn the skills that propel them to the top of their companies?" In pursuit of answers, these authors sought out top executives across the U.S. and asked them about the work experiences that had the greatest influence on the direction of their careers. By examining these career profiles and evaluating them in a systematic manner against current research in the fields of learning and human motivation, the authors reveal surprising answers to what actually shapes the managerial lives of individuals with executive leadership potential. Includes bibliography and index.

New
McEvoy, G. M. (1997). **Organizational change and outdoor management education.** *Human Resource Management, 36*(2), 235-250.

Outdoor management education, such as ropes courses, has become popular in recent years, but little empirical evidence exists to prove its effectiveness. This study examined two groups of employees from an information-processing company—one group that received outdoor training and one that did not—to determine whether the training affected learning and behavior. Tables, graphs, and quotes from employees all help illustrate the results, which show that the training did have some positive long-term effects. An appendix of sample questions from the measurement instrument and bibliographical references are included.

New
Morgan, S., & Dennehy, R. F. (1997). **The power of organizational storytelling: A management development perspective.** *Journal of Management Development, 16*(7), 494-501.

Stories can be an effective way to teach skills and information, as the research reviewed in this article shows. Using several stories as examples, including one about McDonald's founder Ray Kroc, the authors list the characteristics of a good story and describe the five-step framework that every learning story should contain: setting, build-up, crisis or climax, learning, and new behavior or awareness. Advice on how to become a better storyteller, such as telling stories in pairs and writing in a journal, is also offered. Includes bibliographical references.

Palus, C. J., Nasby, W., & Easton, R. D. (1991). *Understanding executive performance: A life-story perspective.* Greensboro, NC: Center for Creative Leadership.

What can be discerned about executive performance by studying the person outside the workplace? What can we learn by looking closely at the way an executive relates personal narratives or life-story experiences? The paper is built around the case of Dodge Morgan, who at the age of 54 circumnavigated the world alone in a 60-foot sailboat. Drawing on excerpts from Morgan's personal log, the authors explore the relationships among identity, personality, and executive performance. Includes a bibliography.

New
Parks Daloz, L. A., Keen, C. H., Keen, J. P., & Daloz Parks, S. (1996). **Lives of commitment: Higher education in the life of the new commons.** *Change, 28*(3), 10-15.

In a time when many Americans are drawing away from their communities and social networks, the authors studied over 100 social-change leaders who "have demonstrated commitment to the *common* good." They found that, among other factors, virtually all of these leaders had a critical experience in college or graduate school that helped them understand themselves as part of a wider world. These experiences included having a special teacher or mentor, listening to influential speakers, internships and travel, and taking interdisciplinary courses. The article encourages schools to teach students how to think critically, how to take the perspective of the other and withhold judgment, and how to create a safe and civil space for others.

Quinn, R. E., Faerman, S. R., Thompson, M. P., & McGrath, M. R. (1996). *Becoming a master manager: A competency framework* (2nd ed.). New York: Wiley.

This textbook is for business schools that want to teach more than technical competence. It helps to teach the paradoxical thinking that is required by managers in a rapidly changing world. The Competing Values Model illustrates the struggles between flexibility versus control and focus on internal versus external values. Each chapter describes a different managerial role—mentor, facilitator, monitor, coordinator, director, producer, broker, and innovator. There are activities for learning competencies in each role and for integrating two or more roles. Includes bibliographical references and index.

New
Redding, J. (1997). **Hardwiring the learning organization.** *Training & Development, 51*(8), 61-67.

Redding describes the use of instruments to measure an organization's potential for learning. He advises on the steps of the assessment process: defining the reason for assessment, selecting the right tool, administering the instrument, developing an organizational strategy to building learning capabilities, and planning learning initiatives. A chart provides brief information on 21 instruments, their learning focus, administration, and source information. The article includes references to several books that describe learning initiatives already in place in companies and government agencies.

New
Sternberg, R. J. (1996). ***Successful intelligence: How practical and creative intelligence determine success in life.*** New York: Simon & Schuster.

Sternberg has developed a theory of intelligence called *successful intelligence*, which is the "kind of intelligence used to achieve important goals." He criticizes schools, other organizations, and individuals for using IQ and memorization—which are neither analytical, creative, nor practical—to measure intelligence. His three keys to successful intelligence, each of which makes up a chapter of the book, are: finding good solutions with analytical intelligence, finding good problems with creative intelligence, and making solutions work with practical intelligence. Sternberg gives examples of each, and lists the characteristics of successfully intelligent people. Includes bibliographical references and index.

Van Velsor, E., & Hughes, M. W. (1990). ***Gender differences in the development of managers: How women managers learn from experience.*** Greensboro, NC: Center for Creative Leadership.

Based on studies of 189 male and 78 female managers, this report investigates gender differences in experiential learning. Experiences are categorized into 16 key events, such as assignments, hardships, and dealing with people. From these events, 33 lessons are identified. Compared to men, women more frequently reported learning about their own personal limits and how to recognize and seize opportunities. Men more frequently reported learning technical skills and shouldering responsibility. Men reported more experience with turnaround and start-up assignments. Includes a bibliography.

POWER AND INFLUENCE

Bailey, F. G. (1988). ***Humbuggery and manipulation: The art of leadership.*** Ithaca, NY: Cornell University Press.

Bailey contends that leaders control followers through domination, deception, and cultivation of ignorance. He writes that leadership is by its very nature defiling, that no successful leader can be immaculate, and that the human condition is untidy and most often without reason. He

recommends that followers recognize evil or criminal behavior and offer compassion to those who are corrupted by the exercise of power. Includes bibliography and index.

Bair, M. L., & Mayhew, R. M. (1991). ***Power and leadership: A resource guide*** (Updated ed.). Newark: Delaware Public Administration Institute, College of Urban Affairs and Public Policy, University of Delaware.

This resource guide on women and power and leadership was developed by the Delaware Public Administration Institute for its 1990 *Women's Leadership Retreat* and updated for its *Power and Leadership* symposia. Relevant writings and research are summarized to highlight the following areas of concern: power, gender differences, success and derailment, mentors, changes in society, and the many characteristics of an effective leader. An annotated bibliography suggests further reading materials.

Baker, D. B. (1992). ***Power quotes: 4,000 trenchant soundbites on leadership and liberty, treason and triumph, sacrifice and scandal, risk and rebellion, weakness and war, and other affaires politiques.*** Detroit: Visible Ink Press.

Historical to contemporary quotes on leadership, ethics, and power are arranged by category, then chronologically. An authors' index aids the reader's search for a favorite pundit and includes very brief biographical information. From humor to inspiration, the quotes are reported to be originals or best translated versions. Includes index.

Cialdini, R. B. (1993). ***Influence: Science and practice*** (3rd ed.). New York: HarperCollins College Publishers.

The author conducted interviews with professionals whose work is to gain the compliance of others: sales people, fund-raisers, and advertising executives. He also interviewed those who deal with the seamy side of compliance: police bunco-squad officers and consumer agencies. His research identified six principles of influence: reciprocation, consistency, social proof, liking, authority, and scarcity. Each chapter ends with a summary and a quiz encouraging this to be used as a textbook for the student of philosophy and human behavior. Includes bibliographical references and index.

Cohen, A. R., & Bradford, D. L. (1990). ***Influence without authority.*** New York: Wiley.

Techniques are outlined for motivating peers, superiors, and subordinates to lend support and share resources. Case scenarios exhibit the right and wrong paths to understanding your allies, mutual exchange, building effective relationships, becoming a partner with your boss, and playing hardball. The authors differentiate between manipulation and influence. Includes bibliographical references.

New
Crawford, C. B., & Strohkirch, C. S. (1997). **Influence methods and innovators: Technocrats and champions.** *Journal of Leadership Studies, 4*(2), 43-54.

This articles reports on research of 238 students at a midwestern university who responded to two surveys, *Acceptance of Technological Innovation* and *Survey of Influence Behavior*. The purpose of the research was to study the relationship between technological innovation and methods of influence. The authors tested four hypotheses: 1) innovators would be more likely to use team influence methods than the majority and laggard adopters; 2) innovators would be more likely to use charismatic influence behaviors; 3) innovators would be more likely to use reward/punishment/manipulation influence behaviors; and 4) charisma, reward/punishment, and team influence behaviors predict innovativeness. The findings suggest that innovators will use coercive methods to achieve results and that these innovators do not have any more charisma or team influence than the majority.

New
Daily, C. M., & Johnson, J. L. (1997). **Source of CEO power and firm financial performance: A longitudinal assessment.** *Journal of Management, 23*(2), 97-117.

This article examines the correlation between the power of a CEO and a company's financial performance. The authors measured four kinds of power—structural, ownership, prestige, and expert—held by CEOs at 100 randomly selected Fortune 500 firms from 1987 through 1990. Three measures of firm financial performance were considered—return on equity, return on investment, and a risk-adjusted, market-based measure of performance. When correlated, the authors concluded that this issue is complex and there are too many variables to draw simple conclusions. One apparent conclusion was that CEOs who serve on other boards wield greater power and run more successful companies. Includes bibliographical references.

De Jouvenal, B. (1949). *On power: Its nature and the history of its growth.* New York: Viking.

This is a classic work on the origins of power and the history of its development. Divided into what the author terms as *books*, each section delves into a particular aspect of the use and meaning of power. Book I examines the origins of civil obedience as well as the growth of sovereignty as a divine and political right. Subsequent sections study the notions of the power of command in time of warfare and explore the use of power in control-

ling social order. Later sections discuss how power may appear to change through revolution and new government when in fact its essential nature remains constant. The issue of limited versus unlimited power, as in the choice between liberty or security, is discussed. Includes bibliographical references in notes.

Fairholm, G. W. (1993). *Organizational power politics: Tactics in organizational leadership.* Westport, CT: Praeger.

In a power situation, two or more parties compete for materials, space, or energy. Using power tactics leads to action that will meet the goals of one party. Fairholm identifies 22 power tactics, including: using ambiguity, displaying charisma, legitimizing control, rationalization, and ritualism. He compares ethics, frequency of use, and effectiveness in varying relationships and varying bases of power. Includes bibliographical references and index.

Fiol, C. M. (1991). **Seeing the empty spaces: Towards a more complex understanding of the meaning of power in organizations.** *Organization Studies, 12*(4), 547-566.

Leaders exert power by doing and deciding. They also exert power in the empty spaces, by not doing and not deciding. Fiol uses semiotics, the study of how something comes to mean what it does within a particular context, as a lens for understanding the multiple dimensions of power. Autobiographies of two auto-industry leaders, Henry Ford and Lee Iacocca, are analyzed to illustrate the meaning of power.

Frost, T. F., & Moussavi, F. (1992). **The relationship between leader power base and influence: The moderating role of trust.** *Journal of Applied Business Research, 8*(4), 9-14.

Trust and its effects on a leader's power base and ability to influence subordinates is examined. Frost and Moussavi offer two models differentiating organizational and individual bases of power. Expert, referent, and information power bases have a positive effect on trust. Legitimate, coercive, and reward power bases have a negative effect on trust.

Hagberg, J. O. (1994). *Real power: Stages of personal power in organizations* (Rev. ed.). Salem, WI: Sheffield Publishing.

Personal power is derived from external sources (expertise, titles, degrees, authority) and from internal sources (introspection, personal struggles, accepting and valuing self). Hagberg presents a model of the six stages of personal power: powerlessness, power by association, power by symbols, power by reflection, power by purpose, and power by gestalt. Each stage is demonstrated with applications to life and work situations. Summary pages may be photocopied. Questionnaires allow the reader to evaluate personal stages. This revised edition contains a new introduction, a new chapter called "Beyond Ego and Gender: Leading from Your Soul," and revised surveys. Includes a bibliography.

New
Hillman, J. (1995). *Kinds of power: A guide to its intelligent uses.* New York: Currency.

In this book, Hillman, a renowned psychologist and author, tries to define the nature of power from a philosophical perspective. A series of chapters, including "Authority," "Charisma," "Prestige," and "Leadership," attempt to describe the many forms and nuances of power, but ultimately Hillman believes that power comes from ideas, not money or might. He calls on his readers to recognize that although "powers beyond the human will affect our daily business," our ideas "hold the most direct and immediate sway."

New
Kaplan, R. E. (1996). *Forceful leadership and enabling leadership: You can do both.* Greensboro, NC: Center for Creative Leadership.

Kaplan's previous research on expansive executives (Kaplan, 1990, 1991; Kaplan, Drath, & Kofodimos, 1992) and ongoing consultation with executives has led him to an appreciation for versatility. This report explains his new theory on the opposing virtues of forceful leadership and enabling leadership. Kaplan explains how executives who are forceful, who assert themselves and push others to perform, can avoid becoming tyrannical. And executives who are enabling, who bring out the capabilities in others, can avoid self-effacement. Kaplan has developed the *Executive Roles Questionnaire*, a 360-degree-feedback instrument to identify the forceful and enabling dimensions of an executive's leadership style. Once identified, an executive may learn to de-emphasize one dimension and develop another. Includes bibliographical references.

Kennedy, D. M., & Parrish, M. E. (Eds.). (1986). *Power and responsibility: Case studies.* San Diego, CA: Harcourt Brace Jovanovich.

The essays in this volume seek to illuminate factors of the complex relationship between leaders and followers. The aim is to explain the personality traits of several leaders and the techniques of power-wielding. Nine case studies of the pursuit and exercise of power in modern America are included.

Kotter, J. P. (1978). **Power, success, and organizational effectiveness.** *Organizational Dynamics, 6*(3), 26-40.

Kotter describes power in organizations: how people acquire and manage power, why success in some jobs depends on power-oriented behavior but in other jobs does not, and how and why successful power-oriented behavior can work for or against the overall interests of the organization.

Machiavelli, N. (1513). *The prince.*

Machiavelli wrote this commentary on politics and statesmanship to demonstrate how a new prince, a usurper, could carve out a new principality for himself. It is a lesson in manipulative behavior and abuse of power. For instance, one lesson says that "men ought to be treated well or crushed, because they can avenge themselves of lighter injuries." The cruelty and unscrupulousness of his fictional prince shocked even Machiavelli's contemporaries in 16th-century Italy. It is suspected that Machiavelli wrote this book as political advice for the Medici family who aspired to public office and for whom Machiavelli secretly felt disdain. This leadership classic is of value to everyone who is likely to work for a manipulative leader or be tempted to become one.

Mansfield, H. C., Jr. (1980). *Machiavelli's new modes and order: A study of the "discourses on Livy."* Ithaca, NY: Cornell University Press.

Mansfield discloses and explicates things that Machiavelli thought prudent to conceal and camouflage, and highlights Machiavelli's clever, conspiratorial, philosophical, and humorous strategy. In exploring the extent of Machiavelli's intention and his responsibility for modernity, Mansfield demonstrates "how the control of things not previously or usually thought political is represented in his discussion of political things." Includes bibliographical references and index.

New
Masters, R. D. (1996). *Machiavelli, Leonardo, and the science of power.* Notre Dame, IN: University of Notre Dame Press.

Masters wrote this book to suggest "a return to the naturalistic tradition of Western thought, in which a scientific study of human life is directly related to questions of morality and law." He believes that Niccolo Machiavelli, the 16th-century Florentine politician and author, originated the scientific study of human affairs. Analysis of Machiavelli's life and writings cause Masters to suspect that Machiavelli was strongly influenced by his friendship with artist, engineer, and scientific innovator, Leonardo da Vinci. This analysis suggests that Machiavelli's use of power is often misunderstood as abuse of power. Masters examines the basic social and political relationships of animals and humans to illustrate the natural state of societies and governments defined by Machiavelli. Nineteen pages of illustrations, primarily da Vinci's paintings and technical drawings, support the integration of biology, psychology, philosophy, and human ethology. Includes bibliographical references and index.

McClelland, D. C. (1979). *Power: The inner experience.* New York: Irvington.

The author is primarily concerned with major personal and national motives, such as the need for power, the need for achievement, and the need for affiliation, as they are revealed in personal and group fantasies. Using modern techniques of measurement, he tests and validates the theory of psychosexual and psychosocial development. Detailed findings are provided. National motivational characteristics are explored as to where they fit in a psychosocial power drive. Includes bibliography and index.

Miller, J. B. (1983). **Women and power.** *Social Power, 13*(4), 3-6.

Miller contends that women historically have used power to nurture and support others, and that women fear using power for self-enhancement. She suggests that women's nurturing approach to power may be more beneficial to society as a whole than a traditional self-interest power motive. She encourages women to use power to nurture themselves as well as others.

Pfeffer, J. (1992). *Managing with power: Politics and influence in organizations.* Boston: Harvard Business School Press.

A decision changes nothing unless it is implemented. But getting others to do something they wouldn't ordinarily do requires power. Examples from Lyndon Johnson and Henry Kissinger to Henry Ford show how strong leaders amass the support and resources they need to get things done. Pfeffer explores sources of power in organizations, outlines strategies for effectively using power (including timing, interpersonal influences, and symbolic actions), and show how power is lost. Though power and influence are an organization's "last dirty secret," they provide the means to effect change and bring about innovation. Includes bibliographical references and index.

Pfeffer, J. (1992). **Understanding power in organizations.** *California Management Review, 34*(2), 29-50.

All organizations are political structures where the interdependence of many people is required to get a job done. Power is used by managers to influence behavior, change the course of events, overcome resistance, and to get people to do things that they would otherwise not do. Managers need to recognize varying interests, diagnose different perspectives, be willing to build sources of power, and understand the forces of timing, structure, and commitment. Putting knowledge into action and facing opposition create power that is beneficial to individuals and organizations.

Salancik, G. R., & Pfeffer, J. (1977). **Who gets power— and how they hold on to it: A strategic-contingency model of power.** *Organizational Dynamics, 5*(3), 2-21.

Power adheres to those who can cope with the critical problems of the organization. As such, power is not a dirty secret but the secret of success. This article argues that traditional "political" power, far from being a dirty business, is one of the few mechanisms available for aligning an organization with its own reality.

Schultz, M. C. (1992). **Leadership and the power circle.** *Human Systems Management, 11*(4), 213-217.

An individual's power circle is composed of position, expertise, and referent power. Awareness of one's power-base strengths and weaknesses maximizes effective leadership. Suggesting that power usage is determined by situations rather than preferred style, Schultz concludes that effectiveness is achieved through self-recognition and self-understanding. Strengthening power effectiveness in particular situations enhances one's future power potential in similar situations, leading to enhanced leadership abilities.

Simonton, D. K. (1991). **Personality correlates of exceptional personal influence: A note on Thorndike's (1950) creators and leaders.** *Creativity Research Journal, 4*(1), 67-78.

Leaders exert exceptional personal influence over others in the areas of politics, war, business, and religion. Creators exert a like influence in the arts, humanities, and sciences. Using a 1950 study, which scores personality factors of 48 leaders and 43 creators, four shared dimensions are identified. Industriousness, extraversion, aggressiveness, and intelligence are then measured in a composite archival index to determine differential eminence.

Smither, R. D. (1991). **The return of the authoritarian manager.** *Training, 28*(11), 40-44.

The authoritarian style of management remains an effective alternative in many cases. Following are some situations where authoritarianism is likely to work well: when employees are poorly educated or do not want responsibility for decision making, when productivity is more important than employee satisfaction, and when short-term performance goals must be met. While *authoritarian management* is not a synonym for *oppressive* or *punitive management*, there is no evidence that teamwork or quality circles in themselves will result in improved productivity.

New
Swanson, D. L. (1996). **Neoclassical economic theory, executive control, and organizational outcomes.** *Human Relations, 49*(6), 735-756.

Swanson examines the congruence between executive self-interest and power-seeking behavior. She presents a model of executive control typology that ranges from insecure to manipulative and exploitive behaviors. When executives practice power-seeking and control behavior, their organizations suffer from lack of social integration and cooperative, mutually beneficial interactions. Another model represents the chaos that often results in this situation. Includes bibliographical references.

New
Whicker, M. L. (1996). *Toxic leaders: When organizations go bad.* Westport, CT: Quorum Books.

Whicker discusses the dark side of leadership in this book. She separates leaders into three categories: trustworthy, transitional, and toxic. Part I explains the need for trustworthy leadership and the characteristics that make a leader trustworthy. Part II contrasts trustworthy leaders with toxic and transitional leaders. Parts III and IV give examples of different types of transitional and toxic leaders including: absentee leader, busybody, controller,

enforcer, street fighter, and bully. These snapshots of problem leaders include a thumbnail sketch, hallmark characteristics, likely sources of inadequacy, operational styles, impact on an organization, and ways to protect against them. Part V explains how toxic leaders influence organizational decline and how an organization can regain its health after a decline. Includes bibliographical references and index.

Zaleznik, A. (1993). *Learning leadership: Cases and commentaries on abuses of power in organizations.* Chicago: Bonus Books.

Using 20 case studies, Zaleznik encourages the leader to learn from the mistakes of others, then to learn by doing. Sections address use and abuse of power, rivalry and ambition, the psychodynamics of leadership, and organizations in crisis. Zaleznik states that leadership is continuous on-the-job training. Includes bibliographical references and index.

Zaleznik, A., & Kets de Vries, M. F. R. (1975). *Power and the corporate mind.* Boston: Houghton Mifflin.

The basis for this book is the clinical perspective of psychoanalysis. It continues the work begun with earlier publications and leads the way to further communications on the psychodynamics of leadership and organizations. The authors contend that understanding how leaders accumulate and use power is a special and continuing requirement of a democratic society. Includes bibliographical references and index.

TRAINING, EDUCATION, AND DEVELOPMENT

GENERAL

New
Ames, M. D. (1994). *Pathways to success: Today's business leaders tell how to excel in work, career and leadership roles.* San Francisco: Berrett-Koehler.

This book for young people explains the complex subject of leadership through profiles of 117 successful business men and women. Judi Sheppard Missett, founder and president of Jazzercise, Inc., advises future leaders to be passionate about work and to find a balance between work and personal life. George Fisher, CEO of Eastman Kodak Company, says leaders must dare to dream, do their best, and never stop learning. William G. Mays, president of Mays Chemical Company, Inc., tells future leaders to not be afraid of failure and to keep their integrity. Teachers may use the 14 sets of "energizers,"

exercises and discussion starters, to reinforce leadership lessons.

Argyris, C. (1976). *Increasing leadership effectiveness.* New York: Wiley.

This book is a description and analysis of a learning seminar designed to teach top-level executives over a long period how to modify their approach to the world—shifting from emphases on control, winning, and rationality to concern for valid information, free and informed choices, and expression of feeling. Argyris links his theory of "double loop learning" to the concept of leadership effectiveness. Includes bibliography and index.

New

Barker, R. A. (1997). **How can we train leaders if we do not know what leadership is?** *Human Relations*, *50*(4), 343-362.

> Barker analyzed the literature of leadership and conducted informal surveys on working leaders and students of organizational behavior. He found a broad range of definitions for leadership and many cases in which leadership was not defined at all. He suggests that leadership scholars and practitioners stop categorizing leadership as an ability, behavior, action, role, function, or experience. Leadership is a dynamic process that resembles a river, continuously flowing, forever changing in speed and strength. Leadership happens through mutual influence and community efforts to reach the greatest good. Based on these conclusions, Barker recommends that leadership education focus more on self-awareness than on skills- or goal-orientation.

Bigelow, J. (1995). **Teaching managerial skills: A critique and future directions.** *Journal of Management Education*, *19*(3), 305-325.

> This article begins with a summary and grouping of the current practices in teaching managerial skills within the university setting. Bigelow concentrates this summary on the nine major managerial skills texts. In response to his findings, the author identifies two key issues: 1) skill learning is not carrying over to later practice, and 2) skill practice is more complex and divergent than the current image of skills implies. The critique concludes with a proposal for changes in current university practices.

New

Boatman, S. A. (Ed.). (1992). *Supporting student leadership: Selections from the student development series.* Columbia, SC: National Association for Campus Activities.

> The 41 short articles in this book first appeared from 1980 to 1990 in *Campus Activities Programming*, the official publication of the National Association for Campus Activities. Most of the articles are written for professionals who design and deliver leadership programs in student activities offices. Theoretical essays include: "Preparing to Choose a Leadership Position," "Leadership, Culture and Change on the College Campus," and "Making Sense Out of Chaos: Leading and Living in Dynamic Systems." Program descriptions are included in "Orientation for New Leaders," "Sequential Leadership Development," and "Designing a Leadership Retreat." Students seeking advice on self-development may enjoy reading "Risk-Taking Your Way to Personal Growth" and "Meet the Challenge of the First Step . . . and Enjoy the Success of Finishing."

New

Bracken, D. W., Dalton, M. A., Jako, R. A., McCauley, C. D., & Pollman, V. A. (1997). *Should 360-degree feedback be used only for developmental purposes?* Greensboro, NC: Center for Creative Leadership.

> This book presents papers from a debate at the 1996 annual meeting of the Society for Industrial and Organizational Psychology. Debate centered around the use of 360-degree feedback for development of high-potential employees or using it for making administrative decisions about promotions and pay. The hot issues included: confidentiality, quality of data, positive and negative halo effects, potential for abuse of feedback data, ways to maximize the use of feedback, its value to an organization, and its value to individuals.

New

Brungardt, C. (1996). **The making of leaders: A review of the research in leadership development and education.** *Journal of Leadership Studies*, *3*(3), 81-95.

> Brungardt reviews 70 years of literature that debates the question, "Can leaders be made?" There is abundant theory and research to support the concepts of leadership development, education, and training. Brungardt defines leadership development as "a continuous learning process that spans an entire lifetime." Leadership education "includes learning activities and educational environments that . . . foster leadership abilities." Leadership training "refers to learning activities for a specific role or job." Brungardt examines the literature in two contexts: leadership development theory, which is development throughout a lifetime, and learning leadership theory, which is the role that education plays in leadership development.

New

Burack, E. H., Hochwarter, W., & Mathys, N. J. (1997). **The new management development paradigm.** *Human Resource Planning*, *20*(1), 14-21.

> Increased globalization and technological changes in the last 25 years have required American corporations to integrate business strategies and human resources practices in order to remain competitive. This article defines such integration as management development (MD) and identifies MD features common to world class organizations. The features include: "seamless" or layerless organizational structure, having a global and cross-cultural orientation, emphasizing individual learning, and recognizing core competencies. A model for defining competencies, which the authors believe is central to organizational effectiveness, is also developed.

New
Cohen, N. H. (1995). ***Mentoring adult learners: A guide for educators and trainers.*** Malabar, FL: Krieger.

Cohen's purpose is to "provide pragmatic guidance to those who assume responsibility for the mentor role." The book includes two versions of a self-assessment instrument, *The Principles of Adult Mentoring Scale*, one for postsecondary education and one for business and government. Cohen wants to link knowledge from psychology and interpersonal communications to challenges facing mentors. His intended audience includes college faculty, administration and staff, professionals running intern training programs, and human-resource development specialists in business and government. Chapter subjects include: relationship emphasis, information emphasis, facilitative focus, confrontational focus, mentor model, and protégé vision. Includes bibliographical references and index.

Conger, J. A. (1992). ***Learning to lead: The art of transforming managers into leaders.*** San Francisco: Jossey-Bass.

To fill the leadership void, are companies wasting millions of dollars of valuable assets on ineffectual leadership training? Conger looks at the tremendous emphasis on leadership training and reexamines the question of whether leaders are made or born beginning with a look at leadership training in the time of Plato. Personal growth, conceptual, feedback, and skill-building approaches are examined for their effectiveness in developing leaders. Conger then goes "beyond Myers-Briggs" in defining his view of leadership training in the future. Includes bibliographical references and index.

New
Crotty, P. T., & Soule, A. J. (1997). **Executive education: Yesterday and today, with a look at tomorrow.** *Journal of Management Development, 16*(1), 4-21.

Executive education "yesterday" involved companies sending top-level managers to university-based executive MBA (EMBA) programs. "Today," companies partner with universities to customize executive training or structure their own in-house corporate universities. "Tomorrow," a global focus will drive executive education. To move across cultural boundaries and maximize potential markets, executives will need to develop strong customer relationships and create winning strategies through organizational change. The authors predict that a variety of approaches will be used: university-based MBA and EMBA programs, in-house corporate universities, customized contract programs, distance learning, and technology-based training.

Duke, B. C. (1991). ***Education and leadership for the twenty-first century: Japan, America, and Britain.*** New York: Praeger.

The cultural divergence of East and West are magnified in the field of leadership; not in the educational process of how leadership positions are attained—through quality high school followed by elite public and private universities—but in the skills that are taught. Whereas the West focuses on verbal and intellectual skills and the ability to take decisive action, the East studies self-effacement and the power of working behind the scenes to create a consensus within the group for a given policy or task. Duke asserts that East and West should reevaluate leadership education to formulate compatible styles for our shrinking world. Includes bibliographical references and index.

New
Edwards, M. R., & Ewen, A. J. (1996). ***360-degree feedback: The powerful new model for employee assessment and performance improvement.*** New York: AMACOM.

The authors give a general overview of 360-degree feedback—assessment by self, supervisors, direct reports, peers, and customers—for those unfamiliar with the concept. They discuss the value of this kind of assessment, how to design a feedback project, and how to evaluate the process. The appendix provides more than 100 questions to use when designing a project. They are related to competencies in: organizational skills, organizational climate, communication skills, group effectiveness, coaching, teams, and leadership. The issue of instrument validity is briefly discussed. Includes bibliography and index.

New
Evans, P. (1997). **New horizons for management development.** *efmd FORUM, 97*(2), 22-25.

This article is based on a speech to the 1997 Global Forum on Management Education. Evans, a professor of organizational behavior at INSEAD, likens the dual responsibilities for human resource development to a split egg. The operational functions are the supportive bottom half of the egg. Development of strategies, new products, and emerging leaders are the visible and glamorous top half of the egg. To achieve operational goals, a manager must push responsibility downward, thus empowering employees and making development happen. The ideal split egg creates a balance between providing challenges and managing risks.

New
Fleenor, J. W., & Prince, J. M. (1997). ***Using 360-degree feedback in organizations: An annotated bibliography.*** Greensboro, NC: Center for Creative Leadership.

This book serves as an introduction to the literature on multi-rater assessment tools. In addition to the 56 books and articles described, the authors answer frequently asked questions about 360-degree feedback: the development of the concept, the benefits to individuals and organizations, recommended uses, and future trends. The appendices contain the criteria for selection in this bibliography, related sources, and a glossary. Includes author and title indexes.

New
Freedman, N., & Mitchell, A. (1997). **Leadership training in companies.** *emfd FORUM, 97*(2), 39-44.

This article reports on a meeting of senior management developers from 20 leading companies in the European Union. These training directors shared their program descriptions, benchmarks, models, and concerns. The highlights are featured in this article. Phillips Company employed a transformation program called Operation Centurion to survey employees' perspectives on company leadership, provide 360-degree feedback to managers, and teach a variety of leadership styles. The executives at Swiss bank UBS served as faculty in leadership development programs for high-potential employees. Ericcson offered three-tiered leadership programs and partnered with business schools to deliver one of the tiers.

New
Fritz, S. M., Brown, F. W., Lunde, J. P., & Banset, E. A. (Eds.). (1996). ***Interpersonal skills for leadership.*** Needham Heights, MA: Simon & Schuster Custom.

This book is compiled by the faculty of the Department of Agricultural Leadership, Education, and Community at the University of Nebraska–Lincoln. The authors share ideas for conceptual and experiential learning with others who teach courses in agriculture and food science. There are ideas for teaching active listening skills, goal setting, and conflict management. Other lessons help students understand the nature of self-esteem, power, perception, and values. One chapter focuses on servant leadership and another suggests journaling as a learning experience. Each chapter contains a case study, discussion starters, activities, and references for further reading.

Fulmer, R. M., & Vicere, A. A. (1995). ***Executive education and leadership development: The state of the practice.*** University Park, PA: Penn State Institute for the Study of Organizational Effectiveness.

In a world of constant change, the advantage goes to the organization that learns the fastest. To meet this challenge, organizations are spending $12 billion annually on executive education and leadership development programs in-house, at universities, through consultants, and at nonuniversity training organizations. Based on a survey of education suppliers, interviews with executives, and a review of recent studies, this book summarizes key trends in the field. Includes bibliographical references. Appendices list intellectual resources (people and publications).

New
Fulmer, R. M., & Vicere, A. A. (1996). **Executive development: An analysis of competitive forces.** *Planning Review, 24*(1), 31-36.

In this article, Fulmer and Vicere examine the multibillion-dollar field of leadership development programs and executive education. They describe the main suppliers of leadership programs today—business schools and private firms—and predict new competitors, including companies like IBM that have begun marketing their internal programs to other organizations. The authors conclude that the field is evolving toward a systems perspective with three major trends: more customized strategic programs; shorter, more focused, large-scaled, cascaded programs; and more action-learning projects with measurable results.

New
Gilley, J. W., & Boughton, N. W. (1996). ***Stop managing, start coaching! How performance coaching can enhance commitment and improve productivity.*** Chicago: Irwin.

The authors claim that organizational failure is the result of managerial malpractice—the failure to develop healthy manager-employee relations. But when managers coach rather than control, they support an employee's personal growth and encourage commitment to the organization—and that leads to organizational success. There are four roles for a performance coach to assume. As a trainer, the coach helps an employee build technical skills. A career coach supports an employee's personal goals and encourages growth. In the confronting role, a coach identifies performance shortfalls and strategies for improvement. The mentor helps an employee to develop networks and to become politically savvy. The chapters in this book are devoted to practical suggestions for becoming a performance coach, including the important issue of rewards. Includes index.

Hickman, G. H. (1994). **Practicing what we preach: Modeling leadership in the classroom.** *Journal of Leadership Studies, 1*(4), 135-144.

Hickman illustrates methods for empowering students to share responsibility for classroom teaching, evaluation, and recognition. Shared power, group action, and service to others reinforce classroom instruction in her Foundations of Leadership Studies, Leadership in Formal Organizations, and other undergraduate courses. Examples are a *Leadership Jeopardy* game, interviews, one-minute feedback evaluations, and random matching of famous leaders and followers.

New
Kelly, J. M., & Grose, P. G., Jr. (1997). **Case teaching and why it works in leadership education.** *Leadership Journal: Women in Leadership—Sharing the Vision, 1*(2), 21-30.

Dismissing "high-tech management education packages," the authors argue that case teaching, in which "class discussions approximate a single-subject meeting where one urgent problem is resolved," is the most effective way to teach leadership skills. In this article they describe the role of the teacher in the case method and give examples of programs where it has been used successfully. They then offer a sample case, a problem faced by a county administrator, complete with teaching notes and possible student solutions.

New
Lepsinger, R., & Lucia, A. D. (1997). *The art and science of 360 feedback.* San Diego, CA: Pfeiffer.

Written by feedback consultants, this book offers advice to leaders planning to implement such a 360-degree-feedback program in their organization. There are sections on choosing a feedback method, selling the idea in your organization, gathering and presenting feedback, and follow-up. Appendices include examples of 360 feedback, sample worksheets for feedback and interpretation, and a 360 feedback administration flowchart.

Lewis, C. T. (1995). **The grammar of leadership education.** *Journal of Leadership Studies, 2*(1), 3-12.

Leadership is a fuzzy, complex, and ever-changing concept that is not easily explained. To help educators differentiate between leadership as a noun and leadership as a verb, leadership in theory and leadership in practice, Lewis suggests a grammatical framework. Teaching leadership theory includes teaching ethical, philosophical, and historical issues as well as the various forms of leadership. Theory should be a prerequisite to learning the skills and behaviors that contribute to the practice of leadership.

New
Maby, R., & Brady, G. (1996). **Sports related leadership.** *Journal of Leadership Studies, 3*(1), 131-137.

This article examines how different leadership theories have been applied to the field of athletic leadership, primarily among coaches. Trait, behavioral, situational, and path-goal theories had particular impact on the development of Chelladurai and Carron's sports-specific Multidimensional Theory of Sports Leadership (*Journal of Sport Psychology, 6,* 167-176). Based on this theory, the Leadership Scale for Sports (*Journal of Sport Psychology, 2,* 34-45) measures: 1) an athlete's preference for specific coaching/leadership behavior, 2) an athlete's perception of his or her coach's leadership behavior, and 3) the coach's perception of his or her own leadership behavior.

New
Marquis, B. L., & Huston, C. J. (1996). *Leadership roles and management functions in nursing: Theory and application* (2nd ed.). Philadelphia: Lippincott.

This is a textbook for students of nursing administration and leadership. It is divided into units covering advocacy, conflict resolution, ethical issues, time management, staffing, motivating, and controlling. The authors walk through the evolution of leadership styles from trait theories to visioning to the integrated leader. Decision-making tools such as decision grids and pay-off tables are provided. Each chapter contains learning exercises to enhance critical-thinking skills and promote discussion.

Marsick, V. J., & Cederholm, L. (1988). **Developing leadership in international managers: An urgent challenge!** *Columbia Journal of World Business, 23*(4), 3-11.

Managers working in the international marketplace are challenged with new ways of leading, decision making, and doing business. In light of these demands, the authors draw on a model developed by a Swedish research institute to describe the principles and advantages of "Action Learning." This article "introduces both theory and experience with Action Learning as a means to develop transformational leaders in the global market." The authors cite evidence that Action Learning is an effective and viable model for developing international managers.

McCall, M. W., Jr. (1992). **Executive development as a business strategy.** *Journal of Business Strategy, 13*(1), 25-31.

McCall asserts that leadership development training should be among every corporation's top five priorities. Elements of leadership development are: succession planning, talent identification, matching talent with opportunity, coaching, and feedback. Job rotation is valuable when learning is increased and when measurement and rewards are used to encourage growth.

New
McDermott, L. (1996). **Wanted: Chief executive coach.** *Training & Development, 50*(5), 67-70.

Most senior executives do very little coaching, although the author considers it an essential part of leading an organization. This article details the reasons executives most often give for not practicing coaching and lists the qualities and behaviors of the ideal executive coach. Quotes and stories from famous coaches of sports teams, including Phil Jackson, Tommy Lasorda, and Don Shula, are used to illustrate how many different styles of coaching there are and how effective coaching can be.

Moulton, H. W., & Fickel, A. A. (1993). *Executive development: Preparing for the 21st century.* New York: Oxford University Press.

Corporations, executives, and directors of executive programs share responsibility for the development of today's and tomorrow's leaders. To meet that responsibility, Moulton and Fickel suggest processes for lifelong learning to achieve the competencies required to meet the economic, social, technological, political, and ethical issues of the future. They summarize past and present changes in the business environment, indicators of future changes, and the developmental influences on executives' success or derailment. Includes bibliographical references and index.

New
Nirenberg, J. (1997). *Power tools: A leader's guide to the latest management thinking.* New York: Prentice Hall.

Nirenberg wrote this book for managers who are tired of quick fixes that promise to solve organizational problems but don't. In an overview of management fads and common wisdom, he synthesizes management thinking into a few basic principles. He describes, in depth, seven management techniques and tools that evolved from customized solutions for unique problems: self-managing work teams, systems thinking, quality, reengineering, authentic communication, a Japanese management model, and a new business paradigm influenced by technology and changing work roles. Nirenberg provides a framework to help the reader determine the most appropriate tool or technique for his or her own organization. At the end of the book, an annotated compendium describes more than 100 tools and techniques. Includes bibliographical references and index.

Nygren, D. J., & Ukeritis, M. D. (1992). **Nonprofit executive leadership education study.** *Theological Education, 24*(1), 117-131.

This study summarizes current leadership programs offered for the training of nonprofit executives. Forty-five programs for religious, educational, philanthropic, and other nonprofit management are identified. College and university certificate and master's programs and specialized shorter programs are detailed. Past and future trends of nonprofit-leadership education are addressed, and the authors analyze whether the trends are being addressed by existing leadership programs.

New
Odenwald, S. B., & Matheny, W. G. (1996). *Global impact: Award winning performance programs from around the world.* Chicago: Irwin.

The authors identify results-oriented HRD training programs around the world. The case studies include: Glaxo Wellcome, Inc.'s adoption of corporate values (Canada); SmithKline Beecham's Information Resources Competency Development (U.S.); Amil's virtual university program for learning managers (Brazil); ISS's action-learning program for executives (Denmark); Teva Pharmaceutical Industries, Ltd's Passage program for young professionals (Israel); ISCOR, Ltd's diversity training program (South Africa); Samsung's cross-cultural training programs (Korea); and Omron Corporation's international training system (Japan).

Palus, C., & Drath, W. (1995). *Evolving leaders: A model for promoting leadership development in programs.* Greensboro, NC: Center for Creative Leadership.

Palus and Drath focus on a problem that many leadership educators encounter. Because the importance of leadership development is largely implied and not specified, it is difficult to design and evaluate programs that seek to promote it. The model presented in this report specifies how programs can influence a key aspect of leadership development—the psychological development of the individual. Includes bibliographical references.

Passow, A. H. (1988). **Styles of leadership training . . . and some more thoughts.** *Gifted Child Today, 11*(6), 34-38.

The first part of Passow's article addresses the need for developing a clear conception of leadership as it relates to university training. He outlines the areas for which leaders in the field of educating the gifted and talented need insight and understanding. The second portion of the article focuses on the process of training gifted students for leadership.

Pearson, A. W. (1993). **Management development for scientists and engineers.** *Research Technology Management, 36*(1), 45-48.

Career development of R&D managers is contrasted to the career development of executives in general. Studies indicate that personal challenges, career moves, transitions across boundaries, start-ups, interpersonal relationships, and training are relevant in both cases. R&D managers indicate a desire for early and frequent training in the areas of personal skills, team building, team roles, feedback, and communication.

Porter, L. W., & McKibbin, L. E. (1988). *Management education and development: Drift or thrust into the 21st century?* New York: McGraw-Hill.

Based upon interviews from an extensive sampling of respondents—students, faculty, curriculum coordinators, business owners, managers, and corporate executives— the current direction of management education and development was examined in light of the changes anticipated in society over the next 30 years. The particular areas examined were business-education degree programs, student composition, faculty, special areas of research, and lifelong learning programs targeted for top-level managers and executives. Includes bibliography and indexes.

New
Rameau, C., & Borges, A. (1996). **Looking back and looking forward.** *emfd FORUM, 96*(2), 13-17.

Speeches by the former dean and present dean of INSEAD trace the development and future of European management education. Rameau describes how, in the past 30 years, European schools have grown to rival American MBA programs, while focusing on general and international management. Borges outlines what European programs must do in the future, from continuing to stress interpersonal relationships to developing more partnerships with businesses.

New
Robinson, J. (1996). *Coach to coach: Business lessons from the locker room.* San Diego, CA: Pfeiffer.

John Robinson, former football coach of the University of Southern California and the Los Angeles Rams, compares his coaching experiences to corporate coaching. He pays homage to his early mentors, from whom he learned about challenge, persistence, authority, and winning. In football and in business, Robinson recommends that a successful coach have vision, love what he or she does—the process, not just the result, and build a cohesive team. Robinson's 18-year coaching record includes five conference championships, six college-bowl wins, four players who won the

Heisman Trophy, and several conference and national Coach of the Year awards. This book is part of the Warren Bennis Executive Briefing Series.

Ruderman, M. N., & Ohlott, P. J. (1994). *The realities of management promotion.* Greensboro, NC: Center for Creative Leadership.

This report describes a study of how 64 management promotions were made at three Fortune 500 companies. Interviewers asked questions of the person promoted, the immediate boss, the approving boss, and a human resource representative. What they learned was that there is no such thing as a typical promotion. Managers typically rationalized a promotion based on a candidate's personal attributes. The study suggests that promotions actually result from a mix of personal attributes, organizational needs, and a candidate's proximity to the decision-maker. Includes bibliographical references.

New
Sharma, B., & Roy, J. A. (1996). **Aspects of the internationalization of management education.** *Journal of Management Development, 15*(1), 5-13.

This paper examines the expansion in number and content of management programs with a global focus. The authors report on efforts to internationalize curricula, course contents, modes of delivery, and research. Some examples of successful efforts are: international internships and faculty exchanges, multicultural case studies and simulations, and partnerships between business schools in different countries.

Smith, A. (1993). **Management development evaluation and effectiveness.** *Journal of Management Development, 12*(1), 20-32.

Training is a dynamic activity with often unexpected outcomes and unintended consequences. Smith suggests that evaluation be used as feedback for increasing the effectiveness of future training rather than as a scientific measurement of previous training. She tested her theory with a key group of mental-health nurses using a diary evaluation to create qualitative feedback on long-term management training.

Swatez, M. J. (1995). **Preparing leadership students to lead.** *Journal of Leadership Studies, 2*(2), 73-90.

As a new area of formal education, leadership studies suffers from a small identity crisis among the uninformed. Are leadership students expected to be offered executive or entry-level jobs upon graduation? Of course, they must earn their ranks like any other employees in an organization. How do educators train leadership students for practical careers? Two effective methods of teaching are modeling leadership in the classroom and experiential education. Example and experience teach students to practice their leadership skills at any level.

Ulmer, W. F. (1994). **Missing links in the education of senior leaders.** *Public Manager, 23*(2), 9-12.

In order for managerial performance to create organizational rejuvenation, the education of senior leaders should be examined. Development programs for executives should include three critical elements that are rarely given serious attention: 1) the role of personality and self-awareness; 2) an enlargement of the conceptual model of leader behavior; and 3) an improved approach to the evaluation of individuals, teams, and organizations. Ulmer is the retired president and CEO of the Center for Creative Leadership.

Verlander, E. G. (1992). **Executive education for managing complex organizational learning.** *Human Resource Planning, 15*(2), 1-18.

Learning to manage the speed, direction, and intensity of inevitable change will determine future business winners and losers. The challenge to leadership is to increase learning skills through on-the-job training, job rotation, and management development programs. This article discusses practical changes in management development programs to improve their quality and impact, including design, development, and delivery.

Vincent, A., & Seymour, J. (1995). **Profile of women mentors: A national survey.** *SAM Advanced Management Journal, 60*(2), 4-10.

The results of a national survey on mentoring are discussed. The survey addressed gender, race, education, salary, experience, and age factors within a mentoring-protégé relationship. Among the findings were: 1) women are as willing to mentor as men, 2) previous mentors or protégés are more willing to enter subsequent mentoring relationships, and 3) female mentors have primarily female protégés whereas male mentors have both female and male protégés. Other findings and the population for the survey are also discussed.

New
Waldroop, J., & Butler, T. (1996). **The executive as coach.** *Harvard Business Review, 74*(6), 111-117.

Coaching requires finding the correct "balance between carrot and stick." This article offers executives advice on how they can best help their managers change negative behavior. Readers are told how to tell when a manager needs coaching—for example, how to decide whether a behavior is changeable or if it is a character trait. Waldroop and Butler also identify what skills are needed

in a coach, such as the ability to be a teacher, not a judge. Finally, they offer suggestions on what coaching techniques work best, including setting microgoals and using script writing and role plays.

New
Witherspoon, R., & White, R. P. (1997). *Four essential ways that coaching can help executives.* Greensboro, NC: Center for Creative Leadership.

This report elaborates on the coaching relationship between consultants and their clients: chief executives, board members, and senior managers of organizations. As a coach, the consultant's role is to provide focused learning regarding a client's specific task, his or her present job, a future job, or the client's long-range goals. These learnings are categorized into four executive coaching roles: coaching for skills, coaching for performance, coaching for development, and coaching for the executive's agenda. As the authors describe each role, they also provide an example that includes a situation, a process, and results. Includes bibliographical references.

COURSE AND PROGRAM DESCRIPTIONS

New
Arches, J., Darlington-Hope, M., Gerson, J., Gibson, J., Habana-Hafner, S., & Kiang, P. (1997). **New voices in university-community transformation.** *Change, 29*(1), 36-41.

CIRCLE (Center for Immigrant and Community Leadership and Empowerment) is a joint venture between the Massachusetts Office for Refugees and Immigrants and the University of Massachusetts. Campuses in Boston, Lowell, and Amherst plan collective leadership programs for students, faculty, and neighborhood "newcomers." The Lowell CIRCLE joins political science faculty with Asian-American and Latino citizens who are eager to strengthen their civic involvement and influence. The Amherst CIRCLE hosts the Giving SEED (Students for Education, Empowerment, and Development), a program for Cambodian youth. The Boston CIRCLE partners university and community personnel in advisory activities. All CIRCLEs offer mentors, ethnic studies, service learning, and skill building for community building.

New
Ashcroft, J. C. (1997). **Creating a new distance education model by embracing change.** *Leadership Journal: Women in Leadership—Sharing the Vision, 1*(2), 49-56.

The advances made in technology and its availability over the past two decades have made distance learning a popular and effective educational method, and Ashcroft argues that this is especially true among women. This article explains why distance learning appeals to women, describes how schools with distance programs accommodate changing markets, and addresses specific issues such as TQM, desktop publishing, and the importance of communication and collaboration for distance students. Includes bibliographical references.

Bailey, J. (1994). **Innovations in leadership development.** *emfd FORUM. Focus: Business Driven Management Development, 94*(3), 48-50.

Five leadership development programs in Australia are described: The Williamson Foundation program for corporate and community leaders; the International Business Development Programme that combines academic and business involvement with action learning to prepare global leaders; Adventure Learning that uses outdoor activities to teach competencies to senior executives; a master's degree program at the Swineburne University of Technology taught by "pracademics" from the corporate world; and a master's degree program at the Royal Melbourne Institute of Technology for corporate leaders.

New
Bales, K. (1997). **Leadership development as an institutional initiative.** *Leadership Journal: Women in Leadership—Sharing the Vision, 1*(2), 103-108.

The Excellence in Leadership program at Ball State University, started four years ago, is a cocurricular collaboration between student affairs and academic affairs. Students in the program incorporate classes and seminars on leadership throughout their four years of study and apply the skills they learn to leading campus and community activities. In this article Bales, the program's director, explains the theories behind the program, its components, student reactions, and the challenges of expansion. Includes bibliographical references.

New
Bricker's international directory: University-based executive development programs (29th ed.). (1998). Princeton, NJ: Peterson's.

This directory is designed to help upper-level management and executives select management programs at leading universities worldwide. Most programs run four weeks or less, some are longer, and some are offered in split sessions with classes offered weeks or months apart. The programs are listed under subject headings such as General Management, Leadership, Business Environment and Global Concerns, Business Strategy, Technology Management, Government and Nonprofit Management, and Executive MBA Programs. Information includes

program objectives, location, duration, profile of participants, methods of instruction, calendar of sessions, tuition, faculty, special features, and the name of the official contact person. Includes institution, geographic, and subject indexes.

New
Brownfain, E., & Churgel, S. (1997). *EBTD directory: Experience-based training and development programs.* Boulder, CO: Association for Experiential Education.

This directory lists organizations that provide experience-based programs for human resource development and organizational change. Such organizations offer programs that create situations to help participants discover their own insights into challenging business situations. Many of the programs have been accredited by the Association for Experiential Education. Some of the organizations listed are: Breckenridge Outdoor Education Center in Breckenridge, Colorado; Corporate Adventure Training Institute in St. Catherines, Ontario; Project Adventure in Portland, Oregon; and Outward Bound with several locations. Includes a bibliography.

Buckner, J. K., & Williams, M. L. (1995). **Applying the competing values model of leadership: Reconceptualizing a university student leadership development program.** *Journal of Leadership Studies, 2*(4), 19-34.

This study assesses eight leadership roles of university students, using an adapted version of Quinn's Competing Values Model (in *Beyond Rational Management: Mastering the Paradoxes and Competing Demands of High Performance*, 1988). This model integrates typical organizational effectiveness criteria, such as: participation, flexibility, innovation, goal clarity, measurement, and internal/external focus. Results indicate that student leaders see themselves as mentors to others within their groups rather than brokers to those outside the group. Position, gender, and type of club influence the leadership roles assumed. The model and results are considered for purposes of reconceptualizing and improving student leadership programs.

Catalyst. (1993). *Mentoring: A guide to corporate programs and practices.* New York: Author.

This book reports on Catalyst's research of women's mentoring programs. Interviews with executives and a review of the literature indicate that formal programs and informal mentoring benefit both female employees and their organizations. This book describes a typical mentoring program and offers guidelines for starting a new one, as well as pitfalls to avoid. Descriptions of ten successful programs include AT&T's Early Career

Advisory Program, Liz Claiborne's Career in Management, and Procter & Gamble's Corporate Mentoring Program.

New
CivicQuest. (1996). *Learning leadership: A curriculum guide for a new generation: Grades K-12.* College Park, MD: Center for Political Leadership and Participation. Call (301) 929-2134 for information.

This book is the result of a two-year field test of a curriculum model for teaching leadership to high school students. This field test, called CivicQuest, was a joint project of the Center for Political Leadership and Participation at the University of Maryland at College Park and the John F. Kennedy High School in Silver Spring, Maryland. It was funded by the Dwight D. Eisenhower Leadership Development Program and the U.S. Department of Education. The curriculum model contains eight modules: Leadership History and Theory, Leadership Competencies–A, Leadership Contexts, Moral and Ethical Dimensions of Leadership, Leadership Competencies–B, Leading Individuals and Groups, Service Learning, and Experiential Learning. There are five to ten lessons in each module. A significant finding of the field test was that young people needed to begin leadership studies before high school. In response, the project sponsors held a leadership institute for K-12 teachers who, in turn, developed lesson plans for younger students. Thirty-one of those lesson plans are included in this book.

The Corporate University guide to management seminars. (1993). Point Richmond, CA: Corporate University Press.

This guide describes more than 750 university- and institution-based management programs. Entries detail the program focus, subject matter, intended audience, cost, and location of each program. A special feature is the Editors Choice, a short list of programs recognized for excellence. This guide serves as a supplement to the Corporate University's *The Evaluation Guide to Executive Programs,* which has more detailed descriptions of longer executive programs that are offered primarily by universities.

Clark, K. E. (1985, March). **Teaching undergraduates to be leaders.** *American Association of Higher Education Bulletin,* pp. 11-14.

This article explores the current situation in the education process of developing leaders. Research and workshops conducted at the Center for Creative Leadership are described, along with several important course offerings at various colleges and universities. The article calls "for colleges to challenge students to develop their capabilities to the fullest, to learn how organizations function and can

be led, and to understand the necessity for accommodating the interest of others . . . ."

New
Clawson, J. G., & Doner, J. (1996). **Teaching leadership through aikido.** *Journal of Management Education, 20*(2), 182-205.

Clawson and Doner teach a two-hour aikido session in many of the leadership courses in the Darden School's executive education and MBA programs at the University of Virginia. Students come to class dressed in loose-fitting clothing, ready to learn the Eastern philosophy behind this defensive martial art. Through relaxation and breathing exercises, students become centered. They practice staying centered as classmates push them physically. To illustrate the concept of ki, the harmony of mind and body, students are asked to have positive thoughts, then negative thoughts, while being pushed. Inevitably, the negative thoughts weaken students and they become vulnerable to the pushing. The next module teaches students to sense the energy of others. Finally, students realize how to harmonize with the energy of others. The authors report that participants find the physical metaphor of aikido a powerful tool to become centered around purpose and principles, clarify a vision, sense danger, and convert challenges into positive energy.

Cooper, S. E., & Smirga, W. G. (1992). **Developing and marketing tomorrow's leaders in today's colleges.** *Journal of College Student Development, 33*(3), 275-277.

Valparaiso University's Student Leadership Development Program permits students to interact with campus leaders, provides student networks, develops leadership skills, and aids with the creation of a leadership development transcript to show future employers. For a $5.00 registration fee per module, a student may participate in 12 modules each semester. An evaluative survey of 96 participants found that reactions to the program were positive.

Dixon, N. M. (1993). **Developing managers for the learning organization.** *Human Resource Management Review, 3*(3), 243-254.

Rapidly changing technology, social trends, and global competition are forcing organizations to learn their way out of problems rather than depend on known solutions. Often management training programs rely on experts to provide ready-made answers. Dixon recommends training programs that develop a manager's ability to reason by: situating learning in real work, defining a less central role for experts, providing spaced rather than compressed time frames, and offering learning in a community rather than individually. She recommends five programs that embody these elements.

Downham, T. A., Noel, J. L., & Prendergast, A. E. (1992). **Executive development.** *Human Resource Management, 31*(1&2), 95-107.

Successful two-week executive development programs at TRW, Inc., and General Electric are founded on action learning. Participants develop real products, services, or strategies, while working on customer satisfaction and total quality management. The emphasis is on teamwork and personal relationships.

Drew, S. A. W., & Davidson, A. (1993). **Simulation-based leadership development and team learning.** *Journal of Management Development, 12*(8), 39-52.

Two-day microworld computer simulation exercises promote organizational change and learning. A microworld provides a practice field for learning new ways of management and a computer provides data for rapid feedback. An effective microworld includes: customer service, total quality, realism, rules and structure, and development of individual and team capacities. Results of a computer microworld program designed for a North American telecommunications organization are reported.

Fagan, M. M., Bromley, K., & Welch, J. (1994). **Using biographies to teach leadership.** *Journal of Leadership Studies, 1*(4), 123-134.

The authors team-teach Profiles in Leadership, a freshman course at Kentucky Wesleyan College. Each semester features six or more biographies of leaders such as Golda Meir, Charles Darwin, and Edward R. Murrow. Subject specialists are invited to lead seminars. For instance, a biology professor leads the discussion on Louis Pasteur. Classroom studies are supplemented by related activities. Stargazing augments the lesson on Galileo Galilei and a ride in a Model T adds interest to the lesson on Henry Ford. Through biographical study, the authors assert that one can learn about the accomplishments of leaders as well as the criticisms they faced, their dedication and sacrifice, creativity, and failures.

New
Fanning Leadership Center. (1996). *Youth leadership in action: A community focus: Program planning guide.* Athens: Fanning Leadership Center, University of Georgia. Call (706) 542-1108 for information.

This guide is written for local organizers of the Fanning Leadership Center's Youth Leadership in Action program but would be helpful to any organizer of youth leadership programs. There is an outline of eight learning modules that focus primarily on skill building. The guide also contains a planning section with schedules, sample letters, and evaluation forms. Other helpful materials include icebreakers, mentoring strategies, suggestions for journal

keeping, and case scenarios to spark group discussion. Separate participant workbooks may be purchased.

New
Fanning Leadership Center. (1997). *Community leadership program: Planning guide* (1997-1998 series ed.). Athens: Fanning Leadership Center, University of Georgia. Phone: (706) 542-1108.

This guide is written for local coordinators of the Fanning Leadership Center's Community Leadership Program but would be helpful for anyone planning a grassroots leadership program. The role of program coordinator and descriptions of supporting committees are outlined with task lists and a timeline for completing tasks. An outline of the 12-module Community Leadership Program, sample letters, meeting agendas, and evaluation forms are included. Additional books are available for instructors and participants.

Galagan, P. A. (1990). **Execs go global, literally.** *Training & Development Journal, 44*(6), 58-63.

The University of Michigan's Global Leadership Program is a cross-cultural, action-learning experience for top executives. For five weeks, teams of American, Japanese, and European executives learn global business strategies for joint ventures and alliances. Participants gain understanding of geopolitical forces and their relationship to business. Teams participate in negotiation workshops, outdoor challenges, and business-opportunity assessments in foreign countries.

Genovese, M. A. (1994). **Teaching political leadership: An introduction.** *Journal of Leadership Studies, 1*(3), 95-103.

One approach to teaching political leadership is outlined in this 13-week course syllabus. Genovese favors using films to spark class discussion and explains why he shows a segment of *I, Claudius* each week. The 13-part film series deals with a variety of leadership issues such as the limits and possibilities of leadership, change, ethics, corruption, and rebellion. In addition to the video series and discussion, Genovese lectures on theory and history. Students do a research paper on the impact of leadership on a specific policy or a profile of a political leader.

New
Gettysburg leadership model. (1996). Gettysburg, PA: Eisenhower Leadership Program at Gettysburg College. Call Tom Dombrowsky at (717) 337-6321 for information.

The 12 learning modules in this book may be used separately to teach specific leadership topics or sequentially to create an undergraduate leadership program. They are: Team Dynamics, Collaboration, Communication, Positional Leadership, Followership, Problem Solving, Decision Skills, Change, Innovation, Trust, Ethics, and Diversity. The modules last from one to three hours and include film clips, reading recommendations, activities, and scenarios for discussion. Several activities utilize an electronic carpet that serves as a maze with "mines" or "hot squares." There are instructions for replicating maze activities by taping a grid to the floor. A copy of the *Student Leadership Inventory* (Rosenbach, Sashkin, & Harburg) and instructions are included so that student scores may be compared before and after participation.

New

Glasman, N. S. (1997). **An experimental program in leadership.** *Peabody Journal of Education, 72*(2), 42-65.

During the 1994-1995 school year, the University of Judaism in Los Angeles offered an experimental program in educational administration with a focus on leadership skills. This article describes the content of the program and its evaluations, which were largely positive. Program objectives, student performance, and the outlines of specific courses are also given here. The author hopes that the description of this program can serve as a model for leadership development programs at other universities. Includes bibliographical references.

Gregory, R. A., & Britt, S. K. (1987, Summer). **What the good ones do: Characteristics of promising leadership development programs.** *Campus Activities Programming, 20,* 33-35.

This article reports the results of a survey conducted by the Center for Creative Leadership of the leadership education efforts of over 1,300 higher-education institutions nationwide. The study showed almost 500 leadership programs offered by the nation's colleges and universities.

New

Healey, B. J. (1997). **Leadership in community health.** *Journal of Leadership Studies, 4*(2), 159-168.

Healey presents a case study of the King's College graduate health care administration program. He argues for the expansion of preventive health care programs such as public education about HIV and high-risk behaviors. The King's College program focuses on preventive medicine and its connection with computers and the media. It has produced a videotape for use in area schools, helped to form a proactive regional wellness council, and implemented a number of community programs. All students in the program are required to develop and implement a community wellness program.

New

Heimovics, D., Taylor, M., & Stilwell, R. (1996). **Assessing and developing a new strategic direction for the executive MBA.** *Journal of Management Education: Special Issue: Evolution and Revolution in Management Education: The Joys and Challenges of Change, 20*(4), 577-594.

This is a report of the two-year planning process that resulted in significant changes at the Bloch School of Business and Public Administration at the University of Missouri–Kansas City. Following gifts of a new building and eight endowed professorships, the school was challenged to update its program. Faculty, student, and business advisory groups identified the primary areas that today's executives need to address: leadership skills that encourage innovation; economic changes and global competition; flat, networked organizations; strategic thinking; technical tools for handling rapidly changing information; just-in-time learning; entrepreneurship; and relations between rational production systems and unpredictable people systems. In response, the school developed a new, four-module curriculum: 1) tools of competitive analysis, 2) managing people and systems, 3) the enterprise and its environment, and 4) strategic leadership.

New

Hickman, G. R., & Creighton-Zollar, A. (1997). **Teaching leadership for a diverse society: Strategies, challenges, and recommendations.** *Journal of Leadership Studies, 4*(1), 90-106.

During the 1994-1995 school year, two pilot courses were taught at the University of Richmond's Jepson School of Leadership. These courses attempted to prepare students to lead in a diverse society by incorporating materials, activities, and teaching methods that dealt with diversity into an introductory leadership studies course. Students in the courses were later surveyed about their responses to the program, and the article includes quotes from the students and tables of survey responses. The authors also offer seven recommendations on how to best incorporate diversity into an introductory leadership course, including: generate a diverse student mix, use a group assignment strategy, use demographic information, and use facilitation to increase group effectiveness. Includes references.

New

Howe, W., & Freeman, F. (1997). **Leadership education in American colleges and universities: An overview.** *Concepts & Connections: A Newsletter for Leadership Educators, 5*(2), 5-7.

The authors report on their 1996 survey, intended to determine the range and scope of leadership courses and programs on college and university campuses. About one-fourth are single academic courses and one-fourth are offered through student-affairs programs. Almost two-thirds are focused on undergraduates and two-thirds award academic credit. More than half teach a balance of theory and application. When compared to a similar survey conducted by the Center for Creative Leadership in 1986, it appears that leadership education has grown by 20% over ten years.

New
Howe, W. S., III. (1997). **Approaching leadership through problem solving.** *Leadership Journal: Women in Leadership—Sharing the Vision, 1*(2), 115-128.

A professor at the University of Richmond's Jepson School of Leadership, the author describes the course he teaches on problem solving that brings "students face-to-face with *real* leadership problems in *real* leadership contexts." He describes the research, mainly from medical schools, that inspired him to focus a course on case-study problems and then outlines the course objectives, assignments, resources, speakers, evaluation methods, and offers a day-by-day class schedule. Includes bibliographical references.

New
Keys, J. B. (1995). **Centres of excellence in management education.** *Journal of Management Development, 14*(5), 3-4.

Keys is guest editor of this special issue that focuses on organizations that provide innovative leadership and management development programs. The featured organizations include: the School of Management Studies at Templeton College, Oxford University; MIT Organizational Learning Center; Inter Cultural Management headquartered in Paris; the Center for Creative Leadership; the Center for Leadership at the University of Tampa; and the College of Business Administration at the University of Hawaii. Keys is Director of the Center for Managerial Learning and Business Simulation at Georgia University. Each article describes one center's history, structure, focus, research, and plans for the future.

New
Lamond, D. A. (1995). **Using consulting projects in management education: The joys and jitters of serving two masters.** *Journal of Management Development, 14*(8), 60-72.

Lamond reports on an action-learning approach used in the MBA program at the Macquarie University Graduate School of Management, New South Wales, Australia. Students assume roles as consultants to the executives of client companies. Working in project teams, each student

contributes eight 40-hour weeks to perform industry analysis, organizational analysis, and problem solving. Many of the involved students are experienced managers sponsored in the MBA program by their employers. Their consulting projects usually benefit their own companies. Others are arranged in the local business community. Includes bibliographical references.

New
Lankford, D. (1997). **License to lead: Instilling decision making skills in our young people.** *Schools in the Middle, 6*(3), 32-33.

This brief article describes NASSP's License to Lead program designed for middle-school students. The nine 30-minute segments present ethical dilemmas that may be easily understood by young people. There are no easy answers. The program's purpose is to teach adolescents how to make tough decisions and how to apply that process to leadership and to daily situations. License to Lead is available from NASSP. Phone: (800) 253-7746.

Learn, grow, become (2nd ed.). (1995). Stillwater: Oklahoma Department of Vocational and Technical Education, 1500 West Seventh Avenue, Stillwater, OK 74074-4364. Phone: (800) 654-4502.

Organizational membership and participation is an integral part of instruction in vocational and technical programs. Oklahoma's program provides a model for leadership development through cocurricular activities in Future Business Leaders of America, Technology Student Association, Health Occupations Students of America, Future Farmers of America, Future Homemakers of America, DECA, and the Vocational Industrial Clubs of America. Each club has a customized edition of *Learn, Grow, Become* filled with instructions for teaching leadership skills, experiential learning activities, skill-based competitions, assessments, and assignments.

New
Meister, J. C. (1994). ***Corporate quality universities: Lessons in building a world-class work force.*** New York: Irwin.

Business organizations are changing from pyramids with thinkers on top and doers on the bottom to flattened organizations. Employees at all levels are required to solve problems and respond to customers with speed and efficiency. These employees are expected to have interpersonal and creative thinking skills as well as basic education and technological competency. Training these employees requires a large commitment, financial and strategic. Some insightful organizations provide continuous education in the form of corporate universities. Their programs are as varied as the companies who support them. Meister reports on corporate universities at Motorola, General Electric, Saturn, IBM, Xerox, McDonald's, and Disney. Smaller companies such as IAMS Company (pet products) and Sun Microsystems have also adopted the corporate university training system with success. Includes bibliographical references and index.

Moulton, H. W. (1995). *The evaluation guide to executive programs* (11th ed.). Point Richmond, CA: Corporate University Press.

This guide evaluates 160 executive programs offered by universities and reputable private institutions. To meet criteria for inclusion, the programs must be at least one week in length, regularly scheduled, in existence for at least two years, and open to private, public, and nonprofit sectors. In addition to descriptive data, comments from human resource professionals and program participants are provided. A faculty strength grid indicates instructors' currency and depth of knowledge, teaching experience, dedication to the learning process, and academic credentials. All program evaluation information is also available on ExecuSource software from Corporate University Press. For an annual directory of 880 short programs, check the annual *Corporate University Guide to Management Seminars.*

Murphy, J., & Hallinger, P. (1987). *Approaches to administrative training in education.* Albany: State University of New York Press.

This book is directed at a variety of audiences: leadership academics, students of educational administration, professors, staff developers, practitioners, policymakers, and staff members of principal centers. Practical information is provided on a wide selection of training programs. Presenting a diversity of training models, the authors have attempted to build upon what has been learned in the past by placing these models into a historical perspective. Those involved in implementing and developing administrative training programs throughout the sphere of educational administration should find this text of special interest. Includes bibliographical references and index.

New
Peak, M. H. (1997, February). **Go Corporate U!** *Management Review, 86,* 33-37.

Corporate training departments look to academia for employee education. They form partnerships with local colleges, networks of colleges, and training organizations to customize programs. Lessons are taught in traditional classrooms and via technology—interactive desktop, self-study, and distance-learning methods. Peak describes the philosophies behind McDonald's Hamburger University,

Sears University, Motorola University, and other proactive programs.

New
Perreault, G. (1997). **The interdisciplinary nature of leadership studies.** *Leadership Journal: Women in Leadership—Sharing the Vision, 1*(2), 109-114.

Written by the director of Leadership Studies at the University of Northern Iowa, this article describes the courses offered there and then looks more broadly at the place of leadership studies in a college curriculum. The author believes that leadership cannot be taught within one discipline but should be taught in a comprehensive framework that focuses on both academic content and learning processes. The article is intended to help educators designing a leadership studies program respond to outside objections, such as the argument that leadership is simply a set of skills and not an academic subject. Includes bibliographical references.

Perrin, K. (Ed.). (1985). *National leadership training center: Leadership curriculum guide.* Reston, VA: National Association of Secondary School Principals.

This curriculum guide is designed to assist educators in the preparation and implementation of leadership training programs aimed at secondary-school students. The guide is composed of the following sections: self-awareness, leadership, goal setting, communication, organization, group process, problem solving, and evaluation. A variety of exercises that correspond to chapter topics are also included.

New
Phelps, B. (1997). *In pursuit of the White Stag: A design for leadership* (2nd ed.). Livermore, CA: TechPros, 1044 Wagoner Drive, Livermore, CA 94550. Phone: (510) 606-9445.

This book describes the White Stag Leadership Development Program, a week-long summer camp run by Explorer Post 122 of the Monterey Bay Area Boy Scout Council. It is based on the premise that every individual is in a state of continuous growth and that leadership development is a long-range process. The book describes the program's methods and content, assessment and evaluation instruments, program history and traditions, and a calendar for program planning. A companion book, *Manager of Learning: Resources for Leadership,* includes learning modules for training White Stag staff. Although the White Stag books were prepared for a one-week outdoor learning experience for a special audience, the lessons could be used in any youth leadership development situation.

Phi Theta Kappa. (1993). *Leadership development program.* Jackson, MS: Phi Theta Kappa.

> Phi Theta Kappa, the international honor society of two-year colleges, created this extensive program and certifies faculty from community, technical, and junior colleges to teach it on their campuses. Fifteen modules address leadership skills and issues through a learn-by-doing philosophy. Classic leadership case studies, debates, exercises, role plays, simulations, films, and surveys are included in each module. Sample module titles are: Your Personal Leadership Philosophy, Conceiving and Articulating a Vision, and Using Logic and Creativity in Decision Making. Includes bibliographical references.

New

Pickert, S. M. (1992). **Using simulations to teach leadership roles.** *Teaching Education,* 5(1), 37-42.

> Pickert describes her course in international and multicultural education at the Catholic University of America. Her students participate in a series of three simulations of organizational situations that involve policy-making: school board meetings, congressional committees that deal with educational issues, and international conferences. The content of each simulation is based on current events and, therefore, changes each year. The students research background information, interview experts, conduct simulated meetings, defend positions, and vote on policies. Lessons they learn include: dealing with the tension between their opinions of good educational practice and the opinions of special interest groups, preparing clear and concise statements, compromising with those who have diverse viewpoints, and understanding the nature of influence.

Powell, S. R. (1993). **The power of positive peer influence: Leadership training for today's teens.** *Special Services in the Schools,* 8(1), 119-136.

> Powell, the president of the Princeton Center for Leadership Training, reports on one of the center's programs, The Peer Group Connection. In this program, high school students receive training to serve as mentors and role models for younger students. The program stresses competence, confidence, connectedness, and understanding. Class credits are awarded for participation.

New

Reed, T. K. (1997). **Developing an introductory course for the study of leadership: A sample syllabus.** *Leadership Journal: Women in Leadership—Sharing the Vision,* 1(2), 129-136.

> Based on an introductory course on leadership from Columbia College in South Carolina, this article stems from a theoretical model of how to teach students about leadership. The model is made up of four quadrants: a knowledge base, knowledge about self, interactive skills, and practical applications. A sample syllabus for a leadership studies course—including course objectives, sample journal entries and learning contracts, and suggested books and articles—is also given.

Rural Organizations and Services Branch, Ontario Ministry of Agriculture and Food. (1993). *Core curriculum of leadership.* Ontario: Author.

> This loose-leaf notebook was developed from a strategic plan to provide relevant resources on 14 areas of leadership skills and knowledge. Each area is defined by a rationale and supported by an outline of skills, knowledge, and attitudes. It is intended to serve as a launching point for assessment of training needs or program development. For more information, contact Rural Organizations and Services Branch, Ontario Ministry of Agriculture and Food, P.O. Box 1030, Guelph, Ontario N1H 6N1.

New

Schwartz, M. K., Axtman, K. M., & Freeman, F. H. (1998). *Leadership education: A source book of courses and programs* (7th ed.). Greensboro, NC: Center for Creative Leadership.

> The 7th edition contains more than 200 examples of leadership majors and minors, academic leadership courses, and cocurricular programs. Course syllabi are from departments of education, business, agriculture, nursing, physical education, political science, and others. Cocurricular courses include campus programs for women, a portfolio program, citizen leadership training, and youth programs. Nonacademic examples are also included to provide a lens for viewing the continuation from leadership studies to lifelong learning. Programs for professionals and for grassroots leaders provide this focus.

SERVE (SouthEastern Regional Vision for Education). (1994). *Leadership for collaboration: Participant's workbook.* Greensboro: University of North Carolina at Greensboro School of Education.

> This workbook supports a team-building, leadership, and collaboration training program for those involved in the care and education of young children. Families, educators, caregivers, health care workers, and policymakers learn to work in teams and share resources. Instructions for getting started and training activities as well as sample overheads, handouts, partnership agreements, and evaluation tools are included. Examples of successful collaboration programs illustrate actual mission statements, histories, and unique applications. For more

information, contact SERVE, 41 Marietta Street, N.W., Suite 1000, Atlanta, GA 30303. Phone: (800) 659-3204 or (404) 577-7737.

New
Stumpf, S. A. (1995). **Applying new science theories in leadership development.** *Journal of Management Development*, *14*(5), 39-49.

Stumpf is cofounder of the nonprofit MSP Institute, Inc., which creates simulations for teaching organizational management. The institute's approach to leadership development is consistent with "new science" (Wheatley, 1992) theories for learning to lead complex organizations in turbulent environments. Stumpf explains how the institute applies quantum mechanics, self-organizing systems, and chaos theory to activity-based leadership lessons. One example of this application is the LOMA Middle Management Workshop on Leadership, a five-day program for mid-level managers in the life insurance industry.

Stumpf, S. A., & Dutton, J. E. (1990). **The dynamics of learning through management simulations: Let's dance.** *Management Games and Simulations*, *9*(2), 7-15.

Stumpf and Dutton attempt to convey the sense of learning and excitement following participation in a behavioral simulation. Using a dance metaphor, they describe how simulations work and how participants learn individually, with partners, or in a group. The speed and the lead change throughout the event. From this behavioral experience, participants gain new insights, confidence, and relationships. Then they leave exhausted but excited.

New
Vicere, A. A. (1996). **Executive education: The leading edge.** *Organizational Dynamics*, *25*(2), 67-81.

To illustrate the importance of innovative, hands-on executive education, the author profiles three different training programs: the Center for Creative Leadership's LeaderLab®, AT&T's Leadership Development Program, and ARAMARK's Executive Leadership Institute. The content and impact of these programs are discussed, as well as their implications for other executive education initiatives.

Wagner, R. J. (1992). ***Annotated bibliography for experience-based training and development and outdoor training.*** Whitewater: Wisconsin University–Whitewater, Center for Research in Experiential Education. (ERIC Document No. ED345900).

This annotated bibliography contains 65 entries on outdoor experiential training, including journal articles, conference papers, newspaper and magazine articles, television broadcasts, books, and unpublished manu-

scripts. Most items are descriptions or evaluations of programs and models of outdoor-based experiential training for personal development. Objectives stated include team building, personal growth, development of wilderness skills, leadership training, development of communication and human relations skills, improved self-esteem, and building group trust.

New
Woyach, R. B. (1997). **Portfolios as means for promoting continuity in leadership development.** *Journal of Leadership Studies*, *4*(2), 144-158.

Woyach describes a portfolio program that has been implemented in three high schools in Oakland County, Michigan. This portfolio program is intended to enhance student leadership abilities and display students' progress in learning the skills and competencies of civic leadership. This article describes the learning objectives and the components of the portfolios. Some examples of learning objectives are: active listening, time management, envisioning, and willingness to take responsibility. Examples of components include a cover letter, table of contents, and section introductions. Woyach gives tips for designing portfolio assessments and advising students.

Wren, J. T. (1994). **Teaching leadership: The art of the possible.** *Journal of Leadership Studies*, *1*(2), 73-93.

Wren shares the most recent version of his introductory leadership course at the University of Richmond's Jepson School of Leadership Studies. This Foundations course is a prerequisite for the curriculum, which pursues leadership from a liberal arts perspective. The article is a discussion of course structure and student competencies and does not include a syllabus.

Wren, J. T. (1995). **The problem of cultural leadership: The lessons of the dead leaders society and a new definition of leadership.** *Journal of Leadership Studies*, *2*(4), 122-139.

Wren reports on a course titled Historical Perspectives on Leadership, which became fondly known as The Dead Leaders Society. Discussion of Native American groups prior to the European contract led to discussion on substitutes for leadership, which then led to a new theory on cultural norms that substitute for leadership. This theory was applied to the rapid social change of the roaring twenties: postwar peace, urbanization, industrialization, the jazz movement, women's suffrage, and the idolization of sports heroes. From a study of leadership in a historical context emerged a new theory to challenge traditional views and provide a rich experience for students and professor.

PROGRAM ASSESSMENT

New
Barnett, B. G. (1995). **Portfolio use in educational leadership preparation programs: From theory to practice.** *Innovative Higher Education, 19*(3), 197-206.

Barnett describes the benefits of using portfolios in assessing leadership development, as well as academic achievement, for future school administrators. A portfolio contains a select sample of artifacts and attestations that reflect the depth of a person's learning over time. It may include examinations, documents of in-class and field-based experiences, journals, case studies, term papers, budgets, audio- or videotapes, letters of recommendation, professional development plans, awards, and transcripts. This collection of evidence may be useful in obtaining licensure, self-development and reflection, evaluation of faculty and programs, and the application of classroom learning to real-life situations. Includes bibliographical references.

New
Brungardt, C., & Crawford, C. B. (1996). **A comprehensive approach to assessing leadership students and programs: Preliminary findings.** *Journal of Leadership Studies, 3*(1), 37-48.

The authors present a framework for evaluating academic leadership programs. The framework is based on a case study of the three-year-old Leadership Studies program at Fort Hays State University. Quantitative and qualitative data are gathered to monitor the impact of program design and delivery as well as the learning outcomes. Student learning is measured from pre-test, in-class, and post-test data. Program impact is measured by student reactions, attitude surveys, behavior tests, results surveys, and follow-up surveys several years after graduation. Because the Fort Hays program was initiated in 1993, the longitudinal data weren't available at the time this article was written.

Cooper, D. L., Healy, M. A., & Simpson, J. (1994). **Student development through involvement: Specific changes over time.** *Journal of College Student Development, 35*(2), 98-102.

How do student-affairs professionals document the effect of cocurricular activities on students' growth and development? The authors used the *Student Developmental Task and Lifestyle Inventory* (Winston, Miller, & Prince, 1987) to measure the changes in 256 students at a Southeastern university. Students were administered the test during freshman orientation and again three years later. When freshman scores were compared to junior scores, students involved in student-affairs programs showed significant change in educational involvement, career planning, lifestyle planning, cultural participation, and academic autonomy. Student leaders showed the greatest changes in the areas of developing purpose and life management.

New
Council for the Advancement of Standards. (1997). **Council for the Advancement of Standards in Higher Education—Student leadership programs: Standards and guidelines.** *Concepts & Connections: A Newsletter for Educators, 5*(2), 17-19.

Newly established standards and guidelines for designing and delivering leadership programs are presented. Two articles in the same issue provide background information. Dennis Roberts describes the evolution of teaching leadership throughout the history of higher education in "The Changing Look of Leadership Programs" (pp. 1, 3, 11-14). Ted Miller describes how and why CAS wrote the standards and how leadership educators should apply them in "Leadership Training Concepts and Techniques: Professional Standards for Student Leadership Programs" (pp. 7-9).

Cusack, S. A., & Thompson, W. J. (1992). **Leadership training in the third age: The research and evaluation of a leadership and personal development program for the retired.** *Journal of Applied Gerontology, 11*(3), 343-360.

The Seniors' Independence Program, sponsored by Simon Fraser University in British Columbia, was developed to increase the number and the ability of skilled senior volunteers to participate in community programs. Evaluations following each of the ten workshops, evaluators' summaries, and pre- and post-test questionnaires form a case-study narrative. A comparison of pre- and post-test scores showed significant improvement in the ability to express ideas comfortably and solve problems in a group.

New
Daugherty, R. A., & Williams, S. U. (1997). **The long-term impacts of leadership development: An assessment of a statewide program.** *Journal of Leadership Studies, 4*(2), 101-115.

This article assesses the long-term impact of a statewide community-based leadership development program. The Oklahoma Family Community Leadership Program (OFCLP) offers workshops to prepare adults for involvement in public-policy decision making. In 30 counties that sponsored the program for at least three years, program agents responded to a survey about: types of community leadership activity, types of OFCLP preparation (workshops, OFCLP materials, and handbooks), most valuable program components, willingness to expand activities, future needs, and long-term impacts. The study found that participants continued their leadership roles beyond their program commitments and that the program's methodology worked well for emerging community issues.

Fertman, C., & Long, J. A. (1990). **All students are leaders.** *School Counselor*, 37(5), 391-396.

The University of Pittsburgh's "All Students Are Leaders" program for 8th and 9th graders is a five-day workshop and a series of one-day workshops during the year to teach leadership concepts. Structured activities assess students' perceptions of their own leadership abilities and teach new attitudes and skills. Areas covered are communication, decision making, stress management, assertiveness, leading meetings, solving problems, and team building. A survey of students after four months in the program indicated that self-concepts of leadership ability jumped from 20% to 80%.

New
Frohlich, N., & Oppenheimer, J. A. (1997). **Tests of leadership solutions to collective action problems.** *Simulation & Gaming*, 28(2), 181-197.

The best way to measure the effectiveness of leadership and the efficacy of leadership solutions has long been debated. This article examines that question in regard to a specific simulation of entrepreneurial leadership. The authors debate the effectiveness of simulations and experiments, and discuss the results of a simulation on communication and collective goods. Includes bibliographical references.

Fuchsberg, G. (1993, September 10). **Executive education: Taking control.** *Wall Street Journal*, pp. R1-R13.

This special *WSJ* report is a survey and evaluation of executive-education courses and programs. It covers university programs as well as seminars and courses outside the university setting. An opening statistical summary tallies the top ten institutions in both these domains and lists the overall top ten most popular courses. An evaluative "report card" on institutions and courses summarizes the judgments of corporate human resources officers who are responsible for buying training for their executives.

Gredler, M. E. (1994). *Designing and evaluating games and simulations: A process approach.* Houston: Gulf.

This book provides a structure for analyzing games and simulations that have no right or wrong answers and no presumed values. The activities discussed here rely on interaction between the participants and situations, crises, and tasks, as well as interaction among the participants themselves. The types of activities discussed are academic

and computer games and simulations of decision making, crisis management, and understanding social systems. Includes bibliographical references and index.

Heifetz, R. A., Sinder, R. M., Jones, A., Hodge, L. M., & Rowley, K. A. (1989). **Teaching and assessing leadership courses at the John F. Kennedy School of Government.** *Journal of Policy Analysis and Management*, 8, 536-562.

The Kennedy School of Government at Harvard University assessed the effectiveness of leadership courses to determine their usefulness in practice. Courses were designed as case studies of traditional leadership traits, situations, and approaches. Traits considered "unteachable," such as wisdom, creativity, and values, were examined. What do students need to learn about these traits and how can they be taught? A survey of graduates resulted in a 56% response that leadership courses were perceived to be the most useful of university courses in actual practice.

New
Holsbrink-Engles, G. A. (1997). **Computer-based role-playing for interpersonal skills training.** *Simulation & Gaming*, 28(2), 164-180.

Role-playing is an important part of interpersonal skills training, but is often too complex for beginners. Computer-based role-playing can simplify the process. In this study one group of students did a conventional role-playing exercise, while a second group did a computer-based role play and then a conventional one. The researchers measured the learning outcomes of the two groups, and conclude that computer role plays can be a useful lead-in to traditional role plays, although not a replacement for them. Includes bibliographical references.

Hunter, J. E., Hunter, R. F., & Lopis, J. E. (1979). **A causal analysis of attitudes toward leadership training in a classroom setting.** *Human Relations*, 32(11), 889-907.

This research article presents an analysis of the interrelationships of various student attitudes in a leadership training program.

Hynes, K., Feldhusen, J. F., & Richardson, W. B. (1978). **Application of a three-stage model of instruction to youth leadership training.** *Journal of Applied Psychology*, 63(5), 623-628.

This study examined the cognitive, behavioral, and attitudinal effects of a three-stage leadership training program consisting of 12 instructional units administered to high school vocational-education students. Results of the one-way analysis of variance indicated that leadership training was effective in improving leadership knowledge as measured by a mastery test. Additional results and measurements of the *Ideal Leader Behavior Description Questionnaire* are discussed.

Lawrence, H. V., & Wiswell, A. K. (1993). **Using the work group as a laboratory for learning: Increasing leadership and team effectiveness through feedback.** *Human Resource Development Quarterly, 4*(2), 135-148.

Managers from a municipal government participated in a field study to determine the effects of training on managers' interactions with work groups. *SYMLOG® (System for the Multiple Level Observation of Groups)* was used for pre- and post-test measurement of individual and group dominance versus submissiveness, friendliness versus unfriendliness, and accepting versus opposing task orientation of established authority. Feedback-skills training generated higher post-test scores in the areas of dominance and friendliness.

Lombardo, M. M., & McCall, M. W., Jr. (1981). *Leaders on line: Observations from a simulation of managerial work.* Greensboro, NC: Center for Creative Leadership.

Leadership makes the most sense when viewed in its environmental and organizational context. This premise forms the basis for the design of a complex simulation for use in this research. This paper addresses issues of measurement: focusing on major organizational problems as the unit of analysis, the impact of different external environments on managerial behavior, and the role of coupling and decoupling strategies in managerial action. Includes a bibliography.

McCauley, C. D., & Hughes-James, M. W. (1994). *An evaluation of the outcomes of a leadership development program.* Greensboro, NC: Center for Creative Leadership.

This research report describes an evaluation study of the Chief Executive Officer Leadership Development Program, which was designed for school superintendents. The program combines a six-day classroom experience, a follow-up year working on personal goals and learning projects, support from an executive facilitator, and reflective journal writing. Thirty-eight Florida superintendents participated in this study. Pre- and post-program assessments and end-of-program interviews provided evaluation data. In addition, five superintendents were studied more in depth. The participants' outcomes, the contributions of various portions of the program, and the variations among individual outcomes are analyzed. Includes bibliographical references and index.

New
Phillips, J. J. (1996). **Meeting the ROI challenge: A practical approach to measuring the return on investment in training and development.** *European Forum for Management Development, 96*(3), 24-28.

For years, executives assumed that the results of training could not be measured. But growing training budgets and an emphasis on accountability across organizations have increased interest in measuring the return on investment (ROI). Phillips offers an ROI process model that includes: methods for collecting post-program data, how to isolate the effects of training, converting the data to monetary value, how to identify intangible benefits, and a simple formula for calculating the ROI.

Preston, J. C., & Chappell, K. E. (1990). **Teaching managers leadership.** *Leadership and Organization Development Journal, 11*(5), 11-16.

Three training methods were evaluated in this study. Students took a pre-training test and a post-training test to measure interpersonal leadership skills. One group received computer-based training (CBT). A second group received modified CBT, and a third group received traditional workshop training. Post-training tests indicated that all training increased skills, regardless of the training method.

Rossing, B. E. (1987). *Wisconsin CES Leadership Impact Study.* Madison: University of Wisconsin–Extension. (ERIC Document No. ED300588).

This is a report of a study on the impact of Wisconsin Cooperative Extension Service programs on leaders and the organizations and communities they serve. A total of 344 community leaders were selected, representing areas of the state where Extension had recently served. The survey results produced some of the following conclusions: leaders assisted by Extension reflect positive changes in leadership skills, Extension rated as an important influence, and Extension provides assistance and education regarded as important. Based on survey findings, recommendations are made for continued program planning and leadership training.

New
Santora, J. C. (1996). **Looking Glass, Inc.: A classroom experience.** *Journal of Leadership Studies, 3*(1), 158-165.

Santora describes his experience with the in-basket business simulation Looking Glass, Inc.® (LGI; Center for Creative Leadership, 1989). He explains the division of roles and the logistics of space, equipment, and time. His students found the simulation very relevant to their classroom learning although it was difficult to accomplish in several classes ranging from 45 minutes to two-and-a-half hours. The frenetic pace and observational demands on the facilitator were the biggest problems. Santora recommends using LGI at the end of a semester, videotaping the simulation to provide feedback later, and investing the necessary time on logistics.

Singleton, T. M. (1978). **Managerial motivation development: A study of college student leaders.** *Academy of Management Journal, 21*(3), 493-498.

This study measured the results of a special managerial-motivation development training course taught at Georgia State University during the spring quarter of 1975. The study was initiated to examine the impact of a formal managerial-motivation training program upon campus student leaders. The study attempts to measure the impact of the training upon the motive to manage of the training subjects.

Spindler, C. J. (1992). **University-based public sector management development and training.** *Public Productivity & Management Review, 15*(4), 439-448.

Spindler explores university-based leadership development programs for state and local government officials. Research results indicate that there is no uniform agreement on what leadership development is, on the essential elements of such a program, or on the necessary qualifications of trainers. Diversity in clientele, delivery, and financing affect each program's philosophy. Spindler suggests that further research on leadership development programs would be beneficial.

Tharenou, P., & Lyndon, J. T. (1990). **The effect of a supervisory development program on leadership style.** *Journal of Business and Psychology, 4*(3), 365-373.

One hundred male supervisors of a government railway department participated in a study of the effect of training on supervisory consideration and structure. Half the supervisors attended a 22-week course in human relations and structuring skills. Skills of both groups were evaluated by subordinates pre- and post-training. Analysis indicated enhanced consideration and structure after training.

New
Young, D. P., & Dixon, N. M. (1996). *Helping leaders take effective action: A program evaluation.* Greensboro, NC: Center for Creative Leadership.

This is an evaluation of the Center for Creative Leadership's LeaderLab® program. Conducted over a six-month period, LeaderLab guides self-awareness of one's behaviors, encourages change, and supports action plans for change. To evaluate LeaderLab, researchers collected quantitative data from the *Impact Questionnaire* administered before and after the program and qualitative data

from telephone interviews with participants, co-workers, and LeaderLab process advisors. Results indicate that a long-term, action-oriented program does help participants to improve their leadership effectiveness. The most significant changes appeared in the areas of: interpersonal relations, organizational systems, coping with emotional disequilibrium, listening, vision, and balancing work and family responsibilities. Includes bibliographical references and index.

TRAINING MODELS

Anderson, L. R. (1990). **Toward a two-track model of leadership training: Suggestions from self-monitoring theory.** *Small Group Research, 21*(2), 147-167.

Because leaders have personality differences, leadership training should be conducted by different techniques. Anderson suggests a two-track model to meet the training needs of two leadership types. Track I trains high self-monitoring leaders to modify their behavior to accomplish tasks or meet social situations. Type II trains low self-monitoring leaders to change organizational structure to match their own behavior.

New
Antonioni, D. (1996). **Designing an effective 360-degree appraisal feedback process.** *Organizational Dynamics, 25*(2), 24-38.

Based on focus-group, survey, and interview research of four companies, this article offers a series of guidelines to companies planning to implement 360-degree-feedback programs. The author recommends that companies define specific desired outcomes before they implement a program, that they develop their own appraisal instrument, and that they provide follow-up support to help employees implement recommended changes.

New
Astin, H. S., Astin, A. W., & Others. (1996). *A Social Change Model of leadership development guidebook.* Version III. Los Angeles: UCLA Higher Education Research Institute.

The Social Change Model proposes that leadership is a process occurring at three levels: individual, group, and community. The model's seven critical values for leadership development are dubbed the 7 Cs. At the individual level, they are: *C*onsciousness of self, *C*ongruence, and *C*ommitment. Group values are: *C*ollaboration, *C*ommon purpose, and *C*ontroversy with civility. The critical value at the community and society level is *C*itizenship. This guidebook shares ideas for applying this model to service-oriented leadership development programs, primarily on college and university campuses. The collaborative research effort to develop this model was funded by the Dwight D. Eisenhower Leadership Development Program and the U.S. Department of Education.

New

Carol, L. (1997). **KIVA: A leadership initiative and technique.** *Journal of Leadership Studies*, *4*(2), 116-118.

KIVA is a group management technique adopted from an ancient ceremonial tradition of the Pueblo tribe. It allows large groups to examine transcendent issues surrounding a concept, program, project, or problem, and it can be used to identify and refine leadership initiatives. Often used as a convening mechanism, it works best when: 1) group members have different levels of responsibility in a hierarchy, 2) members represent three institutional sectors, and 3) multiple members have private perspectives. Details are provided on how to arrange a KIVA and what is necessary for its success. For example, Carol recommends pre-selecting a topic and using a time frame.

Christensen, C. R., Garvin, D. A., & Sweet, A. (1991). *Education for judgment: The artistry of discussion leadership.* Boston: Harvard Business School Press.

Harvard faculty members from diverse disciplines share their reflections on teaching when discussion is the pivotal element. Divided into five parts, the book provides a philosophical and intellectual framework for leading discussions, suggestions for skills development, challenges and tools to overcome them, ethical issues, and autobiographical essays from novices and experienced professors. Includes bibliographical references and index.

Cockrell, D. (Ed.). (1991). *The wilderness educator: The Wilderness Education Association curriculum guide.* Merrillville, IN: ICS Books.

Written as a textbook for W.E.A.'s National Standard Program for expedition leaders, this book outlines wilderness-education theories and principles. Chapters written by practitioners include such subjects as: judgment and decision making, group dynamics, environmental ethics, rations planning, adventure skills, and emergency procedures. How to prepare, market, administrate, and evaluate a wilderness expedition are discussed in depth. Includes an index.

Cowan, D. A. (1992). **Understanding leadership through art, history, and arts administration.** *Journal of Management Education*, *16*(3), 272-289.

In academics, leadership and business students are rarely exposed to the contextual richness of history and the perceptual stimulation of art. Cowan offers a model of a

business course project integrating several concepts to offset the effects of overrestrictive mind-sets. Students who participated in his project claimed to find new insight, appreciate creativity, relate abstract concepts to real-world situations, and see the big picture.

New

Dalton, M. A., & Hollenbeck, G. P. (1996). *How to design an effective system for developing managers and executives.* Greensboro, NC: Center for Creative Leadership.

A model for executive development evolved from the Center's program, Tools for Developing Successful Executives, and the shared experience of 1,000 corporate partners. This six-step model can be used by human resource professionals to design a new program or evaluate an existing one. The steps are: 1) find and use organizational support for creating a process, 2) define the program purpose and the behaviors to be developed, 3) use feedback as the baseline for executive development, 4) define and communicate the critical role of the manager, 5) write the development plan, and 6) make the program accountable. Includes bibliographical references.

Davies, G., Smith, M., & Twigger, W. (1991). **Leading people: A model of choice and fate for leadership development.** *Leadership and Organization Development Journal*, *12*(1), 7-11.

The authors define leadership as a psychological process of accepting responsibility for task, self, and the fate of others. They offer a model of four levels of responsibility based on the number of people and the length of time involved. Leaders choose to accept responsibility or not and choose how to discharge responsibility based on past experiences and personal preferences. In training simulations, leaders can practice relevant behaviors, receive feedback, and learn to be aware of their choices.

Farquhar, K. (1992). **Teaching leadership: Preparing graduate students for "taking charge."** *Journal of Management Education*, *16*(3), 354-370.

Because managers progress through a series of new assignments and promotions during the course of their careers, Farquhar proposes that management schools offer instruction on transitional skills. She identifies the different experiences of entering and established managers, the process of taking charge, and the implications for leadership curricula. A framework for teaching strategies suggests content themes, case studies, instruments, experiential activities, and reading materials.

Fleming, R. (1992). **An integrated behavioral approach to transfer of interpersonal leadership skills.** *Journal of Management Education, 16*(3), 341-353.

Fleming proposes an alternative approach, based on behavioral principles, for improving the transfer of "soft management" skills from the classroom to the job. Currently, students use case studies, simulations, mentoring, and internships. The proposed approach integrates field training with classroom instruction, modeling, role-playing, and feedback.

Gehrs, L. M. (1994). **The relationship between literature and leadership: A humanities-based approach for studying leadership.** *Journal of Leadership Studies, 1*(4), 145-158.

Because the function of literature is to reflect the nature of society and human relationships, it is easily adaptable to lessons on leadership. Gehrs, a graduate of the Jepson School of Leadership at the University of Richmond, demonstrates two ways to use literature in a leadership class. First, she explains how literature can teach general concepts and competencies. Her second method employs the literary genres of poetry, story, drama, and tragedy to evoke emotional responses and encourage new ways of looking at the world.

New
Hashem, M. (1997). **The role of faculty in teaching leadership studies.** *Journal of Leadership Studies, 4*(2), 89-100.

Hashem focuses on the question of whether leadership can be taught and discusses the role of faculty in teaching leadership studies. He examines the questions of why, when, what, and how to teach leadership. Hashem also addresses the three basic elements of leadership: leaders, followers, and context. His interactive approach to teaching leadership is based on six important elements: instructional integrity, intellectual humility, relevant equality and shared power, critical thinking, self-directed humor, and class structure.

Heron, J. (1989). *The facilitator's handbook.* New York: Nichols.

As the author defines it, a facilitator is one who is less concerned with formal teaching than with eliciting active self-directed learning from participants, thus "enabling them to take more responsibility for what they learn and how they learn it." Heron provides a model for facilitating experiential learning groups. Within his framework, he surveys the many options available to facilitators for managing the learning process in groups.

New
Johnson, C. (1997). **A leadership journey to the East.** *Journal of Leadership Studies, 4*(2), 82-88.

Directed toward trainers and teachers, this article describes a Taoist perspective of leadership. A historical overview of this Eastern philosophy is presented, with suggestions for introducing Taoist principles to students of leadership. Taoism prescribes that leadership should be minimal and that leaders should model their own behavior on principles found in nature. For example, leaders should be like uncarved blocks of wood, shapeless and simple. They should reject wealth, status, and cleverness. Johnson describes how he presents Taoism inductively in the classroom with a focus on nature.

Jordon, D. (1989). **A new vision for outdoor leadership theory.** *Leisure Studies, 8*(1), 35-47.

The author reviews and groups 12 models of leadership according to trait, behavioral, group, and situational theories. Based on these theories, she develops an outdoor-leadership model that encompasses the unique demands of outdoor recreation leadership.

New
Karp, H. B. (1996). *The change leader: Using a Gestalt approach with work groups.* San Diego, CA: Pfeiffer.

This workbook helps readers learn to be champions of change by using a Gestalt approach. This approach is based on a clinical theory that people can make better choices for themselves and take full responsibility for their choices. Nine chapters address awareness, negotiation, power, commitment, and resistance. Each chapter concludes with several change-leader activities.

Keys, B., & Wolfe, J. (1990). **The role of management games and simulations in education and research.** *Journal of Management, 16*(2), 307-336.

This review article summarizes how the management-gaming movement has evolved to its current state. The authors define terms and parameters for the management-gaming field and briefly review the history of business gaming. Several learning models applicable to the experiential nature of gaming are explained. Included in the review are studies on the learning value of educational games and projections of future developments in the field.

New
Komives, S. R., Woodard, D. D., & Associates. (1996). *Student services: A handbook for the profession* (3rd ed.). San Francisco: Jossey-Bass.

This comprehensive overview of student services in higher education describes an inclusive, empowerment-based model of leadership as an essential competency for skillful professional practice in student affairs. Other competencies include counseling, consultation, and program development. Chapters also address the theoretical basis of the profession, and organizing and managing programs and services. The third edition contains new chapters on the nature and use of theory, cognition and learning, identity development, and working with a diverse, multicultural population. Includes index.

Linowes, R. G. (1992). **Filling a gap in management education: Giving leadership talks in the classroom.** *Journal of Management Education*, *16*(1), 6-24.

As an experiential learning exercise, giving speeches in the classroom teaches students to practice these leadership skills: demonstrating an understanding of other people's motives, taking charge of a group, taking responsibility, and addressing a challenging opposition. Guidelines are offered for topics, time limits, scenarios, and providing feedback. Locker-room talks provide a forum for discussing a wide variety of the challenges of leadership.

McElroy, J. C., & Stark, E. (1992). **A thematic approach to leadership training.** *Journal of Managerial Issues*, *4*(2), 241-253.

Seven popular theories that focus on leadership behavior are merged into one model. General leadership skills are identified within transactional, conditional, and transforming themes. The authors outline details of themes and skills and recommend which approach to use for various levels of management training.

Miles, J. C., & Priest, S. (Eds.). (1990). *Adventure education.* State College, PA: Venture.

Adventure education involves the planning and implementation of programs designed to put people into challenging situations. Through the process of taking risks, participants learn about the world and about their own potential. This introduction to adventure education is a collection of essays written by practitioners. Five models of successful programs are featured. Experts discuss philosophical foundations, history, program management, ethics, and safety. Includes bibliographical references.

Muntz, P. H. (1990). *Leadership development approaches.* Springfield, VA: ERIC Document Reproduction Service. (ERIC Document No. ED314698).

Muntz has compiled student leadership development ideas from colleges and universities. Outlined are formats for leadership programs, including credit and noncredit classes, workshops, retreats, internships, outdoor-leadership training, and community service. Also included

are methods for selecting participants, titles, and locations of programs; marketing methods; and an eight-step model for setting up a leadership training program.

Phipps, M. (1988). **Experiential leadership education.** *Journal of Experiential Education*, *11*(1), 22-28.

The National Outdoor Leader School (NOLS) and the Wilderness Education Association (WEA) have identified a need for affective leadership. People skills are as important as technical skills in the safety and success of expeditions. Phipps offers a model of situational leadership based on levels of task and relationship behavior compared with the maturity of followers. Another model suggests the stages of group development. Styles of leadership and the stages of group development change continually during an expedition due to changing situations and follower readiness to perform tasks and accept responsibility.

Priest, S. (1988). **Outdoor leadership training in higher education.** *Journal of Experiential Education*, *11*(1), 42-46.

Based on programs used in New Zealand, Australia, Britain, Canada, and the U.S., Priest has developed a model for outdoor-leadership selection and training at the university level. Candidates would be selected for their personal attributes: physical and mental fitness, empathy, motivational philosophy, and healthy self-concept. Training modules would consist of organizational, risk-control, instructional, group-management, problem-solving, and environmental skills. Certification would be awarded for technical and safety skills.

Roberts, D., & Ullom, C. (1989). **Student leadership program model.** *NASPA Journal*, *27*(1), 67-74.

Leadership programs in academic curricula prepare students to assume future leadership roles in society. Roberts and Ullom offer a model curriculum to teach leadership concepts, personal skills, organizational skills, and contemporary issues. They recommend that experiential opportunities in campus and community service be included. Examples are cited from among the existing leadership programs in 600 colleges and universities. A checklist for implementing a student leadership program is offered.

Schatz, M., & Currie, D. M. (1995). **The bricks, mortar, and architecture of the MBA program: Dealing with the issue of leadership.** *Journal of Leadership Studies*, *2*(3), 42-67.

The authors state that MBA programs were the educational darlings of the 1980s, turning out experts in mergers, acquisitions, and takeovers. Ten years later, business needs have changed. Businesses are now seeking leaders who can respond to diminishing authority and global competition. In response, they recommend a redesign of MBA program curricula. To hold together MBA bricks (basic business principles), they apply mortar (learning experiences such as a leadership laboratory, international exchange projects, assessments, teamwork, simulations, and case studies). For easy reference, they lay out the integrated curriculum in chart form.

Stumpf, S. S., Dunbar, R. L. M., & Mullen, T. P. (1991). **Developing entrepreneurial skills through the use of behavioral simulations.** *Journal of Management Development, 10*(5), 32-45.

The authors discuss the use of simulations to teach the sense-making and opportunity-seeking processes of entrepreneurship. This paper outlines typical simulation goals and objectives, setup, facilitation, and feedback. A research study identified several entrepreneurial behaviors: identifying constraints, creating vision, innovation, resiliency, and tolerance.

Tetrault, L. A., Schriesheim, C. A., & Neider, L. L. (1988). **Leadership training interventions: A review.** *Organization Development Journal, 6*(3), 77-83.

This article is a review of the five major leadership models used in leadership training interventions: Blake and Mouton's (1978) Managerial Grid; Hersey and Blanchard's (1977) Situational Leadership model; Leader Match concept by Fiedler, Chemers, and Mahar (1976); Graen's (1975) Leader-Member Exchange; and Vroom and Yetton's Contingency model (1973). The authors discuss the degree of effectiveness these individual programs offer, as well as the drawbacks associated with these specific models. The larger question regarding the effectiveness of leadership training in general is addressed.

VanGundy, A. B. (1987). *Creative problem solving.* New York: Quorum Books.

An excellent resource for creativity trainers, this text facilitates the design and teaching of creative problem solving. Games, exercises, personal inventories, group and individual assessments are included to provide trainers with a wide range of models by which to structure workshops and test their effectiveness. These models and formats focus on using both rational and intuitive thinking skills in exploring and applying creativity to problem solving as well as to personal and professional goals, short-term objectives, and long-range planning.

TRAINER AND EDUCATOR RESOURCES

New
The 1998 annual (30th ed.). (1998). San Francisco: Jossey Bass/Pfeiffer.

This series, formerly called the *Annual Handbook for Group Facilitators*, has been issued each year since 1972. Now in two volumes, the set includes descriptions of 24 new experiential learning activities, seven new assessment instruments, and 20 presentation resources for human resources development practitioners. All material is written by practicing trainers and consultants. *Volume I: Training* is intended for individual and group trainers. *Volume II: Consulting* is intended for organizational consultants.

New
Adams, S. (1996). ***The Dilbert principle: A cubicle's eye view of bosses, meetings, management fads and other workplace afflictions.*** New York: HarperBusiness.

The creator of Dilbert cartoons shares his irreverent view on leadership and management. Adams draws on his nine years of experience as a "necktie-wearing, corporate victim assigned to cubicle 4S700R" to poke fun at leadership gone awry. Fans submit incredible examples of bad bosses that further fuel Adams's cartoons and anecdotes. Highlighted are humorous looks at business communication, great lies of management, employee strategies, and change.

New
Antal, J. F. (1995). ***Infantry combat—the rifle platoon: An interactive exercise in small-unit tactics and leadership.*** Novato, CA: Presidio Press.

Using an interactive fiction approach, this book sets the scene for an infantry battle and allows the reader to assume the role of U.S. Army second lieutenant Steve Davis. Davis's platoon is airlifted into the Middle East to defend Wadi Al Siree against a larger and better-armed enemy. At 31 points, the reader decides which strategy to follow or rolls dice to determine the enemy's strategy. The odds are five to one against a victory for the U.S., but the reader who trusts his or her troops and gathers intelligence information will survive and win. Maps and appendices provide background information for those not familiar with infantry combat and weapons. The author is the commanding officer of a tank battalion in Korea.

Baker Library. (1993). ***Harvard Business School core collection: An author, title, and subject guide, 1993.*** Boston: Harvard Business School Press.

The core collection contains over 3,500 titles that reflect the research, teaching, and general business reading interests of the Harvard Business School. Graduate textbooks, faculty publications, biographies, corporate histories, and business classics are included with full bibliographical information. Books are indexed by geographic area, detailed subject, name, and title.

Bianchi, S., Butler, J., & Richey, D. (1990). *Warmups for meeting leaders.* San Diego, CA: University Associates.

A group that is warmed up becomes involved, focused, and committed. This "how-to" book lists over 100 warm-up activities and includes graphics that can be made into overhead slides. It teaches how to develop new warm-up activities and how to make them work effectively. There also are assessment surveys and a list of resources on group activities. Includes bibliography and index.

New
Bowen, D. D., Lewicki, R. J., Hall, F. S., & Hall, D. T. (1997). *Experiences in management and organizational behavior* (4th ed.). New York: Wiley.

This book contains 65 exercises for use in management education. Of particular interest are: *The Henderson Account*, a role play to develop communication and group decision-making skills; *Analysis of Personal Power*, a questionnaire; *The Culture Quiz Sweepstakes*, a quiz for teams; and *Krunchian Aircraft Co., Ltd.*, a role play to explore cultural differences. Most exercises are complete with handouts. Some recommend reading materials to complete the experience. Includes bibliographical references.

New
Bozeman, W., & Wright, R. H. (1995). **Simulation applications in educational leadership.** *Journal of Educational Technology Systems, 23*(3), 219-231.

This article reports on the educational value of simulations in general and their value as tools to train school administrators specifically. Simulations are used as simplified representations of real-life situations for the purpose of learning new skills in a safe environment. Multimedia simulations have the added benefit of testing new learnings and providing immediate feedback. The authors describe their experience in designing and producing an interactive computer simulation that provides a series of decision-making experiences for graduate students in educational administration.

Brown, J. C. (1994). **Leadership education through humanistic texts and traditions:** *The Hartwick Classic Leadership Cases.*™ *Journal of Leadership Studies, 1*(3), 104-116.

The Hartwick Classic Leadership Cases are based on the premise that the essential subject matter of leadership is

human relationships and that they can best be studied in the collective wisdom of the human race. Brown, who is the case-study series editor, describes nine case studies and how to use them. Rather than one leadership lesson per study, each case examines skills, character, and context. Accompanying each case are teaching notes and discussion questions as well as correlated reading material from a recent book or article describing a modern leader who exemplifies the same qualities as the leader in the case. Summaries include capsules of relevant leadership and management theories that link traditional learning to this humanities approach.

Christopher, E. M., & Smith, L. E. (1987). *Leadership training through gaming.* New York: Nichols.

Leadership skills are imperative for the successful manager. This book has been specifically written for those who use simulation and role-play games for leadership training. Each chapter pinpoints certain games that have been shown to be most effective in drawing out the significant aspects of leadership qualities in its participants. By placing the various activities within both an international and theoretical context, the kind of learning experience they are likely to produce can be measured. The possible roadblocks and dead ends in each simulation are also examined. Includes bibliography and index.

New
Clemens, J. K., & Albrecht, S. (1995). *The timeless leader.* Holbrook, MA: Adams Publishing.

Clemens and Albrecht share some of the leadership lessons developed at the Hartwick Humanities in Management Institute. Shakespeare's *Henry IV* and *Henry V* teach us about mentors and protégés, listening, trust, inspiration, and the language of leadership. *Cleopatra* is an example of a woman leading in a male-dominated society, collaboration, and intercultural understanding. Other lessons are derived from Plato's allegory of the cave, Captain Ahab's maniacal obsession with Moby Dick, Martin Luther King, Jr.'s dialogue that inspired change, Winston Churchill's persuasive rhetoric skills, and Mahatma Gandhi's example of ethics and humility.

Colorado Parks and Recreation Association, Recreational Services Section. (1990). *Planning a workshop.* Wheat Ridge, CO: Recreation Services Section.

Colorado Parks and Recreation created this tool for developing, organizing, and implementing workshops. Arranged in a timetable format, it details how to select topics, speakers, and facilities; how to budget expenses and set participant fees; how to develop a flyer and publicity; and how to evaluate the success of a workshop. Continuing Education Unit (CEU) qualifications and application process are explained. Sample forms include speaker agreement, revenue report, evaluation, and CEU application.

New

Consalvo, C. M. (1993). *Experiential training activities for outside and in.* Amherst, MA: HRD Press.

Thirty-six activities are intended to add fun to training sessions while helping participants change their awareness and behaviors. The *Egyptian Mummy* and *King Tut* exercises are used to practice trust. *Bureaucratic Maze* and *Jigglers and Bursters* are group juggling exercises that require teamwork and creative problem solving. Many of the exercises require physical strength, but there are also nonphysical roles for observers and coaches. Each exercise includes suggestions for debriefing and variations.

New

Craig, R. L. (Ed.). (1996). *The ASTD training and development handbook: A guide to human resource development* (4th ed.). New York: McGraw-Hill.

Fifty-one human resource developers from major corporations contribute essays describing the best practices in the field. James DeVito of Johnson & Johnson writes about the learning organization. Robert Hayles explains The Pillsbury Company's diversity training and development program. Jeffrey Howell and Larry Silvey of Arthur Andersen Worldwide Organization describe interactive multimedia training systems. Donald Conover discusses AT&T's leadership development program. Edward Bales shares Motorola University's experience with business and education partnerships. Includes bibliographical references and index.

New

Czarniawska-Joerges, B., & Guillet de Monthoux, P. (Eds.). (1994). *Good novels, better management: Reading organizational realities in fiction.* Newark, NJ: Gordon & Breach.

Authors from ten countries contribute essays on the use of fiction to teach management, each describing a novel about business and society in the late 19th century. The stories tell of the tensions that occurred as industrialism brought conflict between big business and family-owned shops, between economics and humanitarianism, and between company loyalty and abuse of power. The editors believe that fiction provides a mirror of the human condition and makes visible otherwise invisible thoughts and feelings. Some of the novels discussed are: Emile Zola's *The Ladies' Paradise*, H. G. Wells's *The History of Mr. Polly*, Miguel de Cervantes's *Don Quixote*, and Rosa Montero's *My Beloved Master*. Includes bibliographical references.

Darnay, B. T. (Ed.). (1997). *Consultants and consulting organizations directory* (17th ed.). Detroit: Gale.

Over 23,000 independent consultants and consulting firms are briefly listed in this two-volume set. There are descriptive entries for firms involved in business management, human resources development, education, and personal development. Information includes the names of the principals, year founded, seminars, videos, publications, unique services, SIC codes, fax and toll-free numbers, e-mail and website addresses, and their ability to handle international clients. Volume 2 contains geographic, firm, and activities indexes with cross-references to main listings. All information is verified.

De Ciantis, C. (1995). *Using an art technique to facilitate leadership development.* Greensboro, NC: Center for Creative Leadership.

This report is a description of the touchstone exercise, an activity in which leadership program participants create an artwork that represents their vision and purpose as leaders. De Ciantis describes how the exercise is conducted, provides examples of touchstones produced in programs at the Center for Creative Leadership, and considers the effectiveness of the activity as a means of defining ourselves as leaders. The appendix contains useful information on how anyone can conduct a touchstone exercise. Includes bibliographical references.

Drury, J. K., & Bonney, B. F. (1992). *The backcountry classroom: Lesson plans for teaching in the wilderness.* Merrillville, IN: ICS Books.

Designed for instructors of the Wilderness Education Association's curriculum, this reference tool consists of 40 self-contained lesson plans. Each describes the goal, objectives, body of knowledge, timing, safety measures, and materials required for teaching a specific topic. Lessons include: environmental ethics, group development, decision making, leadership, and risk management.

Dunbar, R. L., Stumpf, S. A., Mullen, T. P., & Arnone, M. (1992). **Management development: Choosing the right leadership simulation for the task.** *Journal of Management Education, 16*(2), 220-230.

Leadership simulations recreate companies, their key success factors, profit-and-loss dynamics, and environmental relationships. Participation in simulations provides diagnostic information on these strategic management elements. The authors offer guidelines for choosing a simulation appropriate for your managers. Some factors to consider: similarities to or differences from your company, skills diagnosed and developed, team building, and cultural or international issues. Nine large-scale simulations are briefly described.

Egan, G. (1988). ***Change-agent skills A: Assessing and designing excellence.*** San Diego, CA: University Associates.

A companion to *Change-agent Skills B: Managing Innovation and Change*, this book has been developed for executives, trainers, managers, consultants, or any individual who may play a role in the assessment and design for planning within a business or organization. The author has created a model known as "Model A." When applied to assessing any or all dimensions of an organization—operations, personnel, facilities, marketing, or resources—it provides a map pinpointing the weaknesses and strengths of present business functions. The results sift through in such a way that the key objectives of an organization's mission are given in a point-by-point outline useful for future planning. Includes bibliography and index.

Egan, G. (1988). ***Change-agent skills B: Managing innovation and change.*** San Diego, CA: University Associates.

A companion to *Change-agent Skills A*, this volume offers a plan for stimulating innovation and change within an organization or business. The author has developed a model that incorporates three stages of the process of cultivating change and innovation. The stages are: assessing the current scene—recognizing problems and blind spots; the preferred scene—considering the spectrum of possibilities and translating ideas into a workable agenda; and getting there—choosing strategies, formulating plans, and moving from transition to action. Includes bibliography and index.

New

Eitington, J. E. (1996). ***The winning trainer: Winning ways to involve people in learning*** (3rd ed.). Houston: Gulf.

Participative training methods, such as icebreakers, small-group exercises, role plays, simulations, puzzles, instruments, problem solving, in-basket, and team building, are covered in this how-to manual for group-in-action trainers. Chapters include techniques for using each method, ideas for involving all participants, and samples of activities. There are also suggestions for training methods with less participant involvement: case studies, films, and lectures. A 4-D model illustrates four steps of the training cycle: 1) determine need, 2) design programs, 3) deliver programs, and 4) discern differences (evaluation). The appendices contain 97 handouts and worksheets, which may be photocopied or made into transparencies. Includes a glossary, bibliographical references, and index.

New

Ellet, W., & Winig, L. (Eds.). (1996). ***A critical guide to management training videos and selected multimedia, 1996.*** Boston: Harvard Business Reference.

This book intends to lighten the costly and time-consuming process of selecting training videos. It objectively evaluates new releases using criteria suggested by trainers. Films are rated on a four-star basis according to: support of training objectives; quality of production, acting, and script; portrayal of women and minorities; support materials; and value for the money. There are films on change management, communication skills, diversity, innovation, leadership, team building, and more. A small sample of CD-ROM training products is included. Each review includes a brief description of the reviewer's background. Includes a source directory and an index.

New

Feinberg, R. A. (1996). **Leadership education and the cinematic experience: Using film to teach leadership.** *Journal of Leadership Studies, 3*(4), 148-157.

Feinberg shares his favorite films for teaching leadership in the classroom. Fellini's *Orchestra Rehearsal*, a film about an old orchestra rebelling against a new conductor, illustrates the relationship between leaders and followers. *Space Camp*, a film about young misfits accidentally launched into space, enhances a lesson on teamwork. Feinberg uses Mel Gibson's version of *Mutiny on the Bounty* to teach students about followers' dependency on a leader's positional power and ethics. Other favorites include: *Lord of the Flies, Boyz N the Hood, Dave, Tommy Boy, A League of Their Own, Toy Story,* and *Working Girl.*

New

Fenwick, W. E., & Steffy, B. E. (1997). **Using film to teach leadership in educational administration.** *Educational Administration Quarterly, 3*(1), 107-115.

The authors like to use film as a teaching tool because it presents a longitudinal view of leadership in context. It illustrates the consequences of a leader's decisions and behaviors. Students can observe and discuss the development of relationships. Fenwick and Steffy briefly describe ten films and the leadership lessons they contain: *Nixon* (1985), *Gandhi* (1982), *Joan of Arc* (1985), *Malcolm X* (1993), *The Last Emperor* (1987), *Patton* (1969), *Inherit the Wind* (1960), *Matewan* (1987), *Lawrence of Arabia* (1962), and *Viva Zapata!* (1952).

Fox, H., & Others. (1991). ***Nonformal education training module.*** Peace Corps, Information Collection and Exchange, 1990 K Street, N.W., 8th Floor, Washington, DC 20526. (ERIC Document No. ED347390).

This document provides training ideas for use by Peace Corps volunteers, but much of the material would be valuable for anyone in a training role. It contains ten sessions, each designed to fit into a three-hour period. Some of the session topics are: helping people identify their needs, facilitation skills, the use of games, planning, and evaluation. Each session comes complete with step-by-step instructions, rationale, objectives, handouts, and related references. Three appendices contain additional warm-ups and evaluation activities.

Greenblat, C. S. (1988). ***Designing games and simulations: An illustrated handbook.*** Newbury Park, CA: Sage.

This handbook will be invaluable to anyone involved with the design and model development of simulation and game formats. The author presents four case studies and provides examples of over 70 games and simulations. Practical advice is given on making decisions, setting objectives, constructing and modifying a model, preparing it as a product, designing the operator's manual, arranging for publication, and pre-testing. The approach of the manual is systematic and comprehensive. The author has distilled the complexity of model development, design, and application into one package. Extensive references, models, and a listing of periodicals and organizations are included.

New
Harris, P. R. (1995). ***Twenty reproducible assessment instruments for the new work culture.*** Amherst, MA: HRD Press.

These instruments are intended to support individual and team development by improving self-awareness and communication skills. Examples are: *Leadership Motivation Inventory* to determine personal needs and goals, *Values Imprint Survey* to understand priorities and prejudices, *Force Field Analysis Inventory* to examine the forces that bring change, and *Team Synergy Analysis Inventory* to judge group cooperation. Very brief instructions are provided for administration and scoring. All of the instruments may be reproduced for training or educational activities.

Hartwick Humanities in Management Institute. (no date). ***Hartwick classic leadership cases.***™ Available to the academic community for $3.95 per case and $9.95 per teaching note, plus shipping and handling. Contact Hartwick Humanities in Management Institute, Hartwick College, Oneonta, NY 13820. Phone: (800) 942-2737.

Mankind's greatest literary, philosophical, biographical, historical, dramatic, and artistic works are used to teach lessons on leadership issues. Each one of the 76 available cases contains excerpts from a great text or film, a contemporary article that mirrors the leadership lesson, and a brief review of relevant leadership theory. Most cases are less than 30 pages and require one hour of student preparation. Extensive teaching notes are available for all cases. Homer's *Iliad* teaches conflict resolution, followership, and power. Martin Luther King, Jr.'s "Letter from a Birmingham Jail" teaches charisma, negotiation, and vision. *Spider Old Woman*, a tale from the Hopi, teaches female leadership, mentoring, and empowerment. Herman Melville's *Billy Budd* teaches crisis management, decision making, and ethics. Shakespeare's *Richard II* teaches goal setting, strategy, and leadership failure. Mahatma Gandhi teaches charisma, followership, and servant leadership. For a complete description of cases and their lessons on leadership, contact the Hartwick Humanities in Management Institute.

Jolles, R. L. (1993). ***How to run seminars and workshops: Presentation skills for consultants, trainers, and teachers.*** New York: Wiley.

Instead of *what* to teach, this book suggests *how* to teach. It claims to give too many ideas, so that a trainer may absorb what is needed for a particular audience, topic, trainer personality, and style. The author uses real-world situations and solutions to illustrate ways of solving the puzzles that each trainer faces in every new session. Includes an index.

Jones, K. (1989). ***A sourcebook of management simulations.*** New York: Nichols.

This sourcebook is composed of ten complete simulations. In Part 1 the author describes his rationale and provides detailed information on organizing the sessions. The ten simulations are presented in Part 2. Each simulation is preceded by "facilitator's notes," which indicate the types of management skills to be exercised. Some of the skills covered include: decision making, planning, evaluation, strategy, interpersonal communication, and interviewing.

Jones, K. (1994). *Simulations: A handbook for teachers and trainers* (3rd ed.). New York: Nichols.

This book first introduces the reader to the basic processes and terminology of simulations. It covers the topics of simulation design, choosing a simulation, how to effectively use simulations, and issues in using simulations for assessment. There are examples to help teachers and trainers use this experiential learning mode to full advantage. Includes bibliography and index.

New
Jones, K. (1997). *Icebreakers: A sourcebook of games, exercises, and simulations* (2nd ed.). Houston: Gulf.

This book includes advice on when and how to use icebreakers and 66 icebreaking activities in three categories: games in which participants have a duty to win, exercises dealing with problems, and simulations involving roles. Facilitator guidelines note the required time, materials, procedure, and debriefing instructions for each activity. Includes reproducible handouts and bibliographical references.

Keys, J. B., Edge, A. G., & Wells, R. A. (1992). *The multinational management game: A game of global strategy.* Boston: Irwin.

In this simulation, a fictional company, MMG, is used to teach decision-making skills. It is based on data from research of North American, Asian, and European marketing, manufacturing, and finance. A two-hour introductory session is required for team assignments. The following one-hour sessions require teams to make decisions on price, advertising, R&D, expenditures, and expansions based on growth trends, inflation, competition, and tariffs. Depending on the complexity of decision making, the simulation can be completed in 6 to 15 sessions. As business and management professors, the authors of this simulation suggest using it in courses on strategic management or international business. Includes bibliographical references and index.

New
Keys, J. B., Fulmer, R. M., & Stumpf, S. A. (1996). **Microworlds and simuworlds: Practice fields for the learning organizations.** *Organizational Dynamics, 24*(4), 36-49.

According to the authors, most organizations have "learning disabilities," barriers that prevent managers from learning, including horizontal and vertical fragmentation. But managers can use the risk-free environment of *simuworlds*, derived from competitive business games, and *microworlds*, which evolved from in-basket simulations, to achieve the "big picture learning" often missing in large companies. A number of specific simulations are profiled, and stories of individual companies and managers illustrate the concepts.

Krug, S. E. (1993). *Psychware sourcebook: A reference guide to computer-based products for assessment in psychology, education and business* (3rd ed.). Champaign, IL: MetriTech.

This sourcebook briefly describes 533 computer-based test interpretation (CBTI) products, including intended use, applications, delivery systems, price, supplier, and hardware needed. A few of the topics covered by these products are: career and vocational issues, cognitive ability, interests and attitudes, motivation and needs, and structured interviews. Samples of most products are presented in the Appendix.

New
Malone, P. (1991). *Myers-Briggs goes to the movies: A guide to screen characters and Myers-Briggs Type Indicator®.* Melbourne: Spectrum.

In 16 popular movies, Malone finds characters with personalities to match each of the 16 MBTI personality types. Tom Cruise's character, Maverick, in *Top Gun* (1989) is an ESTJ confident of his exuberant charm and risk-taking talent. Humphrey Bogart as Sam Spade in *The Maltese Falcon* (1941) is an INTP, a loner who is stimulated by a mystery and methodically gathers information to solve it. Other characters include Mad Max as an ISTP and Eliza Doolittle as an ESFJ. Following his discussion of these sympathetic characters, Malone suggests 16 less appealing characters who are "trapped" in their personality types. Examples of these are the telekinetic teenager in *Carrie* (1986), an INFJ, and Gordon Gecko in *Wall Street* (1987), an ENTJ.

New
Marcic, D. (1995). *Organizational behavior: Experiences and cases* (4th ed.). St. Paul, MN: West Publishing.

Marcic has compiled 90 exercises, instruments, and cases from a variety of sources. These tools support lessons in ethics, decision making, communication, group dynamics, influence, diversity, power, conflict management, learning organizations, and cross-cultural sensitivity. Some popular leadership exercises found in this book are: *Tower Building, Prisoner's Dilemma, Ugli Orange,* and *Border Dispute.* There are adapted versions of inventories to determine leadership style, level of empowerment, and style of conflict resolution. Cases focus on ethical issues, organizational design, diversity problems, and corporate culture.

McLean, J. (Ed.). (1994). *Training and development organizations directory* (6th ed.). Detroit, MI: Gale Research.

This directory lists 2,600 training and development organizations and 12,000 programs, seminars, and workshops. The reader may search by subject heading to find information on assessment instruments, citizen involvement, crisis management, and 2,000 other types of training activities. There are also indexes for geographical location, personal name, and company name.

New
Mohrman, S. A., & Mohrman, A. M., Jr. (1997). *Designing and leading team-based organizations: A workbook for organizational self-design.* San Francisco: Jossey-Bass.

This workbook for leaders who are establishing or refining team-based organizations is composed of nine modules—including designing team structures, designing management and leadership roles, building a decision-making framework, and managing and improving performance—that give the reader a series of steps to follow. Each module includes charts, definitions, and exercises to complete. A leader's/facilitator's guide that accompanies the workbook is also available.

Munson, L. S. (1992). *How to conduct training seminars: A complete reference guide for training managers and professionals* (2nd ed.). New York: McGraw-Hill.

The explosion of new technology on the business scene has transformed the ways in which training seminars are planned and executed. In this edition, Munson explains how to organize and staff a training department and where to go for top-level outside help; what computers can do to aid development and delivery of programs; how to employ video technology in the critical new fields of programmed learning, role-playing, and video dramatizations; and how to expand your training function through teleconferencing techniques. Also included are: professional tips for successful program presentation, advice on evaluating seminars and overall training performance, and eight steps to vital training seminars. Includes bibliographical references and index.

Murray, J. L. (1994). *Training for student leaders.* Dubuque, IA: Kendall/Hunt.

This book is intended to be used as a textbook for classroom instruction or a supplement to cocurricular leadership training. Murray has experience teaching leadership skills in both arenas. He draws from several disciplines as he presents traditional management and leadership theories, skills and behaviors, and the philosophy of leadership as service. Chapters address the issues of self-analysis, communication, group dynamics, ethics,

and goal setting. Within each chapter, Murray includes a test and several activities to practice new skills. He also suggests opportunities for students to gain leadership experience in campus activities.

Nadler, L., & Nadler, Z. (1987). *The comprehensive guide to successful conferences and meetings.* San Francisco: Jossey-Bass.

An invaluable resource for anyone who must plan, organize, and conduct a meeting or conference. The elements involved in coordinating such an event are covered here in great detail. Such considerations include the design of the conference, handling related events and activities, site selection, meeting and function rooms, presenters and speakers, use of audiovisuals, food and beverage functions, arranging exhibitions, effective marketing, public relations, developing a budget, and preparing a participant program book. This guide unravels the complexities of managing a large-scale event, while providing a step-by-step plan to ensure a successful and well-run conference. Includes bibliography and index.

National Association for Community Leadership. (1993). *Taking leadership to heart.* Indianapolis, IN: National Association for Community Leadership.

A community-trusteeship curriculum was established to teach community leaders to work for the common good. In addition to the *where* and *what* of civic education, and the *how* of leadership skills training, trusteeship provides the *why*, the motivation for serving the basic needs of others. Included is a trainer manual with course text, transparencies, and a 60-minute trainer video. Also included are a presentation video with brief messages to begin each class, and participant folders with handouts and readings.

Newstrom, J. W., & Scannell, E. E. (1980). *Games trainers play: Experiential learning exercises.* New York: McGraw-Hill.

Trainers manage the content, process, and environment of learning situations. Exercises, illustrations, and activities are among the games trainers use to present learning situations. In this collection, the format outlines each game's objective, procedure, or method of instruction, discussion questions, approximate time, and materials required. Supporting materials may be photocopied for handouts or made into overhead transparencies. For more games, see Scannell and Newstrom's *More Games Trainers Play* (1983), *Still More Games Trainers Play* (1991), and *Even More Games Trainers Play* (1994). Each book in the series contains about 100 different games to be used in lessons on problem solving, communication, leadership, and team building.

New

Nilson, C. D. (1993). *Team games for trainers.* New York: McGraw-Hill.

Nilson argues that games support learning and presents 100 games that trainers can use to enhance group learning. The games are divided into three sections: team building, team function, and team maintenance. Each game is described in a structured format that lists the objectives, procedures, materials, and approximate time needed for each activity. This makes it easy to target where a particular group needs to work—communication, conflict resolution, or building a vision. There are also discussion questions and tips for team training. Includes an index.

NSIEE. (1991). *Combining service and learning: A resource book for community and public service.* Raleigh, NC: National Society for Internships and Experiential Education.

This resource book is a cooperative project of 93 organizations that integrate learning with community and public-service experiences. Volume I outlines the history and future of the service-learning movement, theories, principles of good practice, and guides for policymakers, educational institutions, and program directors. Volume II offers 55 in-depth profiles of college, K through 12, and community-based programs. It also contains practical advice on management, recruitment, orientation, evaluation, and legal issues. Volume III contains an annotated bibliography of service-learning literature. Includes an index.

Pfeiffer, J. W., & Ballew, A. C. (1988-1989). *UA training technologies.* San Diego, CA: University Associates.

This set consists of seven volumes covering the following topics for use in human resources development: structured experiences; instruments; lecturettes, theories, and models; role plays; case studies, simulations, and games; design skills; and skills for presentation and evaluation. An index to all volumes is included.

Pfeiffer, J. W., & Jones, J. E. (Eds.). (1985). *Handbook of structured experiences for human relations training.* San Diego, CA: University Associates.

A complementary series to the annuals, this series now contains ten volumes, with the last volume published in 1985. Each contains structured experiences designed to promote varied learning experiences and to be useful in a variety of settings. Includes bibliographies.

New

Pfeiffer, J. W., & Nolde, C. (Eds.). (1991). *The encyclopedia of team-building activities.* San Diego, CA: Pfeiffer.

This book contains 55 activities to help HRD professionals teach team building as opposed to team development. Exercises include *Images: Envisioning the Ideal Team; The Car: Feedback on Team-Membership Styles; The Gold Watch: Balancing Personal and Professional Values; Nominations: Analyzing Trust Within a Team; Kaleidoscope: Team Building Through Role Expansion; Control or Surrender: Altering Approaches to Problem-Solving;* and *Project Colossus: Examining Group Dynamics.* Most exercises can be done in one to two hours and require no special materials except a flip chart and the handouts provided in the book. Includes bibliographical references.

Pierce, J. L., & Newstrom, J. W. (1994). *Leaders and the leadership process: Readings, self-assessments, and applications.* Boston: Irwin.

This book was created for the undergraduate course in leadership in the management and organization department at the University of Minnesota at Duluth. To give students a feel for the breadth and richness of the leadership mosaic, the faculty culled readings from history, organizational theory, and academic literature. The readings are organized for lessons on: definitions of leadership, influence, traits, behaviors, situations, followers, substitutions for leadership, charisma, and emerging issues. Lessons are enhanced by self-assessments, case studies, and a point/counterpoint argument titled "Does Leadership Really Make a Difference?" All pages are perforated for easy removal and photocopying.

Powers, B. (1992). *Instructor excellence: Mastering the delivery of training.* San Francisco: Jossey-Bass.

Based on 20 years of research in the field, Powers has developed a set of performance standards to achieve and evaluate instructor excellence. Novices and professional trainers can adopt his techniques for preparation, presentation, generating participation, and sequencing. Managers of trainers can learn how to observe, give feedback, reward performance, and ensure success. Includes bibliographical references and index.

New

Reference guide to handbooks and annuals: Volumes I-X and '72-'97 annuals. (1997). San Francisco: Pfeiffer.

This is a guide to the Pfeiffer series of human resource development materials—the ten volumes of *A Handbook of Structured Experiences for Human Relations Training* and 29 years of the Pfeiffer *Annuals.* There is an introduction on the use and impact of experiential learning.

Activities are organized by classification: individual development, communication, problem solving, groups, teams, facilitating, and leadership. Very brief information tells each activity's title, author, publication date, primary objectives, time required, and source. Includes glossary and name, title, and keyword indexes.

Rohnke, K. (Ed.). (1977). *Cowstails and cobras.* Hamilton, MA: Project Adventure.

This is an outdoor educator's volume that can easily apply to numerous group situations. Ropes courses and initiative games are the focus of this easy-to-use guide. Illustrations and photographs make it easy to understand the narrative directions. *The Blind Polygon* works wonders with a group of 40 student leaders! *Cowstails & Cobras II* was published in 1989. Includes bibliographical references.

New
Rollins, P. C. (1997). **Hollywood takes on the White House.** *World & I, 12*(7), 56-65.

Rollins reviews five films that depict real and fictional U.S. chief executives and their presidential character. *Wilson* (1944) shows Woodrow Wilson as a paragon of integrity, self-sacrifice, and family values. In *Dr. Strangelove; or How I Learned to Stop Worrying and Love the Bomb* (1964), President Merkin Muffley is an ineffective intellectual who cannot control his military advisors and nuclear weapons. *Nixon* (1995) portrays Richard Nixon as a tragic leader and complex personality with both base and noble qualities. *The American President* (1995) takes a delightful peek at the personal side of President Shepherd's romantic interests. More dramatically, this president faces ugly opposition with strength of character. The handsome, young President Whitmore in *Independence Day* (1996) demonstrates integrity, collaboration with his constituents, and courage—characteristics that help him to save the world from annihilation.

New
Sikes, S. (1995). *Feeding the zircon gorilla: And other team-building activities.* Tulsa, OK: Learning Unlimited.

This book contains 38 activities for small to large groups of any age—children through adults. The learnings range from simple to sophisticated. *Don't Touch Me* sets up a shifting paradigm as participants switch places without bumping into others. In *The Group Leader*, a sighted leader guides a blindfolded team though a physical task. *Oogly* is a cornstarch batter that replicates change. When pounded forcefully, it offers resistance. Provide too much energy and it fractures. Provide too little energy and it drools. Handouts in the book may be photocopied.

Silberman, M. L. (1990). *Active training: A handbook of techniques, designs, case examples, and tips.* New York: Lexington Books.

Adults learn best through an active approach, by doing. This guide is intended to help the novice trainer and the seasoned professional design and deliver training courses for active learning. Over 200 techniques are offered to get participant involvement, maximize retention, find alternatives to lecturing, invite feedback, control the pace of a session, and sequence activities for maximum impact. Includes bibliographical references and index.

Simonds, P. W. (1988). *A beginner's guide to leadership training programs.* Columbia, SC: National Association for Campus Activities (NACA) Educational Foundation.

This guide examines three important areas of student leadership training. It first presents a brief history of leadership theory and leadership training programs for higher education. Second, information is provided on what other colleges and universities have done in the past with leadership training programs. Last, a general guide is offered as a tool for the development of a variety of leadership training experiences for potential college student leaders. Exercises and training in decision making, problem solving, conflict resolution, consensus building, and group building are included. This is an excellent beginner's manual to leadership development. Includes bibliography and index.

Smitter, R. (1995). **Criteria for selecting case studies of leadership.** *Journal of Leadership Studies, 2*(2), 146-152.

The use of case studies in business and leadership classrooms is popular because it gives students a chance to grapple with real-life leadership problems. Smitter's criteria for selecting cases include the following questions: Does it portray leadership as a position or relationship? Does it cast leadership as a transaction or transformation? Does it define leadership as a process or single event? Does it raise issues of ethics, vision, or diversity? Does it suggest change? What forms of power are available? How are followers portrayed?

Snyder-Nepo, N. (1993). *Leadership assessments: A critique of common instruments: Leadership paper #4.* College Park: University of Maryland National Clearinghouse for Leadership Programs.

Participants at the 1991 Invitational Leadership Symposium responded to a survey on assessments appropriate for use in college and university leadership courses and programs. The survey revealed that educators didn't know of many instruments and felt that the ones they knew were either too expensive or had a bias toward the experienced business leader. This report introduces a model for leadership assessment and a description of 37 examples. Cost, scoring, reliability and validity, and an overall evaluation of each assessment can help educators make an appropriate choice.

New
Thiagarajan, S., & Thiagarajan, R. (1995). *Diversity simulation games: Exploring and celebrating differences.* Amherst, MA: HRD Press.

This book contains instructions for five simulations that focus on cross-cultural differences. They are brief—30 minutes total time for instruction, play, and debriefing. *Brief Encounters* simulates the misinterpretations that occur during a first-contact experience with another culture. *Chatter* teaches students to accept differences in conversation and behavior during cross-cultural communication. *Exclude* allows students to experience the frustration of being the one left out of a group activity. *Reincarnation* examines the differences among people that contribute to their triumphs and traumas. *Same Difference* helps students identify their commonalities with people in several groups.

New
Thompson, T. A., Purdy, J. M., & Fandt, P. M. (1997). **Building a strong foundation: Using a computer simulation in an introductory management course.** *Journal of Management Education, 21*(3), 418-434.

The authors build a case for using computer simulations to provide an overview of managerial concepts and theories early in an undergraduate business management curriculum. Realistic work scenarios illustrate the interdependence of decisions and their effects. Students practice behaviors and teamwork. Some students experience management situations for the first time and learn about their personal strengths and weaknesses. The authors identify seven criteria for evaluating computer simulations. A chart briefly evaluates eight computer simulations that may be considered for an introductory management course.

New
Uhlfelder, H. F., & Burden, J. S. (Eds.). (1995). *The advanced team guide: Tools, techniques, and tips for experienced teams.* Atlanta, GA: Miller Howard Publishers.

This guide is written in a simple format to help organizations who are planning to build teams or are seeking ways to improve teamwork. There is advice on assessment, feedback, diversity among members, and group dynamics. Case studies, brief exercises, and suggested readings reinforce lessons in personality types, team unity, and role responsibility.

New
Van Velsor, E., Leslie, J. B., & Fleenor, J. W. (1997). ***Choosing 360: A guide to evaluating multi-rater feedback instruments for management development.*** Greensboro, NC: Center for Creative Leadership.

An increasingly popular vehicle for getting feedback from one's boss, peers, and subordinates is the multiple-perspective, or 360-degree, feedback instrument. This book, which updates *Feedback to Managers, Volume 1* (1991), presents a step-by-step process that shows how to evaluate multiple-feedback instruments intended for management development. Issues addressed include instrument development, validity and reliability, feedback display, scoring strategies, and cost. Includes bibliographical references.

Van Wart, M., Cayer, N. J., & Cook, S. (1993). ***Handbook of training and development for the public sector: A comprehensive resource.*** San Francisco: Jossey-Bass.

This book is a train-the-trainer text for schools of public administration, and for human resource development personnel in local, state, and federal departments. HRD faces new challenges: doing more with fewer staff members; agency reorganization; and providing training in communication, quality management, and employee enrichment, as well as traditional skills training. Sections of the book address designing programs, gaining an understanding of instructional methods, and conducting and evaluating programs. Includes bibliographical references and index.

VanGundy, A. B. (1992). ***Idea power: Techniques and resources to unleash the creativity in your organization.*** New York: AMACOM.

Businesses need to develop new and creative approaches for keeping pace with technological advances, information overload, and increasing production costs. To respond, VanGundy presents an introduction to business creativity and creative problem solving. He outlines training methods, course design, retreat planning, and idea-generation techniques. Resource materials, such as movies, books, and cassettes, are listed. Includes bibliography and index.

Welsh, T. M., Johnson, S. P., Miller, L. K., & Merrill, M. H. (1989). **A practical procedure for training meeting chairpersons.** *Journal of Organizational Behavior Management, 10*(1), 151-166.

Based on their case study that compared the performance of two undergraduate chairperson trainees, the authors provide a practical approach for training that is intended to improve chairperson performance and increase participant satisfaction.

Wheelan, S. A. (1990). *Facilitating training groups: A guide to leadership and verbal intervention skills.* New York: Praeger.

Intended as a guide for trainers, this book describes three group models: T-groups, personal growth groups, and skills training groups. It details the theories, goals, and leadership skills of each model. Strategies for matching a model to a given population are offered with intervention techniques for helping a group set and achieve goals. There are practice exercises to reinforce the lessons. Includes bibliographical references and index.

Yukl, G. (1990). *Skills for managers and leaders: Text, cases and exercises.* Englewood Cliffs, NJ: Prentice Hall.

Designed as a text for leadership courses, this book examines 12 leadership skills. Students learn to understand concepts, recognize ineffective behavior, and practice effective behavior. Composite cases, inspired by events in real organizations, are designed to facilitate discussions. Role plays, quizzes, and student assessments are included in each chapter. An instructor's manual is available with additional exercises.

Zorn, T. E., & Violanti, M. T. (1993). **Measuring leadership style: A review of leadership style instruments for classroom use.** *Communication Education, 42*(1), 70-78.

The authors review seven leadership instruments appropriate for classroom use. The reviews do not critique the research base of the instruments (although they do state that all of them have "adequate reliability and validity") but rather provide information that would be useful to the instructor in selecting an instrument for classroom use (for example, cost, norms, time requirements, scoring, and interpretation).

MOTIVATION AND SELF-DEVELOPMENT

Ambrose, D. (1991). *Leadership: The journey inward.* Dubuque, IA: Kendall/Hunt.

Leaders are, at their core, ordinary people with fears, concerns, and challenges. In leaders and all people, a journey inward or self-discovery can increase personal effectiveness. Ambrose offers suggestions for making such a journey.

Bellman, G. M. (1993). *Getting things done when you are not in charge.* San Francisco: Berrett-Koehler.

This sequel to *The Quest for Staff Leadership* is focused toward middle managers, advisors, functional experts, and support personnel. Chapters offer practical advice on handling office politics, effecting change, and earning the respect of top management. Bellman teaches those in supporting roles to empower themselves, increasing their contributions professionally while achieving satisfaction personally. Includes bibliographical references and index.

Bennis, W., & Goldsmith, J. (1994). *Learning to lead: A workbook on becoming a leader.* New York: Addison-Wesley.

This workbook walks the reader through the core competencies of life with discussion of basic principles, exercises for self-improvement, and assessment to measure your progress. Chapters address integrity, trust, goal setting and achievement, reflection, learning from failure, and commitment. The authors expect those readers who respond to activities and assessments with honest answers to become capable leaders of organizations that share a common vision, have empowered members at every level, and promote continuous learning. At the end of the book, an annotated bibliography by A. Khoo and H. Im suggests 20 books for further leadership studies. These books were identified as favorites in a survey of top-level managers and academicians in the field of leadership research. Includes an index.

Brim, G. (1992). *Ambition: How we manage success and failure throughout our lives.* New York: BasicBooks.

How do we deal with success and failure, winning and losing, triumphs and disaster? Brim draws on the latest psychological and social research and real-life case studies to explore how we strive for growth and mastery. His research shows that our capacity to change across our entire lives is much greater than we used to believe. To remain happy, Brim asserts that we must prefer to live our lives at the "just manageable" level of difficulty and that our actions should have four elements: our desired goals; our aspirations—ideal, minimum, and realistic—for what we will achieve; a timetable for achieving our goals; and means for achieving our goals. Includes bibliographical references and index.

Campbell, D. P. (1984). *If I'm in charge here, why is everybody laughing?* (2nd ed.). Greensboro, NC: Center for Creative Leadership.

This book examines a number of questions: How can leaders bring out the best in the people they work with? What are the best ways to overcome opposition? Why are friendships so special to people in charge? Campbell issues a call to take up the challenge of leadership, which can be demanding, enriching, and exhilarating. This is a book full of useful tips for people who are in charge, who make things happen, and who want to have an impact on their world.

Collins, S. (1995). *Our children are watching: Ten skills for leading the next generation to success.* Barrytown, NY: Barrytown, Ltd.

Drawing on her own life experiences and many that have been shared by the participants in her seminars, Collins concludes that parenting is the ultimate leadership experience. She tells compelling stories to teach parents, educators, business managers, and government officials how to progress from childlike following-behavior to adult leadership-behavior. Her ten skills for success include: focusing on successes, imagining positive outcomes, and deleting mental obstacles.

Conger, J. A. (1994). **Personal growth training: Snake oil or pathway to leadership?** *Organizational Dynamics,* *22*(1), 19-30.

Conger comments on a new wave of leadership training called personal growth training, a combination of psychological exercises and outdoor adventure. Different from traditional leadership training, which teaches cognitive skills and provides feedback, personal growth training encourages participants to examine their values, take risks, and assume greater responsibility for their own lives and for their organizations. Conger reflects on his own self-examination and cliff-jumping experiences and his ability to use his new-found personal growth in his work.

Covey, S. R. (1989). *Seven habits of highly effective people: Restoring the character ethic.* New York: Simon & Schuster.

Covey defines habit as a combination of knowledge, skill, and desire; or the what to do, why, how, and want to do. He suggests a shift away from personality ethics, such as public image, superficial solutions, and the pursuit of success. He recommends living with a character ethic based on integrity, dignity, growth, and quality. His seven habits are based on the fundamental principles of human effectiveness. Includes indexes.

Fiedler, F., & Chemers, M. M. (1977). *Improving leadership effectiveness: The Leader Match concept* (2nd ed.). New York: Wiley.

The authors tell how to identify your leadership style and match it with the situation in which you perform best. They offer guidelines on how to change a situation to strengthen your leadership effectiveness.

New
Frigon, N. L., Sr., & Jackson, H. K., Jr. (1996). *The leader: Developing the skills and personal qualities you need to lead effectively.* New York: AMACOM.

This workbook is designed for those beginning leadership positions in business, community, or personal situations. Its building blocks for learning to be a leader are: 1) leadership principles, which include integrity, consideration, and teamwork; 2) leadership traits, which include initiative, ethical behavior, and dependability; and 3) leadership skills, which include planning, decision making, communication, coaching, and knowledge. Diagrams and activities throughout the book guide the reader through each building block. In the appendices are a Leadership Self-Assessment to take at the beginning of the workbook and a Leadership Plan to complete after the book is read. Includes bibliographical references and index.

Haas, H. G., & Tamarkin, B. (1992). *The leader within: An empowering path of self-discovery.* New York: HarperCollins.

Based on his own experience as CEO of Sealy, Inc., and leadership instructor at the University of Chicago Graduate School of Business, Haas weaves a tapestry of leadership theories, skills, and characteristics. Interviews with 150 corporate leaders provide composite stories of the road to leadership and the pitfalls along the way. He predicts that the major challenges for leaders in the 1990s will be human capital issues, environmental responsibility, government/industry relations, global strategies, and a continuously changing culture.

Hallstein, R. W. (1992). *Memoirs of a recovering autocrat: Revealing insights for managing the autocrat in all of us.* San Francisco: Berrett-Koehler.

We all wish to gain control of our careers and our personal lives. Yet controlling behaviors are often the same autocratic behaviors that are ineffective at work and at home. In confessional vignettes, Hallstein shows how one autocrat recovered from the need to always be right and to always be in control. Includes an index.

Heim, P., & Chapman, E. N. (1990). *Learning to lead: An action plan for success.* Los Altos, CA: Crisp.

This self-improvement program for managers who want to become leaders is intended for at-home study or a workshop. The self-paced format is designed "to be read with a pencil." Exercises and assessments facilitate reader participation and feedback. Leadership skills emphasized in this program are personality, power, vision, decision making, and risk taking.

Hitt, W. D. (1988). *The leader-manager: Guidelines for action.* Columbus, OH: Battelle Press.

This is about the practical actions for any leader-manager who aspires to be more effective. The author's approach is based upon the premise that all managers have a "certain amount" of leadership potential and that this potential can be more fully developed. The focus is upon assessing where you happen to be along the leadership continuum and then using the plan of action designed here to develop your attributes. Hitt suggests that "with concerted effort over about a two-year period . . . an individual manager should be able to improve his or her position." Includes bibliography and indexes.

New
Jaffe, D. T., Scott, C. D., & Tobe, G. R. (1994). *Rekindling commitment: How to revitalize yourself, your work, and your organization.* San Francisco: Jossey-Bass.

Organizational change typically begins in the middle levels of an organization. New ideas and enthusiasm flow upward and then spread throughout an organization. The authors promote the individual commitment of change leaders at all levels of an organization. They suggest that such empowerment leads to self-development, innovation, and action. Some new roles for change leaders are: crisis spotter, idea generator, sponsor, tinkerer, and process leader. Includes bibliographical references and index.

New
Jaworski, J., & Flowers, B. S. (Eds.). (1996). *Synchronicity: The inner path of leadership.* San Francisco: Berrett-Koehler.

Jaworski describes his early years, which were filled with dramatic peaks and valleys until a personal crisis alerted him that he was living an unfulfilled life. At that point, he embarked on a journey to find his life's meaning and discovered synchronicity—the connectedness of people and events that enrich your life if you let go of control. He recommends that all leaders adopt a synchronistic mind-set to see the importance of relationships, commit to one's passion, and use the flow of energy that results. Jaworski teaches these lessons as founder of the American Leadership Forum, founder of the Centre for Generative Leadership, and member of MIT's Center for Organizational Learning. Peter Senge writes a moving introduction to this book. Includes index.

Kaplan, R. E., Drath, W. H., & Kofodimos, J. R. (1985). *High hurdles: The challenge of executive self-development.* Greensboro, NC: Center for Creative Leadership.

The authors of this 40-page report conducted a study to explore self-development and the particular challenges to its path faced by executives. The report explores the premise that executives, unlike most professionals throughout an organization, tend to be exempt from coming to terms with their limitations and are further shielded from self-examination by staffs who shy away from opportunities to offer useful criticism. A combination of 40 executives and experts on executives were extensively interviewed. After carefully analyzing over 400 pages of transcripts, the authors found distinct patterns in what executives considered difficult about their positions and in whether or not they attempted personal change. Includes a bibliography.

Karnes, F. A., & Bean, S. M. (1994). *Leadership for students: A practical guide for ages 8-18.* Waco, TX: Prufrock Press.

This guide appeals to the energy and creativity of young people seeking to learn leadership skills. Readers first assess their own strengths and weaknesses to reinforce a positive self-image. They are encouraged to seek opportunities at school, in clubs, and through community service to practice new skills. Keeping a journal provides practice for writing articles or letters to newspaper editors. Students learn where to seek opportunities for public speaking, chairing committees, advocating environmental protection, and service to community. Organizations that offer these leadership opportunities and youth training programs are listed in a resource section. Includes bibliographical references.

New
Malone, P. B., III. (1986). *Love 'em and lead 'em.* Annandale, VA: Synergy Press.

Malone shares his personal philosophy that leading people is more difficult than it used to be. He believes that participative leadership (shared authority) is the most effective leadership style. Leaders must know themselves and develop their own leadership philosophies. Malone's practical experience in the military and his academic research provide a solid background in behavioral science. He adds a lighthearted tone and original cartoons to soften his serious message. Includes bibliographical references.

New

Malone, P. B., III. (1990). *Abuse 'em and lose 'em.* Annandale, VA: Synergy Press.

There are two ways to learn how to lead. One is to examine the right way as illustrated in Malone's *Love 'Em and Lead 'Em* (1986). The other is to study the wrong way as outlined in this book of "18 leadership styles that were made in Hell." With humor and insight, Malone describes flawed leadership, its causes, and its cures. He encourages readers to learn from the mistakes of his fictional characters, Richard Devious, Ignacio Incompetenti, Bella Cose, and Pam Demonium. Includes bibliographical references.

Manz, C. C. (1993). *Self-leadership: A skill-building series.* King of Prussia, PA: Organization Design and Development.

Based on Manz's *Mastering Self-leadership,* this three-part workbook series may be used for self-training or leadership development training sessions. *Becoming a Self-manager: Skills for Addressing Difficult, Unattractive, But Necessary Tasks* has tips for focusing attention and keeping priorities in order and self-observation and self-reward activities. *Redesigning the Way You Do Your Job: Skills for Building Natural Motivation into Your Work* focuses on building enjoyment into work. *The Art of Positive Psyching: Skills for Establishing Constructive Thinking Patterns* recommends strategies for managing beliefs and assumptions, developing constructive self-talk, and developing effective scripts for life. Each workbook includes questionnaires and facilitator guides.

New

McLean, J. W., & Weitzel, W. (1991). *Leadership: Magic, myth, or method?* New York: AMACOM.

McLean and Weitzel encourage all readers to be skeptical about the idea of heroic leadership and instead build the skills necessary to practice leadership. Myths are a convenient excuse for playing it safe and avoiding leadership opportunities. Examples are: leadership is complicated, leaders are charismatic, and leaders are never wrong. The authors outline leadership myths over time and across cultures to illustrate their differences and similarities. From the mix, they suggest six principles, six skills, and six methods to apply new skills to the practice of leadership. They offer the acronym ROPE to remind leaders to welcome Risks, take advantage of Opportunities, be Participants, and generate Energy. Includes bibliographical references and index.

Miller, S., Wackman, D. B., Nunally, E. W., & Miller, P. A. (1988). *Connecting with self and others.* Littleton, CO: Interpersonal Communication Programs.

To some degree we are always engaged in the "dance" of connecting or disconnecting with others. What makes this "dance" so engaging? Drawing on years of research and testing, these authors present strategies, models, and maps to clarify the time, energy, space, and choices that together form the actions we take in our relationships with others. The threefold model of awareness, skills, and options in communicating and building relationships with others is set within a practical framework that shows the paths we travel in our various communication efforts.

New

Murphy, E. C. (1996). *Leadership IQ: A personal development process based on a scientific study of a new generation of leaders.* New York: Wiley.

This book contains a leadership assessment and development program based on Murphy's consulting work with clients such as IBM, AT&T, Xerox, and McDonald's. He suggests that readers first take the *Leadership IQ Self-Assessment* at the back of the book to identify competencies and weaknesses. The remainder of the book explains eight roles of an intelligent leader: selector, connector, problem-solver, evaluator, negotiator, healer, protector, and synergizer. Those who wish to build strength in those roles may do the skill-building exercises. Includes bibliographical references and index.

New

Napolitano, C. S., & Henderson, L. J. (1998). *The leadership odyssey: A self-development guide to new skills for new times.* San Francisco: Jossey-Bass.

The authors say that their book is "designed to be *used* as well as read," and they begin by dividing leadership into three domains—self-leadership, people leadership, organizational leadership—and describing specific skills and attributes within each area, such as having focus, engaging in dialogue, facilitating learning, and promoting a corporate culture. Readers can then evaluate their own skills using the included skills-assessment kit, which includes forms, directions, and instructions on how to analyze the data. The book's final section contains developmental exercises readers can use to address skills deficits and enhance their existing strengths. Includes bibliographical references.

New
Segal, M. (1997). ***Points of influence: A guide to using personality theory at work.*** San Francisco: Jossey-Bass.

Segal profiles the work of nine personality theorists, including Freud, Jung, Skinner, and Bowen, with a specific emphasis on how understanding these theories can help managers influence behavior and effect change in the workplace. Each profile includes examples of work situations in which that theory would apply and real-life stories of how leaders have benefited from understanding a particular behavior and its motivations. The conclusion helps integrate these nine theories into a cohesive picture of how the organizational implications of personality theory can help leaders understand their followers, take action, and increase their own self-awareness.

Smith, M. (1993). ***Changing course: A positive approach to a new job or lifestyle.*** San Diego, CA: Pfeiffer.

Information, tips, and 24 exercises define areas for change and growth in career or personal development. This guide may be used as a participant text in outplacement programs, change-management courses, or career development programs.

New
Stewart, T. (1996, January 15). **You Inc.: The organizational chart.** *Fortune*, pp. 66-67.

This article takes the viewpoint that every worker is actually self-employed: we are each the chief executive officer of a small company that is our life. A necessary component of *You Inc.* is a board of directors that should include spouses, peers, your boss, colleagues, and family members. These people fill roles such as COO, general counsel, VP for marketing, and chief technology officer.

Stumpf, S. A., & Mullen, T. P. (1992). ***Taking charge: Strategic leadership in the middle game.*** Englewood Cliffs, NJ: Prentice Hall.

This guide is intended for middle managers who wish to develop their strategic leadership skills. Identification of vision, mission, goals, and objectives is illustrated by real examples from actual companies. Assessment of one's personal preference for communication, decision making, and creativity provides a starting point for learning alternative behaviors. The authors suggest ways to create opportunities to practice and refine new leadership skills.

New
Toogood, G. N. (1997). ***The inspired executive: The art of leadership in the age of knowledge.*** New York: Carroll & Graf.

The author discusses his premise of communications value added (CVA), or knowledge and the ability to communicate it. CVA is actually Toogood's advice for great public speaking summed up in seven principles. This how-to book is sprinkled with stories of successful executives and their memorable speeches. Includes an index.

Van Maurik, J. (1994). ***Discovering the leader in you.*** New York: McGraw-Hill.

This book is based on the premise that leadership is emotional, not logical—an attitude, not a position. Van Maurik defines leadership as "something you choose to do through a process of action and self-discovery." He presents classic management theories and definitions of leadership to highlight skills and behaviors to practice when learning leadership. At the end of each chapter are a summary and a quiz, making this book suitable for individual use or a classroom text. Includes bibliographical references and index.

New
Waitley, D. (1995). ***Empires of the mind: Lessons to lead and succeed in a knowledge-based world.*** New York: William Morrow.

Denis Waitley is author and narrator of numerous personal development books and audiotapes. In this book, he offers strategies for the development of self-leadership. Chapters suggest ways to welcome change, responsibility, passion, and knowledge. Waitley offers techniques for building integrity, power, and winning habits. He lists action ideas for practicing service to others, a positive attitude, and resilience.

Woodcock, M., & Francis, D. (1991). ***The self-made leader: 25 structured activities for self-development.*** King of Prussia, PA: Organization Design and Development.

For workshops and training sessions, activities are planned to help managers and supervisors learn about themselves and exploit their potential. Hour-and-a-half activities include personal assessments, lecturettes, scoring assessments, review of findings, small-group exercises, and full-group discussions. Areas covered include: interpersonal style, influence style, listening skills, and situational organizing. In each chapter are directions for the facilitator, reproducible questionnaires, and masters for overhead transparencies.

Woyach, R. B. (1993). ***Preparing for leadership: A young adult's guide to leadership skills in a global age.*** Westport, CT: Greenwood Press.

High school and college students who serve in leadership positions can learn how to work more effectively in their current positions and prepare themselves for future leadership roles. Woyach explains that leadership is not a position of power; it is a relationship among people. A leader creates and shares a vision, builds consensus among members, resolves conflicts, and ensures that the group has all it needs to achieve success. The steps to achieve these skills are effectively defined in text, flowcharts, graphs, and cartoons. Includes bibliographical references and index.

New

Zinober, J. W., & Richard, L. R. (1996). **Your leadership report card: How do you stack up?** *Law Practice Management, 22*(7), 30-37.

This article includes a self-administered and self-scored test for leaders of law firms. Individuals respond to A-, B-, C-, and F-level descriptions of 12 leadership behaviors such as establishing a mission, coaching others, listening, being accountable, taking risks, and building teams. There are no data on the development of the instrument. The authors suggest that individuals with low scores on their report cards seek leadership training and development.

JOURNALS AND NEWSLETTERS

The leadership journals and newsletters described in this section are frequently browsed for articles included in the bibliography. They range from scholarly journals that report cutting-edge research to magazines that are a source of book synopses and conference notices. Brief descriptions include contact information.

ACROSS THE BOARD

This magazine, published ten times a year, supports the Conference Board's goal to improve the business enterprise system and to enhance the contribution of business to society. It includes book reviews and a Manager's Tool Kit section that introduces new books and technology.

Conference Board
845 Third Avenue
New York, NY 10022-6679
Phone: (212) 759-0900
Fax: (212) 980-7014
E-mail: atb@conference-board.org
Website: http://www.conference-board.org

ADMINISTRATIVE SCIENCE QUARTERLY

This refereed quarterly journal publishes dissertation research and other fresh scholarly views in organization studies. The journal sponsors the ASQ Award for Scholarly Contribution. Includes book reviews and annual author and title indexes.

Cornell University
20 Thornwood Drive, Suite 100
Ithaca, NY 14850-1265
Phone: (607) 254-7143
Fax: (607) 254-7100
Website: http://www.gsm.cornell.edu/ASQ/asq.html

ALE NEWSLETTER

This is the quarterly newsletter of the Association of Leadership Educators. There are articles on teaching models, development opportunities, and association news.

Association of Leadership Educators
Christine Townsend, Editor
Texas A&M University
Department of Agricultural Education
College Station, TX 77843-2116

CALIFORNIA MANAGEMENT REVIEW

This quarterly journal serves as a bridge between those who study management and those who practice it. Each year, the Andersen Consulting Award is given to the author(s) of the article judged to have made the most important contribution to improving the practice of management.

S549 Haas School of Business #1900
University of California
Berkeley, CA 94720-1900
Phone: (510) 642-7159
Fax: (510) 642-1318

E-mail: cmr@haas.berkeley.edu
Website: http://haas.berkeley.edu/News/cmr

CASE RESEARCH JOURNAL

Each issue of this refereed quarterly journal contains about eight cases. These teaching cases are based on research in actual organizations and in all business disciplines.

North American Case Research Association, Inc.
P.O. Box 6406
Columbus, GA 31917-6405
Website: http://www.siu.edu/departments/ats/NACRA

CONCEPTS AND CONNECTIONS

This thematic newsletter is published several times a year. Each issue spotlights a successful campus leadership course or program. Leadership education as a discipline is examined through surveys of practice, historical context, standards and guidelines, updates on new research, funding ideas, conference notices, and book reviews.

National Clearinghouse for Leadership Programs
1135 Stamp Student Union
University of Maryland at College Park
College Park, MD 20472-4631
Phone: (301) 314-7164
Fax: (301) 314-9634
E-mail: nclp@umdstu.umd.edu
Website: http://www.inform.umd.edu/OCP/NCLP/

THE DIVERSITY FACTOR

This quarterly journal aims to introduce new ideas and stimulate learning about diversity in organizations. Articles present data, best practices, cases, and societal issues. Includes book reviews and information about other training resources.

P.O. Box 3188
Teaneck, NJ 07666-9104
Phone: (201) 833-0011
Fax: (201) 833-4184

EDUCATIONAL LEADERSHIP

Published eight times a year, this magazine is intended for leaders in K-through-12 education, but may be helpful to all who are interested in curriculum development and supervision in schools. Includes book reviews and Portfolio, a showcase of images that inspire, amuse, or provoke.

Association for Supervision and Curriculum Development
1250 North Pitt Street
Alexandria, VA 22314-1453
Phone: (703) 549-9110
E-mail: el@ascd.org
Website: http://www.ascd.org

ENTREPRENEURSHIP THEORY & PRACTICE

This is the official refereed journal of the U.S. Association for Small Business and Entrepreneurship. It features current research as well as articles on educational techniques and government policy. Includes cases and book reviews.

Baylor University
Hankamer School of Business
The John F. Baugh Center for Entrepreneurship
Speight Avenue at 5th Street
Waco, TX 76798-8011
Website: http://hsb.baylor.edu/html/cel/ent/public.htm

EXECUTIVE EXCELLENCE

This monthly periodical promotes personal and organizational leadership based on constructive values, sound ethics, and timeless principles. Leading authors contribute brief articles that are often summaries of newly released books. Includes additional brief book reviews.

Executive Excellence Publishing
1344 East 1120 South
Provo, UT 84606-6379
Phone: (800) 300-3454
E-mail: eecirc@juno.com
Website: http://www.eep.com

FAST COMPANY

This bimonthly magazine is geared to a new generation of business people. Articles on leadership, personal success, change, and learning have a fresh focus on social justice and workplace democracy.

Subscriptions
P.O. Box 52760
Boulder, CO 80321-2760
Phone: (800) 688-1545
Website: http://www.fastcompany.com

GENERATOR: JOURNAL OF SERVICE-LEARNING AND YOUTH LEADERSHIP

This journal, published two to three times per year, is dedicated to developing service-oriented youth leaders by supporting the organizations that encourage them. There

are profiles of successful programs, guides to resources and technical assistance, and articles about leadership written by K-through-12 authors.

National Youth Leadership Council
1910 West County Road B
St. Paul, MN 55113-1337
Phone: (800) FON-NYLC or (612) 631-3672
Fax: (612) 631-2955

HARVARD BUSINESS REVIEW

HBR is a bimonthly publication for professional managers. In addition to essays on improving business functions, there are stories on the human side of management. Includes book reviews, cartoons, and case studies. Includes an annual index. Comprehensive indexes are published periodically.

60 Harvard Way
Boston, MA 02163-1000
Phone: (617) 496-1449
Fax: (617) 495-9933
E-mail: hbr_editorial@hbsp.harvard.edu
Website: http://www.hbsp.harvard.edu

HRMAGAZINE

This monthly magazine aims to support the work of the human resource management profession. A regular feature is HR Pulse, a call-in survey on a hot topic and results of the previous month's survey. The website adds new material each month to supplement the topics covered in the printed issue.

Society for Human Resource Management
1800 Duke Street
Alexandria, VA 22314-3499
Phone: (703) 548-3440
Fax: (703) 836-0367
TDD: (703) 548-6999
E-mail: hrmag@shrm.org
Website: http://www.shrm.org/hrmagazine

HUMAN RELATIONS

This refereed monthly journal is based on the belief that social scientists in all fields should integrate their work to understand the complexities of human problems. Papers are on theoretical developments, qualitative and quantitative data, presentation of new methods, empirical research, and book reviews.

Plenum Publishing Corporation
233 Spring Street
New York, NY 10013-1578
Phone: (800) 221-9369 or (212) 620-8468

Fax: (212) 647-1898
E-mail: info@plenum.com
Website: http://www.catchword.com or
http://www.tavinstitute.org/hr

HUMAN RESOURCE DEVELOPMENT QUARTERLY (HRDQ)

HRDQ is a quarterly, refereed journal of the American Society for Training and Development and the Academy of Human Resource Development. It links HRD theory and application from the fields of economics, education, management, and psychology. Includes book reviews and an annual index.

Jossey-Bass Inc., Publishers
350 Sansome Street
San Francisco, CA 94104-1342
Phone: (888) 378-2537
Fax: (800) 605-2665
E-mail: subinfo@jbp.com
Website: http://www.josseybass.com

JOURNAL OF LEADERSHIP STUDIES

This refereed journal is published quarterly for those who teach, study, or practice leadership. The articles include examples of curriculum, teaching techniques, suggestions for evaluation, and trends in leadership education. Includes book reviews and annual author, title, and subject indexes.

Baker College Center for Graduate Studies
1050 West Bristol Road
Flint, MI 48507-5508
Phone: (810) 766-4105
E-mail: journal@baker.edu
Website: http://www.baker.edu/departments/BCLI/jls-main.htm

JOURNAL OF MANAGEMENT EDUCATION

This bimonthly journal supports management education in the academic classroom and the corporate setting. The articles cover such areas as entrepreneurship, public administration, management consulting, communication, and organizational behavior. There are original simulations and suggestions for using activities, films, and other instructional materials.

Sage Publications, Inc.
2455 Teller Road
Thousand Oaks, CA 91320-2234
Phone: (805) 499-0721
Fax: (805) 499-0871
E-mail: order@sagepub.com

Website: http://www.sagepub.com or
http://universe.cwru.edu/jme

LEADER TO LEADER

This quarterly publication from the Peter F. Drucker Foundation focuses on leadership development and organizational change. Peter Drucker and Frances Hesselbein contribute to most issues. Other articles are written by prominent authors, often summarizing newly released books. Includes annual author and subject indexes.

Jossey-Bass Inc., Publishers
350 Sansome Street
San Francisco, CA 94104-1342
Phone: (888) 378-2537
Fax: (800) 605-2665
E-mail: subinfo@jbp.com
Website: http://www.josseybass.com

LEADERSHIP IN ACTION

This quarterly newsletter aims to help practicing leaders and those who train and develop practicing leaders. It provides them with insights gained in the course of the Center for Creative Leadership's educational and research activities. It is also a forum for the exchange of ideas between practitioners and CCL staff and associates.

Jossey-Bass Inc., Publishers
350 Sansome Street
San Francisco, CA 94104-1342
Phone: (888) 378-2537
Fax: (800) 605-2665
E-mail: subinfo@jbp.com
Website: http://www.josseybass.com

LEADERSHIP INSIGHTS

This newsletter, published three times per year, is for community leaders in Georgia and across the nation. Articles discuss leadership issues in general and Georgia-based leadership programs specifically. There are ideas for civic groups, extension programs, and youth leadership.

Fanning Leadership Center
The University of Georgia
Hoke Smith Annex
Athens, GA 30602-4350
Phone: (706) 542-1108
Fax: (706) 542-7007
E-mail: leadership@flc.uga.edu
Website: http://www.uga.edu/~flc

A LEADERSHIP JOURNAL: WOMEN IN LEADERSHIP—SHARING THE VISION

Published twice a year, this refereed journal contains articles on practical applications for and current research of interest to women leaders. Contributing authors are from the academic, corporate, and government sectors around the world. Includes book reviews.

The Leadership Institute
Columbia College
P.O. Box 3815
Columbia, SC 29230-9963
Phone: (803) 786-3729
Fax: (803) 786-3806

LEADERSHIP QUARTERLY: AN INTERNATIONAL JOURNAL OF POLITICAL, SOCIAL AND BEHAVIORAL SCIENCE

This quarterly refereed journal is dedicated to advancing theory, research, and applications concerning leadership. Contributors are from many disciplines, and each issue offers diverse perspectives or comparative studies. Includes an annual index.

JAI Press Inc.
55 Old Post Road, #2
P.O. Box 1678
Greenwich, CT 06839-1678
Phone: (203) 661-7602
Fax: (203) 661-0792
Website: http://www.jaipress.com or http://www.som.binghamton.edu/yammar.htm

LTI LEADER

High school seniors publish this periodical as one project of the Leadership Training Institute at John F. Kennedy High School. Articles include opinion pieces, descriptions of other institute projects, spotlights on leadership around the world, and school news. The editors hope that other high schools will replicate the work of the institute and this periodical.

Leadership Training Institute
John F. Kennedy High School
1901 Randolph Road
Silver Spring, MD 20902-1498
Phone: (301) 649-8232

NASSP BULLETIN

Published nine times a year, this journal features subjects of interest to middle school and high school administrators. There are articles on ethical issues, technology, and the professional development of teachers and administrators. Includes research briefs, book reviews, and an annual index.

National Association of Secondary School Principals
1904 Association Drive
Reston, VA 20191-1537
Phone: (800) 253-7746
Fax: (703) 476-5432
Website: http://www.nassp.org

NONPROFIT MANAGEMENT AND LEADERSHIP

This quarterly refereed journal is sponsored by the Mandel Center for Nonprofit Organizations at Case Western Reserve University and the Centre for Voluntary Organisation at the London School of Economics and Political Science. The papers emphasize human resources, resource development, financial management, change, and organizational effectiveness. Winter and summer issues feature case studies of ethical and strategic dilemmas.

Jossey-Bass Inc., Publishers
350 Sansome Street
San Francisco, CA 94104-1342
Phone: (888) 378-2537
Fax: (800) 605-2665
E-mail: subinfo@jbp.com
Website: http://www.josseybass.com

NONPROFIT WORLD: THE NATIONAL NONPROFIT LEADERSHIP AND MANAGEMENT JOURNAL

This bimonthly journal is dedicated to building a strong network of professionals in the nonprofit world. The articles discuss funding, legal issues, staff development, and governance. A catalog lists books, videos, and software.

The Society for Nonprofit Organizations
6314 Odana Road, Suite 1
Madison, WI 53719-1141
Phone: (800) 424-7367
Fax: (608) 274-9978
Website: http://danenet.wicip.org/snpo

NSEE QUARTERLY

This newsletter seeks to advance the understanding of experiential education theory and practice. Contributing authors are from all educational levels as well as from business, government, and nonprofit sectors. There is a calendar of opportunities for professional development.

National Society for Experiential Education
3509 Haworth Drive, Suite 207
Raleigh, NC 27609-7229
Phone: (919) 787-3263
Fax: (919) 787-3381
E-mail: info@nsee.org
Website: http://www.nsee.org/quarter.htm

ORGANIZATIONAL DYNAMICS: A QUARTERLY REVIEW OF ORGANIZATIONAL BEHAVIOR FOR PROFESSIONAL MANAGERS

This refereed quarterly journal links leading-edge thought and research in the fields of organizational behavior and organization development. Each issue features a case study describing a company in the process of change and a field report that presents new research. Includes book reviews.

American Management Association International
P.O. Box 319
Saranac Lake, NY 12983-0319
Phone: (518) 891-5510
Website: http://www.amanet.org/periodicals/od

PERSONNEL PSYCHOLOGY: A JOURNAL OF APPLIED RESEARCH

This refereed quarterly journal publishes applied psychological research on personnel problems facing public- and private-sector organizations. Articles are on all areas of human resources including training and development, feedback, and leadership. Includes extensive book reviews and an annual index.

Personnel Psychology, Inc.
745 Haskins Road, Suite D
Bowling Green, OH 43402-1600
Phone: (419) 352-1562

PHI DELTA KAPPAN

Published ten times per year, this periodical contains articles concerned with educational research, service, and leadership. Regular features address federal and state education policies, legal issues, and new technology.

Phi Delta Kappan International, Inc.
408 North Union
P.O. Box 789
Bloomington, IN 47402-0789
Phone: (800) 766-1156
Fax: (812) 339-0018
E-mail: kappan@pdkintl.org
Website: http://www.pdkintl.org/kappan/kappan.htm

PUBLIC ADMINISTRATION REVIEW

This bimonthly journal features articles on public administration from local to global levels. Many articles are concerned with ethical issues, diversity, reform, and leadership. Includes book reviews and annual author and subject indexes.

American Society for Public Administration
1120 G Street, N.W., Suite 700
Washington, DC 20005-3885
Phone: (202) 393-7878
Fax: (202) 638-4952
E-mail: info@aspanet.org
Website: http://www.aspanet.org

RESEARCH TECHNOLOGY MANAGEMENT

Published six times per year, this journal discusses management issues for technical industries such as aerospace, automotive, chemical, computer, and electronics. Articles are on standards, innovation, business issues, government policy, and global cooperation. Includes book reviews. Some articles are available on audiotape.

Sheridan Press
P.O. Box 465
Hanover, PA 17331-0465
Phone: (202) 296-8811
Website: http://www.iriinc.org/v0000007.htm

THE SERVANT LEADER

This newsletter, published twice a year, focuses on the Greenleaf Center's work in servant leadership. Articles describe how companies apply the philosophy to practice and improve their bottom lines. Educators share ideas for teaching servant leadership. Includes book reviews, conference notices, and other learning resources.

Robert K. Greenleaf Center for Servant-Leadership
921 East 86th Street, Suite 200
Indianapolis, IN 46240
Phone: (317) 259-1241
Fax: (317) 259-0560
E-mail: greenleaf@iquest.net
Website: http://www.greenleaf.org

SIMULATION AND GAMING: AN INTERNATIONAL JOURNAL OF THEORY, PRACTICE, AND RESEARCH

This quarterly journal publishes original activities and reviews of board games, computer simulations, role plays, and other active learning products. There are research-based, empirical, and conceptual essays on the use of simulation and gaming in the classroom—often for the business classroom. Includes an annual index.

Sage Publications, Inc.
2455 Teller Road
Thousand Oaks, CA 91320-2234
Phone: (805) 499-0721
Fax: (805) 499-0871
E-mail: order@sagepub.com
Website: http://www.sagepub.com

STUDENT LEADER

This quarterly magazine helps campus leaders prepare to serve in student government, Greek organizations, and clubs. Featured are articles on ethical solutions for common problems, tips for public relations, national polls, and stories of successful student leadership.

Oxendine Publishing
P.O. Box 14081
Gainesville, FL 32604-2081
Phone: (352) 373-6907
Fax: (352) 373-8120
Website: http://www.studentleader.com

TRAINING MAGAZINE

This monthly magazine features articles for and by corporate training consultants. There are book reviews, many training tools advertised, and, in the January issue, a four-year conference-planning calendar.

Lakewood Publications, Inc.
Lakewood Building
50 South Ninth Street, Suite 400
Minneapolis, MN 55402-3165
Phone: (612) 333-0471
Fax: (612) 333-6526
Website: http://www.trainingsupersite.com

TRAINING & DEVELOPMENT

This monthly magazine addresses training concerns from multicultural issues to career development. Regular features include a trends update, information about new technology, Training 101 essays, tips for building a consulting business, and book reviews. The Marketplace is a directory of tools, seminars, and job ads.

American Society for Training & Development Inc.
1640 King Street, Box 1443
Alexandria, VA 22314-2043
Phone: (703) 683-8100
E-mail: mailbox@astd.org
Fax: (703) 683-8103
Website: http://www.astd.org

INSTRUMENTS

The items in this section measure a variety of leadership skills and styles. They range from brief, self-scored tests to ones administered by certified facilitators and accompanied by detailed, computer-generated profiles and action plans. An increasing number are 360-degree instruments that provide feedback from one's peers, direct reports, and superiors. Whenever possible, the descriptions include reference to critical reviews and support materials such as leader's guides or articles that describe using an instrument for development. Each entry, as applicable, includes:

- The instrument's purpose and scales to be measured.
- Administration.
- Brief information about the instrument's development, validity, and reliability; also a statement about the completeness of technical information received upon request.
- Author, publication date, and source. For source contact information, refer to the directory of Instruments and Exercises Vendors.
- Cost.
- Time necessary to administer the instrument.
- Number of items.
- Intended audience.
- Leadership Lesson—a subject descriptor.

To ensure that we included only valid and reliable instruments, the editors made every effort to get detailed information about the psychometric properties of each one that we considered. We requested information about the development of the scales and questions, validity and reliability studies, and norm data. The results we received can be categorized four ways:

- We received no information and could not include an instrument.
- We received little information and included the instrument with a disclaimer.
- We received incomplete information and included the instrument with a disclaimer.
- We received detailed information and indicate this in the description.

The editors recommend that facilitators gather detailed information about the psychometric properties of any instrument used for development purposes. If little or no information exists, one should use caution.

New
16PF® FIFTH EDITION HUMAN RESOURCE DEVELOPMENT REPORT

This test identifies personality factors by analyzing adjectives that describe human behavior. It focuses on five dimensions of management: leadership, interacting with others, making decisions, initiative, and personal adjustment. IPAT recommends using this tool to forecast a candidate's management potential and style.

Administration: Use on-site scoring software or return the answer sheet to IPAT for a five-page computer-generated report and narrative interpretation.

Development, Validity, and Reliability: The editors received detailed information about the psychometric properties of this instrument. The *Human Resource Development Report* is generated from the *16PF*, a standardized and validated personality questionnaire with a strong research base and norms for many populations, that has been in use for over 40 years.

Author and Source: (1994), IPAT
Cost: Ten tests: $12.50; 25 answer sheets: $12.50; *Report Manual*: $18; mail, phone, or fax scoring: $25 to $28; scoring software: $195
Time: 35 to 60 minutes
Number of Items: 185
Audience: Managers
Leadership Lesson: Personality

New
ACCESS MANAGEMENT SURVEY (AMS)

This survey measures managerial effectiveness in providing the necessary supports, both social and technical, to facilitate employee involvement in decision making and problem solving. There are 25 situations, each with two alternative responses. Managers rank how characteristic each response is of their own behaviors. Participant and feedback responses are applied to a "Star Chart" to reveal how well the manager handles employee access to problems, people, information, support systems, and solutions. Employees complete the feedback companion *Survey of Employee Access,* which is available separately.

Administration: This paper-and-pencil survey may be self-administered and self-scored. Interpretive information is included in the test booklet.

Development, Validity, and Reliability: The editors received incomplete information about the psychometric properties of this instrument. The scoring and interpretive section of the test booklet describes earlier research on the effects of employee involvement. Validity and reliability

data are presented without supporting documentation. No norms are provided.

Author and Source: Jay Hall (1989, 1993, 1995), Teleometrics International
Cost: $8.95
Time: 20 to 30 minutes
Number of Items: 25
Audience: Managers
Leadership Lesson: Empowerment

ATTITUDES TOWARD WOMEN AS MANAGERS (ATWAM)

The authors note that "because attitudes are pervasive and powerful influences on behavior, it is important to consider their role in the treatment—both by men and by other women—of women in managerial positions." They developed this instrument to overcome some reported deficiencies of previous instruments designed to measure these attitudes (e.g., ease of faking and tendency to respond in socially desirable ways). It consists of 12 items, with three possible responses for each item.

Administration: This self-scored instrument can be administered in a group setting or individually. Brief interpretation and feedback instructions are given.

Development, Validity, and Reliability: The editors received incomplete information about the psychometric properties of this instrument. Development of the instrument is briefly described and test-retest and internal-consistency reliability measures are reported. Norms for industry (manager and nonmanager) and student samples are presented for male and female groups.

Author and Source: Edward B. Yost & Theodore T. Herbert (1985). In L. D. Goodstein & J. W. Pfeiffer (Eds.), *The 1985 Annual: Developing Human Resources* (pp. 117-127). San Diego, CA: University Associates.
Cost: May be reproduced for educational use
Time: 15 minutes
Number of Items: 12 (two items are not scored)
Audience: General
Leadership Lesson: Women's Leadership

New
ATTRIBUTES OF LEADER BEHAVIOR QUESTIONNAIRE—FORM II

This test is based on the authors' syncretic model of charismatic and transformational leadership, which is a combination of existing models in one set of hypothesized causal and moderating relationships. There are six attributes of leader behavior: displays empathy, dramatizes mission, projects self-assurance, enhances image, assures followers of competency, and provides opportunities to experience success. Included in the same model but in a companion test, the *Follower Belief Questionnaire—Form II*, are key follower beliefs: inspiration, awe, and empowerment.

Administration: Both paper-and-pencil tests are written in language for the follower. Subject response is to be reverse-scored.

Development, Validity, and Reliability: The editors received incomplete information about the psychometric properties of this instrument. Scales were developed through literature review, expert judging, and factor analysis. Internal-consistency reliability coefficients are provided. Construct validity was tested by comparison with other instrument scales. There are no norms reported for these new tests.

Author and Source: Orlando Behling and James M. McFillen (1996). Behling, O., & McFillen, J. M. (1996), A syncretical model of charismatic/transformational leadership. *Group & Organization Management, 21*(2), 163-191. Contact the authors at the Department of Management, Bowling Green State University, Bowling Green, OH 43403. Phone: (419) 372-2946.
Cost: None
Time: 15 minutes total
Number of Items: 18 and 15
Audience: Managers, supervisors
Leadership Lesson: Charisma

BENCHMARKS®

This questionnaire is completed by a manager and his or her co-workers (peers, direct reports, boss) and measures a wide spectrum of management behaviors. The authors note that "it was developed from studying how managers develop rather than what they do." It is designed to help find trouble spots in potentially derailing managers and to suggest ways to build on strengths. Results are presented in three sections: 1) 16 skills that are predictive of success in organizations, 2) six derailment scales, and 3) handling challenging jobs. For all scales the respondent's score is compared to others' ratings and to Center for Creative Leadership norms. *Benchmarks* has been translated and adapted for use by participants in the UK and France. It is also available in multiple languages to allow English-speaking managers feedback from international raters. For a comprehensive review of this instrument, refer to J. B. Leslie & J. W. Fleenor (1998), *Feedback to Managers: A Review and Comparison of Multi-rater Instruments for Management Development* (3rd ed.), Greensboro, NC: Center for Creative Leadership.

Administration: Scoring is by computer. Participants receive detailed feedback information and a development guide for using the feedback to enhance their develop-

ment. Facilitators must attend a two-day certification workshop. *Benchmarks* is also available on the Internet.

Development, Validity, and Reliability: The editors received detailed information about the psychometric properties of this instrument. *Benchmarks* is based on extensive research on managers' developmental experiences. Items and scales were constructed based on this research and factor analysis. Reliability indices include test-retest, alpha, and interrater agreement. Several validity studies are reported using the following as criteria: assessment of promotability, performance evaluations, and a three-point measure—derailed/no change/promoted. A 1993 validity study conducted with a group of upper-level corporate managers found significant relationships between *Benchmarks* scales and ratings of executive performance. Normative comparisons are available for upper- and middle-level private- and public-sector managers as well as for managers in Asia, Australia, Belgium, Canada, Europe, France, Germany, Italy, Latin America, the Netherlands, Saudi Arabia, Sweden, Switzerland, the UK, and Venezuela.

Author and Source: Michael M. Lombardo & Cynthia D. McCauley (1988, 1990, 1993, 1994), Center for Creative Leadership
Cost: $245 (paper-and-pencil) or $275 (online)—includes one self-test, 11 observer tests, scoring, and development guide
Time: 30 to 40 minutes
Number of Items: 164
Audience: Executives, managers
Leadership Lesson: Leadership Development

New
THE BIRKMAN METHOD®

Participants respond to 125 statements about how they see most people and the same 125 statements about how they see themselves. They then respond to 48 possible career choices. The results are intended to link one's basic perceptions and values to career potential. There are ten scales attributed to the relative influence of social desirability: empathy, thought, esteem, change, authority, advantage, acceptance, activity, structure, and freedom. One report, the *Leadership Style Grid*, indicates a participant's style of leadership goals (direct or indirect involvement, task- or relationship-orientation), leadership styles (objective or subjective), environmental needs (objective or subjective), and leadership style when under stress.

Administration: Facilitators must complete Birkman Certification Training. The test may be administered by paper-and-pencil with computer scoring or administered and scored via Windows-based software, *Birkman 2000*SM.

Development, Validity, and Reliability: The editors received detailed information about the psychometric properties of this instrument. *The Birkman Method: Reliabilities and Validities Supplement* (1995) reports internal-consistency and test-retest reliability, and construct validity via correlation with a variety of personality and vocational-interest tests. Large cultural, gender, and ethnic norms are provided.

Author and Source: Roger W. Birkman (1950, 1951, 1952, 1954, 1956, 1967, 1972, 1991), Birkman International, Inc.
Cost: Test: $2.25; individual reports: $27.50 to $175; group reports are also available
Time: 60 to 90 minutes
Number of Items: 298
Audience: Managers
Leadership Lesson: Personality

CAMPBELL-HALLAM TEAM DEVELOPMENT SURVEY™ (TDS™)

Team members, team leaders, and outside observers respond by agreement or disagreement with statements related to interaction of team members, the guidance and direction of the team leader, and the team's ability to perform. Key strengths and weaknesses are assessed including: mission clarity, innovation, satisfaction, shared responsibility, communication, and unity. Individual and team profiles are generated by computer-scoring. A *Facilitator's Guide* offers detailed guidance for providing feedback and discussing results.

Administration: Instruments are computer-scored at NCS. Teams regroup for distribution of feedback, discussion, and action planning.

Development, Validity, and Reliability: The editors received detailed information about the psychometric properties of this instrument. The *TDS* manual reports several reliability and validity studies and provides a description of the instrument's development process. Norms are presented and discussed in the manual.

Author and Source: David Campbell & Glenn Hallam (1992, 1995), NCS Workforce Development
Cost: $15 per team member; $60 per team report
Time: 25 minutes
Number of Items: 166
Audience: Intact groups
Leadership Lesson: Teams

CAMPBELL LEADERSHIP INDEX™ (CLI®)

This is a self-other 100-adjective checklist. Respondents are asked to indicate on a six-point scale how descriptive each adjective is of them or of the leader they are rating.

The individual's self-evaluation of leadership characteristics is compared with the evaluations of others, thus allowing the individual to see patterns of leadership strengths and possible weaknesses. The *CLI* profile presents 22 standardized scoring measures within five orientations: leadership, energy, affability, dependability, and resilience. For a comprehensive review of this instrument, refer to J. B. Leslie & J. W. Fleenor (1998), *Feedback to Managers: A Review and Comparison of Multi-rater Instruments for Management Development* (3rd ed.), Greensboro, NC: Center for Creative Leadership.

Administration: Scoring is performed by NCS using optically scanned answer sheets. Before purchasing the *CLI,* users must complete a qualification form or attend an NCS certification workshop. Participants receive a lengthy feedback report including graphs that display both self-report and observer ratings on orientations, scales, and items. A *Development and Planning Guide* offers background information and assists respondents in interpreting and using their feedback. A detailed administrative and interpretive manual is available for trainers.

Development, Validity, and Reliability: The editors received detailed information about the psychometric properties of this instrument. Test-retest, internal-consistency, and interrater reliability studies are reported. Three major validity studies have been completed, as well as a research study comparing male and female responses.

Author and Source: David Campbell (1988, 1991), NCS Workforce Development
Cost: $195—includes one self-test, five observer tests, and development planning guide
Time: 20 to 30 minutes
Number of Items: 100
Audience: General
Leadership Lesson: Leadership Effectiveness

New
CHANGE ABILITATOR™

This instrument is based on research from the University of Texas about reaction to change. It is a revision of a previous instrument, the *Stages of Concern Questionnaire.* People whose team or organization is experiencing change commonly go through six predictable stages of concern. In the information stage, people need a general description about the change. Then, they often react as though the change is a personal threat. Next, people need detailed information about operational issues. Stage four is when change is accepted in small groups. Next, people must support the change at the organizational level. Stage six involves people who want to rewrite the change to suit their own goals. This instruments identifies employees and managers in each stage so that their concerns can be met.

Administration: This paper-and-pencil test includes a self-scoring profile form and guidelines for developing a personal action plan. The *Leader's Guide* contains interpretive information and suggestions for training with confidential scores and shared scores.

Development, Validity, and Reliability: The editors received incomplete information about the psychometric properties of this instrument. It is a newer version of the *Stages of Concern (SoC) Questionnaire,* which was based on research described in G. E. Hall, A. A. George, & W. L. Rutherford (1979), *Measuring Stages of Concern about the Innovation: A Manual for the Use of the SoC Questionnaire,* Austin, TX: Southwest Educational Development Laboratory. This older instrument reportedly has been extensively tested. The *Facilitator's Guide* reports internal reliability coefficients ranging from .64 to .83 and test-retest correlations. Validity studies included external construct correlation. About 1,500 teachers and school administrators provided norms. Since 1981, the *SoC* has been used as a data-gathering instrument in more than 100 doctoral dissertations.

Author and Source: LHE, Inc. (1994), HRD Press
Cost: Questionnaire: $7.95; *Leader's Guide*: $34.95
Time: 15 minutes
Number of Items: 30
Audience: General
Leadership Lesson: Change

New
CHANGE AGENT QUESTIONNAIRE (CAQ)

The *CAQ* measures personal philosophy about change and one's strategies for effecting change in others. It contains 45 alternative sets of attitudes to be ranked on a 10-point scale. In the scoring and interpretation section of the test booklet, concern for conformity and concern for commitment are applied to a grid format. When participants complete their grids, they learn about their one dominant and four back-up styles of change orientation.

Administration: This paper-and-pencil test may be self-administered and self-scored.

Development, Validity, and Reliability: The editors received incomplete information about the psychometric properties of this instrument. It was developed from the work of Herbert Kelman (1961), "The Induction of Conformity and Commitment," *Proceedings,* International Congress of Applied Psychology, and R. R. Blake & J. S. Mouton (1964), *The Managerial Grid*. Reliability and construct validity coefficients are briefly discussed. Limited norms are reported for individuals in science and

technology, manufacturing, semipublic businesses, sales, finance, human service, government, and law enforcement.

Author and Source: Jay Hall & Martha S. Williams (1969, 1973, 1988, 1994, 1995), Teleometrics International
Cost: $8.95
Time: 20 to 30 minutes
Number of Items: 45
Audience: General
Leadership Lesson: Change

CHANGE STYLE INDICATOR (CSI)

The *CSI* is designed to capture an individual's preferences in approaching change. Results place the respondent on a continuum that ranges from a *conserver* orientation to an *originator* orientation. Conservers prefer a gradual but continuous approach to change, whereas originators prefer a quicker and more radical approach. Stronger scores at either end of the continuum represent strength of preference, not degree of effectiveness or proficiency. The *CSI* can assist in understanding one's response to new situations and to changes in existing situations.

Administration: The *CSI* is a self-scoring instrument. The *User's Guide* contains both transparency masters and a PowerPoint presentation on the rationale and use of the instrument.

Development, Validity, and Reliability: Test-retest reliability data are reported in the *User's Guide*. Instrument validation was by expert panel (for item-content wording and content) and by comparison with other personality-style instruments.

Author and Source: W. Christopher Musselwhite & Robyn P. Ingram (1995), Aviat
Cost: $13.95—includes test and *Style Guide; Facilitator's Guide*: $125
Time: 15 minutes
Number of Items: 22
Audience: General
Leadership Lesson: Change

New
CHOICES™

This questionnaire measures learning agility, the ability to learn and benefit from experience. The authors identify four factors that correlate learning agility to high performance: 1) people agility—knowing oneself and remaining cool under pressure; 2) results agility—getting results in first-time or difficult situations; 3) mental agility—being comfortable with complexity, ambiguity, and explaining one's thinking to others; and 4) change agility—being curious, creative, and interested in building new skills. This test is part of the Leadership Architect® Suite, a set of tools for training needs analysis and succession planning.

Administration: The questionnaire is self-scored and self-interpreted. It is also available in a computerized version and as a set of cards.

Development, Validity, and Reliability: The editors received detailed information about the psychometric properties of this instrument. The four factors were originally developed from Lombardo's research on learning from experience, then tested in different organizations. Internal-consistency reliability is reported. A criterion validity study showed significant relationships between the factors and independent ratings of performance and potential. Limited norms are provided for gender, age ranges, and level of management.

Author and Source: Michael M. Lombardo & Robert W. Eichinger (1997), Lominger Limited, Inc.
Cost: $25—includes test and *User's Manual*
Time: 30 minutes
Number of Items: 81
Audience: High-potential managers
Leadership Lesson: Learning

COACHING PROCESS QUESTIONNAIRE (CPQ)

The *CPQ* assesses a manager's current coaching skills, from the recognition of employee achievements to the setting of goals for employee development. Four key elements of coaching are measured: diagnostic skills, coaching techniques, coaching qualities, and the ability to structure a coaching session. Self-evaluation, employee feedback, and comparison with a normed sample provide an indication of strengths and weaknesses. The interpretive notes include suggestions for improvement.

Administration: Self-scoring questionnaire.

Development, Validity, and Reliability: The editors received little information about the psychometric properties of this instrument. Reliability coefficients and norm groups are mentioned, without supporting documentation, in a brief letter from the publisher.

Author and Source: (1992), TRG Hay/McBer
Cost: Ten self-tests with interpretive notes: $60; ten other tests: $25
Time: 30 to 40 minutes
Number of Items: 40
Audience: Managers
Leadership Lesson: Coaching

New
COACHING SKILLS INVENTORY

This test is designed as a two-step process. Prior to training, participants take Part A to identify their strengths and weaknesses. Following training, participants take Part B to assess new coaching skills. In both parts, there are 18 coaching scenarios with four alternative actions. Participants choose the actions they would be most likely to take when opening a coaching meeting, getting agreement, exploring alternatives, getting a commitment to act, handling excuses, and closing the meeting.

Administration: The tests are self-scored. Interpretation and guidelines for improving coaching skills are provided in the test booklets.

Development, Validity, and Reliability: The editors received incomplete information about the psychometric properties of this instrument. The *Facilitator's Guide* describes scale development via expert panel and factor analysis, and provides reliability data for each of the six scales. Limited sample norms are provided for supervisors and managers in the pharmaceutical industry.

Author and Source: Kenneth R. Phillips (1987, 1991), HRDQ
Cost: Five participant booklets (A or B): $35; *Facilitator Guide*: $18
Time: 30 minutes—each part
Number of Items: 18—each part
Audience: Supervisors, managers, team leaders, facilitators
Leadership Lesson: Coaching

COMPASS: THE MANAGERIAL PRACTICES SURVEY

This instrument is designed to provide managers with information about their current behaviors on the job and to help them identify their strengths and expand their repertoire of effective management practices. Based on a 15-year research program, *COMPASS* measures 14 categories of management and leadership behaviors. These are: informing, clarifying, monitoring, planning, problem solving, consulting, delegating, inspiring, recognizing, rewarding, supporting, mentoring, networking, and team building. For a comprehensive review of this instrument, refer to J. B. Leslie & J. W. Fleenor (1998), *Feedback to Managers: A Review and Comparison of Multi-rater Instruments for Management Development* (3rd ed.), Greensboro, NC: Center for Creative Leadership.

Administration: Facilitators must be certified at a certification workshop provided by Manus. *COMPASS* is computer-scored by the vendor. A manual provides interpretive assistance and instrument background. Development and planning guides help participants understand feedback and make action plans for improvement.

Development, Validity, and Reliability: The editors received detailed information about the psychometric properties of this instrument. This instrument is research-based, with scales verified through factor analysis. Test-retest, internal-consistency, and interrater reliability information is provided, and three validation studies are reported. The norm group is a sample of 1,025 managers.

Author and Source: Gary Yukl (1984, 1988, 1990, 1995), Manus
Cost: $185 to $295 per participant
Time: 30 minutes
Number of Items: 94
Audience: Managers
Leadership Lesson: Leadership Development

New
THE COMPREHENSIVE LEADER: A NEW VIEW OF VISIONARY LEADERSHIP

The authors' premise is that at the heart of leadership is knowledge—about oneself, others, one's organization, and the world. Visionary leadership develops comprehensive knowledge and builds a future based on that knowledge. These two behaviors and four levels of knowledge are assessed in this 360-degree inventory. Participants respond to how well their behaviors match 40 statements of knowledge-based behavior. Others provide feedback on the same 40 items to create a comprehensive leadership profile.

Administration: This instrument may be self-administered and self-scored, but HRDQ recommends that a facilitator assist with interpretation and follow-up training. Training suggestions and transparency masters are included in the *Facilitator's Guide.*

Development, Validity, and Reliability: The editors received little information about the psychometric properties of this instrument. Initial instrument development by literature review, content analysis, and expert judgment is briefly described. Scale and overall reliability is reported in the .67 to .89 range. No validity data are available at this time. A *Technical Development Update* contains scoring norms based on a limited number of managers.

Author and Source: Eileen Russo & Laurie Ribble Libove (1996), HRDQ
Cost: Five participant booklets: $40; five feedback forms: $15; *Facilitator Guide*: $40
Time: 90 minutes

Number of Items: 40
Audience: Managers, executives, team leaders
Leadership Lesson: Vision

New
CONFLICT MANAGEMENT SURVEY (CMS)

The *CMS* assesses one's interpretation of conflict and subsequent handling of it. The survey contains 60 alternative sets of attitudes to be ranked on a 10-point scale. In the scoring and interpretation section of the test booklet, concern for personal goals and concern for relationships are applied to a grid format. After participants complete their grid, they learn their one dominant and four back-up styles of conflict management. Associates may respond to the feedback companion survey, *Conflict Management Appraisal,* which is available separately.

Administration: This paper-and-pencil test may be self-administered and self-scored.

Development, Validity, and Reliability: The editors received incomplete information about the psychometric properties of this instrument. The author briefly describes the development of the five scales via factor analysis and comparison to several personality tests. Reliability for the five scales is reported to range from .70 to .87. A single norm group of mixed populations is provided.

Author and Source: Jay Hall (1969, 1973, 1986, 1996), Teleometrics International
Cost: $8.95
Time: 30 to 45 minutes
Number of Items: 60
Audience: General
Leadership Lesson: Conflict Management

New
CREE QUESTIONNAIRE

This is a psychological test that measures an individual's creative-innovative potential. It has been used with a variety of populations, including managers and professionals. It provides scores on the following dimensions: social orientation—dominance and independence; work orientation—unstructured and under pressure; internal functioning—high energy, spontaneous, ideational; and interests—theoretical, artistic, and mechanical.

Administration: This paper-and-pencil instrument is hand-scored. Facilitators must have completed appropriate coursework in psychology or education and have some technical knowledge of instrument construction and use.

Development, Validity, and Reliability: The editors received detailed information about the psychometric properties of this instrument. The *Interpretation and Research Manual* describes the development of the questionnaire based on a limited sample of creative and noncreative engineers and a sample of 1,016 male subjects in a variety of jobs. Data are provided for factor analysis of original and revised scales. Scale validity was tested through correlation with other instruments. Norms are available for executives, professionals, technical managers, sales managers, and line managers. Predictive validity was examined using earning and job performance criteria.

Author and Source: T. G. Thurstone & John Mellinger (1996), NCS Workforce Development
Cost: 25 test booklets: $42; 25 scoring sheets: $34.75; *Interpretation and Research Manual*: $19.75
Time: 20 minutes
Number of Items: 145
Audience: Executives, line managers, technical managers
Leadership Lesson: Creativity

New
DENISON LEADERSHIP DEVELOPMENT SURVEY

This 360-degree instrument is based on the Denison Model, which is built on four traits of organizational culture and 12 leadership skills that impact organizational performance. Participants indicate how accurately 96 statements reflect their leadership effectiveness. Peers, direct reports, and superiors respond to the same statements to identify areas of strength and weakness.

Administration: Send self- and other surveys to Aviat for scoring. Receive a summary feedback report and guide for planning actions for development. The *Facilitator's Guide* includes instructions for delivering feedback and prescriptive guidelines for individual improvement.

Development, Validity, and Reliability: The editors received incomplete information about the psychometric properties of this instrument. The *Facilitator's Guide* describes the development from the Denison Model that is also the basis for the *Denison Organizational Culture Survey*. A sample of 220 self-assessments and more than 1,000 feedback-givers provides validation data. Analysis using Cronbach's Alpha established reliability in the .78 to .94 range. Factor analysis found internal consistency.

Author and Source: Daniel R. Denison & William S. Neale (1996), Aviat
Cost: $150—includes one self-survey, ten surveys for other, report, and action-planning guide; *Facilitator's Guide*: $125
Time: 20 minutes
Number of Items: 96
Audience: Managers
Leadership Lesson: Leadership Effectiveness

New
DENISON ORGANIZATIONAL CULTURE SURVEY

This instrument measures the underlying beliefs, values, and assumptions held by members of an organization. Participants indicate how accurately 60 statements reflect their organization's culture in four areas: 1) involvement—teamwork, empowerment, and development; 2) consistency—agreement, core values, and integration; 3) adaptability—customer focus, change, and learning; and 4) mission—vision, goals, and strategy. Aviat suggests using this instrument to benchmark an organization's culture to high- and low-performing organizations, to examine subcultures, to determine steps for performance improvement, or to manage transition during mergers or acquisitions.

Administration: Send to Aviat for scoring. Receive a summary report for a group or for the entire organization.

Development, Validity, and Reliability: The editors received incomplete information about the psychometric properties of this instrument. The development of the Denison Model, upon which this instrument is based, is described in the *Facilitator's Guide* and in D. R. Denison & A. K. Mishra (1995), "Toward a Theory of Organizational Culture and Effectiveness," *Organization Science,* 6(2), 204-223. A sample of top executives in 764 organizations provided support for the four scales. Factor analysis and multidimensional scaling support the construct validity of the instrument. Validity was demonstrated by a correlation between the four culture traits and high-performing organizations. Reliability is not directly addressed in the documentation provided.

Author and Source: Daniel R. Denison & William S. Neale (1994), Aviat
Cost: Test booklet and scoring: $12.95; report: $50; *Facilitator's Guide*: $125
Time: 15 minutes
Number of Items: 60
Audience: Intact work groups or an entire organization
Leadership Lesson: Organizations

DEVELOPMENTAL ADVISING INVENTORY: COLLEGIATE EDITION (DAI)

This inventory is designed to help college students understand the developmental tasks they face in this period of their lives. In the *Advisor's Guide* author Dickson states, "The *Developmental Advising Inventory (DAI)* is an assessment tool based primarily on the theory of young adult development outlined by Arthur W. Chickering (1969) and several other developmental psychologists. The major developmental tasks are conveyed through a wellness model with nine dimensions: intellectual, life planning, social, physical, emotional, sexual, cultural, spiritual, and political." Becoming an effective leader is assumed to require growth along all of these dimensions.

Administration: A 116-page *Advisor's Guide* (1993) provides theoretical background, detailed instructions for administration of the *DAI*, interpretation guidelines, an Applications section describing various campus settings in which the *DAI* may be used, and a history of the instrument's development. A *Student Guide* (1989, 1993) is available to help students use inventory results in their development planning. The inventory may be hand- or computer-scored.

Development, Validity, and Reliability: The authors received detailed information about the psychometric properties of this instrument. It was prenormed on a sample of 1,551 college and university students. The 1992 revision included an initial validation sample of 767. Internal-consistency reliability coefficients as well as construct and content validity studies are reported in the *Advisor's Guide* and in G. L. Dickson & T. R. McMahon (1991), "The *Developmental Advising Inventory*: A New Approach to Academic Advising," *NACADA Journal, 11*(1), 34-50.

Author and Source: Gary L. Dickson & Timothy R. McMahon (1989, 1992), Developmental Advising Inventories
Cost: 25 tests: $31.25; 25 answer sheets: $25; *Student Guide*: $1.75; *Advisor's Guide*: $15
Time: 30 minutes
Number of Items: 135
Audience: College students
Leadership Lesson: Self-development

DEVELOPMENTAL CHALLENGE PROFILE®: LEARNING FROM JOB EXPERIENCES (DCP)

This instrument is based on the concept that on-the-job experience is the best management-development tool. Managers can use it to identify the challenges in their existing jobs and to learn to see those challenges as growth opportunities. The content of the instrument is derived from the Center for Creative Leadership studies of how successful executives develop through job experiences. The *DCP* is intended to be used in conjunction with the *Benchmarks*® instrument or other developmental training programs.

Administration: This paper-and-pencil test is self-administered, and the completed questionnaire is sent to the Center for Creative Leadership for scoring and a computer-generated summary report.

Development, Validity, and Reliability: The editors received detailed information about the psychometric

properties of this instrument. The development of the instrument as well as internal-consistency and test-retest reliability figures are reported in the *Manual and Trainer's Guide*. Several validity studies are also discussed. Norms are provided for group characteristics and developmental components.

Author and Source: Marian N. Ruderman, Cynthia D. McCauley, Patricia J. Ohlott, & Morgan W. McCall, Jr. (1993, 1995), Center for Creative Leadership
Cost: Test and report: $20; *Manual and Trainer's Guide*: $15
Time: 20 to 30 minutes
Number of Items: 113
Audience: Executives, managers, and supervisors
Leadership Lesson: Leadership Development

New
DIMENSIONS OF LEADERSHIP PROFILE®

This instrument assesses leadership characteristics from two points of view—personal and situational. Participants rank the importance of five statements in 12 sets. Their scores are then plotted on a Leadership Wheel to learn their strengths in four areas: 1) character—enthusiasm, integrity, and self-renewal; 2) analysis—fortitude, perceiving, and judgment; 3) accomplishment—performing, boldness, and team building; and 4) interaction—collaborating, inspiring, and serving others.

Administration: This paper-and-pencil test may be self-administered and self-scored.

Development, Validity, and Reliability: The editors received incomplete information about the psychometric properties of this instrument. A research report describes development via a literature review and cluster analysis in a research sample. Internal-consistency reliability is reported to range from .61 to .86. Some validity data is provided. Limited gender, age, educational level, and occupational norms are available.

Author and Source: Miriam E. Kragness (1994), Carlson Learning Company
Cost: $12
Time: 15 to 30 minutes
Number of Items: 60
Audience: General
Leadership Lesson: Leadership Styles

EDUCATIONAL ADMINISTRATOR EFFECTIVENESS PROFILE (EAEP)

The *EAEP* is a self-other instrument designed to help educational administrators diagnose their administrative strengths and weaknesses as a guide to self-development. Eleven categories of administrative behavior are assessed:

setting goals and objectives, planning, making decisions and solving problems, managing business and fiscal affairs, assessing progress, delegating responsibilities, communicating, building and maintaining relationships, demonstrating professional commitment, improving instruction, and developing staff.

Administration: The *EAEP* is sold as a kit, which contains a self-description form, five description-by-others forms, scoring worksheets, item-by-item feedback, and a self-development guide. Feedback data include a graphic profile indicating relative strengths and weaknesses. A *Leader's Guide* gives additional background and administrative information.

Development, Validity, and Reliability: The editors received detailed information about the psychometric properties of this instrument. Internal-consistency and interrater reliability figures are reported in a 1987 study. Convergent and criterion validity information is provided. Scale norms based on a group of 100 administrators are also available.

Author and Source: Human Synergistics International (1984, 1988), Human Synergistics, Inc.
Cost: $45
Time: 30 to 45 minutes
Number of Items: 120
Audience: Educational administrators
Leadership Lesson: Educational Leadership

EMPOWERMENT PROFILE

This instrument is based on the Dimensional Empowerment Model that depicts eight dimensions of empowerment: autonomy, centrality, involvement, control, influence, resources, climate, and strengths. Participants respond to each question twice, once for themselves and once for their employees to gain the total picture of empowerment at work.

Administration: Background information and suggestions for training are available in the *Facilitator Guide*.

Development, Validity, and Reliability: The editors received little information about the psychometric properties of this instrument. Items come from a literature review and interview data. Reliability coefficients are mentioned in the *Facilitator Guide*. The authors state that "the instrument displays content validity in that it adequately covers the subject it purports to cover." No norms are provided.

Author and Source: John E. Jones & William L. Bearley (1988), HRDQ
Cost: Five participant booklets: $35; *Facilitator Guide*: $25
Time: 25 to 30 minutes

Number of Items: 99
Audience: Supervisors, managers, executives
Leadership Lesson: Empowerment

ENTREPRENEURIAL QUOTIENT (EQ)

The *EQ* identifies and measures an individual's ability to embrace change, innovation, improvement, and reform. Managerial traits measured are: risk tolerance, creativity, strategic thinking, and goal orientation. Personality traits measured are: extroversion, intuition, thinking, and perceiving. When the above traits are charted with an individual's ability to adapt, an entrepreneurial tendency may be identified and strengthened.

Administration: Using the diskette provided, a Windows-based program scores the instrument and prints an *EQ Guide*, a 16- to 20-page narrative report. Scoring by fax or mail is also available.

Development, Validity, and Reliability: The editors received detailed information about the psychometric properties of this instrument. This instrument was developed using expert judgments, interviews, analysis of related instruments, and statistical analysis. Scale reliability data and predictive validity studies are reported in the *User's Manual*. Subgroup standardized scores are presented.

Author and Source: (1994), Wonderlic Personnel Test, Inc.
Cost: $125—includes five tests, user's manual, and scoring software
Time: 25 to 35 minutes
Number of Items: 100
Audience: General
Leadership Lesson: Entrepreneurial Leadership

New
EXCELLENT MANAGER® PROGRAM

This 360-degree feedback instrument informs managers about their performance and employee perceptions of their leadership style. It is based on situational-leadership research that suggests leaders need a battery of four styles: directing, coaching, supporting, and delegating. The instrument also measures a manager's commitment to employees, customers, self-development, tasks, and the organization.

Administration: Participants and feedback-givers return their surveys to NCS, which prepares a detailed report. Participants then use their feedback report and the *Development Planning Guide* to make action plans for improvement.

Development, Validity, and Reliability: The editors received incomplete information about the psychometric properties of this instrument. A 1988 report by Bob Gable discusses the development of items and content validity through a literature review and construct validity through factor analysis. Internal-consistency reliabilities range from .83 to .89. Norms are provided for a sample of 1,520 individuals.

Author and Source: Keilty, Goldsmith, and Company (1987, 1988, 1991), NCS Workforce Development
Cost: $95
Time: 30 minutes
Number of Items: 66
Audience: Managers
Leadership Lesson: Leadership Styles

New
EXECUTIVE PROFILE SURVEY

This test is based on ten years of research to identify empirically the major self-attitudes, self-beliefs, and values patterns shared by executives. Eleven scales reflect the core of the occupational self-concept of 2,000 top-level executives, including bank presidents, Fortune 500 CEOs, newspaper editors, and college presidents. The scales are: ambition, assertiveness, enthusiasm, creativity, spontaneity, self-reliance, consideration, flexibility, emotional control, practicality, and efficiency.

Administration: This test can be completed with very little supervision. When complete, the answer sheet is sent to IPAT for machine-scoring. The interpretive report supports professional career counseling and is not intended for self-counseling.

Development, Validity, and Reliability: The editors received incomplete information about the psychometric properties of this instrument. Full details are in the *Perspectives on the Executive Personality* guide, which was unavailable to the editors at press time. IPAT reports that reliabilities range from .81 to .90, with a median of .85.

Author and Source: Virgil R. Lang (1978, 1983), IPAT
Cost: Ten reusable test booklets: $20; ten machine-scorable answer sheets: $10; guide: $18
Time: 45 minutes
Number of Items: 94
Audience: Executives
Leadership Lesson: Leadership Skills

New
INSIGHT INVENTORY®

Participants respond to 32 adjectives to describe their behavior at work and again to describe their behavior outside work. The scores reveal a profile of how individu-als get their own way (direct or indirect), respond to people (reserved or outgoing), pace activities (urgent or steady), and deal with details (unstructured or precise).

Administration: This paper-and-pencil test may be self-administered and self-scored.

Development, Validity, and Reliability: The editors received detailed information about the psychometric properties of this instrument. A *Technical Manual* describes development by factor analysis with large samples. Reliability measures include test-retest (.54 to .82) and internal consistency (.71 to .85). Comparisons of this test to the *Myers-Briggs Type Indicator*®, the *Sixteen Personality Factors*, and the *Self-Directed Search* personality and interest tests determined construct validity on all four scales. Norms are reported for adults, college students, high school students, and youth leadership camp participants. Norms are also provided by gender.

Author and Source: Patrick G. Handley (1988, 1990, 1991, 1995), HRD Press
Cost: Test A (with interpretive guide): $11.95; Test B (abbreviated version): $6.50; training manual and 45-minute video: $250
Time: 15 minutes
Number of Items: 64
Audience: General
Leadership Lesson: Self-development

INSTRUCTIONAL LEADERSHIP EVALUATION AND DEVELOPMENT PROGRAM (ILEAD)

ILEAD is a set of instruments used by school administrators, teachers, and students. It is designed to identify and measure school climate and leadership practices that are associated with measurable improvements in student achievement. Scales reported include: instructional leadership, commitment, personal values, motivational factors, and school district culture.

Administration: Completed answer sheets must be sent to MetriTech for scoring. Schools are then sent interpretive reports.

Development, Validity, and Reliability: The editors received detailed information about the psychometric properties of this instrument. Instrument development as well as reliability and validity studies are reported in journal articles. Validity measures include construct and criterion validity. The norm group is from schools in the Midwest.

Author and Source: Larry A. Braskamp & Martin L. Maehr (1985, 1988), MetriTech, Inc.
Cost: Contact the publisher
Time: Varies with each instrument
Number of Items: Varies with each instrument

Audience: K-through-12 students, teachers, and administrators
Leadership Lesson: Educational Leadership

INTERPERSONAL INFLUENCE INVENTORY (III)

This inventory helps individuals determine their interpersonal influence style by assessing the behaviors they use when they attempt to influence others. Inventory items are based on a behavior model that suggests a mix of open and candid behavior coupled with consideration of others. Four influence patterns are derived: assertive, passive, openly aggressive, and concealed aggressive. The author suggests that awareness of influence style has become increasingly important as organizations shift from being hierarchical to more collaborative.

Administration: This is a self-scored instrument. A *Facilitator Guide* discusses its background, provides guidelines for administration and interpretation, and offers suggestions for using it in training.

Development, Validity, and Reliability: The editors received incomplete information about the psychometric properties of this instrument. The *Facilitator Guide* discusses scale development via expert panel and factor analysis, and provides reliability data for each of the four scales. Limited sample norms are provided for retail management supervisors and managers. No validity data are reported.

Author and Source: Rollin Glaser (1983, 1986, 1990, 1993, 1995), HRDQ
Cost: Five tests: $27; *Facilitator Guide*: $20
Time: 60 to 90 minutes
Number of Items: 40
Audience: General
Leadership Lesson: Influence

INVENTORY OF BARRIERS TO CREATIVE THOUGHT AND INNOVATIVE ACTION

This test identifies internal and external factors that inhibit one's ability to create and innovate. Six categories of barriers are measured: concept of self, need for conformity, ability to abstract, ability to use systematic analysis, task achievement, and physical environment. The author hypothesizes that creative and innovative behavior will increase as a result of feedback from this instrument and subsequent awareness of personal inhibitors.

Administration: This test is self-administered and self-scored.

Development, Validity, and Reliability: The editors received little information about the psychometric properties of this instrument. Its development was based upon the work of Carl Rogers. Test-retest reliability is reported. Construct and content validity are briefly mentioned. No norms are available.

Author and Source: Lorna P. Martin (1990). In J. W. Pfeiffer, *The 1990 Annual: Developing Human Resources* (pp. 131-141). San Diego, CA: University Associates.
Cost: May be reproduced for educational use
Time: 20 minutes
Number of Items: 36
Audience: General
Leadership Lesson: Creativity

LEAD—LEADER EFFECTIVENESS AND ADAPTABILITY DESCRIPTION

The purpose of this inventory is to evaluate an individual's leadership style in terms of flexibility and adaptability. It describes this style in terms of *telling, selling, participating,* or *delegating* and indicates whether the style is appropriate in various situations. *LEAD Self* provides self-perception and feedback. *LEAD Other*, completed by the leader's associates, provides a group profile of the leader's style.

Administration: *LEAD* is a short self-scoring instrument. Software is available for in-house administration, scoring, and profiles.

Development, Validity, and Reliability: The editors received little information about the psychometric properties of this instrument. Reliability coefficients and a single-study criterion validity coefficient are reported in a data sheet.

Author and Source: Paul Hersey & Kenneth H. Blanchard (1989, 1993), HRD Press
Cost: Tests: $3.95; scoring: $2.95; profile: $2.95
Time: 10 minutes
Number of Items: 12
Audience: Managers
Leadership Lesson: Flexibility

LEADER ATTRIBUTES INVENTORY (LAI)

The *LAI* is designed to assess 37 attributes (characteristics, knowledge, skills, and values) related to successful performance as a leader in vocational education. Examples of attributes measured are "Insightful—reflects on the relationship among events and grasps the meaning of complex issues quickly," and "Personal integrity—speaks frankly and honestly and practices espoused values." This instrument is available in self-rating and rating-by-other versions. See also the *Leader Effectiveness Index*, described later in this section, which is a companion instrument to the *LAI*.

Administration: Three to five subordinates complete the other form. An administrator's guide includes scoring and interpretation information.

Development, Validity, and Reliability: The editors received detailed information about the psychometric properties of this instrument. Items were developed from the literature and interviews with experts. Reliability was assessed using test-retest, interrater, and internal-consistency methods. Face, content, and concurrent validity studies are reported in the manual. Limited norms are available for several educational-institution types.

Author and Source: Jerome Moss, Jr., Qetler Jensrud, Barry Johansen, & Hallie Preskill (1994, 1996), National Center for Research in Vocational Education (NCRVE)
Cost: 50 tests: $14; administrator's guide: $19.50; technical manual: $12.50
Time: 15 minutes
Number of Items: 37
Audience: Vocational education teachers and administrators
Leadership Lesson: Educational Leadership

LEADER BEHAVIOR ANALYSIS II™ (LBAII)

This self-other instrument provides leaders with information about their own and others' perceptions of their leadership styles. Items are presented in the form of typical job situations in which the leader and staff member would be involved together. Respondents select one of four leader decisions that would best describe the target leader's behavior in that situation. There are four leadership-style scales and two scales that measure flexibility and effectiveness. A related instrument, the *Supervisor Behavior Analysis II*, changes item wording slightly to reflect the level of supervisory responsibility. For a comprehensive review of this instrument, refer to J. B. Leslie & J. W. Fleenor (1998), *Feedback to Managers: A Review and Comparison of Multi-rater Instruments for Management Development* (3rd ed.), Greensboro, NC: Center for Creative Leadership.

Administration: The instrument is self-scored. Separate scoring forms are required. Usually the individual's boss, subordinates, and two associates complete the other version of the instrument. Directions are provided for interpreting responses.

Development, Validity, and Reliability: The editors received detailed information about the psychometric properties of this instrument. The *LBAII* is based on the situational leadership model of Hersey and Blanchard. A Blanchard report, *Research on the LBAII*, provides information on development, reliability, and validity. Reliability indices are provided, and one validity study is

reported using the Wilson *Multi-Level Management Survey* as a comparison. No norms are reported.

Author and Source: Kenneth H. Blanchard, Ronald K. Hambleton, Drea Zigarmi, & Douglas Forsyth (1985, 1991), Jossey-Bass/Pfeiffer
Cost: Test: $4.95; scoring: $4.95; profile: $4.95
Time: 20 minutes
Number of Items: 20
Audience: Managers
Leadership Lesson: Leadership Styles

LEADER EFFECTIVENESS INDEX (LEI)

The *LEI* provides a multi-rater assessment of the effectiveness of leadership performance in vocational education. It asks for ratings of individuals on the following tasks: "1) inspire a shared vision and establish standards that help the organization; 2) foster unity, collaboration, and ownership, and recognize individual and team contributions; 3) exercise power effectively and empower others to act; 4) exert influence outside of the organization; 5) establish an environment conducive to learning; and 6) satisfy the job-related needs of members of the organization as individuals." A seventh item asks for a rating of the leader's overall effectiveness. The *LEI* is a companion instrument to the *Leader Attributes Inventory*, described earlier in this section.

Administration: Three to five subordinates or peers who know the ratee well complete the form. The *LEI* produces a single score. Individualized feedback reports contain charts comparing this score with national norms.

Development, Validity, and Reliability: The editors received detailed information about the psychometric properties of this instrument. The six tasks were synthesized from the literature and from later validation studies. Construct validity was assessed with two studies, and several reliability measures are reported. Norms for several vocational education groups are available.

Author and Source: Jerome Moss, Jr. (1994, 1996), National Center for Research in Vocational Education (NCRVE)
Cost: 50 tests: $14; administrator's guide: $19.50; technical manual: $12.50
Time: 5 minutes
Number of Items: 7
Audience: Vocational education teachers and administrators
Leadership Lesson: Educational Leadership

LEADER REWARD AND PUNISHMENT QUESTIONNAIRE (LRPQ)

This questionnaire is designed to measure four leader-behavior variables related to the leader's use of reward and punishment. The four factors are: 1) performance-contingent reward behavior (the leader rewards high performance); 2) performance-contingent punishment (the leader punishes low performance); 3) noncontingent punishment (the leader's punishments are unrelated to performance); and 4) noncontingent reward (the leader's rewards are unrelated to performance).

Administration: This paper-and-pencil test is administered by a facilitator.

Development, Validity, and Reliability: The editors received detailed information about the psychometric properties of this instrument. The four scales were developed through factor analysis. Scale reliabilities are reported. Criterion validity was supported with the finding that contingent-reward leaders had the most satisfied, productive subordinates. Norms are provided for six sample groups.

Author and Source: P. M. Podsakoff, W. D. Todor, R. A. Grover, & V. L. Huber (1984), "Situational Moderators of Leader Reward and Punishment Behaviors: Fact or Fiction?" *Organizational Behavior and Human Performance, 34,* 21-63. Contact Philip Podsakoff, Department of Management, School of Business, Indiana University, Bloomington, IN 47405. Phone (812) 855-9209.
Cost: Contact the authors for availability and research use
Time: 10 minutes
Number of Items: 23
Audience: General
Leadership Lesson: Leadership Effectiveness

LEADERSHIP DEVELOPMENT REPORT (LDR)

The *LDR* is an interpretive report derived from two general personality measures, the *Jackson Personality Inventory (JPI)* and the *Personality Research Form (PRF).* Hagberg and Jackson developed and elaborated the implications of high and low scores on these two personality questionnaires as they would affect managerial behavior. The *LDR* provides information for managers seeking individual career guidance.

Administration: Tests must be administered and interpreted by a certified individual, although the actual taking of the tests does not require supervision. Answer sheets are faxed to Sigma Assessment Systems. A computerized report is sent to the participant's counselor who reviews the report with the participant in a confidential feedback session.

Development, Validity, and Reliability: The editors received detailed information about the psychometric properties of the two origin instruments. Extensive research work has been published for the individual instruments used to generate the *LDR.* Norms are based on the responses of 1,500 male and female executives.

Author and Source: Richard A. Hagberg & Douglas N. Jackson (1993), Sigma Assessment Systems, Inc.
Cost: $90
Time: 45 minutes per test
Number of Items: *JPI*: 320; *PRF*: 352
Audience: Executives, managers
Leadership Lesson: Leadership Development

LEADERSHIP INVENTORY

This 360-degree-feedback instrument focuses on thoughts and behaviors that result in others' accepting direction and working together. There are ten scales, including: influences others to accomplish the unit's objectives, maintains the wholeness and integrity of the unit, builds trust, and models ethical behavior.

Administration: This instrument is self-administered and self-scored.

Development, Validity, and Reliability: The editors received incomplete information about the psychometric properties of this instrument. Development, reliability, and limited validity data are reported in a paper available from Stephen Stumpf.

Author and Source: Stephen A. Stumpf (1993, 1995). Available from the Center for Leadership, University of Tampa, 401 West Kennedy Boulevard, Tampa, FL 33606-1490. Phone: (813) 253-6221. Fax: (813) 258-7408.
Cost: $5
Time: 20 to 30 minutes
Number of Items: 50
Audience: General
Leadership Lesson: Leadership Skills

LEADERSHIP OPINION QUESTIONNAIRE (LOQ)

This instrument measures consideration and structure, two factors that evolved from the Ohio State leadership studies. It is a self-report format in which respondents indicate how frequently they feel they should do what is described in each item. A high score on the consideration scale suggests an emphasis on the group-process and human-relations aspects of managing, while a high structure score reflects a need to actively direct and structure tasks and activities. The *Examiner's Manual* suggests that the *LOQ*, which is completed by the supervisor, may be used in conjunction with a companion instrument, the *Supervisory Behavior Description*

Questionnaire, which is completed by subordinates on how their managers behave. Users should be aware that these are separate instruments, not different versions of the same instrument.

Administration: Facilitators must have completed appropriate coursework in psychology or education and have some technical knowledge of instrument construction and use. The instrument may be scored by hand or computer. An *Examiner's Manual* (1989) provides a description of the *LOQ* and information on usage, development, reliability, and validity.

Development, Validity, and Reliability: The editors received detailed information about the psychometric properties of this instrument. The instrument grew out of a long history of leadership research at The Ohio State University. The dimensions were developed and refined using factor-analytic techniques. Internal-consistency and test-retest reliability coefficients are reported in the manual, along with reviews of construct and criterion validity studies.

Author and Source: Edwin A. Fleishman (1960-1969, 1989), NCS Workforce Development
Cost: Package of 25 test booklets: $40; *Examiner's Manual*: $19.75; scoring software: $129
Time: 10 to 15 minutes
Number of Items: 40
Audience: Supervisors, managers
Leadership Lesson: Interpersonal Relations

LEADERSHIP ORIENTATIONS

Leadership Orientations comes in two forms: 1) a brief self-report, self-scoring instrument; and 2) a longer, self-and-other feedback instrument that enables respondents to compare their self-perception with the perceptions of colleagues. Both versions are based on the *four-frame* model developed by Bolman and Deal. It measures individuals' orientations toward one of four *frames* or *lenses* for understanding leadership and organizations: 1) a structural lens that views leaders as analysts and social architects, 2) a human resource lens that views leaders as catalysts and servants, 3) a political lens that views leaders as advocates and negotiators, and 4) a symbolic lens that views leaders as poets and prophets. This instrument has been used in a number of populations including corporate managers inside and outside the U.S., higher education administrators, school leaders, and health care administrators.

Administration: The self-report version may be self-scored. A two-page handout provides directions for self-scoring and includes a graphic display of the results. The self-and-other version provides stronger data, but requires computer scoring to produce individualized portraits. One

special feature is that respondents are encouraged to divide raters into different role groups so that participants receive both individual and cohort results. There are supplemental materials to help them interpret results.

Development, Validity, and Reliability: The editors received incomplete information about the psychometric properties of this instrument. *Leadership Orientations* was originally developed for research on leadership and has been used in a number of published research studies. The authors report that the internal reliability of the scales is very good and that the instrument has been validated against a number of other leadership instruments.

Author and Source: Lee G. Bolman & Terrence E. Deal (1990, 1995). Available from Lee G. Bolman, Bloch School of Business, University of Missouri–Kansas City, 5100 Rockhill Road, Kansas City, MO 64110. Phone: (816) 235-5407. Fax: (816) 235-2947. E-mail: lbolman@cctr.umkc.edu
Cost: The instrument is available for free if used for research or self-scored. Scoring and analysis are available for $25 per self-report (regardless of the number of other responses).
Time: 15 minutes
Number of Items: 6 forced-choice items
Audience: General
Leadership Lesson: Self-development

LEADERSHIP/PERSONALITY COMPATIBILITY INVENTORY (L/PCI)

This inventory is designed to help managers understand how the compatibility between basic personality style and leadership role may affect leadership effectiveness. A personality inventory measures four dominant personality types: bold, expressive, sympathetic, or technical. A leadership role inventory measures leadership characteristics: active/competitive, persuasive/interactive, precise/systematic, and willing/steady.

Administration: The two parts of the *L/PCI* are self-administered and self-scored. Interpretations are provided on the back of the scoring sheets. Data from the two inventories are plotted on a compatibility graph.

Development, Validity, and Reliability: The editors received little information about the psychometric properties of this instrument. Internal-consistency reliability is reported only for the personality-style section. Validity studies were reportedly done, but no specific data are provided.

Author and Source: James H. Brewer (1990, 1994), Associated Consultants in Education
Cost: $6.95
Time: 30 minutes

Number of Items: Part one—32; Part two—16
Audience: General
Leadership Lesson: Personality

LEADERSHIP PRACTICES INVENTORY (LPI)

This instrument is based on the premise that leadership is an observable, learnable set of practices and that those with the desire and persistence to lead can improve their leadership skills. The five practices measured are: challenging the process, inspiring a shared vision, enabling others to act, modeling the way, and encouraging others. According to the authors, "The *LPI* helps you discover to what extent you have incorporated these five practices into your everyday behavioral repertoire." The two forms of the instrument (self-assessment and observer) allow self-evaluation and evaluation by others. For a comprehensive review of this instrument, refer to J. B. Leslie & J. W. Fleenor (1998), *Feedback to Managers: A Review and Comparison of Multi-rater Instruments for Management Development* (3rd ed.), Greensboro, NC: Center for Creative Leadership. Variations of this instrument include: *LPI-Delta* to assess changes in leadership practices, *Team LPI* to measure behaviors common to high-performing teams, and *LPI-Individual Contributor* to help nonmanagers assess their behaviors and develop leadership strengths. A student version is described in this book.

Administration: The *LPI* can be self-scored or computer-scored. The computer scoring generates a feedback printout. A facilitator's manual provides interpretive and background information, and a development guide helps individuals use the feedback provided.

Development, Validity, and Reliability: The editors received detailed information about the psychometric properties of this instrument. Its development was based on a program of research by Kouzes and Posner. Reliability was determined using test-retest, internal-consistency, and interrater methods. Validity was tested against an independent measure of leadership effectiveness. Feedback scales were verified with factor analysis. Norms have been developed for a number of populations.

Author and Source: Barry Z. Posner & James M. Kouzes (1988, 1993, 1997), Jossey-Bass/Pfeiffer
Cost: Test and participant's manual: $12.95; observer test: $3.95; *Facilitator's Guide* and software: $140
Time: 10 minutes
Number of Items: 30
Audience: Managers
Leadership Lesson: Leadership Skills

LEADERSHIP PRACTICES INVENTORY–STUDENT (LPI-STUDENT)

This is an instrument designed for assessing and studying leadership in college students. It can be used alone or with an *other* version for constituent feedback. It grew out of the original *Leadership Practices Inventory* developed by Kouzes and Posner, which rests on a model of effective leadership based on specific behaviors of people when they are at their personal best as leaders. The premise for the development of a student version is that leadership assessment techniques that are appropriate for business and public-sector organizations are probably not appropriate in the college environment. *LPI-Student* measures five scales: challenging the process, inspiring a shared vision, enabling others to act, modeling the way, and encouraging the heart.

Administration: The *Student's Workbook* contains a scoring guide, interpretation, and suggested actions. The *Facilitator's Guide* contains background information, workshop designs, and masters for overheads.

Development, Validity, and Reliability: The editors received detailed information about the psychometric properties of this instrument. It was developed with a population of outstanding student leaders, then pilot-tested and validated on additional student-leader groups. Test-retest and internal reliabilities are available in the *Facilitator's Guide*. Criterion validity was measured by comparing instrument scores to leader-effectiveness assessments. Norms are reported for presidents of Greek organizations, resident assistants, peer educators, student body presidents, orientation advisors, high school students, and by gender. Several articles describing the development and use of the instrument are available.

Author and Source: Barry Z. Posner & Barbara Brodsky (1992, 1998), Jossey-Bass/Pfeiffer
Cost: Self test: $2.50; observer test: $1.50; *Student's Workbook*: $7.50; *Facilitator's Guide*: $19.95
Time: 20 minutes
Number of Items: 30
Audience: Students
Leadership Lesson: Leadership Skills

LEADERSHIP QUESTIONNAIRE

This questionnaire is based on the Conger-Kanungo scale of charismatic leadership, which includes three stages. The first is environmental assessment—the ability to recognize opportunities and constraints in the environment. The next stage is vision formulation—the ability to create and communicate an inspirational vision. The final stage is implementation—the leader's perceived personal risk and extraordinary behavior.

Administration: This test is self-administered and self-scored.

Development, Validity, and Reliability: The editors received detailed information about the psychometric properties of this research instrument. An initial questionnaire was based on the authors' manager behavior descriptions, combined with items from other instruments. Factor analysis supported the behavioral dimensions proposed by the authors' model. Reliability data are provided, as well as the results of concurrent and discriminant validity studies, in an article by Conger and Kanungo.

Author and Source: (1994). Available from Jay A. Conger, Executive Director, The Leadership Institute, School of Business Administration, 308-D Bridge Hall, University of Southern California, Los Angeles, CA 90089-1421. Phone: (213) 740-4318. Fax: (213) 740-0200. E-mail: jconger@sba.usc.edu. Also available in J. A. Conger & R. N. Kanungo (in press), *Charismatic Leadership in Organizations,* Thousand Oaks, CA: Sage.
Cost: This is a research instrument; contact the authors.
Time: 10 minutes
Number of Items: 25
Audience: Managers
Leadership Lesson: Charisma

New
LEARNING STYLES QUESTIONNAIRE

This questionnaire helps individuals learn about their preferences for four learning styles. *Activists* are dominated by immediate experiences, get excited by new challenges, and are bored with implementation. *Reflectors* collect data, analyze experiences, and are cautious to act on new learnings. *Theorists* prefer logical, complex, integrated learning based on sound principles and systems thinking. *Pragmatists* seek out new ideas to put into practice.

Administration: This instrument is self-administered and self-scored. Interpretive and usage guidelines are in the test booklet. The *Facilitator Guide* contains suggestions for training.

Development, Validity, and Reliability: The editors received incomplete information about the psychometric properties of this instrument. The *Facilitator Guide* briefly discusses the theories of learning styles that led to the authors' model. Reliability was established by test-retest correlation of .89. Construct validity has not been established. A wide variety of occupational norms, including supervisory and management groups, are reported, as are cultural and gender norms.

Author and Source: Peter Honey & Alan Mumford (1986, 1989, 1995), HRDQ
Cost: Five tests: $27; five workbooks: $30; *Facilitator Guide*: $35
Time: 90 minutes
Number of Items: 80
Audience: General
Leadership Lesson: Learning

LEAST PREFERRED CO-WORKER SCALE (LPC)

This self-report instrument is primarily for research use. It attempts to measure whether a leader is primarily relationship-oriented or task-oriented. The format is somewhat unusual in that the items involve describing someone with whom the respondent *least* likes to work. The relative negativity of these scores determines whether the individual is seen as relationship-oriented (less negative) or task-oriented (more negative). The *LPC* grew out of Fiedler's development of a contingency theory of leadership (see Fiedler & Chemers, *Leadership and Effective Management*, Glenview, IL: Scott Foresman, 1974).

Administration: The overall *LPC* score is a simple sum of the item scores.

Development, Validity, and Reliability: The editors received incomplete information about the psychometric properties of this instrument. Reliability measures using internal-consistency and test-retest procedures are reported. Predictive validity studies seem to show that task-motivated leaders perform well in very favorable or very unfavorable situations, while relationship-oriented leaders do best in moderately favorable situations, an outcome consistent with Fiedler's contingency model.

Author and Source: Fred E. Fiedler (1967, 1984). In Fred E. Fiedler & Martin M. Chemers, *Improving Leadership Effectiveness: The Leader Match Concept* (2nd ed.), 17-27. New York: Wiley, 1984.
Cost: May be used as a research instrument
Time: 5 minutes
Number of Items: 18
Audience: General
Leadership Lesson: Interpersonal Relations

LEATHERMAN LEADERSHIP QUESTIONNAIRE (REVISED) (LLQ)

The *LLQ* seeks to assess an individual's knowledge of 27 leadership skill areas including: assigning work, coaching, giving feedback, performance appraisal, and managing change. It was designed to be, among other things, a paper-and-pencil alternative to assessment centers for leadership selection, training, or program evaluation. The companion feedback instrument is for superiors, subordinates, peers, and customers to rate participants in the same 27 skill areas.

Administration: No special training is needed to administer the *LLQ*. It takes three to five hours to complete, but may be given in two sessions. Scoring is done by the publisher and both individual and aggregate feedback reports are provided.

Development, Validity, and Reliability: The editors received little information about the psychometric properties of this instrument. Item development was through an expert panel and site samples. Reliability and validity studies are described in a separately published *LLQ Research Report.*

Author and Source: Richard W. Leatherman (1987, 1992), International Training Consultants, Inc.
Cost: $1,500—includes administrator's manual, ten reusable tests, ten self-development manuals, ten answer sheets with scoring service, and a research report
Time: 3 to 5 hours
Number of Items: 339
Audience: Managers, team leaders
Leadership Lesson: Leadership Skills

LIFE STYLES INVENTORY® (LSI)

This instrument was developed "to assist individuals in identifying and understanding their thinking patterns and self-concept." The 12 scales (thinking styles) that make up the instrument are: humanistic-encouraging, affiliative, approval, conventional, dependent, avoidance, oppositional, power, competitive, perfectionistic, achievement, and self-actualization. For a comprehensive review of this instrument, refer to J. B. Leslie & J. W. Fleenor (1998), *Feedback to Managers: A Review and Comparison of Multi-rater Instruments for Management Development* (3rd ed.), Greensboro, NC: Center for Creative Leadership.

Administration: The *LSI* is available in a self-form and a form that allows rating by others. It may be self-scored or scored by Human Synergistics. A *Leader's Guide* covers administration, scoring, and interpretation, and a *Self-development Guide* tells how to use the instrument and its scores. No special certification is required to administer the instrument.

Development, Validity, and Reliability: The editors received detailed information about the psychometric properties of this instrument. Reliability data include internal consistency and interrater figures. Validity studies are reported in the manual and in others' research. The 240 items and the 12 resultant scales are conceptually based on Maslow's hierarchy of needs (security versus

satisfaction) and on several other research themes that differentiate a people versus a task orientation. The scale was normed on a sample of over 9,000 adults.

Author and Source: J. Clayton Lafferty (1989), Human Synergistics, Inc.
Cost: $51—includes one self-test, five other tests, a *Self-development Guide*, scoring instructions, and a *Profile Supplement; Leader's Guide: $125*
Time: 30 minutes
Number of Items: 240
Audience: General
Leadership Lesson: Self-development

MANAGEMENT APTITUDE TEST (MAT)

The *MAT* measures an individual's ability to perform day-to-day management responsibilities such as decision making, problem solving, administration, supervisory skills, planning, organizing, public relations, financial skills, and communication. Candidates respond to situational questions that assess mental abilities and business knowledge. This test is used primarily for employee screening.

Administration: The test is administered and interpreted by a facilitator. Scoring may be done via a toll-free telephone call or with Quanta software, which is available from NCS.

Development, Validity, and Reliability: The editors received detailed information about the psychometric properties of this instrument. Test items were developed using data from a literature review and job analysis using managers from a number of industries. Norms from a sample of 364 managers are available.

Author and Source: (1993), NCS Workforce Development
Cost: $33 to $35; Quanta software: $89
Time: 90 minutes
Number of Items: 45
Audience: Managers
Leadership Lesson: Leadership Skills

New
MANAGEMENT SUCCESS PROFILE (MSP)

This tool is used to identify leadership and management potential. Questions fall into ten scales: work background, leadership, management responsibility, productivity, customer-service orientation, practical thinking, adaptability, coaching, business ethics, and job commitment. Candidness and accuracy measures are included. An NCS computerized report indicates positive and negative behavior indicators, suggested interview questions, and an overall score called the Management Potential Index.

Administration: This test is administered by a human resources professional. Test results may be phoned or faxed to NCS or scored in-house with NCS software.

Development, Validity, and Reliability: The editors received incomplete information about the psychometric properties of this instrument. A report from Gary Behrens describes a validation study with 47 executives and managers at a drilling company. Brief data are reported for correlation of the scales by factor analysis and performance ratings. No development or reliability information is available.

Author and Source: (1996), NCS Workforce Development
Cost: $28 to $31
Time: No time limit
Number of Items: 156
Audience: Supervisors, managers, team leaders
Leadership Lesson: Leadership Development

MANAGERIAL COMPETENCY QUESTIONNAIRE (MCQ)

This instrument defines a competency as an underlying characteristic in a person's behavior and asserts that there is a link between competencies and performance. The *MCQ* tests seven competencies that are presumed to be critical to outstanding performance in managerial roles. These competencies are rated according to the frequency with which the manager has practiced them in the past six months: achievement orientation, developing others, directiveness, impact and influence, interpersonal understanding, organizational awareness, and team leadership. This instrument is an updated and revised version of the *Managerial Competency Assessment Questionnaire*.

Administration: Managers, colleagues, and employees may administer their own tests. Scoring is done by a neutral third person.

Development, Validity, and Reliability: The editors received little information about the psychometric properties of this instrument. Reliability coefficients and norm groups are mentioned, without supporting documentation, in a brief letter from the publisher.

Author and Source: McBer & Company (1994, 1997), TRG Hay/McBer
Cost: Ten questionnaires with interpretive notes: $60; ten feedback questionnaires: $25; ten development guides: $45
Time: 30 to 40 minutes
Number of Items: 56
Audience: Managers
Leadership Lesson: Leadership Skills

MANAGERIAL PHILOSOPHY SCALE (MPS)

The *MPS* is based on Douglas MacGregor's Theory X and Theory Y view of human motivation described in his book, *The Human Side of Enterprise* (McGraw-Hill, 1960). Theory Y suggests that employees are motivated by intrinsic rewards and typically desire more self-control. Theory X proponents believe that employees need to be controlled by extrinsic rewards and punishments. *MPS* test-takers agree or disagree with assumptions and generalizations about people in work settings to reveal attitudes affecting the superior-subordinate relationship. Subordinates complete the feedback companion instrument, the *Reality Check Survey*, which is available separately.

Administration: Both instruments are self-administered. Scoring and interpretation are done by the manager or a third party.

Development, Validity, and Reliability: The editors received little information about the psychometric properties of this instrument. Internal-consistency reliability and construct validity coefficients are briefly mentioned, but not documented, in the test booklet. Norms for a managerial population are available.

Author and Source: Jacob Jacoby & James R. Terborg (1975, 1980, 1986, 1989, 1994, 1995), Teleometrics International
Cost: $8.95
Time: 15 to 30 minutes
Number of Items: 36
Audience: Managers
Leadership Lesson: Theory X and Theory Y

MANAGERIAL STYLE QUESTIONNAIRE (MSQ)

Measures managerial style in six dimensions: coercive, authoritative, affiliative, democratic, pace-setting, and coaching. The employee version of the *MSQ* provides the manager feedback from his employees or peers. "The purpose of the *MSQ* is to stimulate thinking about which styles are currently used, and which can be used most effectively to deal with various situations." The test is available in a Spanish translation.

Administration: This test is self-administered and self-scored. A separate publication, *The MSQ Profile and Interpretive Notes*, contains the scoring key, profile, definitions, and normative data.

Development, Validity, and Reliability: The editors received incomplete information about the psychometric properties of this instrument. The *MSQ*'s development is based on an earlier instrument used since the 1970s. Test-retest reliability and construct validity data are presented in the *MSQ Trainer's Guide*. Criterion validity and norms are briefly mentioned.

Author and Source: McBer & Company (1980, 1994), TRG Hay/McBer

Cost: Ten self tests and profiles with interpretive notes: $60; ten feedback tests: $25; *MSQ Trainer's Guide*: $25

Time: 20 minutes

Number of Items: 36

Audience: Executives, managers, supervisors

Leadership Lesson: Leadership Styles

MANAGERIAL WORK-VALUES SCALE (MWVS)

Originally developed to measure the work values of medical doctors, the instrument was later revised to measure managers' work values. It focuses on nine values: creativity, economics, independence, status, service, academics, security, collegiality, and work conditions. A paired-comparison format is used to establish the relative strengths of the values for the individual.

Administration: This self-scoring instrument can be self-administered or given in a group setting. An interpretation sheet provides a ranking of values and a brief explanation of each value; a short Action Plan section provides guidelines for change.

Development, Validity, and Reliability: The editors received incomplete information about the psychometric properties of this instrument. Test-retest reliability figures are provided, as is a brief discussion of concurrent and content validity.

Author and Source: T. Venkateswara Rao (1991). In J. W. Pfeiffer, *The 1991 Annual: Developing Human Resources* (pp. 163-177). San Diego, CA: University Associates.

Cost: May be reproduced for educational use

Time: 20 to 30 minutes

Number of Items: 36

Audience: Managers

Leadership Lesson: Values

New
MATRIX

This instrument measures nine influence tactics: rational persuasion, inspirational appeal, consultation, ingratiation, personal appeal, exchange, coalition, pressure, and legitimation. Self-reported scores are compared to feedback from others to create an influence-behavior profile. A companion workbook contains interpretive information and dozens of exercises to help participants learn about types of power and appropriate times to use each influence tactic. For a comprehensive review of this instrument, refer to J. B. Leslie & J. W. Fleenor (1998),

Feedback to Managers: A Review and Comparison of Multi-rater Instruments for Management Development (3rd ed.), Greensboro, NC: Center for Creative Leadership.

Administration: Facilitators must be certified at a certification workshop provided by Manus. *Matrix* is computer-scored by the vendor. A manual provides interpretive assistance and instrument background. A workbook helps participants understand their feedback and plan actions for improvement.

Development, Validity, and Reliability: The editors received incomplete information about the psychometric properties of this instrument. *Matrix* was developed from the *Influence Behavior Questionnaire*. A preliminary report on the development and validation of that instrument is available from Manus. It describes the scale development through author research, literature on influence behavior, factor analysis, and content validity. Internal-consistency and test-retest stability reliability data range from .56 to .90. Two validity studies examined the correlation between *IBQ* scales and various criteria of leadership effectiveness.

Author and Source: Gary Yukl, Rick Lepsinger, & Toni Lucia (1997), Manus

Cost: $300 to $365 per participant

Time: 20 minutes

Number of Items: 45

Audience: Executives, managers, supervisors

Leadership Lesson: Influence

MULTIFACTOR LEADERSHIP QUESTIONNAIRE (MLQ)

The *MLQ* measures transformational and transactional leadership skills as developed and defined by James MacGregor Burns, Bernard Bass, and others. Five scales reflect transformational leadership and three reflect transactional leadership. Additionally, there is a "non-transactional leadership" scale and three organizational-outcome scales. The transformational scales are idealized influence (attributions), idealized influence (behaviors), inspirational motivation, intellectual stimulation, and individualized consideration. The transactional scales are contingent reward, active management-by-exception, and passive management-by-exception. The three organizational-outcome scales are extra effort, effectiveness, and satisfaction. For a comprehensive review of this instrument, refer to J. B. Leslie & J. W. Fleenor (1998), *Feedback to Managers: A Review and Comparison of Multi-rater Instruments for Management Development* (3rd ed.), Greensboro, NC: Center for Creative Leadership. This instrument is available in 11 languages. A

Team MLQ is also available for assessing the leadership style of a work team.

Administration: This instrument is completed by a manager and a full range of raters (higher organizational level, same organizational level, lower organizational level, and don't want organizational level to be known). Vendor scoring provides an extensive, tailored interpretive report, including graphics and suggestions for improving leadership. Contact Mind Garden about using the *MLQ* as a research instrument.

Development, Validity, and Reliability: The editors received detailed information about the psychometric properties of this instrument. The *MLQ* is based on many studies of managers in varied kinds of organizations. The feedback scales were developed through factor analysis. Reliability studies include test-retest, internal-consistency, and interrater. A number of validity studies are reported. Over 75 academic research studies have been completed and others are underway. Cross-national validity of the *MLQ* is discussed in B. M. Bass (1997), "Does the Transactional-Transformational Leadership Paradigm Transcend Organizational and National Boundaries?" *American Psychologist, 52*(2), 130-139.

Author and Source: Bernard M. Bass & Bruce J. Avolio (1985, 1989, 1990, 1995), Mind Garden, Inc.
Cost: $125—includes self-test, six feedback tests, computer-scoring, and interpretive report
Time: 10 minutes
Number of Items: 45
Audience: Executives, managers, supervisors
Leadership Lesson: Transformational Leadership

New
MYERS-BRIGGS TYPE INDICATOR® STEP II (MBTI)

This instrument is used in some organizations for leadership development purposes. It is based on Jung's theory of types, measuring four bipolar aspects of personality: Extraversion-Introversion, Sensing-Intuition, Thinking-Feeling, and Judging-Perceiving. Combining these four dimensions yields 16 possible types. Each of the four personality dimensions is further examined by five component parts which, when analyzed, suggest one's styles of communication, problem solving, decision making, change management, and conflict management.

Administration: Facilitators must meet educational requirements or attend a certification workshop. Completed tests are returned to CPP for computer-scoring and generation of profile reports. Software for in-house scoring and reporting is available.

Development, Validity, and Reliability: The editors received detailed information about the psychometric properties of this instrument. A number of reliability studies for this well-established instrument are available, including test-retest, internal-consistency, and alternate form methods. Validity information (content, criterion, and construct) is reported in a number of studies. Multiple norm groups are provided.

Author and Source: Isabel Briggs Myers & Katherine C. Briggs (1991), Consulting Psychologists Press, Inc.
Cost: 25 reusable tests: $34.10; five profile reports: $71.20; *Administrator's Manual*: $42.10; *Descriptions of Sub-scales:* $13
Time: 30 to 40 minutes
Number of Items: 131
Audience: General
Leadership Lesson: Personality

New
NEGOTIATING STYLE PROFILE (NSP)

NSP measures an individual's preferred style of negotiating. Participants learn about five styles: defeating the other party at any cost, collaborating for a win-win outcome, accommodating the other party's needs, withdrawal from the negotiation, and meeting the other party halfway. Feedback is available when using the optional *NSP-Other* test.

Administration: HRDQ recommends using this tool as a learning exercise before a training session on conflict management.

Development, Validity, and Reliability: The editors received incomplete information about the psychometric properties of this instrument. The test items and five scales were analyzed by an independent research group and tested on a sample of managers in the retail industry. Factor loadings for each item are reported. Scale reliability is in the .60 to .71 range. Norms are provided by gender and for individuals in a variety of service and manufacturing industries.

Author and Source: Rollin Glaser & Christine Glaser (1983, 1986, 1989, 1991, 1996), HRDQ
Cost: Five tests: $33; *Facilitator Guide*: $25
Time: 15 to 25 minutes
Number of Items: 30
Audience: General
Leadership Lesson: Negotiation

NETWORKING SKILLS INVENTORY (NSI)

The *NSI* is designed to measure networking behaviors at the individual, group, or organizational level. Networking behaviors are translated into three dimensions that correspond to Kotter's three bases for building influence: attaining relevant information, creating and maintaining good working relations, and establishing a good track record. The test aims to identify areas for improving networking behaviors and, in turn, improving an individual's, a group's, or an organization's base of power.

Administration: The inventory is self-scored. Scores are plotted on a triangular graph representing the three influence bases. Brief interpretation instructions are provided.

Development, Validity, and Reliability: The editors received incomplete information about the psychometric properties of this instrument. It was developed from interviews with networking "experts" and from the work of John Kotter on networking. Content validity is based on expert rater acceptance of items as being important networking behaviors. Construct validity was assessed from factor analysis. The authors report moderate internal-consistency reliability. Scale scores for a single norm group are provided.

Author and Source: Beverly Byrum-Robinson & David Womeldorff (1990). In J. W. Pfeiffer, *The 1990 Annual: Developing Human Resources* (pp. 153-168). San Diego, CA: University Associates.
Cost: May be reproduced for educational use
Time: 20 minutes
Number of Items: 24
Audience: Managers
Leadership Lesson: Influence

New
ORGANIZATIONAL CHANGE-READINESS SCALE

This instrument measures the ability of an organization to manage change and plan improvement actions. The focus is on individual perceptions of organizational barriers and supports. The instrument is based on a model of change-readiness with five dimensions: 1) structure—vision and flexibility; 2) technology—innovation and knowledge; 3) climate; 4) systems—flow of information and measuring the change; and 5) people—consensus, rewards, and tolerance.

Administration: This instrument is intended to be used as a training module. Participants score their own surveys and create individual force-field diagrams. A facilitator pools the results to create a group force-field diagram, initiates dialogue, and promotes action planning.

Development, Validity, and Reliability: The editors received incomplete information about the psychometric properties of this instrument. This is a redevelopment of the *Organizational Change-Readiness Survey* (Organization Development and Design, 1985). The new version is based on a review of the literature and results of an expert

panel. Reliability is reported in the .71 to .82 range. Content validity is determined by intercorrelation among the five dimensions in a sample of 88. There are no norms reported. The author states that the test is designed to create internal norms unique to each organization.

Author and Source: John E. Jones & William L. Bearley (1996), HRD Press
Cost: Test booklet: $6.50; *Facilitator's Guide*: $24.95
Time: 120 minutes
Number of Items: 76
Audience: Intact work groups
Leadership Lesson: Change

New
PERSONAL PROFILE SYSTEM®

This instrument provides a framework for understanding human behavior, in general, and the participant's behavior, specifically. Participants make selections in 28 sets of adjectives that describe their most- and least-characteristic behaviors. When the scores are charted and interpreted, participants learn about their tendencies for dominance, influence, conscientiousness, and steadiness.

Administration: This paper-and-pencil test may be self-administered, self-scored, and self-interpreted.

Development, Validity, and Reliability: The editors received incomplete information about the psychometric properties of this instrument. A research report describes this test's development from W. M. Marston's research in *The Emotions of Normal People* (1928) and Carlson Learning Company's more recent literature review and data collection. Scale reliability is reported as internal consistency ranging from .72 to .92. Validity data are limited. Gender, educational level, employment, and ethnic norms are provided for a sample of 812.

Author and Source: (1994), Carlson Learning Company
Cost: $12
Time: 30 minutes
Number of Items: 28
Audience: General
Leadership Lesson: Self-development

New
PERSONAL STYLE INVENTORY (PSI)

This instrument helps individuals understand their preference for rational or intuitive styles in a variety of situations. Participants rank how often they use certain behaviors at work. The results indicate a tendency to plan for the future by developing proposals or generating scenarios, using insight versus analysis to solve problems, and approaching work with an orientation toward procedure or people. Training suggestions in the *Trainer's*

Manual and *Strategy Profile* are designed to improve one's flexibility and appreciation for the diverse styles of co-workers.

Administration: This paper-and-pencil test may be self-administered, self-scored, and self-interpreted. The support materials help to facilitate a one-day workshop.

Development, Validity, and Reliability: The editors received incomplete information about the psychometric properties of this instrument. *PSI* items and structure were derived from a philosophical model , expert panel judgments, and factor analysis. Convergent and discriminate validity data are provided. Reliability is not directly addressed. Norms are reportedly available.

Author and Source: William M. Taggart & Barbara Taggart-Hausladen (1993), Psychological Assessment Resources
Cost: $125—includes 25 tests and manuals; *Trainer's Manual:* $29
Time: 10 to 15 minutes
Number of Items: 30
Audience: General
Leadership Lesson: Intuition

PERSONNEL RELATIONS SURVEY (PRS)

The *PRS* is designed to assess managers' communication tendencies with their subordinates, colleagues, and superiors. It employs a paired-choice format that yields scores on two dimensions. The exposure dimension indicates the manager's willingness to reveal ideas and feelings. The feedback dimension measures the manager's willingness to solicit others' ideas and feelings. Results are tabulated in three Johari Windows (Luft, 1969) to determine the balance of communication skills with subordinates, colleagues, and superiors. The feedback companion instrument, *Management Relations Survey,* is available separately.

Administration: Both instruments are self-administered. Scoring and interpretation are done by the manager or a third party.

Development, Validity, and Reliability: The editors received little information about the psychometric properties of this instrument. The *PRS* is based on Joseph Luft and Harry Ingham's model of interpersonal competence. Internal-consistency reliability and construct/concurrent validity coefficients are briefly discussed, but not documented, in the test booklet. Norms for a managerial population are reported.

Author and Source: Jay Hall & Martha S. Williams (1967, 1980, 1986, 1987, 1994, 1995), Teleometrics International
Cost: $8.95

Time: 15 to 30 minutes
Number of Items: 60
Audience: Managers
Leadership Lesson: Interpersonal Relations

POWER BASE INVENTORY

This instrument measures the following managerial power styles: information giving, expertise, goodwill, authority, reward, and discipline. Power is defined as the ability to influence people, either by personal power or position power. Individuals select whichever of two statements is more descriptive of the reasons why subordinates might comply with their wishes or beliefs.

Administration: The *Power Base Inventory* is self-scored and graphed on a chart in the test booklet. Eleven pages of interpretation and usage guidelines are also provided in the booklet.

Development, Validity, and Reliability: The editors received incomplete information about the psychometric properties of this instrument. It uses a forced-choice format and is based on B. H. Raven's studies of power bases. Internal-consistency and test-retest reliability coefficients are reported. Convergent validity and preliminary external validity data are also reported.

Author and Source: Kenneth W. Thomas & Gail Fann Thomas (1985, 1991), XICOM
Cost: $6.25
Time: 30 minutes
Number of Items: 30
Audience: General
Leadership Lesson: Power

POWER MANAGEMENT INVENTORY (PMI)

When using power, a manager may be motivated by a need to control employees, a desire to benefit the common good of the organization, or a desired to be liked by others. That same manager may employ a power style that is autocratic, collaborative, or weak. This instrument is designed for managers to rate their own motives and styles and to compare their self-scores to those of their employees. The feedback companion instrument, *Power Management Profile,* is available separately.

Administration: Both instruments are self-administered. Scoring and interpretation are done by the manager or a third party.

Development, Validity, and Reliability: The editors received detailed, but somewhat dated, information about the psychometric properties of this instrument. This forced-choice instrument was developed from the three power styles identified by McClelland and Burnham. It was designed to assess both power motivation as well as power practices. Internal-consistency reliability and construct and discriminant validity data are reported and discussed briefly in the test booklet and at greater length in a 1981 report available from the publisher. Norms for a managerial population in technology, manufacturing, sales, finance, human service, government, and law enforcement are available.

Author and Source: Jay Hall & James Hawker (1981, 1988, 1995), Teleometrics International
Cost: $8.95
Time: 15 to 30 minutes
Number of Items: 70
Audience: Managers
Leadership Lesson: Power

PRAXIS® FOR MANAGERS

This Windows-based multi-rater feedback instrument measures and evaluates 16 skill areas in four categories: task management, team development, business values, and leadership. Skills are described in behavioral terms and data are collected from the perspectives of bosses, peers, and direct reports. The instrument's open architecture allows customers to customize items, demographics, score areas, graphics layout, report narratives, and company-specific norms. Feedback indicates management strengths, opportunities for development, skills that co-workers believe are most important for managers, and suggested activities for action planning. A personalized report delivers both graphic profiles and detailed, plain-English narratives that provide individualized feedback. For a comprehensive review of the 1990 edition, refer to E. Van Velsor & J. B. Leslie (1991), *Feedback to Managers, Volume II: A Review and Comparison of Sixteen Multi-rater Instruments,* Greensboro, NC: Center for Creative Leadership.

Administration: *PRAXIS* uses personal computers or paper-and-pencil forms to collect and analyze information. A facilitator guide helps trainers lead a management training course using the feedback. Acumen provides quarterly Train-the-Trainer sessions to train and certify qualified professionals to deliver *PRAXIS* workshops.

Development, Validity, and Reliability: The editors received detailed information about the psychometric properties of this instrument. Internal-consistency and interrater reliability measures are provided. Criterion validity was assessed using leadership effectiveness ratings, appraisal ratings, and promotion rates. The *Technical Report on Methods and Validity* (1995) provides detailed development, reliability, and validity data.

Author and Source: Christopher W. Guest, Peter D. Gratzinger, & Ronald A. Warren (1990, 1993, 1996), Acumen International
Cost: $200; scoring software: $3,500
Number of Items: 116
Audience: Executives, managers, teams
Leadership Lesson: Leadership Skills

PRINCIPAL'S POWER TACTICS SURVEY

This instrument was developed to assess the power strategies used by elementary school principals from the perspective of the teachers. Position power and personal power are the primary scales of the survey. Subscales making up the position-power scale are assertiveness, sanctions, and upward appeal. Subscales making up the personal-power scale are ingratiation, rationality, exchange, and coalition.

Administration: This is a paper-and-pencil test.

Development, Validity, and Reliability: The editors received incomplete information about the psychometric properties of this instrument. Internal-consistency reliability figures of .84 are reported for the two major scales. Content validity was assessed through teacher judgments of items. Instrument development is reported in R. G. Landry, A. W. Porter, & D. K. Lemon (1989), *Educational and Psychological Measurement, 49*(1)*,* 221-226.

Author and Source: Richard G. Landry, Ann W. Porter, & Donald K. Lemon (1986). In A. Porter (1986), *School Climate and Teachers' Perceptions of Principals' Use of Power Strategies*, University of Michigan, available from University Microfilms, Ann Arbor, MI (Order No. DA8702460).
Cost: This is a research instrument. Contact the authors.
Time: 20 minutes
Number of Items: 35
Audience: Principals
Leadership Lesson: Power, Educational Leadership

THE PROFILOR®

A customizable multi-rater feedback instrument, *The PROFILOR* measures 24 management skills, including: analyze issues, build relationships, and lead courageously. The authors state that they have "developed a new skills model based on the manager's current role which requires such skills as fostering teamwork, participative management, championing change, and displaying organizational savvy." The three-part feedback consists of a summary, detailed information, and a development plan. Optional skill areas that may be included at the organization's request are: recognize global implications, value diversity, leverage networks, and innovate. Questionnaires and feedback are available in multiple languages. For a comprehensive review of this instrument, refer to J. B. Leslie & J. W. Fleenor (1998), *Feedback to Managers: A Review and Comparison of Multi-rater Instruments for Management Development* (3rd ed.), Greensboro, NC: Center for Creative Leadership. *The PROFILOR® for Individual Contributors* is recommended for professionals who do not have direct responsibility for managing people.

Administration: Scoring is done by Personnel Decisions, Inc. (PDI). Feedback may be provided by PDI or by feedback-givers trained and certified by PDI.

Development, Validity, and Reliability: The editors received detailed information about the psychometric properties of this instrument. This test grew out of PDI's model of management performance and an earlier instrument, the *Management Skills Profile*. Internal-consistency and interrater reliability data are presented in *The PROFILOR® Technical Summary*. Content and criterion validity studies are also presented in this document. The norm group consists of managers who have taken the instrument since its implementation in 1991.

Author and Source: (1991), Personnel Decisions, Inc.
Cost: $275—includes one self- and ten other-rater forms, scoring, feedback report, development guide, and development plan
Time: 30 to 45 minutes
Number of Items: 135
Audience: Managers
Leadership Lesson: Leadership Skills

New
PROSPECTOR™

This multi-rater questionnaire is designed to measure an individual's ability to learn and take advantage of the growth experiences that facilitate leadership development. There are 11 dimensions: seeks opportunities to learn, acts with integrity, adapts to cultural differences, is committed to making a difference, seeks broad business knowledge, brings out the best in people, is insightful, has courage to take risks, seeks and uses feedback, learns from mistakes, and is open to criticism. For a comprehensive review of this instrument, refer to J. B. Leslie & J. W. Fleenor (1998), *Feedback to Managers: A Review and Comparison of Multi-rater Instruments for Management Development* (3rd ed.), Greensboro, NC: Center for Creative Leadership.

Administration: Facilitators must meet qualification requirements. The *Trainer's Guide* includes suggestions for giving feedback and planning development. Return completed tests to CCL for computer-scoring and computer-generated report.

Development, Validity, and Reliability: The editors received detailed information about the psychometric properties of this instrument. Initial instrument items were based on interviews with corporate executives experienced in identifying people who would be successful in international settings. Cluster and factor analysis identified eleven factors to be included in the final instrument. Alpha reliability coefficients are presented in the *Users Guide*. Content validity was established, and several concurrent validity studies are reported, including the criteria of executive potential, current performance, and the supervisor's ratings of the manager's ability to learn from experience. Differentiated scale norms based on a research sample are provided.

Author and Source: Morgan W. McCall, Jr. (1994, 1995), Center for Creative Leadership
Cost: $195; *Trainer's Guide*: $30
Time: 10 minutes
Number of Items: 48
Audience: Managers
Leadership Lesson: Learning

RAHIM LEADER POWER INVENTORY (RLPI)

This instrument was constructed using the five bases of leader power suggested by French and Raven: coercive, reward, legitimate, expert, and referent. Subordinates rank a superior's ability and willingness to influence in 29 situations. Compliance with the superior's wishes is measured in five items. A high score indicates a superior's perceived broad base of power and his or her subordinates' likeliness to comply.

Administration: No administrative details are provided in the article describing the inventory.

Development, Validity, and Reliability: The editors received detailed information about the psychometric properties of this instrument. Items were developed based on respondent feedback and factor analysis. Construct and criterion validity are reported in the article noted above, while convergent and discriminant validity are reported in a later article. Test-retest and internal-consistency reliability data are also provided, as well as evidence that the inventory is free from "social desirability" response bias.

Author and Source: M. A. Rahim (1988), "The Development of a Leader Power Inventory," *Multivariate Behavioral Research*, *23*(4), 491-503. M. A. Rahim is at the Department of Management, Western Kentucky University, Bowling Green, KY 42101. Phone: (502) 745-2499. Soon to be available from the Center for Advanced Studies in Management, 1574 Mallory Court, Bowling Green, KY 42103. Phone: (502) 782-2601.
Cost: Undetermined at the time of this book's publication
Time: 15 minutes

Number of Items: 29
Audience: Intact work groups
Leadership Lesson: Power

SKILLSCOPE®

This 360-degree-feedback instrument assesses managerial strengths and development needs. Results are summarized in 15 clusters of management skills, presented in a display that indicates whether the skill is a strength, development need, or neither. It compares self-, boss-, and other-ratings. *SkillScope Survey, Feedback Report*, and the *Development Learning Guide* have been translated into Castillian Spanish, Mexican Spanish, German, and French. The *Trainer's Guide* is available only in English.

Administration: Before purchasing, users must offer evidence of skill in giving feedback. *SkillScope* has a simple yes/no checklist format on scannable forms that are scored by the Center for Creative Leadership. A graphic feedback report plots strengths and development needs as seen by the participant and by others. A *Trainer's Guide* provides background information, administrative and interpretive help, psychometric information, and suggested workshop formats.

Development, Validity, and Reliability: Test-retest and internal-consistency reliability studies are reported in the *Trainer's Guide*. Validity was assessed using an independent measure of manager effectiveness.

Author and Source: Robert E. Kaplan (1988, 1996, 1997), Center for Creative Leadership
Cost: $145—includes one self- and nine observer forms, scoring, report, and development planning guide; *Trainer's Guide*: $20
Time: 20 to 30 minutes
Number of Items: 98
Audience: Executives, managers, supervisors
Leadership Lesson: Leadership Skills

SOCIAL SKILLS INVENTORY (SSI)

Social communication is divided into sending skills (expressivity), receiving skills (sensitivity), and controlling skills. Nonverbal communication is classified as emotional, whereas verbal communication is classified as social. Use of these influence strategies is identified: rapport, mirroring, and deception. The author suggests that the *SSI* could be a useful tool in leadership development workshops. He also reports research that suggests high scorers on the *SSI* may be seen as charismatic.

Administration: The *SSI* should be administered by professionals who have a background in psychological testing.

Development, Validity, and Reliability: The editors received detailed information about the psychometric properties of this instrument. Test-retest and internal-consistency reliability figures are reported. Convergent and discriminant validity studies are reported, and factor analysis results confirming the structure of the *SSI* scales are summarized. Norms are based on a college student population.

Author and Source: Ronald E. Riggio (1989), Consulting Psychologists Press
Cost: 25 test booklets and answer sheets: $82; scoring key and manual: $30
Time: 30 to 45 minutes
Number of Items: 90
Audience: General
Leadership Lesson: Communication

STRENGTH DEPLOYMENT INVENTORY® (SDI)

This inventory measures an individual's self-reported style of relating to others under two conditions: when things are going well, and when things are not going well and the respondent is in conflict with others. Scores are plotted on an Interpersonal Interaction Triangle and graphically illustrate the individual's strength of motivation toward four polarities: altruistic-nurturing, assertive-directing, analytic-autonomizing, and flexible-cohering. The 1997 edition also reports on three blends: assertive-nurturing, judicious-competing, and cautious-supporting. The *Feedback Edition* collects data from co-workers. The *Personal Values Inventory* is a simplified version for young people or others who use colloquial English.

Administration: The *SDI* is self-administered. The self-contained form provides instructions for plotting scores as well as text and graphs for understanding and interpreting the results. A *Manual of Administration and Interpretation* provides facilitators and trainers with technical background and other administrative information. There is no special certification required to use and administer the *SDI*.

Development, Validity, and Reliability: The editors received incomplete information about the psychometric properties of this instrument. Test-retest reliability figures are reported in the administration manual and in a separate *Reliability and Validity* brochure. External validity was tested by examining scores of groups presumed to be high on the behaviors measured by one of the scales, but no coefficients were reported.

Author and Source: Elias H. Porter (1973, 1989, 1992, 1997), Personal Strengths Publishing, Inc.
Cost: Test: $9; premier test booklet with exercises: $20; feedback test: $4; administration manual: $30
Time: 20 minutes

Number of Items: 20
Audience: General
Leadership Lesson: Interpersonal Relations

THE STUDENT LEADERSHIP INVENTORY (SLI)

This is the student version of *The Visionary Leader: Leader Behavior Questionnaire* in which items have been rewritten with the assumption that the respondent is not yet in a position of leadership. Students and their peers respond to statements about ability, fairness, communication, credibility, respect, courage, confidence, influence, vision, and principles to determine if the participants exhibit a transactional or a transformational leadership style.

Administration: Answer sheets are returned to Dr. Rosenbach for scoring. Students receive separate reports for their self-test scores and for their observers' scores. A guide book provides instructions for interpreting the reports.

Development, Validity, and Reliability: The editors received little information about the psychometric properties of this instrument. Development, reliability, and validity data are available on the instrument from which the *SLI* was derived, *The Visionary Leader: Leader Behavior Questionnaire*. No data on the *SLI* itself was provided.

Author and Source: Marshall Sashkin & William E. Rosenbach (1995). Available from Dr. William Rosenbach, Department of Management, Gettysburg College, Box 395, Gettysburg, PA 17325.
Phone: (717) 337-6648. Fax: (717) 337-2167. E-mail: william.e.rosenbach@gettysburg.edu
Cost: $3—includes test, scoring, and report; minimum order of $100
Time: 30 minutes
Number of Items: 50
Audience: Students
Leadership Lesson: Vision

SUBSTITUTES FOR LEADERSHIP SCALE–REVISED (SLS-R)

This instrument is a considerably revised version based on one originally developed in 1978 by S. Kerr & J. M. Jermier ("Substitutes for Leadership: Their Meaning and Measurement," *Organizational Behavior and Human Performance, 22*(3), 375-403). It was designed to further test Kerr and Jermier's premise that in certain situations "certain individual, task, and organizational variables act as 'substitutes for leadership,' negating the hierarchical superior's ability to exert either positive or negative influence over subordinate attitudes and effectiveness." The *SLS-R* contains 13 subscales, each reflecting some aspect of the subordinate, task, or organization that may substitute for leader influence.

Administration: This paper-and-pencil test may be administered, scored, and interpreted with information in the article.

Development, Validity, and Reliability: The editors received detailed information about the psychometric properties of this instrument. Scale reliability figures are reported as well as relationships to a number of criterion measures. Test development, validity, and reliability data are further discussed in P. M. Podsakoff & S. B. MacKenzie (1994), "An Examination of the Psychometric Properties and Nomological Validity of Some Revised and Reduced Substitutes for Leadership Scales," *Journal of Applied Psychology, 79*(5), 702-713.

Author and Source: P. M. Podsakoff, B. P. Niehoff, S. B. MacKenzie, & M. L. Williams (1993), "Do Substitutes for Leadership Really Substitute for Leadership? An Empirical Examination of Kerr and Jermier's Situational Leadership Model," *Organizational Behavior and Human Decision Processes, 54*(1), 1-44. Contact Philip Podsakoff, Department of Management, School of Business, Indiana University, Bloomington, IN 47405.
Cost: Contact the authors for availability and research use.
Time: 20 minutes
Number of Items: 74
Audience: General
Leadership Lesson: Substitutes for Leadership Theory

SUCCESS STYLE PROFILE® (SSP)

The *SSP* is a cognitive-styles inventory in which the respondent is asked, "How strong is your *interest, liking,* or *preference* for each of the items below?" It is constructed in a modified paired-comparison format, and offers information on where a person is comfortable operating and the kinds of leadership situations in which the person must stretch. It may also raise awareness of the operating-style differences among people and groups. Output about style information is presented as eight modes of thinking, each resulting from a different configuration of three basic dimensions: perception-conception, logic-feel, and external-internal focus of attention.

Administration: There are two alternatives for using the *SSP:* 1) Facilitators who interpret scores must attend a five-day certification workshop. Performance Support Systems provides computer scoring and individual reports that chart the results. A 37-page booklet and a summary chart of leadership modes are available to assist individuals in interpreting their results. An administrator's handbook and a facilitator's guide are available. 2) The second alternative is self-orientation. Individuals may purchase a set of Signature rank-order cards representing the eight modes to learn about their own leadership style. No data are generated. Facilitators may use the Signature cards for programs based on self-orientation without attending the certification workshop.

Development, Validity, and Reliability: The editors received detailed information about the psychometric properties of this instrument. The premise upon which this instrument was developed is that the behaviors we associate with personality are influenced by a person's thinking style. Test-retest and internal-consistency reliability data are reported in a summary report by Dennis Coates. Criterion validity was assessed using reference groups in specialized occupations, and convergent-construct validity studies are reported.

Author and Source: Dennis E. Coates (1988, 1992), Performance Support Systems
Cost: $55—includes question booklet, scoring, analysis, and cards
Time: 30 to 45 minutes
Number of Items: 96
Audience: General
Leadership Lesson: Leadership Styles

SURVEY OF LEADERSHIP PRACTICES (SLP)

This survey measures leadership effectiveness. It is based on Wilson's model, the Leadership Task Cycle, which includes six competencies: 1) entrepreneurial vision—imagination and risk taking; 2) leadership for change—organizational sensitivity, encouraging participation; 3) gaining commitment—empowering and persuasiveness; 4) monitoring personal impact—feedback; 5) drive—standards of performance, energy, perseverance, and push; and 6) recognizing performance—sharing credit. When there is a balance of high competency across the model, there are two consequences apparent in the test results—residual impact and power. For a comprehensive review of this instrument, refer to J. B. Leslie & J. W. Fleenor (1998), *Feedback to Managers: A Review and Comparison of Multi-rater Instruments for Management Development* (3rd ed.), Greensboro, NC: Center for Creative Leadership. The *Survey of Management Practices* is a similar instrument used to measure management skills such as goal setting and problem solving. The *Survey of Executive Leadership* measures the combined management and leadership skills needed to achieve organizational growth. *Our Team* and *My Team Mates* surveys apply the task cycle theory to team processes.

Administration: Facilitators may be required to attend a qualification workshop. *SLP* is computer-scored. Feedback consists of narrative and graphs, and a personal-planning guide is available. A trainer's guide provides administration, background, and feedback information.

Development, Validity, and Reliability: The editors received detailed information about the psychometric properties of this instrument. Development is based on the authors' Task-Cycle Theory as applied to the leadership process and subsequent factor analysis. Internal-consistency and interrater reliabilities are reported. Criterion validity has been assessed using effectiveness ratings by superiors, direct reports, and peers.

Author and Source: Paul M. Connolly & Clark L. Wilson (1987, 1989, 1995, 1997), Clark Wilson Group, Inc.
Cost: $21 to $28
Time: 30 minutes
Number of Items: 88
Audience: Managers, project leaders
Leadership Lesson: Leadership Skills

SYMLOG®

This self-and-other rating instrument measures adherence to individual and organizational values. Based on the work of Robert F. Bales, it produces scores on three dimensions that have emerged repeatedly in research as critical in understanding individual and group behavior: friendliness versus unfriendliness, dominance versus submissiveness, and accepting versus opposing established authority. For a comprehensive review of this instrument, refer to J. B. Leslie & J. W. Fleenor (1998), *Feedback to Managers: A Review and Comparison of Multi-rater Instruments for Management Development* (3rd ed.), Greensboro, NC: Center for Creative Leadership.

Administration: This instrument may be used for analysis at the individual, group, or organizational level. Facilitators must be certified. SYMLOG Consulting Group offers certification workshops.

Development, Validity, and Reliability: The editors received detailed information about the psychometric properties of this instrument. A review of this instrument (see above) states, "*SYMLOG* is a comprehensive synthesis of findings, theories, and methods from psychology, social psychology, sociology, economics, political science, and several related disciplines." There is much research related to *SYMLOG* development. Interrater reliability data are available, as are several predictive validity studies. There is a large norm group that is an aggregate of a number of samples.

Author and Source: (1983, 1984, 1986, 1990, 1991, 1997), SYMLOG Consulting Group
Cost: Contact the publisher

Time: 20 to 30 minutes
Number of Items: 26 (repeated four times)
Audience: Managers, executives, teams
Leadership Lesson: Values

New
TEAM LEADER SURVEY

In this survey, team leaders rank how well they currently interact with team members. Team members, peers, and managers provide feedback to obtain a team leader effectiveness profile in six skill areas: communication, thinking, administration, influence, interpersonal skills, and change management. Worksheets help participants identify skills they wish to develop and make action plans for development.

Administration: The *Facilitator Guide* contains instructions for scoring, interpretation, and delivering feedback. It also includes an agenda for training, suggested actions for developing each of the six skills, and transparency masters. HRDQ also offers a scoring and feedback service.

Development, Validity, and Reliability: The editors received incomplete information about the psychometric properties of this instrument. The *Facilitator's Guide* discusses the scale development through a research study of employees from organizations that had empowered, participative work environments. Average internal-consistency reliability is .78. No validity data are reported. Limited norms are reported for the final version of the test.

Author and Source: Ann Burress (1994, 1995), HRDQ
Cost: Five participant booklets: $32; five feedback booklets: $15; *Facilitator Guide*: $30
Time: 120 minutes
Number of Items: 36
Audience: Team leaders
Leadership Lesson: Teams

TEAM MULTIFACTOR LEADERSHIP QUESTIONNAIRE (TMLQ)

The *TMLQ* employs the same scales as the *Multifactor Leadership Questionnaire* to measure the transformational and transactional leadership styles of a team (see separate entry in this section for the *MLQ*).

Administration: The instrument is completed by each member of the team. Vendor scoring provides an extensive tailored interpretive feedback report including graphics and suggestions for improving leadership while working in teams.

Development, Validity, and Reliability: The editors received incomplete information about the psychometric properties of this instrument. The publisher states that the *TMLQ* is based on the same research and scale development as the *Multifactor Leadership Questionnaire*. Reliability and preliminary criterion validity data for the *TMLQ* specifically are presented in a manuscript from the authors.

Author and Source: Bernard M. Bass & Bruce J. Avolio (1995, 1996), Mind Garden, Inc.
Cost: $50 per team of ten
Time: 10 minutes
Number of Items: 48
Audience: Intact work groups
Leadership Lesson: Transformational Leadership

New
TEAM PERFORMANCE QUESTIONNAIRE (TPQ)

The purpose of the *TPQ* is to provide team leaders and members with information about their work group characteristics and to identify opportunities for improvement. It is based on Riechmann's Team Performance Model, which describes six characteristics of high-performing teams: leadership, goals and results, collaboration and involvement, competencies, communication processes, and emotional climate.

Administration: Team members complete the questionnaire prior to a three-hour team meeting. An administrator scores the anonymous tests and brings results to the team meeting. At the meeting, team members learn the summary scores and use the workbook to discuss the team's strengths and weaknesses and to plan team goals for improvement.

Development, Validity, and Reliability: The editors received incomplete information about the psychometric properties of this instrument. The author's research on the characteristics of high-performing teams led to the items that make up the *TPQ*. Expert panel and factor analysis were used to determine the content and construct validity of this instrument, but no coefficients or other documentation were presented. Test-retest and internal-consistency reliability correlations are provided. Limited norms are available, but the author states that they may be slightly skewed because some of the teams were known to be high-performing.

Author and Source: Donna Riechmann (1997), DRC Associates
Cost: Test: $4.95; workbook: $19.95; *Facilitator's Guide*: $39.95
Time: 10 minutes
Number of Items: 32

Audience: Teams
Leadership Lesson: Teams

TEAMVIEW/360: EVALUATING TEAM PERFORMANCE

This is a computerized assessment system for intact work teams that generates both individual and team profiles. It is based on the *Individual Behavior Questionnaire (IBQ)*, which assesses perceptions of individual behavioral effectiveness, ranging from cognitive to interpersonal. "Based on *a priori* conceptual schema, the 31 behaviors are grouped into seven categories." These categories are: problem solving, planning, controlling, managing self, managing relationships, leading, and communicating.

Administration: Each team member completes an *Individual Behavior Questionnaire* (which can be printed out by the software) to rate his or her own effectiveness, then uses equivalent Other Rating forms to assess each of the remaining team members. All rating data is then entered into a PC (presumably by a trusted person who is not part of the team) using the software program provided. The software can generate a number of charts, including a team profile and individual profiles, both of which compare self-ratings to ratings by others.

Development, Validity, and Reliability: The editors received incomplete information about the psychometric properties of this instrument. It was designed to assess how effectively the individual is perceived to perform by others compared with a self-assessment of performance. Factor analytic studies to support the instrument's construct validity are summarized. Interrater reliability correlations are presented and discussed.

Author and Source: Michael R. Perrault, Kenneth R. Brousseau, Richard F. Gilmore, Max Mindel, & Marlene A. Benz (1994), Jossey-Bass/Pfeiffer
Cost: $49.95—includes software and one set of Team-Member profiles; additional Team-Member profiles: $29.95
Time: 15 minutes
Number of Items: 31
Audience: Intact work groups
Leadership Lesson: Teams

New
TEAMWORK-KSA TEST

This psychological test provides information about an individual's ability to work in a team setting. Participants respond to multiple-choice questions about hypothetical team situations to determine knowledge, skills, and abilities in five areas: conflict resolution, collaborative

problem solving, communication, goal setting, and planning. Scores in each area identify training needs.

Administration: This test may be administered and scored by hand or on computer. Facilitators must have completed appropriate coursework in psychology or education and have some technical knowledge of instrument construction and use.

Development, Validity, and Reliability: The editors received detailed information about the psychometric properties of this instrument. The *Information Guide* discusses development of scales from a literature review and pilot tests. Internal consistency is reported as .80. Construct, concurrent, and criterion validity studies are reported. Limited norms are reported by race, gender, and educational level.

Author and Source: Michael J. Stevens & Michael A. Campion (1994), NCS Workforce Development
Cost: 10 test booklets: $97.50; *Examiner's Manual*: $19.75; scoring software: $129
Time: 30 to 40 minutes
Number of Items: 35
Audience: Teams
Leadership Lesson: Teams

THOMAS-KILMANN CONFLICT MODE INSTRUMENT (TKI)

This instrument assesses an individual's self-reported behavior in conflict situations. It increases awareness of one's current style and alternative styles that one might practice. Styles of handling conflict include: competing, collaborating, compromising, avoiding, and accommodating. A companion *Facilitator's Guide* provides three workshop formats, three group exercises, and case studies that may be used in conjunction with this instrument.

Administration: The instrument is self-scored and graphed on a chart in the test booklet. Seven pages of interpretation and usage guidelines are also provided in the booklet. A *Facilitator's Guide* includes three workshop formats, group exercises, case studies, and the instrument validity study.

Development, Validity, and Reliability: The editors received incomplete information about the psychometric properties of this instrument. Validity (construct and concurrent) and reliability data are reported in R. H. Kilmann & K. W. Thomas (1977), "Developing a Forced-choice Measure of Conflict-handling Behavior: The 'MODE' Instrument," *Educational and Psychological Measurement, 37*(2), 309-325.

Author and Source: Kenneth W. Thomas & Ralph H. Kilmann (1974), XICOM
Cost: Test: $6.50; *Facilitator's Guide*: $95

Time: 15 minutes
Number of Items: 30
Audience: General
Leadership Lesson: Conflict Management

THE VISIONARY LEADER: LEADER BEHAVIOR QUESTIONNAIRE (LBQ)

This questionnaire is completed by the leader and by the leader's associates. Each item describes a certain leadership behavior, characteristic, or effect a leader might have on the organization. Behavior patterns measured (scales) include clear leadership, communicative leadership, consistent leadership, caring leadership, creative leadership, confident leadership, empowered leadership, visionary leadership, and visionary culture building. Respondents are asked to indicate how true the statement is of the person they are rating. Scores provide information on the extent to which the ratee is a visionary leader, can elicit this response from others, and performs normal leadership functions. For a comprehensive review of this instrument, refer to J. B. Leslie & J. W. Fleenor (1998), *Feedback to Managers: A Review and Comparison of Multi-rater Instruments for Management Development* (3rd ed.), Greensboro, NC: Center for Creative Leadership.

Administration: The instrument is self-scored and results are plotted on a triangular grid. No certification is required to administer it. A *Visionary Leader Trainer Guide* is available that includes background information, technical details, and norms.

Development, Validity, and Reliability: The editors received detailed information about the psychometric properties of this instrument. The *LBQ* is based on behavioral competencies and strategies identified by Warren Bennis in his interviews with successful corporate chief executive officers. Factor analysis was used to verify scale structure and determine construct validity. Internal-consistency reliability and concurrent validity studies are reported in the *Trainer Guide*. This guide also details norms from a variety of sample groups. Additional studies on the current edition are in progress.

Author and Source: Marshall Sashkin (1984, 1985, 1988, 1990, 1995), HRD Press
Cost: $14.95—includes one self-test and three feedback tests; *Trainer Guide*: $24.95

Time: 20 minutes
Number of Items: 50
Audience: Managers
Leadership Lesson: Vision

New
VOICES™

Voices is an electronic 360-degree assessment tool that is customized to fit individual learners. Data can be gathered on 67 core leadership competencies and 19 career stallers to provide continuous feedback from an unlimited number of raters over time. Participants design their own feedback reports to learn about their blind spots, hidden strengths, and relative importance of rated competencies. This tool is part of *The Leadership Architect Suite*, an integrated set of tools that supports training needs analysis and succession planning. For a comprehensive review of this instrument, refer to J. B. Leslie & J. W. Fleenor (1998), *Feedback to Managers: A Review and Comparison of Multi-rater Instruments for Management Development* (3rd ed.), Greensboro, NC: Center for Creative Leadership.

Administration: The customizable, interactive questionnaires and reports require Windows 3.1 or higher and 8 MB RAM. A certified facilitator oversees the administration and interpretation. Certification training is available from Lominger.

Development, Validity, and Reliability: The editors received detailed information about the psychometric properties of this instrument. The competencies measured were originally developed from a content analysis of the literature, then tested in different organizations. Internal-consistency reliability is reported. A criterion validity study showed significant relationships between 47 of the competencies and independent ratings of performance and potential.

Author and Source: Michael M. Lombardo & Robert W. Eichinger (1996), Lominger Limited, Inc.
Cost: Administrative program: $5,000; report writer: $500; tests (self and other): $25 each use
Time: 60 minutes
Number of Items: 86—varies when customized
Audience: Executives, managers
Leadership Lesson: Leadership Development

EXERCISES

This section contains annotations of simulations, training devices, and experiential lessons in leadership development. An educator may use this active learning strategy to introduce a new concept, spark discussion, or change the pace in a classroom—inside or outside. Some items are brief icebreakers, while others are complex experiences that evolve over several days. Most of those that require physical ability are adaptable to meet the needs of participants with physical limitations. Whenever possible, the descriptions include reference to support materials such as leader's guides or articles that describe using an exercise in the classroom. Each entry, as applicable, includes:

- Author, publication date, and source. For source contact information, refer to the directory of Instruments and Exercises Vendors.
- Details for preparation.
- Space and equipment needs.
- Cost.
- Number of participants.
- Time necessary to run the exercise.
- Intended audience.
- Leadership Lesson—a subject descriptor.

New

AFTER NAFTA: A CROSS-CULTURAL NEGOTIATION EXERCISE

This exercise illustrates two styles of negotiating that are effective in cross-cultural situations: 1) logrolling, in which both sides lose a little to gain a lot, and 2) bridging, in which both sides must refocus on their most desirable outcomes. Participants assume roles as the mayors of towns on two sides of the U.S.-Mexico border. Each wants to entice the Japanese Kokishi Company to locate its chemical plant where his voters will benefit from new jobs and tax income. The mayors have strong cultural differences in the areas of individualism versus collectivism, power distance, and uncertainty avoidance. To achieve a win-win outcome, the mayors must overcome cross-cultural miscommunication, must share information, and must learn to trust each other. For more explanation on logrolling and bridging negotiating styles, see J. K. Butler, Jr. (1996), Two integrative win-win negotiating strategies, *Simulation & Gaming, 27*(3), 387-392.

Author and Source: J. K. Butler, Jr. (1996), AFTER NAFTA: A cross-cultural negotiation exercise, *Simulation & Gaming, 27*(4), 507-516.
Preparation: Photocopy role-player handouts
Space or Equipment Needs: Two rooms—one for activity and one for giving private instructions to observers
Number of Participants: Groups of two or three
Time: 60 minutes
Audience: Students, managers
Leadership Lesson: Multicultural Diversity, Negotiation

ALPHA/BETA: EXPLORING CULTURAL DIVERSITY IN WORK TEAMS

This simulation explores the problems that arise when members of two cultures with significantly different social norms must work together productively. Through the exercise and subsequent discussion, participants develop an understanding of the complexities of working in culturally diverse work teams. The two cultures are fictitious, which allows participants to more easily break away from their preconceived notions of appropriate behavior.

Author and Source: S. R. Phillips in J. W. Pfeiffer, *The 1994 Annual: Developing Human Resources* (pp. 37-46). San Diego, CA: Pfeiffer & Company.
Space or Equipment Needs: Pencils, paper, and clipboards for each observer. Large supply of blank paper, 14 magazines, 14 pairs of scissors, glue, tape, and name tags. One large workroom and seven smaller rooms or workstations.
Number of Participants: 35

Time: 120 minutes
Audience: General
Leadership Lesson: Multicultural Diversity, Teams

New

ALPHATEC: A NEGOTIATION EXERCISE WITH LOGROLLING AND BRIDGING POTENTIAL

Students assume the roles of negotiators who are buying and selling integrated circuits. A third student serves as an observer. The negotiators must deal with the issues of trust, information sharing, and a satisfactory outcome for both parties. Because personal promotions are at stake, there is a tendency for negotiators to first seek win-lose situations. The exercise teaches negotiators to use a logrolling technique in which both sides give a little to gain a lot. It also teaches a bridging technique in which both negotiators must overcome initial positions, reveal information, and refocus on the most important issues at stake. Both techniques enable win-win outcomes. Detailed explanation of the two techniques is available in J. K. Butler, Jr. (1996), Two integrative win-win negotiating strategies, *Simulation & Gaming, 27*(3), 387-392.

Author and Source: J. K. Butler, Jr. (1996), ALPHATEC: A negotiation exercise with logrolling and bridging potential, *Simulation & Gaming, 27*(3), 393-408.
Preparation: Photocopy handouts
Number of Participants: Groups of two or three
Time: 60 minutes
Audience: Students, managers
Leadership Lesson: Negotiation

AWAKA: AN EXPLORATION IN DIVERSITY

The Richlanders, who are economically and technologically superior, plan a trip to aid the Awakians with a project. The cultures of the two groups are very different. This provides opportunity for miscommunication and conflict that simulates what naturally occurs when individuals work across cultural boundaries. The simulation's objectives are to: 1) experience issues involved with working across cultural and ethnic boundaries, 2) explore assumptions made about unfamiliar people, and 3) develop an effective process for entering a working relationship with people who are culturally different.

Author and Source: W. C. Musselwhite (1993), Discovery Learning
Preparation: The facilitator must have experience running a simulation and managing a debrief.
Cost: Contact Discovery Learning for licensing or in-house delivery.
Number of Participants: Not specified
Time: 120 minutes

Audience: Managers
Leadership Lesson: Multicultural Diversity, Communication

BAFÁ BAFÁ

This is one of the classic cross-culture simulations. Participants live and cope in a "foreign" culture and then discuss and analyze the experience. *Bafá Bafá* allows participants to explore the social, cognitive, and affective dimensions of interacting with culturally different others. They learn that what seems logical and reasonable to a member of one culture may seem irrational and unimportant to an outsider. In the discussion following the simulation, the "mysteries" of each of the cultures are revealed and participants can see how stereotypes are formed and perpetuated. A variation of this simulation, *Rafá Rafá,* is designed for students in the 5th through 8th grades.

Author and Source: G. Shirts (1977), Simulation Training Systems
Preparation: About 30 minutes are needed to set up the room and game pieces.
Space or Equipment Needs: Two cassette players and a newsprint pad
Cost: $225 (educational version). *Rafá Rafá*: $110.
Number of Participants: Ten to 40
Time: 120 minutes. *Rafá Rafá*: 30 to 40 minutes.
Audience: Students, managers
Leadership Lesson: Multicultural Diversity

BASES OF POWER: DEVELOPING THE GROUP'S POTENTIAL

This exercise is based on the premise that without power, leadership is impossible. Using preliminary readings, discussion, self-analysis, and information sharing, participants are helped to identify their power bases (from among seven possibilities) and discover how they use power. The exercise also points out to group members the different power bases within the group. To wind up the experience, each participant creates an action plan for enhancing his or her power bases.

Author and Source: M. H. Kitzmiller in J. W. Pfeiffer, *The 1991 Annual: Developing Human Resources* (pp. 43-50). San Diego, CA: University Associates.
Number of Participants: All members of an intact work group
Time: 180 to 210 minutes
Audience: Intact work groups
Leadership Lesson: Power

New
BATEC: AN EXPLORATION OF PROJECT LEADERSHIP

BATEC is an interactive behavioral learning activity that simulates a fast-paced research and development project. The project is the development of a superior-quality printing plate that must be ready for market within nine months. At a desktop computer, the project team faces a variety of challenges via on-screen scenarios. They must decide on issues relating to strategy, competition, quality, price, schedule, personnel, and marketing. During the simulation and feedback, participants learn skills to improve team interactions and to enhance strategic planning and problem-solving skills. An earlier version of this activity was titled *RADMIS*.

Author and Source: (1997), Discovery Learning
Space or Equipment Needs: Personal computer and flip charts
Cost: Contact Discovery Learning for licensing or in-house delivery.
Number of Participants: Five to six
Time: One-and-a-half days
Audience: Intact work groups
Leadership Lesson: Decision Making, Teams

BEYOND LIMITS

The purpose of this activity is to assist individuals in exploring their personal limits. To start, participants individually complete a "Limits Checklist" of activities, responding in one of three ways: "I would do this willingly"; "I might do this"; or "I cannot imagine doing this." Scores are derived for five limit areas (e.g., "Low Emotional Expressiveness"), and then individuals complete a limits exercise worksheet and discuss the results with at least one other person. The facilitator emphasizes that it is always possible to choose to venture beyond one's perceived limits and explore new ways of behaving.

Author and Source: M. Woodcock & D. Francis (1991), *The Self-Made Leader: 25 Structured Activities for Self-Development* (pp. 73-81). King of Prussia, PA: HRDQ.
Number of Participants: Groups of three or four
Time: 90 minutes
Audience: General
Leadership Lesson: Self-development

BLIND LEADERSHIP

As described by the authors, *Blind Leadership* "emphasizes the importance of leadership vision to the successful accomplishment of group tasks. In this exercise, a sighted group leader instructs blindfolded subordinates in putting together a Tinkertoy structure." Group leaders are given a picture of a completed Tinkertoy structure and told they may do whatever they wish (except remove blindfolds or touch the Tinkertoys) to get their subordinates to build the structure depicted. The authors note the groups that finish first are usually the ones in which the leader communicated a "vision" of the final structure to the subordinates.

Author and Source: C. P. Lindsay & C. A. Enz (1991), Resource control and visionary leadership: Two exercises, *Journal of Management Education, 15*(1), 127-135.
Space or Equipment Needs: Blindfold for each participant, five sets of Tinkertoys, five pictures of the completed Tinkertoy structure
Cost: Cost of materials
Number of Participants: 20 to 30
Time: 45 to 60 minutes
Audience: General
Leadership Lesson: Communication

New
BORDER DISPUTE

Border Dispute teaches students the appropriate use of competitive and collaborative behaviors and about the dynamics within and between groups. Half the students assume roles as negotiators from the developing country of Arak. The other half are negotiators from the neighboring country of Barkan. Because the neighbors have been squabbling over rights to resources and political jurisdiction, they need to negotiate a treaty before war breaks out. Students pair up to strike the most favorable and honorable deals possible in 30 minutes. The quality of each agreement is measured to determine each student's influence and collaboration skills. A debriefing session helps students understand the benefit of taking risks, the need for flexibility, and the stress caused by time limitations.

Author and Source: G. Whitney in D. Marcic (1992), *Organizational Behavior: Experiences and Cases* (3rd ed.) (pp. 291-293, 392-401). New York: West Publishing.
Preparation: Photocopy handouts
Number of Participants: Groups of two
Time: 50 to 90 minutes
Audience: General
Leadership Lesson: Negotiation

BREAKERS: AN ORGANIZATIONAL SIMULATION FOR VOCATIONAL EDUCATION PROFESSIONALS

Participants in this simulation assume responsibility for operating a fictional technical college serving 10,000 students. There are ten roles consisting of president, vice presidents, deans, and campus administrators. Prior to the actual simulation, participants review orientation materials, including a description of the college, a mission statement, and an organizational chart. Role-playing materials include position descriptions, memoranda, letters, reports, and role-specific mission and program information. A short debriefing guide is provided. The simulation has been field-tested and may be used as a stand-alone experience or in conjunction with a leadership course or program.

Author and Source: C. R. Finch (1992), Item #MDS-278, National Center for Research in Vocational Education (NCRVE)
Preparation: Prepare name tags, office position titles, mail baskets, and office supplies. Ideally, the simulation is run in an office suite or facility where participants can use existing offices, phones, and furniture.
Cost: $33.50
Number of Participants: Ten
Time: Nine to 12 hours
Audience: Students or vocational education professionals
Leadership Lesson: Organizational Behavior

New
BRIEF ENCOUNTERS

Brief Encounters is based on the science fiction theme of first contact with alien beings. Participants are divided into two groups to separately learn the behavior norms of the fictional Pandya and Chola cultures. The groups interact at a brief party organized to exchange cultural values. Cross-cultural differences create difficulties and illuminate the tendency to become ethnocentric. A debriefing session helps participants learn the difference between first impressions and reality. The author suggests varying the cultural norms to fit groups that are diverse in gender or age.

Author and Source: S. Thiagarajan (1995), *Diversity Simulation Games* (pp. 13-21). Amherst, MA: HRD Press.
Preparation: Photocopy handouts
Space or Equipment Needs: Timer and whistle
Number of Participants: 20 or more
Time: 20 minutes
Audience: General
Leadership Lesson: Multicultural Diversity

New
BUREAUCRATIC MAZE

Bureaucratic Maze is a group juggling exercise that demands creative problem-solving and teamwork. Participants form a circle and toss a soft object to someone across the circle. A facilitator slowly adds one more object, then another object, until there are objects for everyone to juggle at once. The goal is to continue juggling without dropping any objects. But that is, of course, impossible. The group must find creative solutions to sustain the juggling for three minutes. The author suggests numerous solutions for group juggling and for follow-up discussions on creativity. A variation of this exercise is *Jigglers and Bursters*, which is played with water balloons (pp. 305-310).

Author and Source: C. M. Consalvo (1993), *Experiential Training Activities for Outside and In* (pp. 219-227). Amherst, MA: HRD Press.
Preparation: Photocopy handouts
Space or Equipment Needs: Stopwatch, soft objects for throwing—one for each participant, and a bag to hold all the objects
Number of Participants: Six to 20
Time: 90 minutes
Audience: General
Leadership Lesson: Problem Solving, Teams

BUSINESS SCRUPLES

In this role-playing game, participants confront and resolve workplace ethical dilemmas. Each participant takes a turn playing each of three roles: employer, employee, or member of society at large. A special scoring system allows participants to compare the ethical standards of these three groups. The objectives of *Business Scruples* are to enable participants to: 1) recognize ethical dilemmas in the workplace, 2) learn how to handle and resolve such dilemmas, and 3) compare individual values to group values.

Author and Source: R. N. Sanyal & J. S. Neves (1993), Business Scruples: Confronting ethical issues in the workplace, *Simulation & Gaming*, *24*(2), 240-247.
Preparation: Prepare business dilemmas on index cards (examples are provided in the article)
Number of Participants: 15 to 30
Time: 30 to 60 minutes
Audience: Students, managers
Leadership Lesson: Ethics

CALLOWAY POWER STATION: ASSESSING TEAM-LEADER EFFECTIVENESS

This case-study exercise provides a forum for participants to evaluate a team leader's effectiveness on several dimensions and to discuss various aspects of team leadership. Participants also have the opportunity "to share their individual views about team leadership and how it affects team functioning." The case centers around a team leader who has been a supervisor for four years. The author suggests that this exercise is best used as part of a leadership development program.

Author and Source: W. N. Parker in J. W. Pfeiffer, *The 1996 Annual: Volume 2, Consulting* (pp. 57-66). San Diego, CA: Pfeiffer & Company.
Number of Participants: 12 to 30
Time: 60 minutes
Audience: Students, managers, intact work groups
Leadership Lesson: Teams

CAN WE SAVE LOGO MOTORS?

The setting for this short simulation is Logo Motors, an organization that manufactures cars, motor bikes, and mopeds; it is in serious financial trouble. A "Committee of Four" has been set up to see if Logo Motors can be saved. The first stage of the simulation involves middle management from the four organizations. The second stage is the meeting of the Committee of Four, which is made up of the bosses from the four organizations. Confidential memos and library documents drive the content of the simulation. Debriefs are held to look at what happened, how the participants made decisions, and how the simulation relates to real-world issues.

Author and Source: K. Jones (1989), *A Sourcebook of Management Simulations* (pp. 54-67). New York: Nichols.
Number of Participants: Eight to 24
Time: 120 to 180 minutes
Audience: Managers, executives
Leadership Lesson: Decision Making

CHOOSING A LEADERSHIP STYLE: APPLYING THE VROOM AND YETTON MODEL

This exercise is one of 48 contained in the above book. It is designed to help participants learn how to diagnose leadership situations and then choose the most appropriate decision-making process for that situation (based on the Vroom and Yetton model). Participants analyze case studies in a group setting and arrive at a consensual decision on the appropriate leadership style. The styles range from making the decision yourself without any additional input, to sharing the problem with your subordinates and coming to a consensus.

Author and Source: R. J. Lewicki, D. D. Bowen, D. T. Hall, & F. S. Hall (1988), *Experiences in Management and Organizational Behavior* (3rd ed.) (pp. 121-131). New York: Wiley.
Preparation: Participants must read an article that describes the Vroom and Yetton model.
Number of Participants: Groups of three to five
Time: 50 minutes
Audience: Students, managers
Leadership Lesson: Leadership Styles

COMMON CURRENCY: THE COOPERATIVE-COMPETITION GAME

Common Currency is designed to teach teams and individuals that competition can create positive energy, even in collaborative situations. Participants are divided into eight teams, each representing a fictional country. The countries learn that their eight currencies will soon be unified, and each one attempts to maximize its wealth. No country knows the value of all the coins, so teams must negotiate, exchanging information and coins, to achieve success. As currency values become apparent, teams employ strategic planning to get bonus points for collecting special combinations. In the debrief, participants discuss the cooperative and competitive tasks and processes within and between teams. They identify the people who have assumed leadership roles. A variation of the game adds the element of change midway to challenge strategic planning and relationship skills.

Author and Source: L. Ukens (1995, 1996), HRDQ
Preparation: The facilitator needs about two hours to read instructions, select debriefing questions, photocopy feedback forms, fill envelopes with coins, assemble flags, and arrange tables.
Space or Equipment Needs: Paper, pencils, two flip charts, markers, calculator
Cost: $250
Number of Participants: 16 to 48
Time: 90 to 180 minutes
Audience: Intact work groups or individuals who compete with each other
Leadership Lesson: Collaboration

THE CRISIS GAME

This game is designed to have participants experience the dynamics of decision making in crisis conditions. A crisis condition is characterized by surprise, threat to vital interests, and incomplete information. The author says that within these conditions the game director can tailor *The Crisis Game* by selecting a specific current crisis that fits the group. The game steps include: an announcement of a crisis condition, distributing a briefing package, group work on policy recommendations, random announcements of both relevant and irrelevant new information, further compression of an already-short time frame, presentation of policy recommendations, and game debriefing. The sample briefing package included in this article is based on an international-relations incident, the Panamanian situation in early 1988, but, as noted above, a crisis situation can be chosen and developed to correspond to any specific setting or group.

Author and Source: H. R. Friman (1991), The crisis game, *Simulation & Gaming*, 22(3), 382-388.
Preparation: Select and prepare a crisis briefing
Number of Participants: Five to 60
Time: 60 to 120 minutes
Audience: Students, managers, executives
Leadership Lesson: Decision Making

CULTURE CLASH: AN ETHICAL INTERCULTURAL SIMULATION

This intercultural ethical simulation is based on a real case of Inuit seal hunters, environmental activists, and animal rights activists. Each group has a sympathetic base for its beliefs. The Inuits' culture and livelihood are threatened. One group of activists rallies for sustainable development while the other protects animals from suffering and death. The conflict among the three groups must be resolved through negotiation. *Culture Clash* provides each group with a briefing on its goals, values, and negotiating style. Through several rounds of negotiation, the groups move from seeing only their differences to a search for common ground.

Author and Source: L. Groff & P. Smoker (1995), Global Options
Preparation: Photocopy handouts
Space or Equipment Needs: Props, such as fur coats, are optional.
Cost: Contact Global Options for information.
Number of Participants: Nine to 18
Time: 180 minutes
Audience: Students, managers, civic leaders
Leadership Lesson: Multicultural Diversity, Ethics, Negotiation

DECISIVE DECISION MAKING: AN EXERCISE USING ETHICAL FRAMEWORKS

This exercise enlightens students about five different ethical frameworks: utilitarianism, self-interest, categorical imperative, legality, and light of day. Each student assumes the role of a seismologist who calculates an 80% chance that a devastating earthquake will hit a major metropolitan area within 48 hours. There are five scenarios that describe the scientist's reaction: confirming the accuracy of the event, informing the media so that evacuation can begin, conforming with company policy, evaluating the cost of destruction versus the cost of chaos, or protecting one's personal interests. Students make individual choices about the most ethical reaction, then form groups to reach consensus. Intragroup and intergroup discussions highlight the values and limitations of each framework.

Author and Source: M. Mallinger (1996), Decisive Decision Making: An exercise using ethical frameworks. *Journal of Management Education, 21*(3), 411-417.
Preparation: Photocopy handouts
Number of Participants: Eight to 30
Time: 60 minutes
Audience: Students
Leadership Lesson: Decision Making, Ethics

DELEGATION: USING TIME AND RESOURCES EFFECTIVELY

This exercise is designed to assist participants in identifying the barriers to delegation, the benefits to delegation, and which kinds of tasks are suitable for delegating. A systematic method of delegating is presented, and each participant has an opportunity to apply this method to those tasks or projects that could be delegated but currently are not. Upon completion of the exercise, participants have action plans for delegating tasks within their own jobs.

Author and Source: M. N. O'Malley & C. M. T. Lombardozzi in J. W. Pfeiffer, *The 1988 Annual: Developing Human Resources* (pp. 81-87). San Diego, CA: University Associates.
Space or Equipment Needs: Pencil for each participant. Paper for group recorders. Newsprint, markers, and masking tape. Meeting room with table and chairs for each group.
Number of Participants: 15 to 30
Time: 135 minutes
Audience: Managers, executives
Leadership Lesson: Communication

DESERT I SURVIVAL SITUATION

This exercise uses the scenario of a plane crash in the desert to teach group-consensus problem solving. Team members work individually and then as a group to assess the survival value of 15 items. Solutions are compared with those of a desert survival expert to initiate discussion of the methods and benefits of team decision making. An optional "scene-setting" video is available to enhance the exercise. An extended version of this, *Desert II Survival Situation*, is designed for those who may have already experienced a shorter simulation, and it encourages more detailed discussion.

Author and Source: Human Synergistics
Space or Equipment Needs: VCR and viewing screen
Cost: Participant booklet: $4.25. *Leader's Guide*: $25. *Observer's Guide*: $5. Enhancement video: $125.

Number of Participants: Small groups
Time: 90 to 150 minutes
Audience: General
Leadership Lesson: Decision Making, Teams

DEVELOPING LEADERSHIP SKILLS

Exploring leadership skills and the learning processes that contribute to developing these skills are two purposes of this exercise. The first phase of this is a Leadership Skills Task, with the groups competing for a $500,000 grant. Each group must make a presentation on how the leaders of the future can be developed. After group presentations, which produce a composite list of leadership skills, individuals prepare their own personal development plan.

Author and Source: M. Woodcock & D. Francis (1991), *The Self-Made Leader: 25 Structured Activities for Self-Development* (pp. 167-171). King of Prussia, PA: HRDQ.
Preparation: Make transparencies
Space or Equipment Needs: Note paper, overhead projector, blank transparencies, transparency pens
Number of Participants: Eight to 21
Time: 150 minutes
Audience: Students
Leadership Lesson: Self-development

DEVELOPING TRUST: A LEADERSHIP SKILL

Establishing trust in relationships is an important leadership skill. This exercise allows participants to analyze and discuss certain behaviors and qualities involved in establishing a climate of trust. Each person completes a trust inventory sheet to assess consistency in exhibiting appropriate behaviors; then each receives feedback from others on how he or she is perceived in relation to these behaviors.

Author and Source: W. J. Bailey in J. W. Pfeiffer & J. E. Jones (1981), *A Handbook of Structured Experiences for Human Relations Training, Volume VIII* (pp. 45-51). San Diego, CA: University Associates.
Number of Participants: Six to 24
Time: 120 minutes
Audience: Intact work groups
Leadership Lesson: Trust

DIVERSOPHY™

Players roll dice and move around a game board, trying to avoid four diversity traps (Ethnocentricity, Stereotypes, Bias, and Assimilation). Players collect diversiCOINS for correct answers to question cards. There are four categories of questions: SMARTS (facts and statistics), CHOICE (business situations that require skilled decision making), SHARE (where players must relate personal diversity experience), and RISK (where chance determines play). Cards address general diversity issues as well as the values and customs of specific ethnic and cultural groups.

Author and Source: George Simons International and Multus, Inc. (1992, 1996), George Simons International
Cost: $199
Number of Participants: Four to six
Time: 75 to 90 minutes
Audience: Managers
Leadership Lesson: Multicultural Diversity

ECO-CYCLIX

This exercise uses both indoor and outdoor components to simulate a worldwide manufacturing operation. It utilizes a matrix organizational structure, financial performance, and a "live market" to focus on key elements for competitive success in the 1990s. Through an accelerated time frame, the simulation offers opportunities to assess the impact of organizational dynamics on strategies, decision making, and actual results. *Eco-Cyclix* can be tailored to meet specific client situations, including alternative use of outdoor features.

Author and Source: C. McEwen (1992), Executive Expeditions
Cost: This is a proprietary simulation. Contact Executive Expeditions for information.
Number of Participants: Not specified
Time: Five to 16 hours
Audience: Managers, executives, intact work groups
Leadership Lesson: Decision Making

New
ECOTONOS

Ecotonos is a multicultural problem-solving simulation. Participants are divided into three groups and assigned different cultural norms. To reinforce cultural identity, each group writes a historical myth. Participants are then mixed into multicultural groups to solve a problem. They make process maps to reflect their group's dynamics and problem-solving strategies. During the large-group debriefing session, all participants gain insights from their own and others' cross-cultural communication skills. Facilitators should have prior experience as participants or observers of this simulation.

Author and Source: Nipporica Associates & D. Hofner Saphiere (1993, 1997), Intercultural Press, Inc.
Space or Equipment Needs: Flip chart, markers, masking tape, paper, and pencils for each group
Cost: $150
Number of Participants: 12 to 50

Time: 180 minutes
Audience: General
Leadership Lesson: Multicultural Diversity, Problem Solving

New
EDGEWORK®

EdgeWork is a business simulation designed to be imbedded in executive training programs that focus on group development, communication, and collaboration. Participants are divided into two groups that run the fictional companies Cheeta Xpress and TELEq. Participants assume the roles of managers, directors, and vice presidents who deal with a buyer-supplier relationship, make long-range plans, make routine decisions, and handle emergencies. During the simulation, participants recognize the need for and learn new skills for communicating across internal and external boundaries. Facilitators must have the background to deliver the product and interpret the results and a knowledge of group dynamics. Certification is required. For more information, call Carolyn Plumb at (336) 288-7210.

Author and Source: (1997), Center for Creative Leadership
Preparation: Participants must read three books that provide background information. The facilitator must read the same three books, become familiar with the simulation materials, and set up the rooms.
Space or Equipment Needs: One large and five small conference rooms with tables, chairs, and flip charts. Overhead projector is optional.
Cost: $2,300 for the first kit, $1,800 for additional kits
Number of Participants: Eight to 20
Time: This one-day simulation is often imbedded in a multiple-day program.
Audience: Executive MBA students, executives, intact work groups
Leadership Lesson: Communication, Teams

EFFECTIVE DELEGATION

The action in this role-play exercise centers around a renovation project that involves construction of access ramps for the handicapped. Participants, playing the roles of those who must manage and implement the project, are exposed to the elements of effective delegation. It is designed to help them develop effective delegation skills, from both a manager's and subordinate's perspective. It also offers a chance to practice feedback skills.

Author and Source: R. J. Lewicki, D. D. Bowen, D. T. Hall, & F. S. Hall (1988), *Experiences in Management and Organizational Behavior* (3rd ed.) (pp. 142-148). New York: Wiley.

Preparation: Read introductory material
Number of Participants: Groups of three
Time: 60 minutes
Audience: Managers
Leadership Lesson: Communication

New
THE EGYPTIAN MUMMY TRUST PROGRESSION

Three Egyptian mummy exercises teach trust, but are also used to teach spotting techniques for other activities in the same book. The first exercise is the *Trust Fall*. Participants are paired with other students of the same approximate size. One assumes a stiff-bodied mummy position and the other crouches behind to spot or safely catch the faller. Trust is learned through the careful communication between faller and spotter. In the *Trust Circle*, a mummy participant is passed upright around a tight circle of spotters. This exercise increases the need for communication and cooperation from a pair to a group. The third exercise is *King Tut's Rebirth* in which a mummy is lifted to shoulder height. Because this exercise presents the greatest risk, a group leader emerges to coordinate the effort. It is important to follow the recommended progression and build spotting skills for safety's sake.

Author and Source: C. M. Consalvo (1993), *Experiential Training Activities for Outside and In* (pp. 41-64). Amherst, MA: HRD Press.
Space or Equipment Needs: An open, level activity area. Camera or videorecorder are optional.
Number of Participants: *Trust Fall*: groups of two. *Trust Circle* and *King Tut's Rebirth*: 7 to 13. There should be one trainer for each 12 participants.
Time: 60 to 90 minutes
Audience: General
Leadership Lesson: Trust

New
ELECTRIC MAZE®

The *Electric Maze* is a pressure-sensitive carpet grid with visible and audible alarms. It can be programmed for various action-learning environments to teach communication and teamwork. In the Team Dynamics module, two groups have 20 minutes to get each member safely across the maze without stepping on the hot squares that trigger alarms. Each team is offered $20 million in prize money with deductions taken for time spent—$1 million per minute—and for penalties. For example, crossing the maze in ten minutes wins the team $10 million. Teams learn that hitting hot spots provides necessary information to find the safe path and trying to avoid hot spots wastes valuable time and money. Individuals who break from the team plan and hit hot spots already identified also waste

time and money. Other modules teach coaching and systems thinking skills. A variation of this simulation is *The Sentinel*, a three-dimensional maze built from eight columns that have electric eyes.

Author and Source: Interel
Space or Equipment Needs: 12-foot by 15-foot activity area, markers and flip chart, nine-volt battery
Cost: Small maze: $2,350. Large maze: $2,850. Portable maze: $3,350. Three-dimensional maze: $3,150.
Number of Participants: Four to 24
Time: 85 minutes
Audience: General
Leadership Lesson: Communication, Teams

New
ERA

ERA is a simulation designed to teach leaders in flat organizations how to think strategically, turn strategy into action, and influence others to do the same. Participants assume roles as the top managers of ERA, Inc., a chain of specialty clothing stores. The CEO, CFO, and vice presidents of sourcing, strategic planning, distribution, and advertising must study new opportunities and make decisions that support the corporate vision as well as their own departments. As ERA executives, the participants attend virtual meetings and serve on task forces to practice their skills in gaining commitment for projects and goals. To succeed, the leaders must employ cross-functional cooperation. Following three hours of tactical work, a debrief provides feedback on each leader's consistency of action and contribution to the process. A variation of this simulation is *Academy Electronics and Equipment* geared to leaders in the field of technology.

Author and Source: B. Jockoe, B. Rosenbaum, & S. Rye Wall (1996), Manus Associates
Preparation: The facilitator must be certified by Manus. Certification training is available.
Cost: Contact Manus Associates for information.
Number of Participants: Groups of four to six
Time: This one-day simulation is often imbedded in a multiple-day program.
Audience: Managers, intact work groups
Leadership Lesson: Decision Making, Influence

FAR SIDE EXERCISE

This communication exercise uses cartoons from Gary Larson's *The Far Side*. The goal is for participants to uncover what the cartoon is communicating to the viewer. A combination of individual work, group consensus, and intergroup debate results in some interesting learnings, according to Gilson. He notes that "the exercise begins with an apparent *shared* perception of humor. Very quickly, however, the exercise exposes divergent and distinct patterns of thought and judgment that sensitizes the students to some of the fundamental barriers to effective interpersonal communication."

Author and Source: C. H. J. Gilson (1991), Teaching communications: Take a walk on "The Far Side," *Journal of Management Education, 15*(1), 121-123.
Number of Participants: Any number
Time: Not specified
Audience: General
Leadership Lesson: Communication

FEEDBACK AWARENESS: SKILL BUILDING FOR SUPERVISORS

The purpose of this exercise is to enhance participants' awareness of the impact of feedback, offer feedback guidelines and practice time, and provide participants an opportunity to discuss and identify feedback characteristics and techniques. Participants record their perceptions of a partner's communication style during a brainstorming/discussion period. The perceptions are exchanged during a feedback session, and later shared with the entire group. The author is Senior Trainer at the National Headquarters of the American Automobile Association in Heathrow, Florida.

Author and Source: R. W. Lucas in J. W. Pfeiffer, *The 1992 Annual: Developing Human Resources* (pp. 29-36). San Diego, CA: Pfeiffer & Company.
Preparation: Make posters
Space or Equipment Needs: Newsprint posters, clipboards for each participant, paper, pencils
Number of Participants: 16 to 24
Time: 135 minutes
Audience: Supervisors, managers
Leadership Lesson: Communication

New
THE FLYING STARSHIP FACTORY®

The Flying Starship Factory simulation teaches employees that overcoming one's resistance to change can improve work processes and deliver quality results. During the first factory run, participants make paper stars in a routine assembly line of cutting, folding, and painting. Performance and profitability numbers are computed. Participants then redesign the factory to increase access to information, minimize critical specifications, and form cross-functional work teams. The second factory run usually produces better quality starships and higher profitability. A variation of this simulation is *The Flying Starship: Quest for Quality,* which is designed with a focus on quality production and measurement.

Author and Source: W. O. Lytle (1983), Block Petrella Weisbord
Space or Equipment Needs: Four flip charts, markers, masking tape, calculator, timer, six tables, a chair for each participant
Cost: Small factory: $700. Large factory: $1,050. *Leader's Guide*: $125.
Number of Participants: 12 to 60
Time: Six to 12 hours
Audience: Managers, intact work groups
Leadership Lesson: Change

FOLLOW THE LEADER: AN INTRODUCTION TO SITUATIONAL LEADERSHIP

Situational leadership theory offers a method for managing people whereby a supervisor can adjust his or her leadership style according to what an individual subordinate needs in order to complete a specific task at a specific time. This exercise is designed to allow the participants to experience each of the four basic styles through a task using puzzle pieces. Upon completion, the participants explore the ways in which leadership styles, tasks, and work groups affect one another.

Author and Source: K. S. Brown & D. M. Loppnow in J. W. Pfeiffer, *The 1984 Annual: Developing Human Resources* (pp. 38-43). San Diego, CA: University Associates.
Number of Participants: 16 to 24
Time: 150 minutes
Audience: General
Leadership Lesson: Situational Leadership Style

FOUR FACTORS: THE INFLUENCE OF LEADER BEHAVIOR

R. Rosenthal and L. Jacobson's *Pygmalion in the Classroom* (Holt, Rinehart and Winston, 1968) is the source of the four leadership influence factors that are the basis of this exercise. The goals of the exercise are to acquaint participants with this theory and to "give the participants an opportunity to analyze case studies showing how particular leader approaches to Rosenthal and Jacobson's four factors (climate, feedback, input, and output) can positively or negatively affect followers." Participants analyze the cases separately, discuss them in small groups, and then discuss them with the entire group.

Author and Source: W. N. Parker in J. W. Pfeiffer, *The 1989 Annual: Developing Human Resources* (pp. 39-46). San Diego, CA: University Associates.
Number of Participants: 16 to 24
Time: 105 minutes
Audience: General
Leadership Lesson: Influence

FOURTEEN DIMENSIONS OF DIVERSITY: UNDERSTANDING AND APPRECIATING DIFFERENCES IN THE WORK PLACE

The goal of this exercise is threefold: to help participants understand that diversity is multidimensional and applies to everyone, to assist participants in exploring which of the dimensions of diversity have special relevance to their own identities, and to stimulate appreciation of the value of diversity in the workplace. Using a "diversity diagram" overhead for reference, the facilitator introduces the exercise by explaining that there are certain primary dimensions of diversity (race, age, gender, etc.) that affect the judgments that people make about us, as well as secondary dimensions that are not necessarily part of our "core identity." Participants then fill in a blank diagram indicating which diversity dimensions are part of their core identity, how the importance of the dimensions have changed over time, and what special contributions they bring to the workplace because of their own diversity.

Author and Source: S. Bradford in J. W. Pfeiffer, *The 1996 Annual: Volume 2, Consulting* (pp. 9-17). San Diego, CA: Pfeiffer & Company.
Number of Participants: 15 to 30
Time: 70 to 90 minutes
Audience: General
Leadership Lesson: Multicultural Diversity

New
GLOBAL DIVERSITY GAME

This is a board game intended for use in cross-cultural training programs. Each team moves a game piece to land on a category space and answer a multiple-choice question about global issues. The Demographics category questions are about population, gender, language, and ethnicity. The Jobs category questions relate to workforce trends, management issues, and industry. The Legislation category asks about policies and economic agreements. The Society category poses questions about culture, religion, education, and health care. When teams answer correctly, they receive a colored chip. Teams who collect chips for all four categories travel to the inner circle to win. A facilitator's guide includes suggestions for debriefing.

Author and Source: (1993), Quality Education Development, Inc.
Cost: $195 (for educational institutions)
Number of Participants: Eight to 16
Time: 90 minutes
Audience: Students, managers
Leadership Lesson: Multicultural Diversity

New
GLOBAL SERVICE PROVIDER: MANAGING CHANGE

In this exercise, participants struggle with the ethical dilemmas that arise when the fictional company, Global Service Provider, makes a significant organizational change. Participants form three groups and assume identities as the corporate human resource, operations, and communications departments. Each department is responsible for part of the downsizing and relocating process. Decisions must be made about eliminating jobs, meeting customer needs during the transition period, and the flow of information. This exercise gives participants the opportunity to reflect on their own personal and professional values as they struggle to meet organizational goals.

Author and Source: V. P. Garza, J. Guardia, J. B. Rodgers, C. A. Ross, & J. F. Vogt in *The 1997 Annual: Volume 2, Consulting* (pp. 101-109). San Francisco: Pfeiffer.
Preparation: Photocopy handouts
Space or Equipment Needs: Masking tape, flip charts, and markers for each group
Number of Participants: 15 to 21
Time: 120 minutes
Audience: General
Leadership Lesson: Change, Ethics

New
GLOBALIZATION

This exercise helps participants understand and manage the paradigm of globalization and the tension it creates. Participants are divided into five groups and tagged according to a facet of life affected by globalization: societal, economic, political, technological, or environmental. Groups list the positive and negative forces that globalization has on their facets of life. The participants mix into new groups that include members representing each interest and they explore new perspectives. As they reach understanding of their interconnectedness, they identify two new values and two new behaviors that would benefit themselves as well as others with diverse backgrounds.

Author and Source: B. Jameson in *The 1997 Annual: Volume 1, Training* (pp. 19-31). San Francisco: Pfeiffer.
Preparation: Photocopy handouts
Space or Equipment Needs: Newsprint, flip charts, markers, and masking tape for the facilitator and each group. Name tags, paper, pencils, and clipboards for each participant.
Number of Participants: 25 to 30
Time: 160 minutes

Audience: General
Leadership Lesson: Values

New
THE GOLD WATCH

The Gold Watch helps students examine their personal and professional values as they encounter business associates from other cultures who have different values. Participants are divided into groups to read and discuss a scenario involving a potential large sales order and a bribe with a gold watch. Each group ranks the ethical behavior of the six people involved. Intra- and intergroup discussions reinforce the lesson that values differ among persons and between cultures.

Author and Source: M. R. Lavery in J. W. Pfeiffer (1974), *A Handbook of Structured Experiences for Human Relations Training, Volume X* (pp. 142-147). San Diego, CA: University Associates.
Preparation: Photocopy handouts
Space or Equipment Needs: Newsprint, markers, masking tape, and a clipboard for each group; pencils for all participants
Number of Participants: 12 to 30
Time: 120 minutes
Audience: General
Leadership Lesson: Multicultural Diversity, Ethics

THE GOOD LEADER: IDENTIFYING EFFECTIVE BEHAVIORS

In small subgroups, participants discuss and, if possible, arrive at consensus regarding the characteristics and behaviors that contribute to a leader's effectiveness. Each small group has a recorder and an observer. The recorder captures the subgroup members' ideas on newsprint; the observer makes notes on how leadership evolves in the subgroup, how members respond to the leadership, and how leadership influences the accomplishment of the task.

Author and Source: G. Carline in J. W. Pfeiffer, *The 1992 Annual: Developing Human Resources* (pp. 37-45). San Diego, CA: Pfeiffer & Company.
Preparation: Photocopy handouts
Space or Equipment Needs: Paper, pencil, and clipboard for each observer; flip chart, markers, and masking tape for the facilitator and for each subgroup
Number of Participants: 20 to 28
Time: 135 minutes
Audience: General
Leadership Lesson: Leadership Effectiveness

New
A GROUP LEADERSHIP EXERCISE

This group exercise was designed to be used in a basic communications course. Students are divided into three groups and asked to select a leader. Each leader adopts a different style (laissez-faire, democratic, and authoritarian) as the groups plan the development of a new corporate project. Typically, the groups experience different decision-making and problem-solving styles. Following the exercise, the class discusses the instructor's observations and the students' experiences with the different dynamics in each group.

Author and Source: J. Meyer & J. Stafford (1993), Document No. ED360661, ERIC Document Reproduction Service
Cost: Cost of ERIC document (approximately $5)
Number of Participants: 15 to 21
Time: 20 to 60 minutes
Preparation: Photocopy handouts
Audience: Students
Leadership Lesson: Communication, Leadership Styles

HATS "R" US: LEARNING ABOUT ORGANIZATIONAL CULTURES

Participants in this exercise are assigned to one of four groups, each representing a general type of organizational culture (as identified by T. E. Deal and A. A. Kennedy in *Corporate Cultures: The Rites and Rituals of Corporate Life*, Addison-Wesley, 1982). Each group is briefed on its culture type. Keeping its type in mind, the group must: 1) design a hat that they think their culture would produce, 2) decide on marketing goals, and 3) devise a marketing action plan. If desired, a manager may be designated for each group and asked to function in the way that a manager from that culture would. In subsequent discussions and debriefing, participants explore their learnings about the four culture types and their reactions to the type they were assigned (i.e., did they feel aligned or misaligned with their culture).

Author and Source: C. J. Nagy in J. W. Pfeiffer, *The 1994 Annual: Developing Human Resources* (pp. 93-106). San Diego, CA: Pfeiffer & Company.
Number of Participants: 16 to 24
Time: 150 minutes
Audience: General
Leadership Lesson: Organizational Culture

HOLLOW SQUARE: A COMMUNICATIONS EXPERIMENT

Hollow Square is a useful communication exercise for illustrating the importance of intergroup communication to complete a task. A planning group has access to information regarding the assembly of a puzzle. They are to instruct the implementing team on how to assemble the puzzle. A third group serves as observers of the process. Typically, members of each team make unnecessary and limiting assumptions about the task. The debrief can be very rich with discussion about the planning process, authority relations, and outcomes and communication strategies within and between groups.

Author and Source: A. Shedlin & W. H. Schmidt in J. W. Pfeiffer & J. E. Jones (1974), *A Handbook of Structured Experiences for Human Relations Training, Volume II* (pp. 32-40). San Diego, CA: University Associates.
Preparation: Trace and cut puzzle pieces and divide into envelopes
Space or Equipment Needs: Cardboard for puzzle pieces and envelopes
Cost: Cost of materials
Number of Participants: Any number
Time: 60 to 120 minutes
Audience: Students, managers, executives
Leadership Lesson: Communication, Teams

New
ISLAND COMMISSION

In this exercise, a team practices long-range planning and discovers emergent leadership. A planning commission is simulated when eight persons assume eight different roles: city planner, community action director, chamber of commerce director, corporate manager, organization development consultant, farmer, dentist, and lawyer. This newly organized commission must plan the expenditure of a multimillion dollar, multiyear grant. Their planning is complicated by economic, transportation, educational, housing, employment, and ethical issues. Reaching consensus requires the team to explore their communication, problem-solving, and decision-making skills. One group's experience with *Island Commission* is reported in S. J. Guastello (1995), Facilitative style, individual innovation, and emergent leadership in problem-solving groups, *The Journal of Creative Behavior, 29*(4), 225-239.

Author and Source: P. G. Gillan in J. W. Pfeiffer & J. E. Jones (1974), *A Handbook of Structured Experiences for Human Relations Training, Volume VII* (pp. 99-104). San Diego, CA: University Associates.
Preparation: Photocopy handouts
Space or Equipment Needs: Place card and pencil for each participant; newsprint and marker for each group
Number of Participants: Groups of eight
Time: 120 to 150 minutes
Audience: Civic leaders, intact work groups
Leadership Lesson: Leadership Styles, Teams

JEFFERSON COMPANY EXERCISE

This exercise exposes students to some of the complexity encountered when attempting to implement change in an organization. "It is a role-play exercise, with four characters, designed to show how both employee and management resistance to change can hinder the implementation of an organizational change effort." The setting is a printing company that has recently been sold in a leveraged buyout. The four roles are CEO, sales manager, shop foreman, and union steward.

Author and Source: A. H. Reilly (1992), Understanding resistance to change: The Jefferson Company Exercise, *Journal of Management Education, 16*, 314-326.
Number of Participants: Groups of four or five
Time: 90 to 120 minutes
Audience: Executive MBA students
Leadership Lesson: Change

New
JUNGLE ESCAPE

Jungle Escape is intended as an exercise for existing teams but may be used by other people who want to learn about group dynamics, team leadership, and consensus. The exercise puts teams in an imaginary jungle following a helicopter crash. To escape the jungle, each team must assemble a new helicopter from 93 parts. An observer notes each team's planning and assembly to track the time spent on each process, the contribution of all team members, the problem-solving and decision-making systems, and the group's morale. A team successfully completes the assignment when its helicopter matches the facilitator's sample. During the debriefing, teams evaluate their dynamics to determine if they are fragmented, divergent, or cohesive. They learn the ideal dynamics of effective teams and discuss the changes they can make on real work projects. More than two teams may participate by using additional helicopter kits or by staggering the activity times. The authors recommend including six teams to get a variety of responses.

Author and Source: R. Glaser & C. Glaser (1981, 1984, 1985, 1988, 1990, 1993, 1995), HRDQ
Preparation: The facilitator needs 30 minutes to assemble the display helicopter, set up the room, and make transparencies.
Space or Equipment Needs: Stopwatch for each observer, audiocassette player, flip chart or overhead projector, markers
Cost: $195. Additional helicopter parts: $30. Twelve additional participant booklets: $38.
Number of Participants: Eight to 14
Time: 90 minutes

Audience: Intact work groups
Leadership Lesson: Teams

LEADERSHIP STYLES AND THEIR CONSEQUENCES

The article in which this exercise appears discusses leadership-style theories and offers an integration of the theories by describing the typical characteristics, philosophy, skills, and consequences associated with each major style. The role-play exercise itself serves to portray the major styles and the productivity and satisfaction each is likely to produce. The exercise includes quantitative ratings of productivity and satisfaction for each style—information that provides grist for debriefing.

Author and Source: D. D. Warrick (1981), Leadership styles and their consequences, *Journal of Experiential Learning and Simulation*, *3-4*, 155-172.
Number of Participants: 14 to 18
Time: Not specified
Audience: General
Leadership Lesson: Leadership Styles

LED LIKE SHEEP

This exercise focuses on the link between group decision-making schemes and the type of task assigned. Group decision making is viewed on a continuum relative to the amount of influence or persuasion necessary to arrive at a group decision. Tasks range from those with correct answers to those that have a preferred answer. Each small group is given four tasks that span this range. After completing all of the tasks, the group members relate their observations about their groups and group processes given the different tasks.

Author and Source: D. Dodd-McCue (1991), Led like sheep: An exercise for linking group decision making to different types of tasks, *Journal of Management Education*, *15*(3), 335-339.
Number of Participants: 25 to 40
Time: 75 to 90 minutes
Audience: Students, managers, executives
Leadership Lesson: Decision Making, Teams

New
LIVING ETHICS: MEETING CHALLENGES IN DECISION MAKING

Participants are divided into four groups to study individually and as groups four scenarios of ethical dilemmas in the workplace: pirating a computer program, hiring a friend, a global executive-exchange program, and giving a problem employee a glowing recommendation so that she'll get a new job and become someone else's problem.

With the help of a facilitator, the groups discuss the critical factors in each ethical dilemma, consider possible resolution actions, and select resolutions that are most positive for all parties.

Author and Source: G. J. Duran, E. E. Gomar, M. Stiles, C. A. Vele, & J. F. Vogt in *The 1997 Annual: Volume 1, Training* (pp. 127-135). San Francisco: Pfeiffer.
Preparation: Photocopy handouts
Space or Equipment Needs: Newsprint, flip chart, marker, and masking tape; pencils, paper, and clipboards for each participant
Number of Participants: 16 to 24
Time: 75 minutes
Audience: General
Leadership Lesson: Ethics

New
MARS SURFACE ROVER

This exercise is based on a model of facilitative leadership presented in Rollin Glaser's *Facilitative Behavior Questionnaire* (HRDQ, 1991). The model illustrates a gradual growth from high directive leadership to facilitative leadership without becoming passive. Because this concept is difficult to grasp, *Mars Surface Rover* was created to provide a physical comparison between the three leadership styles. Participants are divided into three teams. Each team's leader receives instructions to behave in a traditional, passive, or facilitative way as his or her team builds a motorized vehicle to explore the surface of Mars. The traditional leader gives orders, while the passive leader offers no information at all. The facilitative leader shares information and encourages all team members to contribute ideas. When the completed vehicles race, it is usually obvious that the one built by the team with a facilitative leader is the best product. *Mars Surface Rover: Team Version* (Glaser, 1997) showcases the benefits of true teamwork relative to group work.

Author and Source: E. M. Russo & M. P. Eckler (1995), HRDQ
Preparation: Make transparencies and set up team supplies
Space or Equipment Needs: Overhead projector, transparency marker, and masking tape; table and chairs for each team (a round table is best)
Cost: $395. Five extra participant booklets: $25. Extra parts box: $95.
Number of Participants: 12 to 18
Time: 120 minutes
Audience: Managers
Leadership Lesson: Leadership Styles

MAYTOWN IN-BASKET

In this exercise, designed for an agricultural education leadership course, students are placed in the role of director of a rural rehabilitation district. The participants have a week to respond to ten in-basket items. The exercise packet consists of an instruction sheet, background information sheets on the Maytown community, biographical sketches of the director and key employees, and the in-basket items. The author states that the goals for the activity are to: 1) discover general management principles through problem solving, 2) examine one's own management style, and 3) plan applications of management principles.

Author and Source: B. Weeks (1991), Document No. ED347317, ERIC Document Reproduction Service
Cost: Cost of ERIC document (approximately $5)
Number of Participants: Variable
Time: One week
Audience: Students
Leadership Lesson: Decision Making

New
MEET DR. CLAY AND DR. GLASS

This exercise was developed as an exam for international exchange students in management. Because it requires creativity and divergent thinking, this exercise benefits ESL students or managers working in cross-cultural situations. The facilitator introduces two candidates for a CEO position, Dr. Clay (a lump of clay) and Dr. Glass (an empty bottle). Students are asked to write lists of leadership qualities present or absent in each candidate. For instance, Dr. Glass may be perceived as rigid, easily broken when stressed, and open to new ideas (through the hole in the top). Dr. Clay may be considered flexible and responsive. The facilitator leads a discussion about desirable leadership attributes.

Author and Source: R. Cunningham (1997), Meet Dr. Clay and Dr. Glass: A leadership exercise, *Journal of Management Education, 21*(2), 262-264.
Space or Equipment Needs: Lump of clay and an attractive, empty glass bottle
Cost: Cost of materials
Number of Participants: Any number
Time: 50 minutes or less
Audience: General
Leadership Lesson: Creativity

MEETING LEADERSHIP

Meetings are a staple fact of organizational life. The rationale for this exercise is that skillful leadership behavior in meetings can increase efficiency and productivity. Participants first get a grounding in group process through reading articles by Likert, Maier, and Klein. They are then divided into groups, and group members rotate through the function of group leader. Group members provide feedback to leaders on their performance. The exercise also provides opportunities for participants to assess their performance as non-leading group members.

Author and Source: G. D. Klein (1994), Meeting leadership, *Journal of Management Education, 18*(3), 375-379.
Preparation: Read the assigned materials
Number of Participants: Even-numbered groups of six to eight
Time: Not specified
Audience: General
Leadership Lesson: Leadership Style

New
MINEFIELD

This exercise provides a learning experience with the same anxiety, excitement, and commitment that accompanies the start-up of an entrepreneurial venture. Students must cross a simulated 50-yard minefield by placing and stepping on anti-mines. The exercise requires students to create a shared vision, share resources, support each other, be persistent, learn from mistakes, keep morale high, and adjust to change—all behaviors that help entrepreneurs develop new ventures. The students also learn about false starts, lack of focus, and instability—challenges that entrepreneurs often encounter.

Author and Source: P. B. Robinson (1996), The MINEFIELD exercise: "The challenge" in entrepreneurship education, *Simulation & Gaming, 27*(3), 350-364.
Preparation: Gather flat rocks or cut wood six inches in diameter to make anti-mines.
Space or Equipment Needs: One anti-mine for each participant
Number of Participants: 15 to 30
Time: 90 to 150 minutes
Audience: Students
Leadership Lesson: Creativity, Change, Entrepreneurial Leadership Style

MY BEST BOSS

This exercise provides participants with the opportunity to examine their own views on positive behavioral leadership characteristics and share and compare them to other participants' views. From the many discussions, participants should arrive at what theory of leadership comes closest to their actual experiences in working with a good boss.

Author and Source: D. T. Hall in R. J. Lewicki, D. D. Bowen, D. T. Hall, & F. S. Hall (1988), *Experiences in Management and Organizational Behavior* (3rd ed.) (pp. 139-141). New York: Wiley.
Space or Equipment Needs: Flip charts, markers, pens, and paper
Number of Participants: Any number
Time: 50 minutes
Audience: General
Leadership Lesson: Self-development

New
NASA MOON SURVIVAL TASK

This survival exercise asks participants to imagine a crash landing on the moon 200 miles from their rendezvous point. Fifteen supply items survived the crash. Each individual ranks the importance of each item. Participants are then separated into small groups who discuss the possibilities and reach consensus on the rankings. During the discussion, some participants will argue for their own position, cave in to pressure from others, or encourage compromise. The groups are scored on the quality of their decisions and do a self-analysis on their members' commitment, conflict, creativity, and consensus. Researchers at the Manned Spacecraft Center of NASA in Houston, Texas, reviewed the exercise and supplied the expert solution and rationales for each ranking.

Author and Source: J. Hall (1963, 1986, 1989, 1994), Teleometrics International
Space or Equipment Needs: Large meeting room for whole group, small meeting rooms for small groups, flip chart, markers
Cost: Participant booklets: $8.95 each.
Number of Participants: Groups of five to seven
Time: 180 minutes
Audience: General
Leadership Lesson: Decision Making, Influence

New
NETWORK™

NetWork is a group-operated drawing device used to teach team leadership, group decision making, the balance between control and support, and techniques for giving descriptive feedback. The device is constructed of a metal frame and control strings that guide a marker over a variety of targets. Participants each control one or two strings to draw together a series of designs such as a figure 8, the group's best guess at the direction of due north, a mathematical sum, or a rendition of the company logo. Variations of this activity include: giving the drawing instructions to only one person who must act as leader, dividing the group into two competitive teams, and

using a coach outside the group to provide information and instructions. Each drawing period is brief to allow time for discussion.

Author and Source: Interel
Space or Equipment Needs: 6-foot by 6-foot indoor activity area
Cost: Floor model: $350. Tabletop model: $250.
Number of Participants: Four to eight
Time: 20 minutes
Audience: Managers, intact work groups
Leadership Lesson: Decision Making, Communication, Teams

New
NEW COMMONS GAME

This game simulates a central problem of human society, which is that interdependent individuals can destroy the society by choosing only those actions that benefit them as individuals while making the world poorer. It demonstrates that people tend to opt for short-term, individual gain at the expense of the collective good. It illustrates the need for rules limiting freedom and autonomy. Players see that some actions are clearly more beneficial to themselves, and also quickly learn that the world suffers when they make self-serving choices. Even though players eventually learn that if enough other people choose the world-preserving action all can enjoy self-benefits without impoverishing the world, it is maddeningly difficult to get agreement on the rules to enforce this world-preserving option.

Author and Source: R. B. Powers (1993), Educational Simulations
Cost: $100
Number of Participants: Six to 24
Time: 90 to 120 minutes
Audience: Students, civic leaders
Leadership Lesson: Ethics, Power

THE ORGANIZATION GAME

This is the third edition of *The Organization Game*, developed to provide a realistic setting in which individuals can experience and experiment with issues of organizational life. Participants actively create an organization, elaborate its rationalization and institutionalization, and develop the mechanisms for adapting to the internal and external forces of change. The challenge is for participants to integrate and apply their knowledge and skills related to individual, interpersonal, group, intergroup, and organizational behaviors. A summary of changes in this third edition is listed on pages 57 and 58 of the *Administrator's Guide*.

Author and Source: R. H. Miles, W. A. Randolph, & E. R. Kemery (1993), *The Organization Game: A Simulation* (3rd ed.). New York: HarperCollins College Publishers.
Space or Equipment Needs: *Participant's Manual* for each participant. Other requirements are described in the *Administrator's Guide*.
Cost: Contact the publisher for information.
Number of Participants: 22 to 32
Time: One day
Audience: General
Leadership Lesson: Organizational Behavior, Change

ORGANIZATIONAL SPIRITUALITY EXERCISE

This exercise was designed: "a) to teach basic concepts of transformational leadership, b) to encourage metaphorical and hermeneutical thinking, and c) to explore the often-neglected spiritual side of work." In the process of thinking about strong or charismatic leaders, students also explore the spiritual nature of transformational leadership and then relate this to current organizational concerns. In order to keep the spiritual content free from parochial religion, students are prohibited from discussing their religious beliefs during the exercise.

Author and Source: R. W. Boozer & E. N. Maddox (1992), An exercise for exploring organizational spirituality: The case of teaching transformational leadership, *Journal of Management Education, 16*, 503-510.
Space or Equipment Needs: Paper and pencils for each participant; blackboard or flip chart and markers for the facilitator
Number of Participants: Any number
Time: 120 minutes
Audience: General
Leadership Lesson: Charismatic Leadership Style, Spirit

OURTOWN

Two community-based agencies are given the task of exploring their mission and purpose, and developing a five-year strategic plan. In the middle of the process, the agencies are merged unexpectedly and the two groups are instructed to continue the task as one group. The purposes of this exercise are to: 1) have participants experience change over which they have no control, 2) understand the characteristics of effective leadership before and after change, and 3) develop awareness of how to lead people as they pass through change-induced personal transitions. A variation of this exercise, *Lakeview*, is designed for public administrators.

Author and Source: W. C. Musselwhite (1991, 1996), Discovery Learning

Preparation: The facilitator must have experience running a simulation and managing a debriefing.
Cost: Contact Discovery Learning for licensing or in-house delivery.
Number of Participants: Eight to 14
Time: 120 minutes
Audience: Students, managers, civic leaders
Leadership Lesson: Change

OUTBACK! A TEAM ADVENTURE

Outback! is one of a number of similarly formatted team-planning and decision-making exercises available from HRDQ. In this particular exercise, the scenario has the participants lost in the Australian outback. After reading introductory material describing the area and their dilemma, the participants must rank—individually and as a team—the survival utility of ten action alternatives and ten daypack items. This and the other exercises are patterned after the NASA exercise that has been around for some years, but *Outback!* provides more scene-setting detail than many other similar exercises. The *Facilitator Guide* is very thorough and provides plenty of information for introducing the simulation, running it, and debriefing it.

Author and Source: R. Glaser & C. Glaser (1993), HRDQ
Space or Equipment Needs: Slide projector is optional
Cost: Five participant booklets: $27. *Facilitator Guide*: $30. Optional color slides: $32.
Number of Participants: Groups of four to six
Time: 120 minutes
Audience: Intact work groups
Leadership Lesson: Decision Making, Teams

PAPER PLANES, INC.

Paper Planes, Inc. helps participants explore work redesign issues, including participation, total quality, customer satisfaction, and systems thinking. In the simulation, employees of a plane manufacturing company have the opportunity to sell as many planes as they can manufacture that meet given quality standards. The prescribed production design consists of a traditional functional division of labor. After evaluating the effectiveness of their efforts, the workers are told to redesign the production process to their own specifications. Both production designs are compared for cost, quality, delivery time, and worker satisfaction.

Author and Source: W. C. Musselwhite (1993), Discovery Learning
Preparation: Facilitator must have experience with simulations and group facilitation.

Cost: Contact Discovery Learning for licensing or in-house delivery.
Number of Participants: Not specified
Time: Five to seven hours
Audience: Managers
Leadership Lesson: Systems Thinking, Participatory Leadership Style

PAT HOWARD ROLE-PLAY

In a group of eight, four students assume roles as supervisors, each with a different leadership style. The other students assume roles as subordinates, each with different abilities, need for consideration, and task orientation. The role-play situation provides an opportunity for each supervisor to interact with each subordinate and practice using the four leadership styles described by the path-goal theory—supportive, directive, participative, or achievement oriented. Subordinates later rate their supervisor on his or her use of each of the four leadership styles.

Author and Source: J. Seltzer & J. W. Smither (1995), A role-play exercise to introduce students to path-goal leadership theory, *Journal of Management Education, 19*(3), 380-391.
Preparation: Photocopy handouts
Number of Participants: Groups of eight
Time: 60 to 90 minutes
Audience: Students
Leadership Lesson: Four Leadership Styles of the Path-Goal Theory

New
PLASCO, INC.

This management simulation creates an environment for top-level executives to interact as they run a fictional plastics manufacturing company called Plasco. Participants assume roles as the CEO, CFO, presidents of three divisions, and vice presidents of products, marketing, administration, planning, operations, and technology. Over 200 items of information pass around the office. Not everyone is privy to all information—collaboration is necessary for success. Over 100 problems, some trivial and some titanic, need to be addressed. Each participant is given more work than can be accomplished. Manus-trained facilitators observe each participant's strategic-thinking, problem-solving, decision-making, cooperation, and influence skills. At the end of the simulation, participants complete a questionnaire that describes what actions they chose to take and how they met their goals. Feedback from peers and the facilitator helps each participant learn about his or her ability to lead in complex environments. A variation of this simulation is *Tower,* geared to the insurance industry.

Author and Source: (1994), Manus Associates
Preparation: Facilitators must be certified by Manus. Certification training is available.
Space or Equipment Needs: Large meeting room to set up a conference room and 18 workstations; four flip charts and markers; overhead projector
Cost: Contact Manus Associates for information.
Number of Participants: 25 or fewer
Time: Three days
Audience: Executives, intact work groups
Leadership Lesson: Decision Making, Problem Solving, Communication, Influence

POSITION POWER: EXPLORING THE IMPACT OF ROLE CHANGE

Changes in the roles of group members can often affect attitudes and performance. For this exercise, each small group is given the same task to reduce their membership by one. Following the loss of one member, they appoint one member to manager status. Each group is then instructed to create one symbol that best illustrates levels within an organization (worker, managerial, executive). The managers are unable to work directly on the task, and the members who were earlier excluded from the groups become the executive committee that decides which group has the winning symbol. Debriefing questions focus on the thoughts and feelings at each stage in the exercise.

Author and Source: P. Cooke & L. C. Porter in J. W. Pfeiffer, *The 1986 Annual: Developing Human Resources* (pp. 51-54). San Diego, CA: University Associates.
Space or Equipment Needs: Newsprint flip chart and markers for each group, a prize for the winning group, and masking tape
Number of Participants: Ten to 35
Time: 180 minutes
Audience: Managers, executives
Leadership Lesson: Power, Change

PRECISION BICYCLE COMPONENTS: EXPLORING THE GLASS CEILING

Participants have to make both individual and group rankings of men and women candidates who are being considered to replace the retiring vice president of operations for the company. Each group has to reach consensus on who will be selected for this position. Following this step, each group explains how it reached its decision; then, the facilitator leads a discussion about the gender differences in managers' developmental job experiences.

Author and Source: L. M. Hite & K. S. McDonald in J. W. Pfeiffer, *The 1995 Annual: Volume 2, Consulting* (pp. 97-116). San Diego, CA: Pfeiffer & Company.

Space or Equipment Needs: Flip chart and markers
Number of Participants: Eight to 40
Time: 105 to 135 minutes
Audience: Students, managers
Leadership Lesson: Gender Diversity

PRISONERS' DILEMMA: AN INTERGROUP COMPETITION

Prisoners' Dilemma, an older game but still popular, deals with the issues of trust, cooperation, competition, and interpersonal and intergroup relations. A team (acting the part of a prisoner charged with a crime) gets the highest payoff if it doesn't confess and the opposing team does confess, a mid-range payoff if both teams confess, a mid-range loss if neither team confesses, and a maximum loss if it confesses and the other team doesn't. The game is introduced as a "win as much as you can" process, but the competing teams usually interpret this to mean "beat the other team" rather than "maximize points."

Author and Source: J. W. Pfeiffer & J. E. Jones (1974), *A Handbook of Structured Experiences for Human Relations Training, Volume III* (pp. 52-56). San Diego, CA: University Associates.
Preparation: Prepare debriefing material
Number of Participants: 16 or fewer
Time: 60 minutes
Audience: General
Leadership Lesson: Trust, Teams

PUMPING THE COLORS

In this highly interactive exercise, teams design and construct a working water-transfer system. Each participant performs a hands-on task that realistically simulates a real-world job, yet cannot be accomplished in the given time frame without successful teamwork. The learning outcome depends more on the objectives of the training session than on the final product produced. Possible objectives include team building, total-quality-management practices, assessing feedback and communication skills, and developing project management skills. A skillful facilitator is required to process the ongoing dynamics at predetermined "break times" during the simulation.

Author and Source: R. G. Shirts (1991), Simulation Training Systems
Preparation: Facilitators must be trained by Simulation Training Systems.
Space or Equipment Needs: Large break-out area, flip chart, and markers for each team
Cost: Price varies depending on the number of participants. Call Simulation Training Systems for details.
Number of Participants: Groups of six to ten

Time: One-half day to two days
Audience: Students, managers
Leadership Lesson: Communication, Teams

New
PYRAMID™

Pyramid is an activity device that allows participants to practice two types of organizational behavior. The device is constructed of four ten-foot poles that suspend a grabber from 16 strings. In phase one, participants assume hierarchical roles to move the grabber and manipulate an object. Information about the assignment flows from the CEO to functional managers, department managers, and, finally, to the string operators who are restricted in several ways. Problems arise from the executives' lack of operator skills and subsequent inability to give clear directions. In phase two, all members receive the same instructions and string operator training. It is recommended to allow at least one day between phases for classroom instruction. Comparing the two phases demonstrates the value of empowerment and self-directed teams.

Author and Source: Interel
Space or Equipment Needs: 16-foot by 16-foot indoor or outdoor activity area
Cost: $650
Number of Participants: Eight to 16
Time: 90 minutes for each phase
Audience: Managers, intact work groups
Leadership Lesson: Empowerment, Self-directed Teams

RHETORIC AND BEHAVIOR: THEORY X AND THEORY Y

Based on Douglas McGregor's delineation of two contrasting views of work motivation (workers are lazy and need to be controlled versus workers are responsible and eager to be involved), this exercise offers participants a chance to compare their X-Y rhetoric with their behavior. In the process, they also have the chance to explore the assumptions (and the behaviors that demonstrate those assumptions) of Theory X and Theory Y. The exercise starts with participants completing an inventory of what they would "say" and another on what they would "do." The participants compare behavior with rhetoric, explore the assumptions in each, then complete role plays to further demonstrate Theory X and Theory Y rhetoric and behavior.

Author and Source: M. Vanterpool in J. W. Pfeiffer, *The 1991 Annual: Developing Human Resources* (pp. 51-64). San Diego, CA: University Associates.
Preparation: Prepare poster
Space or Equipment Needs: Newsprint and markers
Number of Participants: 12 to 20

Time: 150 minutes
Audience: Managers
Leadership Lesson: Communication

ROLE POWER: UNDERSTANDING INFLUENCE

This role-play exercise explores the types of power inherent in different group and organizational roles. It acquaints participants with power strategies that can be used in the decision-making process and helps them understand effective versus ineffective use of power. The role positions are: controller, director of merchandising, personnel director, promotion director, and operations director. In addition to a description of their particular role, all players get a "public knowledge" sheet that summarizes all positions; later in the role play, they are each given a handout that describes the real political power possessed by the different roles.

Author and Source: P. E. Doyle in J. W. Pfeiffer & L. D. Goodstein, *The 1984 Annual: Developing Human Resources* (pp. 26-36). San Diego, CA: University Associates.
Space or Equipment Needs: Paper, pencil, and clipboard for each observer
Number of Participants: 18 to 35
Time: 120 minutes
Audience: General
Leadership Lesson: Power

RUBICON

Rubicon is an intense simulation utilizing both indoor and outdoor activities to focus on leadership, teamwork, and the impact of values on achievement of results. The simulation offers the opportunity for participants to create an organization that supports a complex scenario involving the recovery of vital worldwide technology and the rescue of missing and injured persons. In establishing the organization, participants must create a vision, build a structure, define values and philosophies for operating, develop strategies and plans, and implement rescue and recovery.

Author and Source: C. McEwen (1992), Executive Expeditions
Cost: This is a proprietary simulation. Contact Executive Expeditions for information.
Number of Participants: Not specified
Time: Six to 24 hours
Audience: Managers, executives
Leadership Lesson: Teams, Values

THE RULES OF THE GAME

This is a role-playing exercise designed to help participants explore issues in hierarchical communication within complex organizations. Participants are assigned roles from production worker to president. Those role-playing each level are given a set of cards containing issues that they must rank in order of importance. Each group's goal is to have the issues they identify as most important dealt with at the appropriate organizational level. To do this, they must communicate with the appropriate level either orally or in writing. Observers are assigned to help record interactions and process. A debriefing follows.

Author and Source: L. C. Lederman & L. P. Stewart (1991), The rules of the game, *Simulation & Gaming*, 22(4), 502-507.
Preparation: The facilitator must prepare the message decks. Sample issues are provided in the article.
Number of Participants: 11 or more
Time: 30 to 90 minutes
Audience: Students, managers
Leadership Lesson: Communication

SHALOM/SALAAM: A SIMULATION OF THE MIDDLE EAST PEACE NEGOTIATIONS

Set in the context of a Middle East conflict, this exercise helps participants understand how differences in power can affect negotiation. They observe how the appearance of having greater power may not result in a better outcome. Several leadership styles and their impact on bargaining results are incorporated within the game. It involves multiparty negotiation, which can evolve into coalition negotiation.

Author and Source: G. H. Harel & S. Morgan (1994), SHALOM/SALAAM: A simulation of Middle East peace negotiations, *Simulation & Gaming*, 25(2), 285-292.
Preparation: The facilitator must photocopy handouts, make transparencies, and read articles on the general background of the Arab-Israeli conflict.
Space or Equipment Needs: Conference room, three smaller meeting rooms, overhead projector; each participant contributes $1
Number of Participants: 15 to 24
Time: 90 to 180 minutes
Audience: Students, managers, executives
Leadership Lesson: Power, Negotiation

SITUATIONAL LEADERSHIP SIMULATION GAME

The *Situational Leadership Simulation Game* has been designed to assist participants in understanding the situational leadership theory of four basic styles. Players receive a situation card from which they are to diagnose the maturity level of the group. Once the diagnosis has been made, the players choose from a set of alternative actions. These actions have points applied to them. The objective is to win points with correct answers and to reach the end of a 28-square track.

Author and Source: P. Hersey, K. Blanchard, & L. Peters (1977), HRD Press
Preparation: The facilitator must be familiar with the situational leadership model.
Cost: $69.95
Number of Participants: Two to 20
Time: 60 to 120 minutes
Audience: Students, managers
Leadership Lesson: Situational Leadership Style

STAR POWER

This is a "new world" game in which participants progress from one level of society to another by acquiring wealth through trading. At a point, the society is "frozen" by giving the group with the most wealth the right to make the rules of the game. This usually leads to further differentiation of power and rebellion by the disempowered group. *Star Power* underscores the use and misuse of power and the sometimes divisive influence of social systems.

Author and Source: R. G. Shirts (1969), Simulation Training Systems
Preparation: 30 minutes to set up the game
Cost: $225 (educational version)
Number of Participants: 18 to 35
Time: 120 minutes
Audience: Students, managers, intact work groups
Leadership Lesson: Power

STRATEEGY CLASSIC

StraTEEgy Classic provides a simulated work process that allows participants to experience real-world work decisions and barriers. The scenario involves a design team working on a request from Wall Street. Using a desktop PC, maps, and architectural modeling materials, the team must design a new golf course, do detailed design and modeling of a "signature hole," and develop a computerized growth model of the neighboring urban community. Within this process, participants practice strategy, teamwork, and negotiation skills. Results are quantified, and a debriefing concludes the exercise.

Author and Source: J. Schmidt & A. Pruitt (1995), Executive Expeditions
Space or Equipment Needs: Desktop computer for each team

Cost: This is a customized, proprietary simulation. Contact Executive Expeditions for information.
Number of Participants: Eight to 250
Time: 180 to 240 minutes
Audience: Managers, executives, intact work groups
Leadership Lesson: Decision Making, Negotiation, Teams

STRATEGIC MANAGEMENT SIMULATIONS (SMS)

SMS is a set of three high-level scenarios, each presenting a complex task environment that allows observation of how managers function in realistic settings. Each scenario generates a range of challenges during a few hours. At certain times during each simulation, managers and teams have ample opportunity to engage in strategic planning; at other times emergencies require decisive action. The simulations, which may be used for both training and assessment, provide profiles of manager effectiveness through precise computer-based measurement of various aspects of performance. A computer-generated report provides 60 performance scores. Validation studies have shown these scales to be predictive of executive success.

Author and Source: S. Streufert (1982, 1997), 4615 Custer Drive, Harrisburg, PA 17110. Phone: (717) 531-6022 or (717) 232-0771. Fax: (717) 232-7015.
Preparation: Participants must read several hours of background material. Administrators must attend a one-week training session to obtain certification and licensing privileges.
Cost: This is a proprietary simulation. Contact S. Streufert for information.
Number of Participants: Seven to nine
Time: One day
Audience: Managers, executives
Leadership Lesson: Decision Making, Leadership Effectiveness

STUDENT ACTIVITIES ALLOCATION EXERCISE

The main purpose of this small-group decision-making simulation is to reveal to participants their leadership strengths and weaknesses. The participants are given roles as student government association members at a small private college. The college has received a gift of $50,000, and each member has a separate pet project. The task is for each member to persuade other members that his or her project is the most worthy. The exercise is videotaped. The video playback and accompanying discussion highlight the importance of communication and leadership strategies.

Author and Source: G. Lamacchia Paris (1992), Professor, Department of Literature and Communications, Pace

University, Bedford Road, Pleasantville, NY 10570.
Phone: (914) 773-3955.
Number of Participants: 12 to 21
Time: Three to five hours
Audience: Students
Leadership Lesson: Decision Making, Influence, Communication

TANGRAM: LEADERSHIP DIMENSIONS

Tangram raises issues around various leadership and work-group functions: setting the overall goal, stating specific objectives, planning, communicating, directing, coordinating, and controlling. The exercise involves a group of five or six individuals who are instructed to put together three puzzles with information only their leader possesses. A group of observers gathers information on questions surrounding the issues mentioned above. (See the *Hollow Square* description for a similar exercise.)

Author and Source: E. Casais in J. W. Pfeiffer & J. E. Jones (1981), *A Handbook of Structured Experiences for Human Relations Training, Volume VIII* (pp. 108-119). San Diego, CA: University Associates.
Preparation: Time to trace and cut puzzle pieces
Space or Equipment Needs: Cardboard for puzzle pieces
Number of Participants: Eight to 15
Time: 120 minutes
Audience: General
Leadership Lesson: Communication

TASK FORCE

This business case study deals with team dynamics within a real business situation. The case is based on a successful task force in a Fortune 100 company that was assigned the responsibility of developing a new customer-service department. Participants are given background information, including notes from the first meeting of the original task force. They are asked to rank order—first individually and then as a group—actions and issues in the areas of task force dynamics, equipment, staffing, and training. Scores are compared to the actual process used by the real task force. The real-world nature of this exercise differentiates it from many ranking-type exercises based upon hypothetical disasters.

Author and Source: R. Hill (1994), Aviat, Inc.
Cost: Participant's exercise: $4.95. *Facilitator's Handbook*: $20.
Number of Participants: Small groups
Time: 90 to 120 minutes
Audience: Students, managers
Leadership Lesson: Decision Making, Teams

TEAM INTERVENTIONS: MOVING THE TEAM FORWARD

The facilitator introduces this exercise by presenting a team development model and explains that "certain interventions by the team leader can assist the team in completing the outcomes for each stage of development and moving into the next." Then, by responding to vignettes of teams in various stages of development, each subgroup is provided a framework within which its members can analyze team performance and assess team needs, then suggest leader interventions appropriate for the stage of team development.

Author and Source: C. Kormanski in J. W. Pfeiffer, *The 1996 Annual: Volume 2, Consulting* (pp. 19-26). San Diego, CA: Pfeiffer & Company.
Space or Equipment Needs: Flip chart, markers, masking tape
Number of Participants: Ten to 30
Time: 120 to 150 minutes
Audience: Managers
Leadership Lesson: Teams

New
TEAMTREK™

TeamTrek is a group transport device used to teach communication and teamwork. Up to ten participants strap their feet to 15-foot rubber treads and hold handstraps for control as they move along a course. The team is forced to communicate and compromise in order to move in synchronicity. Additional challenges may be introduced by blindfolding some members, having some face backwards, placing obstacles along the path, prohibiting speaking, and creating competition between two or more teams. One variation is *PlanTrek* in which teams must rescue one member from a distant island. Another is *DiversiTrek* in which team members adopt personal challenges such as sight or hearing impairments, language differences, breathing difficulties, or other physical limitations. Moderate physical activity is required with all *TeamTrek* activities, so participants who cannot trek may serve as coaches.

Author and Source: Interel
Space or Equipment Needs: 30-foot by 60-foot indoor or outdoor activity area and six markers such as orange cones. Optional materials for challenges and variations include team bandannas, blindfolds, earplugs, face masks, ropes, plastic jugs, tables or other barrier items.
Cost: $350 per set of treads
Number of Participants: Five to ten participants per set of treads
Time: 25 minutes

Audience: Managers, intact work groups
Leadership Lesson: Teams, Communication

TEAMWORK

Teamwork is a puzzle-completion game designed to help participants define teamwork and appreciate how team success leads to individual success. It begins with a brainstorming session about teams and teamwork, then continues with the playing of the game. In the recommended configuration, there are two teams of six players each. Each person on a team takes ownership of one puzzle piece and the teamwork principle associated with it, and must try to fit that piece into the puzzle solution. There is a series of three such puzzles that must be solved. After each, the facilitator reviews effective and ineffective team behavior. By the third round, the two teams must work together to reach a win-win solution.

Author and Source: Alban Associates, Inc., Jossey-Bass/Pfeiffer
Space or Equipment Needs: Overhead projector, VCR, viewing screen
Cost: $395. 13 additional participant notebooks: $49.95.
Number of Participants: 12
Time: 180 to 210 minutes
Audience: Students, intact work groups
Leadership Lesson: Teams

New
THUMBS UP, THUMBS DOWN: A CONFLICT-MANAGEMENT ICEBREAKER

This exercise is an icebreaker to open a lesson on conflict and cooperation. Participants pair off, hook fingers, and raise their thumbs. When the facilitator instructs them to get their partners' thumbs down, most participants assume that means to thumb wrestle. The facilitator explains another option, simple and obvious but often overlooked. This exercise teaches participants to approach conflict with a variety of choices.

Author and Source: R. Gaetani in *The 1997 Annual: Volume 1, Training* (pp. 65-67). San Francisco: Pfeiffer.
Number of Participants: Six to 50
Time: 15 minutes
Audience: General
Leadership Lesson: Conflict Management

TINKERTOY POWER

In *Tinkertoy Power*, participants explore issues of resource dependence, power, and ethics as they bargain for resources to build their structure. One of the four groups is considered resource rich and powerful, one resource poor and powerless, and the remaining two about

average. Each group is awarded points for completing its structure. Debriefing discussions may focus on topics such as coalition-building, win-win versus win-lose assumptions, group cohesion and competition, rules and innovation, and power and influence strategies.

Author and Source: C. P. Lindsay & C. A. Enz (1991), Resource control and visionary leadership: Two exercises, *Journal of Management Education*, *15*(1), 127-135.
Space or Equipment Needs: Five sets of Tinkertoys
Cost: Cost of materials
Number of Participants: 12 to 40
Time: 60 minutes
Audience: General
Leadership Lesson: Power, Ethics

New
TOWER BUILDING EXERCISE

Small groups make plans to build paper towers that will be judged on height, stability, beauty, and significance. During the planning and building phases, group dynamics become evident to observers. Who emerges as group leader? Is there any conflict? Does each member contribute? Does the group function well to produce a good product? After judging the completed towers, the groups analyze their ability to succeed as self-managed teams.

Author and Source: D. Marcic (1992), *Organizational Behavior: Experiences and Cases* (3rd ed.) (pp. 127-130). New York: West Publishing.
Space or Equipment Needs: Newspaper to build towers
Number of Participants: Groups of six to eight
Time: 50 minutes
Audience: General
Leadership Lesson: Teams

TURNAROUND

In this simulation, team members work individually, then as a group to reverse the climate and fiscal position of a failing business. Survival of the company depends on the decisions the participants make in six key areas: assumptions and values, problem identification, establishing objectives, action steps, approach to management, and feedback and communication. A leader's guide provides a theoretical base as well as background and administrative information for simulation facilitators.

Author and Source: Human Synergistics
Cost: $21. *Observer's Guide*: $5. *Leader's Guide*: $25.
Number of Participants: Four
Time: Three to four hours
Audience: Students, managers
Leadership Lesson: Decision Making, Problem Solving, Communication, Teams

New
TWELVE ANGRY MEN

This exercise uses the classic film *Twelve Angry Men* (1957) to learn about influence and group dynamics. Participants view a portion of the film to get acquainted with each juror, his attitudes, and his behavior. Each participant makes a private judgment about the impact each juror will have on the group to determine the final verdict in a murder trial. Then, the class discusses the influence rankings and tries to reach consensus. They once again make individual judgments that may or may not align with their group's consensus. The rest of the film contains a dramatic lesson on the impact of one man's influence on a group. Following the film, participants measure their pre-discussion choices, group choices, and post-discussion choices against the film's results. They learn about their own levels of influence, coercion, and submission. The publisher recommends combining this exercise with the instrument *Group Barrier Analysis,* also available from Teleometrics.

Author and Source: J. Hall (1970, 1986, 1994), Teleometrics International
Space or Equipment Needs: *Twelve Angry Men* video, VCR, viewing screen
Cost: Exercise booklet: $9.95. *Leader's Guide*: $24.95.
Number of Participants: Any number
Time: 180 to 210 minutes
Audience: General
Leadership Lesson: Influence

New
UGLI ORANGE CASE

In this exercise, students practice negotiating and learn about trust, influence, and interpersonal communication. Students are divided into groups of three—Dr. Jones, Dr. Roland, and an observer. Separately, the two doctors read handouts that dictate their bargaining positions to buy the entire, but limited, supply of valuable Ugli oranges. Neither knows the other's budget or end product. To succeed, both parties must share confidential information and give a little to gain a lot. Following negotiations, the observers report on each party's level of trust and influence.

Author and Source: R. House in D. Marcic (1992), *Organizational Behavior: Experiences and Cases* (3rd ed.) (pp. 294-296). New York: West Publishing.
Preparation: Photocopy handouts
Number of Participants: Groups of three
Time: 40 minutes
Audience: General
Leadership Lesson: Negotiation, Influence, Trust

VALUE DILEMMAS

This exercise provides an opportunity to debate managerial values and receive feedback on personal style and values orientation. The initial component is a *Value Dilemmas Questionnaire*, which may be completed in the session or overnight (one hour completion time). Pairs of participants then complete an assessment of their partner's values, based on their partner's questionnaire responses, and share their assessments with each other. The process is completed by a final lecturette on choosing values and a sharing of the exercise experience.

Author and Source: M. Woodcock & D. Francis (1991), *The Self-Made Leader: 25 Structured Activities for Self-Development* (pp. 51-59). King of Prussia, PA: HRDQ. Phone: (800) 633-4533.
Number of Participants: Groups of two
Time: 150 minutes
Audience: General
Leadership Lesson: Values

VANATIN: GROUP DECISION MAKING AND ETHICS

The authors state that "the Vanatin case provides an opportunity for group members to struggle with questions of social responsibility and ethics in decision making. The case is centered around a medical product, considered by experts to be injurious to the health of consumers—even to the point of possibly causing death." Seven corporate roles are assigned, and the action takes place in a meeting called by the chairman of the board. Some specific alternatives are presented and discussed; after 45 minutes, a group decision is recorded and a discussion follows.

Author and Source: R. J. Lewicki, D. D. Bowen, D. T. Hall, & F. S. Hall (1988), *Experiences in Management and Organizational Behavior* (3rd ed.) (pp. 175-179), New York: Wiley.
Space or Equipment Needs: Name tags
Number of Participants: Groups of seven
Time: 90 minutes
Audience: General
Leadership Lesson: Decision Making, Ethics

VICE-PRESIDENT'S IN-BASKET: A MANAGEMENT ACTIVITY

This in-basket exercise focuses attention on communication priorities in organizations and increases awareness of the role of delegation. Participants work individually on the items in their in-basket, having gotten instructions that they will likely not be able to finish in the two hours allotted and, thus, will need to assign priorities and decide what to delegate. After individual work is done, participants meet in small groups to discuss their work and feelings. Following this, the facilitator records the groups' priority setting, then shares the "correct" solution. A final discussion focuses on participants' delegating styles and work styles.

Author and Source: A. N. Shelby in L. D. Goodstein & J. W. Pfeiffer, *The 1983 Annual for Facilitators, Trainers, and Consultants* (pp. 49-64). San Diego, CA: University Associates.
Space or Equipment Needs: Felt marker and newsprint pad for the facilitator; ruled paper pads, paper clips, and pencils for each participant
Number of Participants: Four to 25
Time: 210 minutes
Audience: General
Leadership Lesson: Communication, Decision Making

VISIT TO AN ALIEN PLANET

The objective of this game is to expand participants' understanding of the value of others who may differ from the majority culture on such dimensions as age, sex, religion, and cultural background. The scenario is a visiting alien from another planet who wants to take a number of earth volunteers back to her planet. Since only six people may go on the trip, she has asked that a committee of earth people (the simulation participants) make a decision on who should go. It is this committee and its negotiations, along with the wide diversity among the candidate group, that structure this simulation.

Author and Source: R. B. Powers (1993), Visit to an alien planet: A cultural diversity game, *Simulation & Gaming, 24*(4), 509-518.
Preparation: Photocopy handouts
Number of Participants: Several groups of three to eight players each
Time: 60 minutes
Audience: Students, civic leaders
Leadership Lesson: Multicultural Diversity, Communication

VMX PRODUCTIONS, INC.: HANDLING RESISTANCE POSITIVELY

This role-play exercise is designed to increase participants' understanding of the phenomenon of resistance, to explore and compare strategies for dealing with resistance, and to present to participants an effective method for handling resistance. Participants are divided into pairs and go through a series of activities and role plays to demonstrate personal power and resistance. At the end, those who played "resister" roles are asked for their reactions to the power moves of their partners.

Author and Source: H. B. Karp in J. W. Pfeiffer, *The 1988 Annual: Developing Human Resources* (pp. 43-49). San Diego, CA: University Associates.
Space or Equipment Needs: Flip chart and marker
Number of Participants: Groups of two
Time: 90 minutes
Audience: Students, managers
Leadership Lesson: Change

New
WEB OF YARN: SIMULATING SYSTEMS

This exercise encourages systems thinking. Participants form a circle and toss a ball of yarn from person to person, holding on to a piece of yarn each time. After many tosses, a web forms to create a sensory experience of belonging to a system. Members yank their pieces of yarn, drop pieces, and add new members to the web to reinforce their connectedness and dependence on each individual within the system. They also learn about the importance of the flow of information throughout the system.

Author and Source: M. K. Key in *The 1997 Annual: Volume 2, Consulting* (pp. 25-28). San Francisco: Jossey-Bass/Pfeiffer.
Preparation: Print and post two statements
Space or Equipment Needs: Ball of sturdy yarn, newsprint, marker, masking tape
Number of Participants: Ten to 15
Time: 45 minutes
Audience: Students, managers
Leadership Lesson: Systems Thinking, Communication

New
WHAT'S A LEADER?

Students work in small groups to interview as many organizational constituents possible in 30 minutes to gather data on the desired attributes of a new CEO. Points are awarded for gathering data from a variety of constituents such as co-workers, administrators, and faculty. Group leaders and members separate to analyze the data and plan strategies. They regroup to share perceptions and collaborate on the writing of a job advertisement for the new CEO. Ads are compared as the facilitator debriefs the group on the link between leadership concepts, observed behaviors, and personal experiences.

Author and Source: Michael P. Bochenek (1997). Available from Michael P. Bochenek, Assistant Professor, Center for Business and Economics, Elmhurst College, 190 Prospect Avenue, Elmhurst, IL 60126-3296. Phone: (630) 617-3099. Fax: (630) 617-3742.
Space or Equipment Needs: Two meeting rooms, paper, and pencils

Number of Participants: Six to 70
Time: 90 minutes
Audience: Students
Leadership Lesson: Leadership Behaviors

WHERE DO YOU DRAW THE LINE?

This game is designed to get a group involved in a provocative discussion of ethical issues. To play, participants are divided into small groups; then, the groups make judgments about the ethical behavior of individuals and organizations as described in vignettes. These judgments become the basis of the group's "ethical system." In the second phase, the decisions of all the groups are summarized, displayed, and discussed.

Author and Source: R. G. Shirts (1977), Simulation Training Systems
Preparation: 15 minutes to set up the game
Space or Equipment Needs: Overhead projector is optional
Cost: $110 (educational version)
Number of Participants: Five to 35
Time: 50 minutes
Audience: General
Leadership Lesson: Ethics

WORK DIALOGUE: BUILDING TEAM RELATIONSHIPS

Designed for participants who know one another, this team-building exercise is for enhancing work relationships through mutual openness and disclosure. Participants move from interpersonal disclosure in pairs, to a sharing of that process, to discussing the implications coming out of the sharing for team relationships. Several variations of the process are included for groups differing in interpersonal skills and learning needs.

Author and Source: J. Vogt & K. L. Williams in J. W. Pfeiffer, *The 1995 Annual: Volume 1, Training* (pp. 27-31). San Diego, CA: Pfeiffer.
Preparation: Photocopy handouts
Space or Equipment Needs: Flip charts and markers
Number of Participants: 20 or fewer
Time: 150 minutes
Audience: Intact work groups
Leadership Lesson: Communication, Teams

INSTRUMENTS AND EXERCISES VENDORS

To contact a vendor listed in the Instruments and Exercises sections, refer to this directory. A brief description of each vendor's products helps readers decide where to call and request a catalog or find more information about a product. The vendor's address, phone, and fax are provided. E-mail and website addresses are provided when available.

ACUMEN INTERNATIONAL, INC.

Acumen provides multi-rater instruments for career management and organizational change.

3950 Civic Center Drive, Suite 310 North
San Rafael, CA 94903-4174
Phone: (415) 492-9190
Fax: (415) 479-5358
Website: http://www.acumen.com

ASSOCIATED CONSULTANTS IN EDUCATION

This group produces an easy-to-use, inexpensive line of personality assessments called the BEST Instruments.

708 East Northside Drive
Clinton, MS 39056-3438
Phone: (800) 748-9073 or (601) 924-0691
Fax: (601) 924-6378

AVIAT, INC.

Aviat's simulations are designed to promote an understanding of group dynamics. Some simulations come with slides, overheads, or videos. Train-the-trainer sessions are available, but not required.

101 North Main Street, Suite 850
Ann Arbor, MI 48104-1400
Phone: (800) 421-5323
Fax: (313) 663-3670
Website: http://intergalactic.com/aviat.htm

BIRKMAN INTERNATIONAL, INC.

This organization creates assessment tools for selection, team building, coaching, and career guidance. Dr. Roger Birkman's instrument *The Birkman Method*® is the foundation of their work.

3040 Post Oak Boulevard, Suite 1425
Houston, TX 77056-6511
Phone: (713) 623-2760
Fax: (713) 963-9142
E-mail: info@birkman.com
Website: http://www.birkman.com

BLOCK PETRELLA WIESBORD

This organization provides simulations for learning about organizational change.

Marcus Plaza
118 Westfield Avenue, Suite 7
Clark, NJ 07066-2408
Phone: (732) 680-4300
Fax: (732) 680-4304

CARLSON LEARNING COMPANY

Carlson produces learning tools around concepts such as innovation, leadership, diversity, and time management. Their products are sold through independent distributors like Tamco.

c/o Tamco Training and Management Consultants
716 North Church Street
Palestine, TX 75801-2406
Phone: (800) 657-2235

CENTER FOR CREATIVE LEADERSHIP

The Center's goal to link theory with practice is reflected in its publication of training materials. Instruments are designed to measure competencies, development experiences, creativity, and culture. Certification training is available for those who administer the Center's instruments.

One Leadership Place
P.O. Box 26300
Greensboro, NC 27438-6300
Phone: (336) 545-5000
Fax: (336) 282-3284
E-mail: info@leaders.ccl.org
Website: http://www.ccl.org

CLARK WILSON GROUP, INC.

The Wilson Group publishes multi-rater surveys used for leadership development training to change behavior and improve effectiveness on the job.

1320 Fenwick Lane, Suite 708
Silver Spring, MD 20910-3514
Phone: (800) 537-7249 or (301) 587-2591
Fax: (301) 495-5842
E-mail: info@cwginc.com

CONSULTING PSYCHOLOGISTS PRESS

This is the source for the *Myers-Briggs Type Indicator*® and the *Social Skills Inventory*. They also distribute a wide variety of tests for career and organizational development. Some materials are sold only to facilitators who have advanced degrees.

3803 East Bayshore Road
Palo Alto, CA 94303-4300
Phone: (800) 624-1765 or (415) 969-8901
Fax: (415) 969-8608

DEVELOPMENTAL ADVISING INVENTORIES, INC.

This organization supports Greg Dickson's research on student development through cocurricular programs.

P.O. Box 1946
Paradise, CA 95967-1946
Phone: (916) 872-0511

DISCOVERY LEARNING

Their hands-on learning products are designed to support training in creativity, conflict management, communication, change management, leadership development, and team building.

909 North Elm Street, Suite 200
Greensboro, NC 27401-1512
Phone: (336) 272-9530
Fax: (336) 273-4090
E-mail: mwhite@spyder.net

DRC ASSOCIATES

DRC is the source for the *Team Performance Questionnaire.*

P.O. Box 4151
Chapel Hill, NC 27515-4151
Phone: (919) 667-1500
Fax: (919) 956-9630

EDUCATIONAL SIMULATIONS

This company produces simulations for learning about ethics and multicultural diversity.

P.O. Box 276
Oceanside, OR 97134-0276
Phone: (503) 842-7247

ERIC DOCUMENT REPRODUCTION SERVICE

This is the source for ordering ERIC documents. There is a nominal fee.

7420 Fullerton Road, Suite 100
Springfield, VA 22153-2852
Phone: (800) 443-3742 or (703) 440-1400
Fax: (703) 440-1408
E-mail: service@edrs.com

EXECUTIVE EXPEDITIONS

Their four- to sixteen-hour organizational simulations mirror the complex interactions and work processes of service- and manufacturing-based corporations.

131 Village Parkway, Suite 4
Marietta, GA 30067-4061
Phone: (770) 951-2173
Fax: (770) 951-0437
E-mail: ee@execexp.com

GEORGE SIMONS INTERNATIONAL

This is the source for the *Diversophy*™ game.

236 Plateau Avenue
Santa Cruz, CA 95060-6455
Phone and Fax: (888) 215-3117
E-mail: gsimons@euronet.nl
Website: http://www.intl-partners.com

GLOBAL OPTIONS

Global Options is the source for the *Culture Clash* simulation.

8160 Manitoba Street, #315
Playa del Ray, CA 90293-8640
Phone and Fax: (310) 821-1864
Also:
785 Wright Street
Yellow Spring, OH 45387
Phone and Fax: (937) 767-1960

HRD PRESS

Among other human resource development training products, HRD Press distributes a line of *Situational Leadership*® products.

22 Amherst Road
Amherst, MA 01002-9709
Phone: (800) 822-2801 or (413) 253-3488
Fax: (413) 253-3490
E-mail: hrdpress@aol.com
Website: http://www.hrdpress.com

HRDQ

Formerly known as HRD Quarterly, this vendor sells books, instruments, games, simulations, and case studies to support all areas of human resources development.

2002 Renaissance Boulevard, #100
King of Prussia, PA 19406-2756
Phone: (800) 633-4533 or (610) 279-2002
Fax: (800) 633-3683 or (610) 279-0524
E-mail: hrdq@hrdq.com
Website: http://www.hrdq.com

HUMAN SYNERGISTICS, INC.

Their products measure growth and improvement at the individual, team, and organizational level.

39819 Plymouth Road, C-8020
Plymouth, MI 48170-4290
Phone: (800) 622-7584 or (313) 459-1030
Fax: (313) 459-5557
E-mail: info@humansyn.com
Website: http://www.humansyn.com

INTERCULTURAL PRESS, INC.

This is the source for the simulation *Ecotonos*.

P.O. Box 700
Yarmouth, ME 04096-0700
Phone: (800) 370-2665 or (207) 846-5168
Fax: (207) 846-5181
E-mail: interculturalpress@internetmci.com
Website: http://www.bookmasters.com/interclt.com

INTEREL, INC.

Interel provides action-learning devices to aid corporate productivity. The devices are used in training programs for developing leadership, coaching, systems thinking, and teamwork.

140 Carl Street
San Francisco, CA 94117-3906
Phone: (415) 566-0554
Fax: (415) 566-8317
E-mail: sales@interel.com

INTERNATIONAL TRAINING CONSULTANTS, INC.

Training modules come complete with assessments, participant notebooks, and videos. Inexperienced or seasoned trainers may administer their modules on leadership, empowerment, and diversity.

P.O. Box 35613
Richmond, VA 23235-0613
Phone: (800) 998-8764 or (804) 320-2415
Fax: (804) 794-9429

IPAT—INSTITUTE FOR PERSONALITY AND ABILITY TESTING, INC.

IPAT sells psychological testing materials to qualified purchasers in accordance with ethical and professional standards recommended by the American Psychological Association. Workshops are available for introductory through advanced training.

P.O. Box 1188
Champaign, IL 61824-1188
Phone: (800) 225-4728 or (217) 352-4739
Fax: (217) 352-9674.
Website: http://www.ipat.com

JOSSEY-BASS/PFEIFFER

Formerly known as Pfeiffer and University Associates, this vendor offers a large selection of tests, exercises, videos, books, and CD-ROMs for training in leadership and organizational development.

350 Sansome Street, 5th Floor
San Francisco, CA 94104-1342
Phone: (800) 274-4434
Fax: (800) 569-0443
Website: http://www.pfeiffer.com

LOMINGER LIMITED, INC.

Lominger is the source for The Leadership Architect® Suite of leadership development products. This set of instruments, cards, handbooks, and software supports job profiling, development, team building, and succession planning. Facilitators must be certified.

1825 Girard Avenue South
Minneapolis, MN 55403-2944
Phone: (612) 374-1466
Fax: (612) 374-8917
Website: http://www.lominger.com

MANUS

Manus produces simulations, 360-degree-feedback instruments, and complete training programs. They will provide facilitators or train the trainers at certification workshops.

100 Prospect Street
South Tower
Stamford, CT 06901-1641
Phone: (800) 445-0942 or (203) 326-3880
Fax: (203) 326-3890.

METRITECH, INC.

MetriTech specializes in the research and development of assessment and training products for industry and education. Purchasers must meet standards of educational background and professional certification.

111 North Market Street
Champaign, IL 61820-4004
Phone: (800) 747-4868 or (217) 398-4868

Fax: (217) 398-5798
Website: http://www.metritech.com

MIND GARDEN, INC.

Mind Garden products support personal and team development, mentoring skills, and stress management.

1690 Woodside, Suite 202
Redwood City, CA 94061
Phone: (650) 261-3500
Fax: (650) 261-3505
E-mail: mindgarden@msn.com

NATIONAL CENTER FOR RESEARCH IN VOCATIONAL EDUCATION (NCRVE)

NCRVE develops materials for students, teachers, and administrators in vocational education.

Materials Distribution Service
46 Horrabin Hall
Western Illinois University
Macomb, IL 61455-1390
Phone: (800) 637-7652
E-mail: ncrve-mds@wiu.edu

NCS WORKPLACE DEVELOPMENT

NCS publishes psychological assessments for behavioral counseling and organizational development.

P.O. Box 1294
Minneapolis, MN 55440-1294
Phone: (800) 627-7271 or (612) 939-5000
Fax: (612) 939-5199
E-mail: info@ncs.com
Website: http://www.ncs.com

PERFORMANCE SUPPORT SYSTEMS

This organization provides affordable, easy-to-use tools for performance management.

11835 Canon Boulevard, Suite C101
Newport News, VA 23606-2570
Phone: (800) 488-6463 or (804) 873-3700
Fax: (804) 873-3288
E-mail: pss2@aol.com
Website: http://www.2020insight.net

PERSONAL STRENGTHS PUBLISHING, INC.

This vendor's tools are designed to help individuals understand their own behaviors, motivations, relationships, and personal values.

P.O. Box 2605
Carlsbad, CA 92018-2605
Phone: (800) 624-7347 or (714) 734-1360
Fax: (714) 734-1364

PERSONNEL DECISIONS, INC.

PDI's assessments are designed to be used in their executive feedback and coaching programs. Certification training is available for facilitators.

2000 Plaza VII Tower
45 South 7th Street
Minneapolis, MN 55402-1608
Phone and Fax: (612) 339-0927

PRO-ED, INC.

PRO-ED publishes books, journals, and tests for the educational community.

8700 Shoal Creek Boulevard
Austin, TX 78757-6897
Phone: (512) 451-3246
Fax: (800) 397-7633
E-mail: info@proedinc.com
Website: http://www.proedinc.com

PSYCHOLOGICAL ASSESSMENT RESOURCES, INC. (PAR)

PAR's products include assessment instruments, software, books, audiotapes, and videotapes for professionals in psychology, counseling, education, business, and human resources. Purchasers must meet qualification standards.

P.O. Box 998
Odessa, FL 33556-0998
Phone: (800) 331-TEST
Fax: (800) 727-9329
E-mail: custserv@parinc.com
Website: http://www.parinc.com

QUALITY EDUCATION DEVELOPMENT, INC.

This is the source for the *Global Diversity Game.*

41 Central Park West
New York, NY 10023-6002
Phone: (800) 724-2215 or (212) 724-3335
Fax: (212) 724-4913

SIGMA ASSESSMENT SYSTEMS, INC.

Three levels of tests are available. A-level is for business and educational use. B-level is to be administered by qualified psychologists with at least a master's degree. C-level tests must be administered and interpreted by psychologists with a Ph.D.

511 Fort Street, Suite 435
P.O. Box 610984
Port Huron, MI 48061-0984
Phone: (800) 265-1285
Fax: (800) 361-9411
E-mail: sigma@mgl.ca
Website: http://www.mgl.ca/~sigma

SIMULATION TRAINING SYSTEMS

Their one- to two-hour simulations are intended to spark enthusiasm and change the pace in training sessions.

P.O. Box 910
Del Mar, CA 92014-0910
Phone: (800) 942-2900 or (619) 755-0272.
Fax: (619) 792-0743
E-mail: sts@cts.com
Website: http://www.stsintl.com

SYMLOG CONSULTING GROUP

This is the source for SYMLOG® products that are used in leadership training and development, organizational development, team building, and total quality management.

18580 Polvera Drive
San Diego, CA 92128-1120
Phone: (619) 673-2098
Fax: (619) 673-9279
Website: http://www.symlog.com/mainmenu.htm

TELEOMETRICS INTERNATIONAL

Training themes are supported by feedback instruments, exercises, and videos. Materials are available in nine languages.

1755 Woodstead Court
The Woodlands, TX 77380-0964
Phone: (800) 527-0406 or (713) 367-0060
Fax: (713) 292-1324

TRG HAY/McBER AND COMPANY

This subsidiary of the Hay Group of human resource consulting firms produces training materials to identify and develop leadership styles and competencies.

Training Resources Group
116 Huntington Avenue
Boston, MA 02116-5747
Phone: (800) 729-8074 or (617) 437-7080
Fax: (617) 425-0073
E-mail: TRG_McBer@haygroup.com
Website: http://www.haygroup.com/na/service/trg2.htm

WONDERLIC PERSONNEL TEST, INC.

Wonderlic tests are used primarily for selection and promotion evaluations.

1509 North Milwaukee Avenue
Libertyville, IL 60048-1387
Phone: (800) 323-3742 or (708) 680-4900
Fax: (708) 680-9492
E-mail: contact@wonderlic.com
Website: http://222.wonderlic.com

XICOM

XICOM publishes training tools and assessment instruments for personal and organizational development. Topics include leadership skills, conflict management, and corporate culture.

60 Woods Road
Tuxedo, NY 10987-3108
Phone: (800) 759-4266 or (914) 351-4735
Fax: (914) 351-4762

VIDEOS

In this section, there are videos of three different types: feature films, documentaries of actual people or events, and training films made especially for leadership development programs. They are organized by subject. All videos are in color unless otherwise noted. Whenever possible, the descriptions include reference to support materials such as case studies, leader's guides, or articles that describe using a video in the classroom. Following each description is information about:

- Release year—this indicates the release date of the original film, not the year in which the film became available on video.
- Runtime.
- Source.
- Cost.
- Type of Program—feature film, documentary, or training film.
- Other Leadership Lesson—additional subject descriptors.

See the table of contents for an outline of the subject headings or refer to the index for a detailed guide to subjects and titles. To buy or rent a video, contact the distributors listed in the Video Distributors directory. These distributors are your appropriate contacts for copyright information and permission to use videos in the classroom.

CONTENTS

GENERAL LEADERSHIP

THE BOLERO

The lighting and creative camera work in this film are as dramatic as Ravel's music. Brief comments from soloists, concertmaster, and conductor Zubin Mehta give insight into the subtle leadership touches that make a truly great performance (by Los Angeles Philharmonic).

Release Year: 1974
Runtime: 28 minutes
Source: Pyramid Media
Cost: $295
Type of Program: Documentary
Other Leadership Lesson(s): Leader-Follower Relations

BRINGING OUT THE LEADER IN YOU

This film teaches that whatever your task, you may learn how to maximize your leadership potential. There are lessons on how to inspire followers, how to get people involved and committed to a goal, and how to lead people to success.

Release Year: 1991
Runtime: 23 minutes
Source: AMA Video
Cost: $79.95
Type of Program: Training

THE CREDIBILITY FACTOR: WHAT FOLLOWERS EXPECT FROM LEADERS

Credibility is the critical difference between effective and ineffective leaders. James Kouzes and Barry Posner, authors of *The Leadership Challenge,* describe specific practices that build credibility, fulfill followers' expectations, and create trust and productivity.

Release Year: 1990
Runtime: 22 minutes
Source: CRM Films
Cost: $695
Type of Program: Training

New
DILBERT BUSINESS VIDEO

Cartoonist Scott Adams pokes fun at meetings, managing change, quality, and sales. Dilbert, Dogbert, and a cartoon Tom Peters make viewers laugh and initiate discussions about organizational culture. Includes a user's guide.

Release Year: 1994
Runtime: 21 minutes
Source: Media Learning Resources
Cost: $595
Type of Program: Training
Other Leadership Lesson(s): Change, Quality

New
THE EXCELLENCE FILES

Eight case studies demonstrate how innovative companies and a government agency are strengthening community and corporate culture, building teams, competing globally, and managing change. Includes profiles of: Southwest Airlines, Rubbermaid, Defense Personnel Support Center, USAA Property and Casualty Insurance, Timberland, Coca-Cola, Work/Family Directions, and Whole Foods Market.

Release Year: 1997
Runtime: 86 minutes
Source: Enterprise Media
Cost: $795
Type of Program: Training
Other Leadership Lesson(s): Corporate Leadership, Government Leadership

EXCELLENCE IN THE PUBLIC SECTOR

Tom Peters talks about the similarities between public-sector/nonprofit organizations and for-profit organizations. Well-run organizations, often in turnaround situations, provide examples of good management practices.

Release Year: 1989
Runtime: 48 minutes
Source: CRM Films
Cost: $595
Type of Program: Training
Other Leadership Lesson(s): Government Leadership, Nonprofit Leadership

THE FRONT OF THE CLASS: LEARNING TO LEAD

In this humorous take on basic leadership principles for the beginner, a man goes back to his sixth-grade teacher for advice when he has trouble in his first supervisory role. Together, they illustrate the four Fs that make your employees, and therefore you, succeed: First, Fair, Firm, and Flexible.

Release Year: 1995
Runtime: 29 minutes
Source: Coastal Human Resources

Cost: $625
Type of Program: Training

New
GREAT MINDS OF BUSINESS

The editors of *Forbes* present five case studies of innovative business leaders. Featured are Federal Reserve Chairman, Paul Volker; Intel CEO, Andrew Grove; marketing expert, Pleasant Rowland; FedEx leader, Fred Smith; and investment expert, Peter Lynch.

Release Year: 1997
Runtime: Five tapes—30 minutes each
Source: PBS Video–Home Division
Cost: $79.98 for the set
Type of Program: Documentary
Other Leadership Lesson(s): Corporate Leadership

HIGH IMPACT LEADERSHIP: HOW TO BE MORE THAN A MANAGER

This three-tape series discusses leadership in terms of what motivates leaders and how leaders project personal power and achieve goals. Explores the self-mastery techniques effective leaders use. Shows how leaders may empower their followers, use imagery and storytelling to sell their vision to others, and how leaders are responsible stewards of their resources. Mark Sanborn demonstrates how he thinks leaders foster change and tap creativity to liberate themselves and their people from patterns that hold them back.

Release Year: 1990
Runtime: 76, 59, and 96 minutes
Source: CareerTrack Publications
Cost: $199.95 for the set
Type of Program: Training

LEADERSHIP

John Kotter, Konosuke Matsushita Professor of Leadership at Harvard Business School, explains that leadership produces dramatic, adaptive change in order for organizations to thrive in the face of global competition and rapid change. Kotter uses interviews and dramatic vignettes to demonstrate the techniques and philosophies of a successful leader by comparing and contrasting them to the techniques of a successful manager. Includes one facilitator's guide and six viewer's guides.

Release Year: 1990
Runtime: 120 minutes
Source: WingsNet
Cost: $990
Type of Program: Training

THE LEADERSHIP ALLIANCE

Tom Peters explores the subject of successful leadership by visiting four organizations: General Motors Bay City components plant, Johnsonville Foods sausage factory, Harley-Davidson's York motorcycle assembly plant, and the Julia B. Thayer High School. He explains successful leadership as a special kind of alliance between managers and workers that fully engages the talents and potential of everyone in the organization.

Release Year: 1988
Runtime: 64 minutes
Source: WingsNet
Cost: $895
Type of Program: Training
Other Leadership Lesson(s): Corporate Leadership

THE LEADERSHIP CHALLENGE

In 1987 James Kouzes and Barry Posner published a landmark book of the same name. This video is based on their findings and documents their premise that leadership can be found at all levels of the organization. It tells the stories of four manager/leaders from both the corporate and nonprofit sectors, and in the telling reveals the practices Kouzes and Posner believe are common to successful leaders: challenging the process, enabling others to act, modeling the way, inspiring a shared vision, and encouraging the heart. Includes a leader's guide.

Release Year: 1989
Runtime: 26 minutes
Source: Jossey-Bass/Pfeiffer
Cost: $845
Type of Program: Training

New
LEADERSHIP: REACH FOR THE STARS

Apollo 11 astronaut Buzz Aldrin hosts this film about the differences between managers and leaders. Lessons are dramatized by two brothers, one who seeks guidance and the other who has already learned the difference. Between lessons about communicating vision, raising expectations, gaining commitment, and building trust, Aldrin describes the leadership of the Apollo program. From President John Kennedy's vision to the commitment and creativity at every level, the Apollo program is an example of leadership that helps us to realize extraordinary goals.

Release Year: 1997
Runtime: 20 minutes
Source: Coastal Human Resources
Cost: $495

Type of Program: Training
Other Leadership Lesson(s): Vision, Trust, Transformational Leadership

New
LEADERSHIP: WHAT'S TRUST GOT TO DO WITH IT?

This film follows a team leader who is caught between corporate goals and unmotivated employees. He and his team members discover the importance of trust—of being honest, sharing information, keeping promises, and valuing each member's contribution.

Release Year: 1996
Runtime: 19 minutes
Source: CRM Films
Cost: $695
Type of Program: Training
Other Leadership Lesson(s): Trust, Teams and Groups

New
LEADING BY EXAMPLE: MENTORING AND COACHING FOR EFFECTIVE LEADERSHIP

Stephen Covey presents the story of Anne Sullivan to illustrate that a leader's legacy is reflected in the character and competence of followers. Sullivan was a teacher and mentor to only one student, Helen Keller. Through courage, vision, and patience, Sullivan pioneered methods to help her student and other deaf and blind people find expression and purpose. Helen Keller makes an appearance and, through her interpreter, speaks with eloquence about teaching and leadership. Includes a *Leader's Discussion Guide* and participant handouts.

Release Year: 1996
Runtime: 20 minutes
Source: Franklin Covey
Cost: $695
Type of Program: Training
Other Leadership Lesson(s): Educational Leadership, Influence, Women's Leadership

LEADING OUT: A PROFILE OF UNIVERSITY LEADERSHIP

James Laney, President of Emory University, is followed throughout the demands of an academic year. A strong feature of this video is its detail, which allows a thorough view of academic leadership in a particular cultural context. Includes a leader's guide.

Release Year: 1996 (Revised)
Runtime: 45 minutes
Source: James Ault Productions

Cost: $100
Type of Program: Training
Other Leadership Lesson(s): Educational Leadership

LESSONS FROM THE NEW WORKPLACE

A follow-up to *Leadership and the New Science,* this video uses examples from the U.S. Army, the DuPont Corporation, and a public school system to demonstrate the application of Margaret Wheatley's visionary models in organizations. The film stresses the importance of information, relationships, and vision to the new workplace. Includes a leader's guide.

Release Year: 1995
Runtime: 20 minutes
Source: CRM Films
Cost: $845
Type of Program: Training
Other Leadership Lesson(s): Vision, Corporate Leadership, Educational Leadership

MEETINGS, BLOODY MEETINGS

This updated John Cleese video takes a humorous look at meetings that take too much of a manager's time and accomplish too little. It demonstrates, through whimsical drama, techniques for conducting meetings that are shorter and more productive.

Release Year: 1993
Runtime: 30 minutes
Source: Video Arts Inc.
Cost: $870
Type of Program: Training

New
THE MILAGRO BEANFIELD WAR

When a poor citizen kicks the water cutoff that separates the poor New Mexican town of Milagro from its wealthy neighbor, he accidentally irrigates his father's farmland. What ensues is a battle of legal rights, ethics, and a community's will to survive. Sonia Braga displays courage and persistence as she rallies the townspeople of Milagro to demand legal rights to the local water supply.

Release Year: 1988
Runtime: 118 minutes
Source: MCA/Universal Home Video
Cost: $14.98
Type of Program: Feature
Other Leadership Lesson(s): Citizen Leadership, Multicultural Diversity, Hispanic Leadership

New
MILLENNIUM: LEADERSHIP CAPSULES FOR THE 21ST CENTURY

HRD experts join in a series of group discussions on the basics of leadership and management. Four segments are pertinent to leadership training or self-study: Leadership is . . . , The Leader as Coach, The Leader as Mentor, and Providing Performance Feedback. An accompanying *Leader's Guide* suggests discussion starters to expand and reinforce the lessons on tape.

Release Year: 1995
Runtime: Seven segments—15 minutes each
Source: Coastal Human Resources
Cost: $425
Type of Program: Training

MORE BLOODY MEETINGS

This is a companion film to *Meetings, Bloody Meetings.* Where the other film concentrates on the mechanics of meetings, this one focuses on the human factor, including controlling aggression, keeping the group focused on the objective, and preventing dominant group members from overpowering the rest of the group. John Cleese stars.

Release Year: 1986
Runtime: 27 minutes
Source: Video Arts Inc.
Cost: $870
Type of Program: Training

NOTHING IN COMMON

Tom Hanks and Jackie Gleason star in this comedy that can be used as a business parable. It is about the conflict between work and family, and it can also be used as an exploration of leadership styles. A discussion of this film is found in J. M. Banthin and L. Stelzer (1993), "Dilemmas and Choices Facing Contemporary Business People as Revealed in *Nothing in Common*," *Journal of Management Education, 17*(1), 118-123.

Release Year: 1986
Runtime: 119 minutes
Source: Warner Home Video, Inc.
Cost: $19.98
Type of Program: Feature
Other Leadership Lesson(s): Work and Family Balance

New
SISTER ACT

Whoopi Goldberg poses as a nun to escape her mobster boyfriend. While in hiding, her unique vision of music with "soul" jumpstarts the convent's tortured choir. In time, the music's energy revitalizes the connecting church and the surrounding community. Contrasting leadership styles are portrayed by the tyrannical former choir director, the peacekeeping priest, and the competitive Mother Superior.

Release Year: 1992
Runtime: 100 minutes
Source: Buena Vista Home Video
Cost: $19.99
Type of Program: Feature
Other Leadership Lesson(s): Contrasting Leadership Styles, Spirit, Women's Leadership

STAND AND DELIVER

In this fact-based feature film, a high school mathematics teacher takes a class of potential dropouts and transforms them in one year into kids who want to learn and who do learn—at year's end 18 class members are able to pass a tough advanced-placement calculus exam. The story provides a dramatic exposition of the teacher as leader.

Release Year: 1988
Runtime: 105 minutes
Source: Warner Home Video, Inc.
Cost: $14.95
Type of Program: Feature
Other Leadership Lesson(s): Transformational Leadership, Educational Leadership

TAKE ME TO YOUR LEADERS

This program follows several young people who are learning to lead in creative ways—ways that offer hope for the future. James Garner hosts this look at leadership in the making.

Release Year: 1990
Runtime: 47 minutes
Source: Pyramid Media
Cost: $95
Type of Program: Documentary
Other Leadership Lesson(s): Youth Leadership

TOGETHER: VOLUNTEER-TO-VOLUNTEER RELATIONSHIPS

This videotape portrays, through a simulated committee, the many issues involved in leading volunteer teams. Includes a trainer's guide with recommendations for training.

Release Year: 1989
Runtime: 38 minutes
Source: Energize Inc.
Cost: $395

Type of Program: Training
Other Leadership Lesson(s): Citizen Leadership

New
UNITED STATES PRESIDENTS

This series profiles U.S. presidents from George Washington to William Clinton from their youth to their early careers and the years in office. The world events that shaped each presidency and the legacies left by each man are examined.

Release Year: 1995
Runtime: Five tapes—60 minutes each
Source: PBS Video–Home Division
Cost: $99.98 for the set
Type of Program: Documentary
Other Leadership Lesson(s): Political Leadership

YOU GOT TO MOVE

This is a documentary about the personal and social transformation that ordinary people cause when they dare to assume leadership roles. The people of Tennessee's famous Highlander Folk School are featured with their work for union, civil, environmental, and women's rights in the South.

Release Year: 1985
Runtime: 87 minutes
Source: First Run/Icarus Films
Cost: $390
Type of Program: Documentary
Other Leadership Lesson(s): Citizen Leadership, Global and Social Issues

HISTORY AND BIOGRAPHY

New
AMELIA EARHART: THE PRICE OF COURAGE

Kathy Bates hosts this profile of the groundbreaking female aviator. The film highlights Earhart's personal dreams, her remarkable career, and the public's fascination with her accomplishments.

Release Year: 1994
Runtime: 60 minutes
Source: PBS Video–Home Division
Cost: $19.95
Type of Program: Documentary
Other Leadership Lesson(s): Women's Leadership

New
AMERICA'S GREAT INDIAN LEADERS

This film describes the leadership of four 19th-century Native Americans who fought to save their land and their culture: Apache rebel, Geronimo; Comanche leader, Quannah Parker; Chief Joseph of the Nez Perce nation; and the great warrior, Crazy Horse.

Release Year: 1994
Runtime: 65 minutes
Source: Questar Video, Inc.
Cost: $29.95
Type of Program: Documentary
Other Leadership Lesson(s): Native American Leadership

New
CONQUERORS

Military heroes throughout history are portrayed as men of charisma, vision, and fatal flaws. This film explores how the fate of a nation is impacted by the personality of its leader. Peter the Great and Alexander the Great are portrayed as inspired leaders and Napoleon as an idealistic yet self-serving leader.

Release Year: 1997
Runtime: Two tapes—120 minutes each
Source: Discovery Channel Home Video
Cost: $29.95 for the set
Type of Program: Documentary
Other Leadership Lesson(s): Military Leadership

THE FINEST HOURS

This tribute to Sir Winston Churchill documents his rocky diplomatic career and his inspiring passionate leadership in World War II, recalling his words, humor, family life, and patriotic fervor. Narrated by Orson Welles.

Release Year: 1964
Runtime: 116 minutes
Source: Video City Inc.
Cost: $49.95
Type of Program: Documentary
Other Leadership Lesson(s): Political Leadership

FIVE PRESIDENTS ON THE PRESIDENCY

The filmed speeches of Presidents Harry S. Truman, Dwight D. Eisenhower, John F. Kennedy, Lyndon B. Johnson, and Richard M. Nixon are analyzed. Examined are such topics as: presidential power, congressional relations, press relations, foreign policy, the president as politician, and the office in retrospect.

Release Year: 1973
Runtime: 24 minutes
Source: Phoenix Coronet
Cost: $275
Type of Program: Documentary
Other Leadership Lesson(s): Political Leadership

GANDHI

Richard Attenborough's production and Ben Kingsley's award-winning performance highlight this dramatic account of the spiritual leader who inspired nonviolent resistance to British rule in India. The film follows Gandhi's life from his fight against racial inequality in South Africa to his unsuccessful attempts to unite Hindu and Muslim factions into an independent India. Hartwick Humanities in Management Institute offers a case study based on this film.

Release Year: 1982
Runtime: 188 minutes
Source: Columbia Tristar Home Video
Cost: $29.95
Type of Program: Feature
Other Leadership Lesson(s): Transformational Leadership, Ethics and Values, Negotiation, Multicultural Diversity, Spirit

GETTYSBURG

Ted Turner's adaptation of the novel *The Killer Angels* is epic in scale. The greatest and bloodiest battle of the Civil War is realistically portrayed by an all-male cast including over 5,000 reenactors. The human cost of the war is emphasized.

Release Year: 1993
Runtime: 254 minutes
Source: Movies Unlimited
Cost: $119.99
Type of Program: Feature
Other Leadership Lesson(s): Military Leadership

GREAT COMMANDERS

This series was produced by Channel 4 (Great Britain), in association with A&E, Ambrose Video, SBS (Australia), and Sovtelexport (Russia). Each one features a different military leader: Julius Caesar, Horatio Nelson, Georgi Zhukov, Ulysses S. Grant, Napoleon Bonaparte, and Alexander the Great.

Release Year: 1993
Runtime: Six tapes—45 minutes each
Source: Ambrose Video Publishing Inc.
Cost: $79.95 each
Type of Program: Documentary
Other Leadership Lesson(s): Military Leadership

THE HELPING HAND

In this part of the *Walk Through the Twentieth Century* series, Bill Moyers examines how Franklin D. Roosevelt convinced Congress and led the country into his "New Deal."

Release Year: 1984
Runtime: 58 minutes
Source: PBS Video–Educational Division
Cost: $69.95
Type of Program: Documentary
Other Leadership Lesson(s): Political Leadership

New
HENRY V

Kenneth Branagh portrays the young Hal who assumes the British throne and quickly develops into a transformational leader. He learns about the hopes and dreams of his troops and, in turn, gains their trust. His St. Crispian's Day speech before the battle at Agincourt inspires the small, weary foot soldiers to a spectacular victory against impossible odds. Hartwick Humanities in Management Institute offers a case study based on this film.

Release Year: 1989
Runtime: 138 minutes
Source: CBS/Fox Video
Cost: $19.98
Type of Program: Feature
Other Leadership Lesson(s): Transformational Leadership, Trust, Goal Setting, Communication

IN REMEMBRANCE OF MARTIN

This remarkable documentary chronicles the life of Martin Luther King, Jr., through personal comments from family members, former classmates, close friends, and advisors. Archival footage documents King's early civil rights efforts, including the "I Have a Dream" address on the steps of the Lincoln Memorial. Later events in King's life and a brief synopsis of key civil rights decisions of the 1950s and 1960s are also included.

Release Year: 1986
Runtime: 60 minutes
Source: PBS Video–Educational Division
Cost: $59.95
Type of Program: Documentary
Other Leadership Lesson(s): African-American Leadership, Ethnic Diversity

New
JOAN OF ARC

Ingrid Bergman stars as Joan of Arc, the 15th-century peasant girl who practiced leadership without authority. She claimed that divine inspiration drove her to lead French troops to victory in the Hundred Years War. Her claim to divinity caused her to be burned at the stake as a heretic and later canonized as patron saint of France.

Release Year: 1948
Runtime: 100 minutes
Source: Reel
Cost: $45.99
Type of Program: Feature
Other Leadership Lesson(s): Women's Leadership, Servant Leadership, Military Leadership, Vision

New
MANDELA'S FIGHT FOR FREEDOM

Nelson Mandela's life is documented, from his early years as a protester against racial injustices in South Africa to his 26-year imprisonment, and election as president of a new democracy in 1990. Mandela's early leadership helped to create the Youth League of the African National Congress and inspired the black political movement that eventually ended apartheid.

Release Year: 1995
Runtime: 150 minutes
Source: PBS Video–Home Division
Cost: $29.95
Type of Program: Documentary
Other Leadership Lesson(s): Political Leadership

MARTIN LUTHER KING, JR.: FROM MONTGOMERY TO MEMPHIS

This black-and-white film surveys the career of Martin Luther King, Jr., and the nonviolent Civil Rights Movement under his leadership—from the 1955-1956 bus boycott in Montgomery to his assassination in Memphis.

Release Year: 1969
Runtime: 26 minutes
Source: Phoenix Coronet
Cost: $190
Type of Program: Documentary

Other Leadership Lesson(s): Ethnic Diversity, African-American Leadership

NIXON: CHECKERS TO WATERGATE

From the heights of success to the depths of impending impeachment, this powerful visual survey highlights the triumphs and tragedies of Richard Nixon's life and career.

Release Year: 1976
Runtime: 20 minutes
Source: Pyramid Media
Cost: $225
Type of Program: Documentary
Other Leadership Lesson(s): Political Leadership

PATTON

This is a panoramic portrait of General Patton, the brilliant, unstable, and anachronistic World War II tactician.

Release Year: 1970
Runtime: 169 minutes
Source: CBS/Fox Video
Cost: $19.98
Type of Program: Feature
Other Leadership Lesson(s): Military Leadership

THE THIRTY-SECOND PRESIDENT

This segment of the *Walk Through the Twentieth Century* series with Bill Moyers examines Franklin Roosevelt's relationship with the press and the later role played by the media in presidential advertising campaigns.

Release Year: 1984
Runtime: 58 minutes
Source: PBS Video–Educational Division
Cost: $69.95
Type of Program: Documentary
Other Leadership Lesson(s): Political Leadership

TR AND HIS TIMES

In another program from the *Walk Through the Twentieth Century* series, Bill Moyers examines the presidency of Theodore Roosevelt with historian David McCullough. American optimism was high in 1900, but people still had doubts about America's role as a world superpower.

Release Year: 1984
Runtime: 58 minutes
Source: PBS Video–Educational Division
Cost: $69.95
Type of Program: Documentary
Other Leadership Lesson(s): Political Leadership

DIVERSITY

BREAKING THE GLASS CEILING

The BBC produced this video featuring "ceiling breakers" and organizations like the Center for Creative Leadership. It can be used to inspire women to take risks and come up with their own strategies. It can also be presented as an awareness-building program. It includes a 24-minute discussion starter, a 10-minute case study, and a training notes guide.

Release Year: 1993
Runtime: 34 minutes
Source: Reel
Cost: $420.75
Type of Program: Training
Other Leadership Lesson(s): Women's Leadership

BUILDING THE TRANSNATIONAL TEAM

To demonstrate skills for successful international teams, culturally diverse colleagues meet to discuss selecting a Brussels manager. Germany, France, England, America, and Spain are represented. The strong cultural stereotypes act as a discussion starter for further learning.

Release Year: 1993
Runtime: 23 minutes
Source: MultiMedia Inc.
Cost: $695
Type of Program: Training
Other Leadership Lesson(s): Multicultural Diversity

New
CADENCE

Charlie Sheen and Laurence Fishburne star in this story of a white prisoner placed in an all-black Army stockade. The group dynamics change from harassment to unity as the prisoners collaborate on a project and gain respect for their differences. This change is lyrically reflected in the group's willingness and ability to march together in cadence.

Release Year: 1989
Runtime: 97 minutes
Source: Reel
Cost: $14.98
Type of Program: Feature
Other Leadership Lesson(s): Teams and Groups, Ethnic Diversity

CROSS-CULTURAL MANAGEMENT: THE HUMAN SIDE OF INTERNATIONAL MANAGEMENT

Fons Trompenaars discusses why management principles lose effectiveness across cultures. He explains his Seven Dimensions of Culture model, which was based on data from 15,000 managers. In conclusion, he advocates a pay-for-performance system for cross-cultural management.

Release Year: 1994
Runtime: 64 minutes
Source: MultiMedia Inc.
Cost: $695
Type of Program: Training
Other Leadership Lesson(s): Multicultural Diversity

New
DIVERSITY: FOOD FOR THOUGHT

Viewers visit the Diversity Diner where customers learn to appreciate differences on the lunch menu and among co-workers. Conversation revolves around a new "touchy-feely" human resources survey on diversity. After some initial resistance, diners recognize that there are obvious and not-so-obvious differences among members of any workforce. Valuing these differences can decrease discrimination and increase productivity. Includes a leader's guide and participant handbooks.

Release Year: 1997
Runtime: 20 minutes
Source: Coastal Human Resources
Cost: $595
Type of Program: Training

EYES ON THE PRIZE: AMERICA'S CIVIL RIGHTS YEARS, 1954-1965

New national leaders emerged during the civil rights struggle. This inspiring six-part series is a comprehensive look at the people, events, and issues of those years.

Release Year: 1986
Runtime: Six tapes—60 minutes each
Source: PBS Video–Educational Division
Cost: $250 for the set
Type of Program: Documentary
Other Leadership Lesson(s): Ethnic Diversity, African-American Leadership

EYES ON THE PRIZE 2: AMERICA AT THE RACIAL CROSSROADS, 1965-1985

The second award-winning series by the same name continues the chronicle of the American civil rights movement. From community power in the schools to "Black Power" in the streets; from police confrontations in neighborhoods to political confrontation in city government; from Malcolm X to Martin Luther King; it depicts a period of great transformation.

Release Year: 1990
Runtime: Eight tapes—60 minutes each
Source: PBS Video–Educational Division
Cost: $350 for the set
Type of Program: Documentary
Other Leadership Lesson(s): Ethnic Diversity, African-American Leadership

GETTING TO KNOW BARBARA

This segment from a *60 Minutes* production features Barbara Proctor, who was described by Ronald Reagan as an embodiment of America's "spirit of enterprise." Describes this black woman's rise from ghetto impoverishment to her position as head of a multimillion-dollar advertising agency.

Release Year: 1988
Runtime: 12 minutes
Source: Carousel Film and Video
Cost: $125
Type of Program: Documentary
Other Leadership Lesson(s): Entrepreneurial Leadership, Women's Leadership, African-American Leadership

GLORY

Glory is the story of the 54th Massachusetts, the first black volunteer regiment in the Civil War. The transformational leadership that emerges within the ranks and in their young, white commander contrasts with the authoritarian leadership outside the regiment. Hartwick Humanities in Management Institute offers a case study based on this film.

Release Year: 1989
Runtime: 122 minutes
Source: Columbia Tristar Home Video
Cost: $19.95
Type of Program: Feature
Other Leadership Lesson(s): Contrasting Leadership Styles, Teams and Groups, African-American Leadership

GUNG HO

Gung Ho is a comedy pertinent to discussions about cross-cultural leadership. When a Japanese firm takes over a small U.S. auto factory, Michael Keaton tries to keep employees and management from killing each other during the misunderstandings that occur. Directed by Ron Howard.

Release Year: 1985
Runtime: 111 minutes
Source: Paramount Home Video
Cost: $14.95
Type of Program: Feature
Other Leadership Lesson(s): Multicultural Diversity

LAND OF O'S: COMPETING THROUGH DIVERSITY

Barry Stein talks us through this follow-up to *A Tale of "O,"* addressing "real-world" issues. He links diversity with productivity, competitiveness, and bottom-line results. He also shows how to leverage differences to the advantage of both the organization and the individual.

Release Year: 1995
Runtime: 28 minutes
Source: Goodmeasure Direct, Inc.
Cost: $695
Type of Program: Training

New
THE LAST EMPEROR

This is the ironic and true story of Pu Yi, the last emperor of China. Crowned at the age of three before Communist rule, Pu Yi was forced to abdicate his throne and learn Western ways before he reached adulthood. This movie was shot on location in the Forbidden City.

Release Year: 1987
Runtime: 164 minutes
Source: Columbia Tristar Home Video
Cost: $19.98
Type of Program: Feature
Other Leadership Lesson(s): Multicultural Diversity, Biography

LEADERSHIP SKILLS FOR WOMEN

Based on the book by Marilyn Manning and Patricia Haddock, the video shows women how to use their strengths and talents to become the best leaders possible, both on the job and in their personal lives. It interviews women who have strong leadership skills in order to demonstrate how to build teams, motivate, plan, set goals, solve problems, coach, and counsel.

Release Year: 1991
Runtime: 25 minutes
Source: Crisp Publications
Cost: $495
Type of Program: Training
Other Leadership Lesson(s): Gender Diversity,
Women's Leadership

MAKING DIVERSITY WORK

This film helps managers learn about diversity, understand their own beliefs, and teach their employees to do
the same. Practical guidelines help managers and their
employees value differences in order to reach individual,
group, and organizational goals.

Release Year: 1993
Runtime: 31 minutes
Source: AMA Video
Cost: $89.95
Type of Program: Training

MALCOLM X

Spike Lee's tribute to the controversial black activist
features Denzel Washington in the title role. Malcolm X,
a leader in the struggle for black liberation, leaves a
legacy of black nationalism, self-determination, and racial
pride. Winner of several awards.

Release Year: 1992
Runtime: 201 minutes
Source: Warner Home Video, Inc.
Cost: $24.98
Type of Program: Feature
Other Leadership Lesson(s): Charisma, African-
American Leadership, Biography

New
MAURITIUS: CELEBRATING DIFFERENCES

Stephen Covey takes viewers to the small island of
Mauritius, an African nation with five distinct societies.
Franco-Mauritians, British, Indian, Chinese, and Creole
groups live, work, and govern together with respect for
the diversity among them. They find synergy in their
common values while cherishing the richness of their
differences. Includes a *Leader's Discussion Guide* and
participant handouts.

Release Year: 1995
Runtime: 26 minutes
Source: Franklin Covey
Cost: $695
Type of Program: Training
Other Leadership Lesson(s): Multicultural Diversity

NEW SKILLS FOR GLOBAL MANAGEMENT

Stephen Rhinesmith, author of *A Manager's Guide to
Globalization,* presents his concepts with lecture and
graphics. Global competitiveness, complexity,
multicultural teams, and adaptability are among the
challenges Rhinesmith addresses.

Release Year: 1995
Runtime: 35 minutes
Source: MultiMedia Inc.
Cost: $695
Type of Program: Training
Other Leadership Lesson(s): Multicultural Diversity

A PEACOCK IN THE LAND OF PENGUINS

A fable based on the book by Barbara Hateley and
Warren Schmidt (Berrett-Koehler, 1995) takes us to the
Land of Opportunity, where workers and bosses don't
waste time or energy pretending to be something they're
not. They know many types of qualities and strengths are
needed to succeed in turbulent times. They also know that
the most important requirements for success are acceptance and trust, which allow each bird of a different
feather to fly.

Release Year: 1995
Runtime: 10 minutes
Source: CRM Films
Cost: $495
Type of Program: Training

RAINBOW WAR

An animated short film that won several awards, *Rainbow
War* can illustrate issues dealing with differences, whether
cultural, racial, or other. Three kingdoms—Blue, Red, and
Yellow—fight a colorful battle for supremacy, but in the
end, all are winners. Confrontation is transformed into
collaboration, and the colors blend into the world's first
rainbow.

Release Year: 1986
Runtime: 20 minutes
Source: Pyramid Media
Cost: $295
Type of Program: Training

RUNNING WITH JESSE

From the PBS *Frontline* series, this video chronicles Jesse
Jackson's presidential campaign through the eyes of
reporters who accompanied him, his supporters and
detractors. It assesses the hope and hype that accompanied the campaign of this minority contender.

Release Year: 1989
Runtime: 60 minutes
Source: Reel
Cost: $46.75
Type of Program: Documentary
Other Leadership Lesson(s): African-American Leadership, Political Leadership, Biography

A TALE OF "O": ON BEING DIFFERENT

This revised edition provides an objective, animated look at diversity (being different in any way). Rosabeth Moss Kanter and Barry Stein explore the human problem of what it's like to be the few among many by using Xs and Os in an abstract and therefore widely applicable way. By explaining the impact on people's performance in work groups, it makes points that can defuse conflict, promote mutual understanding, and prevent problems before they occur. Includes a training manual.

Release Year: 1993
Runtime: 18 minutes
Source: Goodmeasure Direct, Inc.
Cost: $695
Type of Program: Training

VALUING DIVERSITY®

This seven-part series explores different aspects of managing workplace diversity. For example, in Part Six, *Champions of Diversity,* key people in well-known organizations explain why they champion diversity and how they change themselves and their organizations to do the same.

Release Year: 1990
Runtime: Seven tapes of various lengths

Source: Griggs Productions, Inc.
Cost: Tapes 1-6: $695 each, Tape 7: $995
Type of Program: Training

New
WINDS OF CHANGE: A MATTER OF PROMISE

This series documents the leadership efforts to preserve the sovereignty of the Onandaga, Navajo, Lummi, and Hopi nations.

Release Year: 1990
Runtime: Two tapes—60 minutes each
Source: REEL
Cost: $16.95 for the set
Type of Program: Documentary
Other Leadership Lesson(s): Native American Leadership

New
WOMEN FIRST AND FOREMOST

This series documents the achievements of women who broke ground in previously male-dominated professions. Included are profiles of women in journalism, the arts, medicine, and the military—one from the Revolutionary War.

Release Year: 1995
Runtime: Three tapes—60 minutes each
Source: Monterey Home Video
Cost: $69.95 for the set
Type of Program: Documentary
Other Leadership Lesson(s): Women's Leadership

TEAMS AND GROUPS

THE ABILENE PARADOX

This film deals with the management of agreement in organizations. The theme is that mismanaged agreement is as dangerous to organizational effectiveness as excessive conflict because it can lead the organization toward inappropriate goals.

Release Year: 1985
Runtime: 27 minutes
Source: CRM Films
Cost: $745
Type of Program: Training

New
AMERICA3: THE POWER TO CREATE

This video chronicles the American crew's 1992 victory in the premier international yachting competition, the America's Cup. There is a strong focus on the collaboration of teamwork, talent, and technology that enabled the crew of America3 to turn setbacks into opportunities.

Release Year: 1993
Runtime: 26 minutes
Source: Enterprise Media
Cost: $645

Type of Program: Training
Other Leadership Lesson(s): Diversity

New
CHALK TALK: STANFORD COACHES ON LEADERSHIP AND TEAM BUILDING

Nine Stanford University coaches share 14 strategies for building winning teams such as: inspiring others to believe in themselves, risk taking, and overcoming obstacles. Includes an assessment tool to identify areas for improvement.

Release Year: 1995
Runtime: 20 minutes
Source: WingsNet
Cost: $195
Type of Program: Training
Other Leadership Lesson(s): Motivation

COACHING FOR TOP PERFORMANCE

Viewers learn how to develop a successful work team through a three-part coaching process: educating, developing, and counseling. Examples from the arts, sports, and business demonstrate good coaching skills.

Release Year: 1992
Runtime: 26 minutes
Source: AMA Video
Cost: $89.95
Type of Program: Training

New
COOL RUNNINGS

This film is based on the true story of the Jamaican bobsled team and their first trip to the Olympic Games in 1988. Their coach forges a unified team from four disparate personalities, introduces small achievable goals, and helps to overcome seemingly impossible obstacles. Jamaican-style persistence and heart win them well-deserved respect if not a medal. This Disney movie is made for young audiences, but the leadership lessons may be appreciated by all ages.

Release Year: 1993
Runtime: 98 minutes
Source: Walt Disney Home Video
Cost: $19.99
Type of Program: Feature
Other Leadership Lesson(s): Multicultural Diversity, Goal Setting

DAS BOOT [THE BOAT]

This World War II drama about a German submarine crew reveals various faces of leadership and crew response in the midst of incredible tension and a literal fight for survival.

Release Year: 1982
Runtime: 150 minutes
Source: Columbia Tristar Home Video
Cost: $19.95
Type of Program: Feature
Other Leadership Lesson(s): Military Leadership

DO YOU BELIEVE IN MIRACLES?

Most of this film is footage of the incredible and emotional victory of the U.S. Olympic Hockey team, with play-by-play descriptions. It includes reflections by the coach and players on the role of leadership, team effort, and determination.

Release Year: 1980
Runtime: 24 minutes
Source: corVision Media Inc.
Cost: $295
Type of Program: Documentary
Other Leadership Lesson(s): Coaching

EVERYBODY LEADS: TEAM MEMBERS TALK ABOUT SELF-MANAGEMENT

This production presents an inside view of how an employee-designed workplace uses self-management to make good decisions, respond to technical problems, increase production, handle emergencies, and improve quality. Team members from two different unions discuss the benefits and difficulties of rotating leadership.

Release Year: 1991
Runtime: 26 minutes
Source: Blue Sky Productions
Cost: $595
Type of Program: Training

New
FLIGHT OF THE PHOENIX

The crash of a small plane changes the group dynamics and leadership behavior of the survivors. Hartwick Humanities in Management Institute offers a case study based on this film.

Release Year: 1965
Runtime: 147 minutes
Source: CBS/Fox Video
Cost: $19.98

Type of Program: Feature
Other Leadership Lesson(s): Emergent Leadership

GROUPTHINK (REVISED EDITION)

Even empowered team players are at risk of experiencing groupthink: the natural tendency to agree just for the sake of unity. Groupthink symptoms and solutions are analyzed against a backdrop of historical events, including the Space Shuttle Challenger disaster, where groupthink so tragically influenced the decision to launch.

Release Year: 1991
Runtime: 22 minutes
Source: Excellence in Training Corporation
Cost: $725
Type of Program: Training
Other Leadership Lesson(s): Decision Making

HOOSIERS

Gene Hackman stars in this movie about a small, in-the-dumps high school basketball team that manages to make it to the state finals. It is a classic sports-movie plot, but in this well-acted drama Hackman's character rings true and exemplifies the leadership and team-building power of inspiration and high expectations. Hartwick Humanities in Management Institute offers a case study based on this film.

Release Year: 1986
Runtime: 115 minutes
Source: Reel
Cost: $14.98
Type of Program: Feature
Other Leadership Lesson(s): Transformational Leadership

HOW TO MAKE CROSS-FUNCTIONAL TEAMS WORK

Viewers learn how to set up cross-functional teams in this four-volume video program. Mark Howard shows how to use teams to break up bureaucracy, streamline processes, solve problems. A facilitator's guide and participants' workbooks are available.

Release Year: 1994
Runtime: 188 minutes
Source: CareerTrack Publications
Cost: $249.95
Type of Program: Training

New
INNOVATIVE PROJECT TEAMS

Examples from Duke Power, Ethican Endo-Surgery, and the *Tallahassee Democrat* newspaper demonstrate the difficulties, risks, and benefits of teams. These companies overcame safety, product development, and marketing dilemmas through teamwork. Includes a presenter's guide.

Release Year: 1994
Runtime: 40 minutes
Source: Harvard Business School Publishing
Cost: $495
Type of Program: Training

New
KEEPING THE VISION ALIVE

Cross-country skier Ann Bancroft describes the challenge and adventure of leading her all-women's team across Antarctica to the South Pole. She credits acts of commitment and recommitment, accountability, and celebration with much of their success. A leader's guide suggests training activities and discussion topics.

Release Year: 1995
Runtime: 27 minutes
Source: Excellence in Training Corporation
Cost: $595
Type of Program: Training
Other Leadership Lesson(s): Conflict Management, Vision, Women's Leadership

New
A LEAGUE OF THEIR OWN

This story is about the 1940s All American Girls Professional Baseball League. Tom Hanks as the disinterested coach and Geena Davis as the star player display contrasting leadership styles. We see Hanks's struggle to change from a tyrant in the "no crying in baseball" scene to a supportive coach with the outfielder who forgets to use a relay.

Release Year: 1992
Runtime: 127 minutes
Source: Columbia Tristar Home Video
Cost: $14.95
Type of Program: Feature
Other Leadership Lesson(s): Contrasting Leadership Styles, Women's Leadership, Self-Development

New
LORD OF THE FLIES

When a group of schoolboys are stranded on a remote island, they regress into primitive behavior. The story is one of power struggles and abuse of power as the group wrestles between the immediacy of survival and the long-range plans for building a new society. Hartwick Humanities in Management Institute offers a case study based on this film.

Release Year: 1992
Runtime: 90 minutes
Source: Columbia Tristar Home Video
Cost: $19.95
Type of Program: Feature
Other Leadership Lesson(s): Contrasting Leadership Styles, Ethics and Values, Power

TEAM BUILDING: AN EXERCISE IN LEADERSHIP

Based on the book by Robert Maddux, *Team Building* teaches managers how to transform a group into a team. Using real-world examples, it covers planning, organizing, motivating, controlling, goal setting, improving communication, building trust, and resolving conflict.

Release Year: 1992
Runtime: 25 minutes
Source: Crisp Publications, Inc.
Cost: $495
Type of Program: Training

TEAMS AND ORGANIZATIONAL CHANGE

Jon Katzenbach and Douglas Smith take viewers behind the scenes at the Ritz-Carlton, Magna Metals, and Sealed Air Corporation to show how they successfully implemented a team-based management structure. High-performance teams help failing businesses, improve customer service, and boost productivity in sustainable ways.

Release Year: 1994
Runtime: 40 minutes
Source: Harvard Business School Publishing
Cost: $495
Type of Program: Training

TWELVE O'CLOCK HIGH

A psychological drama that deals with the problems of an Air Force commander who must rebuild a bomber group whose shattered morale threatens the effectiveness of daylight bombing raids. An edited version (34 minutes) is now available, but if you have time for the unedited version, go with it. Hartwick Humanities in Management Institute offers a case study based on this film.

Release Year: 1949
Runtime: 132 minutes
Source: CBS/Fox Video
Cost: $14.98
Type of Program: Feature
Other Leadership Lesson(s): Situational Leadership, Vision, Goal Setting

New
WORKTEAMS AND THE WIZARD OF OZ

Ken Blanchard draws lessons on group dynamics and team leadership from the classic film. Dorothy, the scarecrow, the tin man, and the lion have personal goals yet realize that joining forces will help them succeed. Together they learn about cooperation, mutual support, diversity, openness, facing obstacles, and creative risk taking. Includes a leader's guide and participant's workbook.

Release Year: 1994
Runtime: 18 minutes
Source: CRM Films
Cost: $695
Type of Program: Training

CHARISMA

BEING THERE

Peter Sellers plays a mentally retarded gardener who is suddenly thrust from a protected existence onto the street. From years of watching television he learned a surface comportment; from the household in which he was employed he acquired the art of impeccable dress. These skills, along with his gardening knowledge, serve him well when he stumbles into Washington's political arena, where his simple comments on gardening are taken as metaphorical wisdom and he is seen as a political savant.

Release Year: 1979
Runtime: 130 minutes
Source: CBS/Fox Video
Cost: $19.98
Type of Program: Feature
Other Leadership Lesson(s): Political Leadership

New
DAVE

Kevin Kline is the presidential look-alike hired to cover for the unscrupulous and unconscious leader of the free world. His inside look at national politics inspires him to balance budgets, hold other officials accountable, expose the bad guys, and eventually run for office in his own identity.

Release Year: 1993
Runtime: 110 minutes
Source: Warner Home Video, Inc.
Cost: $19.98
Type of Program: Feature
Other Leadership Lesson(s): Situational Leadership, Ethics and Values

DEMOCRAT AND THE DICTATOR

In this part of the *Walk Through the Twentieth Century* series, Bill Moyers examines the parallels between two charismatic leaders, Franklin Roosevelt and Adolph Hitler, both of whom came to national power in 1933 and died in 1945. Their presence and conflicting ideologies are revealed through their words and gestures.

Release Year: 1984
Runtime: 58 minutes
Source: PBS Video–Educational Division
Cost: $69.95
Type of Program: Documentary
Other Leadership Lesson(s): Biography

New
EXCALIBER

King Arthur envisions Camelot, a kingdom in which power is used to benefit the common good, and the Round Table, a symbol of participatory leadership. Arthur is portrayed as a mortal who struggles with loyalty and betrayal, duty and power. Hartwick Humanities in Management Institute offers a case study based on this film.

Release Year: 1981
Runtime: 140 minutes
Source: Warner Home Video, Inc.
Cost: $19.98
Type of Program: Feature
Other Leadership Lesson(s): Vision, Power

New
HERO

Dustin Hoffman is the reluctant hero who saves plane crash survivors from a fiery explosion. Andy Garcia is the charismatic impostor who takes credit for the heroic deed and infects society with goodness. Geena Davis is the reporter and crash survivor who makes a noteworthy speech about ethics in journalism and then learns first-hand about apparent and genuine heroism.

Release Year: 1992
Runtime: 116 minutes
Source: Columbia Tristar Home Video
Cost: $14.95
Type of Program: Feature
Other Leadership Lesson(s): Ethics and Values

New
THE MAN WHO WOULD BE KING

Rudyard Kipling's story explores a clash of cultures in 19th-century India. Sean Connery and Michael Caine are British con men who travel to nearby Afghanistan to pose as kings and loot the local riches. When Connery convinces himself that he really is Alexander the Great reincarnated, his deception is revealed. Hartwick Humanities in Management Institute offers a case study based on this film.

Release Year: 1975
Runtime: 129 minutes
Source: CBS/Fox Video
Cost: $19.98
Type of Program: Feature
Other Leadership Lesson(s): Situational Leadership

TRIUMPH OF THE WILL: THE ARRIVAL OF HITLER

Hitler's airplane soars through massive cloud formations en route to a party rally in Nuremburg. Cheering masses greet him at the airport and line the streets of Nuremburg as he rides past. This black-and-white film was designed to appeal to the viewer's emotions through a powerful Wagnerian musical score and images that carry symbolic weight. The uncut version uses English subtitles.

Release Year: 1934
Runtime: 115 minutes
Source: International Historic Films
Cost: $24.95
Type of Program: Documentary
Other Leadership Lesson(s): Influence

COMMUNICATION, FEEDBACK, AND NEGOTIATION

THE BUSINESS OF LISTENING

Based on the book by Diane Bone, this film discusses the basics of effective listening, an essential skill for personal and business success. It offers interviews with experts and practical, positive suggestions.

Release Year: 1991
Runtime: 25 minutes
Source: Crisp Publications
Cost: $495
Type of Program: Training

CAN WE TALK?

Communication in management is often a problem, and *Can We Talk?* shows an example of this: a self-absorbed team leader who never takes the time to listen to staff's suggestions. It demonstrates that the best ideas and abilities are plentiful if you know how to listen.

Release Year: 1993
Runtime: 23 minutes
Source: CRM Films
Cost: $745
Type of Program: Training

New
COACHING AND PERFORMANCE FEEDBACK

This tape is intended for self-study or group learning. There are eight scenarios of workplace problems that involve coaching or feedback dilemmas. Actors dramatize three possible solutions for each dilemma. HRD experts discuss the effectiveness of each solution and explain which solutions facilitate support, commitment, listening, and learning. An accompanying guide includes reproducible handouts so that participants can stop the tape, write out the impact and consequence of each solution, then return to the lesson.

Release Year: 1996
Runtime: 94 minutes
Source: Coastal Human Resources
Cost: $425
Type of Program: Training
Other Leadership Lesson(s): Coaching

New
FEEDBACK SOLUTIONS

This series explains how to give and receive feedback through dramatizations and narrated lessons. The workplace scenarios feature a diverse cast of characters in supervisory and management positions. An accompanying workbook supports both classroom training and self-study.

Release Year: 1994
Runtime: Four tapes—60 minutes each
Source: Ash Quarry Productions
Cost: $495 each
Type of Program: Training

New
I KNOW JUST WHAT YOU MEAN! OVERCOMING ROADBLOCKS TO EFFECTIVE COMMUNICATION

Stephen Covey presents a satire to highlight common mistakes made in communication. The scene is a restaurant at lunchtime with several mini-dramas involving work and family issues. We see repeated instances of listening to evaluate, probe, advise, or interpret. It is obvious that communication could be improved by listening to understand instead. Includes a *Discussion Leader's Guide* and participant handouts.

Release Year: 1996
Runtime: 21 minutes
Source: Franklin Covey
Cost: $695
Type of Program: Training

INTERPERSONAL COMMUNICATION SKILLS

Debra Sutch conducts a four-video seminar on communication for teams. She offers advice on how to minimize conflict and build collaboration through effective communication techniques.

Release Year: 1994
Runtime: 263 minutes
Source: CareerTrack Publications
Cost: $249.95
Type of Program: Training

NEGOTIATING CORPORATE CHANGE

This video dramatizes a manager's job as negotiator. Commentary by negotiation experts helps to explain how corporate negotiation is different and how it can be done successfully.

Release Year: 1995
Runtime: 35 minutes
Source: Harvard Business School Publishing
Cost: $695
Type of Program: Training

New
THE PRACTICAL COACH

This film is intended for self-study use by supervisors and middle managers. Through a simple message and a little humor, viewers identify good coaching experiences from their past to develop their own coaching style. The message is that if you let people know that what they do matters to you, coaching can be a rewarding experience for all parties.

Release Year: 1997
Runtime: 24 minutes
Source: CRM Films
Cost: $625
Type of Program: Training
Other Leadership Lesson(s): Coaching

TALKING 9 TO 5: WOMEN AND MEN IN THE WORKPLACE

Miscommunication can result in lower morale, lost productivity, and nonfunctional teams. Deborah Tannen shows how our natural conversational styles differ, affect our work, and affect how others perceive us. *Talking 9 to 5* will help increase awareness and understanding of the different conversational styles.

Release Year: 1995
Runtime: 29 minutes
Source: ChartHouse International Learning Corporation
Cost: $695
Type of Program: Training
Other Leadership Lesson(s): Gender Diversity

CREATIVITY, INNOVATION, AND CHANGE

C AND THE BOX: A PARADIGM PARABLE

Predictable behavior leads to predictable results. This brief session-starter may help people change from their predictable routines to more creative and innovative problem-solving ways. Based on the book of the same name by Frank Prince, it encourages viewers to break out of their self-imposed boundaries and to have fun doing it.

Release Year: 1993
Runtime: 7 minutes
Source: Jossey-Bass/Pfeiffer
Cost: $295
Type of Program: Training

THE ENTREPRENEURS: AN AMERICAN ADVENTURE

This documentary about great entrepreneurs is meant to inspire innovation. Inventors, tough-minded tycoons, and other wizards of free enterprise are featured in this series of six one-hour programs. The series, narrated by Robert Mitchum, contains archival photos, illustrations, and historic film footage of the prototypes of products upon which industrial empires have been built.

Release Year: 1986
Runtime: Six tapes—60 minutes each
Source: Reel
Cost: $101.97 for the set
Type of Program: Documentary
Other Leadership Lesson(s): Entrepreneurial Leadership

THE FIFTH DISCIPLINE: DEVELOPING LEARNING ORGANIZATIONS

Peter Senge presents the importance of organizational learning. He discusses how to foster it through intrinsic rewards, and draws parallels between early individual learning and organizational learning.

Release Year: 1992
Runtime: 70 minutes
Source: ASTD
Cost: $69.95
Type of Program: Training
Other Leadership Lesson(s): Learning and Experience

New
FRAMING THE FUTURE: LEADERSHIP SKILLS FOR A NEW CENTURY

Cultural anthropologist Jennifer James explains the technological forces causing turbulent change in today's workplace. She describes the skills needed to cope with change and embrace discovery.

Release Year: 1996
Runtime: 26 minutes
Source: Excellence in Training Corporation
Cost: $695
Type of Program: Training

New

THE GREEN MOVIE: EMPOWERMENT WITHIN A FRAMEWORK

Creativity trainer Mark Brown explains how to unleash creativity in every employee. He suggests methods for turning ideas into action without creating chaos or losing control. Includes a leader's guide and activity book.

Release Year: 1995
Runtime: 15 minutes
Source: CRM Films
Cost: $695
Type of Program: Training
Other Leadership Lesson(s): Empowerment and Participation

LEADERSHIP AND THE NEW SCIENCE

In this video based on the popular book of the same name, Dr. Margaret Wheatley suggests a new approach with which to break out of limited perspectives and see chaos as a natural force for creating order. With insights into organizational life gleaned from such diverse fields as physics and biochemistry, she asks us to loosen the bonds of our own paradigms and consider other, more productive models for how we work with one another.

Release Year: 1993
Runtime: 23 minutes
Source: CRM Films
Cost: $845
Type of Program: Training

LEADING THE WAY

Robert Gilbreath encourages managers to use vision, planning, and change in their departments in order to choose their future, be proactive, and "change by design, not by default." Gilbreath's four-part Change Map provides the tool to plan, communicate, and implement the change process.

Release Year: 1990
Runtime: 44 minutes
Source: CRM Films
Cost: $695
Type of Program: Training

LIBERATION MANAGEMENT: NECESSARY DISORGANIZATION FOR THE NANOSECOND NINETIES

Tom Peters presents the ideas in his book of the same name, interspersing three case studies at appropriate moments. Dealing with change in the "nanosecond nineties" is a good topic for all audiences in quickly changing times.

Release Year: 1993
Runtime: 60 minutes
Source: WingsNet
Cost: $895
Type of Program: Training

MASTERING CHANGE

Mark Sanborn teaches the fundamental processes of organizational change, planning change, and managing change in this two-volume video set. Managers learn to deal with change skillfully and to lead their teams through turbulent times. Includes a participant workbook.

Release Year: 1994
Runtime: 125 minutes
Source: CareerTrack Publications
Cost: $349.95
Type of Program: Training

THE NEW WORKPLACE

A Native American storyteller uses folktales to deliver the message that change is a positive force in the workplace. There are two versions of her message: one for employees and one for organizational leaders. Includes a facilitator's guide with handouts to be photocopied, discussion questions, group exercises, and a bibliography.

Release Year: 1993
Runtime: Two tapes—23 minutes each
Source: Coastal Human Resources
Cost: $722.50 for the set
Type of Program: Training

New

PARADIGM MASTERY SERIES

Futurist Joel Barker holds a video retreat to discuss the management of organizational change. Participants share their experiences and new revelations about identifying new trends, encouraging those who break out of the boundaries, and harnessing the enthusiasm around new ideas. The retreat is divided into five segments: Change and Leadership, The Paradigm Effect, The Paradigm Curve, Paradigm Partners, and Paradigm Hunting.

Release Year: 1997
Runtime: Five segments—30 minutes each
Source: Video Arts Inc.
Cost: $1,485
Type of Program: Training

RESILIENCE: A CHANGE FOR THE BETTER

Daryl Conner, a specialist in change management, identifies five key characteristics that resilient people have in common. They are positive, focused, flexible, organized, and proactive. He also shows how to cultivate these qualities in yourself and your organization. Includes a leader's guide.

Release Year: 1993
Runtime: 17 minutes
Source: Mentor Media
Cost: $595
Type of Program: Training

New

TEARING DOWN WALLS: MANAGING CHANGE AND DISMANTLING BARRIERS TO BETTER TEAM AND ORGANIZATIONAL PERFORMANCE

Stephen Covey introduces a discussion about the Berlin Wall among those who lived on both sides. The citizens of the divided city explain their feelings of disbelief, anger, and sadness when they lost the freedom to visit family members, hold jobs, and worship on the other side. Over time, the frustration gave way to acceptance. When the wall came down, a deep chasm remained and will take many years to repair. Covey describes this as a metaphor for organizational barriers that create walls between people and departments. Includes a *Discussion Leader's Guide* and participant handouts.

Release Year: 1996
Runtime: 21 minutes
Source: Franklin Covey
Cost: $695
Type of Program: Training with Documentary excerpts
Other Leadership Lesson(s): Organizations

DECISION MAKING, PROBLEM SOLVING, AND CONFLICT MANAGEMENT

APOLLO 13

In *Apollo 13,* it is not only the team in the air but the teams on the ground that have to work together to get the astronauts home alive. A life-threatening problem on the way to the moon engages everyone on board as well as at NASA in many aspects of teamwork. Everyone keeps working until a creative solution is found and the astronauts make it safely home.

Release Year: 1995
Runtime: 135 minutes
Source: MCA/Universal Home Video
Cost: $22.98
Type of Program: Feature
Other Leadership Lesson(s): Teams and Groups

New

APOLLO 13 LEADERSHIP: DOWN-TO-EARTH LESSONS FOR YOU AND YOUR ORGANIZATION

Captain James Lovell, commander of the Apollo 13 mission, and author James Belasco describe the leadership strategies that safely brought the troubled spacecraft home. They explain how leaders can develop a vision, establish shared values, and teach teams to collaborate under stress.

Release Year: 1996
Runtime: 30 minutes
Source: Media Learning Resources
Cost: $595
Type of Program: Training
Other Leadership Lesson(s): Teams and Groups

CAN CONFLICT IMPROVE TEAM EFFECTIVENESS?

Based on the research of Valerie Sessa, this program demonstrates how the effective handling of conflict can improve team performance. Learn how to use perspective taking and tools such as the Information Importance Grid to focus the group on the task instead of on people-oriented conflict.

Release Year: 1996
Runtime: 22 minutes
Source: corVision Media
Cost: $495
Type of Program: Training
Other Leadership Lesson(s): Teams and Groups

COMMAND DECISION

The back-room boys—a general, his staff, and his peers—debate the aerial bombardment of Germany. This is a plainly reproduced version of a determinedly serious play, with a remarkable cast.

Release Year: 1949
Runtime: 111 minutes
Source: MGM/UA Home Video, Inc.
Cost: $19.98
Type of Program: Feature
Other Leadership Lesson(s): Military Leadership

New
CRIMSON TIDE

Gene Hackman is commander of the submarine USS Alabama and Denzel Washington is the executive officer who challenges his authority. The two struggle for control of the sub's crew and nuclear missiles as they disagree about the authenticity of their order to fire the missiles.

Release Year: 1995
Runtime: 116 minutes
Source: Buena Vista Home Video
Cost: $19.99
Type of Program: Feature
Other Leadership Lesson(s): Power, Military Leadership

DEALING WITH CONFLICT AND CONFRONTATION

Dr. Helga Rhode offers a positive way to look at conflict between "position" and "interest." She explains why the "dual concern model" can resolve conflict, and discusses the five classic conflict resolution strategies: yielding, withdrawing, inaction, contending, and problem solving.

Release Year: 1993
Runtime: 205 minutes
Source: CareerTrack Publications
Cost: $199.95
Type of Program: Training

New
THE GOAL

This dramatization of an actual case concerns a plant manager with 90 days to turn around his losing operation or watch his department get downsized. At the same time, his family relationships are suffering and need attention. An old college professor reminds the manager about focusing on basic goals, using appropriate methods to achieve goals, and recognizing the gap between reality and goals.

Release Year: 1995
Runtime: 50 minutes
Source: American Media, Inc.

Cost: $895
Type of Program: Training
Other Leadership Lesson(s): Goal Setting

New
GROUNDHOG DAY

Bill Murray is Phil the Weatherman, caught in perpetual Groundhog Day and can't get out. In this complex but static environment, he tries ingratiation and manipulation to achieve his short-term goals without much success. When he discovers his competencies and changes his interpersonal style, the spell breaks, he gets the girl, and he wakes up to a new day.

Release Year: 1993
Runtime: 103 minutes
Source: Columbia Tristar Home Video
Cost: $14.95
Type of Program: Feature
Other Leadership Lesson(s): Path-Goal Theory, Self-Development

New
THE HUNT FOR RED OCTOBER

Sean Connery stars as a Soviet submarine commander who involves his crew and nuclear weapons in a plot to defect to the West. Scott Glenn as a U.S. Navy commander and Alec Baldwin as a military analyst complete a leadership triad that overcomes cultural differences to pursue a common goal. Hartwick Humanities in Management Institute offers a case study based on this film.

Release Year: 1990
Runtime: 137 minutes
Source: Paramount Home Video
Cost: $14.95
Type of Program: Feature
Other Leadership Lesson(s): Power, Intuition

INTUITION IN BUSINESS

To remain competitive, organizations must learn to use intuition. In this two-part program, Dr. Weston Agor discusses ways in which organizations can learn to accommodate intuitive styles. He also provides examples of how intuition can be used in different business settings. In part two, he explores the exercises that cultivate intuition in people and organizations.

Release Year: 1993
Runtime: 90 minutes
Source: Thinking Allowed
Cost: $49.95

Type of Program: Training
Other Leadership Lesson(s): Intuition

THE KOPPEL REPORT: THE BLUE X CONSPIRACY

In December of 1989, Ted Koppel gave viewers an unprecedented look at decision making during an international crisis. Video Publishing House revised the original to create a crisis management program for business, in which viewers are guided through the stages of a crisis.

Release Year: 1990
Runtime: 57 minutes
Source: WingsNet
Cost: $995
Type of Program: Documentary

A MAJOR MALFUNCTION: THE STORY BEHIND THE SPACE SHUTTLE CHALLENGER DISASTER

Poor leadership and decision making led to the death of seven astronauts. This three-part video case study uses film clips from various investigations and interviews with key players to illustrate the organizational structure and dynamics that led to the disaster. It can be used in many ways, one of which is to prevent similar destructive practices in your own organization. This case study is reviewed by A. T. Lawrence (1994), *Journal of Management Education, 18*(3), 388-396.

Release Year: 1992
Runtime: 42, 50, and 60 minutes
Source: Dr. Mark Maier
Cost: $595
Type of Program: Documentary

MEN AND WOMEN: PARTNERS AT WORK

Through dramatization, interviews, and narration, this film addresses the "myths" of gender differences and the communication problems they cause. It provides a subtle look at stereotypes, which will help prevent miscommunication and sexual harassment.

Release Year: 1992
Runtime: 20 minutes
Source: Crisp Publications, Inc.
Cost: $495
Type of Program: Training
Other Leadership Lesson(s): Gender Diversity

THE MISSILES OF OCTOBER

The Cuban missile crisis of October 16, 1962, is presented in this dramatic reenactment. The film follows the tensions and decisions faced by President Kennedy during the 12-day period when the United States and the Soviet Union confronted each other with nuclear destruction.

Release Year: 1975
Runtime: 155 minutes
Source: MPI Home Video
Cost: $59.95
Type of Program: Feature
Other Leadership Lesson(s): Political Leadership

MUTINY ON THE BOUNTY

Clark Gable stars in this black-and-white adaptation of the 18th-century case in which Fletcher Christian leads a mutiny against the sadistic Captain Bligh. There is also a 1962 version with Marlon Brando and Trevor Howard available from the same source. And there is a 1984 version called *The Bounty* starring Mel Gibson and Anthony Hopkins available from Verstron Video. Hartwick Humanities in Management Institute offers a case study on the 1984 film.

Release Year: 1935
Runtime: 132 minutes
Source: MGM/UA Home Video, Inc.
Cost: $14.95
Type of Program: Feature
Other Leadership Lesson(s): Theory X and Theory Y, Path-Goal Theory

SOLVING CONFLICT

Solving Conflict addresses new managers on an important topic: interpersonal conflict. By dramatizing a conflict and its resolution, the video imparts basic conflict-management skills. Includes a workbook with role-play exercises.

Release Year: 1993
Runtime: 21 minutes
Source: American Media, Inc.
Cost: $695
Type of Program: Training

TWELVE ANGRY MEN

This film depicts a classic courtroom drama of a hasty jury and one member who quietly makes the others consider their preemptive decision. It is a study of personal conviction and courage under heavy pressure. Henry Fonda stars as the informal leader who eventually sways the others to listen to reason. Hartwick Humanities in Management Institute offers a case study based on this film.

Release Year: 1957
Runtime: 95 minutes
Source: MGM/UA Home Video, Inc.
Cost: $19.98

Type of Program: Feature
Other Leadership Lesson(s): Influence, Teams and Groups, Integrity, Courage

EMPOWERMENT AND PARTICIPATION

THE BEST OF MOTIVES

Two videos, *Nobody Ever Tells Us* and *Nobody Ever Asks Us,* illustrate the six skills of motivation. The comedy-drama protagonist learns to provide information, feedback, recognition, and begins to involve, empower, and listen to the people he supervises. Higher productivity and quality result.

Release Year: 1994
Runtime: 30 minutes each
Source: Video Arts Inc.
Cost: $870 each
Type of Program: Training

New
COURAGEOUS FOLLOWERS, COURAGEOUS LEADERS

This film is based on Ira Chaleff's book *The Courageous Follower: Standing Up To and For Our Leaders* (Berrett-Koehler, 1995). In several workplace scenarios, it demonstrates how employees who are not in positions of power may engage in participatory leadership. They must have courage in four areas: serving their leaders by taking initiative, assuming responsibility, challenging their leaders, and leaving a situation in which they cannot support the leader.

Release Year: 1996
Runtime: 23 minutes
Source: CRM Films
Cost: $845
Type of Program: Training

DEAD POETS SOCIETY

Robin Williams is a professor at an exclusive prep school who gets into trouble for encouraging his students to "seize the day." Management and organizational behavior professors may want to use this video to explore issues in leadership, such as ethics, role conflict, autonomy, risk taking, stress, and organizational pressures toward conformity. Hartwick Humanities in Management Institute offers a case study based on this film.

Release Year: 1989
Runtime: 128 minutes
Source: Buena Vista Home Video
Cost: $19.99
Type of Program: Feature
Other Leadership Lesson(s): Contrasting Leadership Styles

THE EMPOWERED MANAGER

A case study with AT&T and Peter Block's interviews demonstrate that more creative leadership is needed to weather today's business environment. Customer-driven economics, competition, and tight budgets signal the need for participatory management. Most viewers will be able to identify with the employees' feelings of resistance toward empowerment.

Release Year: 1993
Runtime: 30 minutes
Source: Excellence in Training Corporation
Cost: $595
Type of Program: Training
Other Leadership Lesson(s): Change

FLIGHT OF THE BUFFALO: SOARING TO EXCELLENCE, LEARNING TO LET EMPLOYEES LEAD

Based on James Belasco's book of the same title, the video encourages corporate leaders to stop leading like buffaloes—making all the decisions and solving all the problems from the front of the herd/the top of the company. Rather, Belasco recommends that leaders take flight, like geese, in an environment that encourages all employees to take responsibility for customer service, planning work processes, and achieving organizational goals. Tapping employees' intellectual capital creates empowerment that helps organizations soar to excellence. Case studies of the Furon Company, the U.S. Naval Depot, and the UCLA Medical Center demonstrate how leaders of three organizations learned to let others lead.

Release Year: 1994
Runtime: 23 minutes
Source: CRM Films

Cost: $695
Type of Program: Training

New
GIVING LEADERSHIP AWAY

A new leader receives a jar of Lego building blocks as a lesson in team leadership. He learns that each decision is like a building block and that sharing decisions (blocks) can build a better project. Throughout the frustrating period of learning about leadership through trial and error, the jar of blocks reminds him to get out of people's way and trust others to make good decisions.

Release Year: 1996
Runtime: 19 minutes
Source: Video Visions
Cost: $695
Type of Program: Training
Other Leadership Lesson(s): Teams and Groups

New
MAX AND MAX: UNLEASHING THE POTENTIAL IN PEOPLE . . . AND DOGS!

Stephen Covey presents a humorous vignette about the parallel experiences of Max, the new employee, and Max, the new hunting dog. Both enter their new situations ready to put their training and innovative ideas to work. But an authoritarian leader imposes limits and stifles their initiative. Covey suggests that creating conditions to release their potential would yield better results for Max and his company and for Max and his owner. Includes a *Discussion Leader's Guide.*

Release Year: 1996
Runtime: 23 minutes
Source: Franklin Covey
Cost: $695
Type of Program: Training

NORMA RAE

Sally Field portrays a textile worker whose life is changed by the arrival of a union organizer. Norma eventually joins his cause and begins to exert strong leadership in her plant. Hartwick Humanities in Management Institute offers a case study based on this film.

Release Year: 1979
Runtime: 115 minutes
Source: CBS/Fox Video
Cost: $19.98
Type of Program: Feature
Other Leadership Lesson(s): Emergent Leadership, Women's Leadership

New
ORPHEUS IN THE REAL WORLD: 26 MUSICIANS, 26 CONDUCTORS

This film documents the participatory leadership style of the New York City-based chamber orchestra, Orpheus. The musicians demonstrate in planning meetings, practice sessions, and concerts why they prefer to share leadership rather than follow the lead of a conductor. They believe that the artistry and energy that emerge from strong personal commitment far outweigh the difficulties of the democratic process. This film inspired the ensemble of researchers and authors of *A Social Change Model of Leadership Development* (Astin & Astin, 1996).

Release Year: 1995
Runtime: 56 minutes
Source: Four Oaks Foundation
Cost: $69.95
Type of Program: Documentary

THE PRACTICALITY OF A RADICAL WORKPLACE

Peter Block explains how stewardship focuses on empowerment as individual and team ownership and responsibility. He also talks about choosing service over self-interest, partnership over parenting, adventure over safety, and defining the stewardship contract.

Release Year: 1994
Runtime: 90 minutes
Source: ASTD
Cost: $69.95
Type of Program: Training

REPOWERED EMPLOYEES

A case study demonstrates the transition of a traditional organization to a more participative one that promotes job ownership and responsibility. This organizational change and the resistance it creates occur in many organizations. Learn how to identify your own resistance. Includes a leader's guide.

Release Year: 1993
Runtime: 26 minutes
Source: WingsNet
Cost: $595
Type of Program: Training

TEACHING THE ELEPHANT TO DANCE . . . TODAY: EMPOWERING CHANGE IN YOUR ORGANIZATION

James Belasco, author of the book of the same title, uses case studies to show how organizations have used his change-management strategies to empower employees and become customer focused. Shorter government and health care versions are available.

Release Year: 1995
Runtime: 40 minutes
Source: CRM Films
Cost: $795
Type of Program: Training
Other Leadership Lesson(s): Change

New
WIN TEAMS: HOW ONE COMPANY MADE EMPOWERMENT WORK

A successful turnaround at General Electric Mobile Communications is described. Team members and supervisors describe the Winshare program and its self-managed teams who have the authority to make job improvement and budget decisions. A leader's guide suggests how to use this film with hourly workers, supervisors, and managers.

Release Year: 1994
Runtime: 26 minutes
Source: Video Visions
Cost: $595
Type of Program: Training
Other Leadership Lesson(s): Teams and Groups

ZAPP! THE LIGHTNING OF EMPOWERMENT

Adapted from William Byham's book of the same name, this video combines animation and live action to demonstrate the energizing force of empowerment. Viewers may discover the four secrets to sustaining a productive workforce and improving quality, productivity, and customer service.

Release Year: 1992
Runtime: 26 minutes
Source: WingsNet
Cost: $895
Type of Program: Training

ETHICS, VALUES, SPIRIT, AND SERVANT LEADERSHIP

BREAKER MORANT

Based on a true story, the film takes place when England was waging the Boer War in Africa. England court-martialed three Australian volunteer soldiers for murdering Boer prisoners, denying that the Aussies were acting under British orders.

Release Year: 1979
Runtime: 107 minutes
Source: Columbia Tristar Home Video
Cost: $9.99
Type of Program: Feature
Other Leadership Lesson(s): Military Leadership

THE CANDIDATE

Robert Redford performs as an idealistic lawyer whose ideals are steadily eroded when he runs for the U.S. Senate. Jeremy Larner, a speech writer for Senator Eugene McCarthy during his presidential campaign, wrote the screenplay.

Release Year: 1972
Runtime: 110 minutes
Source: Warner Home Video, Inc.
Cost: $19.98
Type of Program: Feature
Other Leadership Lesson(s): Political Leadership

CITIZEN KANE

Considered by many to be a perfect film, if not the best American film of all time, *Citizen Kane* is truly a cinematic masterpiece. The emotion-packed story of Charles Foster Kane (allegedly based on the life of William Randolph Hearst) is told with ever-shifting perspective. Directing his own vital performance as well as members of the famous Mercury Players, Orson Welles created an enduring classic of leadership and power. Hartwick Humanities in Management offers a case study based on this black-and-white film.

Release Year: 1941
Runtime: 119 minutes
Source: Movies Unlimited
Cost: $19.98
Type of Program: Feature
Other Leadership Lesson(s): Leader-Follower Relations, Decision Making

ETHICS IN AMERICA

This series features nearly 100 panelists who tackle ethical issues involving loyalty, confidentiality, privacy, truthfulness, and personal ethics. Individual titles are: Do Unto Others; To Defend a Killer; Public Trust, Private Interests; Does Doctor Know Best?; Anatomy of a Corporate Takeover; Under Orders, Under Fire, Parts 1 &

2; Truth on Trial; The Human Experiment; and Politics, Privacy and the Press.

Release Year: 1988
Runtime: 60 minutes each
Source: Annenberg/CPB Multimedia Collection
Cost: $275 for the set
Type of Program: Documentary

New
EXPLORING THE PARADOX OF SERVANT AS LEADER

Leaders from industry, religion, academia, and health care discuss servant leadership. This is their taped discussion during the Greenleaf Center's 1989 conference on servant leadership.

Release Year: 1989
Runtime: 14 minutes
Source: The Robert K. Greenleaf Center
Cost: $25
Type of Program: Training

New
HEART OF TIBET: THE 14TH DALAI LAMA

This profile of the spiritual leader and exiled political leader of Tibet was filmed during a 1989 visit to Los Angeles for a Tibetan Buddhist ritual. It includes an introduction by former president Jimmy Carter and footage of Chinese military abuse in occupied Tibet.

Release Year: 1991
Runtime: 60 minutes
Source: PBS Video–Home Division
Cost: $29.95
Type of Program: Documentary
Other Leadership Lesson(s): Political Leadership, Biography

New
IRWIN MILLER: PORTRAIT OF A TRUSTEE

Irwin Miller is the former CEO of Cummins Engine Company and trustee of many organizations including Yale University, the Ford Foundation, Christian Theological Seminary, AT&T, and the Museum of Modern Art. In this video, he shares his views on trusteeship. Although there is a Christian focus, the program is relevant to nonreligious organizations. There is footage from a 1960s crisis situation at Yale and discussion of the trustees' role in resolving the crisis.

Release Year: 1990
Runtime: 29 minutes
Source: James Ault Productions

Cost: $75
Type of Program: Training
Other Leadership Lesson(s): Citizen Leadership

A MAN FOR ALL SEASONS

This film is a biographical drama concerning 16th-century Chancellor of England, Sir Thomas More, and his personal conflict with King Henry VIII. More chose to die rather than compromise his religious beliefs. It is an exquisitely rich portrayal that received several Academy Awards.

Release Year: 1966
Runtime: 120 minutes
Source: Columbia Tristar Home Video
Cost: $19.95
Type of Program: Feature
Other Leadership Lesson(s): Integrity, Biography

MR. SMITH GOES TO WASHINGTON

This black-and-white Frank Capra film features James Stewart, Jean Arthur, and Claude Rains. Stewart stars as an idealistic young statesman who finds nothing but corruption when he takes his seat in the Senate. The film illustrates how leaders deal with ethical issues and adversity.

Release Year: 1939
Runtime: 130 minutes
Source: Columbia Tristar Home Video
Cost: $19.95
Type of Program: Feature
Other Leadership Lesson(s): Political Leadership

THE PARABLE OF THE SADHU

The first part of this film is a dramatization, based on the article by Bowen McCoy in the *Harvard Business Review,* depicting McCoy's Himalayan adventure. This sets the scene for a discussion of personal and corporate ethics by Arthur Miller, a panel of executives, theologians, business professors, and mountain climbers.

Release Year: 1983
Runtime: 32 minutes
Source: Bureau of Business Practices
Cost: $395
Type of Program: Training

ROBERT K. GREENLEAF: SERVANT-LEADER

This program introduces the viewer to Greenleaf and to the concept of servant leadership. Biographical information about Greenleaf and Greenleaf's own commentary put the subject in historical context and apply it to modern life.

Release Year: 1991
Runtime: 14 minutes
Source: The Robert K. Greenleaf Center
Cost: $25
Type of Program: Training
Other Leadership Lesson(s): Biography

TD INDUSTRIES: SERVANT-LEADERSHIP IN BUSINESS

For an example of a successful company's use of the servant-leadership concept, use this video case study. TD

Industries is a Dallas-based company that has practiced servant leadership for two decades. Both information and inspiration are provided in this overview.

Release Year: 1989
Runtime: 15 minutes
Source: The Robert K. Greenleaf Center
Cost: $25
Type of Program: Training
Other Leadership Lesson(s): Corporate Leadership

POWER AND INFLUENCE

THE BRIDGE ON THE RIVER KWAI

In a World War II jungle POW camp, British prisoner Alec Guinness refuses to build a bridge for the enemy unless his officers supervise the work. After some grumbling the camp commander shrewdly relents, allowing Guinness to get his way while getting the bridge he wanted. Hartwick Humanities Institute in Management offers a case study based on this film.

Release Year: 1957
Runtime: 161 minutes
Source: Columbia Tristar Home Video
Cost: $19.95
Type of Program: Feature
Other Leadership Lesson(s): Charisma, Vision, Integrity, Decision Making

THE CAINE MUTINY

An all-star cast enacts the drama of rebellion against unreasonable authority on the combat vessel Caine in the Pacific during World War II. Humphrey Bogart stars as the paranoid captain in this superb film adapted from Herman Wouk's prize-winning novel.

Release Year: 1954
Runtime: 125 minutes
Source: Columbia Tristar Home Video
Cost: $19.95
Type of Program: Feature
Other Leadership Lesson(s): Authoritarian Leadership

New
THE CHARGE OF THE LIGHT BRIGADE

This is a dramatization of events in the Crimean War. A power struggle between British officers, who are also brothers-in-law and sworn enemies, leads to a disastrous decision. The British cavalry meet their death in the ensuing battle with the Russian troops at Balaclava. Hartwick Humanities in Management Institute offers a case study based on this film.

Release Year: 1968
Runtime: 130 minutes
Source: MGM/UA Home Entertainment
Cost: $19.98
Type of Program: Feature
Other Leadership Lesson(s): Transformational Leadership, Decision Making, Teams and Groups

New
GLENGARRY GLEN ROSS

The dark side of leadership is featured in this drama about real estate salesmen in vicious competition to save their jobs. The film depicts 48 hours from the company hatchet man's delivery of an ultimatum to the win-all/lose-all conclusion. The tone is harsh and the language is strong, but the message is powerful.

Release Year: 1992
Runtime: 100 minutes
Source: Movies Unlimited
Cost: $19.98
Type of Program: Feature
Other Leadership Lesson(s): Dark Side of Leadership, Path-Goal Theory, Ethics and Values

New
MOBY DICK

Captain Ahab exemplifies the autocratic leader in Herman Melville's story about obsession and power. His maniacal search for the white whale that took his leg puts his crew in danger. Refusal to adapt or accept feedback seals Ahab's fate as well as most of his crew's.

Release Year: 1956
Runtime: 116 minutes
Source: MGM/UA Home Video, Inc.
Cost: $19.95
Type of Program: Feature
Other Leadership Lesson(s): Dark Side of Leadership, Goal Setting

POWER PLAY

This is a bloody action film about idealistic reformers of corrupt governments who create even worse havoc than dictatorships. Peter O'Toole plays Colonel Zeller, a morally corrupt tank commander who joins forces with the rebels to overthrow the government, and who then performs atrocities in order to impede the coup d'état leadership.

Release Year: 1978
Runtime: 109 minutes
Source: CBS/Fox Video
Cost: $49.95
Type of Program: Feature
Other Leadership Lesson(s): Dark Side of Leadership

New
WALL STREET

The characters in this drama are caught up in the unethical culture of insider trading. Neophyte stockbroker Charlie Sheen is torn between the glamour of his greedy mentor and the scruples of his blue-collar father. Hartwick Humanities in Management Institute offers a case study based on this film.

Release Year: 1987
Runtime: 126 minutes
Source: CBS/Fox Video
Cost: $19.98
Type of Program: Feature
Other Leadership Lesson(s): Dark Side of Leadership, Decision Making, Ethics and Values

MOTIVATION AND SELF-DEVELOPMENT

EVEN EAGLES NEED A PUSH

In a motivational way, David McNally presents five essential qualities that successful, confident, empowered people have in common: self-appreciation, vision, purpose, commitment, and contribution. His key message is that each of us can develop new strategies that will help us live the life we've always imagined for ourselves.

Release Year: 1992
Runtime: 24 minutes
Source: CRM Films
Cost: $795
Type of Program: Training

IF AT FIRST . . . OVERCOMING THE FEAR OF FAILURE

Fear of failure stifles many individuals and teams. *If at First* shows how to identify and move beyond the fear. Tony Buzan presents examples from 3M, sports, and the MacPhail Center for the Arts.

Release Year: 1994
Runtime: 26 minutes
Source: ChartHouse International Learning Corporation

Cost: $895
Type of Program: Training

IF I CAN DO THIS I CAN DO ANYTHING

The setting of this motivational film is the annual National Handicapped Skiing Championship, articulately hosted by Ted Kennedy, Jr., who himself lost a leg to cancer at 12. Disabled skiers from around the world participate in this event, under the same conditions and on the same slopes as world-class skiers.

Release Year: 1986
Runtime: 30 minutes
Source: American Media, Inc.
Cost: $245
Type of Program: Training

JOSHUA IN A BOX

This is a short animated parable about freedom and control—and much more. A person imprisoned in a box eventually escapes—then becomes a box himself to control another creature.

Release Year: 1981
Runtime: 6 minutes
Source: CRM Films
Cost: $295
Type of Program: Training
Other Leadership Lesson(s): Power

New
LIFE AND WORK: A MANAGER'S SEARCH FOR MEANING

In this video version of the book by the same name, James Autry explains how to integrate life and work. He suggests that viewers nurture their inner selves through meditation and prayer, reading, walking, the arts, and sports. They should invite challenges and seek meaning in all they do. To support their employees and meet organizational goals at the same time, managers must provide a connection between their employees' personal sense of purpose and the organizational mission.

Release Year: 1995
Runtime: 30 minutes
Source: Excellence in Training Corporation
Cost: $695
Type of Program: Training
Other Leadership Lesson(s): Spirit

LOVE AND PROFIT: THE ART OF CARING LEADERSHIP

This is the video version of James Autry's book by the same name. Through poetry and lecture, Autry injects some feeling to the cold business environment. He shows that the qualities of honesty, trust, courage, and self-awareness help turn leadership into an art, filled with mistakes and triumphs but capable of dealing with the whole range of human experience, from bad to good.

Release Year: 1993
Runtime: 30 minutes
Source: Excellence in Training Corporation
Cost: $695
Type of Program: Training
Other Leadership Lesson(s): Spirit

THE MAGNIFICENT SEVEN

John Sturges' Western remake of Kurosawa's *The Seven Samurai* is set in Mexico. Villagers hire gunmen to protect them from the bandits who are destroying their town. Scenes from the movie may be used to illustrate Maslow's theory of motivation (Hierarchy of Needs) and Kipnis, Schmidt, Swaffin-Smith, and Wilkinson's work on influencing strategies. Discussion on using this film in the classroom is in A. Huczynski (1994), "Teaching

Motivation and Influencing Strategies Using *The Magnificent Seven*," *Journal of Management Education, 18*(2), 273-278.

Release Year: 1960
Runtime: 126 minutes
Source: CBS/Fox Video
Cost: $19.98
Type of Program: Feature
Other Leadership Lesson(s): Influence

THE MAN WHO PLANTED TREES

The award-winning animated version of Jean Giono's book is inspiring. It beautifully illustrates the importance of individual action on larger goals: the small wins that lead to big successes. It is the story of a widowed peasant who plants 100 trees a day for 30 years, even though he knows only a tenth will survive. His devotion to detail and his generosity of heart turn a wasteland into a living ecosystem.

Release Year: 1987
Runtime: 30 minutes
Source: Direct Cinema Limited
Cost: $95
Type of Program: Training
Other Leadership Lesson(s): Goal Setting

PLACES IN THE HEART

The theme of emergent leadership characterizes this movie about a Texas widow and her extended family. Under her growing strength, they work together to raise a successful cotton crop and save her farm during the Depression.

Release Year: 1984
Runtime: 113 minutes
Source: CBS/Fox Video
Cost: $19.98
Type of Program: Feature
Other Leadership Lesson(s): Emergent Leadership, Women's Leadership

SPEED, SIMPLICITY, AND SELF-CONFIDENCE: JACK WELCH TALKS WITH WARREN BENNIS

Jack Welch, the iconoclastic CEO of General Electric, talks candidly with Warren Bennis about elements that translate directly into measurable improvement in performance. Explores the concept and realities of boundaryless behavior.

Release Year: 1993
Runtime: 30 minutes
Source: American Media, Inc.

Cost: $695
Type of Program: Training

THE SPIRIT OF PERSONAL MASTERY

After Peter Senge's introduction, Joel Suzuki tells a story of a master violin maker that exemplifies personal mastery. Personal mastery is one of five disciplines that can transform an organization by increasing its capacity to learn. This story illustrates the concept by showing that the desire for a shared vision will only have depth and power if it embraces personal visions, those that are truly meaningful to each individual.

Release Year: 1994
Runtime: 7 minutes
Source: ChartHouse International Learning Corporation
Cost: $395
Type of Program: Training

SURVIVAL RUN

Harry Cordellos, a blind marathon runner, and a sighted partner run the grueling Dipsea course near San Francisco. This award-winning video shows a highly motivated team that overcomes seemingly insurmountable risks and difficulties to achieve their goal.

Release Year: 1979
Runtime: 12 minutes
Source: Pyramid Media
Cost: $295
Type of Program: Training
Other Leadership Lesson(s): Teams and Groups

VALUING RELATIONSHIP®

This three-part series identifies *relationship* as a kind of ecological system—an integrated living organism where no one part is as important as the whole and the dynamic relationship of the parts. It integrates science and the insight of human resource management and organizational development. Organizational Energy, Personal Patterns, and Interpersonal Synergy are the three titles. Includes a facilitator's guide.

Release Year: 1993
Runtime: 30 minutes each
Source: Griggs Productions, Inc.
Cost: $685 each
Type of Program: Training
Other Leadership Lesson(s): Organizations

YOU

This film combines the thought-provoking narration of William Schallert with a series of fascinating and humorous scenes of a baby exploring a roomful of "treasure." Viewers are encouraged to recapture the good qualities of their childhood and put them to use in adulthood.

Release Year: 1980
Runtime: 4 minutes
Source: Bureau of Business Practice
Cost: $225
Type of Program: Training

VIDEO DISTRIBUTORS

AMA VIDEO
American Management Association
P.O. Box 1026
Saranac Lake, NY 12983-9957
Phone: (800) 262-9699

AMBROSE VIDEO PUBLISHING, INC.
28 West 44th Street, Suite 2100
New York, NY 10036-6600
Phone: (800) 526-4663 or (212) 768-7373
Fax: (212) 768-9282
E-mail: ambrosevid@aol.com
Website: http://www.ambrosevideo.com

AMERICAN MEDIA, INC.
4900 University Avenue
West Des Moines, IA 50266-6769
Phone: (800) 262-2557

ANNENBERG/CPB MULTIMEDIA COLLECTION
P.O. Box 2345
South Burlington, VT 05407-2345
Phone: (800) 532-7637
Website: http://www.learner.org/info/search/

ASH QUARRY PRODUCTIONS, INC.
12444 Ventura Boulevard, Suite 203
Studio City, CA 91604-2409
Phone: (800) 717-0777 or (818) 761-4448
Fax: (818) 761-7277
E-mail: info@ashquarry.com
Website: http://www.ashquarry.com

ASTD
Mobiltape Company Inc.
24730 Avenue Tibbitts, Suite 170
Valencia, CA 91355-4768
Phone: (800) 369-5718 or (805) 295-0504
Website: http://www.mobiltape.com

JAMES AULT PRODUCTIONS
P.O. Box 493
Northampton, MA 01601-0493
Phone: (413) 587-9871
Fax: (413) 584-6907

BLUE SKY PRODUCTIONS INC.
5918 Pulaski Avenue
Philadelphia, PA 19144-3823
Phone: (800) 358-0022 or (215) 844-4444

BUENA VISTA HOME VIDEO
350 South Buena Vista Street
Burbank, CA 91521-7145
Phone: (818) 562-3568

BUREAU OF BUSINESS PRACTICE
24 Rope Ferry Road
Waterford, CT 06386-9985
Phone: (800) 243-0876
Fax: (860) 437-3555

CAREERTRACK PUBLICATIONS
3085 Center Green Drive
Boulder, CO 80301-5408
Phone: (800) 334-1018
Fax: (303) 443-6347
Website: http://www.careertrack.com

CAROUSEL FILM AND VIDEO
260 Fifth Avenue, Suite 405
New York, NY 10001-6408
Phone: (212) 683-1660
E-mail: carousel@pipeline.com

CBS/FOX VIDEO
1330 Avenue of the Americas
New York, NY 10019-5400
Phone: (800) 800-2369 or (212) 373-4800
Website: http://www.foxstore.com

CHARTHOUSE INTERNATIONAL LEARNING CORPORATION
221 River Bridge Circle
Burnsville, MN 55337
Phone: (800) 328-3789 or (612) 890-1800
Fax: (612) 890-0505
E-mail: info@charthouse.com
Website: http://www.charthouse.com

COASTAL HUMAN RESOURCES
3083 Brickhouse Court
Virginia Beach, VA 23452-6854
Phone: (800) 285-9107 or (757) 498-9014
Fax: (757) 498-3657
E-mail: sales@coastal.com

COLUMBIA TRISTAR HOME VIDEO
SONY Pictures Plaza
10202 West Washington Boulevard
Culver City, CA 90232
Phone: (310) 244-4000
Fax: (310) 280-2485
Website: http://207.217.51.31/cgi-bin/CTHV. storefront

CORVISION MEDIA INC.
1359 Barclay Boulevard
Buffalo Grove, IL 60089
Phone: (800) 537-3130
Fax: (847) 537-3353
E-mail: corvision@aol.com
Website: http://www.corvision.com

CRISP PUBLICATIONS, INC.
1200 Hamilton Court
Menlo Park, CA 94025-9600
Phone: (800) 442-7477 or (650) 323-6100
Fax: (650) 323-5800
Website: http://www.crisp-pub.com

CRM FILMS
2215 Faraday Avenue
Carlsbad, CA 92008-7295
Phone: (800) 421-0833 or (760) 431-9800
Fax: (760) 931-5792
E-mail: sales@crmfilms.com
Website: http://www.crmfilms.com

DIRECT CINEMA LIMITED
P.O. Box 10003
Santa Monica, CA 90410-9003
Phone: (800) 525-0000

DISCOVERY CHANNEL HOME VIDEO
Phone: (800) 889-9950
Website: http://shopping.discovery.com

WALT DISNEY HOME VIDEO
500 South Buena Vista Street
Burbank, CA 91521
Phone: (818) 562-3560
Website: http://www.disney.com/disneyvideos

ENERGIZE INC.
5450 Wissahickon Avenue
Philadelphia, PA 19144
Phone: (800) 395-9800 or (215) 438-8342

ENTERPRISE MEDIA
91 Harvey Street, 3rd Floor
Cambridge, MA 02140-1718
Phone: (800) 423-6021 or (617) 354-0017
Fax: (617) 354-1637

EXCELLENCE IN TRAINING CORPORATION
11358 Aurora Avenue
Des Moines, IA 50322-7907
Phone: (800) 747-6569 or (515) 276-6569
Fax: (515) 276-9476

FIRST RUN/ICARUS FILMS
153 Waverly Place
New York, NY 10014-3872
Phone: (800) 876-1710 or (212) 727-1711
Fax: (212) 989-7649
E-mail: info@frif.com
Website: http://www.echonyc.com/~frif/

FOUR OAKS FOUNDATION
635 Madison Avenue
New York, NY 10022-1009
Phone: (212) 753-6677
Fax: (212) 752-2483

FRANKLIN COVEY
2200 West Parkway Boulevard
Salt Lake City, UT 84119-2099
Phone: (800) 654-1776
Website: http://www.franklincovey.com

GOODMEASURE DIRECT, INC.
One Memorial Drive, 16th Floor
Cambridge, MA 02142-1313
Phone: (617) 662-1871
Website: http://www.goodmeasure.com

THE ROBERT K. GREENLEAF CENTER
921 East 86th Street, Suite 200
Indianapolis, IN 46240-1841
Phone: (317) 259-1241
Fax: (317) 259-0560
Website: http://greenleaf.org

GRIGGS PRODUCTIONS, INC.
2046 Clement Street
San Francisco, CA 94121-2118
Phone: (800) 210-4200 or (415) 668-4200
Fax: (415) 668-6004

HARVARD BUSINESS SCHOOL PUBLISHING
60 Harvard Way 230-5
Boston, MA 02163-1001
Phone: (800) 545-7685
Fax: (617) 495-6985
Website: http://www.hbsp.harvard.edu

INTERNATIONAL HISTORIC FILMS, INC.
P.O. Box 29035
Chicago, IL 60629-0035
Phone: (773) 927-2900
Website: http://www.ihffilm.com

JOSSEY-BASS/PFEIFFER
350 Sansome Street
San Francisco, CA 94104-1342
Phone: (800) 274-4434
Fax: (800) 569-0443
Website: http://www.pfieffer.com

DR. MARK MAIER
Chair, Organizational Leadership
Chapman University
333 North Glassell Street
Orange, CA 92866-1099
Phone: (714) 744-7692
Fax: (714) 744-3889

MCA/UNIVERSAL HOME VIDEO
100 Universal City Plaza
Universal City, CA 91608-9955
Phone: (818) 777-1000
Fax: (818) 866-1483
E-mail: store@universalstudios.com
Website: http://store.universalstudios.com

MEDIA LEARNING RESOURCES
919 Conestoga Road
Building II, Suite 304
Bryn Mawr, PA 19010-1352
Phone: (800) 474-1604 or (610) 527-9400
Fax: (610) 527-9401

MENTOR MEDIA
275 East California Boulevard
Pasadena, CA 91106-3615
Phone: (800) 359-1935 or (626) 449-8900
Fax: (626) 449-2624
E-mail: info@mentmedia.com
Website: http://www.mentmedia.com

MGM/UA HOME VIDEO, INC.
2500 Broadway
Santa Monica, CA 90404
Phone: (310) 449-3000
Website: http://www.mgmhomevideo.com

MONTEREY HOME VIDEO
28038 Dorothy Drive, Suite 1
Agoura Hills, CA 91301-2625
Phone: (800) 424-2593 or (818) 597-0047
Fax: (818) 597-0105

MOVIES UNLIMITED
3015 Darnell Road
Philadelphia, PA 19154-3295
Phone: (800) 523-0823
Fax: (215) 637-2350
E-mail: movies@moviesunlimited.com
Website: http://www.moviesunlimited.com

MPI HOME VIDEO
16101 South 108th Street
Orland Park, IL 60462-5305
Phone: (708) 460-0555
Fax: (708) 873-3177

MULTIMEDIA INC.
15 North Summit Street
Tenafly, NJ 07670-1008
Phone: (800) 682-1992
Fax: (201) 569-7599

PARAMOUNT HOME VIDEO
Bluhdorn Building
5555 Melrose Avenue
Los Angeles, CA 90038-3197
Phone: (213) 956-3952
Website: http://www2.paramount.com/homevideo

PBS VIDEO
1320 Braddock Place, Suite 200
Alexandria, VA 22314-1698
Phone: (800) 344-3337 (Educational Division)
Phone: (800) 531-4727 (Home Division)
Website: http://www.pbs.org

PHOENIX CORONET
2349 Chaffee Drive
St. Louis, MO 63146-3306
Phone: (800) 221-1274 or (314) 569-2839
Fax: (314) 569-2834

PYRAMID MEDIA
P.O. Box 1048
Santa Monica, CA 90046-1048
Phone: (800) 421-2304 or (310) 828-7577
Fax: (310) 453-9083
E-mail: sales@pyramedia.com
Website: http://www.pyramedia.com

REEL
2655 Shattuck Avenue
Berkeley, CA 94704-3237
Phone: (510) 549-3333
Website: http://www.reel.com

QUESTAR VIDEO, INC.
P.O. Box 11345
Chicago, IL 60611-0345
Phone: (800) 544-8422 or (312) 266-9400
Fax: (312) 266-9523

THINKING ALLOWED
2560 Ninth Street, Suite 123
Berkeley, CA 94710-2563
Phone: (800) 999-4415 or (510) 548-4415
Website: http://www.thinking-allowed.com

VIDEO ARTS INC.
8614 West Catalpa Avenue
Chicago, IL 60656-1116
Phone: (800) 553-0091 or (312) 693-9966

VIDEO CITY INC.
6851 McDivett Drive
Bakersfield, CA 93301-2004
Phone: (805) 397-7955

VIDEO VISIONS
P.O. Box 42185
Atlanta, GA 30311-0185
Phone: (404) 521-3456
Fax: (404) 755-2054

WARNER HOME VIDEO, INC.
4000 Warner Boulevard
Burbank, CA 91522
Phone: (818) 954-6000
Website: http://whv1.warnerbros.com

WINGSNET
930 North National Parkway, Suite 505
Schaumburg, IL 60173-5934
Phone: (800) 824-8889 or (847) 517-8744
Fax: (800) 517-8744 or (847) 517-8752
E-mail: admin@wingsnet.net
Website: http://www.wingsnet.net

INTERNET RESOURCES

The Internet is a favorite source among information seekers. However, it is also a rapidly changing medium in which addresses change and sites disappear without warning. That said, we offer here some unique sites that provide free resources, search tools, and links that are useful to the leadership educator. Each of these sites was verified in March 1998. Websites for organizations, conferences, journals, and vendors are listed elsewhere in the book and not repeated in this section.

The other part of this section is a list of online discussion groups, usually called lists or listservs. Lists are a valuable source of information because they connect participants to the best resource of all—knowledgeable people. We have included some lists to which we belong and some with which we are less familiar. In each case, subscription information is provided. To find a list that fits your special interests, check the Liszt website described in the first part of this section.

CONTENTS

WEBSITES

New
ACADEMY OF MANAGEMENT ONLINE

In addition to Academy of Management membership information, there is a list of 18 listserv discussion groups open to all interested people. Topics include Conflict Management, Entrepreneurship, Management Education and Development, the Public and Nonprofit Sector, and Organizational Behavior. Follow the links for descriptions and subscription information.

Address: http://www.aom.pace.edu

New
ADVANCING WOMEN IN LEADERSHIP

This site contains a refereed online journal about women in society in general, and in leadership positions specifically. Full-text articles identify barriers faced by professional women and functional approaches to dismantling these barriers. Also available are a chat room, women's news, financial advice, a career center for job searches and resume posting, and links to related sites for professional women.

Address: http://www.advancingwomen.com

New
ANBAR ELECTRONIC INTELLIGENCE: MANAGEMENT COOL SITES

This site provides links to "cool sites" in areas of management such as Asia Pacific management, top management, personnel and training, and management of quality. Each cool site is evaluated by five criteria: style, structure, ease of use, quality of information, and usefulness to the practitioner. A Management Library for subscribers only has abstracts and full-text articles from 400 international management journals.

Address: http://www.anbar.co.uk/coolsite/management/ management.htm

New
APPLICATIONS OF THE SOCIAL CHANGE MODEL OF LEADERSHIP DEVELOPMENT

The National Clearinghouse of Leadership Programs and the Higher Education Research Institute created this site to share examples of programs based on the *Social Change Model of Leadership Development* (Astin & Astin, 1996). There is a brief explanation of the model built on seven Cs—consciousness of self, congruence, commitment, collaboration, common purpose, contro-versy with civility, and citizenship—as well as information for ordering a copy of the guidebook.

Address: http://www.inform.umd.edu/OCP/NCLP/ scmhome.htm

New
THE BEACON PROJECT

This site allows nonprofit leaders to volunteer their time and knowledge online though the *e-corps*. A discussion forum provides a place for emerging leaders to pose questions and for experienced leaders to respond with answers and advice. There is also an electronic cohort service that assigns experienced leaders to nonprofit organizations seeking advice and a knowledge bank for sharing articles of interest. Links to nonprofit resources on the Internet, including journals and the results of surveys of nonprofit leaders, are also provided.

Address: http://www.beaconproject.org

New
BIOGRAPHY

Sponsored by *Biography Magazine,* this searchable site contains brief biographical sketches of 20,000 people. Visitors may search by name or index to find information about celebrities, businesspeople, scientists, authors, politicians, athletes, artists, musicians, and even mythical and fictional characters. Many of the brief descriptions contain links to more detailed information. Some items have video clips.

Address: http://www.biography.com

New
CINEMATIC TICKLERS

Cinematic ticklers are excerpts from television shows and feature films that may stimulate student interest in course material covered in organizational management classes. This site includes an article about the selection, presentation, and discussion of ticklers as well as a list of class-tested examples. For instance, a one-minute scene from *Beauty and the Beast* illustrates team dynamics and feedback and a six-minute excerpt from *Desk Set* demonstrates the management of change. Visitors to the site are invited to share their favorite cinematic ticklers.

Address: http://www.public.asu.edu/~dwightsd/ cinemati.htm

New
CIVICSOURCE

CivicSource, a project of the James MacGregor Burns
Academy of Leadership at the University of Maryland, is
a source for links and announcements related to curricular
and cocurricular leadership education. A resources grid
helps visitors find reading materials and organizations
that support leadership studies.

Address: http://civicsource.org

COMMUNITY COLLEGE WEB

Use the resource search function to link to leadership and
community-service-related programs, organizations, and
information. Some examples are: the Academy for
Community College Leadership Advancement, Innovation and Modeling (ACCLAIM); the National Institute for
Leadership Development; and the New York University
Center for Urban Community College Leadership. Links
are also provided to the web sites of 815 community
colleges.

Address: http://www.mcli.dist.maricopa.edu/cc/gen.html

New
CREATIVITY WEB

The Creativity Web is a source for articles, ideas, products, and quotations about creativity and innovation.
There are basic descriptions of brain theories and links to
more detailed information. An idea bank invites visitors
to "deposit" problems, which are "withdrawn" by others
and "redeposited" when solved. There are also descriptions and source information for books and videotapes
that help teach creativity in the workplace.

Address: http://www.ozemail.com.au/~caveman/Creative

ERIC/AE TEST LOCATOR

This searchable database contains brief descriptions and
source information for more than 10,000 tests, surveys,
and questionnaires, including leadership-related items.
Users can search the ETS Test Collection, The Buros
Institute of Mental Measurements directory, and a
database of the names and addresses of over 900 major
commercial test publishers.

Address: http://www.ericae.net/testcol.htm

New
THE EUROPEAN CASE CLEARING HOUSE (ECCH)

ECCH is a nonprofit organization that acts as a source of
"case study material for management education and

training." This site provides links to the world's business
schools and their case collections. There are more than
14,000 titles searchable by subject.

Address: http://www.ecch.cranfield.ac.uk

New
FOUNDATION CENTER

The Foundation Center is the source for grant seekers.
This site enables searching by keyword as well as links to
relevant foundations, corporate grant makers, community
foundations, and grant-making charities.

Address: http://www.fndcenter.org

New
HUMAN RESOURCES INNOVATIVE PRACTICES LABS

This site contains a benchmarking study being conducted
by ProSci. Human resource managers, project teams, and
consultants are asked to complete a 30-minute questionnaire about ten areas of practice in human resources.
Participants will receive a free copy of the results.

Address: http://www.prosci.com/iplabs/general12.htm

New
INNOVATION

The articles in this free online journal address innovation
in both business and education. Some past articles address
entrepreneurship, community colleges, and creativity
games. Each issue also includes a Company Watch,
Reader Responses, and a Calendar of Events and Conferences. Back articles are archived, and no subscription is
required.

Address: http://www.innovating.com

New
INTERNATIONAL REGISTRY FOR GLOBAL LEADERSHIP

The International Registry for Global Leadership is
maintained by the Leadership Institute of Columbia
College, publisher of the print journal, *A Leadership
Journal: Women in Leadership—Sharing the Vision.* The
site is intended "as a resource for leaders around the
world to foster linkages and to share information."
Registry members submit descriptions of their work and
opportunities for professional development. Visitors are
invited to contact Registry members for further
information.

Address: http://www.colacoll.edu/leader/lead2.htm

New
LISZT

Liszt is a searchable directory of discussion lists around the world. Its purpose is to help visitors identify, research, and join discussion lists in their areas of interest. Data are verified on an ongoing basis to maintain currency. A sample search for "leadership" yielded a match of 75 discussion lists.

Address: http://www.liszt.com

New
MANY PATHS QUOTES ON LEADERSHIP

Many Paths offers 400 quotations to inspire personal and spiritual growth. Visitors may search by keyword or use the index to find quotations on leadership, learning, human nature, problem solving, mastering change, and life management. Words of wisdom are from such varied sources as Winston Churchill, Frederick Nietsche, William Penn, Frank Lloyd Wright, and Booker T. Washington.

Address: http://www.net-quest.com/~gdotao

New
NATIONAL SERVICE-LEARNING COOPERATIVE CLEARINGHOUSE

This site provides information on organizations, people, publications, and information sources related to service learning, primarily at the K-through-12 level. Includes a bibliography organized by subject, back issues of newsletters, a listserv, searchable databases of programs and events, and links to over 100 other service sites on the Internet.

Address: http://www.nicsl.coled.umn.edu

New
QUOTATIONS

This collection contains 18,000 quotations organized by topic, including a section on leadership, and a selection of quotes by great leaders such as Winston Churchill, Henry Ford, and Martin Luther King, Jr. More quotes are added regularly.

Address: http://www.geocities.com/~spanoudi/quote.html

New
THE SOCIETY FOR ORGANIZATIONAL LEARNING (SOL)

The SOL site is based on the integrated theories and practices of leading, learning, and working together. There is an idea exchange where visitors may contribute original ideas or rate others' ideas. The ideas with the highest ratings rise to the top of the page. The Practice Field button leads visitors to news about conferences, projects, and teaching tools. The Community button links to notices for upcoming events and to practitioners and scholars in the field of organizational learning. The Research button opens a bibliography of working papers with first chapters available online. Audio clips feature Peter Senge addressing questions about organizational learning.

Address: http://www.learning.mit.edu

STUDENT AFFAIRS VIRTUAL COMPASS

This site maintains a list of over 600 listserv discussion groups and websites for student affairs professionals, faculty, graduate students, and others involved or interested in higher education. Sites and listservs are organized into topics including Diversity Issues, Student Activism, and Graduate Study. Users can subscribe or unsubscribe to any of the listservs through this site.

Address: http://www.studentaffairs.com

New
TRAINING AND DEVELOPMENT RESOURCE CENTRE

This site aims to be a "virtual" gold mine of resources for the human resources development (HRD) community. There is a bookstore for viewing the recommendations offered on several discussion groups as well as a link to Amazon.com for direct ordering. There is also a career center for resume and job postings, glossaries of HRD terms, and links to related sites.

Address: http://www.tcm.com/trder

THE TRAINING REGISTRY

An online training catalog, this site contains links to training providers, products, facilities, supplies, job opportunities, publications, and popular speakers.

Address: http://www.tregistry.com

New
WORKSHOPS BY THIAGI, INC.

This site contains free training games and articles about using games for improving human performance in organizations. There are also quotes about games and tips for training techniques.

Address: http://www.thiagi.com

New
WORLD LECTURE HALL

Maintained by the University of Texas at Austin, this is a link to faculty pages that share class materials such as syllabi, assignments, lecture notes, exams, and multimedia textbooks in many disciplines. There are 38 links to management courses including Kevin Holsapple's Critical Thinking and Decision-making at the University of Phoenix, John Lawler's International Human Resources Development at the University of Illinois, and Ray Luechtefeld's Introduction to Organizational Behavior at Boston College. Other disciplines with course offerings include communication, education, and cultural studies.

Address: http://www.utexas.edu/world/lecture/man/index.html

LISTSERV DISCUSSION GROUPS

AEDNET (ADULT AND CONTINUING EDUCATION)

Adult and continuing education is the focus of this discussion list. It provides researchers, practitioners, and graduate students with the opportunity to discuss important topics and concerns in an online environment.

Address: listproc@pulsar.acast.nova.edu
Message: subscribe AEDNET your e-mail address

New
AOM-LDSHP

This is the discussion group for the Leadership Division of the Academy of Management. It is open to all interested people but serves primarily for announcements about the activities of AoM.

Address: AoM-Ldrshp@sting.isu.edu
Message: subscribe AoM-Ldrshp Your Name

CRITICAL-MANAGEMENT

This list supports critical discussion, reflection, and research in the fields of business, management, and organizational studies. It encourages debate from a range of disciplines and perspectives in challenging orthodox approaches to management research and education.

Address: mailbase@mailbase.ac.uk
Message: join critical-management Your Name

New
EMPOWERMENT-DISC

This is a new forum for the discussion of empowerment and self-actualization. The moderator hopes that the group will exchange ideas and interact with others who are committed to success.

Address: majordomo@empowerment-now.com
Message: subscribe empowerment-disc

HRD-L

This is a discussion group for issues relative to human resource development including research, best practices, case studies, and teaching methods.

Address: majordomo@mjrdomo.trends.ca
Message: subscribe HRD-L Your Name

HRNET

The Human Resources Network (HRNET) is the electronic bulletin board and communications forum of the Human Resource Division of the Academy of Management. All who are interested in research and the practice of human resource management may participate.

Address: listserv@cornell.edu
Message: subscribe HRNET Your Name

New
INFLUENCE

This moderated list was created to help people increase healthy influence skills as opposed to using a manipulative influence style. In addition to discussion about influence on the Internet, in business, in the media, and in communities, the group is collaborating on a book about its experiences using a healthy-style of influence.

Address: majordomo@po.databack.com
Message: subscribe Influence

LDRSHP

This is an open discussion for the exchange of ideas about all aspects of leadership. Topics such as servant leadership, transformational leadership, the development and practice of leadership, and research are discussed.

Address: listserv@listserv.indiana.edu
Message: subscribe LDRSHP Your Name

New
LEADING

This listserv was developed as a result of discussions around *The Social Change Model of Leadership Development* (Astin & Astin, 1996). The list aims to share applications, exercises, theory, and research on relevant leadership topics.

Address: lists@msc.tamu.edu
Message: subscribe leading

LEADRSHP

Discussions on this list cover all aspects of leadership, from the role of vision to responsibilities of followers. Students in leadership classes at Texas A&M University, where the listserv originates, join the discussion as part of their class assignments.

Address: leadrshp@listserv.tamu.edu
Message: subscribe LEADRSHP Your Name

LEARNING-ORG

This discussion group is on the emerging topic of the learning organization, and is based on the work of Peter Senge as described in his book, *The Learning Organization.*

Address: majordomo@world.std.com
Message: subscribe learning-org

New
LSJ

This is the Leadership Studies Journal online discussion group. It was created to focus on the development of leadership courses and programs in colleges and universities. It aims to provide a link between people interested in leadership studies and a resource for sharing information about successful programs.

Address: listproc@lists.colorado.edu
Message: subscribe LSJ

MANAGEMENT-RESEARCH

This is a discussion of issues related to management research, including its methodology and development, research training, networking, and dissemination of research. Leadership topics are among the issues discussed.

Address: mailbase@mailbase.ac.uk
Message: join management-research Your Name

MGTDEV-L

Participants discuss topics of interest to those involved in management development. Most members are in a university setting.

Address: listserv@miamiu.acs.muohio.edu
Message: subscribe MGTDEV-L Your Name

New
OBTS-L

This is a listserv for the Organizational Behavior Teaching Society, although other interested persons may subscribe. The listserv is used to post conference notices, job openings, calls for papers, discussions of textbooks and teaching ideas, and debates on the subject of organizational behavior.

Address: listserv@bucknell.edu
Message: subscribe OBTS-L

PUBSEC (PUBLIC SECTOR MANAGEMENT ISSUES)

Launched in January 1996, this list "is intended as an experimental vehicle for discussion of issues of public sector management, reform and commercialisation."

Address: listproc@das.gov.au
Message: subscribe PUBSEC your e-mail address

STAFF-DEVELOPMENT

This list provides a forum for the discussion of issues and activities related to the field of staff development in higher education, including curriculum development, learning, teaching, and assessment.

Address: mailbase@mailbase.ac.uk
Message: join staff-development Your Name

TRDEV-L

This list provides a forum for the exchange of information on human resources training and development. The primary focus is to stimulate research collaboration and provide assistance in training and development for the academic and professional communities. This list generates a lot of mail, but it is indexed in folders so that subscribers may easily select messages to read or ignore.

Address: listserv@lists.psu.edu
Message: subscribe TRDEV-L

New
URBAN LEADERS

This list discusses a wide variety of issues important to leaders in urban communities and African-American leadership. There are job postings, conference notices, ideas for funding sources, and alerts to very current news items. This list is a strong networking tool and, as such, generates a lot of personal messages.

Address: majordomo@panix.com
Message: subscribe urban-leaders Your Name

ORGANIZATIONS

The items in this section support leadership education as member associations, institutes, and funding sources. Descriptions include:

• The organization's mission or purpose.
• The audience it serves.
• Examples of programs offered or programs funded.
• Publications.
• Meetings.
• Contact information.

CONTENTS

ASSOCIATIONS AND INSTITUTES

New
THE ALABAMA'S WOMEN'S LEADERSHIP DATABASE (AWLDB)

Sponsored by the Legislative Women's Caucus and authorized by the Alabama legislature in 1994, the AWLDB identifies and trains qualified women who are interested in serving on public boards in Alabama. The AWLDB offers educational programs on the basics of leadership and board service, and provides lists of women who have received training to the appointing authorities for their consideration when appointments are being made.

Address: Judson College, P.O. Box 120, Marion, AL 36756-0120
Phone: (334) 683-5109
Website: http://home.judson.edu/women.html

AMERICAN COUNCIL OF YOUNG POLITICAL LEADERS

The council is an educational-exchange organization formed to enhance foreign-policy understanding and exposure among rising young American political leaders and their counterparts around the world. The council offers practical education programs, annual foreign-policy and democracy conferences, and election-study programs. International exchanges are two- and three-week study programs in which delegates participate in private cabinet- and ministry-level meetings and in sessions with local officials in host countries. The U.S. Election Study Program is held every other November for political leaders from 60 to 70 countries to observe the American electoral process at the local, state, and national levels.

Address: 1612 K Street, N.W., Suite 300, Washington, DC 20006-2802
Phone: (202) 857-0999
Fax: (202) 857-0027
E-mail: acypl@erols.com

AMERICAN HUMANICS, INC. (AH)

The innovative program at AH prepares university students for leadership careers in nonprofit youth and human-service agencies. It develops and certifies entry-level professionals for organizations such as Boy and Girl Scouts, the American Red Cross, 4-H, and YMCA/YWCA. One thousand students on 40 campuses participate in classroom instruction, field trips, workshops, career counseling, job fairs, and 300-hour internships. Additional benefits are scholarships and low-interest

student loans and career placement services upon graduation.

Publications: *Student Leadership Association Co-curricular Manual*; *Internship Model Manual*; *Humanics: The Journal of Leadership for Youth and Human Service* quarterly; annual report; brochures
Meetings: American Humanics Management Institute annual meeting for students, faculty, and agency heads
Address: 4601 Madison Avenue, Suite B, Kansas City, MO 64112-3011
Phone: (816) 561-6415 or (800) 343-6466
Fax: (816) 531-3527
E-mail: ahservices@msn.com
Website: http://www.humanics.org

AMERICAN LEADERSHIP FORUM (ALF)

Composed of a network of chapters across the U.S., the forum seeks out proven leaders and brings them together. Twenty-five men and women who represent various sectors of society are selected from each chapter each year to participate in the Fellows training program of 20 two-day sessions. Each class works on a real community problem to practice collaborative problem solving. Following graduation from the one-year program, Senior Fellows remain in the network to share ideas for solutions to social problems in the ALF community.

Publications: *Leadership Readings;* research reports
Address: P.O. Box 3689, Stanford, CA 94309-3689
Phone: (650) 723-6127
Fax: (650) 723-6131
E-mail: alsnatl2@leland.stanford.edu

AMERICAN SOCIETY FOR TRAINING AND DEVELOPMENT, INC. (ASTD)

ASTD is an international association for people with training and human resource development responsibilities in business, industry, government, and public service. Organized in 1943, ASTD has over 65,000 members in chapters throughout the world. Members are encouraged to join a professional practice network and an industry group to receive information on activities of specific interest. For a fee, members may access the ASTD Online database with current listings of training events and course materials. The Member Information Exchange is a computerized information network for HRD professionals to share their expertise.

Publications: *The Value of Differences* diversity action plan; *Training & Development* monthly journal; *Techni-*

cal Skills and Training magazine; *Training & Development Literature Index*; *Human Resource Development Quarterly*; *INFO-LINE* monthly publication for trainers
Meetings: National and regional conferences
Address: 1640 King Street, Box 1443, Alexandria, VA 22313-2043
Phone: (703) 683-8100
Fax: (703) 683-8103
E-mail: csc@astd.org
Website: http://www.astd.org

AMERICAN YOUTH FOUNDATION

The American Youth Foundation is a nonprofit organization, incorporated in Missouri, Michigan, and New Hampshire, whose purpose is to develop the leadership capacities of young people by helping them achieve their personal best, lead balanced lives, and serve others. The Youth Leadership Compact program puts together diverse students to carry out action plans at their home schools while networking with 30 other schools. Other programs for K-through-12 students include summer resident and day camps and the STREAM Urban Adventure Center, complete with a climbing wall and group challenge course. Adult programs include Renewal for Women, Elderhostel, and a Leaders Institute for professional development. The *I Dare You* Leadership Award each year recognizes 8,000 high school juniors and seniors who demonstrate personal integrity, balanced living, and leadership potential.

Publications: *Leader's Resource Guide*
Meetings: Four sessions each summer
Address: 1315 Ann Avenue, St. Louis, MO 63104
Phone: (314) 772-8626
Fax: (314) 772-7542
E-mail: mail@ayf.com
Website: http://www.ayf.com

New
THE ASPEN INSTITUTE

The institute is an international, nonprofit, educational institution dedicated to enhancing leadership qualities through informed dialog. Executive seminars on topics such as ethics, leading change, and democracy are offered at facilities in Aspen, Colorado, and Maryland's Eastern Shore and at affiliated centers in Germany, France, and Italy. Additional policy programs examine current issues including international security, population and consumption, and philanthropy.

Publications: Reports from policy programs
Address: 1333 New Hampshire Avenue, N.W., Suite 1070, Washington, DC 20036
Phone: (202) 736-5800

Fax: (202) 467-0790
Website: http://www.aspeninst.org

ASPIRA ASSOCIATION, INC.

In Spanish, *aspirar* means to aspire to something greater. In that spirit, the Latino organization ASPIRA is dedicated to promoting youth leadership and education for Puerto Rican and other Latino youth. The ASPIRA Public Policy Leadership Program combines seminars, local community internships, and internships with policymakers in Washington, DC. ASPIRA/AmeriCorps trains and places young people to work as tutors and mentors to secondary school students in return for a stipend and college scholarship. Over 17,000 Latino youth and their families are touched by ASPIRA programs in six states, Puerto Rico, and Washington, DC.

Publications: *ASPIRA News* quarterly newsletter; training manuals; reports
Address: 1444 I Street, N.W., Suite 800, Washington, DC 20005-2210
Phone: (202) 835-3600
Fax: (202) 835-3613
E-mail: aspira@aol.com
Website: http://www.incacorp.com/aspira

New
ASSOCIATION FOR EXPERIENTIAL EDUCATION (AEE)

AEE is a nonprofit organization with roots in adventure education, committed to the development, practice, and evaluation of experiential learning. Members from 25 countries work in education, recreation, outdoor adventure programming, mental health, youth service, management development training, corrections, programming for people with disabilities, and environmental education. AEE accredits adventure programs.

Publications: *Journal of Experiential Education; Adventure Program Risk Management Report; Manual of Accreditation Standards;* other books; directories
Meetings: Annual regional and international conferences
Address: 2305 Canyon Boulevard, Suite100, Boulder, CO 80302-5651
Phone: (303) 440-8844
Fax: (303) 440-9581
E-mail: info@aee.org
Website: http://www.princeton.edu/~rcurtis/aee.html

ASSOCIATION OF LEADERSHIP EDUCATORS (ALE)

ALE is a national organization of 250 professionals in teaching, research, and extension programs in public and private institutions of higher education and the corporate sector. Its goals are to strengthen the leadership skills and competencies of professional educators and to strengthen and broaden the knowledge base that supports research, teaching, and extension programs in leadership. Two awards each year recognize excellence in teaching leadership and leadership contributions to the organization.

Publications: *ALE Newsletter* quarterly; conference proceedings; membership directory
Meetings: Annual conference
Address: c/o Dr. Karen Zotz, North Dakota State University, Human Development, 311 Morrill Hall, P.O. Box 5437, Fargo, ND 58105-5437
Phone: (701) 231-7171
Fax: (701) 231-8378
Website: http://www.aces.uiuc.edu/~ALE

BATTELLE SEATTLE RESEARCH CENTER

As a nonprofit international technology company, Battelle combines research on human performance with understanding of technology systems to design organizational training programs. Services include: leadership institutes that present models of effective leadership, one-on-one coaching, and individual and group assessments.

Publications: Books; research reports
Address: Professional Services, 4000 N.E. 41st Street, P.O. Box 5395, Seattle, WA 98105-5428
Phone: (800) 426-6762
Fax: (206) 528-3554
Website: http://www.seattle.battelle.org

New
THE JAMES MacGREGOR BURNS ACADEMY OF LEADERSHIP

The academy fosters future generations of political leaders through education, service, and research. Founded to encourage political participation at all levels, it is an academically sanctioned program to support emerging leaders seeking public office. Programs include the W. K. Kellogg Leadership Studies Project, the College Park Scholars in Public Leadership, The Ireland-U.S. Leadership Project, the Rising Stars High School Leadership Conference, Team Maryland—a scholar-athlete leadership program, CivicQuest—a curriculum for high schools, Congressional and White House internships, political campaign training, and for-credit courses. A new initiative is the National Issues Project, led by former U.S. Senator Bill Bradley, which seeks to revitalize a civil society.

Publications: *Government by the People* by James MacGregor Burns; *A History of National Service;*

International Directory of Women's Political Leadership; Learning Leadership: A Curriculum for a New Generation for K through 12 curriculum; alumni newsletters
Meetings: Annual Leadership Educators Conference
Address: University of Maryland, 1107 Taliaferro Hall, College Park, MD 20742-7715
Phone: (301) 405-5751
Fax: (301) 405-6402
E-mail: email@academy.umd.edu
Website: http://academy.umd.edu/academy

New
THE BUSINESS ENTERPRISE TRUST

A national, nonprofit organization, the trust promotes social leadership in business by conferring the annual Business Enterprise Awards on people who combine sound management with social conscience. The trust also produces educational materials, including case studies, videos, and books.

Publications: *Prism* quarterly newsletter; *Aiming Higher* by David Bollier; business school cases
Meetings: Annual awards ceremony
Address: 204 Junipero Serra Boulevard, Stanford, CA 94305-8006
Phone: (415) 321-5100
Fax: (415) 321-5774
E-mail: bet@betrust.org
Website: http://www.betrust.org

New
CAMPUS OUTREACH OPPORTUNITY LEAGUE (COOL)

Founded in 1984, COOL promotes college and university students' involvement in community service on a volunteer basis. This organization, directed by recent graduates, offers training programs, resources, peer consulting for ongoing support, awards, and an e-mail discussion group. Students involved in COOL are expected to organize volunteer service programs at their own schools and assume leadership roles on the COOL board of directors or at COOL events.

Publications: *What's COOL* quarterly newsletter; campus organizing manuals; resource books
Meetings: Annual national conference on student community service
Address: 1531 P Street, N.W., Suite LL, Washington, DC 20005-1909
Phone: (202) 265-1200
Fax: (202) 265-3241
E-mail: homeoffice@cool2serve.org
Website: http://www.cool2serve.org

CATALYST

Founded in 1962, Catalyst is a nonprofit organization with a dual mission—to enable women in business and the professions to achieve their maximum potential and to help employers capitalize on the talents of their female employees. Research is conducted on workplace barriers, leadership development opportunities, women's representation on corporate boards, and women as organizational change agents. Advisory staff work with organizations wishing to implement work/life supports, mentoring programs, and flexible work arrangements. Catalyst's Corporate Board Placement, a confidential service, helps companies identify and recruit women board members. An Information Center screens periodicals, books, and statistical fact sheets to compile data on women's workplace issues. Each March, the Catalyst Award is presented to corporations or professional firms that demonstrate outstanding achievement in promoting women's career and leadership development. Winners in 1997 were Sara Lee and Procter & Gamble.

Publications: *Perspective* monthly newsletter; *Mentoring: A Guide to Corporate Programs and Practices*; *The Catalyst Census of Female Board Directors*; *Info Briefs*; research reports
Meetings: Regional conferences cosponsored by major corporations
Address: 120 Wall Street, New York, NY 10005
Phone: (212) 514-7600
Fax: (212) 514-8470
E-mail: info@catalystwomen.org
Website: http://www.catalystwomen.org

CENTER FOR CHRISTIAN LEADERSHIP

Based at the Dallas Theological Seminary, the center's vision is to develop leaders who change lives. Elective courses include Leadership Development and Character Development for Small Groups, Advanced Leadership Development, Dynamics of Leadership, Personal Assessment and Ministry Vision, Leadership Evaluation and Development, and independent study to conduct research. The center follows the philosophy of servant leadership using a biblical focus on character, vision, and skill.

Meetings: One-day conferences
Address: 3909 Swiss Avenue, Dallas, TX 75204-6411
Phone: (214) 841-3515
Fax: (214) 841-3534
Website: http://www.dts.edu/dts/catalog/general/ccl-intr.htm

CENTER FOR CIVIC LEADERSHIP

The center is supported by Princeton Project 55, a nonprofit organization established by the Princeton University Class of 1955 to mobilize Princeton alumni and students to strengthen national institutions and values. The Public Interest Program places Princeton students and recent graduates in summer internships and full-year fellowships with public-interest organizations throughout the U.S. The Character Education program promotes honesty, responsibility, perseverance, and respect for self and others through community service, classroom instruction, media campaigns, regional conferences, publications, and a clearinghouse of effective programs and materials. Other programs include Mentoring, Service Exchange Program, and the Time/Dollar Program.

Address: 32 Nassau Street, Princeton, NJ 08542-4503
Phone: (609) 921-8808
Fax: (609) 921-2712
E-mail: pp55@aol.com

New
CENTER FOR CREATIVE CHURCH LEADERSHIP

Founded with the vision of assisting, training, and serving more effective church leaders, the center serves clergy from all denominations. Training is based on the Creative Church Leader Model, a tools-based approach to ministry developed by the center. The Association for Creative Church Leadership, a part of the center, is made up of individuals with different skill levels in the Creative Church Leadership Model, ranging from those with a basic understanding to qualified trainers.

Address: Long View House, 1722 Niblick Avenue, Lancaster, PA 17602-4826
Phone: (717) 299-5811
Fax: (717) 299-5588
E-mail: sixhats@aol.com

CENTER FOR CREATIVE LEADERSHIP (CCL)

Founded in 1970 by the Smith Richardson Foundation, Inc., CCL is an international, nonprofit educational institution whose mission is to advance the understanding, practice, and development of leadership for the benefit of society worldwide. There are offices in New York, San Diego, Colorado Springs, and Brussels and headquarters in Greensboro, North Carolina. CCL's research focuses on assessment for development, learning and the lessons of experience, executive development, leadership and creativity, teamwork, and simulation design. The Leadership Development Program (LDP)™ enables leadership growth by developing personal awareness. LeaderLab® is a multisession program that facilitates lasting behavioral change using analysis of current work situations, coaching over six months, and action planning. Other programs include the Entrepreneurial Leadership Program, Leading Creatively, The African-American Leadership Program, and The Women's Leadership Program.

Publications: *Leadership in Action* quarterly journal; guidebooks; research reports; instruments; simulations; annual report; directories of programs and products
Meetings: Conferences held periodically for program alumni, professionals in leadership research, and human resource professionals
Address: One Leadership Place, P.O. Box 26300, Greensboro, NC 27438-6300
Phone: (336) 545-5000
Fax: (336) 282-3284
E-mail: info@leaders.ccl.org
Website: http://www.ccl.org

CENTER FOR DEMOCRACY AND CITIZENSHIP

The center is dedicated to the advancement of democracy in the U.S. and abroad and to the study and advancement of education for effective public-spirited action on public problems. It undertakes projects in areas of research, teaching, and outreach through civic-leadership training. From 1993 to 1995 the center joined the Whitman Center at Rutgers University to launch a national campaign called The New Citizenship for the purpose of reinvigorating civic leadership. The center also sponsors civic-education programs for youths, health professionals, low-income parents, and government employees, and organizes a community-located learning center in St. Paul called the Jane Addams School for Democratic Education.

Publications: *Building America: The Democratic Promise of Public Work; Free Spaces: The Sources of Democratic Change; Public Life* quarterly newsletter; annual report
Meetings: Annual May conference; annual fall training institute
Address: Hubert H. Humphrey Institute of Public Affairs, University of Minnesota, 301 19th Avenue South, Minneapolis, MN 55455-0429
Phone: (612) 625-0142
Fax: (612) 625-3513
Website: http://www.hhh.umn.edu/bulletin/centers/democ-citizen.html

CENTER FOR EFFECTIVE ORGANIZATIONS (CEO)

CEO is a research center that conducts intensive studies of key management issues, organizational diagnosis, and experimental programs with corporate sponsors. Its objective is to bridge the gap between theory and practice of the design and management of work organizations. Areas of interest include leadership, labor-management relations, organizational development and design, work design, employee involvement, and reward systems.

Publications: Books, articles, and chapters for general and technical/academic audiences; research reports; annual report
Meetings: Annual Human Resource Executive Seminar; global conference on organizational change
Address: Marshall School of Business, University of Southern California, Los Angeles, CA 90089-1421
Phone: (213) 740-9814
Fax: (213) 740-4354
E-mail: ceo@usc.edu
Website: http://www.marshall.usc.edu/ceo

CENTER FOR LEADERSHIP DEVELOPMENT

The Center for Leadership Development is sponsored by the American Council on Education (ACE). It seeks to strengthen the nation's colleges and universities by providing a forum for discussion of leadership development and by sponsoring programs on institutional improvement. The center identifies new leaders and promotes the creation of new leadership models. The ACE Fellows Program prepares promising leaders in higher education for roles in change management. The Department Leadership Program offers workshops for department chairs to enhance their leadership effectiveness. The Project on Leadership and Institutional Transformation is studying 26 institutions that are undergoing significant change.

Publications: Books on leadership, grants, board governance, higher education teaching and administration; annual report
Meetings: Annual conference
Address: American Council on Education, One DuPont Circle, N.W., Suite 800, Washington, DC 20036-1193
Phone: (202) 939-9420
Fax: (202) 785-8056
E-mail: web@ace.nche.edu
Website: http://www.acenet.edu/programs/CLD/home.html

CENTER FOR LEADERSHIP EXCELLENCE OF THE CATHOLIC HEALTH ASSOCIATION

The center is a focal point for leadership development within the Catholic health care ministry. A research project, *Transformational Leadership for the Healing Ministry: Competencies for the Future*, identified the unique competencies of leadership in Catholic health care. LEAD—Leadership Enrichment through Assessment and

Development—is the center's core program. The Advanced Institute is a forum for experienced leaders that offers 80 hours of instruction over a three-year period.

Publications: *A New Vision of Leadership* videotape and facilitator's guide; *Dossier* 360-degree feedback instrument; *Leadership Development Exchange* directory of programs; *Healthcare Leadership: Shaping a Tomorrow*; *Ministry Perspectives* quarterly newsletter
Meetings: Annual assembly; conferences; seminars
Address: 4455 Woodson Road, St. Louis, MO 63134-3797
Phone: (314) 427-2500
Fax: (314) 427-0029
Website: http://www.chausa.org

CENTER FOR LEADERSHIP STUDIES

This research and educational institution aims to contribute to the understanding of and to identify the importance of the full range of leadership and its applications. The center focuses on the evolution from a transactional style to a transformational style of leadership. The Executive Series of Leadership Development Programs includes one- to six-day workshops offered internationally. Past programs trained community leaders in the southern tier region of New York and partnered college-age emerging leaders with senior leaders in profit and nonprofit organizations.

Publications: *Bass and Stogdill's Handbook of Leadership*; *Leadership and Performance Beyond Expectations*; *Leadership Quarterly* journal; *The Next Module* quarterly newsletter; books; research reports
Address: State University of New York–Binghamton, P.O. Box 6015, Binghamton, NY 13902-6015
Phone: (607) 777-3007
Fax: (607) 777-4188
E-mail: cls@binghamton.edu
Website: http://www.som/binghamton.edu/cls

New
CENTER FOR ORGANIZATION REFORM

The center provides consultation to school districts in Washington State in the areas of site-based management, renewal, and increased organizational effectiveness. It also serves as a professional-development center that sponsors periodic institutes and specialized training in the areas of organizational change and reform and as a resource center for research.

Address: Gonzaga University, AD Box 25, Spokane, WA 99258-0001
Phone: (509) 328-4220 x3592
Fax: (509) 324-5812

CENTER FOR STRATEGIC URBAN COMMUNITY LEADERSHIP

The center is dedicated to the improvement of urban communities throughout the Northeastern U.S. by educating leaders about community-academia partnerships for dealing with race relations and urban development. The future of urban communities belongs to leaders who break the political, social, and cultural barriers that have previously impeded their access to leadership positions. The Hispanic Women Leadership Institute begins with self-examination, then shifts to community concerns. The Leadership Management for Urban Executives Institute trains African-American, Latino, and Asian fellows who aspire to careers in key national, state, and regional programs. The Latino Fellows Public Policy Summer Leadership Institute provides ten weeks of leadership development and public-policy training to Latino students enrolled in New Jersey colleges.

Publications: *The Center Focus* quarterly newsletter
Address: School of Social Work, Rutgers—the State University of New Jersey—Camden Campus, 327 Cooper Street, Camden, NJ 08102-1519
Phone: (609) 225-6348
Fax: (609) 225-6500
Website: http://crab.rutgers.edu/Camden/CFSUCL/

New
CENTER FOR WOMEN'S GLOBAL LEADERSHIP

Founded in 1989, the center seeks to develop an understanding of the ways in which gender affects the exercise of power and conduct of public policy internationally. Its goals are to build international linkages among women in local leadership, and to promote visibility and increase participation of women in public deliberation and policy-making. The center sponsors an annual two-week Women's Global Leadership Institute for women leaders at the grassroots and national levels, runs numerous strategic planning programs, and cosponsors regional workshops and institutes.

Publications: *Global Center News* newsletter; reports; some publications available in Spanish
Address: 27 Clifton Avenue, New Brunswick, NJ 08901-1529
Phone: (908) 932-8782
Fax: (908) 932-1180
E-mail: cwgl@igc.apc.org
Website: http://feminist.com/cfwgl.htm

CITIZEN LEADERSHIP INSTITUTE

Created with a grant from the W. K. Kellogg Foundation, the institute was charged with developing a citizen leader model to be integrated into the curriculum of Florida's 28 community colleges. The model's basic premise is that citizen leaders exist in all communities and that colleges can help these leaders recognize and accept responsibility at the community, state, and national levels. A 30-hour core and 30 stand-alone courses may be taught as for-credit or across-the-curriculum noncredit courses. The introductory program builds a foundation on awareness, communication, and understanding of government agencies. An advanced leadership program assists citizens in becoming change agents. In-house and contract training are available for colleges outside Florida.

Publications: *Leader Letters* quarterly newsletter
Meetings: Annual Public Policy Institute
Address: Gulf Coast Community College, 5230 West U.S. Highway 98, Panama City, FL 32401-1058
Phone: (904) 747-3216
Fax: (904) 872-3836
Website: http://www.gc.cc.fl.us/leader/leadhome.htm

New
COMMUNITY DEVELOPMENT INSTITUTE (CDI)

The primary focus of this nonprofit organization is building organizational capacity and training indigenous leaders in diverse urban communities. The CDI's Management Services Division provides technical assistance, training, and consultation to community-based organizations, foundations, and local governments. The Program Services Division oversees the CDI's community service projects, including the Leadership Training Academy for middle school and high school youths, the Black Male Rebirth Program, and a youth entrepreneurial program.

Address: 321 Bell Street, P.O. Box 50099, East Palo Alto, CA 94303-0099
Phone: (415) 327-5846
Fax: (415) 327-4430

COMMUNITY DEVELOPMENT SOCIETY (CDS)

CDS is a professional association offering a global perspective on community development. Members believe that the human dimension is the most critical aspect of community and that communities can thrive through improvement of individual, organizational, and problem-solving skills. CDS integrates knowledge from many disciplines with community development theory, research, teaching, and practice in both the public and private sectors. Networking opportunities are available through local chapters and special-interest groups. A certificate program rewards experience, education, and achievement.

Publications: *Journal of the Community Development Society* semiannual journal; membership directory and handbook
Meetings: Annual conference
Address: 1123 North Water Street, Milwaukee, WI 53202
Phone: (414) 276-7106
Fax: (414) 276-7704
Website: http://comm-dev.org

COMMUNITY RESOURCE CENTER, INC. (CRC)

This center is dedicated to social, economic, and political change leading to: 1) inspired individual and collective commitment and action; 2) equal opportunity and access for all people; 3) embracing diversity, dignity, and respect for human rights; and 4) a renewed sense of community. To achieve these goals, CRC provides leadership training, technical assistance, and consultation to individuals and community-based organizations in Colorado and across the country. The Colorado Nonprofit Leadership and Management Program is a year-long leadership training program for senior staff and board members of nonprofit agencies. GRASSROOTS FIRST is a statewide initiative to empower local leaders to affect public policy. The Rural Cultural Facilities Leadership Program assists smaller communities to develop and sustain grassroots leadership development programs. CRC has also developed a three-phase Grassroots Leadership Development Program Model.

Publications: *1997-1998 Colorado Grants Guide*
Address: 1245 East Colfax Avenue, Suite 205, Denver, CO 80218-2218
Phone: (303) 860-7711
Fax: (303) 860-7723
E-mail: crcamerica@mho.net
Website: http://www.crcamerica.org

CONFERENCE BOARD

For 70 years, the Conference Board's twofold purpose has been to improve the business enterprise system and to enhance its contribution to society. To accomplish this, the organization provides forums for executives from all industries to exchange ideas on business policy and practices. Recent forum topics include: Developing the Global Information Society, Rewriting the Rules of Human Resources, and Business and Economic Outlook: How Will the Century Close? A research program identifies and reports on key areas of changing management concern, opportunity, and action. Recent research reports include *Value-Creating Growth: Goals, Strategies, Foundations* and *Perspectives on a Global Economy.* The Ron Brown Award for Corporate Leadership is given each year to honor outstanding achievements in employee and community relations. Winners for 1997 were IBM Corporation for its diversity programs and Levi Strauss and Company for its antiracism initiative. Affiliate branches are located in Ottawa, Ontario, and Brussels.

Publications: *Across the Board* magazine ten times a year; regular reports on human resources and economics issues; *West Point Story: What Makes a Successful Leader in the Military and Business Worlds; The Rush to Leadership Training; Leadership: One Thing Missing*
Meetings: Conferences
Address: 845 Third Avenue, New York, NY 10022-6601
Phone: (212) 759-0900
Fax: (212) 980-7014
E-mail: info@conference-board.org
Website: http://www.conference-board.org

CONGRESSIONAL YOUTH LEADERSHIP COUNCIL

This educational organization is committed to fostering and inspiring young people to achieve their full leadership potential through experiential training programs in the nation's capital. Over 400 members of the U.S. Congress serve on the Board of Advisors, volunteer their time to lecture, and provide students with short-term work experience in their offices.

Publications: *Youth Leadership News* newsletter three times a year
Meetings: National Young Leaders Conference, Washington Journalism Conference, Presidential Youth Inaugural Conference
Address: 1511 K Street, N.W., Suite 812, Washington, DC 20005-1498
Phone: (202) 638-0008
Fax: (202) 638-4257
E-mail: cylc@cylc.org
Website: http://www.cylc.org

CORO

CORO is a private, nonprofit, nonpartisan institution that conducts education and research in the field of public affairs through training centers in San Francisco, Los Angeles, St. Louis, Kansas City, and New York. CORO concerns itself with the integrity of a community as a whole. Programs for youths, adults, teachers, community leaders, women, and minorities train individuals for leadership roles in the public sector. Experiential programs range from eight weeks to nine months, part-time and full-time. The Leadership–New York program identifies and prepares the next generation of civic, public, private, and nonprofit leaders who will bring New York City into the 21st century.

Publications: *CORO: Creation-Concepts-Connection* oral history book
Address: One Whitehall Street, 10th Floor, New York, NY 10004-2109
Phone: (212) 248-2935
Fax: (212) 248-2970
Website: http://www.coro.org

CREATIVE EDUCATION FOUNDATION, INC. (CEF)

The foundation encourages and stimulates creativity in learning and decision making through conferences, public programs, contract education, publishing, grant making, and an online bulletin board for members. Programs include the Leadership Development Program, Developing Group Leadership Skills, and leadership programs for ages 13 to 18. CEF has a library of 2,500 volumes and 1,500 doctoral dissertations on microfiche.

Publications: *Creativity in Action* monthly newsletter; *Journal of Creative Behavior* quarterly; resource catalog; books; videos; audiotapes
Meetings: Annual Creative Problem Solving Institute
Address: 1050 Union Road, Buffalo, NY 14224-3402
Phone: (716) 675-3181
Fax: (716) 675-3209
E-mail: cefhq@cef-cpsi.org
Website: http://www.cef-cpsi.org

THE PETER F. DRUCKER FOUNDATION FOR NONPROFIT MANAGEMENT

The foundation believes that a healthy society requires three sectors: a public sector of effective governments, a private sector of effective businesses, and a social sector of effective community organizations. To this end, the foundation helps the social sector achieve excellence in performance and build responsible citizenship through seminars and video teleconferences. Guided by the writing of Peter Drucker, it helps nonprofits convert good intentions into results and make innovation part of all strategy. The Peter F. Drucker Award for Nonprofit Innovation, accompanied by a $25,000 prize, is presented each year to a nonprofit organization that has demonstrated innovation in a program or project. The foundation believes that the social sector offers the greatest opportunities for contribution and faces the greatest challenges.

Publications: *The Drucker Foundation News* quarterly newsletter; *Leader of the Future* (1996); *Leader to Leader* quarterly journal; videotapes; audiotapes
Meetings: Two conferences each year
Address: 320 Park Avenue, 3rd Floor, New York, NY 10022-6839
Phone: (212) 224-1174
Fax: (212) 224-2508

E-mail: info@pfdf.org
Website: http://www.pfdf.org

EISENHOWER WORLD AFFAIRS INSTITUTE

As a living memorial to President Dwight D. Eisenhower, the institute seeks to advance Eisenhower's belief that knowledge and understanding are vital to improving relations among peoples and nations of the world. Public-policy and educational programs are designed to increase understanding of the presidency and world affairs. The Dwight D. Eisenhower Leadership Development Program designed a prototype curriculum for secondary, under-graduate, and graduate leadership courses. This collaborative effort between the institute, Gettysburg College, and Johns Hopkins University's Paul Nitze School of Advanced International Studies aims to stimulate theoretical and practical study as well as improve methods for teaching critical leadership skills. The institute awards scholarships and fellowships to students, teachers, and researchers.

Publications: *The Papers of Dwight D. Eisenhower* multivolume reference work; *The Eisenhower Legacy* three-part television documentary series; *Lessons and Legacies: Farewell Addresses from the Senate*
Address: 918 16th Street, N.W., Suite 501, Washington, DC 20006-2902
Phone: (202) 223-6710
Fax: (202) 452-1837

New
EUROPEAN FOUNDATION FOR MANAGEMENT DEVELOPMENT (EFMD)

This foundation, efmd, is Europe's forum for information, networking, and worldwide cooperation in innovation and best practices in management education. Members are business school educators and HRD professionals. In 1997, efmd established EQUIS, the European Quality Improvement System, for assessment and accreditation of management development institutions.

Publications: *efmd Bulletin; efmd FORUM* journal published three times a year; *Guide to European Business Schools and Executive Centres; efmd Guide to the EC*
Meetings: Periodic conferences
Address: Rue Washington 40, Brussels, B-1050 Belgium
Phone: +32-2-648 03 85
Fax: +32-2-646 07 68
E-mail: info@efmd.be
Website: http://www.efmd.be

New
EXECUTIVE EDUCATION NETWORK (EXEN)

EXEN is a distance-learning option for management development programs. Programs from U.S. business schools and other educational institutions are delivered live, via satellite, to corporate locations. Examples are: Influence and Leadership from Babson College, Creative Leadership from the Center for Creative Leadership, the Program for Strategic Leadership from Penn State, International Business Leadership from the University of North Carolina–Chapel Hill, The Leadership Series with Warren Bennis from the University of Southern California, and Corporate Entrepreneurship from the University of Texas–Austin.

Address: 1303 Marsh Lane, Carrollton, TX 75006-5430
Phone: (800) 483-3936
Fax: (800) 200-0051
Website: http://www.exen.com

FANNING LEADERSHIP CENTER

This center recognizes leadership development as the driving force of local development and quality-of-life issues facing each community, region, state, and beyond. It is a collaborative effort with the University of Georgia, Carl Vinson Institute of Government, Cooperative Extension Service, Georgia Center for Continuing Education, Institute of Community and Area Development, and Small Business Development Center. Its mission is to facilitate leadership development through a central source of information, identification of leadership needs and trends, program development, applied research, and education of community leaders. Among the many local and statewide programs are: Adult Community Leadership Program, Youth Leadership in Action, Leadership PLUS, and High Performance School Teams Leadership Institute.

Publications: *Leadership INSIGHTS* quarterly newsletter.
Address: Hoke Smith Annex, The University of Georgia, Athens, GA 30602-4350
Phone: (706) 542-1108
Fax: (706) 542-7007
E-mail: leadership@flc.uga.edu
Website: http://www.uga.edu/flc/home.htm

FUND FOR AMERICAN STUDIES

Four summer institutes on the campus of Georgetown University provide students with for-credit courses on the U.S. government, economics, and ethics. They include classroom instruction, internships, and lectures by Washington insiders. Students visit the White House,

State Department, Federal Reserve, and several embassies for site briefings. Students majoring in political science, economics, business, and journalism are invited to apply for the institute.

Address: 1526 18th Street, N.W., Washington, DC 20036-1306
Phone: (202) 986-0384
Fax: (202) 986-0390
Website: http:www.aipes.org/tfas.htm

New
FUTURE LEADERS OF AMERICA (FLA)

FLA exists to provide leadership training to academically talented Latino youth. As ninth-grade students, the future leaders attend a six-day entry-level program to learn public speaking, assertiveness, goal setting, and time management. Older students attend advanced programs to learn about community problems and to write proposals for solutions. Follow-up seminars are held in Washington, DC, and at major universities in California. The goal is to create new role models—citizens with the desire and ability to lead by example. The New Citizens Youth Leadership Program helps to integrate new Spanish-speaking citizens into their schools and communities.

Address: 1110 Camellia Street, Oxnard, CA 93030-2823
Phone and Fax: (805) 485-5237
E-mail: flainc@msn.com

GRANTSMANSHIP CENTER

This training organization offers leadership development for the nonprofit sector. Since it was formed in 1972, the center has trained more than 65,000 staff members of public and private agencies in grantsmanship, program management, and fund-raising.

Publications: *Program Planning & Proposal Writing* university text and prototype for proposal writing; *The Grantsmanship Center Magazine* free newsletter
Address: 1125 West Sixth Street, 5th Floor, P.O. Box 17220, Los Angeles, CA 90017-0220
Phone: (213) 482-9860
Fax: (213) 482-9863
E-mail: norton@tgci.com
Website: http://www.tgci.com

GRASSROOTS LEADERSHIP

Grassroots Leadership provides leadership training to traditionally disempowered communities in the South. Programs include year-long training for individuals and custom-designed projects for organizations.

Address: 1515 Elizabeth Avenue, P.O. Box 36006, Charlotte, NC 28236-6006
Phone: (704) 332-3090
Fax: (704) 332-0445
E-mail: grasslead@aol.com
Website: http://www.grasslead.org

THE ROBERT K. GREENLEAF CENTER

The center's goals are to deepen the ideas of Robert K. Greenleaf and the principles of servant leadership through the preservation and promotion of his writings. This is intended to fundamentally improve the caring and quality of all institutions. The servant leader concept emphasizes increased service to others, a holistic approach to work, and promoting a sense of community and the sharing of power in decision making. Workshops offered include Personal Journey Through Servant-Leadership and Servant-Led Boards.

Publications: *The Servant Leader* quarterly newsletter; *Insights on Leadership* by Larry Spears; *On Becoming a Servant-Leader* by Robert K. Greenleaf; other books; videotapes; audiotapes
Meetings: Annual international conference; workshops; symposia
Address: 921 East 86th Street, Suite 200, Indianapolis, IN 46240
Phone: (317) 259-1241
Fax: (317) 259-0560
Website: http://greenleaf.org

HAAS CENTER FOR PUBLIC SERVICE

Established in 1985, the Haas Center represents Stanford University's commitment to education for civic responsibility. Center programs include local, national, and international volunteer work, partnerships with government agencies and school systems, the Visiting Mentor Program, Stanford in Washington, and a clearinghouse for public-service opportunities. Forty courses across the curriculum support the center's study-service connection. For example, the English Department's Community Service Writing Program matches 400 freshmen with community agencies that need articles, grant proposals, and brochures. Courses in American Studies, Anthropology, Education, History, Public Policy, and Urban Studies also integrate public-service activity with academic studies.

Publications: *Academic Study and Public Service: Making the Connection*; *Linking Service with Academic Study: The Faculty Role*; *The Commons* quarterly newsletter
Address: Stanford University, 562 Salvatierra Walk, Stanford, CA 94027-8620

Phone: (650) 723-0992
Fax: (650) 725-7339
E-mail: info@haas.stanford.edu
Website: http://haas.stanford.edu

HARTWICK HUMANITIES IN MANAGEMENT INSTITUTE

This nonprofit research, education, and publishing organization encourages and supports the study of mankind's greatest literary, philosophical, biographical, historical, dramatic, and artistic works as sources of knowledge of leadership.

Publications: Forty-six different *Hartwick Classic Leadership Cases*; *Teaching Notes* and video to accompany each case
Address: Hartwick College, Oneonta, NY 13820
Phone: (607) 431-4952 or (800) 94-CASES
Fax: (607) 431-4954
E-mail: hhmi@hartwick.edu
Website: http://www.hartwick.edu/hhmi

HEARTLAND CENTER FOR LEADERSHIP DEVELOPMENT

The center developed as an outgrowth of Visions from the Heartland, a grassroots futures project. Its programs now serve community leaders throughout the U.S. and Canada who are facing the challenges of rural community survival. Workshops, seminars, in-depth retreats, and customized programs focus on economic diversity, pitfalls to avoid in economic development, and leadership lessons. The Helping Small Towns Survive Institute is an intensive, five-day training program for professionals working in small-town and rural community development.

Publications: *Clues to Rural Community Survival*; *Ten Ideas for Recruiting New Leaders*; *The Entrepreneurial Community: A Strategic Leadership Approach to Community Survival*; other field research reports
Address: 941 O Street, Suite 920, Lincoln, NE 68508-3649
Phone: (402) 474-7667
Fax: (402) 474-7672
E-mail: mw4137@aol.com
Website: http://www.4w.com/heartland

HIGHLANDER RESEARCH AND EDUCATION CENTER

Founded in 1932, the Highlander Center is a nonprofit organization that seeks to empower people to take democratic leadership toward fundamental social change in communities throughout Appalachia and the Deep South. Based on the principle that institutional change can only be effective when solutions come from the people experiencing the problem, it provides educational programs that allow people to analyze their problems, test their ideas, learn from the experiences of others, and strengthen their organizations. The Southern and Appalachian Leadership Training program is designed to serve emerging leaders who are actively working on social justice issues, and the Youth Leadership Development Program holds a summer workshop and recruits and supervises youth interns. Workshops, technical assistance, fellowships, participatory learning, and peer interaction help participants to learn from collective experience.

Publications: *Highlander Reports* bimonthly newsletter; *Environment and Development in the USA: A Grassroots Approach to Education Presented Through a Collection of Writings*; working papers; songbooks; videotapes; audiotapes
Address: 1959 Highlander Way, New Market, TN 37820-4939
Phone: (423) 933-3443
Fax: (423) 933-3424
E-mail: HREC@igc.apc.org

HISPANIC LEADERSHIP INSTITUTE

The institute is a partnership between Valle del Sol, Inc., Arizona State University Research Center, and Arizona State University College of Extended Education. Its purpose is to promote the participation of Hispanics in leadership roles and to increase Hispanic participation in the development of public policy. Evening classes teach leadership theory and skills, ethics, communication, and diversity issues. Team projects put participants to work on community issues. Continuing Education Units are awarded upon completion of the 15-week institute.

Address: Arizona State University, Downtown Center, 502 East Monroe Street, Suite 250, Phoenix, AZ 85004-2337
Phone: (602) 965-3046
Fax: (602) 965-3660

New
HUMAN RESOURCE PLANNING SOCIETY (HRPS)

This nonprofit organization is dedicated to providing current perspectives on complex and challenging human resource and business issues. Members are scholars, HRD practitioners, and consultants around the world. They have access to competency and certification workshops as well as research reports on high-performance work systems and future challenges in the field.

Publications: *Human Resource Planning* quarterly journal

Meetings: Annual conference
Address: 317 Madison Avenue, Suite 1509, New York, NY 10017-5201
Phone: (212) 490-6387
Fax: (212) 682-6851
E-mail: info@hrps.org
Website: http://www.hrps.org

IC² INSTITUTE

This institute is a major research center for the study of innovation, creativity, and capital. Key research and study concentrations include creative and innovative management, entrepreneurship, technology transfer, global networking, economic modeling, and evaluation of attitudes and opinions on key issues. University of Texas students can earn a master's degree in Science and Technology Commercialization at the institute.

Publications: *Industrial Innovation: Productivity and Employment*; *Small Business and the Entrepreneurial Spirit*; books; policy papers; research articles
Meetings: Conferences; workshops
Address: University of Texas–Austin, 2815 San Gabriel Street, Austin, TX 78705-3596
Phone: (512) 475-8900
Fax: (512) 475-8901
Website: http://www.utexas.edu/depts/ic2/main.htm

INDEPENDENT SECTOR (IS)

This organization represents the nonprofit sector of our society, which includes over 600,000 organizations, 800 of which are members. IS encourages the philanthropy and volunteer action that impact the educational, scientific, health, welfare, cultural, and religious life of the nation. To preserve and enhance this nonprofit initiative, IS educates the public about the role of the nonprofit sector and conducts research on its usefulness to society. It engages in government relations to gain public-policy support and encourages effective leadership of nonprofit organizations. Each year, IS awards the John W. Gardner Leadership Award for service in the voluntary sector—in 1997 the award went to Millard Fuller, the founder and president of Habitat for Humanity International.

Publications: *Give Five* newsletter; books; research reports; videos
Meetings: Annual conference
Address: 1828 L Street, N.W., Suite 1200, Washington, DC 20036-5107
Phone: (202) 223-8100
Fax: (202) 416-0580
E-mail: info@indepsec.org
Website: http://www.indepsec.org

New
INDIAN DISPUTE RESOLUTION SERVICES, INC. (IDRS)

IDRS is a national nonprofit Native American organization founded by a consortium of five prominent Native American organizations with the purpose of strengthening tribes' and tribal organizations' capacity to govern themselves; resolve internal and external conflict; and control, manage, and enhance their own destinies. IDRS offers mediation, facilitation, and arbitration services, and assistance in strategic planning and organizational development. Training programs offered include workshops on Leadership Training, Leadership and Violence Prevention, Mediation, and Negotiation.

Address: 1029 K Street, Suite 38, Sacramento, CA 95814-3816
Phone: (916) 447-4800
Fax: (916) 447-4808
E-mail: IDRS@tomatoweb.com
Website: http://www.tomatoweb.com/idrs

INROADS, INC.

INROADS is a career-development organization that places talented minority youths in summer jobs to prepare them for future corporate and community leadership. Over 6,000 African-American, Hispanic, and Native American high school and college students with 3.0 or better grade-point averages receive internships. Over 700 business and engineering corporate sponsors hire interns for two or three summers and often offer permanent positions following graduation. Professional training seminars include time management, business presentation skills, team building, and decision making.

Publications: *INROADS* quarterly newsletter; annual report
Address: 10 South Broadway, Suite 700, St. Louis, MO 63102-1734
Phone: (314) 241-7488
E-mail: info@notes.inroadsinc.org
Website: http://www.inroadsinc.org

INSTITUTE FOR CONSERVATION LEADERSHIP

The mission of the institute is to train and empower volunteer leaders and to build volunteer institutions that protect and conserve the earth's environment. To accomplish this mission, the institute develops and conducts training programs; and designs and facilitates meetings, retreats, and conferences. It also provides consulting and technical assistance to help groups and individuals address critical leadership and organizational development needs such as fund-raising, board development, strategic planning, and recruiting and involving volunteers.

Address: 6930 Carroll Avenue, Suite 420, Tacoma Park, MD 20912-4432
Phone: (301) 270-2900
Fax: (301) 270-0610
E-mail: toicl@aol.com

INSTITUTE FOR CREATIVE DEVELOPMENT (ICD)

The institute is a nonprofit think tank and educational center dedicated to exploring the kinds of thinking, feeling, and imagining needed for our society's vital future. A major focus is to explore and teach new leadership skills to meet the challenges of the future. The institute's broad definition of leadership includes parents, service people, executives, and educators. All program participants face questions of purpose—both personal and cultural—to grow personally and professionally and to contribute to society. The institute's Creative Systems Theory is taught in a year-long Intensive workshop over ten weekends and in five-day Mini-Intensives.

Publications: Books; articles; videotapes
Address: P.O. Box 51244, Seattle, WA 98115-1244
Phone and Fax: (206) 526-0580
Website: http://www.creativesystems.org

INSTITUTE FOR EDUCATIONAL LEADERSHIP

Programs at national, state, and local levels support and enhance the capabilities of educators and policymakers. The institute acts as an educational forum for information exchange among government, nonprofit, and business sectors. Seminars are designed to train education leaders in federal policy processes.

Publications: Newsletter three times a year; policy reports
Meetings: Washington Policy Seminars
Address: 1001 Connecticut Avenue, N.W., Suite 310, Washington, DC 20036-5541
Phone: (202) 822-8405
Fax: (202) 872-4050
E-mail: iel@iel.org
Website: http://www.iel.org

THE INTERNATIONAL UNIVERSITY CONSORTIUM FOR EXECUTIVE EDUCATION (UNICON)

UNICON is a nonprofit organization dedicated to advancing the field of university-sponsored executive education through innovative processes for developing leaders and their organizations. Educational institutions

and corporate representatives share dialog on leadership development informally and at annual meetings. Their focus is on benchmarking and best practices, staff development, return on investment, and market research. UNICON members are located in North America, Europe, Australia, and Asia.

Publications: Member directory; brochure
Meetings: Annual spring and fall conferences
Address: 123 Cross Hill Road, Millington, NJ 07946-1412
Phone: (908) 903-1180
Fax: (908) 903-1180

KANSAS LEADERSHIP FORUM

The Kansas Leadership Forum is a set of network activities designed to serve and assist those Kansas professionals and volunteers involved in providing youth and adult leadership development activities. By linking people working in the field of leadership, the forum serves as a vehicle for the exchange of ideas, information, and knowledge about leadership education and development.

Publications: Publication series; *The Kansas Directory of Leadership Education: 1993-1994*
Meetings: Annual conference
Address: c/o Cheryl Rude, Director of Leadership Studies, Southwestern College, 100 College Street, Winfield, KS 67156-2499
Phone: (316) 221-8381
Fax: (316) 221-8390

KANSAS STATE UNIVERSITY CENTER FOR LEADERSHIP

The center is actually a network of leadership educators who serve the needs of the academic community and local and state business communities. It is designed to encourage an interdisciplinary approach to leadership issues and to foster communication and collaboration among faculty and staff interested in leadership. Currently, the center offers a wide range of programs from quality management to team building and other organizational development issues.

Address: Department of Management, College of Business Administration, Kansas State University, Calvin Hall, Manhattan, KS 66506
Phone: (913) 532-4359
Fax: (913) 532-7024
E-mail: niehoff@business.cba.ksu.edu

LEADERSHAPE, INC.

LeaderShape, Inc., is a nonprofit organization committed to developing young adults who will lead with integrity. One program, the LeaderShape Institute, is a six-day session in which students create visions, build teams, implement action plans, utilize ethics in decision making, and evaluate their personal strengths and weaknesses. Students create LeaderShape Projects to work on when they leave to effect extraordinary improvement in their organizations within the following year. Carpe Diem is a one-day course based on the same principles but in an abbreviated format. The Team Challenge Course is a four-hour outdoor team-building experience intended to reinforce trust, communication, risk taking, and self-esteem.

Address: 1801 Fox Drive, Suite 101, Champaign, IL 61820-7255
Phone: (217) 351-6200
Fax: (217) 355-0910
E-mail: lead@leadershape.org
Website: http://www.leadershape.org

New
LEADERSHIP AMERICA, INC.

Each year, Leadership America, a nonprofit training organization, brings 100 women from diverse backgrounds together for a series of three intensive sessions based around a single theme. In 1997 this theme was "Countdown to the Millennium," and sessions were held in Washington, DC; San Francisco, California; and Dallas, Texas. Graduates of the program are eligible for membership in the Leadership America organization, which provides a continuing network of resources and contacts. Scholarships are available.

Meetings: Annual conference
Address: 700 North Fairfax Street, Suite 610, Alexandria, VA 22314-2040
Phone: (703) 549-1102
Fax: (703) 836-9205
E-mail: info@leadershipamerica.com
Website: http://www.leadershipamerica.com

New
THE LEADERSHIP CENTER

The Leadership Center is a nonprofit professional education and development center designed to help organizations manage change and expand the boundaries of leadership. It offers training workshops for all levels of managers and human resources professionals, provides forums to exchange dialogue, conducts research on emerging trends in leadership, and recognizes exceptional

leadership in the New York City area. Some programs are: Vision Workshop for Entrepreneurial Leaders, Meeting the Challenges of Managing Technical People, Global Leadership Program, and Executive Coaching for Performance and Development.

Address: Robert J. Milano Graduate School of Management and Urban Policy, The New School, 80 Fifth Avenue, Suite 800, New York, NY 10011-8002
Phone: (212) 229-8969
Fax: (212) 807-1913

LEADERSHIP INTO THE NEXT CENTURY (LINC)

LINC is a nonprofit leadership education organization that aims to enhance current leaders in every sector and educate the next generation of leaders in families, institutions, communities, nations, and the world. Activities include interactive conferences, a leadership knowledge bank, individual leadership enhancement coaching, and the Leadership Education for Our Next Generation program.

Publications: *21st Century Leadership—Dialogues with 100 Top Leaders*
Address: 57 Lakeshore Drive, Irvine, CA 92604-3324
Phone: (714) 552-4821
Fax: (714) 857-8000

New
THE LEARNING INSTITUTE FOR NONPROFIT ORGANIZATIONS

The institute promotes educational programs designed to increase the capacity of nonprofit organizations and the communities served by them. Those encouraged to attend programs include nonprofit leaders, staff, board members, and volunteers interested in developing nonprofit organizations. The institute encourages a team of people from the same organization to attend each workshop in order to add long-term value to a shared team-learning experience.

Publications: Informational brochure
Meetings: Distance Education Series—6 programs
Address: 6314 Odana Road, Suite 1, Madison, WI 53719-1129
Phone: (800) 214-8326
Fax: (608) 274-9978
E-mail: li@uwex.edu
Website: http://www.uwex.edu/li

MANDEL CENTER FOR NONPROFIT ORGANIZATIONS

The center is sponsored by three professional schools of Case Western Reserve University: the Mandel School of

Applied Social Sciences, the Weatherhead School of Management, and the School of Law. The mission of the Mandel Center is to foster excellence in the education and leadership of nonprofit organizations. It conducts research and training for students, staff, and trustees in human services, the arts, education, community development, and religion. Programs include the Master of Nonprofit Organizations, an advanced professional degree; the Certificate in Nonprofit Management for the practicing manager; the Executive Education program of workshops for practicing managers; and The Distinguished Public Lecture Series.

Publications: *Nonprofit Management and Leadership* quarterly journal; *Nonprofit Notes* newsletter; discussion paper series; book chapters; journal articles
Address: Case Western Reserve University, 10900 Euclid Avenue, Cleveland, OH 44106-7164
Phone: (216) 368-2275
Fax: (216) 368-8592
Website: http://www.cwru.edu/msass/mandelcenter

MEN'S RESOURCE CENTER

The center offers community-based and national workshops on social issues faced by men. Their focus is to support men's growth and development and to challenge men's violence. Building Men's Community is a national effort to build a male-affirmative, pro-feminist, culturally diverse men's group that takes an active role in transforming local communities. Leadership training in the High School Education Project prepares young adults to lead violence-prevention workshops in high schools, teaching teens to channel energy into healthy and humane relationships. Similar workshops are offered on college campuses and in professional organizations.

Address: 30 Boltwood Walk, Amherst, MA 01002
Phone: (413) 253-9887

New
MEXICAN AMERICAN LEGAL DEFENSE AND EDUCATION FUND (MALDEF)

MALDEF was founded in 1968 to protect and promote the civil rights of Latinos living in the U.S. It secures rights in employment, education, political access, and language. The organization achieves its objectives through litigation, advocacy, community education, leadership training, and scholarship awards. Two programs are the Parent Leadership Program that engages parents in school improvement, and the MALDEF Leadership Development Program that prepares mid-career professionals and grassroots Latinos for board membership and local government positions.

Publications: *Leading Hispanics* newsletter; annual report
Address: 634 South Spring Street, 11th Floor, Los Angeles, CA 90014-1974
Phone: (213) 629-2512
Fax: (213) 629-0266
E-mail: maldefone@aol.com
Website: http://www.maldef.org

MILLER CENTER OF PUBLIC AFFAIRS

The Miller Center is a nonprofit research institute dedicated to scholarship on the American presidency and the enhancement of the structure and functioning of that office. As the only university-based nonpartisan institution with an exclusive focus on the presidency, the Miller Center brings together academics and public servants to serve the scholarly community, the government, and the public. Research programs cover the institution of the presidency, domestic and foreign policy issues, and the process of governance. Seven commission studies have made recommendations on presidential disability, presidency and science advising, the presidency and the press, the presidential nominating process, presidential transitions and foreign policy, and the selection process of vice-presidents.

Publications: *Presidential Portraits*; *Miller Center Report* quarterly; some 300 scholarly and edited books; research reports
Meetings: Miller Center Forums; Monticello Conversations; Rotunda Lectures
Address: The University of Virginia, 2201 Old Ivy Road, P.O. Box 5106, Charlottesville, VA 22905-5106
Phone: (804) 924-7236
Fax: (804) 982-2739
E-mail: miller-center@virginia.edu
Website: http://www.virginia.edu/~miller

NATIONAL ASSOCIATION FOR CAMPUS ACTIVITIES (NACA)

Over 1,200 institutions of higher learning and associate members share ideas for the development of extracurricular and cocurricular activities, including student leadership development. NACA maintains a library and a hall of fame, compiles statistics, and bestows awards. Their Student Leadership Scholarship Endowment funds four $500 scholarships to student leaders in the Southeast who hold significant leadership positions on campus and have made significant volunteer contributions on or off campus. NACA Educational Foundation conducts leadership education research and hosts a National Summer Leadership Symposium.

Publications: *Beginner's Guide to Leadership Programs*
Meetings: Annual meeting
Address: 13 Harbison Way, Columbia, SC 29212-3401
Phone: (803) 732-6222
Fax: (803) 749-1047
Website: http://www.naca.org

NATIONAL ASSOCIATION FOR COMMUNITY LEADERSHIP (NACL)

Over 450 local community-leadership programs and 2,300 individuals in the U.S., Australia, Canada, and England share ideas to strengthen and transform communities through leadership development. The network headquarters in Indianapolis creates, gathers, and distributes information, and provides training. A toll-free hotline connects members to a clearinghouse for advice and materials from successful programs. Two awards are given each year to recognize excellence in community leadership—The Distinguished Leadership Award to a program graduate and the Preceptor Award to a program director. Initiated in 1995, LEADERSHIP USA is a year-long program for 75 individuals. Participants who represent diversity in gender, ethnicity, geographic locality, and volunteer involvement identify and design solutions for social problems that transcend local interests.

Publications: *Leadership News* quarterly newsletter; resource directory; *Taking Leadership in Hand: The Program Development Guide*; *Taking Leadership to Heart: The Community Trusteeship Curriculum*; *Community Trusteeship Trainer Video*; annual report
Meetings: Annual conference; seminars
Address: 200 South Meridian Street, Suite 250, Indianapolis, IN 46225-1015
Phone: (317) 637-7408
Fax: (317) 637-7413
Website: http://www.communityleadership.org

NATIONAL ASSOCIATION FOR FAMILY AND COMMUNITY EDUCATION (NAFCE)

The 37,000 grassroots volunteers who belong to NAFCE are committed to strengthening families as the foundation for a healthy and prosperous society. To accomplish this, NAFCE carries out educational, leadership development, public-policy, and community service programs. The Family Community Leadership Program teaches parents and children leadership qualities including self-esteem, enriched family life, and community involvement. It aims to prepare a generation of responsible, loyal, mature, and informed leaders.

Publications: Annual report; brochure
Meetings: Annual conference

Address: 1973 Burlington Pike, P.O. Box 835, Burlington, KY 41005-0835
Phone: (606) 586-8333
Fax: (606) 586-8348
Website: http://www.nafce.org

New
NATIONAL ASSOCIATION FOR STUDENT PERSONNEL ADMINISTRATORS (NASPA)

NASPA serves college and university student affairs administrators through professional development opportunities and information on current issues. It shares program and administration models of collaborative efforts between academic and student affairs. It also promotes diversity and internationalism in the profession.

Publications: *NASPA Journal: The Journal of Student Affairs Administration, Research, and Practice* quarterly; books; videotapes
Meetings: Annual conference
Address: 1875 Connecticut Avenue, N.W., Suite 418, Washington, DC 20009-5737
Phone: (202) 265-7500
Fax: (202) 797-1157
E-mail: office@naspa.org
Website: http://www.naspa.org

NATIONAL ASSOCIATION OF SECONDARY SCHOOL PRINCIPALS (NASSP)

The association serves leaders at the secondary school level—administrators, educators, and students. A resource center develops and distributes leadership training guides, professional education programs, and student activity materials. Publications report on research and share success stories. A new program, the NASSP-Earth Shuttle motivates students through experiential education across the curriculum. Students study space technology at the Kennedy Space Center, the environment at Discovery Island, life science at Sea World, and history at Colonial Williamsburg. These programs feature real-world applications of classroom concepts and leadership skills training. Programs for administrators include Leader 123 for principals and the Superintendent Leadership Development Program. NASSP also sponsors scholarships, awards for outstanding leadership, international exchange programs for administrators and students, National Student Leadership Week, and summer leadership camps for students.

Publications: *National Leadership Camp Curriculum Guide*; *NASSP Resource Guide*; *NASSP Bulletin*; *Curriculum Report* bimonthly; *NASSP NewsLeader* newsletter; *Leadership for Student Activities* monthly; books
Meetings: Annual conference; seminars

Address: 1904 Association Drive, Reston, VA 20191-1537
Phone: (703) 860-0200
Fax: (703) 476-5432
E-mail: nassp@nassp.org
Website: http://www.nassp.org

NATIONAL CENTER FOR NONPROFIT BOARDS (NCNB)

NCNB's mission is to improve the effectiveness of nonprofit organizations by strengthening their boards of directors. The Board Development Program helps nonprofits design and conduct workshops and retreats. The Board Information Center provides information and advice on nonprofit governance. The membership program offers significant discounts on publications, workshops, and board development programs, a subscription to NCNB's periodical, and a toll-free access to the Board Information Center.

Publications: *A Snapshot of America's Nonprofit Boards: Results of a National Survey*; *Board Members* bimonthly; books; the Nonprofit Governance Series; audiotapes; videotapes; resource kits
Meetings: Annual National Leadership Forum
Address: 2000 L Street, N.W., Suite 510, Washington, DC 20036-4907
Phone: (202) 452-6262 or (800) 883-6262
Fax: (202) 452-6299
E-mail: ncnb@ncnb.org
Website: http://www.ncnb.org

NATIONAL CIVIC LEAGUE (NCL)

The National Civic League advocates a new civic agenda to create communities that work for everyone. Founded in 1894 by Theodore Roosevelt and other turn-of-the-century progressives, NCL's philosophy is based on the power of collaborative problem solving among business, nonprofit and government sectors, and among people with diverse perspectives. The Civic Assistance Program helps communities develop consensus on a vision, goals, and action plans; helps them enhance regional economic development strategies; and helps them share responsibility for action on critical issues.

Publications: *National Civic Review* quarterly journal; *Civic Action* bimonthly newsletter; annual report; NCL Press publishes models for local governments and books about leadership in a civil society
Meetings: Annual National Conference on Governance
Address: 1445 Market Street, Denver, CO 80202-1728
Phone: (303) 571-4343
Fax: (303) 571-4404

E-mail: ncl@ncl.org
Website: http://www.ncl.org/ncl

NATIONAL CLEARINGHOUSE FOR LEADERSHIP PROGRAMS (NCLP)

The goal of this organization is to have on file a copy of every higher education leadership course and program in the U.S. All educators are invited to send in their materials and NCLP members are eligible to receive copies upon request. Their publications board invites educators to send papers on program evaluation, civic leadership, and other topics of interest for the Leadership Education and Leadership Scholar Series.

Publications: *Concepts & Connections: A Newsletter for Leadership Educators* published three times a year; *Leadership Assessments: A Critique of Common Instruments; The Social Change Model of Leadership Development*
Meetings: Leadership Symposium annual conference
Address: 1135 Stamp Student Union, University of Maryland, College Park, MD 20472-4631
Phone: (301) 314-7174
Fax: (301) 314-9634
E-mail: nclp@umdstu.umd.edu
Website: http://www.inform.umd.edu/ocp/nclp

NATIONAL COMMUNITY FOR LATINO LEADERSHIP (NCLL)

Eight organizations that support leadership development for Latino youth, college students, and mid-career professionals form this network. NCLL acts as a clearinghouse for leadership models and community advocacy programs and it submits policy analysis to the electronic network, LatinoNet. NCLL evaluates the impact of leadership development programs in the U.S. and Puerto Rico. Most of the programs sponsored by NCLL member organizations address civic education, analytical and communication skills, and internships with policy-making or advocacy groups. The network organizations are ASPIRA, La Casa de Don Pedro, Inc., Congressional Hispanic Caucus Institute, Inter-University Program, Latino Research/Latino Leadership Opportunity Program, LULAC National Educational Service Centers, Mexican American Legal Defense and Educational Fund, National Urban Fellows, Inc., and the Southwest Voter Registration Education Project.

Address: 4539 North 22nd Street, Suite 202, Phoenix, AZ 85016-4661
Phone: (602) 468-1908
E-mail: ncllpd96@aol.com

NATIONAL FORUM FOR BLACK PUBLIC ADMINISTRATORS (NFBPA)

NFBPA is a professional membership organization dedicated to the advancement of black leadership in the public sector. Through research, networking, training, and mentoring programs, it strengthens the position of blacks in public administration and grooms young, aspiring administrators for senior positions. Special programs like the Executive Leadership Institute polish the managerial skills of successful black managers seeking executive appointments in public service. The Mentor program matches emerging black leaders with seasoned executives to facilitate career planning, skills enhancement, and networking support. The Bridges Summer Internship Program provides exposure to state and local government agencies for students planning careers in public service. Members gain access to a toll-free JOBS-HOTLINE which provides an up-to-date listing of public-management job opportunities in municipal and state agencies.

Publications: *The Forum* quarterly; *Membership Directory*
Meetings: Annual conference
Address: 777 North Capitol Street, N.E., Suite 807, Washington, DC 20002-4239
Phone: (202) 408-9300
Fax: (202) 408-8558
Website: http://www.nfbpa.org

NATIONAL HISPANA LEADERSHIP INSTITUTE (NHLI)

NHLI is a nonpartisan, nonprofit organization committed to the education and leadership development of Hispanic women. Its mission is to help dedicated Hispanic women who have demonstrated community leadership realize their leadership potential, to promote the advancement of the Hispanic community, to create a national network for positive change, and to support and nurture Hispanic leadership. The NHLI fellowship program is held in four segments over a nine-month period. The first, held at the San Juan Bautista retreat center in California, focuses on community building. The second, held at Harvard's Kennedy School of Government, presents an overview of public management. The third, held at the Center for Creative Leadership, focuses on creative goal setting and action planning. The final segment, held in Washington, DC, explores the national political agenda, policy development, and the legislative process. Graduates of the program serve on local, state, and national boards and commissions, hold elected office, and act as mentors for other professional Hispanic women.

Publications: *NHLI News* quarterly newsletter
Address: 1901 North Moore Street, Suite 206, Arlington, VA 22209-1706
Phone: (703) 527-6007
Fax: (703) 527-6009
E-mail: NHLI@aol.com
Website: http://www.incacorp.com/nhli

New
NATIONAL INITIATIVE FOR LEADERSHIP AND INSTITUTIONAL EFFECTIVENESS (NILIE)

NILIE's purpose is to conduct research and disseminate information on strategies to link leadership to institutional effectiveness, and to use quality initiatives to improve student success. NILIE offers three customized organizational climate surveys and various organizational study instruments to community colleges, colleges, and universities throughout North America.

Meetings: Annual conference
Address: North Carolina State University, 300 Poe Hall, Box 7801, Raleigh, NC 27695-7801
Phone: (919) 515-6289
Fax: (919) 515-6305
Website: http://www2.ncsu.edu/cep/acce/nilie/index.html

NATIONAL LEAGUE OF CITIES (NLC)

The league's Leadership Training Institute exists to provide newly elected local officials with the knowledge and skills needed to help them respond proactively to the changing needs of their communities. Short-term seminars address consensus-building skills, media relations, meeting facilitation, neighborhood empowerment, and creative programs for confronting crime. A leadership lab program, The Practice of Political Leadership: Turning Campaign Promises into Effective Governing, combines classroom instruction and experience. Research initiatives, networking opportunities, and information sharing are available to local government leaders in cities that belong to the National League of Cities.

Meetings: Leadership Summit annual conference
Address: 1301 Pennsylvania Avenue, N.W., Suite 600, Washington, DC 20004-1763
Phone: (202) 626-3000
Fax: (202) 626-3043
Website: http://www.nlc.org/ltiNST.htm

NATIONAL OUTDOOR LEADERSHIP SCHOOL (NOLS)

Since 1965, NOLS has been providing teenagers and adults with the opportunity to learn wilderness skills, leadership, and practical outdoor conservation. Mountaineering, kayaking, and horsepacking expeditions are conducted on public lands around the world—in the Rocky Mountains, Grand Canyon, Indian Himalayas, Australia, Alaska, Mexico, Chile, and Kenya. Courses for various ages and skill levels run ten days to three months. The curriculum in every course covers safety and judgment, leadership and teamwork, outdoor skills, and environmental studies. NOLS students may earn college credits at the University of Utah or by making arrangements for independent study at their home schools.

Publications: *Soft Paths* available in book or video; *The NOLS Cookery*; *The Leader* alumni newsletter
Address: 288 Main Street, Lander, WY 82520-3128
Phone: (307) 332-6973
Fax: (307) 332-1220
E-mail: admissions@nols.edu
Website: http://www.nols.edu

NATIONAL SOCIETY FOR EXPERIENTIAL EDUCATION (NSEE)

As a community of individuals, institutions, and organizations, this society is committed to fostering the effective use of experience as an integral part of education, to empower learners, and to promote the common good. Its goals are: 1) to advocate the use of experiential learning throughout the educational system and the larger community, 2) to enhance the professional growth and leadership development of its members, 3) to disseminate information on principles of good practice and on innovations in the field, and 4) to encourage the development and dissemination of research and theory related to experiential learning.

Publications: *NSEE Quarterly*; *The National Directory of Internships*; *Combining Service and Learning: A Resource Book for Community and Public Service*; other books; resource papers
Meetings: Annual national conference
Address: 3509 Haworth Drive, Suite 207, Raleigh, NC 27609-7229
Phone: (919) 787-3263
Fax: (919) 787-3381
E-mail: info@nsee.org
Website: http://www.nsee.org

New
NATIONAL TRAINING AND INFORMATION CENTER (NTIC)

A nonprofit resource center for grassroots community groups, NTIC offers intensive four-day leadership/organizer training sessions to church groups, clubs, nonprofits, and other civic organizations whose goal is to gain power through organizing. The center also provides

consulting and technical assistance, and does research on issues including community leadership, board training, coalition building, and negotiation.

Publications: *Disclosure: The National Newspaper of Neighborhoods*, bimonthly; *Basics of Organizing*; other books, reports
Address: 810 North Milwaukee, Chicago, IL 60622-4103
Phone: (312) 243-3035
Fax: (312) 243-7044
E-mail: HN1742@connectinc.com

New
NATIONAL TRUST FOR THE DEVELOPMENT OF AFRICAN-AMERICAN MEN

The National Trust is a national, nonprofit organization that addresses the development, needs, and challenges of African Americans, especially males, in the areas of health, leadership training, education, economic development, and crime prevention. The Leadership Curriculum consists of Trust Philosophy, Leadership Skills, Community Organization, and Community Development. All training is based on an African view that uses African history and culture to instill self-esteem and responsibility.

Address: 6811 Kennilworth Avenue, Riverdale, MD 20737-1333
Phone: (301) 887-0100
Fax: (301) 887-0405
E-mail: mendezjr@msn.com
Website: http://www.tnt.org

NATIONAL YOUTH LEADERSHIP COUNCIL (NYLC)

The council develops service-oriented youth leaders by supporting individuals, organizations, and communities that encourage youth service and leadership. With regional centers in Arkansas, Michigan, New Mexico, Pennsylvania, South Carolina, and Washington state, it coordinates the National Service-Learning Initiative. This project works with 34 model K through 8 "Generator Schools" throughout the country, which are dedicated to demonstrating the promise of service learning. NYLC runs an annual summer camp, the National Youth Leadership Project, which trains young people to lead service-learning initiatives in their own schools and communities, and offers one- to three-day Youth Leadership Development Seminars.

Publications: *Update: A Newsletter for Service-Learning and Youth Leadership*; *Generator* semiannual journal of service learning; *Learning By Giving*; *Growing Hope: A Sourcebook on Integrating Youth Service into the School Curriculum*

Meetings: Annual national conference
Address: 1910 West County Road B, St. Paul, MN 55113-5448
Phone: (612) 631-3672 or (800) FON-NYLC
Fax: (612) 631-2955
E-mail: nylcusa@aol.com
Website: http://www.nylc.org

NONPROFIT MANAGEMENT AND LEADERSHIP PROGRAM

The Nonprofit Management and Leadership Program offers courses for practicing managers, professionals, board members, and other leaders of nonprofit and voluntary organizations. These leaders must bridge the gap between service as a mission and fiscal accountability as a bottom line. They may attend one-day, noncredit courses including Effective Group Process, the Effective Board-Staff Partnership, and Accessing Federal Grants; or they may attend semester-long, for-credit courses including Leadership and Management in Nonprofit Organizations.

Address: University of Missouri–St. Louis, 8001 Natural Bridge Road, St. Louis, MO 63121-4499
Phone: (314) 516-6713
Fax: (314) 516-5268
E-mail: npml@umslvma.umsl.edu

New
HUGH O'BRIAN YOUTH LEADERSHIP FOUNDATION (HOBY)

Founded in 1958 by actor Hugh O'Brian, HOBY seeks, recognizes, and develops leadership potential in high school sophomores by sponsoring annual state and international leadership seminars. Over 14,000 students each year attend the weekend workshops, which bring them together with recognized business and community leaders. Community Leadership Workshops and scholarships for alumni are also offered.

Publications: *Alumni Directory*; *The Ambassador* semiannual newsletter; annual report; brochures
Meetings: Annual World Leadership Congress
Address: 10880 Wilshire Boulevard, Suite 1103, Los Angeles, CA 90024-4112
Phone: (310) 474-4370
Fax: (310) 475-5426
Website: http://www.hoby.org

New
OHIO STATE UNIVERSITY LEADERSHIP CENTER

The center strives to be a point of collaboration for leadership development efforts and to develop a more

interdisciplinary and interdepartmental approach to leadership education. It also serves the needs of Ohio citizens. Periodic seminars are offered for community leaders, and a resource library of books, journals, videotapes, and curriculum models is available for OSU students and staff and community members. The Center also has an ongoing research agenda focused on leadership, management, and human resource development.

Publications: *Leadership Link* quarterly newsletter
Address: 109 Agricultural Administration Building, 2120 Fyffe Road, Columbus, OH 43210-1084
Phone: (614) 292-3114
Fax: (614) 292-9750
E-mail: earnest1@osu.edu
Website: http://www.ag.ohio-state.edu/~leaders

OMICRON DELTA KAPPA

This national leadership honor society recognizes college students who exhibit superior scholarship, leadership, and exemplary character. Students must rank in the top third of their class and achieve distinction in athletics, campus or community service, social or religious activity, campus government, journalism, public speaking, or the creative arts. Society members are eligible to attend leadership workshops and for scholarships.

Publications: *The Omicron Delta Kappa Manual*; newsletter
Meetings: Biennial national convention; regional meetings
Address: University of Kentucky, 118 Bradley Hall, Lexington, KY 40506-0058
Phone: (606) 257-5000
Fax: (606) 323-1014
E-mail: odknhdq@pop.uky.edu
Website: http://www.uky.edu/OtherOrgs/ODK

OUTWARD BOUND

This nonprofit, educational organization uses experience-based programs to teach leadership skills. Students learn when they engage in and reflect on challenging environments, which require them to make choices, take responsible action, and work with others. Part of a global network, Outward Bound programs are available in 40 wilderness locations in 20 countries. Programs for individuals include dogsledding, rock climbing, whitewater rafting, and canyon exploration. Organizational groups may arrange contract programs to learn team-building skills. Urban education programs bring experience-based learning to classrooms across the U.S. Special courses are available for at-risk youths, and academic credit is available for many Outward Bound programs. The Kurt Hahn Leadership Center in North

Carolina trains instructors of experiential/adventure-based education programs.

Publications: Course catalog; annual report
Address: Route 9D, R2 Box 280, Garrison, NY 10524-9757
Phone: (800) 243-8520 or (914) 424-4000
Fax: (914) 424-4280
Website: http://www.outwardbound.org

THE PENN STATE INSTITUTE FOR THE STUDY OF ORGANIZATIONAL EFFECTIVENESS (ISOE)

Founded in 1993, ISOE is an industry-supported, interdisciplinary research-and-development center devoted to the study of organizational effectiveness, leadership, and global competitiveness. Faculty from Penn State and other universities team with organizational leaders around the world to investigate ideas and information on organizing and leading organizations. Current research is focused on executive/leadership development, global organizational structures, and continuous improvement and innovation. ISOE also supports faculty and doctoral research in the field of organizational effectiveness.

Address: Smeal College of Business Administration, Pennsylvania State University, 310 Business Administration Building, University Park, PA 16802-3003
Phone: (814) 865-3435
Fax: (814) 865-3372

PEW PARTNERSHIP FOR CIVIC CHANGE

This national program is funded by the Pew Charitable Trusts to address problems in smaller American cities. It sponsors projects of collaboration between public, private, and nonprofit sectors in communities; identifies strategies for systemic change in urban issues; and suggests new models of citizen leadership for strengthening communities. At the Pew Civic Entrepreneur Institute, participants learn about collaborative leadership among diverse groups and techniques to mobilize community assets.

Publications: *Community Matters* quarterly newsletter; *Leadership Collaboration Series* research reports
Address: 145-C Ednam Drive, Charlottesville, VA 22903-4629
Phone: (804) 971-2073
Fax: (804) 971-7042
E-mail: mail@pew-partnership.org
Website: http://www.pew-partnership.org

PHI THETA KAPPA, INC.

Phi Theta Kappa is the international honor society for two-year colleges. With funding from the W. K. Kellogg

Foundation, it has developed the Leadership Development Program, a humanities-based curriculum. Eleven skill modules incorporate readings from classic literature, films, discussion groups, and experiential activities. Additional modules teach students to identify their own leadership philosophies, maintain leadership journals, and create five-year plans. Although this program was created for junior-college students, Phi Theta Kappa encourages all leadership instructors and program directors to use this program in part or in full.

Publications: *Leadership Development Program Teacher's Manual*
Meetings: Training for instructors
Address: 1625 Eastover Drive, Suite 415, Jackson, MS 39211-6461
Phone: (800) 946-9995 or (601) 957-2241
Fax: (601) 957-2312

POINTS OF LIGHT FOUNDATION

The foundation engages citizens to work together to solve critical social problems. From grassroots to corporate organizations, volunteer efforts are supported through 500 volunteer centers, networking opportunities, resources, and recognition for programs that make a difference. There are several grant-making programs to help communities mobilize their own resources, administer AmeriCorps programs, and participate in the Presidents' Summit for America's Future.

Publications: *Leadership* quarterly magazine; *Learning from Leaders Resource Directory*; *Today's Heroes* video; books; catalog of recognition items
Meetings: National Community Service Conference
Address: 1737 H Street, N.W., Washington, DC 20006-3912
Phone: (202) 223-9186
Fax: (202) 223-9256
E-mail: volnet@aol.com
Website: http://www.pointsoflight.org

POYNTER INSTITUTE FOR MEDIA STUDIES

This school promotes integrity among media professionals and encourages journalism that informs citizens and enlightens public discourse. Research, educational programs, and conferences support journalists and journalism students in all types of media—print, television, radio, photo, and electronic. Programs include a six-month Leadership Development Program, Leadership for Middle Managers, Improving Diversity, Ethical Decision Making, and Leadership and Craft Skills for Newspaper Editors. Fellowships are available for journalism students and teachers. An extensive library supports the study of visual journalism, the influence of news reporting, media ethics, and media leadership. The library's special collection includes "NewsLeaders," a videotape archive of interviews with print and broadcast journalists.

Publications: *Eyes on the News* research report; *Poynter Report* quarterly newsletter; occasional papers include "A Call to Leadership"; videotapes include "Journalism and Justice: The Media and the O. J. Simpson Case"; books
Address: 801 Third Street South, St. Petersburg, FL 33701-4920
Phone: (813) 821-9494
Fax: (813) 821-0583
E-mail: info@poynter.org
Website: http://www.poynter.org

PRINCETON CENTER FOR LEADERSHIP TRAINING

The center's mission is to increase opportunities for young people to succeed in school and in life. To achieve this mission, the center helps students develop effective leadership skills and trains teams of educators, parents, and members of the community to work collaboratively to improve the education environment. Team Mentoring for Youth programs include The Peer Group Connection, which transforms peer pressure into a positive force, and Gesher L'Kesher, which helps Jewish adolescents build bridges connecting them to their heritage. Partners in Learning Services programs help school-based leaders design teams and manage school reform efforts. Programs are designed to reduce isolation, foster communication, improve morale, increase competence, and build confidence in all members of the school community.

Meetings: Annual Urban/Suburban Conference
Address: 12 Vandeventer Avenue, Princeton, NJ 08542-6921
Phone: (609) 844-1040
Fax: (609) 252-9393

PUBLIC HEALTH LEADERSHIP INSTITUTE

The institute is sponsored by the Centers for Disease Control and Prevention at the University of California–Berkeley. Its mission is to strengthen America's public-health system by enhancing the leadership capacities of senior public-health officials. Each year, 50 city, county, and state health officials participate in the year-long program. The institute also holds interactive electronic seminars and writes case studies.

Meetings: American Public Health Association annual meeting
Address: 2020 Milvia Street, Suite 411, Berkeley, CA 94704-1103

Phone: (510) 649-1599
Fax: (510) 649-1296

PUBLIC LEADERSHIP EDUCATION NETWORK (PLEN)

Network members are 19 women's colleges working together to educate women for public leadership. Students learn about the policy process in PLEN sessions in Washington, DC, and in programs on their own campuses. In the Women and Congress seminar, female members of Congress instruct students on the role of women in the lawmaking process. Women and the Law: A Public Leadership Career Conference introduces law students to women lawyers who use their legal education to influence public policy. Other programs include a Women and International Policy seminar and a Public Policy Internship semester.

Publications: *Preparing to Lead: The College Women's Guide to Internships and Other Public Policy Learning Opportunities in Washington, DC*; *Learning to Lead: An Inventory of Learning Experiences at PLEN Colleges*
Address: 1001 Connecticut Avenue, N.W., Suite 900, Washington, DC 20036-5524
Phone: (202) 872-1585
Fax: (202) 457-0549
E-mail: plen@clark.net
Website: http://www.plen.org

REFLECTIVE LEADERSHIP CENTER

Reflective leadership is informed by a sense of history, oriented toward the future, imbued with ethics and vision, and strong on follow-through and diversity. Reflective leadership is central to the Hubert H. Humphrey Institute's mission of education for public responsibility in a highly complex, specialized, and technical society. Seminars and workshops on leadership, public affairs, and societal change are designed for experienced practitioners with diverse ethnic and occupational backgrounds. All programs link theory and practice through role plays, simulations, small groups, journal writing, retreats, private study, presentations, and discussions.

Publications: Leadership annotations; working papers; books; articles
Meetings: Leadership for the Common Good seminars held January through June
Address: Hubert H. Humphrey Institute of Public Affairs, University of Minnesota, 301 19th Avenue South, Room 55, Minneapolis, MN 55455
Phone: (612) 625-7377
Fax: (612) 625-3513
E-mail: sanderson@hhh.umn.edu

Website: http://www.hhh.umn.edu/bulletin/centers/
reflect.html

THE SOCIETY FOR NONPROFIT ORGANIZATIONS

The society exists to foster the betterment of individual
nonprofit organizations, regardless of their size and
mission, and to foster a sense of community within the
nonprofit sector. To promote excellence in leadership and
governance practices, the society conducts research on
emerging trends and provides training and information to
its members. Resources available to members include a
monthly funding alert on grant opportunities, tax and
legal updates, a directory of services and products, and a
professional network of colleagues throughout the
voluntary sector. Society members are eligible for group
discounts on publications, long-distance telephone
charges, travel, office supplies, and other services.

Publications: *Nonprofit World* bimonthly journal
Address: 6314 Odana Road, Suite 1, Madison, WI
53719-1141
Phone: (800) 424-7367
Fax: (608) 274-9978
E-mail: snpo@danenet.wicip.org
Website: http://danenet.wicip.org/snpo

New
STENNIS CENTER FOR PUBLIC SERVICE

The mission of the Stennis Center is to promote and
strengthen public-service leadership in the U.S. The
center provides training and development in three broad
areas: 1) attracting talented young people to public
service; 2) enhancing the ability and commitment of
senior congressional staff to service the institution of
Congress and its members in a world of rapid change; and
3) improving the quality, character, and performance of
state, local, and other appointed and elected officials. The
center is an independent agency of the federal legislative
branch and is governed by a board of trustees appointed
by the Democratic and Republican leaders in the U.S.
House of Representatives and U.S. Senate.

Publications: Annual report; *Implications of a Global
Economy for Congressional Operations: New Staff Roles
to Foster Institutional Innovation & Effectiveness;
Beyond Vicious Circles: Toward a Restoration of Stew-
ardship and Public Trust in Congress*
Address: P.O. Box 9629, Mississippi State, MS 39762-
9629
Phone: (601) 325-8409
Fax: (601) 325-8623
Website: http://www.stennis.gov

STUDENTS IN FREE ENTERPRISE (SIFE)

This organization builds collegiate SIFE Teams, composed of faculty and students who practice and teach free
enterprise. Students learn communication skills, creativity, team building, and management skills to become
future business leaders. They create public-service
announcements, guest editorials, billboards, posters, and
pamphlets. They teach elementary school children about
basic economic concepts and the role of the entrepreneur.
Student entrepreneurs own and operate campus snack
bars, computer shops, and book stores. SIFE Teams enter
their outreach projects into national competition for
awards and recognition by a panel of business leaders.

Publications: *SIFElines* newsletter
Address: The Jack Shewmaker Center, 1959 East Kerr
Street, Springfield, MO 65803-4775
Phone: (417) 831-9505
Fax: (417) 831-6165
E-mail: sifehq@aol.com
Website: http://www.sife.org

SUPPORT CENTER FOR NONPROFIT MANAGEMENT

The Support Center offers workshops and consulting
services, conducts research, and publishes materials to
help nonprofit organizations manage more efficiently and
effectively. Workshops include Building Board Diversity,
The Basics of Grassroots Fundraising, and Finding It on
the Internet.

Publications: *Strategic Planning for Non-Profit Organi-
zations: A Practical Guide and Workbook*
Address: 706 Mission Street, 5th Floor, San Francisco,
CA 94103-3113
Phone: (415) 541-9000
Fax: (415) 541-7708
E-mail: supportcenter@supportcenter.org
Website: http://www.supportcenter.org/sf

TRUSTEE LEADERSHIP DEVELOPMENT (TLD)

TLD is a national leadership center offering consultation,
training, and resources to individuals and organizations
committed to service and leadership in the not-for-profit
sector. It provides customized workshops that assist participants in self-assessment and the inner work of leadership. Organizational development work includes cultural
assessment, history, mission, and strategic planning.

Publications: *TLD Trustee Education Manual*; *TLD
Individual and Community Trusteeship Manual*; videotapes include *Trustee Leadership Development: Building
the Capacity to Serve and to Lead*

Address: 719 Indiana Avenue, Suite 370, Indianapolis, IN 46202-3176
Phone: (317) 636-5323
Fax: (317) 636-0266

New
UNITED NATIONAL INDIAN TRIBAL YOUTH, INC. (UNITY)

UNITY is a national organization serving Native American and Alaska Native youths ages 15 to 24. The UNITY Network, which consists of 167 youth councils in 30 states, develops leadership, instills cultural pride, and promotes self-sufficiency through conferences, regional training, workshops, and seminars. Youth councils allow young people to develop leadership skills, help others, and become effective team players.

Publications: *UNITY Healthy Lifestyles Catalog; Give It Your Best: Profiles of Native American Athletes; UNITY News* quarterly newspaper
Meetings: Annual conference
Address: 4010 Lincoln Boulevard, Suite 202, P.O. Box 25042, Oklahoma City, OK 73125-0042
Phone: (405) 424-3010
Fax: (405) 424-3018
Website: http://www.unityinc.org

WASHINGTON CENTER FOR INTERNSHIPS AND ACADEMIC SEMINARS

The center was founded to provide promising college students with real-world work experience and professional contacts through internships and academic seminars. Internships are full-time, entry-level jobs in the Washington area, which earn up to 17 college credits. Academic seminars are one- to three-week workshops combining lectures, panel discussions, site visits, briefings, and Mentor-for-a-Day programs with journalists, lawyers, executives, policymakers, diplomats, financial experts, and members of Congress. Some seminar subjects are: Leadership 2000—Access Your Future; Women as Leaders; Global Village—World Politics and Economics; Leadership for America's Cities; and Campaign '96, held on-site at the Democratic and Republican national conventions.

Publications: *Capital News* quarterly newsletter
Address: 1101 14th Street, N.W., Suite 500, Washington, DC 20005-5601
Phone: (800) 486-8921
Fax: (202) 336-7609
Website: http://www.twc.edu

WELLSPRING, INC.

This nonprofit organization serves primarily clergy, educators, business, and professional people associated with a series of experiential learning opportunities designed to help people in middle- to upper-level management positions within the Lutheran community to become more effective leaders. In addition to a series of challenging leadership development experiences, Wellspring also offers an electronic network, opportunities for research and mentoring, and a bookstore offering a wide selection of books and other materials focused on leadership at special discounts.

Address: 6315 Grovedale Drive, P.O. Box 10415, Alexandria, VA 22310-0415
Phone: (301) 753-1812
Fax: (703) 922-6047
E-mail: donaldz7@aol.com

New
WESTERN STATES CENTER

The mission of Western States Center is to build and invigorate democracy in eight states: Alaska, Idaho, Montana, Nevada, Oregon, Utah, Washington, and Wyoming. They are dedicated to three levels of strategy: 1) strengthening grassroots organizing and community-based leadership, 2) building broad-based progressive coalitions, and 3) encouraging a new generation of citizen leaders to run for public office. The Community Leadership Training Program provides assistance to grassroots efforts in low-income and rural communities and communities of color. The Western Progressive Leadership Network supports groups that work for policy reform.

Publications: *Western States Center News* quarterly newsletter
Address: P.O. Box 40305, Portland, OR 97240-0305
Phone: (503) 228-8866
Fax: (503) 228-1965

New
THE WALT WHITMAN CENTER FOR THE CULTURE AND POLITICS OF DEMOCRACY

The Walt Whitman Center is dedicated to sustaining democratic theory and extending democratic practice by encouraging innovative political and cultural activity; providing intellectual leadership and incentives, both within and outside the scholarly community; and by fostering research, pilot projects, and opportunities for practical democratic experience. The Whitman Center sponsors research, conferences, and visiting speakers. The Center focuses on the civic infrastructure on which democracy depends, and attempts to look beyond formal political structures.

Publications: Working papers in the area of democratic theory and practice; articles
Address: Department of Political Science, Rutgers—the State University of New Jersey—Douglass Campus, 409 Hickman Hall, New Brunswick, NJ 08903
Phone: (732) 932-6861
Fax: (732) 932-1922
Website: http://www.cpn.org/sections/affiliates/whitman_center.html

WILDERNESS EDUCATION ASSOCIATION

The purpose of the WEA is to promote the professionalism of outdoor leadership, thereby improving the safety of outdoor trips and enhancing the conservation of the wild outdoors. Strategies to achieve professionalism include the Outdoor Leadership Certification Program, curriculum development, program consulting, and research. Backpacking, rafting, and mountaineering courses are available for college credits, for trainer certification, and for short-term, low-impact sessions. Participants learn judgment and decision making, group dynamics, wilderness skills, environmental ethics, and emergency procedures.

Publications: *WEA Legend* newsletter; *The Backcountry Classroom: Lesson Plans for Teaching in the Wilderness*; catalog
Meetings: Annual conference

Address: 1105 Otter Creek Road, Nashville, TN 37220-1708
Phone: (615) 331-5739
Fax: (615) 331-9023
E-mail: wea@edge.net
Website: http://www.ebl.org/wea

WOMEN IN GOVERNMENT RELATIONS

This organization is committed to the professional and educational development of women who work in government relations. Its Women in Leadership certificate program combines bimonthly classes, a weekend retreat, and a five-day blitz of research and reporting on public-policy issues. In addition to developing leadership skills and networking, participants learn the roles of government, business, labor, nonprofit, and media and their effects on the legislative and regulatory process. The LEADER Foundation offers an intern program; a career awareness program for female, inner-city, at-risk, high school students; LEADERship Lectures; and mid-career fellowships.

Publications: *On the Record* bimonthly newsletter
Meetings: Headliner luncheons; Congressional receptions
Address: 1029 Vermont Avenue, N.W., Suite 510, Washington, DC 20005-3517
Phone: (202) 347-5432
Fax: (202) 347-5434
E-mail: wgr@earthlink.net

FOUNDATIONS

MARY REYNOLDS BABCOCK FOUNDATION, INC.

The foundation concentrates on assisting people in the Southeastern U.S. to build just and caring communities that nurture people, spur enterprise, bridge differences, foster fairness, and promote civility. It provides funds in three areas. The Organizational Development Program supports about 100 nonprofit organizations. The Community Problem Solving Program assists local communities with rebuilding efforts. The Grassroots Leadership Development funding area supports grassroots efforts to influence state policy. In 1998, the foundation expects to fund five grassroots groups with two-year grants of up to $75,000. In 1999, similar grants will be made to an additional five groups.

Publications: Annual report; guidelines
Address: 102 Reynolda Village, Winston-Salem, NC 27106-5123

Phone: (336) 748-9222
Fax: (336) 777-0095
E-mail: info@mrbf.org

BLANDIN FOUNDATION

Newspaper pioneer Charles Blandin created this foundation to promote the well-being of mankind. It supports programs that address the causes of problems and advance the viability of rural communities throughout Minnesota and in the Grand Rapids, Minnesota, metropolitan area. The Blandin Community Leadership Program encourages shared leadership within and between communities in rural Minnesota through the training and development of local leaders. The National Youth Leadership Council receives funding for ongoing programs.

Publications: Annual report
Address: 100 Pokegama Avenue North, Grand Rapids, MN 55744-2739

Phone: (218) 326-0523
Fax: (218) 327-1949
E-mail: bldnfdtn@uslink.net
Website: http://www.blandinfoundation.org

THE BUSH LEADERSHIP FELLOWS PROGRAM

As an arm of the Bush Foundation, this program awards grants to individuals for mid-career development. Men and women, ages 28 to 54, who live and work in Minnesota, North Dakota, South Dakota, or northwestern Wisconsin, may apply for stipends for educational programs and self-designed internships. These career-development experiences enable fellows to assume greater leadership roles within their communities and professions.

Address: E-900 First National Bank Building, 332 Minnesota Street, Saint Paul, MN 55101-1316
Phone: (612) 227-0891
Fax: (612) 297-6485

JESSIE BALL duPONT FUND

The fund has a special interest in issues important to the American South. It supports 350 institutions whose eligibility was determined by Mrs. duPont's prior personal philanthropic decisions. These institutions generally fall into six categories: education, arts and culture, historic preservation, human services, health, and religion. In 1996 the fund supported a new Nonprofit Agencies Initiative, a four-day residential leadership development institute created by the Center for Creative Leadership. Agnes Scott College received $150,000 to support the Atlanta Semester, a curricular offering in leadership and social change. Grants made in 1996 totaled $11.5 million.

Publications: *Notes from the Field* published twice a year highlighting one of the Fund's program areas; annual report; informational brochure; application guidelines
Address: 225 Water Street, Suite 1200, Jacksonville, FL 32202-4424
Phone: (904) 353-0890
Fax: (904) 353-3870
Website: http://www.dupontfund.org

New
FOUNDATION FOR THE MID SOUTH

Formed in 1990, this nonprofit organization seeks to help the states of Arkansas, Louisiana, and Mississippi share resources and leadership across geographical, political, and provincial boundaries. To achieve this goal, the foundation makes grants in four areas: community development, organization and program development, African-American faith-based grants, and leadership development. The Leadership Development Grants Program awards $1,500 for one-year self-initiated experiential learning. Young people are encouraged to apply for this opportunity to work with mentors, serve their communities, and learn to be change agents.

Publications: Annual report; guidelines; newsletter
Address: 308 East Pearl Street, 4th Floor, Jackson, MS 39201-3406
Phone: (601) 355-8167
Fax: (601) 355-6499
E-mail: llilly@fndmidsouth.org
Website: http://www.fndmidsouth.org

GE FUND

Formerly the General Electric Foundation, the GE Fund seeks to educate—grade school through graduate school and beyond. The fund supports educational programs that develop resourceful leaders who grow the economy and foster respect for others. The College Bound Leader program combines academic courses and mentoring for high school students and leadership training for their principals. To increase business and management faculty opportunities for women and minorities, the GE Fund provides forgivable loans for graduate study. The University of Pittsburgh's Katz Graduate School of Business received a grant for an innovative curriculum based on internationalism, ethics, organizational transformation, and managing strategic performance. Total giving in 1996 was $28.4 million.

Publications: Annual report
Address: 3135 Easton Turnpike, Fairfield, CT 06431
Phone: (203) 373-3216
Website: http://www.ge.com/fund

THE WILLIAM RANDOLPH HEARST FOUNDATIONS

The foundations give to programs that aid poverty-level and minority groups, educational programs, health-delivery systems, and cultural programs. Nonprofit human-service agencies may apply for technical assistance and financial support for management training and leadership development.

Publications: Application guidelines
Address: 888 Seventh Avenue, 45th Floor, New York, NY 10106-0057
Phone: (212) 586-5404

EWING MARION KAUFFMAN FOUNDATION CENTER FOR ENTREPRENEURIAL LEADERSHIP INC.

The foundation's mission is to research the unfilled needs of society and to develop, implement, and fund break-through solutions that have a lasting impact and offer people hope for the future. Their Center for Entrepreneurial Leadership Inc. was established in 1992 to stimulate the growth and development of entrepreneurship in both the for-profit and nonprofit sectors. An Entrepreneurial Training Institute teaches strategic development to existing or emerging entrepreneurs and also teaches about the free-enterprise system to students from kindergarten through high school. The institute supports applied research, curriculum development, support systems, and evaluation.

Publications: Reports; curricula; brochure; annual report
Address: 4900 Oak Street, Kansas City, MO 64112-2776
Phone: (816) 932-1000
Fax: (816) 932-1100
E-mail: infocel@emkf.org
Website: http://www.emkf.org/entrepreneurship

W. K. KELLOGG FOUNDATION

For over 50 years, the foundation has helped people help themselves and improve their quality of life. It provides seed money to organizations and grants to persons and programs concerned with the application of existing knowledge. The foundation supports emerging and existing leaders by providing them with broadened perspectives about local and national issues, improving their skills, and facilitating creative solutions. International leadership grants are awarded to people and programs in Africa, the Caribbean, Latin America, and the U.S. In 1997, leaders and leadership programs received $21 million. Some examples are: the Kellogg National Leadership Program—$3,237,000 for development of leadership skills and increased knowledge on national and international issues; Center for Ethical Leadership—$100,000 to provide leadership education for citizens of all ages; Americans for Indian Opportunity—$3,300,000 to prepare Native American leaders; and the University of Massachusetts—$153,100 to strengthen the civic engagement and leadership of college students.

Publications: *International Journal* twice yearly; annual report; program information guidelines
Address: One Michigan Avenue East, Battle Creek, MI 49017-4058
Phone: (616) 968-1611
Fax: (616) 968-0413
Website: http://www.wkkf.org

LILLY ENDOWMENT INC.

The endowment exists to support the causes of religion, education, and community development, with special emphasis on programs that benefit youth and leadership development within the nonprofit sector. Although the endowment supports occasional national and international efforts, its focus is primarily on its hometown, Indianapolis, and its home state, Indiana. Grants paid in 1996 totaled $166.6 million.

Publications: Grantmaking Guidelines; annual report; Religion Division—*Initiatives*
Address: P.O. Box 88068, Indianapolis, IN 46208-0068
Phone: (317) 924-5471
Fax: (317) 926-4431

JOHN D. AND CATHERINE T. MacARTHUR FOUNDATION

The foundation is dedicated to improving the human condition by creating sustainable change and reducing inequities in the distribution of power and resources. It makes grants in the areas of health, education, the environment, population, international peace, and individual creativity. In Chicago, Illinois, and Palm Beach County, Florida, the foundation supports community development and cultural affairs. These two locations serve as test sites for programs that build the capacity of individuals and institutions and programs that address the problems of urban areas throughout the U.S. In 1996 grants totaled $142.6 million.

Publications: Annual *Report on Activities*; *Programs and Policies*
Address: 140 South Dearborn Street, Suite 1100, Chicago, IL 60603-5285
Phone: (312) 726-8000
Fax: (312) 917-0334
E-mail: 4answers@macfdn.org
Website: http://www.macfdn.org

New
MEADOWS FOUNDATION, INC.

The Meadows Foundation exists to help people and institutions of Texas improve the quality of life for themselves and for future generations. It supports work in the arts, civic affairs, education, and health and human services. It also supports efforts to eliminate ignorance and hopelessness. Some programs that received significant grants in 1996 were leadership-related. Texas A&M Research Foundation received $203,500 in support for an interdisciplinary program that provides community leadership training to clergy and laity. Lamar University received $110,000 toward renovation of a residence hall for high school students attending the Texas Academy of Leadership in the Humanities. The YWCA of San Antonio received $81,000 to incorporate an entrepreneurship training program for low-income women.

Publications: Annual report; program policy statement; application guidelines
Address: Wilson Historic Block, 3003 Swiss Avenue, Dallas, TX 75204-6090
Phone: (214) 826-9431
Website: http://www.mfi.org

CHARLES STEWART MOTT FOUNDATION

The major concern of this foundation is maintaining the well-being of a community through partnerships among individuals, families, neighborhoods, and governments. Fundamental to Mott grant making are nurturing strong individuals to ensure a well-functioning society, encouraging responsible citizen participation, promoting the empowerment of all individuals, and respecting the diversity of life. Leadership development initiatives that received funding in 1996 include: Consensus Organizing Institute—$100,000 to support a national community organizing intermediary focusing on neighborhood leadership; Grass Roots Leadership—$100,000 to design and support a training program for community organizers in the Southeastern U.S.; Creative Expression Dance Studio, Inc.—$36,000 to support a leadership development program for underprivileged minority girls.

Publications: *Facts on Grants*; *Mott Exchange* quarterly newsletter; brochures; annual report
Address: 1200 Mott Foundation Building, Flint, MI 48502-1851
Phone: (810) 238-5651
Fax: (810) 766-1753
Website: http://www.mott.org

THE DAVID AND LUCILLE PACKARD FOUNDATION

Support is given to projects for youth, education, management assistance, conservation, and population issues, primarily in the San Francisco area. In 1996, Volunteer Service of Santa Cruz received $15,000 to support meetings on volunteer management and leadership. The Planned Parenthood Federation of America received $50,000 for the Planned Parenthood Leadership Institute, and the Institute for Educational Leadership received $15,000. A new initiative enables community foundations to find better ways to address the management needs of nonprofits in their regions.

Publications: Annual report
Address: 300 Second Street, Suite 200, Los Altos, CA 94022-3632
Phone: (415) 948-7658
Website: http://www.cs.virginia.edu/packard

New
THE Z. SMITH REYNOLDS FOUNDATION

This general-purpose foundation was established in 1936 for the benefit of the people of North Carolina. It concentrates on helping to develop new programs in community and economic development, the environment, precollegiate education, issues affecting minorities, and issues affecting women. Recipients in 1997 included: American Grassroots Unlimited, Inc.—$30,000 for an internship program to develop the next generation of natural resource managers and policymakers; the Center for Diversity Education—$15,000 for diversity programs in Charlotte schools; Eastern Carolina University—$35,000 for assessment and leadership development programs for future educators and practicing school administrators; Leadership Winston-Salem—$20,000 for a youth program; and $15,000 was given to support the 1997 conference of Southern Women in Public Service.

Publications: Annual report includes guidelines
Address: 101 Reynolda Village, Winston-Salem, NC 27106-5199
Phone: (800) 443-6069 or (336) 443-8319
Fax: (336) 725-6069
E-mail: info@zsr.org
Website: http://www.zsr.org

ROCKEFELLER BROTHERS FUND

The fund seeks to improve the well-being of all people through support of efforts in the U.S. and abroad that contribute ideas, develop leaders, and encourage institutions in the transition to global interdependence. It aims to: 1) counter world trends of resource depletion, arms buildup, protectionism, and isolation through grant making to programs that educate individuals, groups, and the public; 2) identify and train leaders; and 3) provide a leadership network. Some examples of leadership grants given in 1997 include: $200,000 to the Southern Education Foundation for the Teachers as Leaders Initiative; $35,000 each to several New York groups that provide leadership development training to parents involved in school reform; and $50,000 each to several New York groups that provide leadership development training for young people.

Publications: *Global Interdependence and the Need for Social Stewardship;* annual report; guidelines brochure; occasional papers

Address: 1290 Avenue of the Americas, New York, NY 10104-0233
Phone: (212) 373-4200
Fax: (212) 315-0996
E-mail: bshute@rbf.org
Website: http://www.rbf.org/rbf

U.S.–JAPAN FOUNDATION

The foundation's mission is to promote a greater mutual knowledge between the U.S. and Japan and to contribute to programs concerning bilateral policy issues. Areas receiving support include leadership development programs for K-through-12 teachers and collaborative efforts between American and Japanese organizations. Representatives from academia, business, government, and the media join forces to conduct research and carry out programs in finance, crisis management, and environmental protection. In 1997, the Center for Strategic and International Studies was awarded $110,000 for the U.S.-Japan Parliamentary Exchange: Leadership in the 21st Century. The Social Science Education Consortium was awarded $296,000 for the Japan Studies Leadership Program.

Publications: Quarterly newsletter; annual report
Address: 145 East 32nd Street, New York, NY 10016-6055
Phone: (212) 481-8753
Fax: (212) 481-8762
E-mail: 73232.332@compuserve.com

New
US WEST FOUNDATION

This company-sponsored foundation gives to programs in the US West calling areas, which are located in Arizona, Colorado, Iowa, Idaho, Minnesota, Montana, North Dakota, Nebraska, New Mexico, South Dakota, Oregon, Utah, Washington, and Wyoming. They support programs that improve education, celebrate diversity through artistic and cultural expression, support human services, and enhance communities. In 1998, they are seeking to fund programs that provide young people with leadership opportunities in civic involvement, creative problem solving, and community improvement.

Publications: Multiyear report; newsletter
Address: 7800 East Orchard Road, Suite 300, Englewood, CO 80111-2526
Phone: (303) 793-6648
Website: http://www.uswest.com/com/communities/foundation

THE THOMAS J. WATSON FOUNDATION

The Thomas J. Watson Fellowship Program enables college graduates with leadership potential to spend a year of independent study and travel abroad. This opportunity for *Wanderjahr* allows students to thoroughly explore a particular interest, test aspirations and abilities, and develop a sense of international concern. Fellowships of $19,000 are awarded to students who demonstrate integrity, potential for creative achievement, and excellence within a chosen field. Applicants must be nominated by one of 51 participating colleges.

Publications: Informational brochure
Address: 217 Angell Street, Providence, RI 02906-2120
Phone: (401) 274-1952
Fax: (401) 274-1954

CONFERENCES

The conferences described here include regularly scheduled events that offer workshops, nationally recognized speakers, resource exhibitions, service-learning opportunities, and presentations of scholarly papers. Information is provided about:

- The host organization.
- Audience.
- When—some are regularly scheduled for a particular season or month. Specific dates of future conferences are given if known at the time of this book's publication.
- Where—some are always in one location. Many change locations each year; specific locations for future conferences are given if known at the time of this book's publication.
- Cost—information is often based on previous conferences and is intended only as a ballpark figure to help with budget planning.

Many conferences offer discounts for members, students, early registration, groups, and one-day tickets. In every case, we verified that there are plans to continue this conference in the future.

AEE CONFERENCES

AEE sponsors eight regional conferences throughout the year and one annual international conference for professionals in experiential education. They all provide professional development renewal, networking opportunities, and workshops on outdoor adventure education programs, youth service, management development training, programs for people with disabilities, and environmental education. For more information, contact the Director of Conferences, Association for Experiential Education, 2305 Canyon Boulevard, Suite 100, Boulder, CO 80302. Phone: (303) 440-8844. Fax: (303) 440-9581. E-mail: info@aee.org. Website: http:// www.princeton.edu/~rcurtis/aee.html

Host Organization: Association for Experiential Education (AEE)
Audience: Professionals in the field of experiential and adventure education
When: Each fall—1998 is November 5-8
Where: Location varies—1998 in Lake Tahoe, CA
Cost: $260 to $360—does not include meals or lodging

ALANA STUDENT LEADERSHIP CONFERENCE

This weekend conference promotes a multicultural environment at SUNY–Oswego and other northeastern schools. Speakers who represent African, Latino, Asian, and Native American (ALANA) communities introduce global perspectives on peace, justice, policy, and culture. There are also crafts workshops, movies, cultural music and dancing, and a job fair. For more information, contact LEAD Center, 214 Hewitt Union, SUNY–Oswego, Oswego, NY 13126. Phone: (315) 341-3203. Fax: (315) 341-2924.

Host Organization: LEAD Center, State University of New York–Oswego
Audience: Students and educators from the northeastern U.S.
When: Each September—1998 is September 24-27
Where: State University of New York, Oswego, NY
Cost: $15 to $20—includes one banquet

ALE ANNUAL CONFERENCE

ALE challenges educators to stretch beyond existing boundaries in practicing and teaching leadership, to bring ideas and enthusiasm to the conference, and to take home inspiration and personal renewal. The conference appeals to various interest groups with programs on graduate and undergraduate curricula, youth leadership development, business leadership, theory and concepts, and practical tips. Participants may attend concurrent sessions, work-

shops, papers presentations, roundtable discussions, an awards ceremony, and social events. Conference proceedings are published. For more information, contact Nancy Huber, University of Arizona, 228 Forbes Building, Tucson, AZ 85721. Phone: (520) 621-5430. E-mail: nhuber@u.arizona.edu. Website: http:// www.aces.uiuc.edu/~ALE

Host Organization: Association of Leadership Educators (ALE)
Audience: Leadership educators in academic studies, extension service, community education, and training and development
When: Each July
Where: Location varies—1998 in Charleston, SC
Cost: $125 to $160—includes some meals, not lodging

ALLIANCE FOR P.E.O.P.L.E. ANNUAL CONFERENCE

This three-day conference on organizational excellence features concurrent sessions on teams, leadership, change, learning, 360-degree feedback, vision, and the virtual workplace. There are sector-based debriefings at the end of the first two days, a video and book store, and a notebook with session-related information provided by the speakers. Clemson University's 21st Century Organizational Excellence Award is presented to one company each year. For more information, contact Professional Development, Clemson University, P.O. Box 912, Clemson, SC 29633-0912. Phone: (800) 258-1017. Website: http://hubcap.clemson.edu/~elliot/ management.html

Host Organization: Clemson University Alliance for P.E.O.P.L.E.
Audience: Executives, managers
When: Each spring
Where: Location varies
Cost: $845 to $1,295—includes some meals, not lodging

ANNUAL HUMAN RESOURCES CONFERENCE AND EXPOSITION

This four-day conference addresses the real-world challenges faced by human resources professionals. Sessions offer practical solutions on leading organizational change, mining intellectual capital, aligning workforce competencies with training needs, identifying opportunities for growth and leadership, developing strategic plans for organizational learning, and team building. Keynote speakers in 1998 included Christopher Reeve and Robert Reich. For more information, contact AMA, HR Conference, 1601 Broadway, New York, NY

10019. Phone: (800) 262-9699 or (212) 903-7935. Fax: (212) 891-0368. E-mail: cust_serv@amanet.org. Website: http://www.amanet.org

Host Organization: American Management Association (AMA)
Audience: Human resources professionals
When: Each April—1999 is April 18-21
Where: Location varies—1999 in Anaheim, CA
Cost: $1,180 to $1,370—includes some meals, not lodging

New
ANNUAL MIDWEST LEADERSHIP CONFERENCE

This one-day event focuses on practical application and best practices in the human side of management. Sessions are designed to help participants become better teachers and trainers. There are workshops for novice and experienced educators based on models of interactive teaching methods. And there are workshops to introduce experiential exercises, technology, and cooperative learning techniques. Participants are eligible for CEUs from Purdue University. For more information, contact Bill Krug, Program Chair, Midwest Leadership Conference, Purdue University, Department of Organizational Leadership and Supervision, 1420 Knoy Hall of Technology, West Lafayette, IN 47907-1420. Phone: (765) 494-5614. Fax: (765) 496-2519. E-mail: wgkrug(tm)ech.purdue.edu

Host Organization: Department of Organizational Leadership, Purdue University
Audience: Leadership educators, trainers, and practitioners from the midwestern U.S.
When: Each March
Where: Purdue University, West Lafayette, IN
Cost: $50—includes lunch

ANNUAL STUDENT LEADERSHIP CONFERENCE

This day-long interactive conference for students features the Leaders for Life series, which showcases outstanding business, political, entertainment, community, and education leaders who share their experiences. Over 40 sessions examine the issues of vision, challenge, diversity, freedom, and common ground. For more information, contact the Student Activities or Residence Life/Housing offices at any of the host schools for registration information. Or contact Dr. Vicki L. McNeil, Associate Vice President for Student Affairs, Box 13, Office of Student Affairs, Danna Center, Loyola University, New Orleans, LA 70118. Phone: (504) 865-3030. Fax: (504) 865-3025.

Host Organizations: Loyola University, Tulane University, Delgado Community College, Xavier University, Our Lady of Holy Cross College, Southern University–New Orleans, and the University of New Orleans
Audience: Students from southern U.S.
When: Each March
Where: New Orleans, LA
Cost: $10—includes meals

New
ASTD INTERNATIONAL CONFERENCE AND EXPOSITION

This conference is for HRD professionals interested in training and development issues, tools, and technology. There are 250 concurrent sessions in seven areas: learning technologies, management and leadership development, managing change, measuring and evaluating training and performance, performance improvement, training basics, and workplace issues. There are also plenary speakers, in-depth pre-conference workshops, and more than 500 booths exhibiting resources. For more information, contact ASTD, P.O. Box 3005, Milwaukee, WI 53201. Phone: (414) 272-8575. Fax: (414) 272-1734. Website: http://www.astd.org

Host Organization: American Society for Training and Development (ASTD)
Audience: Human resources professionals
When: Each May—1999 is May 22-27
Where: Location varies—1999 in Anaheim, CA
Cost: $745 to $995; student rates and one-day passes are available

BLACK STUDENT LEADERSHIP CONFERENCE

This is a forum for the discussion of issues germane to the development, enhancement, and effectiveness of black student leaders. Opening and closing keynote speakers, theatrical performances, and concurrent sessions address the diverse cultural heritage and leadership needs of the global black community. This event lasts one-and-one-half days. For more information, contact Phyllis Slade-Martin, Office of African American Studies, George Mason University, MS 5A4, Fairfax, VA 22030-4444. Phone: (703) 993-4080.

Host Organization: African American Studies, George Mason University
Audience: Students, professionals, and community leaders from the middle-Atlantic states
When: Each November
Where: George Mason University, Fairfax, VA
Cost: $25 to $50—includes some meals

New
CONFERENCE ON WOMEN'S LEADERSHIP IN THE OUTDOORS

The focus of this conference is on learning leadership through experiential education, indoors as well as out. The theme of the 1997 conference was "Leadership and Education in the Outdoors: An Exploration of Gender, the Feminine, and Feminist Concerns." Workshop topics included: competence for girls and women; girls in gangs: an epidemic in violence; a history of women adventurers; and society and body image. Work exchange, child care, and scholarships are available. For more information, contact Lisa Foisy, North Carolina Outward Bound School, 2582 Riceville Road, Asheville, NC 28805. Phone: (704) 299-3366 x112. Fax: (704) 299-3928. E-mail: info@ncobs.org

Host Organization: North Carolina Outward Bound School
Audience: Female college students and working women
When: Each fall
Where: Location varies throughout the U.S. and Canada
Cost: $80—includes meals, not lodging

New
COOL NATIONAL CONFERENCE ON STUDENT COMMUNITY SERVICE

The COOL Conference is a meeting place for college students dedicated to service. Students of differing backgrounds and affiliations are encouraged to unite in the challenge of creating new and better communities. Highlights of the conference are: a keynote speaker, workshops, an opportunities fair, swap shop, idea boards, films, and work on a local service project. At the Oxfam Hunger Banquet, a drawing determines who enjoys a gourmet meal, who eats beans and rice, and who waits in line for plain rice and water. For more information, contact COOL, 1531 P Street, N.W., Suite LL, Washington, DC 20005. Phone: (202) 265-1200. Fax: (202) 265-3241. E-mail: homeoffice@cool2serve.org. Website: http://www.cool2serve.org

Host Organization: Campus Outreach Opportunity League (COOL)
Audience: College students and student affairs professionals
When: Each spring
Where: On various college and university campuses
Cost: $95 to $215—includes some meals and optional free lodging

THE PETER F. DRUCKER FOUNDATION FOR NONPROFIT MANAGEMENT FALL CONFERENCE

This conference focuses on issues of importance to leadership in nonprofit organizations. Nationally recognized leaders from business, government, and the social sector share ideas on designing and delivering service, developing partnerships, and accountability. Each year, one organization with an exceptional program or project is recognized with the Peter F. Drucker Award for Nonprofit Innovation and a $25,000 prize. Most conference sessions are audiotaped and available for purchase after the conference. For more information, contact the Peter F. Drucker Foundation for Nonprofit Management, 320 Park Avenue, 3rd Floor, New York, NY 10022-6839. Phone: (212) 224-1174. Fax: (212) 224-2508. E-mail: info@pfdf.org. Website: http://www.pfdf.org

Host Organization: The Peter F. Drucker Foundation for Nonprofit Management
Audience: Social-sector leaders from the U.S. and abroad
When: Each fall
Where: Alternates each year between the East Coast and West Coast
Cost: $300—includes some meals, not lodging

New
HRPS ANNUAL CONFERENCE

This human resources conference offers fast-paced, interactive sessions and provides immediate opportunities to analyze and practice new learnings. The 1998 conference theme was "The New Business Fabric—Blending Competition with Commitment." Speakers included Dave Ulrich from the University of Michigan, Jerome Adams of Shell Oil, Pat Canavan of Motorola, Victoria Guthrie from the Center for Creative Leadership, Cal Wick of Wick & Company, and more. For more information, contact Dillian Waldron, Human Resource Planning Society, 317 Madison Avenue, Suite 1509, New York, NY 10017. Phone: (212) 490-6387. Fax: (212) 682-6851. Website: http://www.hrps.org

Host Organization: Human Resource Planning Society (HRPS)
Audience: Human resources professionals from around the world
When: Each March—1999 is March 28-31
Where: Location varies—1999 in San Diego, CA
Cost: $1,550 to $1,750—includes some meals, not lodging

INTERNATIONAL CONFERENCE ON SERVANT-LEADERSHIP

This annual conference addresses the link between servant leadership and business, education, health care, religious organizations, and personal growth. Keynote speeches for 1998 include Lea Williams's research on servant leadership in the African-American community, John Bogle's description of servant leadership as a wise investment at the Vanguard Group, Jim Kouzes's invitation to make a journey and find your voice, and Frances Hesselbein's organizational perspective. Pre-conference workshops offer orientation sessions for those not familiar with the work of Robert K. Greenleaf and the theory of servant leadership. For more information, contact Kelly Tobe, The Robert K. Greenleaf Center, 921 East 86th Street, Suite 200, Indianapolis, IN 46240. Phone: (317) 259-1241. Fax: (317) 259-0506.

Host Organization: The Robert K. Greenleaf Center
Audience: General
When: August 6-8, 1998
Where: Indianapolis, IN
Cost: $400 to $500—includes some meals, not lodging; one-day tickets are available; pre-conference is $195

INTERNATIONAL LEADERSHIP CONFERENCES

The International Leadership Conferences (ILC) provide a forum for youth to develop self-esteem, competence, and the skills needed to lead others. Located at rustic educational facilities, all participants leave behind familiar routines and the comforts of home, while sharing in community chores. ILC aims to cultivate students' mental, physical, social, and spiritual capacities through experiential learning and recreation. High school juniors and seniors with leadership experience or leadership potential are selected and sponsored by schools, civic organizations, corporations, and religious organizations. Individuals may apply by paying their own tuition or securing a sponsor. For more information, contact the ILC Registrar, American Youth Foundation, 1315 Ann Avenue, St. Louis, MO 63104. Phone: (314) 772-8626. Fax: (314) 772-7542.

Host Organization: American Youth Foundation
Audience: High school students from the U.S. and around the world
When: There are three 7-day sessions and one 11-day session each summer
Where: Camps are located in New Hampshire, Michigan, and California
Cost: $550 to $725—includes meals and lodging

New
INTERNATIONAL STUDENT LEADERSHIP CONFERENCE AND COMMUNITY INTERNATIONAL PROGRAMS WORKSHOP

This is a conference for students and a workshop for the professionals and volunteers who run programs for students in international education. Students' sessions are on cross-cultural communication, career planning, leadership skills, and program ideas. Workshops for program planners are on connecting international students with local communities, sharing resources, and increasing intercultural exchange and understanding. For more information, contact Melissa Groom, Colorado State University, Fort Collins, CO. Phone: (970) 491-4818. E-mail: melissa@holly.colostate.edu

Host Organization: Colorado State University
Audience: Students, student affairs professionals, and community volunteers
When: Each April
Where: Colorado State University, Fort Collins, CO
Cost: $25

KANSAS HIGH SCHOOL LEADERSHIP CONFERENCE

Over 250 students and advisors attend workshops facilitated by activity advisors and college student leaders and hear a nationally recognized keynote speaker. This is a one-day conference. For more information, contact the Continuing Education Office, Kansas State University, Manhattan, KS 66506-1412. Phone: (913) 532-5566.

Host Organization: Kansas State University and Kansas High School Activity Association
Audience: High school students and activity advisors from the state of Kansas
When: Each winter
Where: Kansas State University, Manhattan, KS
Cost: $17—includes lunch

LEADERSHIP EDUCATORS CONFERENCE

This is a forum for the exchange of ideas on new developments in leadership education as taught in the classroom and experienced in extracurricular activities. The three-day conference features a variety of plenary sessions, panel discussions, workshops, and small, interactive discussion groups. Researchers, educators, student affairs professionals, leadership practitioners, and students participate in the presentations and networking opportunities. For more information, contact the James MacGregor Burns Academy of Leadership, University of Maryland, 1107 Taliaferro Hall, College Park, MD 20742. Phone: (301) 314-7884. E-mail: umdconf@accmail.umd.edu.

Website: http://academy.umd.edu/Academy/
Conferences.htm

Host Organization: James MacGregor Burns Academy
of Leadership at the University of Maryland and the
Jepson School of Leadership Studies at the University of
Richmond
Audience: Educators who teach leadership in academic
courses and who direct leadership programs in student
affairs departments
When: Each summer
Where: University of Maryland, College Park, MD, or
the University of Richmond, VA
Cost: $400—includes some meals, not lodging

LEADERSHIP INSTITUTE

The goal of the Leadership Institute is to provide a
learning opportunity for those who hold leadership
positions or teach leadership in higher education. Two
days of presentations focus on issues of individual
development, humor, culture, organizations, politics, and
symbolism. Two days of "reflection-on-purpose" afford
participants the opportunity to enjoy the park's numerous
waterfalls, gorges, forests, and recreational activities. For
more information, contact Tom Burks, Leadership and
Management Institute, Middle Tennessee State University, Box 602, Murfreesboro, TN 37132. Phone:
(615) 898-5786. Fax: (615) 898-5668. E-mail:
tburks@mtsu.edu

Host Organization: Middle Tennessee State University
Audience: Faculty, deans, administrators, and presidents
from institutions of higher education—limited to 50
people
When: Each spring
Where: Fall Creek Falls State Park, Pikeville, TN
Cost: $495—includes meals, not lodging

LEADERSHIP SUMMIT

In response to changing social, political, and economic
conditions, this summit provides a forum for local leaders
to investigate ways for improving local government.
Structured learning experiences, networking, and in-depth
dialogues help local leaders to improve their leadership
skills and to discover new opportunities for building their
communities. This two-and-one-half-day event schedules
time to reflect, relax, and recharge. For more information,
contact Leadership Training Institute, National League of
Cities, 1301 Pennsylvania Avenue, N.W., Washington,
DC 20004. Phone: (202) 626-3181. Fax: (202) 626-3043.

Host Organization: National League of Cities
Audience: Mayors, city council members, city managers,
and state league executive directors—limited to 125
people

When: Each year—late summer
Where: Location varies
Cost: $400 to $550—does not include meals or lodging

NACL ANNUAL LEADERSHIP CONFERENCE

This conference aims to energize civic leaders for the
roles they play in strengthening and transforming communities. Participants are encouraged to make new connections, to explore community trusteeship, and to enrich
their personal and professional selves. Workshops cover a
wide range of interests from program marketing and
unique programs for special groups to program evaluation
and a festival of training films. Highlights of each
conference are a leadership-resource fair, sharing of
success stories, and an awards ceremony. Audiotapes of
most sessions are available for purchase. For more
information, contact the National Association for Community Leadership, 200 South Meridian Street, Suite 340,
Indianapolis, IN 46225. Phone: (317) 637-7408.
Fax: (317) 637-7413. Website: http://
www.communityleadership.org

Host Organization: National Association for Community
Leadership (NACL) and corporate sponsors
Audience: Civic leaders and leadership development
professionals from the U.S., Canada, Great Britain, and
Australia
When: Each April
Where: Location varies
Cost: $350 to $500—includes some meals, not lodging

New
NASPA INTERNATIONAL SYMPOSIUM ON STUDENT SERVICES AROUND THE WORLD

This conference offers interest sessions on a wide variety
of subjects: diversity, international programs, student
leadership, staff development, and technology issues such
as computer-mediated conferencing and distance learning.
There are also keynote speakers, workshops, a career
services center, exhibits, a bookstore, a technology center,
and several receptions. For more information, contact
NASPA, 1875 Connecticut Avenue, N.W., Suite 418,
Washington, DC 20009. Phone: (202) 265-7500. Fax:
(202) 797-1157. E-mail: office@naspa.org. Website:
http://www.naspa.org

Host Organization: National Association of Student
Personnel Administration (NASPA) and National Council
on Student Development (NCSD)
Audience: Student services professionals
When: Each spring
Where: Location varies
Cost: $175 to $365—does not include meals or lodging;
pre-conference is $50 to $90

New
NATIONAL COMMUNITY SERVICE CONFERENCE

This is an annual training event for leaders in the field of volunteer management. There are more than 100 workshops on topics such as collaboration, community leadership development, diversity, employee volunteerism, mentoring, personal development, technology, and service learning. Participants may choose to attend introductory, intermediate, or advanced level sessions. Outside the classroom, participants may visit local model programs and engage in community service projects. For more information, contact The Points of Light Foundation, 1737 H Street, N.W., Washington, DC 20006. Phone: (202) 223-9186. Fax: (202) 223-9256. E-mail: volnet@aol.com. Website: http://www.pointsoflight.org

Host Organization: The Points of Light Foundation
Audience: Volunteer managers, nonprofit and service organization staff and board members, business and government managers, communities of faith leaders
When: Each June
Where: Location varies
Cost: $365 to $545—includes some meals, not lodging

NATIONAL CONFERENCE FOR COLLEGE WOMEN STUDENT LEADERS

This conference serves as a forum for women student leaders to discuss the challenges they face in their leadership roles, to learn new strategies for dealing with those challenges, and to meet professional women who serve as role models. Participants are encouraged to use their campus leadership experiences as the foundation for continuing leadership roles at the community, state, and federal levels. About 600 students attend each conference. For more information, contact the National Association for Women in Education, 1325 18th Street, N.W., Suite 210, Washington, DC 20036-6511. Phone: (202) 659-9330.

Host Organization: The National Association for Women in Education (NAWE)
Audience: Women students who are currently in leadership roles on campus
When: Each June
Where: Washington, DC
Cost: $295—includes some meals and lodging

NATIONAL CONFERENCE ON GOVERNANCE

For over 100 years, the National Civic League has held an annual conference and membership meeting showcasing community-building efforts. The three-day conference is attended by leaders from the public, private, and nonprofit sectors to discuss current innovations in local and state governance. A keynote speaker and plenary sessions feature experts with community revitalization success stories to share. The 1998 theme is Building a Healthier Community. For more information, contact the National Civic League, 1445 Market Street, Suite 300, Denver, CO 80202-1728. Phone: (303) 571-4343. Fax: (303) 571-4404. Website: http://www.ncl.org/ncl

Host Organization: National Civic League
Audience: Local, state, and federal government policymakers, members of the voluntary sector, citizen activists, and academics
When: Each fall—1998 is November 12-14
Where: Washington, DC, area
Cost: $295—includes some meals, not lodging

NATIONAL LEADERSHIP CONFERENCE ON STUDENT GOVERNMENT

This is a four-day working conference for student leaders in Greek organizations, residence halls, campus union programming, and student government. Faculty members facilitate small-group discussions and roundtables to solve problems in multicultural issues, prevention of burnout, faculty-student relations, hidden agendas, motivating volunteers, and conflict resolution. At the idea-and-material exchange, groups share promotional materials, newspapers, judicial procedures, student government constitutions, and sweatshirts. For more information, contact Pat Bosco, Office of the Vice President for Institutional Advancement, 122 Anderson Hall, Kansas State University, Manhattan, KS 66506-0119. Phone: (800) 432-8222 or (913) 532-6237. Fax: (913) 532-6108.

Host Organization: The Center for Leadership Development, Kansas State University
Audience: Campus student leaders and their advisors—limited to 175 people
When: Each October
Where: St. Louis, MO
Cost: $295—includes some meals, not lodging

NATIONAL LEADERSHIP FORUM

This three-day conference addresses the issues of importance to the management and governance of nonprofit organizations: board composition and structure, leadership development, fund-raising, and the changing nature of volunteerism. A journalistic account of the proceedings is featured in the December issue of *Board Member*. For more information, contact National Center for Nonprofit Boards, 2000 L Street, N.W., Suite 510, Washington, DC 20036. Phone: (202) 452-6262. Fax: (202) 452-6299. Website: http://www.ncnb.org

Host Organization: National Center for Nonprofit Boards
Audience: Executives, staff members, and board members of nonprofit organizations
When: Each November—1998 is November 15-17
Where: Washington, DC
Cost: $400—includes some meals, not lodging

NATIONAL LEADERSHIP INSTITUTE CONFERENCE

At this conference, professionals who are experienced in leading organizations or teaching leadership models share their expertise. Participants learn practical skills and discover new tools in one area each conference. In 1998, the focus is on coaching. This is a three-day event. Submissions for presentations are accepted nine months prior to each conference. For more information, contact the National Leadership Institute, University of Maryland University College, University Boulevard at Adelphi Road, College Park, MD 20742-1668. Phone: (301) 985-7195.

Host Organization: The National Leadership Institute at the University of Maryland University College and Personnel Decisions, Inc.
Audience: Executives, managers, HRD professionals, organizational development consultants from the private and nonprofit sectors, and university professors who teach organizational psychology or business
When: Biennial—next is October 1998
Where: University of Maryland, College Park, MD
Cost: $595 to $695—includes some meals, not lodging

NATIONAL LEADERSHIP SYMPOSIUM

The National Leadership Symposium is a scholarly program designed to promote a greater understanding of critical issues and evolving models centered on college student leadership programs—curricular, cocurricular, and community-based. Each conference, participants are invited to bring working papers on leadership topics of interest to share with colleagues. For more information, contact Sharon LaVoy, NCLP, 1135 Stamp Student Union, University of Maryland, College Park, MD 20742. Phone: (301) 405-0799. Fax: (301) 314-9634. E-mail: nclp@umdstu.umd.edu. Website: http://www.inform.umd.edu/OCP/NCLP

Host Organization: National Association for Campus Activities (NACA) Educational Foundation and the National Clearinghouse for Leadership Programs (NCLP)
Audience: Faculty, student affairs professionals with significant experience in leadership education; graduate students may participate as symposium associates
When: Each summer

Where: Location varies
Cost: $325—includes meals and lodging

NATIONAL SERVICE-LEARNING CONFERENCE

This event promotes service learning as a way to build citizenship and academic skills while renewing communities. Conference features include: school site visits, service projects, service fair, more than 100 workshops, exhibit booths, and special youth activities. Young people are encouraged to get involved as planners, leaders, and participants. For more information, contact the National Youth Leadership Council, 1910 West County Road B, St. Paul, MN 55113. Phone: (612) 631-3672. Fax: (612) 631-2955. Website: http://www.nylc.org

Host Organization: National Youth Leadership Council
Audience: Educators, students, policymakers, and citizens who are involved in leadership education through service learning
When: Each spring
Where: Location varies
Cost: $199 to $350—includes some meals, not lodging

NEW WAYS OF LEARNING AND LEADING IN THE CLASSROOM AND THE WORKPLACE

This weekend-long conference is an exchange of ideas, successes, and challenges focused on broad issues in the field of leadership education. Presentations at the 1998 conference included: collaboration and culture clashes in corporate mergers, successful cross-functional teams in higher education and the workplace, women leading change, leadership and spirituality, synergistic learning teams, and teaching cultural sensitivity through art. There is a concurrent mini-conference for student leaders. For more information, contact the Center for Inclusive Leadership and Social Responsibility, Pine Manor College, 400 Heath Street, Chestnut Hill, MA 02167. Phone: (617) 731-7620. Fax: (617) 731-7185. E-mail: inclusive@pmc.edu. Website: http://www.pmc.edu

Host Organization: Center for Inclusive Leadership and Social Responsibility at Pine Manor College
Audience: Educators, business leaders, and community leaders
When: Each spring
Where: Pine Manor College, Chestnut Hill, MA
Cost: $200 to $225—includes meals and lodging; day rates and special discounts are available

New
NILIE CONFERENCE

This conference features skill-building workshops for career development, leadership and technology, leadership styles, image control, and community. There are also forum presentations, a keynote address, and social activities. Three David Pierce Leadership Awards recognize teams, department chairs, and instructors for incorporating innovative strategies that manage change in their institutions. For more information, contact NILIE, College of Education and Psychology, NC State University, 300 Poe Hall, Box 7801, Raleigh, NC 27695-7801. Phone: (919) 515-9366 or (919) 515-5832. Fax: (919) 515-6305. E-mail: nilie@poe.coe.ncsu.edu. Website: http://www2.ncsu.edu/ncsu/cep/2/nilie_conf/index.html

Host Organization: National Initiative for Leadership and Institutional Effectiveness (NILIE), North Carolina State University
Audience: Leaders and educators in the public and private sectors
When: Each spring
Where: Location varies
Cost: $275 to $350—includes some meals, not lodging

NSEE NATIONAL CONFERENCE

This conference caters to those who are new to the field of experiential education and those who have many years of experience. Workshops and roundtables feature ways to build bridges between schools and communities, school-to-work initiatives, and academic skills in experiential programs. A resource center, site visits, and poster sessions with models on display run throughout the four-day conference. For more information, contact the Registration Coordinator, NSEE National Conference, 3509 Haworth Drive, Suite 207, Raleigh, NC 27609-7229. Phone: (919) 787-3263. Fax: (919) 787-3381. Website: http://www.nsee.org

Host Organization: National Society for Experiential Education (NSEE)
Audience: College faculty, directors of experience-based learning programs, administrators, researchers, and the business and agency staff who host interns
When: Each fall—1998 is October 21-24
Where: Location varies—1998 in Norfolk, VA
Cost: $250—includes some meals, not lodging

SDSU LEADERSHIP INSTITUTE

An intensive weekend program exposes students and advisors to issues on leadership, current affairs, and personal and professional growth. Workshops on motivation, creativity, meeting management, vision, goal setting,

communication, and multicultural diversity encourage participants to find leadership opportunities in their own communities. For more information, contact David Robertson, Coordinator, Student Leadership Programs, San Diego State University, 5500 Campanile Drive, San Diego, CA 92182-7440. Mail code: 7440. Phone: (619) 594-5221. Fax: (619) 594-1045. E-mail: david.robertson@sdsu.edu. Website: http://www.sa.sdsu.edu/src/leadership_home.html

Host Organization: San Diego State University
Audience: Student leaders and faculty/staff advisors from the western U.S.
When: Each fall—1998 is November 20-22
Where: San Diego, CA
Cost: $80 to $100—includes some meals, not lodging

New
JOHN BEN SHEPPERD LEADERSHIP FORUM

This conference trains "young, emerging leaders about the issues of Texas." Awards are presented to three outstanding Texas leaders in three areas: elected, public administration, and citizen leadership. There are speakers, breakout sessions, and panels of experts. For more information, contact the John Ben Shepperd Leadership Institute, University of Texas–Permian Basin, 4901 East University Boulevard, Odessa, TX 79762-0001. Phone: (915) 552-2850. Fax: (915) 552-2851. E-mail: jbs@utpb.edu

Host Organization: John Ben Shepperd Leadership Institute
Audience: Citizens, public administrators, and elected officials who contribute to or are interested in public issues that affect Texas
When: Each fall—1998 is September 25-27
Where: Location rotates among Texas cities—1998 in Odessa
Cost: $75—includes some meals, not lodging

New
SHRM ANNUAL CONFERENCE

Since 1948, this conference has brought HRD professional together for professional development activities and a resources exposition. Executive track and masters series sessions are for senior HR executives. Tools-of-the-trade sessions feature fundamental skills and knowledge refreshers. More-to-life-than-work sessions help participants enhance their personal and professional experiences. There are also sessions focused on consulting work, technology, best practices, and school-to-work initiatives. Keynote speakers at the 1998 conference included General Colin Powell (Ret.), Dr. Jennifer James,

David Ulrich, and Bill Cosby. For more information, contact the Society for Human Resource Management, 1800 Duke Street, Alexandria, VA 22314. Phone (800) 283-7476 or (703) 548-3440. Fax: (703) 836-0367. Website: http://www.shrm.org

Host Organization: Society for Human Resource Management (SHRM)
Audience: Human resources professionals
When: Each June
Where: Location varies
Cost: $710 to $1,020—includes some meals, not lodging

New
SOUTHERN WOMEN IN PUBLIC SERVICE

This bipartisan conference aims to improve the quality, integrity, and effectiveness of government by tapping the talents of women currently serving and opening doors for emerging leaders who wish to make a difference through public service. Each year, the Lindy Boggs Award is presented to the woman from the South who has demonstrated ideals of patriotism, courage, integrity, and leadership in public service. For more information, contact the Stennis Center for Public Service, Box 9629, Mississippi State, MS 39762. Phone: (601) 325-8409. Fax: (601) 325-8623. Website: http://www.stennis.gov

Host Organization: Stennis Center for Public Service
Audience: Southern women who support or are in government leadership positions at the local, state, and national levels
When: Each spring
Where: Location varies among southern cities
Cost: $194 to $254—includes some meals, not lodging

STUDENT CONFERENCE ON LEADERSHIP AND SOCIAL RESPONSIBILITY

Wells College provides the opportunity for high school girls to consider new models of leadership and to understand their own capacities for exercising leadership. Workshops provide information and practice on: leadership development, problem solving, goal setting, action planning, and styles of leadership. Participants make action plans for leadership development in their own high schools. For more information, contact Terry Martinez, Conferences Services and Leadership Programs, Wells College, Aurora, NY 13026. Phone: (315) 364-3399. Fax: (315) 364-3423.

Host Organization: Wells College
Audience: Female high school students who are nominated by their guidance counselors
When: Each summer

Where: Wells College, Aurora, NY
Cost: $150—includes meals and lodging

New
STUDENT LEADERSHIP TRAINING CONFERENCE

This conference includes keynote speakers and breakout sessions on such topics as advising challenges, communication skills, ethical leadership, follow-through, innovation, motivation, service learning, and team building. *New Student Leader* and *Seasoned Student Leader* awards are presented to conference participants nominated by their advisors. For more information, contact the Campus Activities Center, University of South Carolina, Russell House University Union 035, Columbia, SC 29208. Phone: (803) 777-5781.

Host Organization: University of South Carolina–Columbia
Audience: Student leaders and advisors from the southeastern U.S.
When: Each spring
Where: University of South Carolina, Columbia, SC
Cost: $20 to $30—includes lunch

THE WAVE

The Wave consists of a fall conference and a spring seminar. In the fall, 300 students gather for discussions on current leadership issues, workshops, keynote speakers, and networking sessions. In the spring, students participate in an outdoor adventure program to learn team-development strategies. At both Wave events, the registration fee is used to reserve a space and is refunded on the day of the event. For more information, contact the office of student activities at participating schools.

Host Organization: The Ocean State Leadership Consortium
Audience: Students from the ten colleges and universities in Rhode Island
When: Each fall and spring
Where: University of Rhode Island, Kingston, RI
Cost: $5—includes dinner

WEA NATIONAL CONFERENCE FOR OUTDOOR LEADERSHIP

This annual three-day conference focuses on existing wilderness-education programs and provides a forum to display and examine them. Workshops are offered in outdoor leadership, skill development, design of programs, and career issues. The Paul Petzoldt Award is presented each year to a professional who has made an outstanding contribution to the field of wilderness education. Pre-conference certification workshops are available for an extra fee. For more information, contact the Wilderness Education Association, Department of Natural Resource Recreation and Tourism, Colorado State University, Fort Collins, CO 80523. Phone: (970) 223-6252. Fax: (970) 223-6252.

Host Organization: Wilderness Education Association (WEA) and university or state park cohosts
Audience: Educators, students, trainers
When: Each winter
Where: Usually at a university campus or state park
Cost: $60 to $120—includes some meals, not lodging

WOMEN'S LEADERSHIP CONFERENCE FOR COLLEGE AND UNIVERSITY STUDENTS

Young women and men who support women's leadership attend this one-day conference. They learn new leadership skills, explore issues unique to female leaders, and receive encouragement to aspire to leadership positions. Keynote speakers and plenary sessions are videotaped for the conference video collection. Some session topics are third-wave feminism, activism, and leadership in a global community. For more information, contact the Women's Center, George Mason University, Fairfax, VA 22030-4444. Phone: (703) 993-2896.

Host Organization: The Women's Center, George Mason University
Audience: College students from the middle-Atlantic states
When: Each spring
Where: George Mason University, Fairfax, VA
Cost: $15 to $35—includes meals

INDEXES

CONTENTS

AUTHOR INDEX

Golding, W., *The lord of the flies*, 28
Goldsmith, J., *Learning to lead: A workbook on becoming a leader*, 197
Goldsmith, M.
  The leader of the future: New visions, strategies, and practices for the next era, 6
  The organization of the future, 62
Goldstein, H., *The essence of leadership: The four keys to leading successfully*, 8
Gomar, E. E., *Living Ethics: Meeting Challenges in Decision Making*, 256
Goodsell, C. T., *Public administration illuminated and inspired by the arts*, 112
Goodwin, V. L., *A cognitive interpretation of transactional and transformational leadership theories*, 21
Goss, T., *The reinvention roller coaster: Risking the present for a powerful future*, 83
Gouillart, F. J., *Champions of change: A global report on leading business transformation*, 137
Graef, C. L., *The situational leadership theory: A critical view*, 17
Graen, G. B., *Relationship-based approach to leadership: Development of leader-member exchange (LMX) theory of leadership over 25 years: Applying a multi-level multi-domain perspective*, 19
Graham, J. W.
  Mission statements: A guide to the corporate and nonprofit sectors, 61
  Servant-leadership in organizations: Inspirational and moral, 150
Gratzinger, P. D., *Praxis for Managers*, 234
Gray, J. W., *Skills for leaders*, 118
Gredler, M. E., *Designing and evaluating games and simulations*, 181
Green, J. C., *Board performance and organizational effectiveness in nonprofit social services organizations*, 75
Green, M. F.
  Investing in higher education: A handbook of leadership development, 93
  Leaders for a new era: Strategies for higher education, 93
Green, S. G., *A test of the situational theory*, 16
Greenberg, J., *Managing behavior in organizations: Science in service to practice*, 61
Greenblat, C. S., *Designing games and simulations: An illustrated handbook*, 191
Greene, D., *Defining the leadership role of school boards in the 21st century*, 91
Greenleaf, R. K., *Servant leadership: A journey into the nature of legitimate power and greatness*, 151
Greenstein, F. I.
  The hidden-hand presidency: Eisenhower as leader, 35
  Leadership in the modern presidency, 105
  The president who led by seeming not to: A centennial view of Dwight Eisenhower, 35
  The two leadership styles of William Jefferson Clinton, 36
Greenwood, R. G., *Leadership theory: A historical look at its evolution*, 13
Greer, J. T., *Leadership in empowered schools: Themes from innovative efforts*, 98
Gregersen, H. B., *Participative decision-making: An integration of multiple dimensions*, 140
Gregory, R. A., *What the good ones do: Characteristics of promising leadership development programs*, 175
Gresso, D. W., *Cultural leadership: The culture of excellence in education*, 92
Griesinger, D. W., *Board performance and organizational effectiveness in nonprofit social services organizations*, 75
Grobler, P. A., *In search of excellence: Leadership challenges facing companies in the new South Africa*, 28
Groff, L., *Culture Clash: An Ethical Intercultural Simulation*, 248
Grose, P. G., Jr., *Case teaching and why it works in leadership education*, 168
Grove, A. S., *Only the paranoid survive: How to exploit the crisis points that challenge every company and career*, 83
Grover, H. L., *Transition leadership and legacies*, 112
Grover, R. A., *Leader Reward and Punishment Questionnaire (LRPQ)*, 224

Grude, K. V., *The project manager as change agent: Leadership, influence and negotiation*, 139
Guarasci, R., *Democratic education in an age of difference: Redefining citizenship in higher education*, 93
Guardia, J., *Global Service Provider: Managing Change*, 253
Guastello, S. J., *Facilitative style, individual innovation, and emergent leadership in problem solving groups*, 22
Guest, C. W., *Praxis for Managers*, 234
Gueths, J., *The academic intrapraneur: Strategy, innovation, and management in higher education*, 96
Guillet de Monthoux, P., *Good novels, better management: Reading organizational realities in fiction*, 189
Gullatt, D. E., *Teachers taking the lead*, 93
Guns, B., *The faster learning organization: Gain and sustain the competitive edge*, 61
Guy, M. E., *Three steps forward, two steps backward: The status of women's integration into public management*, 50
Gyatso, T. (Dalai Lama XIV), *Freedom in exile: The autobiography of the Dalai Lama*, 36

H

Haas, E. F., *Political leadership in a Southern city: New Orleans in the progressive era, 1896-1902*, 105
Haas, H. G., *The leader within: An empowering path on self-discovery*, 198
Habana-Hafner, S., *New voices in university-community transformation*, 171
Hackel, S. W., *The staff of leadership: Indian authority in the missions of Alta California*, 56
Hackman, J. R., *Groups that work (and those that don't): Creating conditions for effective teamwork*, 69
Hackman, M. Z.
  Leadership: A communication perspective, 129
  Perceptions of gender-role characteristics and transformational leadership behaviours, 119
Hagan, C. M., *Management practice, organization climate, and performance: An exploratory study*, 147
Hagberg, J. O., *Real power: Stages of personal power in organizations*, 161
Hagberg, R. A., *Leadership Development Report (LDR)*, 224
Hahn, R., *Getting serious about presidential leadership: Our collective responsibility*, 94
Halberstam, D., *The best and the brightest*, 36
Hale, G. A., *The leader's edge: Mastering the five skills of breakthrough thinking*, 140
Haley, A., *The autobiography of Malcolm X*, 37
Hall, B. P., *Leadership through values: A study in personal and organizational development*, 151
Hall, D. T.
  Choosing a Leadership Style: Applying the Vroom and Yetton Model, 247
  Effective Delegation, 250
  Experiences in management and organizational behavior, 188
  My Best Boss, 257
  Unplanned executive transitions and the dance of the subidentities, 94
  Vanatin: Group Decision Making and Ethics, 266
Hall, F. S.
  Choosing a Leadership Style: Applying the Vroom and Yetton Model, 247
  Effective Delegation, 250
  Experiences in management and organizational behavior, 188
  Vanatin: Group Decision Making and Ethics, 266
Hall, G. E., *Becoming a principal: The challenges of beginning leadership*, 96
Hall, J.
  Access Management Survey (AMS), 212
  Change Agent Questionnaire (CAQ), 215
  Conflict Management Survey (CMS), 217
  NASA Moon Survival Task, 258
  Personnel Relations Survey (PRS), 233

TITLE INDEX

M

Machiavelli, Leonardo, and the science of power, Masters, R. D., 162

Machiavelli's new modes and order: A study of the "discourses on Livy," Mansfield, H. C., Jr., 162

The MADD queen: Charisma and the founder of Mothers Against Drunk Driving, Weed, F. J., 127

The Magnificent Seven, 303

A Major Malfunction: The Story Behind the Space Shuttle Challenger Disaster, 296

Making common sense: Leadership as meaning-making in a community of practice, Drath, W. H., & Palus, C. J., 19

The making of the corporate acolyte: Some thoughts on charismatic leadership and the reality of organizational commitment, Hopfl, H., 125

Making differences matter: A new paradigm for managing diversity, Thomas, D. A., & Ely, R. J., 44

Making diversity happen: Controversies and solutions, Morrison, A. M., Ruderman, M. N., & Hughes-James, M. W., 43

Making Diversity Work, 285

The making of a fearful leader: "Where's the rest of me?", DeMause, L., 35

The making of leaders: A review of the research in leadership development and education, Brungardt, C., 165

Making leadership effective: A three stage model, Neider, L. L., & Schriesheim, C. A., 22

Making many Penny's: New management challenge, Maccoby, M., 158

Malcolm X, 285

Man for All Seasons, 300

The Man Who Planted Trees, 303

The Man Who Would Be King, 290

Management of the absurd: Paradoxes in leadership, Farson, R. E., 6

Management Aptitude Test (MAT), NCS Workforce Development, 228

Management in developing countries, Jaeger, A. M., & Kanungo, R. N., 29

Management development: Choosing the right leadership simulation for the task, Dunbar, R. L. M., Stumpf, S. A., Mullen, T. P., & Arnone, M., 189

Management development evaluation and effectiveness, Smith, A., 170

Management development in Israel: Current and future challenges, Reichel, A., 31

Management development for scientists and engineers, Pearson, A. W., 170

Management education and development: Drift or thrust into the 21st century, Porter, L. W., & McKibbin, L. E., 170

Management ethics: Integrity at work, Petrick, J. A., & Quinn, J. F., 154

Management of organizational behavior: Utilizing human resources, Hersey, P., Blanchard, K. H., & Johnson, D. E., 61

Management practice, organization climate, and performance: An exploratory study, Schuster, F. E., Morden, D. L., Baker, T. E., McKay, I. S., Dunning, K. E., & Hagan, C. M., 147

Management Success Profile (MSP), NCS Workforce Development, 228

Management and theories of organizations in the 1990s: Toward a critical radical humanism, Aktouf, O., 18

Managerial Competency Questionnaire (MCQ), McBer & Company, 229

Managerial dilemmas: Cases in social, legal and technological change, Westin, A. F., & Aram, J. D., 143

Managerial leadership: A review of theory and research, Yukl, G. A., 15

Managerial motivation development: A study of college student leaders, Singleton, T. M., 183

The managerial mystique, Zaleznik, A., 89

Managerial Philosophy Scale (MPS), Jacoby, J., & Terborg, J. R., 229

Managerial promotion: The dynamics for men and women, Ruderman, M. N., Ohlott, P. J., & Kram, K. E., 54

Managerial Style Questionnaire (MSQ), McBer & Company, 229

Managerial Work-Values Scale (MWVS), Rao, T. V., 230

A manager's guide to globalization: Six keys to success in a changing world, Rhinesmith, S. H., 46

The manager's job: Folklore and fact, Mintzberg, H., 9

Managers and leaders: Are they different?, Zaleznik, A., 89

Managers as mentors: Building partnerships for learning, Bell, C. R., 156

Managing across cultures: A learning framework, Wilson, M. S., Hoppe, M. H., & Sayles, L. R., 47

Managing in the age of change: Essential skills to manage today's diverse workforce, Ritvo, R. A., Litwin, A. H., & Butler, L., 46

Managing behavior in organizations: Science in service to practice, Greenberg, J., 61

Managing by storying around, Armstrong, D. M., 127

Managing conflict: Interpersonal dialogue and third-party roles, Walton, R. E., 131

Managing corporate ethics: Learning from America's ethical companies how to supercharge business performance, Aguilar, F. J., 149

Managing cultural differences, Harris, P. R., & Moran, R. T., 45

Managing diversity: A complete desk reference and planning guide, Gardenswartz, L., & Rowe, A., 42

Managing diversity: Human resource strategies for transforming the workplace, Kossek, E. E., & Lobel, S. A., 43

Managing diversity: Lessons from the private sector, Dobbs, M. F., 42

Managing the dream: Leadership in the 21st century, Bennis, W. G., 25

Managing Generation X: How to bring out the best in young talent, Tulgan, B., 12

Managing globalization in the age of interdependence, Lodge, G. C., 30

Managing the hidden organization: Strategies for empowering your behind-the-scenes employees, Deal, T. E., & Jenkins, W. A., 144

Managing the new team environment: Skills, tools, and methods, Hirschhorn, L., 69

Managing organizational change, Connor, P. E., & Lake, L. K., 60

Managing people is like herding cats, Bennis, W. G., 3

Managing as a performing art: New ideas for a world of chaotic change, Vaill, P. B., 12

Managing with power: Politics and influence in organizations, Pfeffer, J., 163

Managing the presidency: Carter, Reagan, and the search for executive harmony, Campbell, C., 103

Managing the problem formulation process: Guidelines for team leaders and facilitators, Volkema, R. J., 142

Managing quality in America's most admired companies, Spechler, J. W., 87

Managing scientists: Leadership strategies in research and development, Sapienza, A. M., 122

Managing with the wisdom of love: Uncovering virtue in people and organizations, Marcic, D., 153

Mandela' Fight for Freedom, 282

Mankiller: A chief and her people, Mankiller, W., & Wallis, M., 37

Mao: A biography, Terrill, R., 40

Mars Surface Rover, Russo, E. M., & Eckler, M. P., 256

Martin Luther King, Jr.: From Montgomery to Memphis, 282

The mask of command, Keegan, J., 36

Mastering Change, 293

Matilda of Tuscany and Daimbert of Pisa: Women's leadership in medieval Italy, 1054-1092, Davis, M. A., Jr., 34

Matrix, Yukl, G. A., Lepsinger, R., & Lucia, T., 230

Mauritius: Celebrating Differences, 285

Maverick: The success story behind the world's most unusual workplace, Semler, R., 147

Max and Max: Unleashing the Potential in People and Dogs, 298

Maximum leadership: The world's leading CEOs share their five strategies for success, Farkas, C. M., 82

Mayoral leadership and economic development policy: The case of Ed Rendell's Philadelphia, McGovern, S. J., 107

Maytown In-Basket, Weeks, B., 257

Measures of leadership, Clark, K. E., & Clark, M. B., 4

Measuring leadership style: A review of leadership style instruments for classroom use, Zorn, T. E., & Violanti, M. T., 197

Meet Dr. Clay and Dr. Glass, Cunningham, R., 257

Meeting God: When organizational members come face to face with the supreme leader, Gabriel, Y., 125

Meeting Leadership, Klein, G. D., 257

The politics presidents make: Leadership from John Adams to Bill Clinton, Skowronek, S., 39

Portfolio use in educational leadership preparation programs: From theory to practice, Barnett, B. G., 180

Portfolios as means for promoting continuity in leadership development, Woyach, R. B., 179

A portrait of youthful leadership, Hamel, A., 94

Position Power: Exploring the Impact of Role Change, Cooke, P., & Porter, L. C., 260

Power: The inner experience, McClelland, D. C., 163

The power of balance: Transforming self, society, and scientific inquiry, Torbert, W. R., 32

Power Base Inventory, Thomas, K. W., & Thomas, G. F., 233

The power broker: Robert Moses and the fall of New York, Caro, R. A., 34

Power and the corporate mind, Zaleznik, A., & Kets de Vries, M. F. R., 164

The power elite, Mills, C. W., 30

The power of followership: How to create leaders people want to follow and followers who lead themselves, Kelley, R. E., 145

Power and leadership: A resource guide, Bair, M. L., & Mayhew, R. M., 160

Power and leadership in pluralist systems, McFarland, A. S., 106

Power Management Inventory (PMI), Hall, J., & Hawker, J., 233

The power of organizational storytelling: A management development perspective, Morgan, S., & Dennehy, R. F., 159

Power Play, 302

The power of positive peer influence: Leadership training for today's teens, Powell, S. R., 178

Power and powerlessness: Quiescence and rebellion in an Appalachian valley, Gavanta, J., 35

Power quotes: 4,000 trenchant soundbites on leadership and liberty, treason and triumph, sacrifice and scandal, risk and rebellion, weakness and war, and affaires politiques, Baker, D. B., 160

Power and responsibility: Case studies, Kennedy, D. M., & Parrish, M. E., 162

Power, success, and organizational effectiveness, Kotter, J. P., 162

Power tools: A leader's guide to the latest management thinking, Nirenberg, J., 169

Powershift: Knowledge, wealth and violence at the edge of the 21st century, Toffler, A., 32

The Practical Coach, 292

A practical procedure for training meeting chairpersons, Welsh, T. M., Johnson, S. P., Miller, L. K., & Merrill, M. H., 196

The practical value of philosophical thought for the ethical dimension, Heslep, R. D., 94

The Practicality of a Radical Workplace, 298

Practicing leadership: Principles and applications, Shriberg, A., Lloyd, C., Shriberg, D. L., & Williamson, M. L., 11

Practicing what we preach: Modeling leadership in the classroom, Hickman, G. R., 168

A pragmatic approach to business ethics, Michalos, A. C., 154

Praxis for Managers, Guest, C. W., Gratzinger, P. D., & Warren, R. A., 234

Precision Bicycle Components: Exploring the Glass Ceiling, Hite, L. M., & McDonald, K. S., 260

Preparing leaders for change-oriented schools, Thurston, P., Clift, R., & Schacht, M., 98

Preparing for leadership: A young adult's guide to leadership skills in a global age, Woyach, R. B., 202

Preparing future leaders today, 57

Preparing leadership students to lead, Swatez, M. J., 170

Preparing to lead: The college women's guide to internships and other public policy learning opportunities in Washington, DC, Compoc, K., Lewis, C., Weaver, M., & Stoneback, S., 157

The president abroad: Leadership at the international level, Kellerman, B., 106

The president who led by seeming not to: A centennial view of Dwight Eisenhower, Greenstein, F. I., 35

The presidential character: Predicting performance in the White House, Barber, J. D., 33

Presidential leadership: Making a difference, Fisher, J., & Koch, J. V., 92

Presidential leadership in the post Cold War era, Hastedt, G. P., & Eksterowicz, A. J., 106

Presidential power and the modern presidents: The politics of leadership from Roosevelt to Reagan, Neustadt, R. E., 107

Presidential style: Personality, biography, and performance, Simonton, D. K., 109

The president's call: Executive leadership from FDR to George Bush, Michaels, J. E., 107

The prince, Machiavelli, N., 162

The Principal as Teacher: A model for instructional leadership, Boyd, B., 91

Principal's Power Tactics Survey, Landry, R. G., Porter, A. W., & Lemon, D. K., 234

Principle-centered leadership, Covey, S. R., 150

Prisoners' Dilemma: An Intergroup Competition, Pfeiffer, J. W., & Jones, J. E., 261

Prisoners of leadership, Kets de Vries, M. F. R., 119

The problem of cultural leadership: The lessons of the dead leaders society and a new definition of leadership, Wren, J. T., 179

Problem-solving discussions and conferences: Leadership methods and skills, Maier, N. R., 141

Proceedings: The 1996 NLI Conference: Leaders and change, National Leadership Institute, 136

Productive workplaces: Organizing and managing for dignity, meaning and community, Weisbord, M. R., 67

Productivity and American leadership: The long view, Baumol, W. J., Blackman, S. A. B., & Wolff, E. N., 25

Profile of women mentors: A national survey, Vincent, A., & Seymour, J., 171

The Profilor, Personnel Decisions, Inc., 234

The project manager as change agent: Leadership, influence and negotiation, Turner, J. R., Grude, K. V., & Thurloway, L., 139

The promotion record of the United States Army: Glass ceilings in the officer corps, Baldwin, J. N., 99

Prospector, McCall, M. W., Jr., 235

Providing a base for executive development at the state level, Van Wart, M., 115

Psychware sourcebook: A reference guide to computer-based products for assessment in psychology, education and business, Krug, S. E., 192

Public administration illuminated and inspired by the arts, Goodsell, C. T., & Murray, N., 112

Public administration and the theater metaphor: The public administrator as villain, hero, and innocent victim, Terry, L. D., 115

Public entrepreneurs: Agents for change in American government, Schneider, M., Teske, P., & Mintrom, M., 114

The public and the paradox of leadership: An experimental analysis, Sigelman, L., Sigelman, C. K., & Walkosz, B. J., 114

Public participation in public decision: New skills and strategies for public managers, Thomas, J. C., 115

Pumping the Colors, Shirts, R. G., 261

Pyramid, Interel, 261

Q

The quickening of America: Rebuilding our nation, remaking our lives, Lappe, F. M., & Du Bois, P. M., 29

R

Rahim Leader Power Inventory (RLPI), Rahim, M. A., 235

Rainbow War, 285

Re: Project team empowerment aboard the Starship Enterprise, Case, R. H., & Singer, J., 143

Reach for the top: Women and the changing facts of work life, Nichols, N. A., 52

SUBJECT INDEX

ORDER FORM

To obtain additional copies of *Leadership Resources: A Guide to Training and Development Tools*, see below.

Readers might also wish to consult

Leadership Education: A Source Book of Courses and Programs (7th edition)

Leadership Education is an essential tool for leadership educators who are planning a course or program, whether it be in higher education, secondary education, or the business, nonprofit, human service, or community sectors.

Drawing on a survey of colleges, universities, professional organizations, corporate universities, training organizations, and other sites, this edition presents selected descriptions of 230 leadership courses and programs that have come into existence or have been significantly revised since the sixth edition of this book was published in 1996.

Each description is richly detailed, including information on purpose, requirements, schedule, assigned readings, and more. In addition, *Leadership Education* features a list of frequently used texts and a complete index to people, institutions, and subjects.

Please copy this form and return to: **Publication, Center for Creative Leadership, P.O. Box 26300, Greensboro, NC 27438-6300**, or call **336-545-2805**, or fax to **336-545-3221**, or E-mail your order via the Center's online bookstore at **www.ccl.org**. Discounts are available for academicians for classroom use, distributors, libraries, bookstores, and nonprofit organizations. For more information, call 336-545-2805.

Quantity

____ *Leadership Resources: A Guide to Training and Development Tools* (7th edition). Stock No. 340. $40.00.
____ *Leadership Education: A Source Book of Courses and Programs* (7th edition). Stock No. 339. $40.00.
____ *Leadership Education/Leadership Resources* Package. Stock No. 722. $70.00.

CCL's Federal ID Number is 237-07-9591.
METHOD OF PAYMENT (ALL orders for less than $100 must be PREPAID.)

❑ My check or money order in the amount of $_____ is enclosed (payable to Center for Creative Leadership).

❑ Purchase Order No. _____ (Must be accompanied by this form.)

❑ Charge my order, plus shipping, to my credit card: ❑ American Express ❑ Discover ❑ MasterCard ❑ VISA

ACCOUNT NUMBER: _____ EXPIRATION DATE: MO. _____ YR. _____

NAME OF ISSUING BANK: _____

SIGNATURE _____

Name _____ **Subtotal** _____

Title _____ **Shipping and Handling**
(add 6% of subtotal with a $4.00 minimum;
add 40% on all international shipping) _____

Organization _____

Mailing Address _____ **Add Sales Tax if resident of**
(street address required for mailing) **CA (7.75%), CO (6.2%), NC (6%)** _____

City/State/Zip _____ **TOTAL** _____

Telephone _____ FAX _____
(telephone number required for UPS mailing) ❑ Please send me your new Publications catalog.